T0213827

Lecture Notes in Computer Science 9253

Commenced Publication in 1973
Founding and Former Series Editors:
Gerhard Goos, Juris Hartmanis, and Jan van Leeuwen

Editorial Board

David Hutchison
  Lancaster University, Lancaster, UK
Takeo Kanade
  Carnegie Mellon University, Pittsburgh, PA, USA
Josef Kittler
  University of Surrey, Guildford, UK
Jon M. Kleinberg
  Cornell University, Ithaca, NY, USA
Friedemann Mattern
  ETH Zurich, Zürich, Switzerland
John C. Mitchell
  Stanford University, Stanford, CA, USA
Moni Naor
  Weizmann Institute of Science, Rehovot, Israel
C. Pandu Rangan
  Indian Institute of Technology, Madras, India
Bernhard Steffen
  TU Dortmund University, Dortmund, Germany
Demetri Terzopoulos
  University of California, Los Angeles, CA, USA
Doug Tygar
  University of California, Berkeley, CA, USA
Gerhard Weikum
  Max Planck Institute for Informatics, Saarbrücken, Germany

More information about this series at http://www.springer.com/series/7409

Hamid Reza Motahari-Nezhad · Jan Recker
Matthias Weidlich (Eds.)

Business Process Management

13th International Conference, BPM 2015
Innsbruck, Austria, August 31 – September 3, 2015
Proceedings

 Springer

Editors
Hamid Reza Motahari-Nezhad
IBM Almaden Research Center
San Jose, CA
USA

Matthias Weidlich
Humboldt-Universität zu Berlin
Berlin
Germany

Jan Recker
Queensland University
Brisbane, QLD
Australia

ISSN 0302-9743   ISSN 1611-3349 (electronic)
Lecture Notes in Computer Science
ISBN 978-3-319-23062-7 ISBN 978-3-319-23063-4 (eBook)
DOI 10.1007/978-3-319-23063-4

Library of Congress Control Number: 2015946592

LNCS Sublibrary: SL3 – Information Systems and Applications, incl. Internet/Web, and HCI

Springer Cham Heidelberg New York Dordrecht London
© Springer International Publishing Switzerland 2015
This work is subject to copyright. All rights are reserved by the Publisher, whether the whole or part of the material is concerned, specifically the rights of translation, reprinting, reuse of illustrations, recitation, broadcasting, reproduction on microfilms or in any other physical way, and transmission or information storage and retrieval, electronic adaptation, computer software, or by similar or dissimilar methodology now known or hereafter developed.
The use of general descriptive names, registered names, trademarks, service marks, etc. in this publication does not imply, even in the absence of a specific statement, that such names are exempt from the relevant protective laws and regulations and therefore free for general use.
The publisher, the authors and the editors are safe to assume that the advice and information in this book are believed to be true and accurate at the date of publication. Neither the publisher nor the authors or the editors give a warranty, express or implied, with respect to the material contained herein or for any errors or omissions that may have been made.

Printed on acid-free paper

Springer International Publishing AG Switzerland is part of Springer Science+Business Media
(www.springer.com)

Preface

BPM 2015 was the 13th International Conference on Business Process Management. It provided a global forum for researchers to meet and exchange views over research topics and outcomes in business process management. BPM 2015 was hosted by the University of Innsbruck and took place August 31 to September 3.

We received 125 full submissions. After a review process involving 17 senior Program Committee (PC) members and 75 PC members, we accepted 30 papers in total, 21 full papers (17 % acceptance rate), seven short papers and two industrial papers, for an overall acceptance rate of 24 %.

This year, we encouraged in particular two types of submissions. First, research that attests to the interdisciplinary nature of BPM and connects to disciplines such as information systems, management and organizational science, data and knowledge management, operations management, service-oriented computing, social computing, cloud computing, big data, and others. Second, research that explicitly examines emerging BPM areas and novel applications of BPM concepts and methods. Out of the submissions on these and the existing traditional subject areas of BPM research, we selected a range of papers addressing topics ranging from process discovery, modeling, and monitoring, to emerging and practical areas of BPM, runtime process management, and process performance aspects.

The selection of this scientific program would not have been possible without the dedicated combined efforts of the PC and the entire reviewer community. We are most grateful to all those involved and in particular to the senior PC members for leading the review process and preparing recommendations to the PC chairs. Of course, all these efforts would have been futile if not for the entire community of BPM researchers that authored submissions to BPM and that led to the enjoyable yet difficult task of selecting papers from the vast set of submissions.

The scientific program in 2015 was complemented by three keynotes, selected to provide a perspective from within the BPM community (Marlon Dumas, University of Tartu), from BPM industry (Gustavo Gomez, Bizagi) and from adjacent areas to the core BPM research community (Munindar Singh, North Carolina State University).

Finally, we would like to thank the BPM 2015 Organizing Committee and in particular the General Chair, Barbara Weber, for their efforts in making this conference possible, and we thank the sponsors, Bizagi, Prologics, Minitlabs, IBM Research, Signavio, Exformatics, and SAP, for their generous support.

We hope that you will enjoy reading the papers that comprise the scientific program of BPM 2015 and we hope that you will be inspired to contribute to the next edition of BPM in 2016.

September 2015

Hamid R. Motahari-Nezhad
Jan Recker
Matthias Weidlich

Organization

BPM 2015 was organized in Innsbruck, Austria, by the University of Innsbruck.

Steering Committee

Wil van der Aalst (Chair)	Eindhoven University of Technology, The Netherlands
Boualem Benatallah	University of New South Wales, Australia
Jörg Desel	University of Hagen, Germany
Schahram Dustdar	Vienna University of Technology, Austria
Marlon Dumas	University of Tartu, Estonia
Mathias Weske	HPI, University of Potsdam, Germany
Michael zur Muehlen	Stevens Institute of Technology, USA
Barbara Weber	University of Innsbruck, Austria

Executive Committee

General Chair

Barbara Weber	University of Innsbruck, Austria

Program Chairs

Hamid R. Motahari-Nezhad	IBM Research, USA
Jan Recker	Queensland University of Technology, Australia
Matthias Weidlich	Humboldt University of Berlin, Germany

Industry Chairs

Jan Mendling	Vienna University of Economics and Business, Austria
Jan vom Brocke	University of Liechtenstein, Liechtenstein

Workshop Chairs

Manfred Reichert	University of Ulm, Germany
Hajo Reijers	VU University Amsterdam, The Netherlands

Tutorial and Panel Chairs

Jakob Pinggera	University of Innsbruck, Austria
Pnina Soffer	University of Haifa, Israel

Demo Chairs

Florian Daniel	University of Trento, Italy
Stefan Zugal	University of Innsbruck, Austria

Doctoral Consortium Chairs

Stefanie Rinderle-Ma	University of Vienna, Austria
Mathias Weske	HPI, University of Potsdam, Germany

Local Organization Chairs

Cornelia Haisjackl	University of Innsbruck, Austria
Ilona Zaremba	University of Innsbruck, Austria

Web and Social Media Chairs

Cornelia Haisjackl	University of Innsbruck, Austria
Jakob Pinggera	University of Innsbruck, Austria
Stefan Zugal	University of Innsbruck, Austria

Publicity Chairs

Amin Beheshti	University of New South Wales, Australia
Henrik Leopold	VU University Amsterdam, The Netherlands
Lucinea Thom	Federal University of Rio Grande do Sul, Brazil
Lijie Wen	Tshingua University, China
Michael zur Muehlen	Stevens Institute of Technology, USA

Senior Program Committee

Florian Daniel	University of Trento, Italy
Jörg Desel	University of Hagen, Germany
Marlon Dumas	University of Tartu, Estonia
Avigdor Gal	Technion, Israel
Akhil Kumar	Penn State University, USA
Marcello La Rosa	Queensland University of Technology, Australia
Hajo A. Reijers	Eindhoven University of Technology, The Netherlands
Stefanie Rinderle-Ma	University of Vienna, Austria
Michael Rosemann	Queensland University of Technology, Australia
Pnina Soffer	University of Haifa, Israel
Jianwen Su	University of California at Santa Barbara, USA
Farouk Toumani	Blaise Pascal University, France
Boudewijn van Dongen	Eindhoven University of Technology, The Netherlands
Jan vom Brocke	University of Liechtenstein, Liechtenstein
Mathias Weske	University of Potsdam, Germany
Roel Wieringa	University of Twente, The Netherlands
Michael Zur Muehlen	Stevens Institute of Technology, USA

Program Committee

Mari Abe	IBM Research, Japan
Alistair Barros	Queensland University of Technology, Australia
Seyed-Mehdi-Reza Beheshti	University of New South Wales, Australia
Boualem Benatallah	University of New South Wales, Australia
Christoph Bussler	Oracle, USA
Jorge Cardoso	University of Coimbra, Portugal
Fabio Casati	University of Trento, Italy
Anis Charfi	SAP Research, Germany
Sarah Cohen-Boulakia	University of Paris-Sud, France
Francisco Curbera	IBM Research, USA
Ernesto Damiani	University of Milan, Italy
Nirmit Desai	IBM Research, India
Remco Dijkman	Eindhoven University of Technology, The Netherlands
Schahram Dustdar	Vienna University of Technology, Austria
Johann Eder	University of Klagenfurt, Austria
Dirk Fahland	Eindhoven University of Technology, The Netherlands
Marcelo Fantinato	University of São Paulo, Brazil
Hans-Georg Fill	University of Vienna, Austria
Luciano García-Bañuelos	University of Tartu, Estonia
Christian Gerth	University of Paderborn, Germany
Claude Godart	Loria, France
Sven Graupner	Hewlett-Packard Laboratories, USA
Paul Grefen	Eindhoven University of Technology, The Netherlands
Daniela Grigori	University of Paris-Dauphine, France
Thomas Hildebrandt	IT University of Copenhagen, Denmark
Rick Hull	IBM Research, USA
Arno Jacobsen	TU Munich, Germany
Leonid Kalinichenko	Russian Academy of Science, Russia
Gerti Kappel	Vienna University of Technology, Austria
Dimka Karastoyanova	University of Stuttgart, Germany
Rania Khalaf	IBM Research, USA
Ekkart Kindler	Technical University of Denmark, Denmark
Agnes Koschmider	Karlsruhe Institute of Technology, Germany
Jochen Kuester	University of Applied Sciences Bielefeld, Germany
Geetika Lakshmanan	IBM Research, USA
Henrik Leopold	VU University Amsterdam, The Netherlands
Frank Leymann	University of Stuttgart, Germany
Chengfei Liu	Swinburne University of Technology, Australia
Peter Loos	Saarland University, Germany
Heiko Ludwig	IBM Research, USA
Shahar Maoz	Tel Aviv University, Israel
Massimo Mecella	Sapienza University of Rome, Italy
Jan Mendling	Vienna University of Economics and Business, Austria

Marco Montali	Free University of Bozen-Bolzano, Italy
Bela Mutschler	University of Applied Sciences Ravensburg-Weingarten, Germany
John Mylopoulos	University of Toronto, Canada
Andreas Oberweis	Karlsruhe Institute of Technology, Germany
Hye-Young Paik	University of New South Wales, Australia
Oscar Pastor Lopez	Polytechnic University of Valencia, Spain
Artem Polyvyanyy	Queensland University of Technology, Australia
Frank Puhlmann	Bosch Software Innovations GmbH, Germany
Mu Qiao	IBM Research, USA
Manfred Reichert	University of Ulm, Germany
Domenico Sacca	University of Calabria, Italy
Shazia Sadiq	The University of Queensland, Australia
Sherif Sakr	The University of New South Wales, Australia
Erich Schikuta	University of Vienna, Austria
Heiko Schuldt	University of Basel, Switzerland
Sergey Smirnov	SAP Research, Germany
Minseok Song	Ulsan National Institute of Science and Technology, Korea
Mark Strembeck	Vienna University of Economics and Business, Austria
Harald Störrle	Technical University of Denmark, Denmark
Keith Swenson	Fujitsu America Inc., USA
Stefan Tai	Technical University of Berlin, Germany
Samir Tata	Telecom SudParis, France
Arthur Ter Hofstede	Queensland University of Technology, Australia
Peter Trkman	University of Ljubljana, Slovenia
Alberto Trombetta	Insubria University, Italy
Aphrodite Tsalgatidou	National and Kapodistrian University of Athens, Greece
Roman Vaculin	IBM Research, USA
Wil van der Aalst	Eindhoven University of Technology, The Netherlands
Irene Vanderfeesten	Eindhoven University of Technology, The Netherlands
Hagen Voelzer	IBM Research, Switzerland
Jianmin Wang	Tsinghua University, China
Ingo Weber	NICTA, Australia
Lijie Wen	Tsinghua University, China
Karsten Wolf	University of Rostock, Germany
Liang Zhang	Fudan University, China
Leon Zhao	City University of Hong Kong, SAR China
Xiaohui Zhao	University of Canberra, Australia

Additional Reviewers

Andrews, Kevin
Awad, Ahmed
Beheshti,
  Seyed-Mehdi-Reza
Bill, Robert
Botezatu, Mirela Madalina
Chiao, Carolina Ming
Claes, Jan
Debois, Søren
Elgammal, Amal
Falkenthal, Michael
Gaaloul, Walid
Hahn, Michael
Hake, Philip
Huma, Zille
Kammerer, Klaus
Knuplesch, David
Koutrouli, Eleni
Kusen, Ema
Leotta, Francesco
Lübbecke, Patrick
Marengo, Elisa
Mayerhofer, Tanja
Mehdiyev, Nijat
Neubauer, Patrick
Pittl, Benedikt

Rodriguez, Carlos
Santoso, Ario
Athanasopoulos, George
Barukh, Moshe Chai
Bhiri, Sami
Bork, Dominik
Busany, Nimrod
Chituc, Claudia-Melania
Conforti, Raffaele
Dumont, Tobias
Eshuis, Rik
Feinerer, Ingo
Görlach, Katharina
Hajimirsadeghi,
  Seyed Alireza
Huemer, Christian
Ishakian, Vatche
Kleinert, Thomas
Kolb, Jens
Kucza, Timo
Köpke, Julius
Lu, Xixi
Mach, Werner
Marrella, Andrea
Mazak, Alexandra
Mundbrod, Nicolas

Pichler, Horst
Rasouli, Mohammad Reza
Rogge-Solti, Andreas
Schobel, Johannes
Shepherd, John
Skvortsov, Nikolay
Slominski, Aleksander
Sun, Yutian
Tsagkani, Christina
Ul Haq, Irfan
Wagner, Sebastian
Weiß, Andreas
Wolters, Dennis
Yin, Peifeng
Yu, Jian
Skouradaki, Marigianna
Slaats, Tijs
Stupnikov, Sergey
Thaler, Tom
Tsarfaty, Reut
Vanwersch, Rob
Wang, Zhaoxia
Wen, Lijie
Wynn, Moe
Yongchareon, Sira

Sponsors

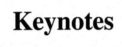

Keynotes

From Models to Data and Back: The Journey of the BPM Discipline and the Tangled Road to BPM 2020

Marlon Dumas

University of Tartu, Estonia
marlon.dumas@ut.ee

Keynote Abstract

It has been over two decades since the first research articles on Business Process Management (BPM) saw light. Much ink has been spilled meantime to build up a discipline out of what is essentially a vision of how work in organizations can be effectively conceptualized and analyzed for the purpose of performance improvement. There is by now a relatively well-established body of methods and tools to instill "process thinking" in organizations and to manage business processes throughout their lifecycle.

A considerable subset of these methods and tools rely on business process models, be it for understanding processes, for preserving and communicating process knowledge, for analyzing, redesigning or automating processes, and even for monitoring them. It is thus not surprising that a lot of research and development in the field of BPM has concentrated on modeling languages, tools and methods, to the extent that the early evolution of the discipline is sometimes associated with the development of modeling languages. Along this line, the discipline has gone through a long convergence and standardization process, starting from proprietary notations such as Event-driven Process Chains (EPCs), moving on to standardization attempts such as UML Activity Diagrams and the XML Process Definition Language (XPDL), followed by a parade of standardization proposals and associated acronyms in the early '00s (WSFL, XLANG, BPML, WSCI to name a few), the rise and fall of the Business Process Execution Language (BPEL), the broad adoption of the Business Process Model and Notation (BPMN), and the somehow failed struggle to reach a standard case management notation (cf. CMMN).

The overwhelming volume of these developments calls for two questions: What have we fundamentally learned from the development of modeling languages, tools and methods? And perhaps more importantly, what have we so far failed to fully comprehend?

Another significant subset of methods and tools in the BPM field rely on data, specifically data collected during the execution of business processes. As processes become increasingly digitized, data is moving from being a (necessary) side-product of the execution of business processes, to becoming a central asset that can be leveraged across all phases of the business process lifecycle. This prospect has fueled a stream of research and development on business process data analytics, starting from dashboards, cockpits and process data warehouses, to the era of process mining methods and tools. Along this line, we have seen emerge a number of methods and tools to summarize process execution data, to generate or enhance models using these data, and to understand how the recorded execution of a business process diverges from its modeled behavior or vice-versa.

Again, the overwhelming volume of developments in this field calls for two questions: What have we fundamentally learned from the development of process mining tools and methods? And perhaps more importantly, what have we so far failed to fully comprehend?

This talk will argue that answers to the above questions can be summarized with two concepts: *variation* and *decisions*, be them offline (e.g. design-time) or online (runtime). Many if not most developments and open challenges in the field boil down to comprehending, analyzing, executing and monitoring business processes with inherently high levels of variation and with complex decisions. Indeed, the discipline has learned to analyze, optimize and automate routine work that involves well-structured data objects and simple choices, even on relatively large scales. But we are yet to learn how to manage large-scale variation, unstructuredness and complex decision spaces. The emergence of the Internet of Things and cyber-physical systems is likely to only heighten the challenge, as in a world where the number of connections increases exponentially, so does the complexity of options and variations that ought to be accounted for. The coming of age of automated decision making, the maturation of natural language processing as well as advances in heterogeneous data analytics, create significant opportunities to address the challenges that lie ahead for the BPM discipline.

For a while, the trend in BPM has been to simplify by standardization, at different levels. Now it's time to learn how to embrace variation and the manifold decisions that arise thereof. One thing for sure: A tangled road lies ahead towards BPM 2020.

NoBPM: Supporting Interaction-Oriented Automation via Normative Specifications of Processes

Munindar P. Singh

Department of Computer Science
North Carolina State University
Raleigh, NC 27695-8206, USA
singh@ncsu.edu

Keynote Abstract

Business and business processes are centuries old social constructions that underlie human society. Business process management or BPM is a modern construction in information technology. The objective of BPM is to support business processes: it has partially succeeded, especially in regards to improving the efficiency of process enactment.

However, BPM embodies a number of restrictive assumptions treated as dogma in current research that limit its applicability. First, BPM is almost entirely characterized in operational terms, that is, describing the steps to be taken and constraints on their ordering and occurrence. Usually, these characterizations are procedural, though occasionally they may be declarative, such as in temporal logic. The underlying modeling primitives in operational characterizations, especially, the procedural forms, are little different from the primitives of any programming language.

Second, BPM is usually treated from a central viewpoint, even when the enactments of the concerned business process are physically distributed. That is, BPM's focus is on technical rather than business aspects. In essence, BPM does not so much support a business process as redefine it in operational terms. That is, it omits a standard of correctness but provides a means to an implementation as an alternative to a standard.

Although BPM has proved effective in IT practice, I claim that it has run its course. I claim that BPM is inadequate for dealing with modern challenges such as processes that incorporate humans and organizations as well as diverse services and devices that reflect the autonomy of humans and organizations.

If we were to rethink the foundations of business processes from first principles, we would understand them as social constructions just as they are—and have been through history. We would establish new computational foundations for business processes that place them as elements of a sociotechnical system. In particular, we would

- specify them via *normative* (not operational) standards of correctness—independent of implementation;

– describe how to verify correctness properties of specifications and evaluate implementations with respect to specifications; and
– enact and govern them in a decentralized manner.

I term this new perspective *NoBPM*. NoBPM is about a computational approach—or, rather, a family of computational approaches—to business processes that seek to, first, capture the essence of what a business process is meant to accomplish for its various participants and, second, to support provably most flexible enactments.

The vision of NoBPM brings forth a number of major research questions.

– What does it mean for a normative process specification to be sound?
– How can we learn such specifications from observations of humans and organizations and their services and devices?
– What does it mean for an autonomous participant to comply with a normative process specification?
– How can we define and ensure a suitable notion of alignment of the various parties involved in a business process?

I describe recent and ongoing research [1–13] that hints at how we may approach the above questions. I offer some suggestions for how the considerable research strength of the BPM community can be directed toward these questions and invite researchers to participate in NoBPM.

Acknowledgments   Thanks to Matteo Baldoni, Cristina Baroglio, and Amit Chopra for helpful discussions about this research.

References

1. Baldoni, M., Baroglio, C., Chopra, A.K., Singh, M.P.: Composing and verifying commitment-based multiagent protocols. In: Proceedings of the 24th International Joint Conference on Artificial Intelligence (IJCAI), pp. 1–8. IJCAI, Buenos Aires, July 2015
2. Chopra, A.K., Dalpiaz, F., Aydemir, F.B., Giorgini, P., Mylopoulos, J., Singh, M.P.: Protos: foundations for engineering innovative sociotechnical systems. In: Proceedings of the 18th IEEE International Requirements Engineering Conference (RE), pp. 53–62. IEEE Computer Society, Karlskrona, Sweden, August 2014
3. Chopra, A.K., Singh, M.P.: Cupid: Commitments in relational algebra. In: Proceedings of the 23rd Conference on Artificial Intelligence (AAAI), pp. 2052–2059. AAAI Press, Austin, Texas, January 2015
4. Chopra, A.K., Singh, M.P.: Generalized commitment alignment. In: Proceedings of the 14th International Conference on Autonomous Agents and MultiAgent Systems (AAMAS), pp. 453–461. IFAAMAS, Istanbul, May 2015
5. Gao, X., Singh, M.P.: Extracting normative relationships from business contracts. In: Proceedings of the 13th International Conference on Autonomous Agents and MultiAgent Systems (AAMAS), pp. 101–108, Paris, May 2014
6. Kalia, A.K., Motahari Nezhad, H.R., Bartolini, C., Singh, M.P.: Monitoring commitments in people-driven service engagements. In: Proceedings of the 10th IEEE International Conference on Services Computing (SCC), pp. 160–167. IEEE Computer Society, Santa Clara, California, June 2013

7. Marengo, E., Baldoni, M., Chopra, A.K., Baroglio, C., Patti, V., Singh, M.P.: Commitments with regulations: Reasoning about safety and control in Regula. In: Proceedings of the 10th International Conference on Autonomous Agents and MultiAgent Systems (AAMAS), pp. 467–474. IFAAMAS, Taipei, May 2011

8. Singh, M.P.: Information-driven interaction-oriented programming: BSPL, the Blindingly Simple Protocol Language. In: Proceedings of the 10th International Conference on Autonomous Agents and MultiAgent Systems (AAMAS), pp. 491–498, May 2011

9. Singh, M.P.: LoST: Local State Transfer—An architectural style for the distributed enactment of business protocols. In: Proceedings of the 9th IEEE International Conference on Web Services (ICWS), pp. 57–64. IEEE Computer Society, Washington, DC, July 2011

10. Singh, M.P.: Semantics and verification of information-based protocols. In: Proceedings of the 11th International Conference on Autonomous Agents and MultiAgent Systems (AAMAS), pp. 1149–1156. IFAAMAS, Valencia, Spain, June 2012

11. Singh, M.P.: Norms as a basis for governing sociotechnical systems. ACM Trans. Intell. Syst. Technol. (TIST) 5(1), 21:1–21:23 (2013)

12. Singh, M.P.: Bliss: specifying declarative service protocols. In: Proceedings of the 11th IEEE International Conference on Services Computing (SCC), pp. 235–242. IEEE Computer Society, Anchorage, Alaska (2014)

13. Singh, M.P., Chopra, A.K., Desai, N.: Commitment-based service-oriented architecture. IEEE Comput. 42(11), 72–79 (2009)

Adaptability, Architecture and CX: The Bizagi Way

Gustavo Ignacio Gomez

Bizagi, UK
Gustavo.Gomez@bizagi.com

Keynote Abstract

Business Process Management Systems (BPMS) have put processes at the centre of the universe. This focus has enabled the creation of formal practice and theories from which IT solutions have benefited enormously during the last 15 years.

By delivering the right information to the right person at the right time, information workers have been empowered by systems that truly understand what they intend to do. And by doing this in a model-driven way whereby the technology adapts itself to this business model - and not the other way around - these new systems have enabled continuous improvement and adaptability: capabilities indispensable to achieving much-desired business agility. Yet despite this, the user experience is often counter-intuitive to the business objectives. Knowledge workers may find themselves asking questions such as:

- Do I really know which process I want to start when I enter my BPMS application?
- Do I need to carry out some analysis before I start?
- Are all process combinations known to me beforehand?
- How smart is the solution at suggesting processes that actually make sense?

Furthermore, what if we wanted to create modern applications that resemble sophisticated web sites such as *amazon.com* or *hotels.com*? Could we build them with a BPMS? If not… why not? What's missing?

Customer experience (CX) is quickly becoming the hottest buzzword in business and industry. How is CX related to BPMS? What makes a great CX anyway?

In this talk, we will explore how by marrying process and data and extending current process technologies with few new concepts we can create fundamentally new, context-sensitive applications that empower knowledge workers like never before, and redefine the boundaries of what a BPMS can do.

Contents

Runtime Process Management

Improving Business Processes: Does Anybody have an Idea?   3
   Rob J.B. Vanwersch, Irene Vanderfeesten, Eric Rietzschel,
   and Hajo A. Reijers

Inspection Coming Due! How to Determine the Service Interval of Your
Processes!   19
   Jonas Manderscheid, Daniel Reißner, and Maximilian Röglinger

Data-Driven Performance Analysis of Scheduled Processes   35
   Arik Senderovich, Andreas Rogge-Solti, Avigdor Gal, Jan Mendling,
   Avishai Mandelbaum, Sarah Kadish, and Craig A. Bunnell

Process Modeling

Specification and Verification of Complex Business
Processes - A High-Level Petri Net-Based Approach   55
   Ahmed Kheldoun, Kamel Barkaoui, and Malika Ioualalen

Concurrency and Asynchrony in Declarative Workflows   72
   Søren Debois, Thomas Hildebrandt, and Tijs Slaats

Detecting Inconsistencies Between Process Models and Textual
Descriptions   90
   Han van der Aa, Henrik Leopold, and Hajo A. Reijers

Process Model Discovery I

Mining Invisible Tasks in Non-free-choice Constructs   109
   Qinlong Guo, Lijie Wen, Jianmin Wang, Zhiqiang Yan,
   and Philip S. Yu

Incorporating Negative Information in Process Discovery   126
   Hernan Ponce-de-León, Josep Carmona,
   and Seppe K.L.M. vanden Broucke

Ensuring Model Consistency in Declarative Process Discovery   144
   Claudio Di Ciccio, Fabrizio Maria Maggi, Marco Montali,
   and Jan Mendling

Business Process Models and Analytics

Avoiding Over-Fitting in ILP-Based Process Discovery   163
Sebastiaan J. van Zelst, Boudewijn F. van Dongen,
and Wil M.P. van der Aalst

Estimation of Average Latent Waiting and Service Times of Activities from
Event Logs.   172
Takahide Nogayama and Haruhisa Takahashi

A Structural Model Comparison for Finding the Best Performing Models in
a Collection   180
D.M.M. Schunselaar, H.M.W. Verbeek, H.A. Reijers,
and W.M.P. van der Aalst

Context-Sensitive Textual Recommendations for Incomplete Process
Model Elements   189
Fabian Pittke, Pedro H. Piccoli Richetti, Jan Mendling,
and Fernanda Araujo Baião

Extracting Configuration Guidance Models from Business Process
Repositories   198
Nour Assy and Walid Gaaloul

BPM in Industry

Web-Based Modelling and Collaborative Simulation of Declarative
Processes   209
Morten Marquard, Muhammad Shahzad, and Tijs Slaats

Case Analytics Workbench: Platform for Hybrid Process Model Creation
and Evolution.   226
Yiqin Yu, Xiang Li, Haifeng Liu, Jing Mei, Nirmal Mukhi,
Vatche Ishakian, Guotong Xie, Geetika T. Lakshmanan, and Mike Marin

A Clinical Pathway Mining Approach to Enable Scheduling of Hospital
Relocations and Treatment Services.   242
Karsten Helbig, Michael Römer, and Taïeb Mellouli

A Framework for Benchmarking BPMN 2.0 Workflow
Management Systems   251
Vincenzo Ferme, Ana Ivanchikj, and Cesare Pautasso

Process Compliance and Deviations

Visually Monitoring Multiple Perspectives of Business Process Compliance . . .   263
David Knuplesch, Manfred Reichert, and Akhil Kumar

Managing Controlled Violation of Temporal Process Constraints. 280
    Akhil Kumar, Sharat R. Sabbella, and Russell R. Barton

Complex Symbolic Sequence Encodings for Predictive Monitoring
of Business Processes 297
    *Anna Leontjeva, Raffaele Conforti, Chiara Di Francescomarino,
    Marlon Dumas, and Fabrizio Maria Maggi*

Emerging and Practical Areas of BPM

Business Process Management Skills and Roles: An Investigation
of the Demand and Supply Side of BPM Professionals 317
    Patrick Lohmann and Michael Zur Muehlen

BPMN Task Instance Streaming for Efficient Micro-task Crowdsourcing
Processes. 333
    *Stefano Tranquillini, Florian Daniel, Pavel Kucherbaev,
    and Fabio Casati*

Goal-Aligned Categorization of Instance Variants in Knowledge-Intensive
Processes. 350
    *Karthikeyan Ponnalagu, Aditya Ghose, Nanjangud C. Narendra,
    and Hoa Khanh Dam*

Process Monitoring

Process Mining on Databases: Unearthing Historical Data from
Redo Logs 367
    *Eduardo González López de Murillas, Wil M.P. van der Aalst,
    and Hajo A. Reijers*

Log Delta Analysis: Interpretable Differencing of Business Process Event
Logs 386
    *Nick R.T.P. van Beest, Marlon Dumas, Luciano García-Bañuelos,
    and Marcello La Rosa*

Fast and Accurate Business Process Drift Detection. 406
    *Abderrahmane Maaradji, Marlon Dumas, Marcello La Rosa,
    and Alireza Ostovar*

Process Model Discovery II

Mining Project-Oriented Business Processes 425
    *Saimir Bala, Cristina Cabanillas, Jan Mendling, Andreas Rogge-Solti,
    and Axel Polleres*

Efficient Process Model Discovery Using Maximal Pattern Mining   441
  Veronica Liesaputra, Sira Yongchareon, and Sivadon Chaisiri

Log-Based Simplification of Process Models   457
  Javier De San Pedro, Josep Carmona, and Jordi Cortadella

Author Index   475

Runtime Process Management

Improving Business Processes: Does Anybody have an Idea?

Rob J.B. Vanwersch[1(✉)], Irene Vanderfeesten[1], Eric Rietzschel[2], and Hajo A. Reijers[3]

[1] Eindhoven University of Technology, Eindhoven, The Netherlands
{r.j.b.vanwersch,i.t.p.vanderfeesten}@tue.nl
[2] University of Groningen, Groningen, The Netherlands
e.f.rietzschel@rug.nl
[3] VU University, Amsterdam, The Netherlands
h.a.reijers@vu.nl

Abstract. As part of process redesign initiatives, substantial time is spent on the systematic description and analysis of the as-is process. By contrast, to-be scenarios are often generated in a less rigorous way. Only one or a few workshops are organized for this purpose, which rely on the use of techniques that are susceptible to bias and incompleteness, e.g. brainstorming. In this paper, we evaluate a new technique for generating process improvement ideas: the RePro (Rethinking of Processes) technique. Its backbone is formed by process improvement principles that guide practitioners in a systematic and comprehensive exploration of the solution space. An experiment was conducted to compare the performance of the RePro technique with traditional brainstorming. Results confirm the potential for using a more advanced technique during process redesign workshops, but also show that the way such a technique is used strongly affects its performance.

Keywords: Process redesign · Process innovation · Improvement principles · Controlled experiment · RePro

1 Introduction

The redesign of business processes has a huge potential in terms of reducing processes' costs and throughput times, as well as improving customer satisfaction [1]. A typical process redesign initiative consists of describing the as-is process, analyzing the as-is to identify process weaknesses, and generating process improvement ideas [2]. Whereas practitioners typically spend a lot of time on describing and analyzing the as-is situation, process improvement ideas are often generated in one or a few workshops using traditional creativity techniques, in particular brainstorming [3 - 5]. Such techniques lack guidance concerning the kind of process alternatives that are worthwhile to consider and do not provide a solution for the personal inertia to search for alternatives that are different from familiar directions [6]. In other words, no safeguard is provided to guarantee a systematic exploration of the full range of redesign possibilities. Consequently, traditional brainstorms are at risk to lead to biased choices and neglect interesting redesign possibilities [4, 6]. As such, the improvement potential of many process redesign initiatives is not fulfilled.

©Springer International Publishing Switzerland 2015
H.R. Motahari-Nezhad et al. (Eds.): BPM 2015, LNCS 9253, pp. 3–18, 2015.
DOI: 10.1007/978-3-319-23063-4_1

As an alternative to traditional creativity techniques, the Rethinking of Processes (RePro) technique was developed [7]. The RePro technique, which primarily supports rethinking care processes, relies on a set of process improvement principles that are rooted in Business Process Redesign (BPR) best practices [8] and TRIZ innovation principles [6]. All RePro principles can be seen as solutions that have been applied previously and seem worthwhile to reproduce in another situation or setting. Examples of these principles are "parallelism" (consider whether tasks in the business process can be executed in parallel) and "reconstruction" (consider reconstructing the physical lay-out of the workplace). The RePro technique contains an application procedure, which allows practitioners to go systematically through the list of principles. In summary, the RePro technique includes two innovations: an integration of two groups of process improvement principles, and an application procedure [7].

Prior research, in the form of a cross-case survey and an applicability check with potential end-users, suggests that the RePro technique provides comprehensive, compact and well-structured support for rethinking care processes [7]. Nonetheless, detailed insights into the benefits of explicitly applying the technique were not obtained.

It is expected that by using the RePro technique effective process alternatives are more likely to be identified as compared to a traditional brainstorm. Through the method-ism of the technique, novice analysts may become less reliant on experienced consultants or domain experts to support them in finding attractive process redesigns.

In order to gain more in-depth insights into the benefits of the technique, experiments offer interesting opportunities for a rigorous evaluation [9]. In the experiment that is reported upon in this paper, we evaluate the RePro technique and compare its performance with traditional brainstorming. By doing so, our work informs research into the effectiveness of process improvement techniques and potentially advances the knowledge base for people being active in process improvement.

This paper is structured as follows. Section 2 provides a summary of the RePro technique. Section 3 outlines the expected effects of using the technique and includes our hypotheses. In Section 4, the experiment is explained. Section 5 presents the results of the experiment, and Section 6 discusses the findings and limitations of our work. We discuss related work in Section 7, and Section 8 summarizes this paper.

2   Background

This section provides a brief summary of the RePro technique. More details about the RePro technique can be found in [7].

After an analysis of the as-is process, the RePro technique supports analysts in a workshop setting to generate process improvement ideas for reducing costs and throughput times, as well as improving customer satisfaction. The RePro technique contains a set of 46 RePro principles and a related application procedure [7]. All RePro principles are organized into 9 categories that address aspects of a process that can be improved. In Table 1, we provide a description of each RePro category, the number of RePro principles per category, and an example of a RePro principle. Descriptions of all 46 principles can be found in [7].

Table 1. RePro categories.

RePro category	Description of RePro category	No. of principles	Example of RePro principle
Customers	Contacts with customers	3	Move controls towards customers
External environment	Collaboration and communication with third parties	2	Consider outsourcing a business process in whole or parts of it
Tasks	The tasks that are part of the process	6	Add tasks to prevent the occurrence of an undesirable situation or to reduce its impact
Task order and timing	The order in which tasks are executed and the more detailed timing of task execution	7	Consider whether tasks may be executed in parallel
Human resources	The number and types of available human resources, and the way they are allocated to tasks	11	Let workers perform as many steps as possible for single orders
Facilities, equipment and material	The number and types of available facilities, equipment and material, and the way these are allocated to tasks	7	Consider changing the number of involved non-human resources
Information	The way information is used or created in the process	5	Consider introducing feedback.
Information and Communication Technology	How information and communication technology is used	2	Consider automating tasks
Physical lay-out	The physical arrangement of the process	3	Make the spatial arrangement flexible

An application procedure based on the nominal group technique [10] and the multi-level design approach [11] guides practitioners in applying the RePro principles. This application procedure contains five steps: (1) introduction and explanation of the procedure, (2) idea generation by each individual based on RePro principles and an analysis of the as-is process, (3) sharing ideas, (4) discussing content, advantages and disadvantages of ideas, and (5) voting and ranking ideas. In this study, the second step, i.e. idea generation, is at the center of attention. During this step, the RePro principles are explicitly considered by each participant taking into account the multi-level design approach (see Figure 1). For the sake of brevity, we use the term RePro technique in the remainder of this paper to refer to this particular step of the technique.

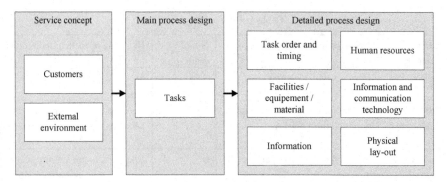

Fig. 1. RePro multi-level design approach.

The RePro multi-level design approach implies that all RePro categories and related principles are assigned to three levels that can be considered successively: (1) *Service concept*: the position of the process in relation to customers and third parties; principles of the customers and external environment category are assigned, (2) *Main process design*: the tasks that have to be executed in order to fulfill customer needs; principles of the tasks category are assigned, and (3) *Detailed process design*: the "when, who, with what, where" aspects of task execution; principles belonging to the remaining categories are assigned. By offering this classification, the RePro technique aims to enable a more systematic exploration of the solution space.

3   Hypotheses

In this section, we formulate hypotheses with regard to the impact of the RePro technique on productivity (i.e. the number of unique process improvement ideas generated by each individual) and participants' satisfaction with and intention-to-use the technique. The correlation between the quantity of ideas and the number of high-quality ideas was so high in other studies that reliance on the quantity of ideas as the sole indicator of productivity has become common practice [12 - 14].

Productivity (H1). The RePro technique might have both stimulating and impeding effects on idea generation productivity. Firstly, we consider two stimulating effects: (1) a more complete exploration of the solution space, and (2) a reduction of cognitive effort required to start a new train of thought. Secondly, we discuss a potential impeding effect: (3) fixation on ideas that conform to examples offered by the technique.

Exploration of the solution space. Prior research suggests that individuals presented with an all-encompassing problem tend to explore only a small fraction of the potential solution space (e.g. [15 - 18]). This is caused by people's tendency to not leave the path of least resistance and reproduce slightly modified or even unmodified ideas that can be directly retrieved from memory [18]. As a result, key solution opportunities are missed. For example, unaided participants in [15] missed on average more than half of the solution categories while generating solutions for a parking as well as a housing problem.

Several studies suggest that problem decomposition into multiple categories might decrease the inclination to explore a small number of dominant solution categories. In the context of a natural environment problem [19], individual brainstormers who received stimulation ideas from a diverse range of solution categories outperformed unaided participants in terms of the diversity and number of ideas generated. Similarly, individual brainstormers in [17] receiving ten potential solution categories were more productive than unaided participants and participants receiving only two solution categories when generating ideas for improving their university.

The RePro technique also offers diverse stimulus ideas in the form of RePro principles. Hence, we expect that the RePro technique facilitates a more complete exploration of the solution space as well.

Cognitive effort required to start new train of thought. As indicated by the results of [17, 19], diverse stimuli do not only increase the diversity of ideas generated, but also increase productivity. The observed productivity increases might be attributable to the fact that diverse stimuli prevent individuals from completely running out of ideas. Given the fact that individual brainstormers in [17, 19] had to work under tight time constraints, it is not likely that this is the only mechanism responsible for the observed productivity increase.

Another mechanism responsible for the observed productivity increase was found in [19]. In a follow-up analysis, the researchers observed that unaided participants needed on average significantly more time for a category change (the next idea is from a different solution category) than for a category repetition (the next idea is from the same solution category). For participants receiving stimuli, this difference was not found. It appeared that stimulation ideas reduce the time for a category change to the level of a category repetition.

Accordingly, we expect that the RePro technique, which offers nine RePro categories, is able to reduce the cognitive effort to start exploring a new category of ideas (i.e. a new train of thought), with a productivity gain as a consequence.

Conformance to technique examples. Previous research indicates that concrete idea examples may constrain the ideas generated by individuals subsequently [20]. More precisely, generated ideas seem to conform to features of examples given prior to a design task [20]. Given ample time, such a conformity effect might also have negative consequences for the number of ideas that an individual is able to generate.

In a more recent study [21], individuals received design heuristics accompanied with application examples prior to a product design task. These design heuristics were conceptually similar to RePro principles, i.e. also contained a title, definition, explanation and example. The results of [21] indicate that multiple applications of the same design heuristic do not yield prescribed solutions. The researchers concluded that this finding supports the level of specificity of heuristics, suggesting that they support exploration without limiting possibilities (e.g. without a conformity effect).

Based on the conceptual similarity between the design heuristics in [21] and the RePro principles, we expect that the negative impact of the RePro technique on productivity due to a conformity effect is limited.

The three arguments above suggest that individuals using the RePro technique should be able to generate more ideas than individual brainstomers, i.e. individuals following the four brainstorming rules (quantity is wanted, freewheeling is welcomed, combine and improve ideas, and self-criticism is ruled out) [22].

Hypothesis 1: The RePro technique supports individuals in generating more ideas as compared to traditional brainstorming.

Satisfaction with and Intention-to-Use the Technique (H2 and H3). Prior research that gives insights into the potential effects of the RePro technique on satisfaction and intention-to-use is limited to case studies. In [23], a goal-driven approach for analyzing and improving business processes was evaluated. During the improvement phase of this approach, 28 process improvement principles were considered. The questionnaire evaluating users' perceptions indicated that users were satisfied with the approach and were willing to use it in future projects. However, the different phases of the approach were not separately evaluated. Consequently, it is hard to draw conclusions regarding users' perceptions of the technique supporting the improvement phase. In [24], professional engineers working on a new outdoor product line were observed while applying the design heuristics as mentioned in [21]. The results of this study were similar to the results in [23]. Given these positive findings and our expectation that users will experience the stimulating effects of the technique as mentioned in the previous section, we expect that users of the RePro technique are more satisfied with their technique than individual brainstormers, and have a positive intention-to-use the technique.

Hypothesis 2: Individuals using the RePro technique are more satisfied with their technique than individuals using traditional brainstorming.

Hypothesis 3: Individuals using the RePro technique have a positive intention-to-use the technique.

4   Research Method

In this section, we outline the set-up of our controlled experiment. In line with [25, 26], we describe the participants, experiment task, factor and factor levels, experiment procedure, response variables as well as the pre-test and pilot of our experiment.

Participants. The participants in our experiment were 89 graduate students in Industrial Engineering at Ghent University. Given the fact that many practitioners involved in generating process improvement ideas are not business process redesign experts, participants in our experiment were not required to be experts. We contend that the selected students are likely to be quite representative for novice process advisors involved in redesigning business processes.

To avoid problems with understanding process models that had to be studied as part of the experiment task, all participants were trained into the EPC process modeling notation prior to this experiment during a university lecture of one hour.

All students received course credit for participation in the experiment. Additionally, the three best performing students received a cash prize (€75, €50, €25).

Experiment Task. We asked participants to generate improvement ideas for the cataract surgery process at a University Medical Center. A cataract leads to a decrease in vision due to a clouding of the lens inside the eye, and is conventionally treated with surgery. The cataract surgery process describes all diagnosis and treatment steps from intake until discharge for cataract patients. As a basis for idea generation, all participants received a case-description of this process. Based on a long-term collaboration with the EyeClinic, we were able to create a real-life case-description together with its employees. The case-description included information about (1) redesign objectives (i.e. reducing costs and throughput-times, and increasing patient satisfaction), (2) redesign limitations (e.g. surgery supervision of assistants is required), (3) process models including projections of actual routing fractions, wait- and process times, and cost information, (4) textual process descriptions, and (5) main problem areas as identified by employees and patients (e.g. scheduling assistants work overtime). As such, the real-life case-description covers the typical inputs for generating process improvement ideas [27, 28].

Prior to the experiment, we conducted a pre-test and pilot study to check the understandability of the case-study description, as well as the time needed to read the description (see last part of this section for more details).

Factor and Factor Levels. The factor considered in this study is the technique used to generate process improvement ideas. Two factor levels are distinguished, resulting in two experiment conditions: *traditional brainstorming (TB)* and *RePro*. Participants were randomly assigned to one of the two conditions, leading to groups of 44 and 45 individuals per condition respectively. Individuals in the TB condition received an instruction document that included the four brainstorming rules formulated in process redesign terminology [22]. Individuals in the RePro condition received an instruction document that, besides these rules, included the list of 46 principles. As illustrated in Figure 2, each RePro principle contained a title, definition, explanation as well as an application example.

---

1. Control relocation: *'Move controls towards the customers'*
By moving checks and other operations that are part of a business process to the customer, cost can be reduced and customer satisfaction might increase. A disadvantage of this solution is a higher probability of fraud.
Example: Ask the patient, instead of the nurse, to pick up the drugs by the hospital pharmacy.

Fig. 2. Example of RePro principle in technique description.

To prevent a positive instrument bias, two reviewers independently checked that all application examples of the RePro principles were unrelated to the cataract surgery process.

Experiment Procedure. The experiment started with a plenary video message of the medical manager of the Eyeclinic. In this video message, the objective of the experiment task and cataract surgery process were briefly discussed. After this video message, all participants received a hand-out, which included a reading guide, a description of the experiment task, the case-description mentioned earlier and a technique description (TB or RePro). The first two steps in the experiment task description instructed participants in both conditions to read the case-description and technique description successively. As part of the RePro technique description, participants had to read a summary of the RePro technique and screen all RePro principles. These principles were investigated in more detail while generating ideas.

After the first two preparatory steps, participants in both conditions were asked to generate as many good process improvement ideas as possible while using the assigned technique. For each idea, all participants had to document the concrete process change as well as its expected effect. Additionally, participants in the RePro condition were asked to indicate which RePro principle inspired them to come up with the suggested improvement. For the complete experiment task, i.e. reading the hand-out, which included the case-description and the technique description, and generating process improvement ideas, all participants had 2 hrs 40 m available. Although this duration can be considered somewhat long, the pilot study revealed that students showed enthusiasm for the "real-life" experiment task and were motivated to keep on generating ideas until the end of the session.

Immediately after finishing the experiment task, participants received a digital, post-experiment questionnaire. Participants had to indicate personal characteristics (e.g. age, sex, and prior experience with cataract surgery processes), whether or not they used the assigned technique, and their satisfaction with the technique. Participants in the RePro condition were additionally asked about their intention-to-use the technique. Participants in the TB condition were not asked a similar question, due to the fact that they lacked detailed information with regard to a relevant benchmark, i.e. the RePro technique. After completing the questionnaire, all participants were debriefed and thanked, and the price winners were announced during a guest-lecture.

Response Variables. *Productivity* was determined by counting the number of unique ideas of each individual. Two reviewers, who where blind to experiment conditions, independently evaluated the entered input of each individual. They were instructed to identify redundant ideas, ideas not describing an improvement action (e.g. the phrase "waiting time before consultation is long" does not describe an improvement action), and ideas containing multiple unrelated ideas. Redundant ideas and ideas not describing an improvement action were eliminated for calculation purposes. Ideas containing multiple unrelated ideas were split for these purposes.

Satisfaction with the provided technique was measured using a single questionnaire item in line with [18]: How satisfied are you with the provided traditional brainstorming / RePro technique? Responses were given on a seven-point Likert scale ranging from "completely dissatisfied" (1) to "completely satisfied" (7).

Intention-to-use the RePro technique was measured using the two items of the Method Evaluation Model [29], which is based on the Technology Acceptance Model. More specifically, we used the following items: (1) I would definitely <u>not</u> use the RePro technique for similar process improvement initiatives (reverse scored); (2) I intend to use the RePro technique in preference to relying on just personal experience and intuition if I have to generate improvement ideas in future similar process improvement initiatives. Responses to both items were given on seven-point Likert scale ranging from "completely disagree" (1) to "completely agree" (7).

Pre-test and Pilot Experiment. Prior to the experiment, a pre-test and pilot experiment were conducted. The pre-test was used to check the understandability of the hand-out material and evaluate the timing of the session. During the pre-test, participants went through the complete experiment procedure as outlined earlier. However, at this stage, the post-experiment questionnaire was not used to measure the constructs as specified above (e.g. satisfaction with the provided technique), but to evaluate and improve the hand-out material. 12 students in Industrial Engineering with at least three-year education experience at Eindhoven University of Technology (TU/e) participated in the pre-test and were randomly assigned to the two experiment conditions. The pre-test led to a more brief description of the post-operative phase of the cataract surgery process, small improvements regarding the readability of process models, and minor textual updates of the hand-out material.

After the pretest, a pilot experiment was conducted to check the understandability of the updated hand-out material, post-experiment questionnaire, and the timing of the complete experiment procedure. 13 third-year undergraduate students in Industrial Engineering at TU/e were randomly assigned to the two conditions. The pilot study revealed that participants were motivated to use all time available to generate improvement ideas and were enthusiastic about the "real-life" experiment task. In addition, minor final textual corrections in the hand-out material were suggested.

5   Results

This section outlines the results of the experiment. Before presenting descriptive statistics and test results regarding our hypotheses, we discuss demographic information as well as data validation measurements and criteria.

Demographics. The average age of participants in our experiment was 22.6 years (std: 0.93 years). About 38% of these were female.

Data Validation Measurements and Criteria. For each of the three productivity correction types (i.e. redundant ideas, ideas not describing an improvement action, and ideas containing multiple unrelated ideas), two reviewers independently checked whether each entered input needed to be corrected or not. Percentages of agreements between the two reviewers were 98.9%, 99.8% and 97.9% respectively. The interrater reliability measurements in terms of Cohen's kappa were high as well: 0.74, 0.75 and 0.77. In total, 89 out of 1401 ideas (6.1%) were corrected.

We also checked whether all participants had used the assigned technique. Seven participants in the TB condition and one participant in the RePro condition indicated in the questionnaire that they had not used the assigned technique. Consequently, eight participants had to be removed. 37 and 44 participants remained in the TB and

RePro condition respectively. Note that none of the participants indicated to have prior experience with or knowledge about cataract surgery processes.

Finally, the reliability of the two-item construct intention-to-use in the question-naire was high: Cronbach's alpha = 0.87.

5.1 Results Hypotheses Testing

This section presents descriptive statistics and test results regarding our hypotheses.

Productivity (H1). Means (avg), standard deviations (std), medians (m), minimum (min) and maximum (max) values for productivity are presented in Table 2. In the TB condition, individuals generated on average 14.57 unique ideas. In the RePro condition, the average number of unique ideas generated was 17.82. Since the data were not normally distributed in the RePro condition ($p < 0.01$ in Shapiro Wilk test), the Mann-Whitney U-test was used to test for differences regarding productivity. No significant difference was found ($p = 0.082$) when using a confidence interval of 95%. As such, we did not find support for hypothesis 1.

Satisfaction with the Technique (H2). As shown in Table 2, the average satisfaction with the technique in the TB condition was 4.7 (on a seven-point Likert scale). In the RePro condition, the average satisfaction with the technique was 5.3. Since the data were not normally distributed in both conditions, we used the Mann-Whitney U-test to test for differences regarding satisfaction with the technique. A significant difference ($U = 1067.50$, $p = 0.013$) offered support for hypothesis 2.

Intention-to-Use the Technique (H3). Table 2 shows that the mean intention-to-use (ITU) of the RePro technique was 5.07 (on a seven-point Likert scale). 82% of the participants had a positive intention-to-use the RePro technique (ITU > 4). The percentages of participants with a neutral (ITU = 4) or negative (ITU < 4) intention-to-use the RePro technique were 14% and 5% respectively. The Wilcoxon Signed Rank test for non-normal distributions revealed that the median intention-to-use was significantly positive ($T = 789.50$; $p < 0.001$). As such, we found support for hypothesis 3.

Table 2. Descriptive statistics regarding productivity, satisfaction with the technique and intention-to-use the technique ($N_{TB} = 37$; $N_{RePro} = 44$).

Measure	TB			RePro		
	Min - Max	M	Avg (std)	Min - Max	M	Avg (std)
Productivity (number of unique ideas generated)	7 - 24	14	14.57 (0.76)	8 - 37	17	17.82 (1.11)
Satisfaction with the technique (seven-point Likert scale)	2 - 7	5	4.70 (0.20)	2 - 7	5.5	5.30 (0.21)
Intention-to-use the technique (seven-point Likert scale)				1 - 7	5.5	5.07 (0.18)

5.2   Results Follow-Up Analysis

The non-normal and double-peaked distribution of the number of unique ideas generated in the RePro condition, led us to investigate the idea generation logs in more detail and conduct follow-up discussions with eight individual participants in this condition[1]. By screening the idea generation logs of the participants and discussing our findings with participants, we identified two different styles of using the RePro technique. Several participants took the RePro principles as a starting point and went through them category-by-category to identify application opportunities. We will refer to this style as *opportunity-centric (OC)* generation. Other participants took the problem areas as identifiable in the case-description as a starting point. For identified process weaknesses, each time they screened the list of RePro principles to identity or label relevant solutions. This implies that the order of the RePro principles being applied did not follow the strict category-by-category application scheme. We will refer to this style as *problem-centric (PC)* generation.

To objectify the classification of participants regarding these two styles, the Adjusted Ratio of Clustering (ARC)[2] was calculated for each participant in the RePro condition. This ratio measures the degree to which consecutive ideas fall in the same RePro category corrected for chance [15, 30]. In this way, we received an indication for the degree of following an *opportunity-centric* category-by-category scheme (high ARC) versus a *problem-centric* approach (low ARC).

Productivity. Correlation analysis between ARC and productivity revealed a positive and significant correlation (Spearman's rho = 0.38; p = 0.012), which indicates that the usage style of RePro is strongly connected to productivity. In order to enable further statistical testing, we analyzed the ARC - productivity scatterplot in line with [31] to identify a cut-off point for classifying participants as adopters of either an OC or PC generation style. This analysis revealed a steep increase of the graph around ARC = 0.75. Hence, we decided to use ARC = 0.75 as cut-off value for classifying participants as being adopters of an OC (ARC >= 0.75) or PC generation (ARC < 0.75) style. Whereas the normality assumption had to be rejected for productivity data in the RePro condition before the ARC classification, the productivity distributions of the two post-hoc groups no longer violated this assumption (p > 0.05 in Shapiro Wilk test). This phenomenon further confirmed that our post-hoc classification was based on a relevant factor and appropriate cut-off value.

---

[1]   We used stratified sampling to gain the best insights into RePro usage styles: 4 individuals with a negative and 4 individuals with a positive intention-to use were randomly selected.

[2]   ARC = (R - E(R)) / (maxR - E(R)), where R is the number of observed RePro category repetitions (the next idea is from same solution category), E(R) is the expected number of RePro category repetitions according to chance, and maxR is the maximum number of RePro category repetitions. maxR = N - k, where N is the total number of ideas generated and k is the number of RePro categories surveyed by a participant. For ARC calculation purposes, redundant ideas as well as ideas not describing an improvement action were included, because these contain information with regard to the order in which RePro principles are considered. All ideas, including ideas containing multiple ideas, were labeled with the RePro principle as indicated by the participant. Based on this label, the related RePro category was determined and ARC calculations were performed.

As shown in Table 3, participants adopting an OC generation style in the RePro condition generated on average 24.77 unique ideas. Participants adopting a RePro PC generation style generated on average only 14.90 unique ideas. Recall that participants using TB generated on average 14.57 unique ideas. Since the normality assumption for each of these three groups was no longer violated, we conducted a one-way ANOVA to test for significant differences. Because the homogeneity of variances assumption was violated as assessed by the Levene Statistic ($p < 0.01$), we relied on the Welch ANOVA and related Games-Howell post-hoc tests. Productivity was significantly different between the three groups, Welch's $F(2, 29) = 8.20$, $p < 0.01$. Games-Howell post-hoc tests revealed that the participants using a RePro OC style generated significantly more ideas than participants in the two other groups (for both groups: $p < 0.01$). Differences between adopters of a RePro PC generation style and participants using TB were not significant ($p = 0.947$).

These results indicate that only adopters of an *opportunity-centric* application scheme of RePro generate more ideas than individual brainstormers. This provides us with an important insight as to the optimal use of the RePro technique, as will be discussed in more detail in the next section.

Table 3. Descriptive statistics regarding productivity for different generation styles ($N_{TB} = 37$; $N_{RePro\_PC} = 31$; $N_{RePro\_OC} = 13$).

Measure	TB			RePro_PC			RePro_OC		
	Min - Max	M	Avg (std)	Min - Max	M	Avg (std)	Min - Max	M	Avg (std)
Productivity	7 - 24	14	14.57 (0.76)	8 - 24	15	14,90 (0.76)	12 - 37	24	24.77 (2.40)

Satisfaction with the Technique. We did not identify a significant correlation between ARC and satisfaction with the RePro technique (Spearman's rho = 0.256; $p = 0.094$). In line with this result, pairwise comparisons of the three groups (i.e. TB, RePro_PC, RePro_OC) as part of the Kruskal Wallis test for multiple sample non-normal data did not reveal a significant differences between the PC (avg = 5.23; std = 0.26) and OC generation style (avg = 5.46; std = 0.39).

Intention-to-Use the Technique. A significant correlation between ARC and intention-to-use the RePro technique was neither identified (Spearman's rho = 0.252; $p = 0.099$). In line with this result, the Mann-Whitney U-test for two-sample non-normal data, did not lead to the identification of a significant difference between the PC (avg = 5.03; std = 0.21) and OC generation style (avg = 5.12; std = 0.38).

6   Discussion

In this paper, we investigated the impact of the RePro technique on productivity, satisfaction with and intention-to-use the technique, and compared its performance with traditional brainstorming.

Regarding productivity, we did not find direct support for our hypothesis that the RePro technique supports individuals in generating more process improvement ideas than traditional brainstormers. However, our follow-up analysis suggests that the usage style of the RePro technique is strongly connected to productivity. In our experiment, adopters of an *opportunity-centric* category-by-category application scheme generated 65-70% more ideas than *RePro* participants adopting a *problem-centric* generation style or participants using traditional brainstorming. These results are in line with [17], where it was found that presenting categories of solutions sequentially supports individuals in generating more ideas. The authors argued that a simultaneous presentation of solution categories may overwhelm individuals and prevent them from focusing attention adequately on each prime. Similarly, a *problem-centric* screening of the complete list of RePro principles is likely to prevent a productivity gain. Further research should investigate the impact of different usage styles of RePro on productivity and other outcome measures in more detail. In further experiments, participants might be more strongly guided to adopt an *opportunity-centric* generation style. For example, by making use of automated tool support the RePro principles can be offered piecemeal, i.e. category-by-category. Outcome effects of the *opportunity-centric* variant can then be investigated while taking into account potential moderators, such as a participant's Personal Need for Structure [32, 33].

In line with our second and third hypotheses, individuals using the RePro technique were more satisfied with the technique than individual brainstormers, and intend to use the technique in future projects. This finding is in line with qualitative evaluation of design heuristics in the context of a product design project [24]. Interestingly, the usage style of the RePro technique did not affect the satisfaction with and intention-to-use the technique. Apparently, participants adopting a *problem-centric* style were still satisfied with the technique and intended to use the technique in future projects, despite the absence of productivity gains. In post-experiment interviews, participants adopting this style mentioned that the RePro technique supported them in coming up with ideas that were different from familiar directions. This finding calls for further research investigating whether other outcomes besides productivity, such as diversity and originality of ideas, explain the satisfaction of these adopters.

Inevitably, there are some limitations to our work. As mentioned earlier, we focused on the quantity of ideas as the sole indicator of productivity. This focus was justified by the fact that the quantity of ideas and the number of high-quality ideas are typically strongly related [12 - 14]. Notwithstanding this, an evaluation of other outcomes, such as the diversity, originality, expected effectivity and feasibility of ideas, can give us additional insights into the effects of the RePro technique.

Also, the use of the Adjusted Ratio of Clustering (ARC) classification mechanism for distinguishing the two RePro generation styles can be further validated. By asking participants in future experiments to indicate their generation style, the results of the classification mechanism can be cross-checked and statistically tested.

Finally, we have to note that our experiment participants were graduate students in Industrial Engineering with basic training in process modeling and analysis. Although these students are likely to be representative for novice process advisors, one should be careful in generalizing our results to the redesign community at large. Based on reviews indicating consistency between findings from artificial laboratory studies and field studies in a number of different domains [34, 35], we do not expect causal inferences to be highly different for real-life settings.

7   Related Work

Besides the RePro technique, several other techniques have been developed that - in contrast to traditional brainstorming - offer guidance regarding the kind of process alternatives that are worthwhile to consider, e.g. techniques relying on BPR best practices (e.g. [8]) and techniques assuming the existence of a repository that includes specifications of numerous existing processes (e.g. [36 - 38]). A complete overview and analysis of these techniques is provided in [28]. As discussed there, many method-development studies do not include an evaluation mechanism or merely provide an illustration of how the technique can be applied. Only a small number of studies (e.g. [6, 23, 39]) includes a case study that investigates the application of the technique in practice [28]. These case studies include an evaluation of the technique, but lack possibilities for comparing the performance of the applied technique with the performance of competing techniques, e.g. brainstorming. Consequently, benefits attributable to the technique are still hard to determine. Although conducting controlled experiments is getting more common in the area of process modeling (e.g. [25, 26]), this study is, as far as we know, the first investigation to report on a controlled experiment in the area of generating process improvement ideas. We contend that our experiment offers an interesting alternative for traditional case studies, and enables a more rigorous evaluation of the benefits attributable to process improvement techniques.

8   Conclusion

Whereas many process improvement techniques have been developed during the last decade, little is known about the effectivity of these techniques. The reported experiment can be seen as the first endeavor to evaluate the performance of process improvement techniques in a controlled environment. In particular, we focused on evaluating the Rethinking of Processes (RePro) technique, which relies on a set of 46 process improvement principles, and compared its performance with traditional brainstorming. The results of the experiment confirm the potential of using a more advanced technique for generating process improvement ideas, but also indicate that the usage style of such a technique strongly affects its performance. Future experiments are recommended to investigate the effects of different usage styles of RePro on outcome measures in more detail.

Acknowledgement. We wish to thank Jan Claes, Frederik Gailly, Steven Mertens and Michaël Verdonck for their support in preparing and executing the experiment at UGent. We also thank Josette Gevers for her advice regarding the research design and Paul Grefen for his input with respect to improving the draft version of this paper. Finally, we are grateful to Frank van den Biggelaar, Rudy Nuijts and all other employees of the EyeClinic for offering us the opportunity to develop a real-life experiment task.

References

1. Van der Aalst, W.M.P.: Business Process Management: a comprehensive survey. ISRN Software Engineering **2013**, 1–37 (2013)
2. Netjes, M., Mans, R.S., Reijers, H.A., van der Aalst, W.M., Vanwersch, R.J.B.: BPR Best Practices for the Healthcare Domain. In: Rinderle-Ma, S., Sadiq, S., Leymann, F. (eds.) BPM 2009. LNBIP, vol. 43, pp. 605–616. Springer, Heidelberg (2010)
3. Netjes, M., Vanderfeesten, I.T., Reijers, H.A.: "Intelligent" Tools for Workflow Process Redesign: A Research Agenda. In: Bussler, C.J., Haller, A. (eds.) BPM 2005. LNCS, vol. 3812, pp. 444–453. Springer, Heidelberg (2006)
4. Limam Mansar, S., Reijers, H.A., Ounnar, F.: Development of a decision-making strategy to improve the efficiency of BPR. Expert. Syst. Appl. **36**, 3248–3262 (2009)
5. Griesberger, P., Leist, S., Zellner, G.: Analysis of techniques for business process improvement. In: 19th European Conference on Information Systems, paper 20. Association for Information Systems (2011)
6. Chai, K.-H., Zhang, J., Tan, K.-C.: A TRIZ-based method for new service design. J. Serv. Res. **8**, 48–66 (2005)
7. Vanwersch, R.J.B., Pufahl, L., Vanderfeesten, I., Mendling, J., Reijers, H.A.: How suitable is the RePro technique for rethinking care processes? Beta working paper no. 468, Eindhoven (2015)
8. Reijers, H.A., Limam Mansar, S.: Best practices in business process redesign: an overview and qualitative evaluation of successful redesign heuristics. Omega **33**, 283–306 (2005)
9. Hevner, A.R., March, S.T., Park, J., Ram, S.: Design science in information systems research. MIS Quarterly **28**, 75–105 (2004)
10. Van de Ven, A.H., Delbecq, A.L.: The effectiveness of nominal, Delphi, and interacting group decision making processes. Acad. Manage. J. **17**, 605–621 (1974)
11. Patrício, L., Fisk, R.P., Cunha, J.F.E., Constantine, L.: Multilevel service design: from customer value constellation to service experience blueprinting. J. Serv. Res. **14**, 180–200 (2011)
12. Parnes, S.J., Meadow, A.: Effects of "brainstorming" instructions on creative problem solving by trained and untrained subjects. J. Educ. Psychol. **50**, 171–176 (1959)
13. Diehl, M., Stroebe, W.: Productivity loss in brainstorming groups: Toward the solution of a riddle. J. Pers. Soc. Psychol. **53**, 497–509 (1987)
14. Stroebe, W., Nijstad, B.A., Rietzschel, E.F.: Beyond productivity loss in brainstorming groups: the evolution of a question. Adv. Exp. Soc. Psychol. **43**, 157–203 (2010)
15. Gettys, C.F., Pliske, R.M., Manning, C., Casey, J.T.: An evaluation of human act generation performance. Organ. Behav. Hum. Perform. **39**, 23–31 (1987)
16. Dennis, A.R., Valacich, J.S., Connolly, T., Wynne, B.E.: Process structuring in electronic brainstorming. Information Systems Research **7**, 268–277 (1996)
17. Coskun, H., Paul, P.B., Brown, V., Sherwood, J.J.: Cognitive stimulation and problem presentation in idea-generating groups. Group Dynamics: Theory, Research, and Practice **4**, 307–329 (2010)
18. Rietzschel, E.F., Nijstad, B.A., Stroebe, W.: Relative accessibility of domain knowledge and creativity: the effects of knowledge activation on the quantity and originality of generated ideas. J. Exp. Soc. Psychol. **43**, 933–946 (2007)
19. Nijstad, B.A., Stroebe, W., Lodewijkx, H.F.M.: Cognitive stimulation and interference in groups: exposure effects in an idea generation task. J. Exp. Soc. Psychol. **38**, 535–544 (2002)
20. Smith, S.M., Ward, T.B., Schumacher, J.S.: Constraining effects of examples in a creative generation task. Mem. Cognit. **6**, 837–845 (1993)

21. Daly, S.R., Christian, J.L., Yilmaz, S., Seifert, C.M., Gonzalez, R.: Assessing design heuristics for idea generation in an introductory engineering course. International Journal of Engineering Education **28**, 463–473 (2012)
22. Osborn, A.F.: Applied imagination. Charles Scribner's Sons, Oxford (1953)
23. Shahzad, K., Giannoulis, C.: Towards a Goal-Driven Approach for Business Process Improvement Using Process-Oriented Data Warehouse. In: Abramowicz, W. (ed.) BIS 2011. LNBIP, vol. 87, pp. 111–122. Springer, Heidelberg (2011)
24. Yilmaz, S., Christian, J.L., Daly, S.R., Seifert, C.M., Gonzalez, R.: Idea generation in collaborative settings. In: Kovacevic, A. et al. (eds.) E&PDE 2011. Creativity in Design Education, pp. 115–120 (2011)
25. Kolb, J., Zimoch, M., Weber, B., Reichert, M.: How social distance of process designers affects the process of process modeling: insights from a controlled experiment. In: 29th Annual Symposium on Applied Computing, pp. 1364–1370. ACM, New York (2014)
26. Weber, B., Zeitelhofer, S., Pinggera, J., Torres, V., Reichert, M.: How Advanced Change Patterns Impact the Process of Process Modeling. In: Bider, I., Gaaloul, K., Krogstie, J., Nurcan, S., Proper, H.A., Schmidt, R., Soffer, P. (eds.) BPMDS 2014 and EMMSAD 2014. LNBIP, vol. 175, pp. 17–32. Springer, Heidelberg (2014)
27. Vanwersch, R.J.B., Shahzad, K., Vanhaecht, K., Grefen, P., Pintelon, L., Mendling, J., Van Merode, G.G., Reijers, H.A.: Methodological support for business process redesign in health care: a literature review protocol. International Journal of Care Pathways **15**, 119–126 (2011)
28. Vanwersch, R.J.B., Shahzad, K., Vanderfeesten, I., Vanhaecht, K., Grefen, P., Pintelon, L., Mendling, J., Van Merode, G.G., Reijers, H.A.: Methodological support for business process redesign in healthcare: a systematic literature review. Beta working paper no. 437, Eindhoven (2013)
29. Moody, D.L.: The method evaluation model: a theoretical model for validating information systems design methods. In: 11th European Conference on Information Systems, paper 79. Association for Information Systems (2003)
30. Roenker, D.L., Thompson, C.P., Brown, S.C.: Comparison of measures for the estimation of clustering in free recall. Psychol. Bull. **76**, 45–48 (1971)
31. Williams, B.A., Mandrekar, J.N., Mandrekar, S.J., Cha, S.S., Furth, A.F.: Finding optimal cutpoints for continuous covariates with binary and time-to-event outcomes. Technical report series no. 79, Health Sciences Research Mayo Clinic Rochester, Minnesota (2006)
32. Rietzschel, E., Slijkhuis, J.M., Van Yperen, M.W.: Task structure, need for structure, and creativity. Eur. J. Soc. Psychol. **44**, 386–399 (2014)
33. Neuberg, S.L., Newsom, J.T.: Personal Need for Structure: Individual differences in the desire for simpler structure. J. Pers. Soc. Psychol. **65**, 113–131 (1993)
34. Anderson, C.A., Bushman, B.J.: External validity of ``trivial" experiments: The case of laboratory aggression. Rev. Gen. Psychol. **1**, 19–41 (1997)
35. Anderson, C.A., Lindsay, J.J., Bushman, B.J.: Research in the psychological laboratory: Truth of triviality? Curr. Dir. Psychol. Sci. **8**, 3–9 (1999)
36. Malone, T.W., Crowston, K., Lee, J., Pentland, B., Dellarocas, C., Wyner, G., Quimby, J., Osborn, C.S., Bernstein, A., Herman, G., Klein, M., O'Donnell, E.: Tools for inventing organizations: toward a handbook of organizational processes. Management Science **45**, 425–443 (1999)
37. Klein, M., Petti, C.: A handbook-based methodology for redesigning business processes. Knowledge and Process Management **13**, 108–119 (2006)
38. Margherita, A., Klein, M., Elia, G.: Metrics-based process redesign with the MIT process handbook. Knowledge and Process Management **14**, 46–57 (2007)
39. Nissen, M.E.: An intelligent tool for process redesign: manufacturing supply-chain applications. International Journal of Flexible Manufacturing Systems **12**, 321–339 (2000)

Inspection Coming Due! How to Determine the Service Interval of Your Processes!

Jonas Manderscheid[1(✉)], Daniel Reißner[1], and Maximilian Röglinger[2]

[1] FIM Research Center, University of Augsburg, Augsburg, Germany
{jonas.manderscheid,daniel.reissner}@fim-rc.de
[2] FIM Research Center, University of Bayreuth, Bayreuth, Germany
maximilian.roeglinger@fim-rc.de

Abstract. Just like cars, processes require a general inspection from time to time. As, in reality, process portfolio managers are in charge of many processes, they do not have enough resources to deeply inspect all processes simultaneously. Nor would this be reasonable from a process performance point of view. Process portfolio managers therefore require guidance on how to determine the service interval of their processes, i.e., when they should analyze which process in depth to find out whether to initiate redesign projects. Despite the profound knowledge on process improvement, monitoring, and controlling, existing approaches are only able to rank processes or redesign projects. They do not indicate when to conduct an in-depth analysis. To overcome this research gap, we propose the critical process instance method (CPIM) that analytically predicts after which number of executed instances a process should undergo an in-depth analysis. The CPIM combines ideas from process performance management, value-based business process management, and stochastic processes. It accounts for variations in process performance induced by the paths and tasks included in a process model as well as by the positive and negative deviance experienced during past executions. For demonstration purposes, we apply the CPIM to an approval process for loan applications from the banking industry including a scenario analysis.

Keywords: Business process management · Deviance · Process decision-making · Process performance management · Stochastic processes

1   Introduction

Process orientation is an accepted paradigm of organizational design with a proven impact on corporate performance [21]. Business process management (BPM) therefore receives constant attention from industry and academia [13], [44]. Global surveys and literature reviews corroborate the interest in BPM in general and business process redesign in particular [27], [35]. As, during the last years, BPM has proposed many approaches to the design, analysis, improvement, and enactment of processes [17], [39], the BPM's focus is shifting towards managerial topics [43]. In this paper, we

©Springer International Publishing Switzerland 2015
H.R. Motahari-Nezhad et al. (Eds.): BPM 2015, LNCS 9253, pp. 19–34, 2015.
DOI: 10.1007/978-3-319-23063-4_2

investigate a novel managerial research question, i.e., how to determine when processes should undergo an in-depth analysis to check whether they require redesign.

This research question bears resemblance to the car industry, as processes, just like cars, require a general inspection from time to time [18]. Whereas car inspections focus on technical issues, an in-depth process analysis needs an economic perspective as well. Process portfolio managers require guidance on how to determine the service interval of their processes, leveraging performance data like a car's mileage from process aware information systems [37], [47]. As process portfolio managers do not have enough resources to analyze all processes simultaneously and as processes should not undergo an in-depth analysis too often, providing such guidance is a worthwhile endeavor [7].

From a literature perspective, the BPM body of knowledge abounds in approaches to process redesign, monitoring, and controlling [35]. Approaches to process monitoring and controlling primarily focus on technically enabling the assessment of the state of a process, e.g., using complex event processing or modelling of control objectives [19], [22], [34]. Most redesign approaches take a single-process perspective, e.g., they propose redesign projects for single processes based on an identified need for redesign [41], [46]. The need for redesign is typically quantified via performance indicators [13], [24]. Very few approaches investigate how to select or schedule redesign projects for multiple processes [10], [23]. Bandara et al. [1] discuss approaches to process prioritization, classifying them as "either of very high level and hence not of much assistance [...] or [...] so detailed that it can take a significant effort to simply identify the critical processes." Some approaches to process prioritization help rank processes or redesign projects [10], [28], [30]. No approach, however, helps determine when processes should undergo the next in-depth analysis to check whether they require redesign.

To address the research gap, we propose the critical process instance method (CPIM) that analytically predicts after which number of executed instances a process should undergo the next in-depth analysis. An in-depth process analysis is a thorough and resource-intense means of identifying variations in process performance and respective root causes (e.g., including simulation and diagnosis, verification, and process mining) [13], [41]. The CPIM builds on knowledge from process performance management and value-based BPM using process cash flows as performance indicators [6], [25]. To predict the risky performance of future process instances in terms of their cash flows, the CPIM draws from stochastic processes, a tool commonly used in financial mathematics [8]. The CPIM is data- and model-driven as it accounts for two types of performance variation, i.e., variation induced by the paths and tasks included in process models and variation induced by positive or negative deviance experienced during past executions. That is, the CPIM uses historical performance data not only to analyze how a process currently performs, but also to forecast future performance. Our contribution is a new method that extends prior work on process performance management and value-based BPM via predictive components based on stochastic processes.

The paper is organized as follows: In section 2, we outline the background with respect to process monitoring and controlling, process performance management, value-based BPM, and stochastic processes. In section 3, we introduce the CPIM and illustrate how it fits into the BPM lifecycle by a general monitoring and controlling cycle. In section 4, we report the results of applying the CPIM to an approval process for loan applications from the banking industry including a scenario analysis. In section 5, we critically discuss results and limitations. We conclude by pointing to future research.

2   Theoretical Background

2.1   Business Process Monitoring and Controlling

From a lifecycle perspective, BPM involves the identification, discovery, analysis, redesign, and implementation plus the monitoring and controlling of processes [13]. Continuous monitoring and controlling as well as adequate redesign are necessary to prevent process performance from degenerating over time. Reasons are the organic nature of processes and the evolving environment [13]. While people are bound in day-to-day operations, processes become more complex and lose performance. Multiple actors and resources influence one another, while being influenced themselves by the technological and organizational environment [3]. The unexpected behavior of employees as well as other kinds of unexpected change let emerge process instances that deviate from the process model [40]. Deviance becomes manifest in better or worse performance compared to the "normal" performance in case of positive or negative deviance. Deviance can be analyzed manually or automated, e.g., using sequence mining [29]. In sum, the organic evolution of processes over time allows for interpreting processes as a specific subset of organizational routines at drift [3].

The key part of process monitoring and controlling is to determine how well is the process performs with respect to defined performance indicators and targets as well as to identify bottlenecks, waste, and deviance [13], [33]. The monitoring and controlling phase can be considered from an operational and a strategic perspective [25]. Operationally, process managers and process-aware information systems continuously observe process performance regarding the target values and undertake corrective actions if necessary without changing the process model [22]. The operational perspective can be linked with each single process instance. The strategic perspective strives for novel process models through redesign, when the target can no longer be reached or critical performance thresholds are violated. In this case, processes must undergo an in-depth analysis whose results serve as input for a subsequent redesign.

2.2   Process Performance Management and Value-Based BPM

To assess the performance of a process, organizations use performance indicators together with desired target values (benchmarks) and admissible value ranges [25]. Process performance indicators can be grouped via the Devil's Quadrangle, a framework comprising a time, cost, quality, and flexibility dimension [32]. The Devil's Quadrangle is so-named because improving one dimension weakens at least one other, disclosing the trade-offs to be resolved during redesign. To resolve the partly conflicting nature of these performance dimensions via integrated performance indicators, the principles of value-based management have been applied to process performance management [6].

Value-based management is a paradigm where all corporate activities and decisions are valued according to their contribution to the company value [15]. A process-related performance indicator that complies with value-based management is the risk-adjusted expected net present value of the process cash flows [6]. This indicator can be decomposed into risky cash flows per process instance [5]. A process model consists of tasks and gateways that define the paths along which a model can be traversed. Each instance follows a distinct path. The instance cash flows result from the tasks included in the paths (e.g., outflows for wages) as well as independently from the paths (e.g., inflows for selling a product). The instance cash flows are risky, i.e., they are beset with variation, as it is unclear ex-ante which path an instance takes and because the cash flows of the tasks show variation themselves (e.g., consulting a customer takes different amounts of time, which causes different outflows) [5]. Task cash flows are risky as they depend on characteristics such as wages, material prices, time, or quality [13], [42]. In line with value-based management, instance cash flows are characterized in terms of their expected value and variance, capturing all path and task information [6]. Bolsinger [5] proposed a method for determining both figures for arbitrary process models. Using the expected value and the variance of instance cash flows is reasonable as, according to the central limit theorem, cumulated instance cash flows are approximately normally distributed for sufficiently many instances and independent from how the cash flows of single instances are distributed [5]. This property holds for the net present value of the process cash flows and the aggregated difference from a performance benchmark, which allows for providing analytical decision support. In sum, instance cash flows are a reasonable value-based performance indicator for monitoring and controlling purposes, whereas more complex value-based performance indicators such as the risk-adjusted expected net present value fit the preparation of investments in process redesign.

2.3   Predicting Process Performance Using Stochastic Processes

The performance data collected during process monitoring and controlling form an essential input for forecasting the performance of future process instances. While redesign projects can be initiated based on the insights from the last in-depth analysis, predicting when a process should undergo the next in-depth analysis requires information about future process executions, i.e., about the risky development of process performance. As this problem is similar to the assessment of risky price movements, we adopt the concept of stochastic processes from mathematical finance.

Stochastic processes are typically used to model the behavior of physical or mathematical systems [36]. This behavior is characterized by transitions among a finite or infinite number of states over time. At a distinct point in time, a system is in a distinct state. As transitions among states occur either at discrete points in time or continuously, there is a distinction between discrete and continuous stochastic processes. Mathematically speaking, a stochastic process is a family of random variables

$\{X_t\}_{t \in T}$ denoting the transition probabilities for different states at time t. Stochastic processes are further classified according to the properties of the transition probabilities and the evolution of states. If transition probabilities do not change over time, the stochastic process is homogenous. If the evolution of a stochastic process is invariant to shifts in time, the process is stationary, i.e., it has a stationary distribution for being in certain recurrent states at time t, if $t \to \infty$ [36]. Otherwise, the stochastic process is non-stationary.

Mathematical finance is a typical application domain of stochastic processes. As financial products can be traded at virtually each point in time such that the value of these products changes continuously, continuous stochastic processes are used to enable risk-neutral assessments of options or other derivatives based on interest rates [4], [9]. Stochastic processes also enable trading strategies based on volatility forecasts or risk management according to the value-at-risk approach [12], [26]. Even portfolio investment strategies are based on stochastic processes [14].

Since the development of process performance is driven by process instances, continuous stochastic processes do not fit the BPM context. Rather, discrete stochastic processes are appropriate, such as shown in the field of stochastic process control, a fundamental concept of six sigma [2]. As all instances of a process follow the same process model, the transition probabilities do not change over time. The stochastic process is homogenous. The number of states depends on the used performance indicator. It is finite for qualitative, ordinally scaled performance indicators (e.g., a customer satisfaction index). In case of quantitative, metrically scaled indicators, such as the risky instance cash flows, the number of states is infinite. Considering stationarity, both cases are possible as shown in stochastic process control [45]. A stochastic process that models aggregated performance (e.g., aggregated difference from a performance benchmark) does not have a stationary distribution as the value range of the aggregated performance increases with an increasing number of executed process instances.

3   The Critical Process Instance Method

3.1   General Setting

The CPIM predicts after which critical number of executed process instances (CPI) a process should undergo the next in-depth analysis. As it is neither possible nor reasonable to work on all processes simultaneously, the CPIM uses an individual process as unit of analysis. The central input of the CPIM is the related process model annotated with cash flows [41]. If available, the CPIM also considers historical process data (e.g., from event logs) to achieve better predictions by catering for deviant behavior. Depending on the available performance data, the risky instance cash flows $\widetilde{CF}$ can be determined based on real values from past executions or be estimated based on process simulation or experts [13], [39], [42]. As discussed in section 2.2, the expected value and the variance of the instance cash flows can be calculated based on Bolsinger [5]. We make the following assumptions:

(A.1) The processes included in the organization's process portfolio can be analyzed independently. Sufficient performance data is available or can be estimated for the process in focus. The CPIM does not consider external events that may trigger an extraordinary, potentially earlier in-depth analysis (e.g., price changes, new competitors).

(A.2) The expected values and variances of the cash flows associated with process tasks are finite and known (or can be estimated). The cash flows of single process instances are independent, i.e., the expected value $E[\widetilde{CF}]$ and variance $Var[\widetilde{CF}]$ of the instance cash flows can be calculated based on Bolsinger [5].

Besides the performance indicator $\widetilde{CF}$, the organization must provide a process-specific performance benchmark β [25]. This benchmark could be any target value set by the management or just the expected value of the instance cash flows.

3.2   The Role of Variation and Deviance

Comparing the cash flows of a specific instance with the performance benchmark provides no information about future process instances. It only shows the difference between that instance and the benchmark, not a trend in process performance. To determine the CPI, the organization must be able to predict process performance. Thus, it should account for two types of performance variation, i.e., variation induced by the tasks and paths included in the process model and variation induced by positive or negative deviance from the process model experienced in the past.

Although handling process instances in a compliant way, the first type of variation results from the process model itself depending on the process paths as discussed in section 2.2. Thus, the planned model-induced cash flows of a process instance $\widetilde{CF}_{\text{Model}}$, i.e., the cash flows that result from executing the process according to its current model, are a random variable whose distribution depends on the control flow of the process model as well as on the risky cash flows that relate to tasks. The expected value and the variance of the model-induced cash flows are shown in Formula (1) and (2).

$$\mu_{\text{Model}} = E[\widetilde{CF}_{\text{Model}}] \qquad (1) \qquad \sigma_{\text{Model}}^2 = Var[\widetilde{CF}_{\text{Model}}] \qquad (2)$$

The second type of variation results from positive or negative deviance experienced during past executions, i.e., behavior not covered by the process model as used in the past. In fact, process users sometimes run a process in a way not intended by the process owner [3]. As, for instance, more or fewer tasks are executed and new process paths emerge, this type of variation results in deviance-induced cash flows $\widetilde{CF}_{\text{Dev}}$. Deviance-induced cash flows take positive or negative values in case of positive or negative deviance, respectively. We consider deviant executions that largely comply with the process model. Deviance can, for example, be identified by analyzing event data from past executions using sequence mining [29]. To use the deviance experienced during past executions as a predictor for future deviance, we make the following assumption:

(A.3) The historic model-induced cash flows $\widetilde{CF}_{\text{Model,hist}}$ and the actual cash flows recorded from past executions $\widetilde{CF}_{\text{Log,hist}}$ feature a strong positive correlation $0 \ll \rho < 1$. Although the process model may have changed over time (e.g., due to the implementation of redesign projects), the process model used in the past only slightly differs from the process model to be used as foundation of future executions. Further, the current process users are about the same as in the past.

Assumption (A.3) implies that the cash flows recorded from past executions result from many instances with compliant and very few instances with deviant behavior. Assuming a strong positive correlation is a reasonable compromise between assuming independence, which would heavily overestimate the variance of the deviance-induced cash flows, and assuming a perfect correlation, which would underestimate the variance of the deviance-induced cash flows. If the recorded cash flows were indeed independent of the historic model-induced cash flows, all process instances would have shown deviant behavior. Perfect correlation would imply that all instances had perfectly complied with the process model. Both options seem unrealistic. We investigate the sensitivity of the CPIM with respect to this parameter in the demonstration section.

On this foundation, the deviance-induced cash flows can be calculated as difference between the cash flows actually recorded for past process executions and the historic model-induced cash flows that should have been recorded based on the process model used in the past [36]:

$$\mu_{\text{Dev}} = \mu_{\text{Log,hist}} - \mu_{\text{Model,hist}} \tag{3}$$

$$\sigma_{\text{Dev}}{}^2 = \sigma_{\text{Log,hist}}{}^2 + \sigma_{\text{Model,hist}}{}^2 - 2 \cdot \rho \cdot \sigma_{\text{Log,hist}} \cdot \sigma_{\text{Model,hist}} \tag{4}$$

As it is not possible to determine the exact correlation ρ mathematically, it must be set outside the CPIM. If an organization cannot access recorded data from event logs at all, only the first type of variation can be used for predicting the development of process performance. The prediction results then are less precise compared to the case where the deviance-induced variation is included as well. Based on this information, we can formulate the risky cash flows of a single instance via a compound random variable:

$$\widetilde{CF} = \widetilde{CF}_{\text{Model}} + \widetilde{CF}_{\text{Dev}} \tag{5}$$

Thus, the performance of a single instance can be predicted based on past and planned cash flows. As the organization is interested in determining the CPI, it must be able to identify trends in process performance. Therefore, the organization needs aggregated information about future process instances. We therefore calculate the aggregated difference $\delta(n)$ from the process benchmark β, shown in Formula (6), as a discrete stochastic process where n refers to the number of executed instances. Remember that the cash flows of instances from the same process are identically distributed as they share the same process model. Thus, the aggregated difference is a sum of independent and identically distributed (iid) random variables and can be treated as a normally distributed random variable for sufficiently many process instances according to the central limit theorem [36]. In addition, the property of identically distributed cash flows results in homogenous transitions. In contrast to many homogenous stochastic processes, the distribution of $\delta(n)$ will be non-stationary as the value range of the aggregated performance increases with the number of executed instances.

$$\delta(n) = \sum_{1}^{n}(\widetilde{CF} - \beta) \tag{6}$$

Hence, the aggregated difference serves as central indicator for determining the CPI.

3.3   Determining the Critical Process Instance

As the instance cash flows follow Formula (5), the value range of the aggregated difference from the process benchmark is cone-shaped, as illustrated in Figure 1 [11]. The cone represents the upper limit $UL(n)$ and the lower limit $LL(n)$ of the aggregated difference's value range after a distinct amount of executed instances n and at a distinct probability. As the aggregated difference is a sum of random variables, the upper and the lower limit increase and decrease with an increasing number of executed instances. That is, the cone is small in the near future after and broadens in the farer future expressed in terms of executed instances.

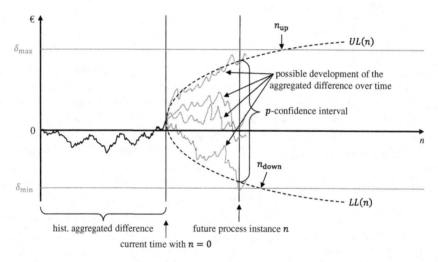

Fig. 1. Determination of the process instances n_{down} and n_{up}

As the aggregated difference from the performance benchmark is risky, it may take any value. Therefore, we use a confidence interval in which the true value of the aggregated difference lies with the probability $p \in]0; 1[$, also known as the confidence level. Consequently, the value of the aggregated difference is outside the confidence interval with a probability of $(1 - p)$. The confidence level must be set by the management. A confidence level p of 95% is typically used in statistics [11]. Transferred to the CPIM, the factual aggregated difference from the performance benchmark then lies outside the upper and lower limits with a probability of 2.5%, respectively. The larger the confidence level, the broader the confidence interval.

The upper limit $UL(n)$ and the lower limit $LL(n)$ of the confidence interval are calculated as shown in Formula (8) and (9) [11]. Based on assumption (A.3), the variables $\widehat{CF}_{\text{Model}}$ and $\widehat{CF}_{\text{Dev}}$ feature the correlation ρ as well because the current process model is very similar to the historical process model. Further, the function $\phi^{-1}(p)$ is the inverse function of the normal distribution for the chosen confidence level. We use this function as the aggregated difference, as specified in Formula (5) follows a normal distribution. Formula (7) represents the diffusion of the stochastic process ξ.

$$\xi = \sigma_{\text{Model}}^2 + \sigma_{\text{Dev}}^2 + 2 \cdot \rho \cdot \sigma_{\text{Model}} \cdot \sigma_{\text{Dev}} \tag{7}$$

$$UL(n) = n \cdot (\mu_{\text{Dev}} + \mu_{\text{Model}} - \beta) + \phi^{-1}(p) \cdot \sqrt{\xi \cdot n} \tag{8}$$

$$LL(n) = n \cdot (\mu_{\text{Dev}} + \mu_{\text{Model}} - \beta) - \phi^{-1}(p) \cdot \sqrt{\xi \cdot n} \tag{9}$$

Besides the performance benchmark, we need thresholds concerning the aggregated difference from the performance benchmark to determine the CPI. The process in focus should undergo an in-depth analysis if the aggregated difference violates one of the thresholds at the given confidence level to check whether the aggregated difference factually violates a threshold. According to [20], [31], and [3], the organization must balance two conflicting goals: Staying competitive by conducting redesign projects earlier vs. avoiding resistance by conducting redesign projects later. Thus, the organization must define two thresholds for the aggregated difference, one upper δ_{max} and one lower δ_{min} threshold. The upper threshold represents the value at which the organization has gathered enough information about positive deviance that could be used to realize first mover advantages or to reflect on a reallocation of resources currently assigned to the process. The lower threshold represents the value at which a negative development of process performance endangers the profitability or competitiveness of the process.

Based on the thresholds and the information about the future development of the aggregated difference, we can determine the CPI after which the aggregated difference falls short of or exceeds the thresholds at the given confidence level. We calculate the number of instances for which the upper and the lower limit of the confidence interval intersect the upper and lower threshold following Formula (10) and (11).

$$n_{\text{down}} = \left\lceil \min\left\{ \left(\frac{+\phi^{-1}(p) \cdot \sqrt{\xi} \pm \sqrt{\phi^{-1}(p)^2 \cdot \xi - 4 \cdot (\mu_{\text{Dev}} + \mu_{\text{Model}} - \beta) \cdot (-\delta_{\text{min}})}}{2 \cdot (\mu_{\text{Dev}} + \mu_{\text{Model}} - \beta)} \right)^2 \right\} \right\rceil \tag{10}$$

$$n_{\text{up}} = \left\lceil \min\left\{ \left(\frac{-\phi^{-1}(p) \cdot \sqrt{\xi} \pm \sqrt{\phi^{-1}(p)^2 \cdot \xi - 4 \cdot (\mu_{\text{Dev}} + \mu_{\text{Model}} - \beta) \cdot (-\delta_{\text{max}})}}{2 \cdot (\mu_{\text{Dev}} + \mu_{\text{Model}} - \beta)} \right)^2 \right\} \right\rceil \tag{11}$$

If the benchmark equals the expected performance of the process, i.e., $\beta = \mu_{\text{Dev}} + \mu_{\text{Model}}$, Formulas (10) and (11) can be simplified as follows:

$$n_{\text{down}} = \left\lceil \left(\frac{\delta_{\text{min}}}{\phi^{-1}(p) \cdot \sqrt{\xi}} \right)^2 \right\rceil \tag{12} \qquad n_{\text{up}} = \left\lceil \left(\frac{\delta_{\text{max}}}{-\phi^{-1}(p) \cdot \sqrt{\xi}} \right)^2 \right\rceil \tag{13}$$

The CPI then equals the smaller number of instances:

$$n^* = \min\{n_{\text{down}}; n_{\text{up}}\} \tag{14}$$

3.4   Integration into the BPM Lifecycle

As mentioned, the BPM lifecycle covers the phases identification, discovery, analysis, redesign, implementation as well as monitoring and controlling. A vital part of monitoring and controlling is "to determine how well is the process performing with respect to its performance measures and performance objectives" [13]. Since the CPIM identifies the critical number of instances, it belongs to the monitoring and controlling phase. We therefore investigate how the CPIM can be integrated into this phase.

First, the CPIM determines the next CPI of a specific process. Therefore, our proposed monitoring and controlling cycle follows an iterative approach, as shown in Figure 2: In the beginning, the expected value and the variance are calculated based on the current process model. If available, the performance data gathered in a preceding in-depth analysis can serve as input. For instance, performance data can be extracted from event logs [38]. These performance data fit past process executions, if the process model has not changed. Otherwise, the performance data from past executions must be collected separately. After that, the process benchmark and the thresholds must be set. Then, the CPI is calculated based on past and planned cash flows, following three steps: First, the past deviance and, second, the intersections between the thresholds and the confidence interval are determined. Third, the CPI is selected. Now, the process is executed until the CPI is reached, before an in-depth analysis is conducted to assess whether the process required redesign. If the in-depth analysis concludes that the process performance is uncritical, the CPIM is applied again. The organization may also adapt the thresholds or the benchmark in response to changes in the corporate environment. Otherwise, a redesign project should be started. No forecast is needed until the redesign is finished.

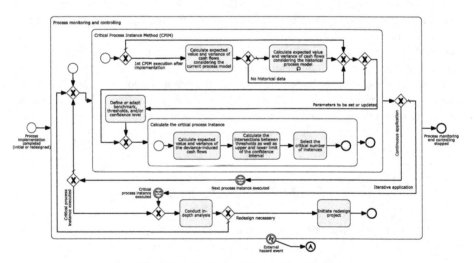

Fig. 2. Monitoring and Controlling Cycle

In cases of IT-supported process performance management or business activity monitoring, the CPIM can be applied continuously, i.e., after each finished process instance. As the performance forecast also grounds on data from past executions, each instance provides knowledge about process performance and deviance. As the deviance-induced cash flows affect the intersection between the thresholds and the confidence interval, they can be used to continuously adjust the scheduling of the next in-depth analysis.

Finally, the CPIM can be used as a tool for process portfolio management, taking a multi-process perspective. When applying the CPIM to multiple processes, the process portfolio manager receives information about the CPI for each process. Hence, the process portfolio manager is not only able to prioritize processes such as already supported by existing approaches, but also to schedule several in-depth analyses, taking into account possible resource restrictions.

4   Demonstration Example

For demonstration purposes, we apply the CPIM to an exemplary approval process for loan applications from the banking industry. We first present the process models that contain the information needed for the calculation, including the properties of the deviance-induced cash flows. We then determine and analyze the CPI using a scenario analysis to discuss the sensitivity of the CPIM.

The approval process for loan applications is an internal back-office process. The planned – historical and future – process model, shown in Figure 3, starts with a request of the bank agency. First, an employee of the loan approval department gathers the necessary customer data. Before the internal assessment, an external rating agency assesses the customer's creditworthiness. If the customer is creditworthy, the application comes to a decision based on the four-eyes-principle. Two independent and positive assessments are required for specifying the contract conditions and accepting the loan application. Otherwise, creditworthiness is denied and the application is declined. As it is for internal use only, we consider a transfer price as cash inflow in addition to cash outflows induced by task processing when calculating the process cash flows.

As it is part of the CPIM, we also include information about the process model and the associated deviant behavior extracted from log data (differing parts are presented in gray and where appropriate with dashed lines in Figure 3). The main difference is that internal creditworthiness assessors consolidate their information before the final judgment and may ask for further customer information one time. Furthermore, the factual task cash flows as well as the particular path probabilities differ from the planned ones.

We analytically calculate the expected values and variances of both process models. As this is a fictitious example, we estimate the distribution properties of the past executions. To visualize the deviance-induced cash flows, we determined the density functions of the process instance cash flows for both process models using simulation. The results in Figure 4 show that simple distributions such as the normal distribution typically do not fit the instance cash flows. It can also be seen that the planned process model overestimated the expected value and underestimated the variation of the instance cash flows. Based on these insights, the model-induced as well as the deviance-induced variation can be calculated and included in the CPIM.

Besides the parameters gathered from process models or logs, the management must set the critical thresholds, the performance benchmark, and the confidence level. It must also determine the correlation between the model-induced cash flows and the cash flows recorded from past executions (e.g., approximating by the fraction of instances adhering to the historical process model or the quotient $\sigma_{Model}/\sigma_{Log}$ as it explains the variance of the cash flows recorded from past executions that cannot be explained by the process model). Since estimation errors can occur in real-world applications (e.g., when reconstructing an event log), we consider different scenarios to evaluate the sensitivity of the CPIM. Table 1 summarizes the results.

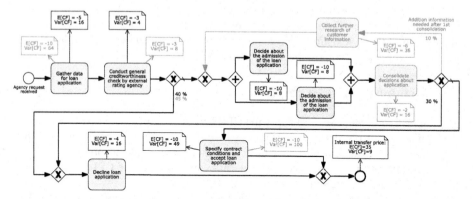

Fig. 3. Process model based on design and log data (deviant tasks and properties in gray)

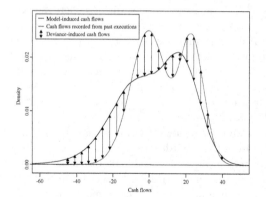

	μ	σ
Model	8.48	213.55
Log	2.83	298.60
Dev	-5.65	$512.15 - 505.04 \cdot \rho$

Fig. 4. Density functions of the process instance cash flows

Table 1. Results of the scenario analysis

No.	ρ	p	β	δ_{min}	δ_{max}	n_{down}	n_{up}	n^*
1	0.70	0.80	8.48	-1,000	1,000	133	n.d.	133
2	0.70	0.80	5.65	-1,000	1,000	238	n.d.	238
3	0.70	0.90	5.65	-1,000	1,000	194	n.d.	194
4	0.70	0.90	2.83	-1,000	1,000	966	1,249	966
5	0.70	0.90	2.83	-500	250	241	78	78
6	0.80	0.90	2.83	-500	250	269	74	74
7	0.80	0.90	1.41	-500	250	n.d.	42	42
8	0.80	0.99	1.41	-500	250	n.d.	18	18
9	0.80	0.99	1.41	-500	1,000	n.d.	191	191

The results can be interpreted as follows (with corresponding scenarios in brackets):

1. The variation of the benchmark confirms that a benchmark close to the actual performance increases the CPI and postpones the next in-depth analysis (3 & 4). Larger differences between the benchmark and the performance lead to unilateral solutions, i.e., one threshold will never be reached (1 & 7). As there is no solution for the calculation of the second intersection, one CPI is not defined ("n.d."). In this case, the process heavily under- or over-performs.

2. The results show that the thresholds have a higher impact on the CPI, if the actual process performance is close to the benchmark, i.e., the process executions meet the process target (4 & 5 and 8 & 9). As the cone of the confidence interval is a concave curve, this is not a counterintuitive observation, but must be remembered by process managers when defining the thresholds.

3. Just like the thresholds, the breadth of the confidence interval expressed by the confidence level influences the CPI (2 & 3 and 7 & 8). An increased confidence level heavily reduces the CPI. A higher confidence level increases the probability that the predicted process performance matches with the real future one.

4. Finally, the demonstration example contains statements about the influence of the correlation between the model-induced cash flows and the cash flows recorded during past executions (5 & 6). A higher correlation implies a lower variance of the deviance-induced cash flows and, therefore, a more distant CPI. It can be seen that the CPI is less sensitive to the correlation compared to other parameters such as the confidence level. The effect of a differing correlation on the CPIM is very limited.

The scenario analysis provides insights into the sensitivity of the CPIM against estimation errors. The assumption of a strong positive correlation between the model-induced cash flows and the cash flows recorded from past executions has a small effect on the CPI. The thresholds and the confidence level affect the CPI much more strongly. Determining these parameters thus requires special care. The process-specific performance benchmark has the greatest effect on the CPI. Therefore, process targets should be very clear and set very mindfully – not just because of the application of the CPIM.

5   Discussion

As the CPIM is beset with limitations, we compile noteworthy discussion points that, e.g., arise from the CPIM's assumptions. The most important point relates to the assumed independence of process instances (A.2). This simplification has weaknesses compared to techniques from time series analysis (e.g., autocorrelation, asymmetric effects), particularly when using deviance-induced cash flows. Deviance-induced cash flows, however, are only an optional input of the CPIM. As event logs are not available for all processes, the CPIM is content with model-induced cash flows that can be estimated by process experts. Thus, the CPIM also applies to processes where no historical data is available, which is not the case for techniques from time series analysis. Moreover, assumption (A.2) enabled building on Bolsinger's results [5]. It cannot be easily assessed how (A.2) influences the results of the CPIM. Thus, a thorough comparison between the CPIM and time series analysis should be conducted in future research.

Further, the CPIM focuses on single processes and abstracts from interactions among processes. In reality, however, we find portfolios of interacting processes. Hence, the CPIM should be extended such that the critical number of instances accounts for interactions among processes. Moreover, the CPIM only incorporates performance data that results from deviance experienced during past executions as well as performance data that can be expected to occur based on the current process model. The CPIM neglects external events that may cause an extraordinary, potentially earlier in-depth analysis. To overcome this drawback, the CPIM may be coupled with complex event processing systems, which already account for external events.

As for the evaluation, the CPIM was applied to only a small example. The sensitivity analysis aimed at testing the CPIM with respect to varying input parameters. Therefore, the results must be critically examined when applying the CPIM in reality. Furthermore, organizations use different process variants in different contexts. According to a higher amount of routing constructs, the variance of the instance cash flows increases and influences the CPI substantially. Conducting in-depth analyses would be impossible. In such cases, it might help split the process model into smaller groups of similar paths regarding a limited set of executed instances.

6   Conclusion

We investigated when a process should undergo an in-depth analysis to check whether it requires redesign. As a first answer, we proposed the critical process instance method (CPIM) that analytically predicts the critical number of executed instances after which a process should undergo the next in-depth analysis. We also sketched how to integrate the CPIM in the process monitoring and controlling phase of the BPM lifecycle, depending on whether a process runs in an automated execution environment. Finally, we demonstrated the CPIM using a sample process from the banking industry.

Future research should address the limitations discussed in section 5 and conduct real-world case studies. Our long-term vision is to extend the CPIM accordingly and to implement it in an automated process execution environment such that it can be applied continuously and simultaneously to multiple interdepending processes to provide process portfolio managers with adequate support for process decision-making.

References

1. Bandara, W., Guillemain, A., Coogans, P.: Prioritizing Process Improvement: An Example from the Australian Financial Services Sector. In: vom Brocke, J., Rosemann, M. (eds.) Handbook on Business Process Management 2, 2nd edn., pp. 289-307. Springer, Heidelberg (2015)
2. Bersimis, S., Psarakis, S., Panaretos, J.: Multivariate Statistical Process Control Charts: An Overview. Qual. Reliab. Eng. Int. **23**, 517–543 (2007)
3. Beverungen, D.: Exploring the Interplay of the Design and Emergence of Business Processes as Organizational Routines. Bus. Inf. Syst. Eng. **6**, 191–202 (2014)
4. Black, F., Scholes, M.: The Pricing of Options and Corporate Liabilities. J. Polit. Econ. **81**, 637–654 (1973)

5. Bolsinger, M.: Bringing Value-Based Business Process Management to the Operational Process Level. Inf. Syst. E-Bus. Manage. **13**, 355–398 (2015)
6. Buhl, H.U., Röglinger, M., Stöckl, S., Braunwarth, K.: Value Orientation in Process Management - Research Gap and Contribution to Economically Well-Founded Decisions in Process Management. Bus. Inf. Syst. Eng. 3, 163–172 (2011)
7. Champy, J., Weger, J.: Reengineering: The Second Time Around. Strat. Ldrsp. **33**, 53–56 (2005)
8. Cox, J.C., Huang, C.: Optimal Consumption and Portfolio Policies when Asset Prices Follow a Diffusion Process. J. Econ. Theory **49**, 33–83 (1989)
9. Cox, J.C., Ingersoll Jr., J.E., Ross, S.A.: A Theory of the Term Structure of Interest Rates. Econometrica **53**, 385–407 (1985)
10. Darmani, A., Hanafizadeh, P.: Business Process Portfolio Selection in Re-Engineering Projects. BPMJ **19**, 892–916 (2013)
11. Dixit, A.K., Pindyck, R.S.: Investment Under Uncertainty. Princeton University Press, Princeton (1994)
12. Dumas, B., Kurshev, A., Uppal, R.: Equilibrium Portfolio Strategies in the Presence of Sentiment Risk and Excess Volatility. J. Finance **64**, 579–629 (2009)
13. Dumas, M., La Rosa, M., Mendling, J., Reijers, H.A.: Fundamentals of Business Process Management. Springer, Heidelberg (2013)
14. El Karoui, N., Peng, S., Quenez, M.C.: Backward Stochastic Differential Equations in Finance. Math. Finance **7**, 1–71 (1997)
15. Forstner, E., Kamprath, N., Röglinger, M.: Capability Development with Process Maturity models–Decision Framework and Economic Analysis. J. Decis. Syst. **23**, 127–150 (2014)
16. Harmon, P.: Business Process Change, 2nd edn. Morgan Kaufmann, Burlington (2010)
17. Harmon, P., Wolf, C.: The State of Business Process Management (2014). http://www.bptrends.com/bpt/wp-content/uploads/BPTrends-State-of-BPM-Survey-Report.pdf
18. Irani, Z., Hlupic, V., Giaglis, G.: Editorial: Business Process Reengineering: A Modeling Perspective. Int. J. Flex. Manuf. Syst. **13**, 99–104 (2001)
19. Janiesch, C., Matzner, M., Müller, O.: Beyond Process Monitoring: A Proof-of-Concept of Event-Driven Business Activity Management. BPMJ **18**, 625–643 (2012)
20. Kettinger, W.J., Grover, V.: Special Section: Toward a Theory of Business Process Change Management. J. Manage. Inf. Syst., 9–30 (1995)
21. Kohlbacher, M., Reijers, H.A.: The Effects of Process-Oriented Organizational Design on Firm Performance. BPMJ **19**, 245–262 (2013)
22. Lakshmanan, G.T., Mukhi, N.K., Khalaf, R., Martens, A., Rozsnyai, S.: Assessing the Health of Case-Oriented Semi-Structured Business Processes., 499–506 (2012)
23. Lehnert, M., Linhart, A., Röglinger, M.: Chopping Down Trees vs. Sharpening the Axe – Balancing the Development of BPM Capabilities with Process Improvement. In: Sadiq, S., Soffer, P., Völzer, H. (eds.) BPM 2014. LNCS, vol. 8659, pp. 151–167. Springer, Heidelberg (2014)
24. Levina, O., Hillmann, R.: Network-Based Business Process Analysis. In: Proceedings of the 2012 45th Hawaii International Conference on System Sciences, HICSS 2012, pp. 4356–4365. IEEE Computer Society (2012)
25. Leyer, M., Heckl, D., Moormann, J.: Process Performance Measurement. In: vom Brocke, J., Rosemann, M. (eds.) Handbook on Business Process Management 2, 2nd edn., pp. 227–241. Springer, Heidelberg (2015)
26. Longin, F.M.: From Value at Risk to Stress Testing: The Extreme Value Approach. J. Bank Financ **24**, 1097–1130 (2000)
27. Luftman, J., Zadeh, H.S., Derksen, B., Santana, M., Rigoni, E.H., Huang, Z.D.: Key Information Technology and Management Issues 2012–2013: An International Study. J. Inform. Technol. **28**, 354–366 (2013)

28. Mansar, S.L., Reijers, H.A., Ounnar, F.: Development of a Decision-Making Strategy to Improve the Efficiency of BPR. Expert Syst. Appl. **36**, 3248–3262 (2009)
29. Nguyen, H., Dumas, M., La Rosa, M., Maggi, F.M., Suriadi, S.: Mining Business Process Deviance: A Quest for Accuracy. In: Meersman, R., Panetto, H., Dillon, T., Missikoff, M., Liu, L., Pastor, O., Cuzzocrea, A., Sellis, T. (eds.) OTM 2014. LNCS, vol. 8841, pp. 436–445. Springer, Heidelberg (2014)
30. Ohlsson, J., Han, S., Johannesson, P., Carpenhall, F., Rusu, L.: Prioritizing Business Processes Improvement Initiatives: The Seco Tools Case. In: Jarke, M., Mylopoulos, J., Quix, C., Rolland, C., Manolopoulos, Y., Mouratidis, H., Horkoff, J. (eds.) CAiSE 2014. LNCS, vol. 8484, pp. 256–270. Springer, Heidelberg (2014)
31. Ortbach, K., Plattfaut, R., Poppelbuss, J., Niehaves, B.: A Dynamic Capability-Based Framework for Business Process Management: Theorizing and Empirical Application. In: Proceedings of the 2012 45th Hawaii International Conference on System Sciences, HICSS 2012, pp. 4287–4296. IEEE Computer Society (2012)
32. Reijers, H.A., Mansar, S.L.: Best Practices in Business Process Redesign: An Overview and Qualitative Evaluation of Successful Redesign Heuristics. Omega **33**, 283–306 (2005)
33. Rosemann, M., vom Brocke, J.: The Six Core Elements of Business Process Management. In: Rosemann, M., vom Brocke, J. (eds.) Handbook on Business Process Management 1, 2nd edn., pp. 105–122. Springer, Heidelberg (2015)
34. Sadiq, W., Governatori, G., Namiri, K.: Modeling Control Objectives for Business Process Compliance. In: Alonso, G., Dadam, P., Rosemann, M. (eds.) BPM 2007. LNCS, vol. 4714, pp. 149–164. Springer, Heidelberg (2007)
35. Sidorova, A., Isik, O.: Business Process Research: A Cross-Disciplinary Review. BPMJ **16**, 566–597 (2010)
36. Stewart, W.J.: Probability, Markov Chains, Queues, and Simulation: The Mathematical Basis of Performance Modeling. Princeton University Press, Princeton (2009)
37. Tsui, E., Malhotra, Y.: Integrating Knowledge Management Technologies in Organizational Business Processes: Getting Real Time Enterprises to Deliver Real Business Performance. J. Knowl. Manag. **9**, 7–28 (2005)
38. van der Aalst, W.M.P.: Process Mining. Discovery, Conformance and Enhancement of Business Processes. Springer, Berlin (2011)
39. van der Aalst, W.M.P.: Business Process Management: A Comprehensive Survey. ISRN Software Eng. (2013)
40. van der Aalst, W.M.P., Jablonski, S.: Dealing with Workflow Change: Identification of Issues and Solutions. Comput. Syst. Sci. Eng. **15**, 267–276 (2000)
41. Vergidis, K., Tiwari, A., Majeed, B.: Business Process Analysis and Optimization: Beyond Reengineering. IEEE Trans. Syst. Man Cybern. C Appl. Rev. **38**, 69–82 (2008)
42. vom Brocke, J., Recker, J., Mendling, J.: Value-Oriented Process Modeling: Integrating Financial Perspectives into Business Process Re-Design. BPMJ **16**, 333–356 (2010)
43. vom Brocke, J., Sonnenberg, C.: Value-orientation in business process management. In: vom Brocke, J., Rosemann, M. (eds.) Handbook on Business Process Management 2, 2nd edn., pp. 101–132. Springer, Berlin (2015)
44. vom Brocke, J., Becker, J., Braccini, A.M., Butleris, R., Hofreiter, B., Kapočius, K., De Marco, M., Schmidt, G., Seidel, S., Simons, A., Skopal, T., Stein, A., Stieglitz, S., Suomi, R., Vossen, G., Winter, R., Wrycza, S.: Current and Future Issues in BPM Research: A European Perspective from the ERCIS Meeting 2010. CAIS **28**, 393–414 (2011)
45. Woodall, W.H.: Controversies and Contradictions in Statistical Process Control. J. Qual. Tech. **32**, 341–350 (2000)
46. Zellner, G.: A Structured Evaluation of Business Process Improvement Approaches. BPMJ **17**, 203–237 (2011)
47. zur Muehlen, M.: Workflow-Based Process Controlling: Foundation, Design, and Application of Workflow-Driven Process Information Systems. Logos, Berlin (2004)

Data-Driven Performance Analysis
of Scheduled Processes

Arik Senderovich[1]([✉]), Andreas Rogge-Solti[2], Avigdor Gal[1], Jan Mendling[2],
Avishai Mandelbaum[1], Sarah Kadish[3], and Craig A. Bunnell[3]

[1] Technion – Israel Institute of Technology, Haifa, Israel
sariks@tx.technion.ac.il, {avigal,avim}@ie.technion.ac.il
[2] Vienna University of Economics and Business, Wien, Austria
{andreas.rogge-solti,jan.mendling}@wu.ac.at
[3] Dana-Farber Cancer Institute, Boston, USA
{sarah_kadish,craig_bunnell}@dfci.harvard.edu

Abstract. The performance of scheduled business processes is of central importance for services and manufacturing systems. However, current techniques for performance analysis do not take both queueing semantics and the process perspective into account. In this work, we address this gap by developing a novel method for utilizing rich process logs to analyze performance of scheduled processes. The proposed method combines simulation, queueing analytics, and statistical methods. At the heart of our approach is the discovery of an individual-case model from data, based on an extension of the Colored Petri Nets formalism. The resulting model can be simulated to answer performance queries, yet it is computational inefficient. To reduce the computational cost, the discovered model is *projected* into Queueing Networks, a formalism that enables efficient performance analytics. The projection is facilitated by a sequence of *folding* operations that alter the structure and dynamics of the Petri Net model. We evaluate the approach with a real-world dataset from Dana-Farber Cancer Institute, a large outpatient cancer hospital in the United States.

1 Introduction

Scheduled processes are pervasive in our lives. In services, manufacturing systems and transportation, one encounters corresponding schedules, such as appointment books, production plans and bus timetables. Typically, it is of central importance for companies to analyze the performance of their processes. Data stemming from event logs of these processes play an increasingly important role in this context [2] and first contributions have been made to investigate scheduled process from a conformance perspective, which is grounded in process mining concepts [22].

While there are powerful methods for performance analysis in prior research, these are bound to different types of limitations. First, analytical work in the area of operations research often does not provide direct techniques to make use

© Springer International Publishing Switzerland 2015
H.R. Motahari-Nezhad et al. (Eds.): BPM 2015, LNCS 9253, pp. 35–52, 2015.
DOI: 10.1007/978-3-319-23063-4_3

of available execution data [15]. Second, process mining methods for performance analysis carry their own limitations. In particular, Petri Net-based techniques discover fine-grained models to capture the process perspective at the individual-case level [18,19], but these analyses are restricted to simulation. Third, queue mining [21] focuses on the resource perspective to efficiently answer performance questions (*e.g.*, delay prediction), while ignoring other aspects of the underlying process, such as the control-flow perspective.

The main purpose of this paper is to provide a flexible, efficient and accurate method for data-driven performance analysis of scheduled processes. We achieve this goal by bridging the gap between the discovery of Petri Net simulation models and queue mining. In contrast to manual modeling that is typically applied in operations research fields (simulation, queueing theory), our approach is driven by data. At the foundation of the approach lies a discovery procedure that utilizes the schedules and execution logs of the underlying process to construct and enrich a novel type of Colored Petri Nets, the Queue-Enabling Colored Stochastic Petri Nets (QCSPN). The proposed formalism is highly expressive and includes stochastic times, scheduling mechanisms and queues.

To reduce the computational effort required to simulate the resulting model, we *project* the QCSPN into the performance-oriented formalism of Queueing Networks. Several types of Queueing Networks and their approximations are well-known for their complexity-reducing characteristics [8]. However, there is a gap of expressiveness between Petri Nets and Queueing Networks, which does not allow for an immediate transformation of one formalism into the other [24]. To close the gap between the two formalisms, we introduce the concept of *folding* that alters the structure and dynamics of the originating Petri Net, thus making the Petri Net projection-ready. We test our approach by conducting a predictive evaluation against a real-world dataset of the Dana-Farber Cancer Institute, a large outpatient cancer hospital in the United States. Our experiments demonstrate the influence of abstraction on prediction accuracy, depending on the correctness of folding assumptions. Moreover, we show that projection of Petri Net models into Queueing Networks can improve accuracy, while benefiting from run-time efficiency.

This paper is structured as follows. Section 2 presents an overview of our approach and a running example. Section 3 presents our data model and the Queue-Enabling Colored Stochastic Petri Nets. Section 4 defines the discovery algorithm for Queue-Enabling CSPNs (QCSPN). Section 5 formalizes the techniques for folding and projecting QCSPNs. Section 6 describes an empirical evaluation of our approach. Section 7 discusses related work before Section 8 concludes.

2   Approach Overview

This section motivates the need for our approach. To this end, we refer to a use-case that is inspired by data from the Dana-Farber Cancer Institute. The outpatient hospital is equipped with a Real-Time Location System (RTLS) that

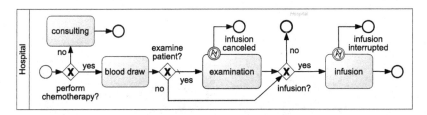

Fig. 1. The main process in Dana-Farber Cancer Institute.

tracks, via 905 sensors, approximately 900 patients per day. These patients are served by 300 healthcare providers (*e.g.*, physicians, nurse practitioners, registered nurses), supported by 70 administrative staff, and occupying 7 floors.

The schedule of an ambulatory patient typically includes a blood draw, an examination by a physician or nurse practitioner, and a chemotherapy infusion (Figure 1). The process may vary among cases, with some patients skipping activities, while others having additional activities (*e.g.*, acupuncture therapy, speech therapy, radiology scans).

Example 1. *Consider two specific patients, pat1 and pat2, and their scheduled routes for the same day. Both patients are to go through a* blood draw *activity that is scheduled to be performed by Registered Nurse Tanya (we write RNTanya, as an abbreviation). Then, pat1 is to go through an* examination *activity, performed by two physicians (medical doctors): MDVictor and MDElaine. Pat2 is also scheduled to go through an* examination, *which includes a speech therapy appointment as a parallel activity; the examination is planned to be carried out by MDElaine, while the speech therapy will be performed by Speech Therapist Brooke (STBrooke).*

Performance questions arise from several perspectives. From the patient's perspective, it is important to predict their length-of-stay to reduce uncertainty about the remainder of their day. From the hospital's perspective, assessing the utilization profiles of resources is a key issue. These questions can be answered either off-line (*e.g.*, the day before) or in real-time. For the off-line scenario, a data-driven simulation model that captures every phase of the process can be invaluable (because run-time is not an issue). This detailed case-level view is not covered by the queueing perspective. For real-time analysis, an efficient and relatively accurate model with a fast response time is required. This excludes simulation as an option, because its run-time may be slower than the required response time. Our approach offers methods to move freely in the spectrum between detailed-complex models and abstract-efficient models.

Figure 2 presents the outline of our approach with section numbers on the arcs. The phases of our approach are depicted by rectangles, modeling formalisms (QCSPN, Queueing Networks) are shown by circles, while the resulting models (after each phase) are shown above the relevant phases.

The approach starts with a data log, which contains details on the scheduled tasks, and on the corresponding actual execution times. As our formalism,

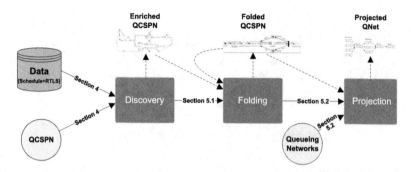

Fig. 2. An outline of our approach.

we adjust Colored Petri Nets [13] to form Queue-Enabling Colored Stochastic Petri Nets (QCSPN) with time distributions, scheduling transitions and queueing stations. In the first phase, the data is used to discover a simulation-ready QCSPN model that represents a schedule in detail. The main drawback of the resulting model is that one 'cannot see the forest for the trees,' meaning that the amount of details cause the QCSPN model to be less effective in terms of run-time complexity.

To resolve this inefficiency, we propose the second and third phases, *folding* and *projection*. An abstracted version of the original QCSPN model is produced by applying a sequence of foldings, which alter the model at the net-level. This phase bridges the expressiveness gap between Petri Nets and Queueing Networks (QNets), thus allowing for the last phase of our approach, which is projection of the QCSPN into Queueing Networks.

3   Models

We introduce a *schedule log*, which serves as the data model, and *Colored Stochastic Petri Nets*, a modeling formalism that is based on Coloured Petri Nets with stochastic delays and scheduling transitions. For the latter, we define Queue-Enabling CSPNs, to be used to construct projection functions from Petri Nets into Queueing Networks.

Data Model. A *schedule log* contains a set of tasks and the actual execution times of these tasks. A *task* is defined as a relation between cases, activities, resources, and times. Let Θ be the universe of tasks, A be the domain of activities, R be the set of resources, $\mathbb{TS}$ be the set of timestamps (Unix time) and I be the set of case identifiers. Then, task information is defined as follows.

Definition 1 (Task Information). *Task information* $\mathcal{I} = \langle \xi, \alpha, \rho, \tau, \delta, \tau_{start}, \tau_{end} \rangle$ *is a tuple satisfying the following requirements:*

- $\xi : \Theta \to I$ *assigns a case identifier to a task.*
- $\alpha : \Theta \to A$ *assigns an activity to a task.*
- $\rho : \Theta \to 2^R$ *assigns a set of resources to a task.*

- $\tau : \Theta \to \mathbb{TS}$ *assigns a timestamp representing the planned start time to a task.*
- $\delta : \Theta \to \mathbb{N}^+$ *assigns a scheduled duration to a task.*
- $\tau_{start} : \Theta \to \mathbb{TS}$ *assigns the observed start time to a scheduled task.*
- $\tau_{end} : \Theta \to \mathbb{TS}$ *assigns the observed end time to a scheduled task.*

Given task information, we can define schedule logs, which will serve us as input.

Definition 2 (Schedule Log). *Let $\Theta_P \subseteq \Theta$ be a set of scheduled tasks. The schedule log is defined as a tuple $\langle \Theta_P, \mathcal{I} \rangle$, which contains all scheduled tasks and their task information.*

Table 1 shows a schedule log for the running example. Notice that the scheduled times and actual times do not necessarily match.

Table 1. Schedule log for the running example.

Case	Activity	Resources	Scheduled Start	Scheduled Duration	Actual Start	Actual End
pat1	Blood-Draw	[RNTanya]	9:00AM	10 (MIN)	9:05AM	9:10AM
pat1	Exam	[MDVictor, MDElaine]	10:00AM	30 (MIN)	9:55AM	10:20AM
pat2	Blood-Draw	[RNTanya]	9:10AM	15 (MIN)	9:15AM	9:27AM
pat2	Exam	[MDElaine]	9:40AM	20 (MIN)	9:30AM	9:45AM
pat2	Speech-Therapy	[STBrooke]	9:40AM	50 (MIN)	9:35AM	10:32AM

Formalism. Regarding our formalism, we build on Colored Petri Nets (CPN) by Jensen [13] to discover, enrich and simulate the scheduled process. To this end, we extend the CPN model with *scheduling transitions* and *distribution functions* of firing delays. Below, we define the structure of the CSPN formalism and specify its state and dynamics (marking and firing semantics, respectively).

Definition 3 (CSPN Structure). *The structure of a CSPN is a tuple $N = \langle \mathcal{C}, P, T, F, N, \mathcal{G}, \mathcal{E}, \mathcal{D}, \mathcal{S} \rangle$ where:*

- $\mathcal{C}$ *is a finite set of non-empty types, called* color sets.
- P *is a finite set of* places.
- $T = T_R \cup T_\Sigma$ *is a finite set of* transitions, *such that T_R is the 'regular' timed transitions, and T_Σ are referred to as 'scheduling' transitions.*
- F *is a finite set of* arcs *representing flow such that: $P \cap T = P \cap F = T \cap F = \emptyset$.*
- $N : F \to P \times T \cup T \times P$ *is a node function.*
- $\mathcal{G} : T \to Expr$ *is a guard function that evaluates to boolean predicates.*
- $\mathcal{E} : F \to Expr$ *is an arc expression function that evaluates to a multi-set of colors.*
- $\mathcal{D} : T_R \to (\mathbb{N}^+ \to [0, 1])$ *are distribution functions of firing delays in seconds that are associated with timed transitions,*
- $\mathcal{S} : T_\Sigma \to \mathbb{TS}$ *are timestamps assigned to scheduling transitions,*

In the remainder of the paper, we adopt the common Petri Net bullet notation for in-places and out-places of transitions. That is, the in-places $\bullet t$ of a transition t are $\{p \in P \mid (p, t) \in F\}$, and the out-places $t\bullet$ are $\{p \in P \mid (t, p) \in F\}$.

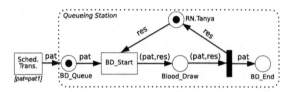

Fig. 3. An illustration of the blood-draw task for pat1; the elements of the queueing station are highlighted with the dashed box.

Figure 3 demonstrates parts of the formalism by showing the CSPN that corresponds to the blood draw task for the first patient *pat1* in our running example. We closely follow the semantics as introduced by Jensen for CPNs [13]. The arc expressions contain variables that can be bound to typed tokens. For example, the variable *pat* can be bound to patient *pat1*. A transition t is *color enabled* in a binding, if the input places •t contain tokens that satisfy the arc expressions and the guard function $\mathcal{G}(t)$ evaluates to true given the binding. The binding by the arc expressions takes care of proper routing of the tokens to their respective output places. In our example, we require the token of *RNTanya* to return to its place so that she can draw blood from the next patient. This is taken care of by the variable *res* in the corresponding arc expressions.

Besides the colors, a token carries an associated time that specifies at which point in time the token becomes *ready* for the next firing. This depends on the global clock g, i.e., the token time must be smaller or equal to g. Transitions are eager to fire, that is, whenever a transition is color enabled and the tokens are ready, it immediately fires. The timestamp ts of each of the produced tokens is set to $g + \Delta(t, g)$, where $\Delta(t, g)$ is the firing delay of t at time g:

$$\Delta(t, g) = \begin{cases} d & \text{if } t \in T_R, \\ \max(g, \mathcal{S}(t)) - g & \text{if } t \in T_\Sigma, \end{cases} \tag{1}$$

Here, d is a realization of the random duration D_t that comes from distribution $\mathcal{D}(t)$. We call a transition t_i with all the probability mass of $\mathcal{D}(t_i)$ on 0 an *immediate* transition and depict it with a bar in the model, as known from the GSPN formalism [4].

Queue-Enabling CSPN. In this part we define the *Queue-Enabling CSPN (QCSPN)*, which is a CSPN with scheduling transitions, queueing stations, and fork/join constructs.

Definition 4 (Queueing Station). *A queueing station is a CSPN, where*

- $P = \{p_q, p_a, p_e, p_{r_1}, ..., p_{r_K}\}$, *with p_q being a queueing place, p_a being the on-going activity place, p_e being the end place and $K \in \mathbb{N}$ being the number of service providing resources per station,*
- $T = \{t_s, t_e\}$ *being the start and end transitions,*

- $F = \{f_{enter}, f_{in_i}, f_{serve}, f_{served}, f_{out_i}, f_{leave}\}$ are the flow arcs with $i = 1, ..., K$ and,
- $N(f_{enter}) = (p_q, t_s)$, $N(f_{in_i}) = (p_{r_i}, t_s)$, $N(f_{serve}) = (t_s, p_a)$, $N(f_{served}) = (p_a, t_e)$, $N(f_{out_i}) = (t_e, p_{r_i})$, $N(f_{leave}) = (t_e, p_e)$.

For example, in Figure 3, the subnet that starts with the queueing place 'BD_Queue' and ends at the 'BD_End' place, is a queueing station. We are now ready to define the Queue-Enabling CSPN (QCSPN).

Definition 5 (Queue-Enabling CSPN (QCSPN)). *A Colored Stochastic Petri Net* $\langle C, P, T, F, N, \mathcal{G}, \mathcal{E}, \mathcal{D}, \mathcal{S} \rangle$ *is called* Queue-Enabling, *if the CSPN contains a single source* p_α, *a single sink* p_ω, *and every other node* ($n \in P \cup T \setminus \{p_\alpha, p_\omega\}$) *of the CSPN belongs to either,*

- *A queueing station, or*
- *An immediate split or join transition* t_i *(with* $| \bullet t_i| = 1 \wedge |t_i \bullet| > 1$ *or* $| \bullet t_i| > 1 \wedge |t_i \bullet| = 1$), *or*
- *There exist a scheduling transition* $t_\Sigma \in T_\Sigma$, *such that* n *is the predecessor place of the scheduling transition or* t_Σ *itself.*

In other words, the QCSPN models represent cases flowing through queueing stations that can be parallel, and are scheduled. In our running example, patient *pat2* has two tasks scheduled in parallel, with the corresponding QCSPN depicted in Figure 4.

4   Discovery of Queue-Enabling CSPN Models

This section is devoted to the discovery and enrichment of Queue-Enabling Colored Stochastic Petri Nets (QCSPN) from the schedule log. To discover the QCSPN, we extend the approach of van der Aalst's work on scheduling with Petri Nets [1] to include scheduling transitions and stochastic times. First, we provide an overview of preprocessing and assumptions required for discovering and enriching the QCSPN model. Then, we demonstrate a three-step discovery algorithm that constructs the QCSPN. Finally, an enrichment procedure of the model from data is described.

Preprocessing and Assumptions. Precedence constraints (synchronization points) are a key feature of scheduled processes, ensuring that cases are not allowed to continue to a new task before a subset of other tasks is performed. To handle parallelism, we apply a *preprocessing* phase in which we detect parallel tasks using interval calculus [5]. Thereby, we assume tasks to be parallel if the intersection of their planned times is not empty. Henceforth, we shall assume the existence of a *parallelism set*, $\Pi \subseteq 2^\Theta$, which contains *sets of tasks* that are scheduled to be performed in parallel. The set Π is a partition of Θ_P, since we assume transitivity of the parallelism property, thus avoiding new splits prior to joining previous splits. Three more assumptions are used in the discovery process, as follows:

- **Work conserving:** Resources become available immediately after the completion of a task.
- **Temporal deviations:** The scheduled tasks may deviate in time only (no activities, resources or routing deviation).
- **Duration dependencies:** Activity durations depend only on the activity and its planned duration (independent of marking components, i.e. case identifier, resources, and scheduled time).

Discovery. The discovery algorithm comprises three steps of linear complexity in the number of tasks in the schedule. The steps are (1) construction of queueing stations, (2) synchronization of parallel tasks, and (3) initialization of the state (marking and global clock). Next, we go over the steps and relate them to the proposed models (Section 3).

Step 1: Construct Queueing Stations. We start by inserting all resource places, $\{p_r \mid r \in R\}$. Then, for each task $\theta \in \Theta_P$ of the schedule log, a corresponding queueing station is created as follows. The activity place is defined as $p_a^\theta, a = \alpha(\theta)$. The resource places that are connected to the starting transitions are $\{p_r \mid r \in \rho(\theta)\}$; the durations of timed transitions t_s^θ are set to be deterministic (*i.e.*, according to plan) with $D_{t_s^\theta} = \delta(\theta)$. Arcs that connect places and transitions receive arc-expressions, which verify that resource tokens and case tokens are separated and routed appropriately. Subsequently, scheduling transitions are inserted to precede queueing places, p_q^θ, to prevent an ahead-of-time arrival into the queueing station. Every scheduling transition $t_\Sigma^\theta \in T_\Sigma$ is assigned with a timestamp $\mathcal{S}(t_\Sigma^\theta) = \tau(\theta)$ according to the earliest start time of the activity. Finally, we add a source and sink place, p_α and p_ω, respectively.

Step 2: Synchronize Parallel Constructs. In this step, we add split and join transitions for every parallelism class in Π. Let $\pi \in \Pi$ be a set of parallel tasks, with $|\pi| > 1$ (parallelism classes may be singletons for sequential tasks). We add a *split* transition t_{sp}^π to the set of transitions and connect it to each scheduling transition $t_\Sigma^\theta, \theta \in \pi$ via a new scheduling place. Then, we add *join* transitions t_j^π after each parallel construct to express the synchronization of the concurrent tasks. Each of the join transitions is assigned with a guard that verifies that joining is performed only for tokens with the same static component, *i.e.*, case identifier. Figure 4 demonstrates a parallel construct for *pat2* from our running example. According to schedule, the patient is to undergo examination and speech therapy in an overlapping period of time.

Step 3: Initialize State. This step sets the initial marking and the global clock. The global clock, which is the dynamic part of the state, is set to zero. For the initial marking, all case tokens start at p_α, while resource tokens reside in their corresponding places. The number of resource tokens in each resource place corresponds to the offered capacity of that resource, which is the maximum number of tasks that a single resource is scheduled to perform at the same time. For our running example, this allows for a nurse to attend multiple infusion patients in parallel. The static marking component of case and resource tokens is their unique identifiers. The timestamp component for case tokens is initialized to be zero. The timestamp component of resource tokens is initialized to the timestamp of the first scheduled task for the corresponding resource.

Enrichment. Once the QCSPN model is discovered from the schedule, we enrich it based on actual execution times per task by replacing deterministic durations with stochastic ones. To this end, we apply the techniques for enhancement of non-Markovian Stochastic Petri Nets with non-parametric kernel density regression [18]. Other model components that are often stochastic, *e.g.*, exception-handling mechanisms and routing, are assumed to be driven by case-information and therefore deterministic. The outcome of the discovery and enrichment steps is a simulation-ready QCSPN model, which we refer to as N_0.

5   Folding and Projection of QCSPN into Queueing Networks

In this section we introduce the concepts of *folding* and *projection* of QCSPNs. First, we define the folding function and provide several examples of foldings. Then, we define the projection function and demonstrate a single projection with the help of a sequence of foldings.

5.1   Folding of QCSPN

Let M_{QCSPN} be the universe of all QCSPN models and let $\mathbb{A}$ be the universe of possible assumptions on the process, (*e.g.*, activity times are exponentially distributed, all parallel tasks start and end at the same time). Note that these process assumptions must not always be realistic, however they can be useful as approximations for performance analysis.

Definition 6 (Folding Function). *A folding function* $\psi_{\mathcal{A}} : M_{QCSPN} \rightarrow M_{QCSPN}$, *creates a new QCSPN model, under a set of assumptions* $\mathcal{A} \subseteq \mathbb{A}$.

Below, we provide several examples of folding functions. For each function, we explain the net-level changes that it requires, and demonstrate it with our running example. We omit the formal proofs that show that the resulting nets are QCSPN, due to space restrictions.

Folding 1: Remove Parallelism (RP) Parallelism is well-known for its negative influence on the analytical tractability of Queueing Networks [9]. This motivates us to consider a folding operation ψ_{RP} that transforms N_0 into a concurrency-free model, $\psi_{RP}(N_0)$. Specifically, ψ_{RP} adds the assumption: "all parallel tasks must start and end at the same time occupying all resources that were scheduled to perform the (originally) parallel tasks."

Without loss of generality, we show the net-level changes that the RP function implies on a single parallel class of tasks, $\pi \in \Pi$. Note that the marking-related elements remain unchanged. For every $\theta \in \pi, |\pi| > 1$, the folding function removes the corresponding queueing station (non-resource places, transitions, flow relation). Moreover, the corresponding split and join transitions $(t^\pi_{split}, t^\pi_{join})$ are also removed from the net.

Subsequently, a single queueing station that corresponds to a new task θ' is created and is connected to all resource places that were connected to the original tasks $\theta \in \pi$. The activity name for the new station is defined as a concatenation (denoted $\uplus$) of all previously parallel activities, $i.e.$, $\alpha(\theta') = \biguplus_{\theta \in \pi} \alpha(\theta)$. The random duration of the timed transition t' that corresponds to the new activity is given as $D_{t'} = \max_{\theta \in \pi}[D_{t^\theta_s}]$, with $D_{t^\theta_s}$ being the random duration of task θ. The scheduling transitions per parallel branch are folded into a single scheduling transition $t^{\theta'}_\Sigma$ with $\mathcal{S}(t^{\theta'}_\Sigma) = \min_{\theta \in \pi}[\mathcal{S}(t^\theta_\Sigma)]$, i.e. the scheduled start time of the new task is the earliest among all start times of the original parallel tasks. Figure 5 shows $\psi_{RP}(N_0)$ for the running example. We observe that for $pat2$, a new task 'Exam_SpeechTherapy' that requires both resources is created. The synchronization constructs for the previous two queueing stations no longer exist.

Folding 2: Remove Shared Resources (RSR) Shared resource possession imposes mathematical difficulties when analyzing queueing systems [12]. Therefore, as a next step towards projection of N_0 into Queueing Networks we apply folding function ψ_{RSR}, which removes shared resources. The underlying assumption for the RSR function is the following: "resources $R' \subseteq R$ that share task θ can be combined into a single resource with $\rho(\theta) = \{ \biguplus_{r \in R'} r \}$". In other words, the set of resources R' becomes a new resource that is added to R. Figure 6 demonstrates the result of $\psi_{RSR}(\psi_{RP}(N_0))$: a new resource *MDElaine_STBrooke* is created for the second task of patient $pat2$.

Folding 3: Fuse Queues (FQ) In this step, we reduce model complexity by fusing queueing stations that perform the same activities and share the same resources. For example, consider two queueing stations that correspond to two tasks, θ_1 and θ_2, such that $\alpha(\theta_1) = \alpha(\theta_2)$ and $\rho(\theta_1) = \rho(\theta_2)$. The fusion merges the queuing, service, and end places, as well as the start and end transitions for the two tasks. Duplicate arcs are removed, as the arc-expressions are equal. Scheduling transitions are not fused and govern the routing of the corresponding patients through the fused queueing stations.

Figure 7 presents $\psi_{FQ}(N_0)$ for $RNTanya$'s two blood draw tasks of our running example. We observe that in the new net, two case tokens can reside in the queueing place and wait for $RNTanya$. Here, if we assume that both patient tokens are *ready*, the conflict between them needs to be resolved. We assume that cases are served according to the earliest-due-date first (EDD) policy, i.e. the case token with the smaller timestamp gets served first. The fuse queues folding does not change the performance characteristics of the QCSPN model. Nevertheless, it is a required step that enables projection into Queueing Networks, since it joins the otherwise scattered queues of activity-resource pairs.

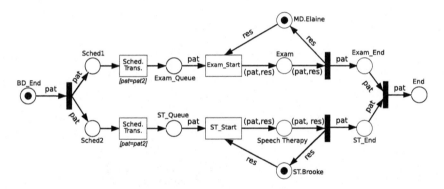

Fig. 4. Parallel examination and speech therapy for pat2.

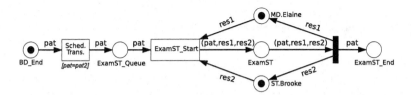

Fig. 5. Folding function: Remove parallelism.

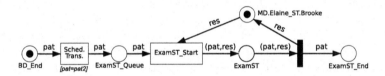

Fig. 6. Folding function: Remove shared resources.

Folding 4: Remove Scheduling Constraints (RSched) The last folding function builds on the assumption that "scheduling constraints are not enforced". In other words, cases that finish service in a certain queueing station are immediately routed to the succeeding station according to schedule. The RSched folding implies a very simple change at the net level: every scheduling transition is turned into an immediate transition with corresponding guards that verify the identity of cases for routing purposes.

5.2 Projection of QCSPN into Queueing Networks.

The intuition behind the idea of projecting QCSPN into Queueing Networks is straightforward. Queueing networks are directed graphs, with vertices being single-station queues and edges being the routing mechanism that communicate customers between these queues[1]. Therefore, as a first step of projection,

---

[1] Due to Queueing Network conventions we write the terms customers and cases interchangeably

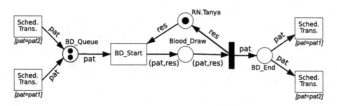

Fig. 7. The result of fusing queues

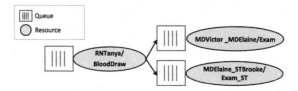

Fig. 8. The result of the projection function: Queueing Network with distinguishable cases.

queueing stations of the originating QCSPN are transformed into vertices of the target Queueing Network. Every vertex of the Queueing Network can be characterized by the number of resources that reside in that vertex, which serve customers according to some service time distribution. These times correspond to the random durations of the timed transitions in the QCSPN. The matching between cases and resources are governed by service policies, *e.g.* first-come-first-served (FCFS) or earliest-due-date first (EDD). At service completion, customers are routed to the next queueing vertex (either deterministically or according to assigned probabilities). The described behavior corresponds in a one-to-one manner to our definition of a QCSPN, and provides the basis for the construction of a projection function. Formally, the projection function is defined as follows.

Definition 7 (Projection Function). *Let M_{QN} be the universe of all Queueing Networks. A projection function $\phi : M_{QCSPN} \rightarrow M_{QN}$ creates a Queueing Network from the originating QCSPN.*

Figure 8 presents a projection function, operated on the folded version of our running example. The folding includes the four foldings of Section 5.1, namely Remove Parallelism, Remove Shared Resources and Fuse Queues, and Remove Scheduling Constraints, in the order of their presentation. The resulting Queueing Network has distinguishable customers, single resource per-station and does not allow for exogenous arrivals (customers start in the system at the time of their arrival).

6   Evaluation

In this section we describe the results of an empirical evaluation of the proposed approach. Here, we aim at demonstrating the usefulness of the method spectrum:

from detailed Petri Net-based simulators, through folded versions of the original model, to predictors that are based on the projected Queueing Network. We start with the main aspects that involve the implementation of our techniques. Then, we describe the dataset and the design of our experiment. We conclude the section with our main results and a discussion of the evaluation.

Implementation. We implemented the model construction, its enrichment with historical data, the simulation semantics, the folding operations and a projection into the Queueing Theory based snapshot predictor. The implementation uses the Python programming language and builds on the open-source SNAKES framework [16]. The implementation is available as a free open-source project.[2]

Data Description. The data that we consider comes from the Dana-Farber Cancer Institute. We combine two datasets into one: the scheduled visits and their corresponding execution times. The former contains a detailed schedule for each day, while the latter is based on Real-Time Location System measurements of that day. Specifically, every patient's path is measured by the RTLS and matched to the originating appointments that reside in the patient's schedule. We utilize a year's worth of data, for year 2014 (222 regular workdays, nearly 140000 scheduled visits), for training the enrichment algorithms and testing our techniques. The training set includes 212 regular workdays, while the test set consists of 10 workdays, selected at random. We excluded special days (*e.g.*, Christmas) with irregularly high or low workloads from the random selection of the test days.

Experimental Setup. The design of our experiment is as follows. We predict the length-of-stay (i.e. the time in process from start to end) for every scheduled patient over the 10 test days. The prediction is then compared against the actual length-of-stay. Patients are assumed to arrive at their real arrival-time, as it is recorded in the data. The *uncontrolled* variables in our experiments are the root of the mean-squared prediction error (RMSE), and the mean error. The former measures the deviation between the predicted value and the actual value of the length-of-stay (LOS), while the latter shows the 'bias' of the predictors. The *controlled* variable is the model that we use for prediction of the LOS. The QCSPN models are discovered from the test day's schedules and are then enriched by the training set.

For prediction, we consider the following five models: the original model (N_0), the no-concurrency model ($\psi_{RP}(N_0)$), the removed shared resources model without concurrency ($\psi_{RP,RSR}(N_0)$), the scheduling transitions and fuse queues model ($\psi_{RP,RSR,FQ,RSched}(N_0)$), and the queueing predictor that corresponds to the projected model ($\phi(\psi_{RP,RSR,FQ,RSched}(N_0))$).

The first four models are based on simulation and therefore, their application to predicting lengths-of-stay is straightforward. Specifically, all test-day patients are placed into the simulator at their corresponding actual arrival time, and their simulated departure times are recorded. The predictor that we use per patient is the average length-of-stay of that patient across 30 runs. On the other hand, the

---

[2] See QueueingCPN project: https://github.com/AndreasRoggeSolti/QueueingCPN

Table 2. Mean Error and RMSE (hours) for length-of-stay predictors.

	N_0	RP	RP&RSR	RSched	Queueing
Mean Error	0.92	0.91	0.88	0.46	-0.42
RMSE	1.97	1.95	1.95	1.82	1.38

queueing predictor does not require simulation, and can be calculated directly as the patient arrives. The justification for using the former quantity is based on the heavy-traffic snapshot principle for networks, a well-known result from Queueing Theory [17]. The predictor was found to be empirically accurate in several recent works on queue mining [20]. The second predictor is a first-order approximation that is based on average durations and stationarity assumptions, in the spirit of the queue-length predictor in [11,21], extended from single-station queues to networks.

Let us examine the queueing predictor in further detail. Let $\langle q_1, ..., q_k \rangle$ be the scheduled path in terms of queueing stations for the patient whose length-of-stay we wish to predict. Denote $S_i, i = 1, ..., k$ the sojourn time (delay and activity duration) of the last patient that went through station q_i (every S_i can be calculated from histories of different patients). Let L_i be the number of patients that currently occupy the ith station (queue and service), upon the patient's arrival, and let μ_i be the service rate of the ith station. The queueing predictor LOS_q is given as follows:

$$
LOS_q = \begin{cases} \sum_{i=1}^{k} S_i & \text{if } S_i > 0, \forall i \\ \sum_{i=1}^{k} \frac{(L_i+2)}{\mu_i} & \text{otherwise.} \end{cases} \tag{2}
$$

As default, we use the well-established snapshot predictor, which uses the sum of recent visits to stations $q_1, ..., q_k$. However, S_i might not exist ($S_i = 0$) for some of the patients, since there is a positive probability that no other patient has visited station q_i before the arrival time of the current patient. For these cases, we resort to the second predictor, which assumes that the queue-length will not change while the patient is in the system. The second predictor assumes that for each station, the patient will wait for the queue to clear up ($L_i + 1$ service terminations), at rate μ_i. Then, the patient enters service and gets served at rate μ_i, hence the total time per station is $\frac{(L_i+2)}{\mu_i}$.

Results. Table 2 presents the results of the empirical evaluation, with time units being hours. The considered measures are Mean Error representing the *bias* of the model, and the Root Mean Squared Error (RMSE) as an indicator for model *accuracy*. We observe that the most accurate predictor in terms of RMSE is the queueing predictor. However, it is characterized with systemic under-estimation of the length-of-stay. The first 3 simulation-based models are less accurate and comparable among each other in terms of their RMSE. These predictors present an over-estimation of the length-of-stay. In contrast, the RSched folding demonstrates improvement in both RMSE and mean error, with respect to other QCSPN models.

Discussion. The empirical evaluation demonstrates that, in terms of RMSE, the efficient queueing predictor is most accurate, when compared to the simulation models. The weakness of the projected model however, is that it cannot be applied to answer performance questions at a granular level. For instance, consider the estimation of individual resource utilization, without relaxing the shared-resources and parallelism assumptions. Classical Queueing Networks are not expressive enough to analyze such questions, without the help of simulation. We also observe that folding of parallelism and shared resources did not have an influence on the simulation model. This can be explained by the fact that our dataset comprises few parallel tasks, and that tasks are executed by single resources.

The mean error measure provides us with additional insights. Since the queueing predictor builds upon the RSched folding, it neglects scheduling delays and thus has a negative mean error. This causes it to under-estimate the length-of-stay. However, this relaxation may also be the reason for its superior accuracy. The latter hypothesis is supported by the fact that the error has decreased due to the removal of scheduling transitions in the RSched model. One may then conclude that, for the process in the Dana-Farber Cancer Institute, scheduling constraints are not strictly binding in the process.

Finally, after an exploratory data analysis, we found that deviations in the order of tasks are not rare. This phenomena explains the inaccuracy of the simulation models, since they assume that the sequence of tasks is not violated. However, the queueing predictors consider only the set of tasks regardless of their execution order, which explains their accuracy.

7 Related Work

We categorize related research to three classes, namely modeling formalisms, abstraction methods, and process mining techniques for performance analysis.

Formalisms. Several modeling formalisms were proposed to extend Petri Net models, such that stochastic elements and queues are included [7]. For example, Queueing Petri Nets (QPN) were developed to accommodate subprocesses that encompass queueing stations [6]. However, their work does not clearly define the allowed structure for the embedded queueing network. This can result in an arbitrary large and complex Queueing Networks within the Petri Net. Our QCSPN formalism is also related to Interval Timed Colored Petri Nets [3]. In this work, we extend this formalism with stochastic durations and scheduling transitions.

Abstraction. Abstraction techniques, such as aggregation at the net level, were applied to conceal insignificant model details with respect to some analysis [23]. Furthermore, simplifying reduction rules that preserve certain properties of the original system were applied to Petri Nets. For instance, Juan et al. considered reduction rules for delay time Petri Nets [14], such that timing and deadlock properties of the model were unchanged. The idea of aggregation is also encountered in the performance analysis of Stochastic Well-Formed Colored Nets [10]. The idea is to construct the symbolic reachability graph and apply an aggregation method to condense the state space for efficient analysis. These techniques are only applicable with exponential delay distributions. Our methods allow for transitions with arbitrary firing distributions, while preserving queueing related properties with scheduling transitions.

Operational Process Mining. As previously mentioned, our work relates to discovery of Petri Net models from execution logs. Rozinat et al. [19] extracted Colored Petri Net models from data by mining control-flow, case, decision and time perspectives. Rogge-Solti et al. [18] extended this framework by considering the Generalized Stochastic Petri Net formalism, with non-Markovian durations of timed transitions. However these two works did not consider the queueing perspective, but rather modeled resource induced delays as stochastic components. On the other side of the abstraction scale, research on queue mining focused on resources, without considering the process perspective [21]. In this paper, we combine the best of both worlds by integrating the queueing perspective with other process mining perspectives. Furthermore, we generalize the approach for discovering scheduled processes presented in [22]. In their work, only a single type of Queueing Networks (Fork/Join network) was considered, while our approach allows for the discovery (through projection) of an arbitrary Queueing Network.

8   Conclusion

In this paper, we address the problem of data-driven performance analysis for scheduled processes. To this end, we develop an approach that combines techniques from Queueing Theory with Colored Petri Nets and define the corresponding class of Queue-Enabling Colored Stochastic Petri Nets (QCSPN). For computational efficiency, we define folding operations that allow us to project the originating QCSPN model into the Queueing Networks formalism. Our approach was implemented and evaluated using real-world data from an outpatient cancer hospital showing the impact of model abstraction on accuracy in terms of root mean-squared error.

We consider the current work as a first step in bringing together process mining techniques that often present a high computational cost (curse of dimensionality), and efficient Queueing Theory-based techniques that ignore elements of the process perspective (curse of simplicity). In future work, we aim to extend our approach towards conformance checking of schedules via discovery of QCSPN models. Understanding where and why patients and resources deviate from schedules is of utmost importance to hospitals and other businesses, and can have an impact on performance analysis. Furthermore, we are interested in developing techniques for predicting case paths, as well as real-time prediction methods as cases progress along these paths.

Acknowledgment. We are grateful to the SEELab members, Dr. Valery Trofimov, Igor Gavako and Ella Nadjharov, for their help with data analysis. We also thank Kristen Camuso, from Dana-Faber Cancer Institute for the insightful data discussions.

References

1. van der Aalst, W.M.P.: Petri net based scheduling. Operations-Research-Spektrum **18**(4), 219–229 (1996)
2. van der Aalst, W.M.P.: Process mining: Discovery, Conformance and Enhancement of Business Processes. Springer (2011)
3. van der Aalst, W.M.P.: Interval timed coloured petri nets and their analysis. In: Ajmone Marsan, M. (ed.) ICATPN 1993. LNCS, vol. 691, pp. 453–472. Springer, Heidelberg (1993)
4. Ajmone Marsan, M., Conte, M., Balbo, G.: A class of generalized stochastic petri nets for the performance evaluation of multiprocessor systems. ACM Trans. Comput. Syst. **2**(2), 93–122 (1984)
5. Allen, J.F.: Maintaining knowledge about temporal intervals. Communications of the ACM **26**(11), 832–843 (1983)
6. Bause, F.: Queueing Petri nets-a formalism for the combined qualitative and quantitative analysis of systems. In: PNPM 1993, pp. 14–23. IEEE (1993)
7. Bause, F., Kritzinger, P.S.: Stochastic Petri Nets. Springer (1996)
8. Bolch, G., Greiner, S., de Meer, H., Trivedi, K.S.: Queueing networks and Markov chains: modeling and performance evaluation with computer science applications. John Wiley & Sons (2006)
9. Boxma, O., Koole, G., Liu, Z.: Queueing-theoretic solution methods for models of parallel and distributed systems. Statistics, and System Theory, Centrum voor Wiskunde en Informatica, Department of Operations Research (1994)
10. Chiola, G., Dutheillet, C., Franceschinis, G., Haddad, S.: Stochastic well-formed colored nets and symmetric modeling applications. IEEE Trans. Comput. **42**(11), 1343–1360 (1993)
11. Ibrahim, R., Whitt, W.: Real-time delay estimation based on delay history. Manufacturing and Service Operations Management **11**(3), 397–415 (2009)
12. Jacobson, P.A., Lazowska, E.D.: Analyzing queueing networks with simultaneous resource possession. Commun. ACM **25**(2), 142–151 (1982)
13. Jensen, K.: Coloured Petri nets: basic concepts, analysis methods and practical use, vol. 1. Springer (1997)
14. Juan, E.Y., Tsai, J.J., Murata, T., Zhou, Y.: Reduction methods for real-time systems using delay time petri nets. IEEE Transactions on Software Engineering **27**(5), 422–448 (2001)
15. Pinedo, M.L.: Planning and Scheduling in Manufacturing and Services. Springer (2005)
16. Pommereau, F.: Quickly prototyping petri nets tools with SNAKES. In: Proceedings of PNTAP 2008, pp. 1–10. ACM (2008)
17. Reiman, M.I., Simon, B.: A network of priority queues in heavy traffic: One bottleneck station. Queueing Systems **6**(1), 33–57 (1990)

18. Rogge-Solti, A., van der Aalst, W.M.P., Weske, M.: Discovering stochastic petri nets with arbitrary delay distributions from event logs. In: Lohmann, N., Song, M., Wohed, P. (eds.) BPM 2013 Workshops. LNBIP, vol. 171, pp. 15–27. Springer, Heidelberg (2014)
19. Rozinat, A., Mans, R.S., Song, M., van der Aalst, W.M.P.: Discovering simulation models. Information Systems **34**(3), 305–327 (2009)
20. Senderovich, A., Weidlich, M., Gal, A., Mandelbaum, A.: Queue mining for delay prediction in multi-class service processes. Tech. rep. (2014)
21. Senderovich, A., Weidlich, M., Gal, A., Mandelbaum, A.: Queue mining – predicting delays in service processes. In: Jarke, M., Mylopoulos, J., Quix, C., Rolland, C., Manolopoulos, Y., Mouratidis, H., Horkoff, J. (eds.) CAiSE 2014. LNCS, vol. 8484, pp. 42–57. Springer, Heidelberg (2014)
22. Senderovich, A., Weidlich, M., Gal, A., Mandelbaum, A., Kadish, S., Bunnell, C.A.: Discovery and validation of queueing networks in scheduled processes. In: Zdravkovic, J., Kirikova, M., Johannesson, P. (eds.) CAiSE 2015. LNCS, vol. 9097, pp. 417–433. Springer, Heidelberg (2015)
23. Smirnov, S., Reijers, H., Weske, M., Nugteren, T.: Business process model abstraction: a definition, catalog, and survey. Distributed and Parallel Databases **30**(1), 63–99 (2012)
24. Vernon, M., Zahorjan, J., Lazowska, E.D.: A comparison of performance Petri nets and queueing network models. University of Wisconsin-Madison, Computer Sciences Department (1986)

Process Modeling

Specification and Verification of Complex Business Processes - A High-Level Petri Net-Based Approach

Ahmed Kheldoun[1(✉)], Kamel Barkaoui[2], and Malika Ioualalen[1]

[1] MOVEP, Computer Science Department, USTHB, Algiers, Algeria
ahmedkheldoun@yahoo.fr, mioualalen@usthb.dz
[2] CEDRIC-CNAM, 292 Rue Saint-Martin, 75141 Cedex 03, Paris, France
kamel.barkaoui@cnam.fr

Abstract. The Business Process Modeling Notation (BPMN) has been widely used as a tool for business process modeling. However, BPMN suffers from a lack of standard formal semantics. This weakness can lead to inconsistencies, ambiguities, and incompletenesses within the developed models. In this paper we propose a formal semantics of BPMN using recursive ECATNets. Owing to this formalism, a large set of BPMN features such cancellation, multiple instantiation of subprocesses and exception handling can be covered while taking into account the data flow aspect. The benefits and usefulness of this modelling are illustrated through two examples. Moreover, since recursive ECATNets semantics is expressed in terms of conditional rewriting logic, one can use the Maude LTL model checker to verify several behavioral properties related to BPMN models.

Keywords: Business process modelling · BPMN · RECATNets · Conditional rewriting logic · Maude language and tool.

1 Introduction

The standard Business Process Modeling Notation (BPMN) [12] has been established as the de-facto standard for modeling business processes. It provides a standard notation easily understandable that supports the business process management while being able to represent complex processes semantics. Nevertheless, despite the various advantages of BPMN, it suffers from a lack of formal semantics which can lead to inconsistencies, ambiguities, and incompletenesses within the developed models. Furthermore, BPMN brings additional features drawn from a range of sources including Workflow Patterns [15] which are able to define: (1) subprocesses that may be executed multiple times concurrently; and (2) subprocesses that may be interrupted as a result of exceptions. These features increase the types of semantic errors that can be found in BPMN models. As a result, many researchers proposed formal methods to build formal description and verification models of business processes. However, one of the weaknesses of

© Springer International Publishing Switzerland 2015
H.R. Motahari-Nezhad et al. (Eds.): BPM 2015, LNCS 9253, pp. 55–71, 2015.
DOI: 10.1007/978-3-319-23063-4_4

these proposals is their lack of support for modeling complex BPMN business processes involving exception, cancellation and multiple instantiation of subprocesses. For that, we need an expressive modeling formalism that allows, on one hand, to specify their dynamic structure, and on the other hand, to check the control-flow correctness of these business processes while taking into account their data flow aspect.

In this paper, we propose the use of Recursive ECATNets [1] to cope with the modeling and verification of complex BPMN models. The Recursive ECATNets model offers practical mechanisms for handling the most advanced BPMN constructs (involving exception, cancellation and multiple instances). Since Recursive ECATNets semantics can be expressed in terms of conditional rewriting logic [10], we can use the Maude LTL model-checker [7] to investigate several behavioral properties of business processes.

The remainder of this paper is organized as follows. Section 2 discusses related work. Section 3 provides an overview about BPMN and Recursive ECATNets. Section 4 presents the suggested approach for the verification of BPMN models. Section 5 presents the mapping rules from BPMN to Recursive ECATNet. Section 6 shows two examples for the proposed mapping. Section 7 presents the formal semantics of the mapping rules. Finally, Section 8 concludes and gives some further research directions.

2   Related Work

Many researchers have tried to deal with formal modeling and verification of business processes using BPMN models. [11] presents an extended survey of the existing verification techniques of BPMN diagrams and compares them with each other with respect to motivations and methods. Nevertheless, none of the cited works take into account the following key features of BPMN : (1) cancellation of subprocesses; (2) parallel multi-instance subprocesses; and (3) exception handling in the context of subprocesses that are executed multiple times concurrently.

Petri nets often are a topic in verification of business processes using BPMN models. In [5], the authors propose a mapping from a core set of BPMN to labelled Petri nets. This output is represented in the PNML language [4] and can subsequently be used to verify BPMN processes by using the open source tool WofBPEL [14]. The proposed mapping for exception handling is very complicated and does not work properly in the case where an activity within the subprocess is enabled multiple times concurrently. In [13], the authors propose a Petri-net-based approach to evaluate the feasibility of a BPMN model. This approach enables to reveal deadlocks and infinite loops. It consists in manually translating the BPMN model to a modified BPEL4WS representation, and then to XML-based representation of Colored Petri nets (CPNXML) that can be verified using CPN Tools. However, only, simple BPMN contructs are taken into account. In [18], an approach is proposed to automatically convert business processes to YAWL (Yet Another Workflow Language) nets [16] and to verify them subsequently by YAWL verification tools like WofYAWL [17]. However, modelling a synchronization of a dynamic number of process instances depending on their termination state can't be done using the multiple instantiation constructors of YAWL where the terminated process instances are synchronized following their number and not following their states. Also, the semantics of YAWL constructors is expressed in terms of Colored Petri nets and in terms of reset nets [6] to describe the cancellation construction. Therefore, regarding BPMN analysis, the *soundness* property is not decidable for YAWL specifications. In contrast, our model allows the modelling of cancellation constructs via cut steps execution while the *soundness* property remains decidable, if the state space generated from the specified model is finite [3]. Table 1 summarizes the BPMN features that are supported by the different semantics discussed above. The advantages of our proposed model are : (1) adequate for handling the most

Table 1. Features supported by BPMN semantics

BPMN 2.0 Object	Dijkman et al. [5]	Ou-Yang & Lin [13]	Ye et al. [18]	This paper
Events				
Start events	X	X	X	X
End events	X	X	X	X
Timer events			X	X
Error events (catch)	X		X	X
Error events (throw)	X		X	X
Cancel events			X	X
Message events	X		X	
Gateways				
Parallel Fork (AND-Split)	X	X	X	X
Parallel Join (AND-Join)	X	X	X	X
Data-based gateway (XOR-Split)	X	X	X	X
Event-based gateway (XOR-Split)	X		X	
Merge gateway (XOR-Join)	X	X	X	X
Activities				
Task (atomic activity)	X	X	X	X
Subprocess	X		X	X
Loop activity	X		X	X
Static Multiple instance activity			X	X
Dynamic Multiple instance activity			X	X
Formal method	PN	CPN	YAWL	RECATNet

advanced BPMN constructs such as multiple instantiation, cancellation of sub-processes and exceptional behaviors (2) providing a hierarchical and modular specification (3) allowing distributed execution of modeling business processes and (4) its semantic may be defined in terms of conditional rewriting logic [10] and therefore the model checker Maude [7] can be used to investigate several behavioral properties.

3   Background

This section gives background on BPMN 2.0 and Recursive ECATNets.

3.1   BPMN Overview

A BPMN process, which is using the core subset of BPMN elements shown in Fig. 1 is referred to as a core BPMN process. In this paper, we only consider the well-formed core BPMN models [5].

Definition 1. *A core BPMN process [5] is a tuple* $B = \langle O, F, Cond, Excp \rangle$ *where :*

- *O is a set of objects which can be partitioned into disjoint sets of activities A, events E and gateways G,*
  - *A can be partitioned into disjoint sets of tasks T and subprocess invocation activities S,*
  - *E can be partitioned into disjoint sets of start events E^s, intermediate events E^i and end events E^e,*
  - *E^i can be partitioned into disjoint sets of intermediate message events E^i_M, intermediate timer events E^i_T and intermediate error events E^i_R,*
  - *E^e can be partitioned into disjoint sets of end non-error events E^e_N and end error events E^e_R,*
  - *G can be partitioned into disjoint sets of parallel fork gateways G^F, parallel join gateways G^J, data-based XOR decision gateways G^D and XOR merge gateways G^M.*
- *$F \subseteq O \times O$ is the control flow relation,*
- *$Cond : F \cap (G^D \times O) \to C$ is a function which maps sequence flows emanating from data-based XOR gateways to conditions[1],*
- *$Excp : E^i \to A$ is a function assigning an intermediate event to an activity.*

3.2   RECATNet Overview

Recursive ECATNets (abbreviated RECATNets) [1][2] are a kind of high level algebraic Petri nets combining the expressive power of abstract data types and Recursive Petri nets [8]. RECATNets are proposed to specify flexible concurrent systems where functionalities of discrete event systems such as abstraction, dynamicity, preemption and recursion are preponderant.

---

[1] A condition C is a boolean function, which operates over a set of propositional variables.

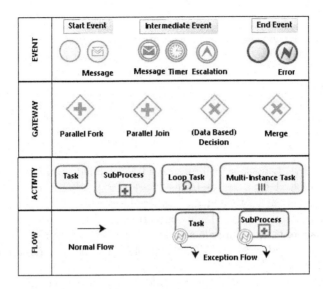

Fig. 1. A core subset of BPMN elements

In what follows, we denote by $Spec = \langle \Sigma, E \rangle$ an algebraic specification of an abstract data type associated to a RECATNet, where $\Sigma = \langle S, OP \rangle$ is its multi-sort signature (S is a finite set of sort symbols and OP is a finite set of operations, such that $OP \cap S = \phi$). E is the set of equations associated to $Spec$. A set of variables associated to $Spec$ is a family $X = (X_s)_{s \in S}$ with X_s being the set of variables of sort s, where $OP \cap X = \phi$. We denote by $T_\Sigma(X)$ the set of Σ-terms with variables in the set X and by $T_{\Sigma,s}(X)$ the set of Σ-terms with variables in the set X_s. The multisets of Σ-terms are denoted by $[T_\Sigma(X)]_\oplus$, where the multiset union operator $(_\oplus)$ is associative, commutative and admits the empty multiset ϕ as the identity element.

Definition 2. *A recursive ECATNet [1] is a tuple* $RECATNet = \langle Spec, P, T,$ *sort*, $Cap, IC, CT, TC, \Omega, I, \Upsilon, ICT, K \rangle$ *where:*

- *$Spec = (\Sigma, E)$ is a many sorted algebra, where the sorts domains are finite (with $\Sigma = (S, OP)$), and X is a set of variables associated to $Spec$,*
- *P is a finite set of places,*
- *$T = T_{elt} \cup T_{abs}$ is a finite set of transitions ($T \cap P = \phi$) partitioned into abstract and elementary ones,*
- *sort: $P \to S$, is a mapping called a sort i.e type assignment,*
- *Cap: is a P-vector on capacity places: $p \in P$, $Cap(p)$: $T_\Sigma(\phi) \to \mathbb{N} \cup \{\infty\}$,*
- *$IC : P \times T \to [T_{\Sigma,sort(p)}(X)]_\oplus$ maps a multiset of terms for every input arc,*
- *$CT : P \times T \to [T_{\Sigma,sort(p)}(X)]_\oplus$ maps a multiset of terms for every output arc (p, t) where $t \in T_{elt}$,*
- *$TC : T \to [T_{\Sigma,bool}(X)]$ maps a boolean expression for each transition,*
- *$\Omega : P \times T_{abs} \to [T_{\Sigma,sort(p)}(X)]_\oplus$ maps a multiset of terms for every starting marking associated to $t \in T_{abs}$ according to place p,*

- $I = I_{cut} \cup I_{pre}$ is a finite set of indices, called termination indices, dedicated to cut steps and preemptions (interruptions) respectively,
- Υ is a family, indexed by I_{cut}, of effective semi-linear sets of final markings,
- $ICT : P \times T_{abs} \times I_{cut} \rightarrow [T_{\Sigma, sort(p)}(X)]_\oplus$ maps a multiset of terms for every output arc (p, t, i) where $t \in T_{abs}$ and $i \in I_{cut}$,
- $K : T_{elt} \rightarrow T_{abs} \times I_{pre}$, maps a set of interrupted abstract transitions, and their associated termination indexes, for every elementary transition.

Let's use the net in Fig. 2(a) to highlight RECATNet's graphical symbols :

1. An elementary transition is represented by a filled rectangle; its name is possibly followed by a set of terms $(t', i) \in T_{abs} \times I$. Each term specifies an abstract transition t', which is under the control of t, associated with a termination index to be used when interrupting t' consequently to a firing of t. For instance, t_{cancel} is an elementary transition, where its firing preempts instances of threads created by the firing of t_1 and the associated termination index is $<1>$.
2. An abstract transition t is represented by a double rectangles; its name is followed by the starting marking $\Omega(t)$. For instance, t_1 is an abstract transition and $\Omega(t_1) = <p_5, Rq>$ means that any thread, named refinement net, created by firing of t_1 starts with one token i.e. Rq in place p_5.
3. Any termination set can be defined based on place marking. For instance, Υ_0 specifies the final marking of threads such that the place p_6 is marked at least by one token.
4. The set I of termination indices is deduced from the indices used to subscript the termination sets and from the indices bound to elementary transitions i.e. interruption. For the example, $I = \{0, 1\}$.

Informally, a RECATNet generates during its execution a dynamical tree of marked threads called *extended marking* [1] which reflects the global state of such net. This latter denotes relation between generated threads, where each one of them having its own execution context.

Let's now consider the net of Fig. 2(a) with initial marking $<p_1, Rq_1> \otimes$ $<p_0, ok>$ to illustrate the firing sequence notion. The graphical representation of any extended marking Tr is a tree where an arc $v_1(m_1) \rightarrow v_2(m_2)$ labelled by t_{abs} means that v_2 is a child of v_1 created by firing the abstract transition t_{abs}, and m_1 (resp. m_2) is the marking of v_1 (resp. v_2). In Fig. 2(b), note that the initial extended marking Tr_0 is reduced to a single node v_0, whose marking is $<p_1, Rq_1> \otimes <p_0, ok>$. From the initial extended marking Tr_0, the abstract transition t_1 is enabled; its firing is achieved as follows: the consumption of tokens specified by the precondition of t_1 (i.e. $IC(t_1)$ from the place p_1) and the creation of a thread modelled by a refinement net, which starts its evolution with an initial marking $\Omega(t_1) = (p_5, Rq)$. The obtained extended marking after firing the abstract transition t_1 is denoted by Tr_1. Note that the extended marking Tr_1 contains a new node v_1 marked by the starting marking $\Omega(t_1)$. Then, the firing of the elementary transition t_2 from the node v_1 of Tr_1 leads to an extended marking Tr_2, having the same structure as Tr_1, but only the marking of node v_1

is changed. From the node v_1 in Tr_2, the cut step τ_0 is enabled; its firing leads to an extended marking Tr_3 by removing the node v_1 and change the marking on its node father i.e. v_0 by adding $ICT(t_1, 0) = (p_4, achieved)$. Also, from the node v_0 in Tr_1, the elementary transition t_{cancel} with associated interruption $(t_1, 1)$ is enabled; its firing leads to an extended marking Tr_4 by removing the node v_1 and changing the marking on its node father, i.e. v_0 by adding $ICT(t_1, 1) = (p_3, cancelled)$.

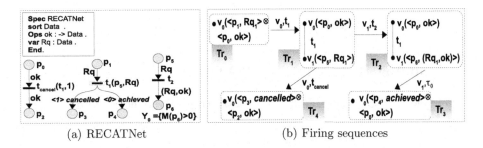

(a) RECATNet   (b) Firing sequences

Fig. 2. Example of a RECATNet and two possible firing sequences

The analysis of a RECATNet is based on constructing its state space, named extended reachability graph, which is used for checking properties such as reachability, deadlock and liveness. Furthermore, RECATNets semantics can be expressed in rewriting logic, and the Maude LTL model checker can be used to check LTL properties.

4   RECATNet Based Model Verification for Business Processes

The proposed approach for the verification of BPMN models is based mainly on Meta-modeling and Model Transformations. It is achieved automatically into three steps : (1) transformation of business processes specified in BPMNs into RECATNets using the ATLAS Transformation Language (ATL) [9] where two meta-models for BPMN and RECATNet are defined (URL: http://recatnets.cnam.fr/), (2) transformation of obtained RECATNets into rewriting logic description using the transformation tool Acceleo (URL: http://www.eclipse.org/acceleo/) (3) checking the properties of business processes expressed as rewrite theories by using the the Maude LTL model checker. This is summarized in Fig. 3.

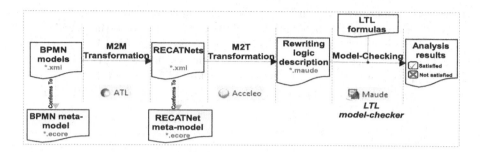

Fig. 3. Overview of the proposed approach

5   Mapping BPMN into RECATNets.

This section presents the mapping rules of the core BPMN models into RECAT-Nets.

5.1   Mapping Events and Gateways

In Fig. 4, we present the mapping of a set of BPMN events and Gateways to RECATNets. A *start event* indicates where a particular process starts. So, in Fig. 4.(a), a *start event* is mapped into an elementary transition with one input place. An *end event* ends the flow of the process. So, in Fig. 4.(b), an *end event* is mapped into one transiton with only one output place. An intermediate event, such *message event* is mapped, in Fig. 4.(c), into an elementary transition with one input resp. output place.

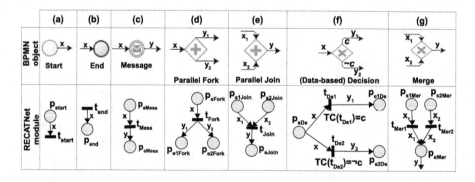

Fig. 4. Mapping Events and Gateways into RECATNets

Gateways are used to control the divergence and convergence of sequence flows in a Process. A *parallel Fork* gateway, known as **AND-Split**, allowing to split one sequence flow into two or more paths that can run in parallel within the process. So, in Fig. 4.(d), a *parallel Fork* gateway is mapped into one elementary transition with only one input place and a set of output places as paths that can run in parallel. A *parallel Join* gateway, known as **AND-Join**, allowing to combine two or more parallel sequence flow paths into one sequence flow path. So, in Fig. 4.(e), a *parallel Join* gateway is mapped into one elementary transition with a set of input places as the number of parallel sequence flow paths to be combined, and one output place. A diverging exclusive *Decision* gateway, known as **XOR-Split**, is used to create alternative paths within a process flow. So, in Fig. 4.(f), a *Decision* gateway is mapped into a set of elementary transitions as the number of alternative paths, sharing in common one input place. To each transition t is associated an additional condition of firing $TC(t)$. A *Merge* gateway, known as **XOR-Join**, is used to combine two or more alternative sequence flow paths into one sequence flow path, but no synchronization is required because no parallel activity runs at the join point. So, in Fig. 4.(g), a *Merge* gateway is mapped into a set of elementary transitions as the number of sequence flow paths to be combined, and one output place.

5.2 Mapping Activities

An activity can be a *task* or a *subprocess*. A *task* is mapped, as shown in Fig. 5.(a), into an elementary transition with one input resp. output place. A *subprocess* may be viewed as an independent BPMN process. In Fig. 5.(b), we depict the mapping of calling a *subprocess* via a subprocess invocation activity. The place $p_{sSubProc}$. resp $p_{eSubProc}$ represents the start. resp end event of the invoked *subprocess*. Also, a semi-linear set of final markings is defined which indicates the end flows of a *subprocess*. For instance, the set $\Upsilon_0 = \{M(p_{eSubProc}) > 0\}$ indicates that a *subprocess* ends when the place $p_{eSubProc}$ is marked. The invocation of a *subprocess* is mapped into an abstract transition $t_{CallSubProc}$ where its starting marking is $\Omega(t_{CallSubProc}) = (p_{sSubProc}, x)$. The firing of the abstract transition $t_{CallSubProc}$ refines the transition by a new sub-net (i.e. creation of new thread, named its child), which starts its own token x in place $p_{sSubProc}$. Once a final marking is reached, according to the semi-linear set of final markings Υ_0 defined above, a cut step closes the corresponding sub-net, and produces tokens in the appropriate output place $p_{eCallSubProc}$ of the abstract transition $t_{CallSubProc}$.

In BPMN, an activity may have attributes specifying its additional behavior, such as looping and parallel multiple instances. Activity looping constructs capture both *While-do* and *do-Until* loops depending on their attribute *TestTime*. In fact, if *TestTime = Before* resp. *TestTime = After* means that the loop condition is evaluated at the beginning resp. at the end of the loop iteration. The Fig. 6.(a) shows the mapping of *While-do* loop activity in RECATNet whereas the Fig. 6.(b) shows the mapping of *do-Until* loop activity in RECATNet. In the obtained RECATNets, when the abstract transition $t_{CallTask}$ is fired, it calls the sub-net associated to the looped *Task*. Parallel multi-instance activity contruct allows for creation a set of activity instances where they executed in parallel. In Fig. 6.(c), we show a mapping of Parallel multi-instance activity. The obtained RECATNet is general where we don't need, a priori, to know the number of

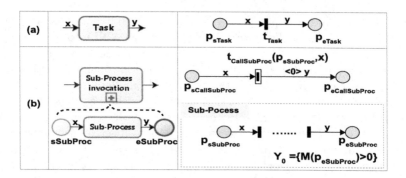

Fig. 5. Mapping Activities into RECATNets

multiple instances of activity. The number of instances may be created dynamically using the elementary transition $t_{addInst}$, where its firing will add a token in place p_{inst}, which can enable the abstract transition $t_{CallTask}$. Each firing of the abstract transition $t_{CallTask}$ will create one instance of the activity $Task$. The elementary transition t_{remove} is used to stop the creation of instances. In the case, where the number of multi-instances (n) running in parallel is known at design time, then the place p_{inst} will be marked by this natural (n).

5.3   Exception Handling

In BPMN, exception handling is captured by exception flow. An exception flow originates from an exception event attached to the boundary of an activity, which is either a task or a subprocess. Fig. 7.(a) depicts the mapping of an exception associated with a task and a subprocess. The RECATNet associated to a subprocess shows the mapping of an exception associated with an atomic activity i.e. $Task$. The occurrence of the exception may only interrupt the normal

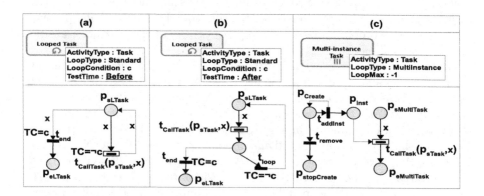

Fig. 6. Mapping Advanced Activities into RECATNets

flow at the point when it is ready to execute the task. Hence, the mapping of an exception associated with a task is an elementary transition t_{exTask} where its firing will avoid to run the atomic activity $Task$ and generates a token represents the type of exception in place p_{exTask}.

For the exception handling associated to a subprocess, the occurrence of the exception event will interrupt the execution of the normal flow within the subprocess, when it is active (running). This mapping is straightforward into RECATNet. Firstly, a semi-linear set of final markings is defined, it indicates the occurring of such exception in a subprocess. For instance, as shown in Fig. 7.(a), the semi-linear set of final markings $\Upsilon_1 = \{M(p_{exTask}) > 0\}$ indicates the occurring of an exception associated to the atomic activity $Task$. So, the subprocess may end with two types of terminations. The first way of termination is when the subprocess ends properly by marking the place $p_{eSubProc}$, which needs to define the set of terminations Υ_0. The second way of termination is when the subprocess ends upon the occurrence of an exception i.e. marking the place p_{exTask} which needs to define the set of termination Υ_1. Secondly, we need to add another output place for the abstract transition, which models the invocation of the subprocess to capture the exception. For instance, as shown in Fig. 7.(a), the asbtract transition $t_{CallSubproc}$, which can invoke the subprocess, has a second output place $p_{sException}$, with index of termination $<1>$. It means that, when the subprocess reachs a final marking in Υ_1, a cut step interrupts the subprocess and produces tokens in the output place $p_{sException}$ associated to the index of termination $<1>$.

5.4   Cancellation Activity

Assume that a subprocess P is nested within another subprocess P' (i.e. P' is the *parent* of P). The execution of P may be cancelled at any point due to the

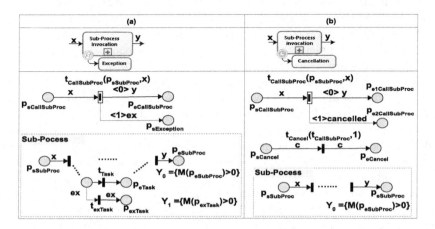

Fig. 7. (a) Mapping exceptions and (b) Mapping cancellation subprocess into RECAT-Nets

cancellation of P', despite whether or not, there is an exception associated with P. This type of construct is very difficult for mapping using other types of Petri nets. But, by using the RECATNets, the mapping becomes straightforward, thanks to the preemption and cut step which are a key features of RECATNet. Fig. 7.(b) depicts the mapping of cancellation subprocess into RECATNet. In fact, in the subprocess P', we need to add an elementary transition t_{Cancel} associated a term $K(t_{Cancel}) = (t_{CallSubproc}, 1)$. The firing of this elementary transition will interrupt all instances of a subprocess P created by firing the abstract transition $t_{CallSubproc}$, with a termination's index $<1>$. After firing this elementary transition, a token $cancelled$ is added to the place $p_{e2CallSubproc}$ for each running instance of subprocess P.

6   Case Studies

In this section, we illustrate our approach for mapping BPMN processes into RECATNets through two examples, where a translation to Petri nets is not feasible.

6.1   Travel Request Process

Fig. 8(a) depicts the business process for Travel Request process. First, the requester enters the information related to the travel, then the administrative department has to manage the bookings for the employee and send the information related to them, once they have been confirmed. The administrative department can manage the car, hotel and flight bookings simultaneously as requested by the employee. When completed, the subprocess finishes. However, many situations can arise during the booking process. Suppose that the administrative department has successfully confirmed the car and hotel booking, but when the flight is going to be booked, an error arises (connection error, etc.). Thus, the sub-process will have to be finished and an exception flow has to be enabled for the main process. In addition, to make the travel request process more flexible, the employee must be able to cancel the booking process at any moment, if necessary.

The RECATNet derived from the travel request process is depicted in Fig. 8(b). The obtained RECATNet contains one abstract transition $t_{CallBook}$, where its firing will call the sub-net models the booking process. As shown in Fig. 8(b), the sub-net associated to the booking process models the car, hotel and flight bookings by three elementary transitions $t_{CarBook}$, $t_{HotelBook}$ and $t_{FlightBook}$. Then to each type of booking is associated an elementary transition to model exceptions. For instance, the elementary transition $t_{FlightBookEx}$ models the exceptions occurred during flight booking. The abstract transition $t_{CallBook}$ has three outgoing labelled arcs. The arc labelled by the termination index $<0>$ means that the bookings process ends successfully. The arc labelled by the termination index $<1>$ $BookError$ means that the bookings process ends with failure and the expected error $BookError$ is returned. The arc labelled

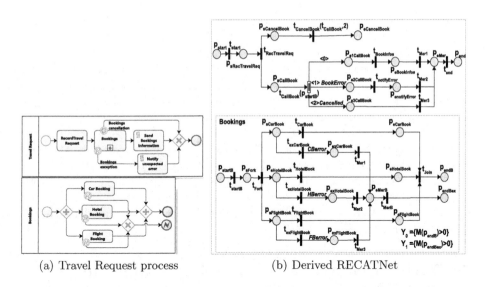

(a) Travel Request process   (b) Derived RECATNet

Fig. 8. Travel Request process and its derived RECATNet

by the termination index $<2>$ *Cancelled* means that the Bookings process is cancelled when firing the elementary transition $t_{CancelBook}$ associated a term $K(t_{CancelBook}) = (t_{CallBook}, 2)$.

6.2   Intelligence Test Process (Cancel Multiple Instance Activity)

The Cancel Multiple Instance Task pattern describes the ability of completing a whole Multiple Instance task by withdrawing all running instances, which have not yet been completed. For instance, the Human Resources Manager

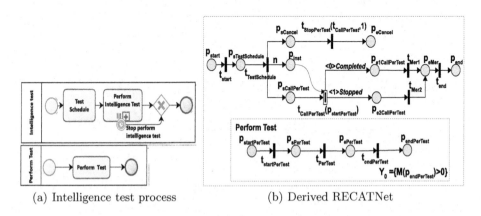

(a) Intelligence test process   (b) Derived RECATNet

Fig. 9. Intelligence test process and its derived RECATNet

established that a group of applicants must face concurrently the same intelligence test. However, the Human Resources Manager must be able to interrupt applicants, when a specific test's time is expired. The business process modelling this example is shown in Fig. 9(a). The RECATNet derived from the intelligence test process is depicted in Fig. 9(b). The abstract transition $t_{CallPerTest}$ is used to call the subnet models the perform test process. The abstract transition $t_{CallPerTest}$ has two outgoing labelled arcs. The arc labelled by the termination index <0> *Completed* means that the perform test process ends successfully. The arc labelled by the termination index <1> *Stopped* means that the perform test process is interrupted. In fact, when firing the elementary transition $t_{StopPerTest}$, associated a term $K(t_{StopPerTest}) = (t_{CallPerTest}, 1)$, it interrupts all running instances which perform test process, created by the abstract transition $t_{CallPerTest}$. This type of BPMN process is not trivial to model by other types of Petri nets.

7   Formal Semantics of the Mapping BPMN into RECATNet

In this section, we formally define the mapping of BPMN to RECATNet. In order to facilitate the definition, we introduce the following functions : The function $in(x) = \{y \in O | (y, x) \in F\}$ returns the input BMPN objects of a BPMN object x, the function $out(x) = \{y \in O | (x, y) \in F\}$ returns the output BPMN objects of a BPMN object x, the function $endsSubProc(S)$ returns the set of end events in a BPMN subprocess associated to invocation activity S, the function $startSubProc(S)$ returns the start event in a BPMN subprocess associated to invocation activity S and the function $getTermIndex()$ returns a natural number represent the index of termination.

Definition 3. *Let $B = \langle O, F, Cond, Excp \rangle$ be a core BPMN process. Without considering activities attributes and the communication between interacting processes, B can be mapped to a RECATNet $= \langle Spec, P, T, sort, Cap, IC, CT, TC, \Omega, I, \Upsilon, ICT, K \rangle$ where:*

start event $start \in E^s$	$P = P \cup \{p_{start}\}$, $T_{elt} = T_{elt} \cup \{t_{start}\}$, $IC = IC \cup \{(p_{start}, t_{start}, token)\}$, $CT = CT \cup \{(t_{start}, p_{(start,y)}, token) | y \in out(start)\}$
end event $end \in E^e$	$P = P \cup \{p_{end}\}$, $T_{elt} = T_{elt} \cup \{t_{end}\}$, $IC = IC \cup \{(p_{(x,end)}, t_{end}, token) | x \in in(end)\}$, $CT = CT \cup \{(t_{end}, p_{end}, token)\}$, $\Upsilon = \Upsilon \cup \{(p_{end} > 0, getTermIndex()) | \exists_{x \in S} : end \in endSubProc(x)\}$
sequence flow $(x, y) \in F$	$P = P \cup \{p_{(x,y)}\}$

fork $x \in G^F$	$T_{elt} = T_{elt} \cup \{t_x\}$, $IC = IC \cup \{(p_{(x,y)}, t_y, token)|y \in in(x)\}$, $CT = CT \cup \{(t_x, p_{(x,y)}, token)|y \in out(x)\}$
join $x \in G^J$	$T_{elt} = T_{elt} \cup \{t_x\}$, $IC = IC \cup \{(p_{(x,y)}, t_y, token)|y \in in(x)\}$, $CT = CT \cup \{(t_x, p_{(x,y)}, token)|y \in out(x)\}$
data-decision $x \in G^D$	$T_{elt} = T_{elt} \cup \{t_{(x,y)}|y \in out(x)\}$, $TC = TC \cup \{(t_{(x,y),Cond(x,y)})|y \in out(x)\}$, $IC = IC \cup \{(p_{(z,x)}, t_{(x,y)}, token)|y \in out(x) \wedge z \in in(x)\}$, $CT = CT \cup \{t_{(x,y)}, (p_{(x,y)}, token)|y \in out(x)\}$
merge $x \in G^M$	$T_{elt} = T_{elt} \cup \{t_{(x,y)}|y \in in(x)\}$, $IC = IC \cup \{(p_{(y,x)}, t_{(x,y)}, token)|y \in in(x)\}$, $CT = CT \cup \{t_{(x,y)}, (p_{(x,z)}, token)|y \in in(x) \wedge z \in out(x)\}$
intermediate event $x \in E^i$	$T_{elt} = T_{elt} \cup \{t_x|in(x) \neq \phi\}$, $IC = \{(p_{(y,x)}, t_x, token)|y \in in(x)\}$, $CT = CT \cup \{(t_x, p_{(x,y)}, token)|y \in out(x)\}$
task $x \in T$	$T_{elt} = T_{elt} \cup \{t_x\}$, $IC = IC \cup \{(p_{(y,x)}, t_x, token)|y \in in(x)\}$, $CT = CT \cup \{(t_x, p_{(x,y)}, token)|y \in out(x)\}$
subprocess $x \in S$	$T_{abs} = T_{abs} \cup \{t_x\}$, $\Omega = \Omega \cup \{(t_x, p_{start}, token)|start = startSubProc(x)\}$, $IC = IC \cup \{(p_{(y,x)}, t_x, token)|y \in in(x)\}$, $ICT = ICT \cup \{(t_x, p_{(x,y)}, index, token)|y \in out(x) \wedge$ $\exists_{cs(p_{end},index)} \in \gamma end \in endsSubProc(x) \wedge end \in E_N^e\}$
exception@task E_R^i@T	$T_{elt} = T_{elt} \cup \{t_{excp}|excp \in E_R^i \wedge in(excp) = \phi \wedge \exists_{y \in T} y = Excp(excp)\}$, $IC = IC \cup \{(p_{(x,y)}, t_{excp}, exception)|y \in T \wedge x \in in(y) \wedge excp \in E_R^i \wedge y = Excp(excp)\}$, $CT = CT \cup \{(t_{excp}, p_{(excp,y)}, exception)|excp \in E_R^i \wedge \exists_{x \in T} x = Excp(excp) \wedge y \in out(excp)\} \cup$
exception@subprocess E_R^i@S	$ICT = ICT \cup \{(t_y, p_{(excp,z)}, index, exception)|y \in S \wedge excp \in E_R^i \wedge y = Excp(excp) \wedge z \in out(excp) \wedge \exists_{cs(p_{end},index)} \in \gamma end \in endsSubProc(y)\} \wedge end \in E_R^e\}$
cancellation@task E_T^i@T	$T_{elt} = T_{elt} \cup \{t_{cancel}|cancel \in E_T^i \wedge in(cancel) = \phi \wedge \exists_{y \in T} y = Excp(cancel)\}$, $IC = IC \cup \{(p_{(x,y)}, t_{cancel}, cancelled)|y \in T \wedge x \in in(y) \wedge cancel \in E_T^i \wedge y = Excp(cancel)\}$, $CT = CT \cup \{(t_{cancel}, p_{(cancel,y)}, cancelled)|cancel \in E_T^i \wedge \exists_{x \in T} x = Excp(cancel) \wedge y \in out(cancel)\}$

cancellation @subprocess $E_T^i @S$	$P = P \cup \{p_{scancel}, p_{ecancel} \mid cancel \in E_T^i \wedge \exists_{y \in S} \, y = Excp(cancel)\}$, $T_{elt} = T_{elt} \cup \{t_{cancel} \mid cancel \in E_T^i \wedge in(cancel) = \phi \wedge \exists_{y \in S} \, y = Excp(cancel)\}$, $IC = IC \cup \{(p_{scancel}, t_{cancel}, cancelled) \mid cancel \in E_T^i \wedge \exists_{x \in S} \, x = Excp(cancel)\}$, $CT = CT \cup \{(t_{cancel}, p_{ecancel}, cancelled) \mid cancel \in E_T^i \wedge \exists_{x \in S} \, x = Excp(cancel)\}$, $\Upsilon = \Upsilon \cup \{(\phi_c, getTermIndex()) \mid \exists_{s \in S} \, \exists_{c \in E_T^i} s = Excp(c)\}$, $ICT = ICT \cup \{(t_y, p_{(cancel,z)}, index, cancelled) \mid y \in S \wedge cancel \in E_T^i \wedge y = Excp(cancel) \wedge z \in out(cancel) \wedge \exists_{cs(\phi_c, index) \in \Upsilon} c = cancel\}$, $K = K \cup \{(t_{cancel}, t_x, index) \mid cancel \in E_T^i \wedge x \in S \wedge x = Excp(cancel) \wedge \exists_{cs(\phi_c, index) \in \Upsilon} c = cancel\}$

8   Conclusion and Future Work

The contribution of this work is a definition of a method allowing the transformation of a subset of BPMN to RECATNets. On the basis of mapping rules for which a formal semantics is established. With this mapping, we can cover a large set of BPMN features like cancellation, multiple instantiation of subprocesses and exception handling while taking into account the data flow aspect.

The formalism of RECATNets benefits from its definition in terms of rewriting logic. A set of rewriting rules has been introduced in [1][2] to express the semantics of RECATNet in termes of rewriting logic. In order to automate this transformation, we have developed a Model-to-Text (M2T) transformation tool based Acceleo generator code. Since we obtain a rewriting logic description from a RECATNet, we can benefit from the use of the LTL model checker of the Maude system for verification purpose. For instance, we can check the liveness and the safety properties on the finite generated state space related to finite BPMN models.

In the future, we plan to complete this work by developing a graphical tool which helps users to visualize the derived RECATNets from their BPMN models. Other ongoing work aims at extending this work by proposing a mapping rules for other BPMN constructs such as transaction, compensation activities...etc.

References

1. Barkaoui, K., Hicheur, A.: Towards analysis of flexible and collaborative workflow using recursive ECATNets. In: ter Hofstede, A.H.M., Benatallah, B., Paik, H.-Y. (eds.) BPM Workshops 2007. LNCS, vol. 4928, pp. 232–244. Springer, Heidelberg (2008)

2. Barkaoui, K., Boucheneb, H., Hicheur, A.: Modelling and analysis of time-constrained flexible workflows with time recursive ECATNet. In: Bruni, R., Wolf, K. (eds.) Web Services and Formal Methods. LNCS, vol. 5387, pp. 19–36. Springer, Berlin Heidelberg (2008)
3. Hicheur, A.: Modélisation et Analyse des Processus Workflows Reconfigurables et Distribués par les ECATNets Récursifs. Ph.D. dissertation. CEDRIC-CNAM, Paris (2009)
4. Billington, J., Christensen, S., van Hee, K.M., Kindler, E., Kummer, O., Petrucci, L., Post, R., Stehno, C., Weber, M.: The petri net markup language: concepts, technology, and tools. In: van der Aalst, W.M.P., Best, E. (eds.) ICATPN 2003. LNCS, vol. 2679, pp. 483–505. Springer, Heidelberg (2003)
5. Dijkman, R.M., Dumas, M., Ouyang, C.: Semantics and Analysis of Business Process Models in BPMN. Information and Software Technology **50**(12), 1281–1294 (2008)
6. Dufourd, C., Finkel, A., Schnoebelen, P.: Reset nets between decidability and undecidability. In: Larsen, K.G., Skyum, S., Winskel, G. (eds.) ICALP 1998. LNCS, vol. 1443, pp. 103–115. Springer, Heidelberg (1998)
7. Eker, S., Meseguer, J., Sridharanarayanan, A.: The Maude LTL Model Checker. Electronic Notes in Theoretical Computer Science **71**, 162–187 (2004)
8. Haddad, S., Poitrenaud, D.: Recursive Petri nets - Theory and application to discrete event systems. Acta Informatica **44**(7–8), 463–508 (2007)
9. Jouault, F., Allilaire, F., Bzivin, J., Kurtev, I.: ATL : A model transformation tool. Science of Computer Programming (EST) **72**(1–2), 31–39 (2008). Special Issue on Second issue of experimental software and toolkits
10. Meseguer, J.: Conditional rewriting logic as a unified model of concurrency. Theoretical Computer Science **96**(1), 73–155 (1992)
11. Morimoto, S.: A survey of formal verification for business process modeling. In: Bubak, M., van Albada, G.D., Dongarra, J., Sloot, P.M.A. (eds.) ICCS 2008, Part II. LNCS, vol. 5102, pp. 514–522. Springer, Heidelberg (2008)
12. O. M. G. (OMG). Business Process Model and Notation (BPMN), Version 2.0. Technical report, January 2011
13. Ou-Yang, C., Lin, Y.D.: BPMN-based business process model feasibility analysis: a Petri net approach. International Journal of Production Research **46**(14), 3763–3781 (2008)
14. Ouyang, C., Verbeek, E., van der Aalst, W.M.P., Breutel, S., Dumas, M., ter Hofstede, A.H.M.: WofBPEL: A tool for automated analysis of BPEL processes. In: Benatallah, B., Casati, F., Traverso, P. (eds.) ICSOC 2005. LNCS, vol. 3826, pp. 484–489. Springer, Heidelberg (2005)
15. Russell, N., ter Hofstede, A., van der Aalst, W., Mulyar, N.: Workflow Control-Flow Patterns: A Revised View. Technical report, BPM Center (2006)
16. van der Aalst, W., ter Hofstede, A.: YAWL: Yet Another Workflow Language. Information Systems **30**(4), 245–275 (2005)
17. Verbeek, H.M.W.E., van der Aalst, W.M.P.: Woflan 2.0 A petri-net-based workflow diagnosis tool. In: Nielsen, M., Simpson, D. (eds.) ICATPN 2000. LNCS, vol. 1825, pp. 475–484. Springer, Heidelberg (2000)
18. Ye, J., Sun, S., Song, W., Wen, L.: Formal semantics of BPMN process models using YAWL. In: Second International Symposium on Intelligent Information Technology Application (IITA), vol. 2, pp. 70–74, December 2008

Concurrency and Asynchrony
in Declarative Workflows

Søren Debois[1]([✉]), Thomas Hildebrandt[1], and Tijs Slaats[1,2]

[1] IT University of Copenhagen, Copenhagen, Denmark
{debois,hilde,tslaats}@itu.dk
[2] Exformatics A/S, 2100 Copenhagen, Denmark

Abstract. *Declarative* or *constraint-based* business process and work-flow notations, in particular DECLARE and Dynamic Condition Response (DCR) graphs, have received increasing interest in the last decade as possible means of addressing the challenge of supporting at the same time flexibility in execution, adaptability and compliance. However, the definition of *concurrent* semantics, which is a necessary foundation for asynchronously executing distributed processes, is not obvious for formalisms such as DECLARE and DCR Graphs. This is in stark contrast to the very successful Petri-net–based process languages, which have an inherent notion of concurrency. In this paper, we propose a notion of concurrency for declarative process models, formulated in the context of DCR graphs, and exploiting the so-called "true concurrency" semantics of Labelled Asynchronous Transition Systems. We demonstrate how this semantic underpinning of concurrency in DCR Graphs admits asynchronous execution of declarative workflows both conceptually and by reporting on a prototype implementation of a distributed declarative workflow engine. Both the theoretical development and the implementation is supported by an extended example; moreover, the theoretical development has been verified correct in the Isabelle-HOL interactive theorem prover.

1 Introduction

The last decade has witnessed a massive revival of business process and workflow management systems driven by the need to provide more efficient processes and at the same time guarantee compliance with regulations and equal treatment of customers. Starting from relatively simple and repetitive business processes, e.g. for handling invoices, the next step is to digitalise more *flexible work processes*, e.g. of knowledge workers [22] that are *distributed* across different departments.

In many business process management solutions, notably solutions employing Business Process Model and Notation (BPMN), a distributed process will be described as a set of pools, where each pool contains a flow graph that explicitly

Authors listed alphabetically. This research is supported by ITU, Exformatics A/S and the Velux Foundation through the Computational Artefacts (CompArt) project (http://www.compart.ku.dk).

© Springer International Publishing Switzerland 2015
H.R. Motahari-Nezhad et al. (Eds.): BPM 2015, LNCS 9253, pp. 72–89, 2015.
DOI: 10.1007/978-3-319-23063-4_5

describes the flow of control between actions at that particular location. However, the explicit design time specification of both distribution and control flow sometimes lead to overly rigid processes; and changes to the distribution and control flow at run time, i.e. delegation of activities to different locations, repetition or skipping of activities, is non-trivial to support. Moreover, flow diagrams describe constraints on the ordering of activities only implicitly. For instance, a simple business rule stating that a bank customer must provide a budget before getting approved for a loan can be checked only by verifying that on every path from the request for a loan to an approval, there is a "receive budget" event. Depending on the exact process language, the complexity of verifying this simple rule ranges from challenging to undecidable.

Towards the challenge of accommodating flexibility and compliance, there has been a renewed and increasing interest in *declarative* or *constraint-based* process notations such as DECLARE [23,24] and Dynamic Condition Response (DCR) graphs [7,13,16]. In a declarative process notation, a process is described by the constraints it must fulfill, while the control flow is left implicit. This means that activities can be carried out in any order and at any location that fulfills the constraints. It also means that compliance rules and constraints are captured explicitly in the model. However, so far constraint-based process notations have only been equipped with sequential semantics allowing only one event to happen at a time. This is in stark contrast to successful Petri Net-based workflow specifications, which have an inherent notion of concurrency.

In the present paper we make the following contributions:

1. We provide an overview of the challenges a notion of concurrency must overcome for an event-based declarative workflow notation.
2. We give a "true concurrency" semantics for DCR graphs by enriching DCR graphs with a notion of *independent events*, and prove that the semantics of a DCR graph in this case gives rise to a labelled asynchronous transition system [25,27]. The development, which is quite technical, has been verified to be correct in the Isabelle-HOL interactive theorem prover[19]; the formalised development is available online [4].
3. We show how this semantic underpinning of concurrency admits practical asynchronous execution of declarative workflows. Essentially, this is achieved by assigning events to location. Thus, we capture asynchronous semantics for the entire spectrum of distributions, spanning from the fully centralized workflow where every event is happening at the same location, to the fully decentralized workflow, where every event is managed at its own location.
4. We demonstrate the practical feasibility of the developed theory by reporting on a prototype implementation of a distributed declarative workflow engine. The prototype is accessible online [3].

Related Work. Concurrency and distribution of workflows defined as flow graphs are well-studied. Declarative modelling and concurrency has been studied in the context of the Guard Stage Milestone (GSM) model [14] and declaratively specified (Business) Protocols [8–10,26]. In the GSM model [14], declarative rules govern the state of Guards, which in turn admits Stages to open and execute.

The declarative rules reference a global state, which executing a Stage might change non-atomically. Stages may run concurrently; to prevent errors of atomicity, a transactional concistency dicipline based on locks is followed. That is, stages can be said to be concurrent if they do not have interferring reads and writes to the global state. Neither (core) DCR graphs nor (core) DECLARE has explicit notions of data, global state or state update. Writes and reads of data must be modelled in DCR graphs as events, and interferrence between such events by relations, i.e. any write event to a data location should explicitly exclude and include every other event representing access to the same location. Thus, dependencies between activities are not expressed implicitly as predicates on a global state, but instead explicitly through relations between activities.

In [8–10,26] protocols are given declaratively as rules governing which actions must and must not be available in a given state. Like GSM, the steps in the protocol entail modifying the global state, and the availability of actions in a particular state is directly expressed as predicates on this state. Unlike GSM, race conditions are resolved by either ordering the types of updates [8], or by projecting the global specification onto subsets of its rules in a way that avoids the problems of non-local state and blindness [10].

The Agent-based approach of [15], while philosophically similar to the present approach, sidesteps the issue of concurrency. Agents manage or invoke services, comprised of tasks; tasks are explicitly declared as being in sequence, in parallel, etc. Before invoking a service, the invoking agent must negotiate the particulars of its usage with the managing agent; this negotiation is specified in part declaratively. It is left to the implementation of agents and services to ensure that concurrency issues do not arise.

Concurrency is less well-studied in the setting of pure declarative formalisms without explicit data and global state, like DECLARE and DCR graphs. We took tentative steps for DCR graphs in [1]. For DECLARE, [11,12] provide pattern based translations of a subset of DECLARE LTL constraints to Petri Nets by giving a net for each constraint. These works do not cover the full expressive power of LTL (in particular, they only cover finitary semantics). In contrast, DCR Graphs are known to be equivalent to Büchi-automata [5,16,18], and thus express infinitary liveness conditions and are more expressive than LTL. [20] offers a fully automatic mapping from Declare to finite state automata to Petri Nets, but disregard the independence relation in their translation. Finally, [21] considers declarative, event-based workflow specifications. Local constraints for each event are derived from a global specification provided in an LTL-like temporal logic. However, the use of the temporal logic makes the setting dependent on an initial calculation of the local constraints, which only provide the independence relation implicitly.

2   Concurrency and Declarative Workflows

In this section, we explain through examples the issues surrounding concurrency in declarative workflow specifications, and give the main gist of our proposed solution. Along the way, we will recall the declarative model of DCR graphs.

2.1   A Mortgage Credit Application Workflow

As our main example, we will use a declarative specification of a workflow from the financial services industry, specifically the mortgage application process of a mortgage credit institution. The example is based on an ongoing project with the Danish mortgage credit institution BRFKredit. For confidentiality reasons, we are unable to present an actual process of BRFKredit; instead, we have distilled down the major challenges discovered in that project into the following wholly fictitious application process.

Mortgage application processes are in practice *extremely* varied, depending on the type of mortgage, the neighbourhood, the applicant, and the credit institution in question. The purpose of the process is to arrive at a point where the activity *Assess loan application* can be carried out. This requires in turn:

1. Collecting appropriate documentation,
2. collecting a budget from the applicant, and
3. appraising the property.

In practice, applicants' budgets tend to be underspecified, so an intern will screen the budget and request a new one if the submitted one happens to be so.

The caseworker decides if the appraisal can be entirely statistical, i.e., carried out without physical inspection, but rather based on a statistical model taking into account location, tax valuation, trade history etc.; or if it requires an on-site appraisal. On-site appraisals are cursory in nature, and do not require actually entering the property. For reasons of cost efficiency, one may not do both on-site and statistical appraisals, not even in the case of an audit. However, if the neighbourhood is insufficiently uniform, a thorough on-site appraisal is required. This thorough appraisal requires physical access to the property, so the mobile consultant performing the appraisal will in this case need to book a time with the applicant.

Appraisals are occasionally audited as a matter of internal controls; an audit may entail an on-site appraisal, which may or may not coincide with an ordinary on-site appraisal. It is customary, however, to consider a statistical appraisal an acceptable substitute for an on-site appraisal during an audit.

2.2   A DCR Formalisation

This textual description of the application process is inherently *declarative*: we have described constraints on the ordering of activities in the process rather than positing a particular sequencing. Thus, this process is naturally described by a declarative process model such as DECLARE or DCR graphs. Presently, we give a DCR graph-based declarative model in Figure 1 on page 76, produced with the tool available at [3].

DCR models are graphical; activities, also known as "events" are represented by boxes, labelled by the name of the activity and the role or participant executing that activity. E.g., the top-right box represents an activity *Collect documents* which is carried out by a caseworker. Activities are colored according to their

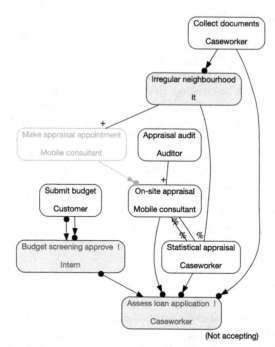

Fig. 1. Declarative DCR model of a mortgage application process

state: grey is not currently executable, red text is required, and greyed out is excluded. Arrows between boxes represent constraints between activities. DCR graphs define in their most basic form only 4 such constraints: Conditions and Responses, Inclusions and Exclusions.

Conditions. A condition, drawn as an arrow with a dot at the head, represents the requirement that the source activity must be executed at least once before the target activity can be executed. In our model, we see, e.g., that *Collect documents* must be executed before *Assess loan application* can be.

Responses. An activity can be required for the workflow to be considered complete, usually called *accepting*. Incomplete or "pending" activities are labelled in red and have an exclamation mark next to them. In the model, the activities *Budget screening approve* and *Assess loan application* are initially pending. A response, represented by an arrow with a dot at the tail, indicates that executing the source activity imposes the requirement to later do the target activity, that is, executing the former makes the latter pending. In the model, when an applicant does *Submit budget*, this imposes the requirement of a subsequent screening, and so there is a response from *Submit budget* to *Budget screening approve*.

Inclusions and Exclusions. An activity is always in one of two states: it is either included or excluded. In diagrams, excluded activities are drawn with a thin gray; regularly drawn activities are included. An excluded activity cannot execute; it cannot prevent the workflow from being accepting, even if it is pending; and it cannot prevent other activities from executing, even if they have conditions on it. For ease of reading, conditions from excluded activities are also drawn with a thin gray, to indicate that they currently do not have effect.

An activity may cause other activities to be included or excluded when it is itself executed. This is indicated diagrammatically with arrows that has "+" and "%" as heads. In the model, the *Irregular neighbourhood* activity—which is an automated activity executed by IT-systems—includes the *Make appraisal appointment*, which is initially excluded; this in turn makes *On-site appraisal* non-executable until the appointment has been made, by virtue of the condition from *Make appraisal appointment* to *On-site appraisal*. Conversely, the *On-site appraisal* and *Statistical appraisal* activities exclude each other: after doing one, one may no longer do the other.

The semantics of a DCR model is the set of (finite and infinite) sequences of activities in which every pending activity is eventually executed. We call such sequences "traces". For finite traces, this means that no activity is pending at the end.

Example 2.1. The model in Figure 1 admits (among infinitely many others), the following three traces. The first is the "happy path", the usual and simplest case. The second is the "happy path" for the less frequent case of an irregular neighborhood. The third is a convoluted special case, with audit and re-submission of a pre-screened budgets.

1. *Collect documents, Submit budget, Statistical appraisal, Budget screening approve, Assess loan application.*
2. *Submit budget, Collect documents, Irregular neighbourhood, Budget screening approve, Make appraisal appointment, On-site appraisal, Assess loan application.*
3. *Collect documents, Submit budget, Statistical appraisal, Irregular neighbourhood, Budget screening approve, Appraisal audit, Make appraisal appointment, Submit budget, On-site appraisal, Budget screening approve, Assess loan application.*

2.3   Concurrency in the Example Workflow

It would appear that certain activities in this workflow could happen concurrently, whereas others are somehow in conflict. It is clear from the textual specification that, e.g., the process of submitting and screening the budget is independent from the appraisal model, and we would expect to be able to execute them concurrently in practice.

Our DCR model of Figure 1 appears to bear out this observation: there are no arrows—and so it would seem no constraints—between *Submit budget* and *Budget screening approve* on the one hand; and *Appraisal audit, On-site appraisal,* and *Statistical appraisal* on the other. This insight begets the question: Exactly when are two activities concurrent? Exactly when will it always be admissible to swap two activities? These questions have practical relevance: E.g., the mobile consultant might be without internet connectivity when he executes the activity *On-site appraisal*; but this is admissible *only* if it is somehow guaranteed that only concurrent activities happen simultaneously.

We proceed to examine what is a reasonable notion of concurrency of activities through a series of examples. We will attempt to obtain a set of principles to help us later judge what is and is not a good definition of "concurrency".

Example 2.2. The traces indicated above gives an indication that there is indeed some form of independence, in that, e.g., in the first trace, the activities *Submit budget* on the one hand and *Statistical appraisal* on the other can be swapped and we still have an admissible trace. In fact, it is not terribly difficult to prove that in any admissible trace, we can always swap adjacent activities when one is among the budget activities and the other is among the appraisal activities, and the trace we then get is still admissible.

The principle we observe here is that adjacent concurrent activities should be able to happen in either order.

Example 2.3. A very easy example of activities that cannot be considered concurrent are ones related by a condition. If one requires the other to have happened previously, clearly they cannot in general happen at the same time. This is the case for, e.g., *Collect documents* and *Irregular neighbourhood*.

The principle we observe here is that concurrent activities cannot enable each other.

Example 2.4. However, clearly not every two activities can be reasonably swapped. For instance, the activies *On-site appraisal* and *Statistical appraisal* are specified to be mutually exclusive (in most cases) in the textual specification, and in the DCR model each excludes the other. If one happens, the other cannot, and so they cannot reasonably be considered concurrent: When they cannot happen one after the other, surely they should not be allowed to happen simultaneously.

The principle we observe here is that concurrent activities cannot disable each other.

Example 2.5. A different way activities can be in conflict is if their executions have mutually incompatible effects on the state of the DCR graph. For instance, the *Appraisal audit* includes *On-site appraisal*, whereas *Statistical appraisal* excludes it. Clearly, *Appraisal audit* and *Statistical appraisal* cannot be executed concurrently: if they were to happen at the same time, what would be the resulting state of *On-site appraisal*—included or excluded?

The principle we observe here is that concurrent activities cannot have incompatible effects on the state of other activities.

Example 2.6. The examples we have seen so far have one thing in common: activities that could not be considered concurrent were related by arrows in the model. Could it be that events not directly related are necessarily concurrent?

No! Consider the events *Irregular neighbourhood* and *On-site appraisal*. These are not directly related: there are no arrows from one to the other. However,

Irregular neighbourhood includes *Make appraisal appointment*, which is a condition for *On-site appraisal*. Thus executing *Irregular neighbourhood* prevents the execution of *On-site appraisal*. Thus we might observe the ordering first *On-site appraisal* followed by *Irregular neighbourhood*, but never the opposite order. In the abstract, like for conditions, one of these activities precludes the execution of the other, and so they cannot be considered concurrent—even though there is no arrow between them.

The principle we observe here we saw already before: concurrent events cannot disable each other.

In subsequent sections, we formalise concurrency of DCR activities in terms of Labelled Asynchronous Transition Systems. We shall see that within the notion of concurrency embodied in those, the handful of examples we have given above in fact embody *all* the ways activities of a DCR graph can be non-concurrent.

3 DCR Graphs

In this Section we define DCR graphs formally. This is a necessary prerequisite for defining concurrency of DCR graph events (activities) in the next Section.

The formalisation here mirrors a mechanised but somewhat less readable formalisation in the proof-assistant Isabelle-HOL [19]; results of the next section are verified to be correct by Isabelle-HOL. The formalisation is available online [4].

We will need the following notation. For a set E we write $\mathcal{P}(E)$ for the power set of E (i.e. set of all subsets of E) and $\mathcal{P}_{ne}(E)$ for the set of all non-empty subsets of E. For a binary relation $\to \subseteq E \times E$ and a subset $\xi \subseteq E$ of E we write $\to \xi$ and $\xi \to$ for the set $\{e \in E \mid (\exists e' \in \xi \mid e \to e')\}$ and the set $\{e \in E \mid (\exists e' \in \xi \mid e' \to e)\}$ respectively. For convenience, we write $\to e$ and $e \to$ instead of the tiresome $\to \{e\}$ and $\{e\} \to$.

In Def. 3.1 below we formally define DCR Graphs.

Definition 3.1 (DCR Graph). *A Dynamic Condition Response Graph (DCR Graph) G is a tuple* $(\mathsf{E}, \mathsf{M}, \mathsf{R}, \mathsf{L}, l)$, *where*

(i) E *is a set of* events *(or activities),*
(ii) $\mathsf{M} = (\mathsf{Ex}, \mathsf{Re}, \mathsf{In}) \in \mathcal{M}(G)$ *is the* marking, *for* $\mathcal{M}(G) =_{def} \mathcal{P}(\mathsf{E}) \times \mathcal{P}(\mathsf{E}) \times \mathcal{P}(\mathsf{E})$ *(mnemonics: Executed, Response-required, and Included),*
(iii) $\mathsf{R} = (\to\bullet, \bullet\to, \to+, \to\%)$ *are the* condition, response, include *and* exclude *relation respectively, with each relation* $\to \subseteq \mathsf{E} \times \mathsf{E}$.
(iv) L *is the set of* labels *and* $l : \mathsf{E} \to \mathsf{L}$ *is a labeling function mapping events to labels.*

For the remainder of this paper, when a DCR graph G is clear from the context, we will assume it has sub-components named as in the above definition; i.e., we will write simply $\bullet\to$ and understand it to be the response relation of G.

An event of a DCR graph is enabled if it is included and every one of its conditions were previously executed:

Definition 3.2. *For an event e of a DCR graph G, we say that e is enabled, written $G \vdash e$, iff $e \in \mathsf{In} \wedge (\mathsf{In} \cap \rightarrow\bullet e) \subseteq \mathsf{Ex}$.*

In the following definitions we then define the result of executing an event of a DCR Graph. Firstly, in Def. *3.3* we define the *effect* of the execution of the event, i.e. which event was executed(Δe), which events are being included(ΔI), which events are being excluded(ΔX) and which events are being made pending(ΔR). We then in Def. *3.4* define how the effect is applied to the (marking of the) DCR Graph to yield a new (marking of the) DCR Graph: Δe is added to the set of executed events, first ΔX are removed from the set of included events and afterwards ΔI are added to the set of included events (meaning that events that are both included and excluded in a single step will remain included), finally Δe is removed from the set of pending responses before ΔR is added to the set of pending responses (meaning that if an event is a response to itself it will remain pending after execution). Finally in Def. *3.5* we define how these two operations are used together to execute an event on a DCR Graph, yielding a new DCR Graph.

Definition 3.3. *The* effect *of the execution of an event e on a DCR Graph G is given by* EFFECT$(G, e) = (\Delta e, \Delta I, \Delta X, \Delta R)$ *where:*

(i) $\Delta e = \{e\}$ the singleton set containing the event being executed,
(ii) $\Delta I = e \rightarrow+$ the events being included by e,
(iii) $\Delta X = e \rightarrow\%$ the events being excluded by e,
(iv) $\Delta R = e \bullet\rightarrow$ the events being made pending by e.

When the DCR Graph G is given from the context we will below write δ_e for EFFECT(G, e).

Definition 3.4. *The* action *effect* $\delta_e = (\Delta e, \Delta I, \Delta X, \Delta R)$ *on marking* $(\mathsf{Ex}, \mathsf{Re}, \mathsf{In})$ *is:*

$$\delta_e \cdot (\mathsf{Ex}, \mathsf{Re}, \mathsf{In}) = \big(\mathsf{Ex} \cup \Delta e, (\mathsf{Re} \setminus \Delta e) \cup \Delta R, (\mathsf{In} \setminus \Delta X) \cup \Delta I\big)$$

The action of effect δ_e on a DCR Graph $G = (E, M, R, L, l)$ is then defined as:

$$\delta_e \cdot (E, M, R, L, l) = (E, \delta_e \cdot M, R, L, l)$$

Definition 3.5. *For a Dynamic Condition Response Graph G and event $G \vdash e$, we define the result of executing e as $G \oplus e =_{def}$ EFFECT$(G, e) \cdot G$.*

Towards defining accepting executions of DCR graphs, we first define the *obligations* of a DCR graphs to be its set of included, pending events.

Definition 3.6. *Given a DCR graph $G = (E, M, R, L, l)$ with marking $M = (\mathsf{Ex}, \mathsf{Re}, \mathsf{In})$, we define the* obligations *of G to be* OBL$(G) = \mathsf{Re} \cap \mathsf{In}$.

Having defined when events are enabled for execution, the effect of executing an event and a notion of obligations for DCR Graphs we define in Def. 3.7 the notion of finite and infinite executions and when they are accepting. Intuitively, an execution is accepting if any obligation in any intermediate marking is eventually executed or excluded.

Definition 3.7 (DCR Semantics). *For a DCR graph G an* execution *of G is a (finite or infinite) sequence of tuples $\{(G_i, e_i, G_i')\}_{i \leq k}$ (for $k \in \mathbb{N} \cup \omega$) each comprising a DCR Graph, an event and another DCR Graph such that $G = G_0$ and for $i < k$ we have $G_i' = G_{i+1}$; moreover for $i \leq k$ we have $G_i \vdash e_i$ and $G_i' = G_i \oplus e_i$. We say the execution is* accepting *if for $i \leq k$ we have for all $e \in \mathrm{OBL}(G_i)$ there is a $j \geq i$ with either $e_j = e$ or $e \notin \mathrm{OBL}(G_j')$. We denote by $\mathsf{exe}(G)$ respectively $\mathsf{acc}(G)$ the sets of all executions respectively all accepting executions of G. Finally, we say that a DCR graph G' is* reachable *from G iff there exists a finite execution of G ending in G'.*

4 Asynchronous Transition Systems and DCR Graphs

With the DCR graphs in place, we proceed to imbue DCR graphs with a notion of concurrency. For this, we use the classical model of asynchronous transition systems [27], here extended with labels as in [25]. As mentioned, the development has been verified in Isabelle-HOL [19]; the formalisation source is available online [4].

Once we embed DCR graphs in labelled asynchronous transition systems, we shall find that the examples of concurrent and non-concurrent activities from Section 2 actually exemplify *independent* and non-independent events. Moreover, the examples will turn out to be exhaustive, in the sense that each example exemplifies one of the properties necessary for events to be (or not to be) independent.

We apply the results of the present section in Section 5, when we present a prototype implementation of a distributed declarative workflow engine. The correctness of this engine hinges on the notion of independence presented here.

First, we recall the definition of labelled asynchronous transition systems [25].

Definition 4.1 (LATS). *A* Labelled Asynchronous Transition System *is a tuple $A = (S, s_0, \mathsf{Ev}, \mathsf{Act}, l, \rightarrow, I)$ comprising states S, an initial state $s_0 \in S$, events Ev, a labelling function $l : \mathsf{Ev} \rightarrow \mathsf{Act}$ assigning labels (actions) to events, a transition relation $\rightarrow \subseteq S \times \mathsf{Ev} \times S$, and an irreflexive, symmetric independence relation I satisfying*

1. *$s \xrightarrow{e} s'$ and $s \xrightarrow{e} s''$ implies $s' = s''$*
2. *$s \xrightarrow{e} s'$ and $s' \xrightarrow{e'} s''$ and eIe' implies $\exists s'''$ such $s \xrightarrow{e'} s'''$ and $s''' \xrightarrow{e} s''$*
3. *$s \xrightarrow{e} s'$ and $s \xrightarrow{e'} s''$ and eIe' implies $\exists s'''$ such $s' \xrightarrow{e'} s'''$ and $s'' \xrightarrow{e} s'''$*

In words, the first property says simply that the LATS is *event-determinate*: an event will take you to one and only one new state. The second says that independent events do not enable each other. The third that independent events can be re-ordered. In the context of DCR graphs, the first property is trivially true, and we have seen an example of the second property holding in Example 2.3, and of the third in Example 2.2.

For the remainder of this section, we establish that a DCR graph G gives rise to a LATS $\mathcal{A}(G)$. Along the way, we shall see how the various definitions we set up to eventually arrive at independence arise from the examples of "obviously concurrent" and "obviously non-concurrent" behaviours we saw in Section 2.

Towards finding a suitable notion of independence, we first define a notion of effect-orthogonality for events of a DCR graph. As we shall see, this orthogonality characterises the situation where the effects of events commute on markings.

Definition 4.2. *We say that events* $e \neq f$ *of a DCR graph* G *are* effect-orthogonal *iff*

1. *no event included by* e *is excluded by* f *and vice versa, and*
2. e *requires a response from some* g *iff* f *does.*

We lift this notion to effects themselves, saying δ_e, δ_f *of* G *are orthogonal iff* e, f *are.*

Here, the first condition says that effect-orthogonal events cannot have conflicting effects. We saw an example of such conflicts in Example 2.5: the *Appraisal audit* includes *On-site appraisal*, whereas *Statistical appraisal* excludes it. The second condition is perhaps less intuitive, saying that if one event makes the other pending, the other event hides this effect by making itself pending. A more intuitive, but also more restrictive alternative, would be to require that neither event has a response on the other.

Proposition 4.3. *Let* δ_e, δ_f *be effects of a DCR graph* G*, and let* M *be a marking for* G*. If* e, f *are orthogonal then* $\delta_e \cdot (\delta_f \cdot M) = \delta_f \cdot (\delta_e \cdot M)$*.*

Proof (in Isabelle). See [4], Lemma "orthogonal-effect-commute".

Next, we define that two events are cause-orthogonal. The intention is that for such event pairs, executing one cannot change the executability of the other.

Definition 4.4. *Events* e, f *of a DCR-graph* G *are* cause-orthogonal *iff*

1. *neither event is a condition for the other,*
2. *neither event includes or excludes the other, and*
3. *neither event includes or excludes a condition of the other.*

We saw examples of all three conditions previously. Specifically, for (1), we saw in Example 2.3 that *Collect documents* is a condition for *Irregular neighbourhood*, and so these activities cannot be considered non-causal. For (2), we saw in Example 2.4 how *On-site appraisal* and *Statistical appraisal* exclude each other and thus cannot be cause-orthogonal. For (3), we saw in Example 2.6 how *Irregular neighbourhood* included a condition of *On-site appraisal*, and thus those two events cannot be cause-orthogonal.

From effect- and cause-orthogonality, we obtain the requisite notion of independence. This explains the contents of the examples we have seen so far: activities that could be considered "concurrent" are independent; those that could not are not.

Definition 4.5. *Given a DCR graph G, we say that events e, f are independent if they are both effect- and cause-orthogonal. We write I_G for the independence relation induced by a DCR-graph G.*

We must of course prove that our proposed independence relation I_G satisfies the conditions for an independence relation of Definition 4.1.

Theorem 4.6. *Let G be a DCR graph. If e, f are independent events of G then any marking in G satisfies the concurrency properties (1–3) of Definition 4.1.*

Proof (in Isabelle). See [4], Theorem "causation-and-orthogonality-entails-independence".

And with that, we arrive at a formal definition of concurrency for the declarative workflow model of DCR graphs: Each DCR graph has an associated independence relation, and thus an associated LATS, which tells us which activities (events) can be considered concurrent and which cannot.

Corollary 4.7. *Let G be a DCR graph. Then $\mathcal{L}(\mathcal{G})$ is a Labelled Asynchronous Transition System when equipped with independence relation I_G. We call this LATS $\mathcal{A}(\mathcal{G})$.*

Proof (in Isabelle). See [4], Theorem "DCR-LATS".

We shall see in Section 5 how Corollary 4.7 and Theorem 4.6 enables a practical distributed implementation of declarative workflows in general, and in particular of our mortgage application example. We conclude this section by noting in Table 1 which events of our running example are in fact independent.

5 A Process Engine for Distributed Declarative Workflows

The previous sections supply an understanding of DCR graphs as labelled asynchronous transition systems and in particular of independence of DCR graph events. With that, the door opens to a distributed implementation of a declarative workflow language. We have implemented such a prototype engine; in this Section, we describe by example the workings of that engine.

The central idea is to exploit the extremely local nature of DCR events in conjunction with the notion of independence. Because of the locality of DCR events, we can partition the set of events of a DCR graph into *components*, assigning each component to a distinct node in a distributed system. The node is responsible for executing the particular event, and for notifying other components of executions, when such executions requires them to update their state.

However, a node cannot freely execute its events; that would leave us open to all the mistakes of non-concurrency exemplified in Section 2. We therefore employ a locking mechanism to ensure that *only concurrent events can be executed simultaneously.*

Table 1. Independence relation for activites of the model of Figure 1.

	Appraisal audit	Assess loan application	Budget screening approve	Collect documents	Irregular neighbourhood	Make appraisal appointment	On-site appraisal	Statistical appraisal	Submit budget
Appraisal audit			x	x	x	x			x
Assess loan application						x			x
Budget screening approve	x			x	x	x	x	x	
Collect documents	x		x			x	x	x	x
Irregular neighbourhood	x		x						x
Make appraisal appointment	x	x	x	x				x	x
On-site appraisal			x	x					x
Statistical appraisal			x	x		x			x
Submit budget	x	x		x	x	x	x	x	

We exemplify this by forming a distributed version of our running example. For ease of presentation, we distribute the workflow over only two nodes: one for the "Mobile consultant" (presumably his mobile device), and one for the rest. However, the principles of distribution employed here apply to arbitrarily fine sub-divisions of DCR graphs, right down to each node hosting only a single event.

Presently, we obtain the two components in Figure 2. The diagram for each component represents remote events as dashed boxes. Moreover each component retains only remote events with which some local event is not independent. For the "Mobile consultant" component (Figure 2), that means that all events related to budgets are gone, as is the initial *Collect documents*. The "other" component (Figure 2) retains all the "Mobile consultant" events, because every event of the Mobile consultant is in fact in conflict with some event local to "other".

The procedure for executing an event, in detail, is as follows. A component wishing to execute an event e must first request[1] and receive locks on all (local and remote) events that are in conflict (i.e., not independent) with e (thus, in particular, on itself). It then queries the state of remote events to determine if e is currently executable. If it is, it instructs remote events affected by firing e to change state accordingly. Finally, it releases all locks.

For example, if the "other" component wishes to execute the *Assess loan application* event in the DCR graphs of Figures 2 and 2, it will first request and receive a lock on *On-site appraisal*; then query the state of *On-site appraisal*;

---

[1] All components request locks in the same fixed order to prevent deadlocks.

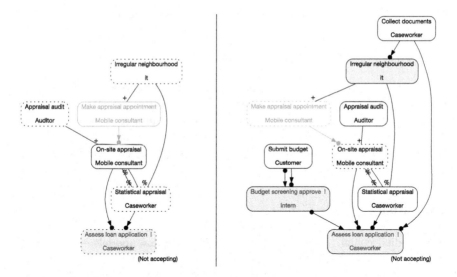

Fig. 2. Component models for the Mobile consultant (left) and for other roles (right).

then find out that that event is not previously executed; and will then release the lock on *On-site appraisal*.

Notice that since this procedure is based on independence, it allows concurrency in the very concrete sense that the "other" component is free to execute any of the events *Collect documents*, *Submit budget*, and *Budget screening approve* **without** communication with the "Mobile consultant" component, because these three events are all independent with all the events of the "Mobile consultant" component. Conversely, any other event requires communication, since these other events are all in conflict with the some event of the "Mobile consultant" component.

Implementation. We have implemented the technique described here in the DCR Workbench, an existing web-based tool for experimenting with DCR graphs; see, e.g., [7]. The diagrams in this paper are all output from this prototype.

The prototype allows specifying components by accepting for each activity an optional indication of a URL at which the event is located. E.g, in the component model for other roles (Fig 2), the remote activity "On-site appraisal" is given as:

```
"On-site appraisal"
  [ role = "Mobile consultant"
    url  = "http://localhost:8090/events/On-site%20appraisal" ]
```

The DCR Workbench then enables starting separate REST services for each such component model. Each service accesses information about state of remote events by issuing a GET to URLs derived from the specified one. E.g., in the other roles component model, "On-site appraisal" is a condition for "Assess loan application"; accordingly, to execute "Assess loan application", the REST service

for that model will query the executed state of "On-site appraisal" by issuing a
GET request to:

```
http://localhost:8090/events/On-site%20appraisal/executed
```

Similarly, PUT requests are used to update the state of remote activities; e.g.,
"Irregular neighbourhood" will, when executed, make "Make appraisal appointment" excluded by issuing an appropriate PUT.The implementation ensures
that before state of remote events is queried or updated, all independent activities are locked. Please refer to the prototype [3] to experiment with declarative
concurrency first-hand!

6   Conclusion

We have studied concurrency of pure declarative workflow models. This problem is important, since its solution is a prerequisite for implementing distributed
engines for declaratively specified workflows. Concretely, we investigated reasonable examples and non-examples of concurrency for the declarative DCR model
by example; we formally added a notion of concurrency between events of DCR
graphs, enriching the standard semantics to a semantics of the classical true
concurrency model of labelled asynchronous transition systems. We backed this
foundational contribution by (a) a formal verification in Isabelle-HOL of the
development [4], and (b) a proof-of-concept implementation of a distributed
declarative workflow engine, available at [3].

6.1   Discussion and Future Work

The present work considers only core DCR Graphs, which can represent only
finite state processes and have no (practical) representation of data, as events
can not be parametrized by data. This consitutes of course a noteworthy gap
between the theory and practice.

The practical commercial use of DCR graphs by Exformatics has succes-
fully employed DCR graphs as a control-flow layer on top of an underlying
database, using database triggers as events signalling changes to data values [6].
Processes dynamically handling multiple instances of business artifacts (e.g. multiple instances of the budget in our running example) with separate life cycles
were realised by different DCR graphs, one for each data object being processed,
interacting via the underlying database. In this case, the present work would
apply to the individual models for each artifact, but not accross the models.

In [5,7], DCR Graphs have been extended to DCR Graphs with sub-
processes, allowing dynamically created multiple instances of sub processes and
thus enabling analysis of processes as described above. We believe that the
present work on concurrency can be lifted to DCR Graphs with sub-processes.
The increased expressiveness however comes at the cost of making the model
Turing complete [5].

Regarding data, we are presently working on extending the work on sub-processes for DCR-graphs [7] to *parametric* sub-processes: Events which take data values as input can spawn a new sub-process as a continuation, whose shape depends on the data inputs (and in particular allows to declaratively "store" the reviewed data in the continuation, as in functional programming languages). This should be compared to declarative models facilitating data and state as side-effects on a global state such as [14].

On a different note, given the similarity of DCR graphs and DECLARE, it is natural to ask whether the presently introduced notion of concurrency and subsequent distribution of executable models can be transferred to DECLARE. To this end, it's important to realise that the present work relies crucially on the notion of "event state" inherent in DCR graphs. Concurrency and independence can be framed in terms of which events may or may not update the states of other events by firing. DECLARE does not come with a similar notion of state, and so it would appear that the present approach does not apply directly. However, there is still hope: Looking at the standard relations of DECLARE instead of LTL in general, it seems plausible that one might define an alternate semantics either by encoding of DECLARE into DCR Graphs or in terms of some similar notion of "activity state"; and then apply the approach of the present paper.

Our work with industry suggests that the flexibility of DCR Graphs is sought for, but the difficulty of presenting and understanding declarative models is a major obstacle to wider adaptation of declarative methodologies. This often stems from fairly small models defining sometimes quite complex behaviour. We believe that the ability to distribute DCR Graphs and understand the independence between events is likely to help presenting the models. For instance, defining independence for DCR graph events as labelled asynchronous transition systems (lats) opens the door to an encoding of DCR graphs into Petri nets using the mapping from lats to Petri nets in [25]. In addition to opening up for the application of the many tools and techniques developed for Petri Nets, it would give a way of deriving flow diagrams from DCR graphs in a concurrency-preserving way, which should be compared to the work in [11].

Finally, the concurrent semantics opens up for possible use of partial-order reduction model checking techniques [2] towards more efficient static analysis of DCR graphs than the current implementations based on verification on Büchi-automata [16–18].

Acknowledgments. The authors gratefully acknowledges helpful comments from Younes Nielsen, Morten Marquard, Nicholas Guenot, and anonymous reviewers.

References

1. Stehr, M.-O., Kim, M., Talcott, C.: Toward distributed declarative control of networked cyber-physical systems. In: Yu, Z., Liscano, R., Chen, G., Zhang, D., Zhou, X. (eds.) UIC 2010. LNCS, vol. 6406, pp. 397–413. Springer, Heidelberg (2010)
2. Baier, C., Katoen, J.-P., et al.: Principles of model checking. MIT Press (2008)
3. Debois, S.: DCR Workbench (2015). http://tiger.itu.dk:8021/static/bpm2015.html

4. Debois, S.: Isabelle-hol formalisation of present paper (2015). http://www.itu.dk/people/debois/dcr-isabelle
5. Debois, S., Hildebrandt, T., Slaats, T.: Safety, liveness and run-time refinement for modular process-aware information systems with dynamic sub processes. In: Bjørner, N., de Boer, F. (eds.) FM 2015. LNCS, vol. 9109, pp. 143–160. Springer, Heidelberg (2015)
6. Debois, S.: Thomas hildebrandt, tijs slaats, and morten marquard. a case for declarative process modelling: agile development of a grant application system. In: EDOC Workshops 2014, pp. 126–133. IEEE, September 2014
7. Debois, S., Hildebrandt, T., Slaats, T.: Hierarchical declarative modelling with refinement and sub-processes. In: Sadiq, S., Soffer, P., Völzer, H. (eds.) BPM 2014. LNCS, vol. 8659, pp. 18–33. Springer, Heidelberg (2014)
8. Desai, N., Chopra, A.K., Arrott, M., Specht, B., Singh, M.P.: Engineering foreign exchange processes via commitment protocols. In: IEEE International Conference on Services Computing (SCC 2007), pp. 514–521. IEEE (2007)
9. Desai, N., Chopra, A.K., Singh, M.P.: Amoeba: A methodology for modeling and evolving cross-organizational business processes. ACM Trans. Softw. Eng. Methodol. 19(2), 6:1–6:45 (2009)
10. Desai, N., Singh, M.P.: On the enactability of business protocols. In: AAAI 2008, pp. 1126–1131. AAAI Press (2008)
11. Fahland, D.: Synthesizing petri nets from LTL specifications - an engineering approach. In: Philippi, S., Pinl, A. (eds.) Proc. of Algorithmen und Werkzeuge Petrinetze (AWPN), Arbeitsbericht aus dem Fach Informatik, Nr. 25/2007, pp. 69–74. Universitt Koblenz-Landau, Germany, September 2007
12. Fahland, D.: Towards analyzing declarative workflows. In: Autonomous and Adaptive Web Services, number 07061 in Dagstuhl Seminar Proceedings. Internationales Begegnungs- und Forschungszentrum fuer Informatik (IBFI). Schloss Dagstuhl, Germany (2007)
13. Hildebrandt, T.T., Mukkamala, R.R.: Declarative event-based workflow as distributed dynamic condition response graphs. In: PLACES. EPTCS, vol. 69, pp. 59–73 (2010)
14. Richard, H., et al.: Introducing the guard-stage-milestone approach for specifying business entity lifecycles (invited talk). In: Bravetti, M. (ed.) WS-FM 2010. LNCS, vol. 6551, pp. 1–24. Springer, Heidelberg (2011)
15. Jennings, N.R., Faratin, P., Johnson, M.J., Norman, T.J., O'Brien, P., Wiegand, M.E.: Agent-based Business Process Management. Int'l. J. of Cooperative Inf. Sys. 05(02n03), 105–130 (1996)
16. Mukkamala, R.R.: A Formal Model For Declarative Workflows - Dynamic Condition Response Graphs. PhD thesis, IT University of Copenhagen, March 2012
17. Mukkamala, R.R., Hildebrandt, T., Slaats, T.: Towards trustworthy adaptive case management with dynamic condition response graphs. In: EDOC, pp. 127–136. IEEE (2013)
18. Mukkamala, R.R., Hildebrandt, T.T.: From dynamic condition response structures to büchi automata. In: TASE, pp. 187–190. IEEE Computer Society (2010)
19. Nipkow, T., Wenzel, M., Paulson, L.C.: Isabelle/HOL: A Proof Assistant for Higher-order Logic. Springer, Heidelberg (2002)
20. Prescher, J., Di Ciccio, C., Mendling, J.: From declarative processes to imperative models. In: SIMPDA 2014, pp. 162–173 (2014)
21. Singh, M.P.: Synthesizing distributed constrained events from transactional workflow specifications. In: Proc. of the Twelfth Int'l Conf. on Data Eng., pp. 616–623. IEEE (1996)

22. Swenson, K.D.: Mastering the Unpredictable: How Adaptive Case Management Will Revolutionize the Way That Knowledge Workers Get Things Done. Meghan-Kiffer (2010)
23. van der Aalst, W., Pesic, M., Schonenberg, H., Westergaard, M., Maggi, F.M.: Declare. Webpage (2010). http://www.win.tue.nl/declare/
24. van der Aalst, W.M.P., Pesic, M.: DecSerFlow: Towards a truly declarative service flow language. In: Bravetti, M., Núñez, M., Zavattaro, G. (eds.) WS-FM 2006. LNCS, vol. 4184, pp. 1–23. Springer, Heidelberg (2006)
25. Winskel, G., Nielsen, M.: Models for concurrency. In: Handbook of Logic and the Foundations of Computer Science, vol. 4, pp. 1–148. OUP (1995)
26. Yolum, P., Singh, M.P.: Flexible protocol specification and execution: Applying event calculus planning using commitments. In: AAMAS 2002, pp. 527–534. ACM (2002)
27. Zielonka, W.: Notes on finite asynchronous automata. Informatique Théorique et Applications **21**(2), 99–135 (1987)

Detecting Inconsistencies Between Process Models and Textual Descriptions

Han van der Aa[1]($\boxtimes$), Henrik Leopold[1], and Hajo A. Reijers[1,2]

[1] Department of Computer Sciences, Vrije Universiteit Amsterdam,
Faculty of Sciences, De Boelelaan 1081, 1081HV Amsterdam, The Netherlands
`j.h.vander.aa@vu.nl`
[2] Department of Mathematics and Computer Science, Eindhoven University
of Technology, PO Box 513, 5600MB Eindhoven, The Netherlands

Abstract. Text-based and model-based process descriptions have their
own particular strengths and, as such, appeal to different stakeholders.
For this reason, it is not unusual to find within an organization descriptions of the same business processes in both modes. When considering
that hundreds of such descriptions may be in use in a particular organization by dozens of people, using a variety of editors, there is a clear
risk that such models become misaligned. To reduce the time and effort
needed to repair such situations, this paper presents the first approach to
automatically identify inconsistencies between a process model and a corresponding textual description. Our approach leverages natural language
processing techniques to identify cases where the two process representations describe activities in different orders, as well as model activities
that are missing from the textual description. A quantitative evaluation
with 46 real-life model-text pairs demonstrates that our approach allows
users to quickly and effectively identify those descriptions in a process
repository that are inconsistent.

1 Introduction

Organizations use business process models for documenting and improving business operations as well as for the specification of requirements for information
systems [18]. As a result, many companies maintain huge process model repositories, often including several hundred or even thousand models [32]. While
process models turn out to be useful artifacts in numerous contexts, many organizations are also aware of their limitations. One major challenge is that process
models are not intuitive to every employee. Particularly business professionals,
those who actually conduct the various process tasks, often do not feel confident
in reading and interpreting process models [7,11]. For this reason, the value of
maintaining text-based business process descriptions alongside model-based ones
has been recognized [24]. A textual description uses natural language to outline
the steps of a business process. While such a description may not be suitable to
exactly represent all complex aspects of a process [3], it has the advantage that it
can be understood by virtually everyone. Companies can thus ensure that information about their processes is widely accessible by using textual descriptions
next to using process models for analytical and technical purposes [1].

© Springer International Publishing Switzerland 2015
H.R. Motahari-Nezhad et al. (Eds.): BPM 2015, LNCS 9253, pp. 90–105, 2015.
DOI: 10.1007/978-3-319-23063-4_6

Despite its merits, the existence of multiple representation formats describing the same process can lead to considerable problems as well. When a text and a process model both describe the same business process, it is crucial to prevent inconsistencies in terms of contradicting information. Inconsistencies occur in particular when documents are being developed or maintained independently from each other [31]. Once conflicts start occurring over time, the effort that is needed to identify and clear up the differences is considerable, even more so when organizations have already built up huge process repositories.

To effectively deal with the problem of inconsistencies between process model and text, we propose in this paper a technique that automatically detects differences between textual and model-based process descriptions. The technique can be used to quickly identify those process models in a collection that are likely to diverge from their accompanying textual descriptions. This allows organizations to focus their efforts on those processes that can be expected to contain such inconsistencies. Focusing on such key processes is crucial for organizations, since few have the resources required to analyze all their processes in detail [11]. Our quantitative evaluation demonstrates that the proposed technique is indeed able to quickly identify the vast majority of problematic processes in a collection of model-text pairs obtained from practice.

The remainder of this paper is structured as follows. Section 2 explains the research problem using an illustrative example. Section 3 discusses related work and identifies the research gap of interest. Section 4 describes the proposed approach for inconsistency detection. In Section 5, we present a quantitative evaluation of the approach. Finally, we conclude the paper and present directions for future research in Section 6.

2   Problem Illustration

To illustrate the challenges that are associated with the endeavor to detect inconsistencies between textual and model-based process descriptions, consider the model-text pair shown in Figure 1. It includes a textual and a model-based description of a bicycle manufacturing process. On the left-hand side, we observe a textual description, which comprises eleven sentences. On the right-hand side, a corresponding model-based description can be seen, expressed in the Business Process Model and Notation (BPMN). The model contains nine activities, which are depicted using boxes with rounded edges. The diamond shapes that contain a plus symbol indicate concurrent streams of action; the diamond shapes containing a cross represent decision points. The gray shades suggest correspondences between the sentences and the activities of the process model.

A closer look at the example reveals that many connections between the two artifacts are evident. For example, there is little doubt that sentence (7) describes the activity *"reserve part"* or that sentence (8) describes the activity *"back-order part"*. In some cases, however, there is clearly an inconsistency between the two process representations. For instance, there is no sentence that is related to the activity *"ship bicycle to customer"*, i.e. that activity is missing from the

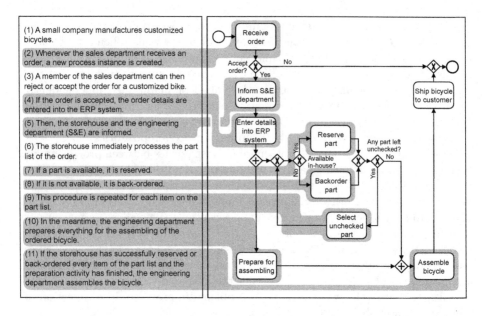

Fig. 1. A textual and a model-based description of a bicycle manufacturing process

textual description. Likewise, we can observe that sentences (4) and (5) occur in a different order than the corresponding activities in the model.

In other cases it is *less* straightforward to decide on the consistency – or lack thereof – between the representations. For example, the text of sentence (9) simply indicates that a part of the process must be repeated. By contrast, the model includes an activity, "*select unchecked part*", which associates an explicit action with this repetition. Whether or not sentence (9) actually describes an activity, and thus should be considered an inconsistency, seems to be open for debate. Ambiguous cases that are already difficult to resolve for human readers pose even greater problems when texts are analyzed in an automatic manner.

The brief illustration of the model-text pair from Figure 1 shows that an appropriate technique for detecting inconsistencies (i) must consider several types of inconsistencies and (ii) must deal with considerable challenges caused by the ambiguous nature of natural language.

3 Related Work

The work presented in this paper relates to two major streams of research: semantic matching and transformations between model and text.

Semantic matching refers to the task of identifying relations between concepts [15]. Particularly in the field of schema and ontology matching it has received considerable attention [10,13,30]. However, in recent years the potential of matching was also recognized in the domain of process modeling [5]. So-called process model matchers are capable of automatically identifying correspondences between the activities of two process models. The application scenarios of these matchers range from harmonization of process model variants [21] to the detection of of process model clones [34]. To accomplish these goals, matchers exploit different process model features, including natural language [12], model structure [9], and behavior [20]. Nevertheless, due to the different nature of our problem, these matchers cannot be applied in a straightforward fashion. Natural language texts neither explicitly provide structural nor behavioral information. Natural language information in texts also differs significantly from what we can find in process model activities. The labels of model activities are shorter than sentences; they also lack the background information and conditional sentences that are provided by natural language texts [23].

The field of transformations between model and text can be further subdivided into two groups. The first group relates to techniques that automatically derive models from natural language text material. Such techniques have been defined for UML class diagrams [4], entity-relationship models [16], and process models [14]. The second group includes techniques that transform a given model into a textual description. Such techniques have been defined for UML diagrams [28], object models [22], and process models [24]. What both groups have in common is that they provide insights on how to move from model to text and vice versa. Among others, they address the problem of inferring structural and behavioral information from textual descriptions. However, to achieve satisfactory results, these techniques require human input. Hence, they are not suitable for supporting the automatic identification of correspondences between a textual and a model-based description.

In summary, we can state that existing techniques do not provide the means to adequately compare textual and model-based process descriptions. In light of this research gap, we define an approach that detects inconsistencies between textual and model-based process descriptions in the subsequent section.

4   Approach

This section describes our approach to identify inconsistent model-text pairs in a process model repository, which consists of various steps. It ultimately provides a quantification of the likelihood that any particular model-text pair contains inconsistencies. Section 4.1 presents an overview of the approach. Sections 4.2 through 4.5 subsequently describe the steps of the approach in detail.

4.1   Overview

As depicted in Figure 2, the first three steps in our approach set out to create an *activity-sentence* correspondence relation between a process model's activities and the sentences of a textual process description. This aligns each process model activity to the sentence that best describes it, if any. To obtain an optimal correspondence relation, we first subject the textual process description and the labels of the activities in the process model to a linguistic analysis. Second, we compute similarity scores between individual activities and sentences, which quantify how well a given sentence describes an activity. Third, we compute an optimal activity-sentence correspondence relation. We do so by complementing the similarity scores with a consideration of the ordering relations that exist between the various process elements. In the fourth and final step, the approach evaluates the quality of the obtained correspondence relation. The quality is here assessed in terms of the similarity between activities and sentences included in the optimal correspondence relation. If this quality is deemed sufficient, we expect that the model-text pair does not contain any inconsistencies. If, however, the correspondence relation has severe quality issues, we predict that the model-text pair contains inconsistencies.

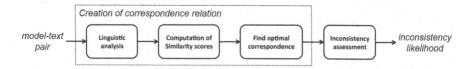

Fig. 2. Outline of the approach

4.2   Linguistic Analysis

In order to create an accurate activity-sentence correspondence for a model-text pair, we first subject the textual process description and the activity labels to a linguistic analysis. In this step we make extensive use of the *Stanford Parser*, a widely employed Natural Language Processing (NLP) tool [27]. It is used to identify base forms of words (i.e. *lemmatization*), and for *part-of-speech* tagging. The latter task assigns a category, i.e. the part of speech, to each word in a text [17]. Common parts of speech include *nouns*, *verbs*, *adjectives*, and *adverbs*.

This step consists of three sub-steps: (i) *anaphora resolution*, (ii) *clause extraction*, and (iii) *text sanitization*. With these three sub-steps, we aim to obtain a representation that accurately reflects the important parts of a sentence, while abstracting from irrelevant details. To illustrate the sub-steps, we consider their impact on sentence (8) from the running example. This sentence is initially represented by the following *bag-of-words*:
{if, it, is, not, available, it, is, back-ordered}.

Anaphora Resolution. A problem that must be tackled when analyzing natural language texts is the resolution of anaphoric references or *anaphors*. Anaphors are usually pronouns (*"he"*, *"her"*, *"it"*) or determiners (*"this"*, *"that"*) that refer to a previously introduced unit. These references represent an important challenge in the context of assessing the similarity between an activity and a sentence. Anaphoric references must be properly resolved in order to correctly determine the object that some action refers to. As an example, consider the sentence *"If it is not available, it is back-ordered"*. Here, the approach has to identify that *"it"* refers to the word *"part"*, which is contained in the preceding sentence. To augment sentences with such important information, we introduce an anaphora resolution technique.

The anaphora resolution technique in our approach sets out to identify the objects contained in a sentence. We identify objects by considering *Stanford Dependencies*, which reflect grammatical relations between words [8]. To identify objects in a sentence, the most important relations to consider include *direct objects* and *nominal subjects*. For instance, in sentence (7) the Stanford Parser identifies the relation *nsubj(reserved, part)*, indicating that the business object *"part"* (acting as the nominal subject in the sentence) is the object being reserved. If all the objects in a sentence are anaphoric references, i.e. the sentence includes only pronouns and determiners, we resolve the references by replacing them with the objects contained in the previous sentence. For sentence (8), this results in: {`if, part, is, not, available, part, is, back-ordered`}.

Relevant Clause Extraction. Sentences in a textual description describe actions that are performed in a process, its flow, and additional information. To accurately align process model activities, it is important to identify (parts of) sentences related to actions, while excluding parts unrelated to these actions from consideration. The most problematic cases are conditional sentences, in which the *dependent clause* that specifies a condition, contains terms similar or equal to those used in activity labels. Consider, for example, sentence (11): *"If the storehouse has successfully reserved or back-ordered every item of the part list and the preparation activity has finished [...]"* When considered naively, this sentence has a high term similarity to the activities *"reserve part"* and *"back-order part"*. However, it is clear that these activities are actually described elsewhere in the description. By focusing only on the *main clause* of such sentences, we therefore remove potential confusion caused by conditional expressions.

In order to differentiate between conditions and main clauses, we use the parse trees generated by the Stanford Dependency Parser. In these trees, conditional expressions are represented as subordinate clauses (SBAR), starting with a conditional term, e.g. *"if"*, *"in case"*, or *"once"*. The parse tree for sentence (8) is shown in Figure 3. By extracting the main clause from this sentence, the following bag-of-words remains: {`part, is, back-ordered`}.

Text Sanitization. The final linguistic analysis sub-step involves text sanitization on both (previously processed) sentences and activity labels. Text sanitization sets out to create a similar and comparable representation of activity labels and sentences, and of their individual terms. Sanitization comprises the removal of stop words and word lemmatization.

First, we remove all *stop words* from each activity label and sentence. Stop words are common words that are of little value when considering similarity between texts (i.e. labels and sentences) [26]. We remove *closed class* determiners, prepositions, and conjunctions (e.g. *"the"*, *"in"*, *"to"*, *"for"*) from the activity labels and sentences. This procedure is in line with many approaches from the domain of process model matching (see e.g. [6,19,36]). Second, we lemmatize the remaining words using the Stanford Parser. The resulting *lemmas* represent grammatical base forms

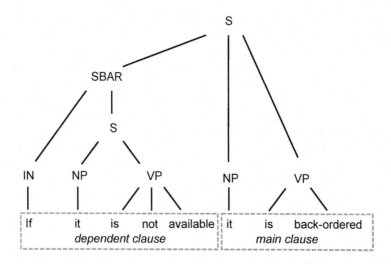

Fig. 3. Simplified parse tree for sentence (8).

of words. By considering lemmas, it is straightforward to determine whether two words have a similar root. E.g. "*sing*", "*sang*", and "*sung*" are all mapped to the common lemma "*sing*" [17].

Text sanitization concludes the linguistic analysis. For sentence (8), this results in the final bag-of-words representation: {part, be, back-order}. The next step takes the processed activity labels and sentences as input, to determine their similarity.

4.3   Computation of Similarity Scores

The ability to judge the similarity between a sentence and an activity is critical to the performance of our approach. A sentence and an activity are considered to be similar if they refer to the same stream of action. To accurately judge this, the variability of natural language expressions contained in the sentences should be taken into account [2]. To deal with this variability, we select a semantic measure to assess the similarity of a sentence to an activity. Specifically, we use a semantic similarity measure proposed by Mihalcea et al. [29] because it combines *word semantic similarity* with *word specificity* scores. The similarity between an activity a and a sentence s is formalized in Equation 1.

$$sim(a, s) = \frac{1}{2} \left(\frac{\sum\limits_{t \in \{a\}} maxSim(t, s) \times idf(t)}{\sum\limits_{t \in \{s\}} idf(t)} + \frac{\sum\limits_{t \in \{s\}} maxSim(t, a) \times idf(t)}{\sum\limits_{t \in \{s\}} idf(t)} \right) \quad (1)$$

Here, $maxSim(t_1, s)$ denotes the maximum semantic similarity between a term t_1 and any term t_2 contained in s.

$$maxSim(t_1, s) = \max\{Lin(t_1, t_2) \mid t_2 \in s\} \tag{2}$$

To compute the semantic similarity $Lin(t_1, t_2)$ between two terms, we employ a WordNet-based implementation of the similarity measure defined by Lin[1]. It is a measure from the domain of information theory, which has been widely adopted for computing semantic similarity. What is more, it has been shown to correlate well with human judgments [25].

To determine the similarity between a sentence and an activity, it is not only important to consider the similarity between individual terms. The relative importance of words or *word specificity* also plays an important role. Common terms have little discriminating power in determining similarity, while more unique terms represent important similarity indicators. For this reason, Equation 1 incorporates the *Inverse Document frequency* (idf) of terms. The idf assigns a low score to terms that occur in a large number of activity labels or sentences and, therefore, have lower discriminating power. The idf for a term t is given by Equation 3, where document collection D comprises all activity labels and sentences.

$$idf(t, D) = \log \frac{|D|}{|d \in D : t \in d|} \tag{3}$$

The similarity between a sentence and an activity plays an important role in the creation of a correspondence relation between a process model and a textual description. To further improve the results, our approach also considers the order in which activities and sentences appear, as detailed in the next section.

4.4   Optimal Correspondence Relation

This section describes how we obtain an optimal correspondence relation between activity set A and sentence set S. To achieve this, we not only consider the similarity of activities and sentences, but also the order in which activities are described the textual description and contained in the process model. We refer to a correspondence relation that respects these orders as *coherent*.

Textual process descriptions generally describe process steps in a chronological order [33]. That means that if activity a precedes activity b in a process, the text describes activity a prior to b. For a process model, these relations are explicitly captured in a *partial order* relation $\leq$. The relation $\leq$ defines for each activity which other activities precede and succeed it. Such an order is only partial (as opposed to a strict order), because processes may contain *alternative* and *concurrent* execution paths. For instance, the process of Figure 1 executes either of the alternative activities *"reserve part"* and *"back-order part"*, depending on the availability of a given part. To construct a partial order, we employ

---

[1] https://code.google.com/p/ws4j/

the behavioral profile computation as defined in [37]. A correspondence relation C between an activity set A and a sentence set S is considered to be coherent if it adheres to the following constraint: Given process model activities a and b, and the sentences s_a and s_b to which they are, respectively, aligned. If activity a is a predecessor of activity b, i.e. $a \leq b$, then sentence s_a should not occur in the text *after* sentence s_b.

The optimal correspondence relation $\hat{C}$ is then the coherent correspondence relation C with the highest total similarity score between the activities and sentences. This is defined in Equation 4.

$$\hat{C} = \underset{C}{\mathrm{argmax}} \sum^{(a,s)\in C} sim(a, s) \tag{4}$$

Because the majority of process models are not purely sequential, finding $\hat{C}$ is not straightforward. Each ordering in which the activities of a process model can be executed must be considered as a possible ordering in which the activities are contained in the textual process description. Given that each of these orderings has a potentially huge set of possible correspondence relations to the sentence set S, this problem calls for an efficient solving approach.

We adopt a *best-first search* algorithm similar to those used in machine translation problems [17]. Instead of aligning one language to another, we here align the activities of A with sentences of S. Intuitively, the best-first search algorithm traverses a search space of partial hypotheses, which consist of activity-sentence alignments between A and S. The algorithm explores the search space by expanding the partial hypothesis with the highest possible score, while it exempts unpromising hypotheses from expansion. Because this approach exempts unpromising hypotheses from expansion, the explored search space is greatly reduced. Since the algorithm merely affects computational efficiency – not the resulting optimal correspondence relation $\hat{C}$ – we abstract from further details for reasons of brevity.[2] Section 4.5 describes how we assess the optimal correspondence relation to quantify the likelihood that it contains inconsistencies.

4.5 Inconsistency Assessment

The optimal correspondence relation $\hat{C}$ represents the best coherent alignment possible between activity set A and sentence set S. If this alignment is of insufficient quality, it can be expected that the model-text pair contains inconsistencies. An inconsistency exists if an activity cannot be coherently aligned to a sentence that refers to the same action. The semantic similarity measure $sim(a, s)$ quantifies this. An optimal correspondence $\hat{C}$ that contains an activity-sentence pair with a low similarity score thus implies that an activity exists that cannot be aligned to a sentence with a similar meaning. This means that the textual and

---

[2] The interested reader is referred to e.g. [17,35] for a detailed description.

model-based descriptions likely contain one or more inconsistencies. As a quantification of this likelihood we define a likelihood indicator ρ as the lowest similarity value found in the optimal correspondence relation. Equation 5 formalizes this concept.

$$\rho = \min\{sim(a, s) \mid (a, s) \in \hat{C}\} \tag{5}$$

Section 5 demonstrates the usefulness of the likelihood indicator ρ and, accordingly, the ability of our approach to identify inconsistent processes in a process model repository.

5   Evaluation

This section presents a quantitative evaluation that demonstrates how well the proposed approach is able to identify inconsistent model-text pairs in a collection. We have manually annotated the inconsistencies in a collection of 46 model-text pairs obtained from practice. This annotation is referred to as the *gold standard* against which we compare the results of our approach. Subsequently, we present the set-up of the evaluation, its results, and a discussion of the strengths and weaknesses of our approach.

5.1   Test Collection

To evaluate our approach, we use an existing collection of pairs of process models and manually created textual descriptions from [14]. The collection contains 46 model-text pairs that originate from different sources including academia, industry, textbooks, and public sector models.[3] The included process models are heterogeneous with regard to several dimensions, such as size and complexity. Also, the corresponding textual descriptions vary in several regards. For instance, they describe the processes from different perspectives (first and third person) and differ in terms of how explicitly and unambiguously they refer to the process model content. Hence, we believe that the collection is well-suited for achieving a high external validity of the results. Table 1 summarizes the main characteristics of the collection and the contained model-text pairs.

We involved three researchers in the creation of the gold standard. Two of them independently identified activity-to-sentence mappings for each model. This yielded an inter-annotator agreement of 92.9%. The biggest cause for discussion was the implicitness of some activity descriptions, such as seen for the *"select unchecked part"* activity in the bicycle manufacturing example. The 27 differences were discussed, involving a third researcher to settle ties.

Out of the 378 activities contained in the process models, five activities are described in the wrong place, whereas 26 activities can be considered to be missing. These lead to a gold standard that consists of 24 correct processes and 22 that contain between one and three erroneously described activities.

---

[3] For more details about the sources of the collection, please refer to [14].

Table 1. Overview of the test collection

ID	Source	P	P_i	Type	A	G	S
1	HU Berlin	4	1	Academic	9.0	6.5	10.3
2	TU Berlin	2	2	Academic	22.5	10.5	34.0
3	QUT	8	0	Academic	6.1	2.0	7.1
4	TU Eindhoven	1	1	Academic	18.0	8.0	40.0
5	Vendor Tutorials	3	2	Industry	5.3	1.3	7.0
6	inubit AG	4	3	Industry	9.0	3.8	11.5
7	BPM Practitioners	1	0	Industry	4.0	1.0	7.0
8	BPMN Practice Handbook	3	3	Textbook	5.0	2.0	4.7
9	BPMN Guide	6	5	Textbook	7.0	3.2	7.0
10	Federal Network Agency	14	5	Public Sector	8.0	3.1	6.4
	Total	**46**	**23**	-	**8.1**	**3.5**	**9.0**

Legend: P = Model-text pairs per source, P_i = Inconsistent pairs per source, A = Activities per model, G = Gateways per model, S = Sentences per Text,

5.2   Setup

To demonstrate the applicability of the approach presented in this paper, we test the following, different configurations:

- **Baseline:** As a baseline configuration, we aligned every activity a to the sentence s with the highest value for $sim(a, s)$. Prior to the computation of the similarity scores, we sanitize all sentences and activity labels.
- **Linguistic analysis:** For this configuration, prior to the computation of similarity scores, we applied all linguistic analysis activities described in Section 4.2. We thus subjected the textual description to text sanitization, resolved anaphoric references, and extracted relevant clauses.
- **Full configuration:** For the full configuration, we performed all linguistic analysis activities *and* included the ordering constraint described in Section 4.4. This configuration computes a correspondence relation between activity set A and sentence set S that achieves a maximal similarity score, while respecting the ordering constraints implied by the partial ordering of the process model.

We assess the performance of each of these configurations with standard information retrieval metrics. More specifically, we calculate *precision* and *recall* by comparing the computed results against a manually created gold standard. For a process collection P, we define a set P_τ as the set of processes with an assigned likelihood indicator ρ in the range $[0.0, \tau]$. P_I is the set of 22 processes that are inconsistent according to the gold standard. Each process in P_I contains at least one activity that is not included in the textual description or has activities that are described in a different order.

For a given P_τ, *precision* describes the fraction of processes a configuration classified as inconsistent that are also contained in P_I. *Recall* represents the fraction of all inconsistent processes from the gold standard which our approach successfully identified. Formally, the metrics are defined as shown by Equations 6 and 7.

$$\text{precision} = \frac{|P_I \cap P_\tau|}{|P_\tau|} \qquad (6) \qquad \qquad \text{recall} = \frac{|P_I \cap P_\tau|}{|P_I|} \qquad (7)$$

5.3   Results

We computed precision and recall scores for different values of threshold τ for each of the three configurations. When the value of τ increases, more model-text pairs are predicted to contain inconsistencies and thus included in P_τ.

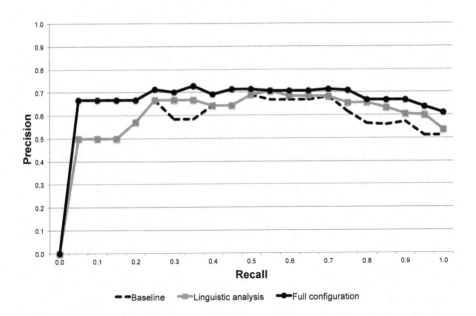

Fig. 4. Precision-recall graph for the performance of the three configurations

The precision-recall graph of Figure 4 shows that the full configuration consistently outperforms the baseline. The curves for the linguistic analysis and full configurations are always equal to or higher than the curve for the baseline configuration. This means that there are numerous cases for which the inclusion of these additional steps improves the results, it furthermore indicates that these steps *never* negatively impact the performance of the approach.

The improved results for the full approach also become apparent when considering the *F-measures* of the configurations. The F-measure represents the harmonic mean between precision and recall. For the baseline configuration, the maximum achieved F-measure equals 0.70. This performance is already promising, signaling that the semantic similarity measure we have selected is able to correctly identify a considerable number of inconsistencies. At this point, the baseline yields a recall of 0.91 against a precision of 0.57. The performance of the approach is further improved by including a linguistic analysis. This configuration achieves a maximum F-measure of 0.74, simultaneously improving both recall (0.96) and precision (0.60) in comparison to the baseline. The full configuration achieves an even higher F-measure of 0.77. It reaches a recall of 0.91 with a precision of 0.68. The full approach thus outperforms the precision of the baseline configuration by 11 percentage points.

The performance of the full approach is also demonstrated when we consider the point at which the approach has successfully identified all 22 inconsistent model-text pairs, i.e. the point when recall equals 1.0. The baseline configuration only reaches this point after considering 43 model-text pairs. It therefore hardly yields any benefits in comparison to a random selection as it makes 21 incorrect predictions. By contrast, the full configuration identifies all inconsistent processes after considering just 36 model-text pairs. Due to our linguistic analysis and the consideration of order, we thereby reduce the number of incorrect predictions by more than 33%.

5.4 Discussion

The evaluation shows that the full approach successfully identifies inconsistent model-text pairs from a collection while limiting the number of false positives. A post-hoc analysis reveals that the approach faces two main types of challenges.

First, the approach sometimes fails to recognize that an activity is contained in a textual description. These cases mainly occur when the description of activities is highly implicit or context-dependent. Consider, for example, an activity labeled *"use other sources"*, as present in a process related to the procurement of information through various channels. The sentence fragment that describes this activity is *"[..] and sometimes you just happen to know somebody"*. Due to its implicit description, aligning that activity to the appropriate sentence is difficult using natural language processing techniques. Similar problems occur when a textual description describes actions using references to earlier parts of the text. Most notably due to the anaphora resolution, the linguistic analysis successfully mitigates the impact of such problematic cases. Consequently, the full configuration of our approach detects inconsistencies more precisely.

Second, the approach, especially the baseline configuration, can return false negatives when it fails to detect inconsistencies in a model-text pair. In these cases, an activity is aligned with a sentence even though the activity is actually missing in the textual description. This happens when a strong semantic similarity between certain terms in an activity label and terms in the sentence exists, although neither this, nor any other sentence in the textual description, is related to the activity. The evaluation results demonstrate that the introduction of ordering constraints successfully avoids a number of such cases. For this configuration, it is no longer sufficient that a sentence just contains words semantically similar to those used in an activity label. Rather, the sentence must also occur in a proper location in the textual description. Hence, the approach including these constraints achieves higher recall values than the baseline configuration.

6   Conclusions

In this paper, we presented the first approach to automatically detect inconsistencies between textual and model-based process descriptions. The approach combines linguistic analysis, semantic similarity measures, and ordering relations to obtain a correspondence relation between the activities of a process model and the sentences of a textual process description. The approach subsequently assesses the quality of the obtained correspondence relation to predict whether or not a model-text pair contains inconsistencies. A quantitative evaluation shows that this approach successfully identifies the majority of incorrect process models, while yielding a low number of false positives. These insights result from a comparison of the predictions made by the approach against a manually constructed gold standard for a collection of real-life process descriptions. The evaluation furthermore reveals that the quality of the results is greatly improved due to the inclusion of tailored natural language processing techniques. By using our approach, organizations can thus quickly gain insights into the processes for which conflicts between the textual and model-based process descriptions are most likely. The effort that is needed to identify differences in large process model repositories is thereby greatly reduced. As such, organizations can focus their redesign efforts on the analysis and improvement of only their most problematic process descriptions.

In future work we set out to further develop approaches aimed at processes described using both models and text. The current approach can be extended by considering information beyond the control-flow dimension of a process. For instance, by deriving *"who does what, to whom, and where"* from sentences, or by comparing a model's conditional branches to the discourse in a textual description. The approach can also be broadened by performing a completeness check, i.e. by verifying whether all described activities are contained in the process model. Furthermore, the activity-sentence correspondence relation we obtain can be used for other purposes. Instead of using them to identify inconsistencies *ex post facto*, correspondence relations can form a basis to directly propagate one-sided process updates. In this way, the consistency between multiple process representations can be ensured, rather than corrected. Finally, we recognize that organizations also capture process information in formats other than the textual and model-based descriptions considered in this paper. Common examples include checklists, rules and regulations, and spreadsheets. In the future, we therefore aim to apply the techniques developed here on a broader spectrum of process representation formats.

References

1. van der Aa, H., Leopold, H., Mannhardt, F., Reijers, H.A.: On the fragmentation of process information: challenges, solutions, and outlook. In: Gaaloul, K., Schmidt, R., Nurcan, S., Guerreiro, S., Ma, Q. (eds.) BPMDS 2015 and EMMSAD 2015. LNBIP, vol. 214, pp. 3–18. Springer, Heidelberg (2015)
2. Achananuparp, P., Hu, X., Shen, X.: The evaluation of sentence similarity measures. In: Song, I.-Y., Eder, J., Nguyen, T.M. (eds.) DaWaK 2008. LNCS, vol. 5182, pp. 305–316. Springer, Heidelberg (2008)
3. Allweyer, T.: BPMN 2.0: introduction to the standard for business process modeling. BoD-Books on Demand (2010)
4. Bajwa, I.S., Choudhary, M.A.: From natural language software specifications to UML class models. In: Zhang, R., Zhang, J., Zhang, Z., Filipe, J., Cordeiro, J. (eds.) ICEIS 2011. LNBIP, vol. 102, pp. 224–237. Springer, Heidelberg (2012)
5. Cayoglu, U., Dijkman, R., Dumas, M., Fettke, P., Garcia-Banuelos, L., Hake, P., Klinkmüller, C., Leopold, H., Ludwig, A., Loos, P., et al.: The process model matching contest 2013. In: 4th International Workshop on Process Model Collections: Management and Reuse (PMC-MR 2013) (2013)
6. Cayoglu, U., Oberweis, A., Schoknecht, A., Ullrich, M.: Triple-s: A matching approach for Petri nets on syntactic, semantic and structural level
7. Chakraborty, S., Sarker, S., Sarker, S.: An exploration into the process of requirements elicitation: A grounded approach. J. AIS **11**(4) (2010)
8. De Marneffe, M.C., Manning, C.D.: The stanford typed dependencies representation. In: Coling 2008: Proceedings of the workshop on Cross-Framework and Cross-Domain Parser Evaluation, pp. 1–8 (2008)
9. Dijkman, R., Dumas, M., Van Dongen, B., Käärik, R., Mendling, J.: Similarity of business process models: Metrics and evaluation. Information Systems **36**(2), 498–516 (2011)
10. Doan, A., Halevy, A.Y.: Semantic integration research in the database community: A brief survey. AI magazine **26**(1), 83 (2005)
11. Dumas, M., Rosa, M., Mendling, J., Reijers, H.: Fundamentals of Business Process Management. Springer (2013)
12. Ehrig, M., Koschmider, A., Oberweis, A.: Measuring similarity between semantic business process models. In: Proceedings of the Fourth Asia-Pacific Conference on Comceptual Modelling, vol. 67, pp. 71–80 (2007)
13. Euzenat, J., Shvaiko, P., et al.: Ontology matching, vol. 18. Springer (2007)
14. Friedrich, F., Mendling, J., Puhlmann, F.: Process model generation from natural language text. In: Mouratidis, H., Rolland, C. (eds.) CAiSE 2011. LNCS, vol. 6741, pp. 482–496. Springer, Heidelberg (2011)
15. Giunchiglia, F., Shvaiko, P., Yatskevich, M.: Semantic matching. In: Encyclopedia of Database Systems, pp. 2561–2566. Springer (2009)
16. Gomez, F., Segami, C., Delaune, C.: A system for the semiautomatic generation of ER models from natural language specifications. Data & Knowledge Engineering **29**(1), 57–81 (1999)
17. Jurafsky, D., Martin, J.H.: Speech & language processing. Pearson Education India (2000)
18. Kettinger, W., Teng, J., Guha, S.: Business Process Change: a Study of Methodologies, Techniques, and Tools. MIS quarterly, pp. 55–80 (1997)

19. Klinkmüller, C., Weber, I., Mendling, J., Leopold, H., Ludwig, A.: Increasing recall of process model matching by improved activity label matching. In: Daniel, F., Wang, J., Weber, B. (eds.) BPM 2013. LNCS, vol. 8094, pp. 211–218. Springer, Heidelberg (2013)

20. Kunze, M., Weidlich, M., Weske, M.: Behavioral similarity – a proper metric. In: Rinderle-Ma, S., Toumani, F., Wolf, K. (eds.) BPM 2011. LNCS, vol. 6896, pp. 166–181. Springer, Heidelberg (2011)

21. La Rosa, M., Dumas, M., Uba, R., Dijkman, R.: Business process model merging: An approach to business process consolidation. ACM Transactions on Software Engineering and Methodology (TOSEM) 22(2), 11 (2013)

22. Lavoie, B., Rambow, O., Reiter, E.: The modelexplainer. In: Eighth International Workshop on Natural Language Generation, Herstmonceux, Sussex (1996)

23. Leopold, H.: Natural language in business process models. Springer (2013)

24. Leopold, H., Mendling, J., Polyvyanyy, A.: Supporting process model validation through natural language generation. IEEE Transactions on Software Engineering 40(8), 818–840 (2014)

25. Lin, D.: An information-theoretic definition of similarity. ICML 98, 296–304 (1998)

26. Manning, C.D., Raghavan, P., Schütze, H.: Introduction to informationretrieval, vol. 1. Cambridge university press Cambridge (2008)

27. Manning, C.D., Surdeanu, M., Bauer, J., Finkel, J., Bethard, S.J., McClosky, D.: The Stanford CoreNLP natural language processing toolkit. In: Proceedings of 52nd Annual Meeting of the Association for Computational Linguistics: System Demonstrations, pp. 55–60 (2014)

28. Meziane, F., Athanasakis, N., Ananiadou, S.: Generating natural language specifications from UML class diagrams. Requirements Engineering 13(1), 1–18 (2008)

29. Mihalcea, R., Corley, C., Strapparava, C.: Corpus-based and knowledge-based measures of text semantic similarity. In: AAAI, vol. 6, pp. 775–780 (2006)

30. Noy, N.F.: Semantic integration: a survey of ontology-based approaches. ACM Sigmod Record 33(4), 65–70 (2004)

31. Rahm, E., Bernstein, P.A.: A survey of approaches to automatic schema matching. The VLDB Journal 10(4), 334–350 (2001)

32. Rosemann, M.: Potential Pitfalls of Process Modeling: Part A. Business Process Management Journal 12(2), 249–254 (2006)

33. Schumacher, P., Minor, M., Schulte-Zurhausen, E.: Extracting and enriching workflows from text. In: 2013 IEEE 14th International Conference on Information Reuse and Integration (IRI), pp. 285–292. IEEE (2013)

34. Uba, R., Dumas, M., García-Bañuelos, L., La Rosa, M.: Clone detection in repositories of business process models. In: Rinderle-Ma, S., Toumani, F., Wolf, K. (eds.) BPM 2011. LNCS, vol. 6896, pp. 248–264. Springer, Heidelberg (2011)

35. Wang, Y.Y., Waibel, A.: Decoding algorithm in statistical machine translation. In: Proceedings of the 35th Annual Meeting of the Association for Computational Linguistics and Eighth Conference of the European Chapter of the Association for Computational Linguistics, pp. 366–372 (1997)

36. Weidlich, M., Dijkman, R., Mendling, J.: The ICoP framework: identification of correspondences between process models. In: Pernici, B. (ed.) CAiSE 2010. LNCS, vol. 6051, pp. 483–498. Springer, Heidelberg (2010)

37. Weidlich, M., Mendling, J., Weske, M.: Efficient consistency measurement based on behavioral profiles of process models. IEEE Transactions on Software Engineering 37(3), 410–429 (2011)

Process Model Discovery I

Mining Invisible Tasks in Non-free-choice Constructs

Qinlong Guo[1], Lijie Wen[1(✉)], Jianmin Wang[1], Zhiqiang Yan[2],
and Philip S. Yu[3,4]

[1] School of Software, Tsinghua University, Beijing, China
guoqinlong@gmail.com, {wenlj,jimwang}@tsinghua.edu.cn
[2] Information School, Capital University of Economics and Business, Beijing, China
zhiqiang.yan.1983@gmail.com
[3] Department of Computer Science, University of Illinois at Chicago, Chicago, USA
[4] Institue for Data Science, Tsinghua University, Beijing, China
psyu@cs.uic.edu

Abstract. The discovery of process models from event logs (i.e. process mining) has emerged as one of the crucial challenges for enabling the continuous support in the life-cycle of a process-aware information system. However, in a decade of process discovery research, the relevant algorithms are known to have strong limitations in several dimensions. *Invisible task* and *non-free-choice construct* are two important special structures in a process model. Mining invisible tasks involved in non-free-choice constructs is still one significant challenge. In this paper, we propose an algorithm named $\alpha^\$$. By introducing new ordering relations between tasks, $\alpha^\$$ is able to solve this problem. $\alpha^\$$ has been implemented as a plug-in of ProM. The experimental results show that it indeed significantly improves existing process mining techniques.

Keywords: Process mining · Non-free-choice constructs · Invisible tasks

1 Introduction

Process mining is an essential discipline for addressing challenges related to Business Process Management and "Big Data" [15]. Nowadays, more and more organizations are applying workflow technology to their information systems, in order to manage their business processes. The information systems are logging events that are stored in so-called "event log". Informally, process mining algorithms are meant to extract meaningful knowledge from event logs, and use this knowledge for supporting or improving the process perspective.

Of the three process mining scenarios (i.e., discovery, conformance checking, and enhancement), discovery of a process model from an event log is the most important. In this paper we focus on the scenario of discovering Workflow nets [8] from event logs. However, the techniques presented in this paper may be adapted for the discovery of other process formalisms.

In many cases, the benefit of process mining depends on the exactness of the mined models [2]. The mined models should preserve all the tasks and the

© Springer International Publishing Switzerland 2015
H.R. Motahari-Nezhad et al. (Eds.): BPM 2015, LNCS 9253, pp. 109–125, 2015.
DOI: 10.1007/978-3-319-23063-4_7

dependencies between them that are present in the logs. Although much research is done in this area, there are still some significant and challenging problems to be solved [2][5]. In this paper, we focus on mining invisible tasks involved in non-free-choice constructs (IT-in-NFC for short). *Invisible tasks* (IT) [4] are such tasks that appear in a process model, while not observable in the corresponding event log. In a Workflow net, places cannot be linked with each other directly, so invisible tasks can be used for bridges between places. Besides, invisible tasks can also be used for expressing routing information. AND construct is that several places are connected to a transition, which has a meaning of parallel construct; XOR construct is that several transitions are connected to a place, which means a choice construct. *Non-free-choice construct* (NFC) [3] is a special kind of choice construct, whether to choose some task is dependent on what have been executed in the process model before (i.e. this choice is not "free"). In other words, NFC means the input places set of two transitions share some common places while they are not same. IT-in-NFC means that a process model contains both IT and NFC. As mentioned in [3][4], both of them are difficult to be discovered from event logs. Moreover, the combination of them (namely, some tasks in NFCs are invisible) even increases the difficulty of mining.

α [8] is a pioneering process mining algorithm which mines the Workflow net by considering relations between tasks in the event log. In order to mine NFCs, α^{++} [3] takes a new relation called *implicit dependency* (i.e. the indirect casual relation between tasks) into consideration based on α. Similarly, $\alpha^{\#}$ [4] is able to mine invisible tasks by considering *mendacious dependency*, which is the improper casual relations caused by invisible tasks. However, none of $\alpha^{\#}$ and α^{++} can properly mine IT-in-NFC. There are several other state-of-the-art mainstream process mining algorithms, such as *Genetic* [6], *Heuristic* [11], *ILP* [12], and *Region* [1]. Each of these algorithms has its own advantages. However, none of them is able to mine IT-in-NFC correctly.

In this paper, $\alpha^{\$}$ algorithm takes both *mendacious dependency* and *implicit dependency* into consideration. However, simple combination of considering these two dependencies cannot guarantee a correct mining result. There will be two significant challenging issues encountered:

1. The *reachable dependency*, which means one task can be executed after the execution of another task directly or indirectly, is a required relation to obtain the *implicit dependency*. However, reachable dependencies are detected by scanning the event log, but invisible tasks are unobservable here. Thus, *reachable dependencies* involved with these invisible tasks cannot be detected without complementation. The details can be found in Subsection 4.3.
2. Non-free-choice constructs, which are discovered after invisible tasks, bring more dependencies (e.g. the *implicit dependency*). These newly added dependencies may make invisible tasks unstructured. Thus, the affected invisible tasks should be split or combined to make the mined model sound. The details can be found in subsection 4.5.

Besides dealing with these issues, $\alpha^{\$}$ algorithm also addresses two drawbacks of *implicit dependencies* and *mendacious dependencies* respectively:

1. *Mendacious dependencies* cannot deal with some invisible tasks spanning one whole branch in a parallel construct.
2. *Implicit dependencies* cannot deal with the Length-1-loop (L1L for short) involved in NFCs.

The remainder of this paper is organized as follows. Section 2 shows a motivating example. Section 3 gives some preliminaries about process mining. In Section 4, we propose $\alpha^\$$ algorithm. Experimental results are given in Section 5. Section 6 concludes the paper and sketches the future work.

2 A Motivating Example

Figure 1 shows a real-life process model in SY company that is the largest construction machinery manufacturer in China. This model depicts the roadheader repairing process in the mine. A roadheader is a piece of excavating equipment consisting of a boom-mounted cutting head, a loading device usually involving a conveyor, and a crawler traveling track to move the entire machine forward into the rock face. For repair, there are three options. One option is that the roadheader is directly repaired underground. This option usually applies to simple repairs. In the other two options, the roadheader has to be repaired on the ground. The difference between the later two options is whether the roadheader should be decomposed before moved up to the ground through the tunnel, and then should be assembled after taken down to the mine.

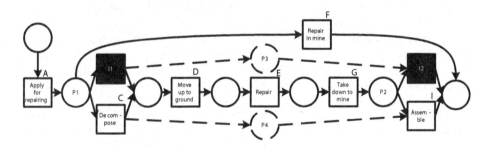

Fig. 1. A process model in SY company

The process model in Figure 1 is modelled in Petri net [8]. There are two invisible tasks (i.e., *I1* and *I2*), which are designed to skip the task *Decompose* and *Assemble* respectively. *I2*, together with *Assemble*, *P2*, *P3*, and *P4* composes a NFC. After *Take down to the mine*, whether *Assemble* is executed is dependent on whether *Decompose* has been executed before.

For convenience, we use the label in the right top of each task as abbreviation, for example *A* is short for *Apply for repairing*. Then [<A,F>,<A,D,E,G>, <A,C,D,E,G,I>] is an example event log corresponding to this model. Despite its apparent simplicity, this model and its corresponding log represent a hard case for all existing techniques. Table 2(c) is an example model similar to this one. $\alpha^\#$ mines a similar model, while the NFC has not been discovered. The models mined by *Genetic* and *Heuristic* are identical, with the ITs not discovered. The models mined by α^{++} and *ILP* are not Workflow nets at all.

3   Preliminaries

Firstly, we discuss event log in detail and give an example. Then we give WF-net and its relevant concepts.

3.1   Event Log

The *event*, which represents a real-life action, is the basic unit of event logs. As defined in Definition 1, each event has several attributes, such as the time (i.e., when the event happens), activity [1] (i.e., what task this event corresponds to).

Definition 1. *(Event, Attribute) Let $\mathscr{E}$ be event universe, i.e., the set of all possible event identifiers. Let AN be a set of attribute names. For any event $e \in \mathscr{E}$ and a name $n \in AN{:}\#_n(e)$ is the value of an attribute n for event e.*

For convenience we assume the following standard attributes: $\#_{activity}(e)$ is the task associated to event e, $\#_{time}(e)$ is the timestamp associated to event e.

Though *time* is an important attribute for an event, we only consider the time order between events in this paper. Namely, the exact start time, end time or duration of an event are not taken in to consideration. The time order between events is enough for $\alpha^\$$ to mine a process model.

An event log consists of cases. Each case consists of ordered events, which are represented in the form of a *trace*, i.e., a sequence of unique events. Moreover, cases, like events, can also have attributes. Each case or event has an attribute of *case id* or *event id* respectively as the unique identifier.

Definition 2. *(Case, Trace, Event log, Simple Event Log) Let $\mathscr{C}$ be the case universe, i.e., the set of all possible case identifiers. For any case $c \in \mathscr{C}$ and name $n \in AN{:}\#_n(c)$ is the value of an attribute n for case c. Each case has a special mandatory attribute trace : $\#_{trace}(c) \in \mathscr{E}^*$. $c = \#_{trace}(c)$ is a shorthand for the trace of case c.*

A trace is a finite sequence of events $\sigma \in \mathscr{E}^*$ such that each event appears only once, where $|\sigma|$ means the number of events contained in trace σ. The order of events in a trace is according to their timestamp, namely $\forall_{1 \le i < j \le |\sigma|} \#_{time}(\sigma_i) \le \#_{time}(\sigma_j)$. An event log is a set of cases $L \subset \mathscr{E}^*$.

Let $\mathscr{A}$ be the set of activity names, A simple trace σ is a sequence of activities, i.e., $\sigma \in \mathscr{A}^*$. A simple even log L is a multi-set of traces over $\mathscr{A}$.

---

[1] In this paper, we use activity and task alternatively.

Since information of time order and activity name of an event are sufficient for $\alpha^{\$}$, the simple event log and trace are used in the rest part of the paper.

Given a set of tasks (say T), an *event log W over T* means the task associated to any event in W is contained in T, i.e. $\forall e \in W : \#_{activity}(e) \in T$.

Table 1 is an example simple event log of the process model in Figure 1. This log contains four cases. For example, for case 1 and case 4, A and F are executed successively. The event log in Table 1 can be shortened as $[< A, F >^2, < A, D, E, G >, < A, C, D, E, G, I >]$, where 2 means $< A, F >$ occurs twice.

As mentioned in [5], dealing with noises in event logs is a challenging issue in process mining domain. However, many log filtering plugins have been implemented in Prom 6 [9]. The plugin *Filter Log with Simple Heuristic* is used for abating noise. By this way, we assume that the event log has no noise.

Table 1. An example simple event log of the process model in Figure 1

Case Id	Event Id	Activity	Case Id	Event Id	Activity	Case Id	Event Id	Activity
1	35654422	A		35654485	G		35654583	G
	35654423	F	3	35654579	A		35654584	I
2	35654481	A		35654580	C	4	35655442	A
	35654483	D		35654581	D		35655443	F
	35654484	E		35654582	E			

3.2 Workflow Net

In this paper, *Workflow net* [8] is used as the process modelling language. Workflow nets as defined in Definition 5, are a subset of labeled Petri nets.

Definition 3. *(Petri net) A Petri net is a triplet $N = (P, T, F)$ where P is a finite set of places, T is a finite set of transitions such that $P \cap T = \emptyset \wedge P \cup T \neq \emptyset$, and $F \subseteq (P \times T) \cup (T \times P)$ is a set of directed arcs, called the flow relation.*

Definition 4. *(Labeled Petri Net) A labeled Petri net is a tuple $L\Sigma = (P, T, F, A, l)$, where (P, T, F) is a Petri net, A is a finite set of task names, and l is a surjective mapping from T to $A \cup \{\tau\}$ (τ is a symbol unobservable to the outside world).*

Definition 5. *(Workflow net). Let $N = (P, T, F, A, l)$ be a labeled Petri net and $\bar{t}$ be a fresh identifier not in $P \cup T$. N is a workflow net (WF-net) if and only if (a) P contains a unique source place i such that $\cdot i = \emptyset$, (b) P contains a unique sink place o such that $o \cdot = \emptyset$, and (c) $\bar{N} = (P, T \cup \{\bar{t}\}, F \cup \{(o, \bar{t}), (\bar{t}, i)\}, A \cup \{\tau\}, l \cup \{(\bar{t}, \tau)\})$ is strongly connected.*

Figure 1 gives an example of a process modelled in WF-net. This model has two IT-in-NFCs. The transitions (drawn as rectangles) $A, C, ..., I$ represent tasks, where hollow rectangles represent visible tasks, and the solid one (i.e. *I1* or *I2*) represents an invisible task. The places (drawn as circles) $P1, P2, ..., P4$ represent conditions. We adopt the formal definitions, properties, and firing rules of WF-net from [7] [8]. For mining purpose, we demand that each visible task (i.e., transition) has a unique name in one process model.

4   The New Mining Algorithm $\alpha^\$$

$\alpha^\$$ is composed of five steps: *Detect Invisible Tasks, Complement Reachable Dependencies, Detect Non-free-choice Constructs, Adjust Invisible Tasks*, and *Construct Workflow Net*. By applying *improved mendacious dependencies*, the first step of $\alpha^\$$ finds invisible tasks from the given event log. In the second step, $\alpha^\$$ complements reachable dependencies related to the found invisible tasks. Then, it discovers NFCs by using *implicit dependencies*. Next, $\alpha^\$$ adjusts the invisible tasks in order to ensure the mined model's soundness. Finally, $\alpha^\$$ constructs the process model based on the relations found in previous steps. Since the last step is identical to other α-*series* algorithms [3][4][8], it would not be elaborated. Initially, basic relations are introduced, then the following subsections elaborate the first four steps and the whole algorithm respectively.

4.1   Basic Relations

α algorithm, which is the forerunner of the α-series algorithms, defined six relations, $>_W, \triangle_W, \Diamond_W, \rightarrow_W, \|_W$, and $\#_W$. $>_W$ expresses two tasks can be executed successively. $\triangle_W$ means a possible length-2-loop structure (i.e. a loop with length 2). $\Diamond_W$ shows two tasks have the $\triangle_W$ relations between each other. $\rightarrow_W$ is referred as the (direct) casual relation. $\|_W$ suggests the concurrent behavior, namely two activity can be executed in any order. Relation $\#_W$ reflects that two tasks never follow each other directly. For example, in the event log in Table 1, $A >_W F$, $A >_W C$, $A \rightarrow_W F$, $G \rightarrow_W I$ hold.

Definition 6. *(Relations defined in α [8], Mendacious dependency [4], Reachable dependency [3]) Let T be a set of tasks, W be an event log over T, a and b be two tasks in T, the relations defined in α algorithm, mendacious dependency, and reachable dependency are defined as follows:*

- $a >_W b \iff \exists \sigma = t_1 t_2 ... t_n \in W, i \in 1, ..., n-1 : t_i = a \wedge t_{i+1} = b,$
- $a \triangle_W b \iff \exists \sigma = t_1 t_2 ... t_n \in W, i \in 1, ..., n-2 : t_i = t_{i+2} = a \wedge t_{i+1} = b,$
- $a \Diamond_W b \iff a \triangle_W b \wedge b \triangle_W a,$
- $a \rightarrow_W b \iff (a >_W b \wedge b \not>_W a) \vee a \Diamond_W b,$
- $a \|_W b \iff a >_W b \wedge b >_W a \wedge a \not\Diamond_W b,$
- $a \#_W b \iff a \not>_W b \wedge b \not>_W a,$
- $a \rightsquigarrow_W b \iff a \rightarrow_W b \wedge \exists x, y \in T : a \rightarrow_W x \wedge y \rightarrow_W b \wedge y \not>_W x \wedge x \not\parallel_W b \wedge a \not\parallel_W y,$
- $a \gg_W b \iff \exists \sigma = t_1 t_2 ... t_n \wedge i, j \in 1, ..., n : i < j \wedge t_i = a \wedge t_j = b \wedge \forall k \in [i+1, ..., j-1] : t_k \neq a \wedge t_k \neq b,$ *and*
- $a \succ_W b \iff a \rightarrow_W b \vee a \gg_W b.$

In $\alpha^\#$ algorithm, *mendacious dependency* $\rightsquigarrow_W$ is proposed to describe the relations reflecting invisible tasks. It is based on six pre-conditions as defined in Definition 6. $A \rightsquigarrow_W D$ holds in the event log in Table 1, because $A \rightarrow_W D$, $A \rightarrow_W C$, $C \rightarrow_W D$, $C \not\parallel_W D$, $C \not\parallel_W A$, and $C \not>_W C$, which means there should be an invisible task between A and D (i.e., the invisible task $I1$ in Figure 1).

Reachable dependency is used to depict the indirect dependency between activities. In α^{++}, reachable dependency is a necessary condition for discovering NFCs. For example, in Table 1, $E \gg_W G$, $C \gg_W I$, and $D \succ_W G$ hold.

4.2 Detecting Invisible Tasks by Improved Mendacious Dependency

The aim of this step is to discover invisible tasks from the given event log. Most invisible tasks can be detected by applying *mendacious dependency* proposed in [4]. However, mendacious dependency cannot deal with some invisible tasks involved in one whole branch of a parallel construct. Thus, we propose an *improved mendacious dependency* to resolve this issue.

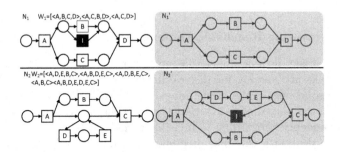

Fig. 2. Two examples for the defect of mendacious dependency

Two examples in Figure 2 show the defect of mendacious dependency. N_1 and N_2 are the original models, N_1' and N_2' are the models mined by $\alpha^\#$ algorithm. In N_1', $\alpha^\#$ didn't discover the invisible task I. This is because that $A \rightarrow_W D$, which is a requirement for discovering task I, does not hold due to the interference from task C in another branch. As for N_2', the disturbance from task B makes $A \not\rightarrow_W C$ hold. This leads to the invisible task I improperly discovered in N_2'. Due to task I, N_2' has less behavior than N_2, e.g., trace $< A, B, C >$ cannot be replayed on N_2'. In order to the overcome this defect, we introduce *Between-Set* and define *improved mendacious dependency*.

Between-Set, which is defined in Definition 7, is to depict the tasks that occur between two tasks. When the two tasks are the endpoints of a parallel construct, the Between-Set is the set of tasks in the parallel branches. For examples in Figure 2, $Between(W_1, A, D) = \{B, C\}$, $Between(W_2, A, C) = \{B, D, E\}$.

Definition 7. *(Between-Set) Let T be a set of tasks, W be an event log over T, a and b be two tasks in T, σ be a trace of W with length n, namely $\sigma \in W$, the Between-Set of a,b (i.e. Between(W,a,b)) can be defined as follows:*
- $Between(\sigma, a, b) = \{\sigma_k | \exists_{1 \leq i < j \leq n}(\sigma_i = a \wedge \sigma_j = b \wedge i < k < j$
$\wedge \nexists_{i < l < j}(\sigma_l = a \vee \sigma_l = b))\}$,
- $\neg Between(\sigma, a, b) = \{\sigma_k | 1 \leq k \leq n\} \backslash Between(\sigma, a, b)$, *and*
- $Between(W, a, b) = \cup_{\sigma \in W} Between(\sigma, a, b) \backslash \cup_{\sigma \in W} \neg Between(\sigma, a, b)$

The *improved mendacious dependency* is defined in Definition 8. We redefine $\rightarrow_W$ and $>_W$ in [4] as $\Rightarrow_W$ and $\geqslant_W$ respectively. Compared with the old ones, $\Rightarrow_W$ and $\geqslant_W$ are able to eliminate the interference of parallel constructs. For instance, in N_1, $A \rightarrow_W D$ does not hold. However, $A \Rightarrow_W D$ holds. In N_2, $A \not\rightarrow_W C$ 'improperly' holds. Nevertheless, $A \geqslant_W C$ holds.

Definition 8. *(Improved mendacious dependency) Let T be a set of tasks, W be an event log over T, a,b be two tasks from T, the* improved mendacious dependency $a \hookrightarrow_W b$ *is defined as follows:*

- $a \geqslant_W b \iff \exists_{x,y \in T}(Between(W,x,y) \subset Between(W,a,b) \wedge$
  $\forall_{m \in (Between(W,a,b) \setminus (Between(W,x,y) \cup \{x,y\}))} \forall_{n \in Between(W,x,y)} m \parallel_W n \wedge$
  $\exists_{\sigma \in W} Between(\sigma,a,b) \subseteq (Between(W,a,b) \setminus (Between(W,x,y) \cup \{x,y\}))),$
- $a \rightrightarrows_W b \iff (a \geqslant_W b \wedge b \not\geqslant_W a) \vee a \Diamond_W b$, *and*
- $a \hookrightarrow_W b \iff \exists_{x,y \in T}(a \rightarrow_W x \wedge y \rightarrow_W b \wedge x \not\parallel_W b \wedge y \not\parallel_W a \wedge a \rightrightarrows_W b \wedge y \not\geqslant_W x).$

4.3   Complementing Reachable Dependencies

Since invisible tasks do not appear in any event log, $>>_W$ and $\succ_W$ related to invisible tasks are missing for discovering NFSs. For example, in Figure 1, the part with solid lines is the model mined by $\alpha^\$$ without this complementing step. NFC (i.e. the dotted edge line part) was not discovered due to incomplete reachable dependencies regarding to invisible tasks.

In order to deal with this incompleteness, we first introduce the definition of *conditional reachable dependency* (CRD for short). Symbol $a>>_\sigma b$ expresses that task a is indirectly followed by task b in trace σ. We artificially add a *starting task* (i.e. $\bot$) and an *ending task* (i.e. $\top$) to each trace in the event log. Namely, for a trace σ with length n, $\#_{activity}(\sigma_0) = \bot$ and $\#_{activity}(\sigma_{n+1}) = \top$.

In Definition 9, there are three kinds of CRDs: *pre-CRD* (i.e. $\succ_{W,Pre=x}$), *post-CRD* (i.e. $\succ_{W,Post=y}$), and *both-CRD* (i.e. $\succ_{W,Pre=x,Post=y}$). $a \succ_{W,Pre=x,Post=y} b$ means there is a trace σ where $a>>_\sigma b$ holds, and x occurs directly before a, y occurs directly after b. For example, in Table 1, $C \succ_{W,Pre=A,Post=\top} I$ holds. The pre-CRD and post-CRD are special cases of both-CRD.

Definition 9. *(Conditional reachable dependency) Let T be a set of tasks, W be an event log over T, a,b be two tasks from T, x,y be two tasks from $T \cup \{\bot\} \cup \{\top\}$. Conditional reachable dependencies are defined as follows:*

- $a \succ_{W,Pre=x} b \iff a \rightarrow_W b \vee (\exists_{\sigma \in W \wedge 1 \leq i \leq |\sigma|} \sigma_i = a \wedge \sigma_{i-1} = x \wedge a>>_\sigma b),$
- $a \succ_{W,Post=y} b \iff a \rightarrow_W b \vee (\exists_{\sigma \in W \wedge 1 \leq j \leq |\sigma|} \sigma_j = b \wedge \sigma_{j+1} = y \wedge a>>_\sigma b),$
- $a \succ_{W,Pre=x,Post=y} b \iff a \rightarrow_W b \vee (\exists_{\sigma \in W \wedge 1 \leq i,j \leq |\sigma|} \sigma_i = a \wedge \sigma_j = b \wedge \sigma_{j+1} = y \wedge \sigma_{i-1} = x \wedge a>>_\sigma b).$

Based on CRDs, the *Reachable dependency related to invisible task* is defined in Definition 10. For two invisible tasks x and y, $x \succ_W y$ holds if there are four tasks a_1, a_2, b_1, and b_2 satisfying $a_1 \rightarrow_W x$, $x \rightarrow_W b_1$, $a_2 \rightarrow_W y$, $y \rightarrow_W b_2$, and $b_1 \succ_{W,Pre=a_1,Post=b_2} a_2$ holds. For an invisible task x, and a task m, $x \succ_W m$ holds if there are two tasks a and b satisfying $a \rightarrow_W x$, $x \rightarrow_W b$, and $b \succ_{W,Pre=a} m$ holds. For instance, the event log in Table 1, $I1 \succ_W E$ holds, because $A \rightarrow_W I1$, and $D \succ_{W,Pre=A} E$ and $I1 \rightarrow_W D$. $m \succ_W x$ is similar to $x \succ_W m$.

Definition 10. *(Reachable dependency related to invisible task) Let T be a set of tasks, W be an event log over T, m be a task from T, x,y be two invisible tasks, the* reachable dependency related to invisible task *is defined as follows:*

$$- \ x \succ_W m \iff \exists_{(a=\perp \lor a \in W) \land b \in W} a \to_W x \land x \to_W b \land b \succ_{W,Pre=a} m,$$
$$- \ m \succ_W x \iff \exists_{a \in W \land (b \in W \lor b=\top)} a \to_W x \land x \to_W b \land m \succ_{W,Post=b} a,$$
$$- \ x \succ_W y \iff \exists_{(a_1=\perp \lor a_1 \in W) \land b_1 \in W \land a_2 \in W \land (b_2 \in W \lor b_2=\top)}$$
$$a_1 \to_W x \land x \to_W b_1 \land a_2 \to_W y \land y \to_W b_2 \land b_1 \succ_{W,Pre=a_1,Post=b_2} a_2.$$

4.4   Detecting Non-free-choice Constructs

After making the reachable dependencies complete, the aim of this step is to discover NFCs. α^{++} algorithm can mine NFCs in most cases. However, α^{++} is not able to mine the length-1-loop construct (L1L for short) involved in NFCs. L1L set, as defined in Definition 11, is a set of tasks, where each task appears at least twice continuously in an given event log. α^{++} excludes all tasks in L1L set when considering implicit dependencies, which impedes discovering the L1L involved in NFCs. For example, Figure 3 shows the defect of α^{++} on dealing with such issue. N_3 and N_4 are the original models which contain NFCs combined with L1L, N_3' and N_4' are models mined by α^{++}. The NFC is not detected in N_3', which makes N_3' have more behavior than N_3: trace ¡A,C,G,F,D,B,E¿ can be replayed on N_3' but cannot be replayed on N_3. Besides, α^{++} does not discover the arcs related to task D, which results in N_4' not sound at all [8].

Definition 11. *(length-1-loop set) Let T be a set of tasks, W be an event log over T, the L1L set is defined as follows:*

$$- \ L1L = \{t \in T | \exists_{\sigma=t_1 t_2 ... t_n \in W; i \in 2,3,...,n} t = t_{i-1} \land t = t_i\}.$$

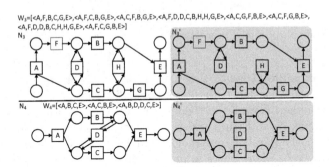

Fig. 3. Defect of α^{++} on mining L1L involved in NFCs

Thus, a set of tasks (called L1L-Free set) is determined before applying α^{++}, in which the tasks should not be excluded when detecting NFCs. L1L-Free set is summarized in Definition 12. Namely, for each such task x of L1L, there exists a pair of tasks a,b parallel with each other. Besides, two *sequence relations* $a \to_W x$ and $x \to_W b$ hold. For example, L1L-Free set of N_3 is {D,H}. For task D, $F \to_W D$, $D \to_W C$, and $F\|_W C$ hold.

Definition 12. *(L1L-Free set) Let T be a set of tasks, W be an event log over T, and L1L be the set of length-1-loop. The L1L-Free set is defined as follows:*

$$- \ L1L\text{-}Free = \{x \in L1L | \exists_{a \in T \land b \in T} (a \to_W x \land x \to_W b \land a \|_W b)\}.$$

4.5   Adjusting Invisible Tasks

In order to construct a sound and accurate process model, this step adjusts the invisible tasks by combining or splitting. Before introducing the details of invisible task adjustment, some auxiliary functions are given.

- MD means the set of improved mendacious dependencies,
- ID means the set of implicit dependencies,
- $MD(t)$ is the set of improved mendacious dependencies related to an invisible task t, and
- $\sigma \uparrow X$ is the projection of σ onto some task set $X \subset T$.

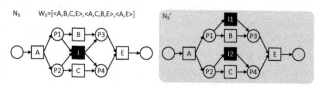

(a) Mined model without combining

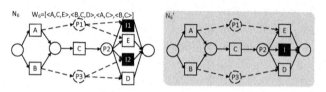

(b) Mined model without spliting

Fig. 4. Example of mined process models without combining or splitting

Combining Invisible Tasks. When there are invisible tasks in different branches of a parallel construct, there is a possibility that invisible tasks should be combined together. However, $\alpha^{\#}$ does not take this situation into consideration. For example, N_5 in Figure 4(a) is a process model with an invisible task I combined with the parallel construct (B,C,P1,P2,P3,P4). N_5' is the process model mined by $\alpha^{\#}$, where there is one invisible task $I1$ or $I2$ in each parallel branch. N_5' has more behavior than N_5, such as traces $< A, C, E >$ and $< A, B, E >$. Definition 13 is used to discover the pairs of combinable invisible tasks.

Definition 13. *(Combinable invisible tasks) Let T be a set of tasks, W be an event log over T, T_I be the set of invisible tasks discovered from W, and trace $\sigma \in W$. The Combinable invisible tasks is defined as follows:*

- $R(t) = \{z | (a, x, y, b) \in MD(t) \wedge (z = x \vee z = y)\}$,
- $P(\sigma, a, b) = \sigma \uparrow (R(a) \cup R(b))$,
- $a \bigotimes_\sigma b \iff |P(\sigma, a, b)| = 0 \vee (|P(\sigma, a, b)|\%2 = 0 \wedge \forall_{1 \leq k < |P|/2}((P(\sigma, a, b)_{2k+1} \in R(a) \wedge P(\sigma, a, b)_{2k+2} \in R(b)) \vee (P(\sigma, a, b)_{2k+1} \in R(b) \wedge P(\sigma, a, b)_{2k+2} \in R(a)))$,

- $a \bigotimes_W b \iff \forall_{\sigma \in W} a \bigotimes_\sigma b$, and
- $Combinable\_Set(W,T_I) = \{(a,b)|a \parallel_W b \wedge a \in T_I \wedge b \in T_I \wedge a \bigotimes_W b\}$.

$R(t)$ is the set of tasks that are related to invisible task t. $P(\sigma, a, b)$ is the projection of trace σ on the task set $R(a) \cup R(b)$. $a \bigotimes_\sigma b$ holds only if either the tasks from R(a) and R(b) alternately occurs in $P(\sigma, a, b)$, or none of tasks in R(a) and R(b) occurs. It means that in one trace, either invisible tasks a and b occur together or none of them occurs. If for any trace $\sigma \in W$, $a \bigotimes_\sigma b$ holds (i.e. $a \bigotimes_W b$), invisible tasks a and b should be combined.

Splitting Invisible Tasks. NFCs are detected after the discovery of invisible tasks, and they would bring extra dependency relations between tasks. This would lead to deadlock when they are involved with invisible tasks in some case. N_6 and N_6' in Figure 4 present an example of this situation. N_6 is the original sound process model, while N_6' is the process model mined without splitting. In N_6', task I is found earlier than the NFC (P1, P2, P3, E, D). Place P1, P3 and the dotted edges are added for constructing the NFC. The new-added dependencies (A,E) and (B,D) make the net not sound. For example, after the execution of $< A, C, I >$ or $< B, C, I >$, there would be a remaining token in P1 or P3. Thus, we should check each invisible task, and split them if necessary.

Definition 14. *(Splittable invisible tasks) Let T be a set of tasks, W be an event log over T. The* Splittable invisible tasks *is defined as follows:*

- $IMD(t) = \{(a,x,y,b) \in MD(t)|\exists(m,n) \in ID : (n = x \vee m = y)\}$, and
- $Splittable\_Set(W,T_I)=\{t \in T_I||IMD(t)| > 1\}$.

For each invisible task t, $IMD(t)$ is the set of mendacious dependencies involved in implicit dependencies (we call this mix dependencies for short). By analyzing the workflow net, we discover that each mix dependency should be expressed as one unique invisible task. If two mix dependencies are expressed in one invisible task, the mined model would not be sound, like the invisible task I in N_6'. Thus, the invisible task t should be split if $|IMD(t)| > 1$.

4.6   The $\alpha^{\$}$ Algorithm

The $\alpha^{\$}$ algorithm is defined in Definition 15. According to the previous sections, the algorithm is luminous. And thus, there is no further explanation.

Definition 15. *Let T be a set of tasks, W be an event log over T. The $\alpha^{\$}(W)$ algorithm is defined as follows:*

1. $T_{log} = \{t \in T|\exists_{\sigma \in W} t \in \sigma\}$,
2. $L1L_{raw} = \{t \in T_{log}|\exists_{\sigma=t_1 t_2 t_3...t_n \in W; i \in 1,2,...,n} t = t_{i-1} \wedge t = t_i\}$,
3. $L1L_{free} = getL1LFree()$,
4. $L1L = L1L_{raw} - L1L_{free}$,
5. $W^{-L1L} = removeL1L(W, L1L)$,

6. $(P_{W-L1L}, T_{W-L1L}, T^I_{W-L1L}, F_{W-L1L}) = \alpha^{\#}_{improved}(W^{-L1L})$,
7. $R_{W-L1L} = getReachableDependency(T^I_{W-L1L}, W^{-L1L})$,
8. $ID_{W-L1L} = \alpha^{++}(P_{W-L1L}, T_{W-L1L}, T^I_{W-L1L}, F_{W-L1L}, R_{W-L1L})$,
9. $(F'_{W-L1L}, P'_{W-L1L}) = addImplicitDependency(F_{W-L1L}, P_{W-L1L}, ID_{W-L1L})$,
10. $(P_W, T_W, F_W) = addL1L(L1L, F'_{W-L1L}, P'_{W-L1L}, T_{W-L1L})$,
11. $(P_W, T_W, F_W) = adjustInvisibleTask(T^I_{W-L1L}, F_W)$, and
12. $\alpha^{\$}(W) = (P_W, T_W, F_W)$.

5   Experimental Evaluation

The $\alpha^{\$}$ algorithm has been implemented as a plug-in in ProM [9]. The ProM 5.2-based implementation of $\alpha^{\$}$, is publicly accessible from GitHub (https://github.com/ guoqinlong/Alpha-Dollar-Process-Mining-Algorithm).

In the evaluation, we compared the performance of $\alpha^{\$}$ with other process mining algorithms: α^{++}, $\alpha^{\#}$, *Genetic*, *Heuristic*, *ILP*, and *Region*. Note that the default mining results of Genetic and Heuristic are Heuristic nets. With the transformation package in ProM, a transformation to Petri net has been implemented. Besides, all algorithms were executed using their default settings.

5.1   Evaluation Based on Artificial Logs

We first focus on artificial examples which demonstrate that $\alpha^{\$}$ significantly improves existing approaches. To illustrate the capabilities of $\alpha^{\$}$, we first show some concrete experimental results in Table 2.

Table 2(a) is an example of an invisible task involved in a parallel construct. In the reference model, two parallel branches share the same invisible task. $\alpha^{\$}$ and *Genetic* managed to mine the proper process model. α^{++} and Heuristic failed to discover the invisible task. $\alpha^{\#}$ managed to mine two invisible tasks, but failed to combine them into one. *ILP* cannot mine a sound process model. Besides, *ILP* also cannot mine proper process models for other examples in Table 2, which will not be elaborated then. The reference model in Table 2(b) has two invisible tasks combined with NFCs. $\alpha^{\$}$ managed to rediscover it. The models mined by $\alpha^{\#}$, *Heuristic* and *Genetic* failed to detect all NFCs, and these three mined models have more behavior than the reference model. α^{++} failed to discover the invisible task. Table 2 is an example of IT-in-NFC. α^{++}, *Genetic* and *Heuristic* failed to mine the invisible task. Two invisible tasks were detected by $\alpha^{\#}$, while the NFC was not discovered. The reference model in Table 2(d) has one invisible task. α^{++}, $\alpha^{\#}$ and *Heuristic* failed to discover the invisible task. Besides, the process model discovered by *Genetic* is not sound.

There are 40 process models in the artificial data set, 30 of which are from the *general significant reference model set* proposed in [13]. Besides, five artificial models (i.e., Artif-1) with IT-in-NFC are supplied in the experimental data set to demonstrate the capabilities of $\alpha^{\$}$ algorithm. Another five artificial models (i.e., Artif-2) are generated by tool *Process Log Generator*(PLG) [17].

Table 2. Four example process models

(a)

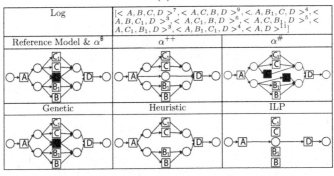

Log	$[< A,B,C,D >^7, < A,C,B,D >^9, < A,B_1,C,D >^4, < A,B,C_1,D >^3, < A,C_1,B,D >^6, < A,C,B_1,D >^5, < A,C_1,B_1,D >^3, < A,B_1,C_1,D >^4, < A,D >^{11}]$
Reference Model & $\alpha^\$$	α^{++} ... $\alpha^{\#}$
Genetic	Heuristic ... ILP

(b)

Log	$[< B,C,D,F,G >^{22}, < A,C,E,F,H >^{17}, < B,C,F,G >^{32}, < A,C,F,H >^{18}]$
Reference Model & $\alpha^\$$	α^{++} ... $\alpha^{\#}$
Genetic	Heuristic ... ILP

(c)

Log	$[< A,C,D >^{22}, < C >^{23}]$
Reference Model & $\alpha^\$$	α^{++} ... $\alpha^{\#}$
Genetic	Heuristic ... ILP

(d)

Log	$[< A,E,F,G >, < A,E,B,C,F,G >^6, < A,E,C,B,F,G >, < A,E,C,F,B,G >^{10}, < A,C,E,F,B,G >^8, < A,C,F,E,B,G >^6, < A,C,E,B,F,G >^4]$
Reference Model & $\alpha^\$$	α^{++} ... $\alpha^{\#}$
Genetic	Heuristic ... ILP

For evaluation of the performance on artificial dataset, two criteria are applied : *Fitness* [10] tests the conformance between the mined model and the given log. The fitness is determined by replaying the log on the model, i.e., for each trace the "token game" is played. If $fitness = 1$ then the log can be parsed by the model without any error; *Model rediscoverability* [13] tests the conformance between the mined model and the original model. Model rediscoverability of a process mining algorithm is measured by the similarity degree between the original model and the model mined by the process mining algorithm.

Table 3. Time expense on experiments in seconds

Mining algorithm	$\alpha^\$$	α^{++}	$\alpha\#$	Genetic	Heuristic	ILP	Region
Artificial logs	14.63	10.33	12.06	122.04	14.95	23.95	47.13

Table 3 shows the time expense on evaluation. As for the artificial logs, the cost of $\alpha^\$$ are more than that of either $\alpha\#$ or α^{++}, yet less than the sum of them. Compared with *Genetic*, the time cost of $\alpha^\$$ is much smaller.

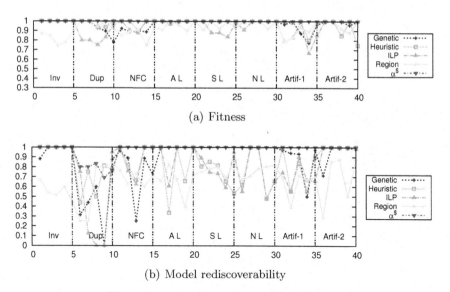

(a) Fitness

(b) Model rediscoverability

Fig. 5. Experiment result on artificial logs

Figure 5(a) shows the fitness result of different process mining algorithms. Since $\alpha^\$$ is based on $\alpha\#$ and α^{++}, $\alpha^\$$ outperforms both of them. For the clearness of the figure, the results of $\alpha\#$ and α^{++} are not listed in Figure 5. In the fitness measurement, 2.5% models mined by $\alpha\#$ and 10.0% models mined by α^{++} do not have a value of 1, but $\alpha^\$$ has a fitness of 1 in all the models. $\alpha^\$$ has a better fitness result than all the other algorithms. Model rediscoverability result is shown in Figure 5(b). Except the process models with duplicate tasks, $\alpha^\$$ is able to mine each process model identical with the original one in the experiment data set, while the other algorithms cannot mine them successfully. $\alpha^\$$ has a better result in model rediscoverability than $\alpha^\#$ and $\alpha^\$$. 47.5% of models mined by $\alpha^\#$ and 32.5% of models mined by α^{++} have a less model rediscoverability than $\alpha^\$$.

5.2 Evaluation Based on Real-Life Log

In this section, we use the event log used in paper [6]. This real-life log shows the event traces (process instances) for four different applications to get a license to ride motorbikes or drive.

Since there is no groundtruth model of the event log, *model rediscoverability* cannot be applied as the evaluation criteria. In this section, two additional quality measures in ProM are applied: precision - a measure how closely the behavior in the log is represented by the Petri net, simplicity - all places, transitions and arcs of the discovered Petri nets are counted and accumulated to a simplicity measure. Additionally, whether the mined model is a WF-net and the time cost of mining are evaluated.

Table 4. Evaluation results of different process discovery algorithms on a real-life log

	$\alpha^\$$	α^{++}	$\alpha^\#$	Genetic	Heuristic	ILP	Region
Fitness	*1.00*	0.95	*1.00*	*1.00*	*1.00*	*1.00*	0.90
Precision	*1.00*	*1.00*	0.84	*1.00*	0.84	0.56	0.91
Simplicity	22	20	22	26	20	*17*	26
Workflow Net	*True*	*True*	*True*	*True*	*True*	False	False
Time(ms)	224	175	185	34301	*102*	470	2786

Table 4 is the evaluation result on the log. Due to strongly unconnected nodes, models mined by ILP and Region are not WF-nets. Only $\alpha^\$$ and Genetic mined process model with both Precision = 1 and Fitness = 1. Other algorithm such as α^{++}, $\alpha^\#$ and Heuristic cannot mine invisible tasks and NFCs simultaneously, which leads either Precision or Fitness less than 1. Though $\alpha^\$$ and Genetic mine the same model, $\alpha^\$$ shows about 2 orders of magnitudes improvement in time costs, and there is no parameter setting needed for $\alpha^\$$.

6 Conclusion and Future Work

A novel process mining algorithm named $\alpha^\$$ is proposed. Using the *improved mendacious dependency* and *implicit dependency*, $\alpha^\$$ is the first algorithm which can adequately mine IT-in-NFC. Experiments show that $\alpha^\$$ can outperform the state-of-the-art mainstream process mining algorithms. The efficiency of $\alpha^\$$ is comparable to the fastest process mining algorithms by far.

Our future work would mainly focus on the following two aspects. One is to enhance mining capability of $\alpha^\$$ on process models with duplicated tasks. The other one is to design a parallel and distributed process mining algorithm based on $\alpha^\$$ to handle huge event logs.

Acknowledgments. This work is supported by National Natural Science Foundation of China (No. 61472207, 61325008). The authors would like to thank Boudewijn van Dongen for his detailed and constructive suggestions.

References

1. van der Aalst, W.M.P., Rubin, V., Verbeek, H.M.W., van Dongen, B.F., Kindler, E., Günther, C.W.: Process mining: a two-step approach to balance between underfitting and overfitting. Software & Systems Modeling **9**(1), 87–111 (2010)
2. van der Aalst, W.M.P., van Dongen, B.F., Herbst, J., Maruster, L., Schimm, G., Weijters, A.J.: Workflow mining: A survey of issues and approaches. Data & knowledge engineering **47**(2), 237–267 (2003)
3. Wen, L., van der Aalst, W.M.P., Wang, J., Sun, J.: Mining process models with non-free-choice constructs. Data Mining and Knowledge Discovery **15**(2), 145–180 (2007)
4. Wen, L., Wang, J., van der Aalst, W.M.P., Huang, B., Sun, J.: Mining process models with prime invisible tasks. Data & Knowledge Engineering **69**(10), 999–1021 (2010)
5. van der Aalst, W.M.P., Weijters, A.J.M.M.: Process mining: a research agenda. Computers in industry **53**(3), 231–244 (2004)
6. Medeiros, A.K., Weijters, A.J., Aalst, W.M.: Genetic process mining: an experimental evaluation. Data Mining and Knowledge Discovery **14**(2), 245–304 (2007)
7. van der Aalst, W.M.P.: The application of Petri nets to workflow management. Journal of circuits, systems, and computers **8**(01), 21–66 (1998)
8. van der Aalst, W.M.P., Weijters, T., Maruster, L.: Workflow mining: Discovering process models from event logs. IEEE Transactions on Knowledge and Data Engineering **16**(9), 1128–1142 (2004)
9. van Dongen, B.F., de Medeiros, A.K.A., Verbeek, H.M.W.E., Weijters, A.J.M.M.T., van der Aalst, W.M.P.: The ProM framework: a new era in process mining tool support. In: Ciardo, G., Darondeau, P. (eds.) ICATPN 2005. LNCS, vol. 3536, pp. 444–454. Springer, Heidelberg (2005)
10. Rozinat, A., van der Aalst, W.M.P.: Conformance testing: measuring the fit and appropriateness of event logs and process models. In: Bussler, C.J., Haller, A. (eds.) BPM 2005. LNCS, vol. 3812, pp. 163–176. Springer, Heidelberg (2006)
11. Weijters, A.J.M.M., van der Aalst, W.M.P., De Medeiros, A.A.: Process mining with the heuristics miner-algorithm. Technische Universiteit Eindhoven, Tech. Rep. WP, 166, pp. 1–34 (2006)
12. van der Werf, J.M.E.M., van Dongen, B.F., Hurkens, C.A.J., Serebrenik, A.: Process discovery using integer linear programming. In: van Hee, K.M., Valk, R. (eds.) PETRI NETS 2008. LNCS, vol. 5062, pp. 368–387. Springer, Heidelberg (2008)
13. Guo, Q., Wen, L., Wang, J., Ding, Z., Lv, C.: A universal significant reference model set for process mining evaluation framework. In: Ouyang, C., Jung, J.-Y. (eds.) AP-BPM 2014. LNBIP, vol. 181, pp. 16–30. Springer, Heidelberg (2014)

14. Günther, C.W., van der Aalst, W.M.P.: Fuzzy mining – adaptive process simplification based on multi-perspective metrics. In: Alonso, G., Dadam, P., Rosemann, M. (eds.) BPM 2007. LNCS, vol. 4714, pp. 328–343. Springer, Heidelberg (2007)
15. van der Aalst, W.M.P.: Process Mining: Discovery, Conformance and Enhancement of Business Processes. Springer, Heidelberg (2011)
16. van der Aalst, W.M.P., Adriansyah, A., van Dongen, B.: Replaying history on process models for conformance checking and performance analysis. Wiley Interdisciplinary Reviews: Data Mining and Knowledge Discovery 2(2), 182–192 (2012)
17. Burattin, A., Sperduti, A.: PLG: a framework for the generation of business process models and their execution logs. In: Muehlen, M., Su, J. (eds.) BPM 2010 Workshops. LNBIP, vol. 66, pp. 214–219. Springer, Heidelberg (2011)

Incorporating Negative Information
in Process Discovery

Hernan Ponce-de-León[1]([✉]), Josep Carmona[2],
and Seppe K.L.M. vanden Broucke[3]

[1] Department of Computer Science and Engineering, School of Science, Helsinki
Institute for Information Technology HIIT, Aalto University, Espoo, Finland
hernan.poncedeleon@aalto.fi
[2] Universitat Politecnica de Catalunya, Barcelona, Spain
jcarmona@cs.upc.edu
[3] Department of Decision Sciences and Information Management,
Faculty of Economics and Business, KU Leuven, Leuven, Belgium
seppe.vandenbroucke@kuleuven.be

Abstract. The discovery of a formal process model from event logs describing real process executions is a challenging problem that has been studied from several angles. Most of the contributions consider the extraction of a model as a *semi-supervised* problem where only positive information is available. In this paper we present a fresh look at process discovery where also negative information can be taken into account. This feature may be crucial for deriving process models which are not only simple, fitting and precise, but also good on generalizing the right behavior underlying an event log. The technique is based on numerical abstract domains and Satisfiability Modulo Theories (SMT), and can be combined with any process discovery technique. As an example, we show in detail how to supervise a recent technique that uses numerical abstract domains. Experiments performed in our prototype implementation show the effectiveness of the techniques and the ability to improve the results produced by selected discovery techniques.

1 Introduction

The digital revolution that is taking place in the last decade is abruptly changing the way organizations, industry and people access, store and analyze the vast amount of digital information currently available. The challenge is to be able to extract value from this information in an effective way. In the context of information systems and business process management, where processes are responsible for the correct undertaking of system functionalities, end-users desire to extract process-oriented aspects that can contribute to a better understanding of the process perspective of the reality observed.

Process Mining is considered to be a viable solution to this problem: by using the *event logs* containing the footprints of real process-executions, process mining techniques aim at discovering, analyzing and extending formal process models

© Springer International Publishing Switzerland 2015
H.R. Motahari-Nezhad et al. (Eds.): BPM 2015, LNCS 9253, pp. 126–143, 2015.
DOI: 10.1007/978-3-319-23063-4_8

revealing the real processes in a system [1]. From its arising around a decade ago, the process mining field has evolved into several directions, with process discovery perhaps being the most difficult challenge demonstrated by the large amount of techniques available nowadays. What makes process discovery hard is the fact that derived process models are expected to be good in four quality dimensions which often are opposed: *fitness* (ability of the model to reproduce the traces in the event log), *precision* (how precise is the model in representing the behavior in the log), *generalization* (is the model able to generalize for behavior not in the log) and *simplicity* (the well-known *Occam's Razor* principle).

Process discovery is a *learning* technique: a set of training examples (traces denoting process executions) are used to derive a process model which encloses the behavior underlying in the training set. Most techniques that have been proposed for process discovery so far assume a positive label in each trace, i.e. the example is an instance of behavior that must be in the process model to be derived. A slight extension of this assumption may be obtained if extra information is considered that enables to weight different traces: for instance, if the frequency of a trace is also considered, there exist some techniques that are able to extract only the most frequent patterns into a process model [2,3].

In literature, very few techniques have been presented that consider the discovery problem as a *supervised learning* task, i.e. using both the real process executions as positive examples, but also incorporating negative examples, that is, traces representing behavior that cannot be executed in the underlying system and should hence not be present in the process model to be derived. Such information might be crucial to derive the right model [4–8]. Clearly, the use of negative information can bring significant benefits, e.g. enable a controlled generalization of a process model: the patterns to generalize should never include the negative behavior. Another benefit is the ability to simplify a model on those parts that do not contribute to differentiate between positive and negative examples. The existence of few techniques for supervised process discovery is due to the fact that most real-life event logs do not provide easy ready-to-use negative examples.

This paper proposes a *novel methodology for supervised process discovery*, and shows how this technique can be adapted to be used in combination with arbitrary process discovery methods. The two main techniques combined to this end are numerical abstract domains [9] and Satisfiability Modulo Theories [10].

We ground the supervisory approach on the duality between the marking equation of a Petri net and the domain of convex polyhedra which has been already exploited for process discovery [11] and which we summarize now informally. The idea of [11] is to transform the traces in the log into points of an n-dimensional space (where n is the number of different activities in the log) and then to find a convex envelope of these points representing the concept to learn. The domain of *convex polyhedra* is used as it is a good compromise between expressivity and complexity of the operations [12]. The final step is to convert the convex polyhedron into a process model (a Petri net [13]) by extracting half-spaces of the polyhedron and transforming them into Petri net places that

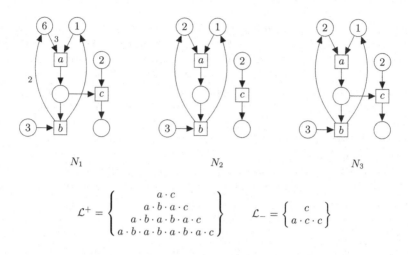

$$\mathcal{L}^+ = \left\{ \begin{array}{c} a \cdot c \\ a \cdot b \cdot a \cdot c \\ a \cdot b \cdot a \cdot b \cdot a \cdot c \\ a \cdot b \cdot a \cdot b \cdot a \cdot b \cdot a \cdot c \end{array} \right\} \qquad \mathcal{L}_- = \left\{ \begin{array}{c} c \\ a \cdot c \cdot c \end{array} \right\}$$

Fig. 1. Three process models to illustrate supervised process discovery.

restrict behavior in the derived Petri net. Remarkably, this approach is among the few ones that can discover the full class of pure P/T-nets, i.e. Petri nets with arbitrary arc weights and tokens. This aspect makes the approach well suited for domains like manufacturing, where the flow relation between activities may be non-unitary. Most of the techniques in the literature do not aim for such a general class of process models.

The technique presented in [11] suffers from two main limitations. First, since it is tailored to P/T nets, the number of half-spaces describing the concept learned are often large and complex which significantly hampers the practical use of the corresponding model to understand the underlying process. Among the problems, we highlight deriving overfitting and/or *spaghetti* models as the most stringent ones. Second, the technique follows a semi-supervised paradigm, i.e. only positive instances of a process are considered. This implies that the model obtained may be accepting behavior that is against the expected functioning of the process represented; in other words: the model is imprecise.

We extend the technique from above by an extra simplification step on the polyhedron before transforming it into a net. The restrictions on the polyhedron can be relaxed as far as they preserve the initial solutions, i.e. the positive traces. Additionally, negative information can be encoded as negative points which must be not enclosed by the polyhedron and thus preventing some of the problems from [11]. This step is automated with the help of SMT instances that enable the rotation and shifting of the polyhedron.

Example 1. Consider the three models of Fig. 1 and the logs $\mathcal{L}^+$ and $\mathcal{L}_-$ representing respectively the observed and the undesired behavior of the system. The model on the left (N_1) represents a system where an action c can only be fired once and when it is preceded by action a^1. N_1 can replay all the traces in $\mathcal{L}^+$, but not those in $\mathcal{L}_-$; we can conclude that it is fitting, precise and generalizes well the intended behavior. N_2 is also fitting, but it is too general since it accepts some of the undesired behaviors in $\mathcal{L}_-$, e.g. action c can be fired independently of the firing of a. Using the approach from [11] both nets could be discovered, but the structure of the latter is simpler (it has less arcs and smaller weights). The problem with the simplification from N_1 into N_2 is that it introduces undesired behaviors as commented previously. With the contributions of this paper net N_3 can be discovered, which is fitting, precise, does not accept any undesired behavior and it is still simpler than N_1.

The remainder of this paper is organized as follows: Section 2 introduces all the necessary background to understand the contribution of this paper. Then in Section 3 the approach for supervised process discovery is presented. A small discussion in Section 4 is devoted to decouple the methods of this paper from the particular discovery technique used. The approach is evaluated in Section 5, and compared with related work in Section 6. Section 7 concludes.

2   Preliminaries

In this section we introduce some basic definitions and ideas used in the subsequent sections.

2.1   Parikh Representation of an Event Log

The behavior of a process is observed as sequences of events from a given alphabet. For convenience, we use T to denote the set of symbols that represent the alphabet of events. A trace is a word $\sigma \in T^*$ that represents a finite sequence of events; $|\sigma|_a$ represents the number of occurrences of a in σ.

A *log* $\mathcal{L}$ is a set of traces from a given alphabet. We say that $\sigma \in \mathcal{L}$ if σ is the prefix of some trace of $\mathcal{L}$. Given an alphabet of events $T = \{t_1, \ldots, t_n\}$, the *Parikh vector* of a sequence of events is a function $\hat{\ } : T^* \to \mathbb{N}^n$ defined as $\hat{\sigma} = (|\sigma|_{t_1}, \ldots, |\sigma|_{t_n})$. For simplicity, we will also represent $|\sigma|_{t_i}$ as $\hat{\sigma}(t_i)$. Given a log $\mathcal{L}$, the set of Parikh vectors of $\mathcal{L}$ is defined as $\Pi(\mathcal{L}) = \{\hat{\sigma} \mid \sigma \in \mathcal{L}\}$.

2.2   Petri Nets and Process Discovery

A *Petri net* [13] is a tuple (P, T, F, M_0) where P and T represent respectively finite and disjoint sets of places and transitions, $F : (P \times T) \cup (T \times P) \to \mathbb{N}$ is the weighted flow relation. A marking M is a function $M : P \to \mathbb{N}$. M_0 is the initial marking that defines the initial state of the Petri net.

The preset and postset of a place p are respectively denoted as $^\bullet p$ and $p^\bullet$ and defined by $^\bullet p = \{t \in T \mid F(t, p) > 0\}$, $p^\bullet = \{t \in T \mid F(p, t) > 0\}$. A Petri

---

[1] Notice that there is a safe Petri net which includes $\mathcal{L}^+$ and excludes $\mathcal{L}_-$: we are using the unsafe models in Fig. 1 just as an illustrative example.

net is said to be *pure* if it does not have any self-loop, i.e. $\forall p \in P : {}^\bullet p \cap p^\bullet = \emptyset$. Henceforth, we will assume that all Petri nets referred to in the paper are pure.

The dynamic behavior of a Petri net is defined by its firing rules. A transition $t \in T$ is *enabled* in a marking M if $M(p) \geq F(p,t)$ for any $p \in P$. Firing an enabled transition t in a marking M leads to the marking M' defined by $M'(p) = M(p) - F(p,t) + F(t,p)$, for any $p \in P$, and is denoted by $M \xrightarrow{t} M'$. A sequence of transitions $\sigma = t_1 t_2 \ldots t_n$ is fireable if there is a sequence of markings $M_1, M_2, \ldots, M_n$ such that $M_0 \xrightarrow{t_1} M_1 \xrightarrow{t_2} M_2 \cdots \xrightarrow{t_n} M_n$. Given a Petri net N, $L(N)$ denotes the language of N, i.e. the set of fireable sequences of transitions. The set of markings reachable from the initial marking M_0 is called the *Reachability Set* of N and denoted as $\mathsf{RS}(N)$.

The Marking Equation: Let us consider a place p with ${}^\bullet p = \{x_1, \ldots, x_k\}$, $p^\bullet = \{y_1, \ldots, y_l\}$ and all flow relations having weight 1. Let us assume that the place contains $M_0(p)$ tokens in its initial marking. Then, the following equality holds for any sequence of events σ:

$$M(p) = M_0(p) + \widehat{\sigma}(x_1) + \cdots + \widehat{\sigma}(x_k) - \widehat{\sigma}(y_1) - \cdots - \widehat{\sigma}(y_l).$$

The previous equation can be generalized for weighted flows:

$$M(p) = M_0(p) + \sum_{x_i \in {}^\bullet p} F(x_i, p) \cdot \widehat{\sigma}(x_i) - \sum_{y_i \in p^\bullet} F(p, y_i) \cdot \widehat{\sigma}(y_i).$$

If we formulate the previous equation for all places in a Petri net, we can compress it using a matrix notation: $M = M_0 + A \cdot \widehat{\sigma}$, where M and M_0 are place vectors and A is the *incidence matrix* with $|P|$ rows and $|T|$ transitions that represents the flow relation of the net. The previous equation is called the *Marking Equation* of the Petri net [13].

The set of solutions for which the following inequality holds

$$M = M_0 + A \cdot \widehat{\sigma} \geq 0 \tag{1}$$

is called the *Potentially Reachable Set* (PRS(N)). All reachable markings of a Petri net fulfill (1). However the opposite is not always true. In general there can be unreachable markings for which (1) also holds, i.e. $\mathsf{RS}(N) \subseteq \mathsf{PRS}(N)$.

Process Discovery: The problem of process discovery requires the computation of a model M that adequately represents a log $\mathcal{L}$. A model M is *overfitting* with respect to log $\mathcal{L}$ if it is too specific and too much driven by the information in $\mathcal{L}$. On the other hand, M is an *underfitting* model for $\mathcal{L}$ if the behavior of M is too general and allows for things "not supported by evidence" in $\mathcal{L}$. Whereas overfitting denotes lack of generalization, underfitting represents too much generalization. A good balance between overfitting and underfitting is a desired feature in any process discovery algorithm [1].

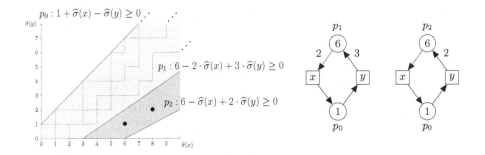

Fig. 2. Walks in the integer lattice and Petri net.

2.3 Convex Polyhedra and Integer Lattices

An n-dimensional convex polyhedron is a convex set of points in $\mathbb{R}^n$. Convex polyhedra admit two equivalent representations: the H-representation and the V-representation [9]. The former denotes a convex polyhedron $\mathcal{P}$ as the intersection of a finite set of half-spaces, i.e.

$$\mathcal{P} = \{x \in \mathbb{R}^n \mid A \cdot x + b \geq 0\} \tag{2}$$

where $A \in \mathbb{R}^{k \times n}$ and $b \in \mathbb{R}^k$ are the matrix and vector that represent k half-spaces. Given a polyhedron $\mathcal{P}$, the set of integer points inside $\mathcal{P}$ are called the Z-polyhedron of $\mathcal{P}$. For the sake of brevity, all polyhedra mentioned in this work will be assumed to be convex.

2.4 Numerical Abstract Domains and Process Discovery

In [11] several techniques are presented for the discovery of Petri nets from Parikh vectors. In particular, given a log $\mathcal{L}$, the set $\Pi(\mathcal{L})$ is used to find A and M_0 in (1) such that the associated Petri net is a good approximation of the process behavior. We now summarize the approach.

Given a Petri net N, by comparing the expressions (1) and (2) we can observe that $\mathsf{PRS}(N)$ is the Z-polyhedron of a convex polyhedron that has two properties: $A \in \mathbb{Z}^{|P| \times n}$ and $M_0 \in \mathbb{N}^{|P|}$. These properties guarantee that the initial marking is not negative and only markings with integral token values are reachable.

The n-dimensional integer lattice $\mathbb{Z}^n$ is the lattice of n-tuples of integers. For describing a log, each lattice point represents a Parikh vector from an alphabet with n symbols and hence the points belong to $\mathbb{N}^n$. A log can be represented as a set of walks in $\mathbb{N}^n$. Every step in a walk moves from one lattice point to another by only increasing one of the components of the n-tuple by one unit.

The link between logs and Petri nets is illustrated in Fig. 2. The figure at the left represents three different walks in a 2-dimensional space. The light grey area represents a polyhedron that *covers* the points visited by the walks. The polyhedron can be represented by the intersection of two half-spaces in $\mathbb{R}^2$:

$$1 + \widehat{\sigma}(x) - \widehat{\sigma}(y) \geq 0$$
$$6 - 2 \cdot \widehat{\sigma}(x) + 3 \cdot \widehat{\sigma}(y) \geq 0$$

The polyhedron can also be represented in matrix notation with a direct correspondence with the marking equation (1) of a Petri net:

$$\begin{bmatrix} 1 \\ 6 \end{bmatrix} + \begin{bmatrix} 1 & -1 \\ -2 & 3 \end{bmatrix} \cdot \begin{bmatrix} \widehat{\sigma}(x) \\ \widehat{\sigma}(y) \end{bmatrix} \geq \begin{bmatrix} 0 \\ 0 \end{bmatrix}$$

The Petri net on the left represents the one obtained from the interpretation of the marking equation. Each face of the polyhedron is represented by a place (row in the matrix). The set of Parikh vectors generated by the Petri net corresponds to the Z-polyhedron of the polyhedron depicted at the left.

In summary, given a set of Parikh vectors from a log, the techniques in [11] find the polyhedron which can finally be translated to a Petri net as shown in the example.

2.5 Inducing Negative Information from a Log or Model

Due to the fact that real-life event logs seldom contain negative information, i.e. behavior that the system should not allow, scholars have proposed alternative ways to induce negative information to guide the learning task. In [8], a technique is proposed to induce so called "artificial negative events" based on the positive information contained in the log. Recent contributions have shown that the obtention of negative information from event logs can be done efficiently in a manner which is robust to differing levels of event log completeness [14]. Finally, when a prescriptive, ground-truth process model is known, negative information can also be appended to the known, positive traces contained in a given event log by replaying the traces over the model and querying the latter to investigate which activities in the activity alphabet are not enabled in a given position in the trace at hand, from which a set of negative traces can be derived.

3 Supervised Process Discovery

In this section we show in detail how to make the approach from [11] supervised. Next section shows how to make an arbitrary discovery technique supervised.

3.1 Stages of the Approach

The proposed approach for supervised process discovery and simplification is illustrated in Fig. 3. The upper part of the figure (enclosed in a round box) represents the approach from [11] from which this work is grounded; the detailed

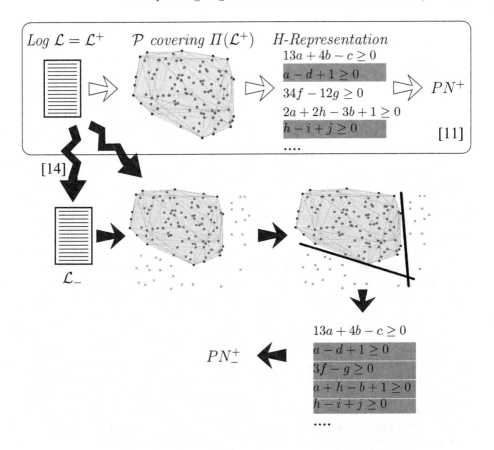

Fig. 3. Flow for supervised process discovery (arrows with black background) compared with the approach in [11] (arrows with white background).

explanation of this is found in Section 2.4. This approach suffers from two short-comings. First, it is exponential on the number of different activities in the log: in [11] a divide-and-conquer strategy is presented that uses sampling and projection to overcome this limitation for large event logs. Sampling and projection techniques alleviate the complexity of the monolithic approach considerably, but on the other hand the quality metrics regarding precision and simplicity may become considerably degraded, thus deriving an underfitting and complex process model. The reason for this is due to the fact that sampling tends to extract an overfitting representation of the samples used, which may be simplified if the whole set of Parikh vectors (instead of using samples) was used to construct the polyhedron. Additionally, the representations for the samples obtained may miss important relations, a problem that causes a precision degradation.

The second limitation of the approach in [11] is the manual selection of the constraints within the H-representation of the polyhedron computed. Only constraints with simple coefficients (those with gray background in Fig. 3) are used, leaving the rest of constraints (half-spaces that mean to separate the observed behavior from the rest of behavior) out of the model, and hence the model derived may be generalizing too much, i.e. may be imprecise. The selection of simple constraints is guided by the assumption that in reality (and specially, in the scope of business process management), process models tend to be defined by simple constructs.

Having only event logs with positive information at our disposal, we use the technique from [14] to extract accurate negative execution traces. The proposed approach inserts the negative Parikh vectors into the n-dimensional space and uses a tailored SMT-based optimization technique to *shift* and *rotate* the half-spaces covering the positive information to simplify and generalize them while keeping the negative information away from the transformed polyhedron (see Sections 3.2 and 3.3). In the figure, it can be seen that $34f - 12g \geq 0$ is a constraint obtained from the polyhedron only covering the positive information. This constraint is then simplified and generalized to $3f - g \geq 0$ which is then considered as a simple constraint, and therefore will be also translated to the final process model. This enables relating in the model activities f and g.

Remarkably, the approach of Fig. 3 can also be applied without any negative information, leading to a simplification (and generalization) of the models derived by the approach presented in [11]. As the shifting and rotation techniques presented in the following sections are implemented as instances of an SMT problem, leaving out the parts related to negative information will enable end users focusing only on simplification of the model in the positive perspective. Next section presents this idea.

3.2   Generalization and Simplification on the Positive Perspective

Section 2.4 explains how to to compute a Petri net containing a set of traces using the minimal convex hull of its Parikh vectors and then extracting its H-representation that can in turn be translated to a Petri net. However, the structure of the obtained model might be too complicated; e.g. actions might consume and produce big amounts of resources. Real-life business process usually have a simpler structure and therefore the discovered models need to be simplified. This task is usually done manually using expert knowledge to detect situations where the net can be simplified. When discovery algorithms based on numerical abstract domains are used, the simplification consists on removing manually inequalities (half-spaces defining the polyhedron) from the H-representation. Since each inequality defines a place in the net, removing them reduces the number of places in the net and simplifies it.

We shift and rotate the polyhedron to obtain simpler inequalities and thus preserve as much as possible the behavior of the system. In Fig. 3 only inequalities in dark background are transformed into places in the final net. Whenever an inequality is removed, the new polyhedron is less restrictive and therefore more points satisfy the set of remaining constraints; in the mined Petri net, more traces are possible, thus generalizing the underlying behavior.

Example 2. Fig. 2 (left) shows a polyhedron (light grey area) defined by the H-representation $\{p_0, p_1\}$, and some of its walks. A more general polyhedron, i.e. one with larger Z-polyhedron (see Section 2.3) is defined by $\{p_0, p_2\}$ (light and dark grey area). Points marked as $\bullet$ are solutions of $\{p_0, p_2\}$, but not of $\{p_0, p_1\}$. The right of the figure shows the Petri nets representing both polyhedra; the sequence $xxxyxxx$ is a trace of the second net, however it cannot be fireable in the first net. This is represented in the left part of the figure by the point $(6, 1)$ which is a solution of $\{p_0, p_2\}$, but not of $\{p_0, p_1\}$.

The approach that we propose in this section simplifies the H-representation of a given polyhedron by modifying its inequalities; this is achieved by trying to reduce the coefficients of each inequality. Each new inequality should accept at least the same solutions as the original one to avoid loosing the fitness of the model. Given an inequality of the form $\alpha_0 + \alpha_1 \cdot x_1 + \cdots + \alpha_n \cdot x_n \geq 0$ we need to find new coefficients $\beta_0, \beta_1, \ldots, \beta_n$ such that:

$$\sum_{i=1}^{n} \beta_i > 0 \text{ and } \beta_0 \geq 0 \qquad \text{(NZ)}$$

for each $0 \leq i \leq n$:
$$|\beta_i| \leq |\alpha_i| \qquad \text{(MIN)}$$

and for all $x_i \geq 0$ with $i \leq n$:

$$(\alpha_0 + \sum_{i=1}^{n} \alpha_i \cdot x_i) \geq 0 \implies (\beta_0 + \sum_{i=1}^{n} \beta_i \cdot x_i) \geq 0 \qquad \text{(PC)}$$

Constraint (NZ) specifies that at least one of the variable's coefficients should be different than zero to eliminate trivial solutions and that the independent coefficient should not be negative since it represents the initial marking. The meaning of constraint (MIN) is that the new inequality should be simpler than the original one, i.e. each transition should consume or produce less tokens. Finally, every solution of the original inequality should also be a solution of the discovered one (PC).

To obtain the H-representation of a polyhedron representing a simpler and more general net, constrains (NZ), (MIN) and (PC) can be encoded using Satisfiability Modulo Theories; we have implemented the proposed encoding using the Z3 SMT solver [15]. For the inequality $6 - 2 \cdot \widehat{\sigma}(x) + 3 \cdot \widehat{\sigma}(y) \geq 0$ the proposed encoding results in:

$$(\beta_1 + \beta_2 > 0) \wedge (\beta_0 \geq 0) \wedge (|\beta_1| \leq 2) \wedge (|\beta_2| \leq 3) \wedge$$
$$\forall \widehat{\sigma}(x), \widehat{\sigma}(y) : (6 - 2 \cdot \widehat{\sigma}(x) + 3 \cdot \widehat{\sigma}(y) \geq 0) \implies (\beta_0 + \beta_1 \cdot \widehat{\sigma}(x) + \beta_2 \cdot \widehat{\sigma}(y) \geq 0)$$

which has as a solution for example $\beta_0 = 6, \beta_1 = -1, \beta_2 = 2$. The original inequality can be thus replaced in the H-representation of the polyhedron by

$6 - \hat{\sigma}(x) + 2 \cdot \hat{\sigma}(y) \geq 0$. The new polyhedron generates a simpler Petri net (less tokens are consumed by x and produced by y), but more traces are accepted as it is shown in Example 2.

Since our approach only simplifies inequations, it might be still necessary to remove some of them manually; in Fig. 3 two inequalities are simplified and remain in the final model, but $13a + 4b - c \geq 0$ cannot be simplified and thus is still removed.

The method that we propose does not sacrifices fitness of the model since the Z-polyhedron obtained by the transformations is a superset of the original one:

Theorem 1. *Let $\mathcal{L}$ be a log, N a fitting model of $\mathcal{L}$ and N' the model obtained by our method, then N' if fitting for $\mathcal{L}$.*

Proof. The proof is immediate by the constraint (PC) in the encoding of the new polyhedron.

Structural Simplification Ratio: Given an inequality $p_i = \alpha_0 + \sum_{i=1}^{n} \alpha_i \cdot x_i \geq 0$ its *structural complexity* is given by $C_{p_i} = \sum_{i=0}^{n} |\alpha_i|$; the complexity of the H-representation of a polyhedron is the sum of the complexity of its inequalities. With this definition the complexity of polyhedra $\{p_0, p_1\}$ and $\{p_0, p_2\}$ are 14 and 12 respectively. Hence we consider the second polyhedron and the corresponding net simpler since its complexity is smaller. The effectiveness of our method is defined as the reduction in the complexity of the new polyhedron.

Example 3. Fig. 1 shows the result of applying our method; the net N_1 has complexity $c_1 = C_{p_0} + C_{p_1} + C_{p_2} + C_{p_3} + C_{p_4} + C_{p_5} = (6 + 2 + 3) + (1 + 1 + 1) + (2 + 1) + (1 + 1 + 1) + (3 + 1) + 1 = 25$ while the net N_2 obtained by our method has complexity $c_2 = C_{p_0} + C_{p_1} + C_{p_2} + C_{p_3} + C_{p_4} + C_{p_5} = (2 + 1 + 1) + (1 + 1 + 1) + (2 + 1) + (1 + 1) + (3 + 1) + 1 = 17$. In this example the efficiency of our method is $100 - 100 \times (c_2/c_1) = 32\%$.

3.3   Improving Generalization and Simplicity via Negative Information

The generalization and simplification method proposed in Section 3.2 may introduce extra behaviors in the discovered model since the new polyhedron covers more points. If we take into account negative information (forbidden traces), the proposed encoding needs to be refined to rule out certain solutions.

We use the method proposed in [14] to generate negative information for our supervised process discovery. This method generates negative traces which are in the frontier of a polyhedron, but since any postfix of a negative trace is also a negative trace, we use extrapolation to generate traces that are not close to the positive behaviors, i.e. the half-spaces defining the polyhedron. If this step is avoided, in most of the cases the method presented in this section does not reduce the complexity of the model discovered simply by using [11] since rotation is very restricted.

In order to avoid the negative traces derived, each of them is converted into its Parikh representation. Each negative point should not be a solution of the new inequality; this can be encoded as follows; for each negative point $(k_1, \ldots, k_n)$:

$$\beta_0 + \sum_{i=1}^{n} \beta_i \cdot k_i < 0 \tag{NP}$$

Going back to Example 2, if we want to simplify inequality p_1 while ruling out the point $(6, 1)$, the new encoding should add the constraint

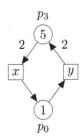

$$(\beta_0 + \beta_1 \cdot 6 + \beta_2 \cdot 1 < 0)$$

which rules out $\beta_0 = 6, \beta_1 = -1, \beta_2 = 2$ as a solution. The method using negative information proposes $5 - 2 \cdot \widehat{\sigma}(x) + 2 \cdot \widehat{\sigma}(y) \geq 0$ as the simplified inequality resulting in the net on the right which does not accept $xxxyxxx$ as a trace.

3.4 Discussion

The approach presented in this section comes with a hidden assumption that we would like to acknowledge here. It is assumed that negative information can be separated from positive information linearly, i.e. by a set of half-spaces representing a convex polyhedron. However, it is clear that geometrically this is not true in general, i.e. there may be negative points inside the polyhedron constructed. Due to the prefix-closed nature of the positive points in the convex polyhedron (see Fig. 2), negative points must be near the polyhedron half-spaces, and not in the center since a negative point cannot be the prefix of a positive point. In case of dealing with negative points inside a polyhedron, the learning can be oriented to not one but a set of convex polyhedron covering only the positive points, and the merge of several models can then be applied.

Another interesting source of negative information apart from the techniques used in this paper is the use of expert knowledge. This has not been considered in this paper, but extracting negative points from such expert knowledge can be done easily and may contribute to improve the method considerably.

4 Supervising Arbitrary Process Discovery Techniques

An important observation can be made at this point of the paper: the techniques presented in the previous section can be applied on top of any Petri net and hence are not dependent on the discovery technique from [11]. In Section 2.4

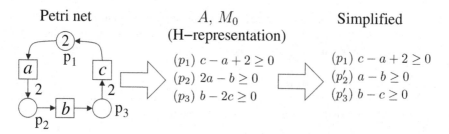

Fig. 4. Supervising the discovery approach from [16].

it has been shown the correspondence between a polyhedron and a Petri net by observing that the H-representation of $\mathcal{P}$ represents the marking equation of the corresponding Petri net N. This correspondence is used in [11] in the forward direction, i.e. for computing N from $\mathcal{P}$. To enable the application of the techniques in the previous section to an arbitrary Petri net N, one can simply use the aforementioned correspondence in the backward direction (to compute $\mathcal{P}$ from N) by taking the adjacency matrix of N and the initial marking and use them as the H-representation of a polyhedron corresponding to N.

Example 4. Fig. 4 (left) shows a Petri net that has been derived with the approach from [16] using the state-based theory of regions. The Petri net accepts traces where after firing a, there might be twice the number of bs, e.g., $ababbbc$. Now imagine that these traces are now forbidden, i.e. they are negative traces and only traces with the same amount of as, bs and cs should be included in the model. The technique presented will derive the inequalities in the right, denoting a Petri net similar to the original but where the weights in the arcs are now unitary and the net is conformant with the negative information provided.

5   Experiments

We run our approach as described in Section 3 on several real-life logs. To illustrate the general applicability of the approach as described in Section 4, we also apply our technique on models obtained by ILP Miner [17]. Results on the effectiveness (reduction in the complexity of the simplified polyhedron with regards to the original one) are reported. We also evaluate the precision of discovered models using the state-of-the-art technique from [18], as well as the generalization using the approach from [14]. Finally we compare our method with AGNEsMiner [8], a supervised technique for process discovery.

5.1   Supervising Process Discovery Techniques

The results of the simplification/generalization approach are shown in Tables 1 and 2. For all the examples the simplification step took less than a minute, showing that the overall performance of the discovery method is not degraded.

Table 1. Experimental results on models mined by the approach of Section 3.

log	total	prec	gen	$\mathcal{L}^+$				$\mathcal{L}^+$ and $\mathcal{L}_-$			
				iter	effec	prec	gen	iter	effec	prec	gen
caise2014	425	0,08	0.56	6	7.41	**0,09**	**0.59**	4	0.31	0,08	0.56
complex	28	**0,32**	0.54	2	2.81	**0,32**	**0.60**	1	0.00	**0,32**	0.54
confdimblocking	15	**1,00**	**0.84**	2	6.25	0,25	**0.84**	1	0.00	**1,00**	**0.84**
documentflow	26	**0,16**	**0.99**	2	11.94	**0,16**	**0.99**	2	7.46	0,15	**0.99**
fhmexamplen5	11	0,32	0.90	3	16.21	0,35	**0.93**	2	2.70	**0,36**	0.90
incident	15	**0,26**	**1.00**	2	17.46	0,22	**1.00**	2	4.76	0,24	**1.00**
purchasetopay	15	0,17	**1.00**	2	4.16	**0,20**	**1.00**	2	2.08	**0,20**	**1.00**
receipt	49	**0,26**	0.62	2	19.31	0,23	**0.69**	3	3.44	0,24	0.62

The following information is given: total number of inequations[2] ("total"), precision ("prec") and generalization ("gen") in the original model[3]; the efficiency ("effec") precision and generalization of the enhanced models when only positive information is used ("$\mathcal{L}^+$") and when negative information is also added ("$\mathcal{L}^+$ and $\mathcal{L}_-$"). Since the SMT encoding gives one solution (not necessarily the minimal one), we applied our method iteratively until the effectiveness between two iterations is not improved; the number of iterations is also reported in the table ("iter").

The results show that the complexity can be reduced up to 20% when only positive information is considered; in all the cases the penalty of this reduction is rather small, since the precision of the new model is similar to the original one (except for *confdimblocking* where a drop in precision occurs). When negative information is added, the effectiveness is reduced (below 8%) but precision values are almost coinciding with the original models. The same remark can be made for generalization: when only positive information is considered, all models exhibit a slight increase. After adding negative information, generalization scores are comparable to the original models. We can conclude that applying the ideas of Sections 3 and 4 results in models which are much simpler without a big impact on precision and which retain original generalization capabilities.

5.2 Empirical Comparison

Few approaches have been proposed in literature towards supervised process discovery (see next Section 6 for an overview on related work). We have chosen to compare our approach with [8], a supervised technique which is also able to utilize artificially generated negative events. Table 3 provides a comparative

---

[2] Although in Section 3 we comment on the fact that inequations can be chosen manually to retain only simple constructs, in the experiments we have avoided such manual selection for the sake of a fair comparison.

[3] As both the numerical abstract domains based miner and ILP Miner discover perfectly fitting models, fitness is not reported in the result tables.

Table 2. Experimental results on models mined by ILP Miner [17].

log	total	prec	gen	$\mathcal{L}^+$				$\mathcal{L}^+$ and $\mathcal{L}_-$			
				iter	effec	prec	gen	iter	effec	prec	gen
caise2014	112	0,17	0.57	7	24.04	0,05	**0.65**	3	9.21	**0,24**	0.58
complex	15	**0,57**	0.56	2	14.89	0,35	**0.75**	2	2.12	0,40	0.58
confdimblocking	10	**1,00**	**0.84**	2	8.33	0,26	**0.84**	2	4.16	0,28	**0.84**
documentflow	128	0,37	0.95	5	10.23	**0,39**	**0.96**	3	2.13	0,36	**0.96**
fhmexamplen5	22	0,38	0.92	2	9.70	**0,42**	**0.94**	2	0.97	0,38	0.92
incident	27	0,25	**0.99**	9	25.25	0,28	**0.99**	4	10.60	**0,29**	**0.99**
purchasetopay	12	**0,35**	**0.99**	3	13.13	0,09	**0.99**	2	12.12	0,20	**0.99**
receipt	35	**0,35**	0.62	6	25.26	0,29	**0.83**	2	3.15	0,32	0.62

Table 3. Fitness, precision, and generalization for supervised techniques.

log	Supervised Polyhedra			Supervised ILP Miner			AGNEsMiner		
	fit	prec	gen	fit	prec	gen	fit	prec	gen
caise2014	**1.00**	0,08	0.56	**1.00**	**0,24**	**0.58**	–	–	–
complex	**1.00**	0,32	0.54	**1.00**	0,40	**0.58**	0.82	**0.71**	0.43
confdimblocking	**1.00**	**1,00**	**0.84**	**1.00**	0,28	**0.84**	**1.00**	**1.00**	**0.84**
documentflow	**1.00**	0,15	**0.99**	**1.00**	**0,36**	0.96	–	–	–
fhmexamplen5	**1.00**	0,36	0.90	**1.00**	0,38	**0.92**	0.94	**0,53**	0.32
incident	**1.00**	0,24	**1.00**	**1.00**	0,29	0.99	0.84	**0,65**	0.63
purchasetopay	**1.00**	0,20	**1.00**	**1.00**	0,20	0.99	0.86	**0,82**	0.26
receipt	**1.00**	0,24	**0.62**	**1.00**	0,32	**0.62**	0.92	**0.81**	0.23

overview of fitness, precision and generalization scores for our approach applied on the numerical abstract domains based miner, ILP Miner, and AGNEsMiner[4].

The following conclusions are derived from the results: first, we note that AGNEsMiner generally performs well on the dimension of precision, although at a cost of deriving models which are not perfectly fitting. In addition, the miner did not succeed to find a model within the allotted time period (one day of calculation, the dash mark "–" represents a time out). In terms of generalization, our proposed approach outperforms AGNEsMiner since the best results are obtained either by the supervised polyhedra or the supervised ILP Miner.

---

[4] Attentive readers will observe that it is in fact possible to apply our supervised simplification approach to models mined by supervised process discovery techniques, e.g. AGNEsMiner. We have not done so in this section, however, to keep the comparison between various supervised discovery strategies pure.

6   Related Work

Very few approaches exist towards supervised process discovery, especially when compared to the multitude of process discovery techniques which work in an unsupervised fashion. Maruster et al. [19] were among the first to investigate the use of supervised techniques (in this case: rule-induction learners) to predict dependency relationships between activities. Instead of relying on negative information, the authors apply the learner on a table of metrics for each activity derived from the positive information.

Ferreira and Ferreira [4] apply inductive logic programming and partial-order planning techniques to derive a process model. Negative information is collected from users and domain experts who indicate whether a proposed execution plan is feasible or not, iteratively combining planning and learning to discover a process model.

Lamma et al. [5–7] apply an extension of logic programming, SCIFF, towards supervised declarative process discovery, i.e. the process model is represented as a set of logic constraints and not as a visual process model as done in this work. The authors assume the presence of negative information.

Similarly, Goedertier et al. [8] represent the process discovery task as a multi-relational first-order classification problem and apply inductive logic programming in their AGNEsMiner algorithm to learn the discriminating preconditions that determine whether an event can take place or not, given a history of events of other activities. These preconditions are then converted to a graphical model after applying a pruning and post-processing step. To guide the learning process, an input event log is supplemented with induced artificial negative events, similar as in this work.

7   Conclusions and Future Work

We have presented a supervised approach based on numerical abstract domains and SMT which is able to simplify and generalize discovered process models based on negative information found in event logs, derived artificially or supplied by domain experts. We believe this contribution opens the door for supervising (either manually or automatically) discovery techniques, a crucial feature for improving the quality of derived process models.

With regard to future work, we plan to pursue to following avenues. First, we have made use of an artificial negative event induction technique in order to derive negative information for a given event log. We plan to investigate the possibilities towards incorporating domain knowledge to simplify and generalize models using our technique. Second, we have assumed that negative information can be separated from positive information in a linear fashion, i.e. by a set of half-spaces representing a convex polyhedron. However, there may be negative points inside the polyhedron constructed. As such, the learning task can be oriented to not one but a set of convex polyhedron covering only the positive points, for which merging methods would need to be investigated. Third we may combine the techniques of this paper with other simplification techniques developed by some of the authors that enrich the model with log-based simulation scores. Finally, we plan to set up a thorough experiment in which we investigate the effects of our approach on models mined by various miners. As we have argued, our approach can be applied on top of any Petri net in order to generalize and simplify it without loss of fitness.

Acknowledgments. This work as been partially supported by funds from the Spanish Ministry for Economy and Competitiveness (MINECO), the European Union (FEDER funds) under grant COMMAS (ref. TIN2013-46181-C2-1-R) and the Academy of Finland projects 139402 and 277522.

References

1. van der Aalst, W.M.P.: Process Mining - Discovery, Conformance and Enhancement of Business Processes. Springer (2011)
2. Günther, C.W., van der Aalst, W.M.P.: Fuzzy mining – adaptive process simplification based on multi-perspective metrics. In: Alonso, G., Dadam, P., Rosemann, M. (eds.) BPM 2007. LNCS, vol. 4714, pp. 328–343. Springer, Heidelberg (2007)
3. Weijters, A.J.M.M., Ribeiro, J.T.S.: Flexible heuristics miner (FHM). In: CIDM, pp. 310–317 (2011)
4. Ferreira, H., Ferreira, D.: An integrated life cycle for workflow management based on learning and planning. International Journal of Cooperative Information Systems **15**(4), 485–505 (2006)
5. Lamma, E., Mello, P., Montali, M., Riguzzi, F., Storari, S.: Inducing declarative logic-based models from labeled traces. In: Alonso, G., Dadam, P., Rosemann, M. (eds.) BPM 2007. LNCS, vol. 4714, pp. 344–359. Springer, Heidelberg (2007)
6. Lamma, E., Mello, P., Riguzzi, F., Storari, S.: Applying inductive logic programming to process mining. Inductive Logic Programming, 132–146 (2008)
7. Alberti, M., Chesani, F., Gavanelli, M., Lamma, E., Mello, P., Torroni, P.: Verifiable agent interaction in abductive logic programming: the sciff framework. ACM Transactions on Computational Logic (TOCL) **9**(4), 29 (2008)
8. Goedertier, S., Martens, D., Vanthienen, J., Baesens, B.: Robust Process Discovery with Artificial Negative Events. Journal of Machine Learning Research **10**, 1305–1340 (2009)
9. Rockafellar, R.T.: Convex Analysis. Princeton University Press (1970)
10. Nieuwenhuis, R., Oliveras, A., Tinelli, C.: Solving SAT and SAT modulo theories: From an abstract Davis-Putnam-Logemann-Loveland procedure to DPLL(t). J. ACM **53**(6), 937–977 (2006)
11. Carmona, J., Cortadella, J.: Process discovery algorithms using numerical abstract domains. IEEE Trans. Knowl. Data Eng. **26**(12), 3064–3076 (2014)
12. Fukuda, K., Picozzi, S., Avis, D.: On canonical representations of convex polyhedra. In: Proc. of the First International Congress of Mathematical Software, pp. 350–360 (2002)
13. Murata, T.: Petri nets: Properties, analysis and applications. Proceedings of the IEEE **77**(4), 541–580 (1989)
14. vanden Broucke, S.K.L.M., Weerdt, J.D., Vanthienen, J., Baesens, B.: Determining process model precision and generalization with weighted artificial negative events. IEEE Trans. Knowl. Data Eng. **26**(8), 1877–1889 (2014)

15. de Moura, L., Bjørner, N.S.: Z3: an efficient SMT solver. In: Ramakrishnan, C.R., Rehof, J. (eds.) TACAS 2008. LNCS, vol. 4963, pp. 337–340. Springer, Heidelberg (2008)
16. Carmona, J., Cortadella, J., Kishinevsky, M.: New region-based algorithms for deriving bounded Petri nets. IEEE Trans. Computers **59**(3), 371–384 (2010)
17. van der Werf, J.M.E.M., van Dongen, B.F., Hurkens, C.A.J., Serebrenik, A.: Process discovery using integer linear programming. In: van Hee, K.M., Valk, R. (eds.) PETRI NETS 2008. LNCS, vol. 5062, pp. 368–387. Springer, Heidelberg (2008)
18. Adriansyah, A., Munoz-Gama, J., Carmona, J., van Dongen, B.F., van der Aalst, W.M.P.: Measuring precision of modeled behavior. Inf. Syst. E-Business Management **13**(1), 37–67 (2015)
19. Maruster, L., Weijters, A., van der Aalst, W., van den Bosch, A.: A Rule-Based Approach for Process Discovery: Dealing with Noise and Imbalance in Process Logs. Data Mining and Knowledge Discovery **13**(1), 67–87 (2006)

Ensuring Model Consistency in Declarative Process Discovery

Claudio Di Ciccio[1]([✉]), Fabrizio Maria Maggi[2], Marco Montali[3], and Jan Mendling[1]

[1] Vienna University of Economics and Business, Vienna, Austria
{claudio.di.ciccio,jan.mendling}@wu.ac.at
[2] University of Tartu, Tartu, Estonia
f.m.maggi@ut.ee
[3] Free University of Bozen-Bolzano, Bolzano, Italy
montali@inf.unibz.it

Abstract. Declarative process models define the behaviour of business processes as a set of constraints. Declarative process discovery aims at inferring such constraints from event logs. Existing discovery techniques verify the satisfaction of candidate constraints over the log, but completely neglect their interactions. As a result, the inferred constraints can be mutually contradicting and their interplay may lead to an inconsistent process model that does not accept any trace. In such a case, the output turns out to be unusable for enactment, simulation or verification purposes. In addition, the discovered model contains, in general, redundancies that are due to complex interactions of several constraints and that cannot be solved using existing pruning approaches. We address these problems by proposing a technique that automatically resolves conflicts within the discovered models and is more powerful than existing pruning techniques to eliminate redundancies. First, we formally define the problems of constraint redundancy and conflict resolution. Thereafter, we introduce techniques based on the notion of an *automata-product monoid* that guarantee the consistency of the discovered models and, at the same time, keep the most interesting constraints in the pruned set. We evaluate the devised techniques on real-world benchmarks.

1 Introduction

The compact and correct representation of behaviour observed in event data of a business process is one of the major concerns of process mining. Various techniques have been defined for generating models that balance criteria such as fitness and completeness. Mutual strengths and weaknesses of declarative and

The research of Claudio Di Ciccio and Jan Mendling has received funding from the EU Seventh Framework Programme under grant agreement 318275 (GET Service). The research of Fabrizio Maria Maggi has received funding from the Estonian Research Council and by ERDF via the Estonian Centre of Excellence in Computer Science.

© Springer International Publishing Switzerland 2015
H.R. Motahari-Nezhad et al. (Eds.): BPM 2015, LNCS 9253, pp. 144–159, 2015.
DOI: 10.1007/978-3-319-23063-4_9

procedural models are discussed in terms of capturing the behaviour of the log in a structured and compact way.

One of the advantages of procedural models such as Petri nets is the rich set of formal analysis techniques available. These techniques can, for instance, identify redundancy in terms of implicit places or inconsistencies like deadlocks. In turn, novel declarative modelling languages like DECLARE have hardly anything to offer as counterparts. This is a problem for several reasons. First, we are currently not able to check the consistency of a generated constraint set. Many algorithms that generate DECLARE models work with confidence and support, often set to values smaller than 1 such that potentially inconsistent constraint sets are returned. Second, it is currently unclear whether a given constraint set is minimal. Since there are constraint types that imply one another, it is possible that constraint sets are generated that are partially redundant. The lack of formal techniques for handling these two issues is unsatisfactory from both a research and a practical angle. It is also a roadblock for conducting fair comparisons in user experiments when a Petri net without deadlocks and implicit places is compared with a constraint set of unknown consistency and minimality.

In this paper, we address the need for formal analysis of DECLARE models. We define the notion of an *automata-product monoid* as a formal notion for analysing consistency and local minimality, which is grounded in automata multiplication. Based on this structure, we devise efficient analysis techniques. Our formal concepts have been implemented as part of a process mining tool, which we use for our evaluation. Using event log benchmarks, we are able to show that inconsistencies and redundancies are indeed likely to occur and that our technique generates constraints sets that are not only consistent, but also substantially smaller than sets provided by prior algorithms.

The paper is structured as follows. Section 2 introduces the problem of inconsistencies and redundancies. In this context, the major concepts of DECLARE are revisited. Section 3 frames the problem. Section 4 defines our formal notion of an automata-product-space, which offers the basis to formalise techniques for checking consistency and local minimality. Section 5 gives an overview of our implementation and the results of our evaluations based on benchmarking data. Section 6 discusses our contributions in the light of related work. Section 7 concludes the paper.

2   Background

This section describes the consistency and minimality problem and revisits the DECLARE concepts.

2.1   The Consistency Problem

In order to illustrate the problem of potential inconsistencies and redundancies, we utilise the event log set of the BPI Challenge 2012 [9]. The event log pertains to an application process for personal loans or overdrafts of a Dutch bank.

Table 1. Semantics of Declare templates as POSIX regular expressions [18]

		Template	Regular expression	Notation
Existence templates	Cardinality templates	$Participation(x)$	`[^x]*(x[^x]*)+[^x]*`	
		$AtMostOne(x)$	`[^x]*(x)?[^x]*`	
	Position templates	$Init(x)$	`x.*`	
		$End(x)$	`.*x`	
Relation templates	Forward-unidirectional relation templates	$RespondedExistence(x,y))$	`[^x]*((x.*y.*)|(y.*x.*))*[^x]*`	
		$Response(x,y)$	`[^x]*(x.*y)*[^x]*`	
		$AlternateResponse(x,y)$	`[^x]*(x[^x]*y[^x]*)*[^x]*`	
		$ChainResponse(x,y)$	`[^x]*(xy[^x]*)*[^x]*`	
	Backward-unidirectional relation templates	$Precedence(x,y)$	`[^y]*(x.*y)*[^y]*`	
		$AlternatePrecedence(x,y)$	`[^y]*(x[^y]*y[^y]*)*[^y]*`	
		$ChainPrecedence(x,y)$	`[^y]*(xy[^y]*)*[^y]*`	
	Coupling templates	$CoExistence(x,y)$	`[^xy]*((x.*y.*)|(y.*x.*))*[^xy]*`	
		$Succession(x,y)$	`[^xy]*(x.*y)*[^xy]*`	
		$AlternateSuccession(x,y)$	`[^xy]*(x[^xy]*y[^xy]*)*[^xy]*`	
		$ChainSuccession(x,y)$	`[^xy]*(xy[^xy]*)*[^xy]*`	
	Negative templates	$NotChainSuccession(x,y)$	`[^x]*(aa*[^xy][^x]*)*([^x]*|x)`	
		$NotSuccession(x,y)$	`[^x]*(x[^y]*)*[^xy]*`	
		$NotCoExistence(x,y)$	`[^xy]*((x[^y]*)|(y[^x]*))?`	

It contains 262,200 events distributed across 24 different possible tasks and 13,087 traces. In general, an *event log* L is as a collection of traces t_i with $i \in [1, |L|]$, which in turn are finite sequences of events $e_{i,j}$ with $i \in [1, |L|]$ and $j \in [1, |t_i|]$. Each event refers to a task. The *log alphabet* $\mathfrak{A}$ is the set of symbols identifying all possible tasks and we write a, b, c to refer to them.

Process mining tools such as MINERful [8] and Declare Maps Miner [15] generate declarative process models in DECLARE from event logs. In essence, these models define a set of declarative constraints that collectively determine the allowed and forbidden traces. Each constraint is defined using a *template* that captures the semantics of the constraint using generic parameters. We generically refer to parameters of templates as x, y, z. Table 1 summarises the available templates. A template is then instantiated by assigning parameters to actual tasks. For instance, $Response(a, b)$ is a constraint imposing that if a is executed, then b must be eventually executed in the future. In this example, a and b are the assigned parameters of $Response(x, y)$. We define $\mathfrak{C}$ as the set of templates and refer to $\mathfrak{C}_{\mathfrak{A}}$ as the set of constraints constructed by considering all possible parameter assignments of the templates in $\mathfrak{C}$ to the tasks in $\mathfrak{A}$.

The main idea of declarative process mining is that overfitting of the discovered models can be avoided by defining thresholds for parameters such as support. The support (*supp*) of a constraint is defined as the number of traces verifying the constraint divided by the total number of traces in the event log. Additional metrics are confidence (*conf*) and interest factor (*IF*), which scale the support by the percentage of traces in which the constraint is triggered, resp. both parameters occur. By choosing a support threshold smaller than 100%, we can easily obtain constraint pairs that are supported by different parts of the log and such that the first contradicts the second. E.g., when using MINERful on the BPIC 2012 event log with a support threshold of 75%, it returns the constraints *NotChainSuccession*(A_PREACCEPTED, W_Completeren aanvrag) and *ChainResponse*(A_PREACCEPTED, W_Completeren aanvrag), which have an empty set of traces that fulfil both. In fact, the first constraint imposes that A_PREACCEPTED can never be directly followed by W_Completeren aanvrag, whereas the second one requires that if A_PREACCEPTED is executed, W_Completeren aanvrag must immediately follow. Clearly, such inconsistent constraint pairs should not be returned. Models with inconsistencies cannot be used for simulation nor execution, and process analysts might be confused by these results.

2.2   The Minimality Problem

The second problem next to consistency is minimality. As observed in [8,20], DECLARE templates can be organised in a hierarchy of constraints, depending on a notion of subsumption. Technically, given the names N_1 and N_2 of two templates $\mathcal{C}, \mathcal{C}' \in \mathfrak{C}$ of the same arity, we say that $\mathcal{C}$ *is subsumed by* $\mathcal{C}'$, written $N_1 \sqsubseteq N_2$, if for every trace t over $\mathfrak{A}$ and every parameter assignment σ from the parameters of $\mathcal{C}$ to tasks in $\mathfrak{A}$, whenever t complies with the instantiation of $\mathcal{C}$ determined by σ, then t also complies with the instantiation of $\mathcal{C}'$ determined by σ. For binary constraints, we write $N_1 \sqsubseteq N_2^{-1}$ if the subsumption holds by inverting the parameters of $\mathcal{C}'$ w.r.t. those in $\mathcal{C}$, i.e., by considering templates $N_1(x, y)$ and $N_2(y, x)$.

For example, *RespondedExistence*(a, b) states that if a occurs in a trace, then b has to occur in the same trace (either before or after a). *Response*(a, b) thus enforces *RespondedExistence*(a, b) by stating that not only must b be executed, but also that it must *follow* a. By generalising, we have then *Response* $\sqsubseteq$ *RespondedExistence*. By the same line of reasoning, we have that *Precedence* $\sqsubseteq$ *RespondedExistence*$^{-1}$.

Based on the concept of subsumption, we can define the notion of relaxation, $\mathscr{R}$. $\mathscr{R}$ is a unary operator that returns the direct parent in the subsumption hierarchy of a given template. If there exists no parent for the given template, then $\mathscr{R}$ returns a predicate that would hold true for any possible trace, i.e., $\top$.

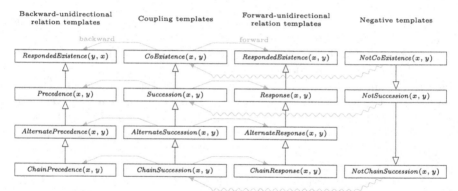

Fig. 1. The subsumption map of DECLARE relation templates

Formally, given a template $\mathcal{C} \in \mathfrak{C}$, we have:

$$\mathscr{R}(\mathcal{C}) = \begin{cases} \mathcal{C}' & \text{if } (i)\ \mathcal{C}' \in \mathfrak{C} \setminus \{\mathcal{C}\},\ (ii)\ \mathcal{C} \sqsubseteq \mathcal{C}',\ \text{and} \\ & \quad (iii)\ \nexists \mathcal{C}'' \in \mathfrak{C} \setminus \{\mathcal{C}, \mathcal{C}'\}\ \text{s.t.}\ \mathcal{C} \sqsubseteq \mathcal{C}'' \sqsubseteq \mathcal{C}' \\ \top & \text{otherwise} \end{cases}$$

We extend the relaxation operator and the subsumption relation also to the domain of constraints: Hence, e.g., $\mathscr{R}(Response(\mathsf{a}, \mathsf{b})) = RespondedExistence(\mathsf{a}, \mathsf{b})$. Figure 1 depicts the subsumption hierarchy for relation templates. The forward and backward components are specified for coupling templates, and the negative templates are linked with their negated counterparts. Note that, in addition to the specified template subsumption, also $Init(x)$ and $End(x)$ are subsumed by $Participation(x)$.

When using MINERful on BPIC 2012 with a support threshold of 75%, it returns the constraints $ChainResponse(\mathsf{A\_SUBMITTED}, \mathsf{A\_PARTLYSUBMITTED})$ and $NotChainSuccession(\mathsf{A\_SUBMITTED}, \mathsf{A\_ACCEPTED})$. The latter constraint is clearly redundant, because the former requires the first task following $\mathsf{A\_SUBMITTED}$ to be $\mathsf{A\_PARTLYSUBMITTED}$. Therefore, no other task but $\mathsf{A\_PARTLYSUBMITTED}$ can directly follow. A fortiori, $\mathsf{A\_SUBMITTED}$ and $\mathsf{A\_ACCEPTED}$ cannot be in direct succession. Clearly, such redundant constraint pairs should not be returned. Models that are not minimal are difficult to understand for the process analysts. Also, redundant constraints do not provide any additional information about the permitted behaviour.

3   Framing the Problem

In Section 2, we have informally introduced the issues of consistency and redundancy in declarative process discovery. We now specify the problem more precisely. Our goal is to define *effective* post-processing techniques that, given a previously discovered DECLARE model M possibly containing inconsistencies and redundancies, manipulate it by removing inconsistencies and reducing redundancies, but still retaining as much as possible its original structure. In this respect, the post-processing is completely agnostic to the process mining algorithm used to generate the model, as well as to the input event log.

This latter assumption makes it impossible to understand how much a variant of the discovered model "fits" with the log. However, we can at least assume that each single constraint in M retains the support, confidence, and interest factor that were calculated during the discovery phase. These values can be used to decide which constraints have to be preferred, and ultimately decide whether a variant M' of M has to be preferred over another one M''. Still, notice that by no means such values can be composed to calculate a global support/confidence/interest factor for the whole model M'. This is only possible if the original log is considered. To see this, consider the case of two constraints C_1, C_2, with support $s_1, s_2 < 100\%$. When the two constraints are considered together, the global support could range from 0 to the minimum of s_1 and s_2, and the exact value could only be determined by computing it directly over the log.

In principle, we could obtain an optimal solution by exhaustive enumeration, executing the following steps. 1. The vocabulary Σ of M is extracted. 2. The set $\mathfrak{C}_\Sigma$ of all possible candidate constraints is built. 3. The set $\mathcal{P}^{\mathfrak{C}_\Sigma}$ of all possible subsets of $\mathfrak{C}_\Sigma$, i.e., of all possible DECLARE models using constraints in $\mathfrak{C}_\Sigma$, is computed. 4. A set $\mathcal{K}$ of candidate models is obtained from $\mathcal{P}^{\mathfrak{C}_\Sigma}$, by filtering away those models that are inconsistent or contain redundant constraints. 5. A ranking of the models in $\mathcal{K}$ is established, considering their similarity to the original, discovered model M.

However, this exhaustive enumeration is in general unfeasible, given the fact that it requires to iterate over the exponentially many models in $\mathcal{P}^{\mathfrak{C}_\Sigma}$, a too huge state space. Consequently, we devise a heuristic algorithm that mediates between optimality of the solution, and performance. In summary, its main features are:

- It produces as output a consistent variant of the initial model M. This is a strict, necessary requirement.
- The algorithm works in an incremental fashion, i.e., it constructs the variant of M by iteratively selecting constraints, and once a constraint is added, it is never retracted from the model. This is done by iterating through candidate constraints in decreasing order of "suitability" w.r.t. the input log, which is computed by considering the support/confidence/interest factor of such constraints. On the one hand, this drives our algorithm to favour more suitable constraints, and remove less suitable constraints in the case of an inconsistency. On the other hand, this has a positive effect on performance, and also guarantees that the algorithm is deterministic.
- Due to incrementality, the algorithm is not guaranteed to produce a final variant that is optimal in size, but we obtain a local minimum. However, our experimental findings show that the algorithm is able to significantly reduce the number of redundant constraints.

4   The Approach

This section describes how we tackle the problem of finding a non-redundant consistent DECLARE model in a way that reduces the intractable theoretical complexity. First, we present the algebraic structure on top of which the check of redundancies and conflicts is performed: It bases upon the mapping of the conjunction of DECLARE constraints to the product of finite state automata (FSAs). Thereafter, we define and discuss the algorithm that allows us to pursue our objective. In particular, we rely on the associativity of the product of FSAs. This property allows us to check every constraint one at a time and include it in a temporary solution. This is done by saving the product of the constraints checked so far with the current one. For the selection of the next candidate constraint to check, we make use of a greedy heuristic, that explores the search space by gathering at every step the constraint that has the highest support, or is most likely to imply the highest number of other constraints. The algorithm proceeds without visiting the same node in the search space twice.

4.1   Declare Models as Automata

As already shown in [7], DECLARE constraints can be formulated as regular expressions (REs) over the log alphabet. The assumption is that every task in the log alphabet is bi-univocally identified by a character. Thus, traces can be assimilated to finite sequences of characters (i.e., strings) and regular languages represent the traces allowed by a DECLARE model.

Using the POSIX wildcards, we can express, e.g., $Init(a)$ as a.*, and $Response(a, b)$ as [^a]*(a.*b)*[^a]*. The comprehensive list of transpositions for DECLARE templates is listed in Table 1 and explained in [18]. Henceforth, we will refer to such mapping as $\mathscr{E}_{\mathrm{Reg}}(C)$, which takes as input a constraint C and returns the corresponding RE: E.g., $\mathscr{E}_{\mathrm{Reg}}(Response(a, b)) =$ [^a]*(a.*b)*[^a]*. Defining the operations of conjunction between DECLARE constraints ($\wedge$) and intersection between REs (&&), $\mathscr{E}_{\mathrm{Reg}}$ is a monoid homomorphism w.r.t. $\wedge$ and &&. In other words, given two constraints C and C', $\mathscr{E}_{\mathrm{Reg}}(C \wedge C') = \mathscr{E}_{\mathrm{Reg}}(C)$ && $\mathscr{E}_{\mathrm{Reg}}(C')$, preserving closure, associativity and the identity element (resp., $\top$ and .*).

Since regular grammars are recognisable through REs [5], an RE can always be associated to a deterministic labelled FSA, which accepts all and only those finite strings that match the RE. Formally, an FSA is a tuple $\mathcal{S} = \langle \Sigma, S, s_0, \delta, S^f \rangle$, where: Σ is the alphabet; S is the finite non-empty set of states; $s_0 \in S$ is the initial state; $\delta : S \times \Sigma \rightarrow S$ is the transition function; $S^f \subseteq S$ is the set of final states. Naming as $\mathscr{A}$ the operation leading from an RE to an FSA, we thus have that a DECLARE constraint can be associated with its corresponding FSA, $A^C = \mathscr{A}(\mathscr{E}_{\mathrm{Reg}}(C))$. Henceforth, we also call A^C the C-automaton. We remark that, by applying $\mathscr{A}$ to the RE of a conjunction of constraints, we obtain an FSA that exactly corresponds to the product $\times$ of the FSAs for the individual constraints [12]: $\mathscr{A}(\mathscr{E}_{\mathrm{Reg}}(C \wedge C')) = \mathscr{A}(\mathscr{E}_{\mathrm{Reg}}(C)) \times \mathscr{A}(\mathscr{E}_{\mathrm{Reg}}(C'))$. Also, we recall that the identity element for FSAs is a single-state automaton whose unique state is both initial and accepting, and has a self-loop for each character in the considered alphabet.

Given a model $M = \{C_1, \ldots, C_{|M|}\}$, we can therefore implicitly describe the set of traces that comply with M as the language accepted by the product of all C_i-automata (for $i \in [1, |M|]$). The language accepted by an FSA A will be denoted as $\mathscr{L}(A)$. In the light of this discussion, our approach searches a solution to the problem of finding a non-redundant consistent DECLARE model within the **automata-product monoid**, i.e., the associative algebraic structure with identity element (the universe-set of FSAs) and product operation $\times$. For the automata-product monoid, the property of commutativity also holds.

4.2   The Algorithm

Algorithm 1 outlines the pseudocode of our technique. Its input is a DECLARE model, M, intended as a set of constraints $C_1, \ldots, C_{|M|}$. For every $C \in M$, we assume that its support, confidence and interest factor are given too, which is the usual condition when M is the output of mining algorithms such as Declare Maps Miner or MINERful. Table 2a shows an example of M, defined on the

---

Algorithm 1. Procedure makeConsistent (M), returning the suboptimal solution to the problem of finding a minimal set of non-conflicting constraints in a DECLARE model.

Input: A log alphabet $\mathfrak{A}$, and a DECLARE model M defined over $\mathfrak{A}$. M is a set of constraints for which support, confidence and interest factor are given

Output: Set of non-conflicting constraint M^{R}

1 $M' \leftarrow$ removeSubsumptionHierarchyRedundancies(M)

2 $M^{\mathrm{S}} \leftarrow \{C \in M' : supp(C) = 1.0\}$ // Non-conflicting constraints

3 $M^{\mathrm{U}} \leftarrow M' \setminus M^{\mathrm{S}}$ // Potentially conflicting constraints

4 $A \leftarrow \langle \mathfrak{A}, \{s_0\}, s_0, \{\bigcup_{\sigma \in \mathfrak{A}} \langle s_0, \sigma, s_0 \rangle, \{s_0\} \} \rangle$ // Automaton accepting any sequence of tasks

5 $M^{\mathrm{R}} \leftarrow \emptyset$ // Set of returned constraints

6 $M^{\mathrm{V}} \leftarrow \emptyset$ // Set of checked constraints

  /* Pruning of redundant constraints from the set of non-conflicting ones   */

7 $M^{\mathrm{S}}_{\mathrm{list}} \leftarrow$ sortBySupportCategoryConfidenceIF(M^{S})

8 **foreach** $C_i^{M^{\mathrm{S}}} \in M^{\mathrm{S}}_{\mathrm{list}}$, with $i \in [1, |M^{\mathrm{S}}_{\mathrm{list}}|]$ **do**

9 $\quad$ $M^{\mathrm{V}} \leftarrow M^{\mathrm{V}} \cup \{C_i^{M^{\mathrm{S}}}\}$ // Record that $C_i^{M^{\mathrm{S}}}$ has been checked

10 $\quad$ $A^{C_i^{M^{\mathrm{S}}}} \leftarrow \mathscr{A}\left(\mathscr{E}_{\mathrm{Reg}}\left(C_i^{M^{\mathrm{S}}}\right)\right)$ // Build the constraint-automaton of $C_i^{M^{\mathrm{S}}}$

11 $\quad$ **if** $\mathscr{L}(A) \supset \mathscr{L}\left(A^{C_i^{M^{\mathrm{S}}}}\right)$ **then**   // If $C_i^{M^{\mathrm{S}}}$ is not redundant

12 $\quad\quad$ $A \leftarrow A \times A^{C_i^{M^{\mathrm{S}}}}$ // Merge the $C_i^{M^{\mathrm{S}}}$-automaton with the main FSA

13 $\quad\quad$ $M^{\mathrm{R}} \leftarrow M^{\mathrm{R}} \cup \{C_i^{M^{\mathrm{S}}}\}$ // Include $C_i^{M^{\mathrm{S}}}$ in the set of returned constraints

  /* Pruning of conflicting constraints   */

14 $M^{\mathrm{U}}_{\mathrm{list}} \leftarrow$ sortBySupportCategoryConfidenceIF(M^{U})

15 **foreach** $C_i^{M^{\mathrm{U}}} \in M^{\mathrm{U}}_{\mathrm{list}}$, with $i \in [1, |M^{\mathrm{U}}_{\mathrm{list}}|]$ **do**

16 $\quad$ resolveConflictAndRedundancy$\left(A, M^{\mathrm{R}}, C_i^{M^{\mathrm{U}}}, M^{\mathrm{V}}\right)$

17 **return** removeSubsumptionHierarchyRedundancies(M^{R})

Algorithm 2. Procedure resolveConflictAndRedundancy $(A, M^{\mathrm{R}}, C, M^{\mathrm{V}})$, adding constraint C to the set of constraint M^{R}, if it has not already been checked (and thus included in set M^{V}), and is not conflicting with the already added constraints, as verified over the corresponding FSA A.

Input: An FSA A, a set of non-conflicting constraints M^{R}, a constraint C, and a list of already checked constraints M^{V}

```
1  if C ∉ M^V then                              // If C was not already checked
2      M^V ← M^V ∪ {C}                          // Record that C has been checked
3      A^C ← 𝒜(ℰ_Reg(C))                        // Build the C-automaton
4      if ℒ(A) ⊃ ℒ(A^C) then                    // If C is not redundant
5          if ℒ(A × A^C) ≠ ∅ then               // If C is not conflicting
6              A ← A × A^C                       // Merge the C-automaton with the main FSA
7              M^R ← M^R ∪ {C}                   // Include C in the set of returned constraints
8          else                                  // Otherwise, resolve the conflict
9              if ℛ(C) ≠ ⊤ then                  // If a relaxation of C, i.e., ℛ(C), exists
10                 resolveConflictAndRedundancy(A, M^R, ℛ(C), M^V)
11             if C is a coupling constraint then
12                 resolveConflictAndRedundancy(A, M^R, fw(C), M^V)
13                 resolveConflictAndRedundancy(A, M^R, bw(C), M^V)
```

---

log alphabet $\{\mathsf{a},\mathsf{b},\mathsf{c},\mathsf{d}\}$. We also assume that the same metrics are defined for those constraints that are not in M, yet are either their subsuming, negated, forward or backward version. Again, this is common in the output of the aforementioned algorithms. For the sake of readability, these additional constraints are not reported in Table 2a. Table 2b shows the output that corresponds to the post-processing of Table 2a. Constraints that are considered as redundant are coloured in grey. Struck-out constraints are those that are in conflict with the others and thus dropped from the returned set.

Given M, the first operation "removeSubsumptionHierarchyRedundancies" prunes out redundant constraints based on the subsumption hierarchy. The procedure considers a removal of the subsuming constraints such that their support is less than or equal to the subsumed one, and the elimination of forward and backward constraints if the related coupling constraint has an equivalent support. Detail of this operations have already been described in [8]. The usefulness of this procedure resides in the fact that it reduces the number of candidate constraints to be considered, thus reducing the number of iterations performed by the algorithm. In Table 2b, this operation is responsible for the dropping of *Participation*(a), due to the fact that *Init*(a) is known to hold true.

Thereafter, we partition M into two subsets, i.e.: *(i)* M^{S}, consisting of those constraints that are verified over the entire event log (i.e., having a support of 1.0), and *(ii)* M^{U}, containing the remaining constraints. The reason for doing this is that the former is guaranteed to have no conflict: Given the fact that constraints are mined using the alphabet of the event log, those that have a support of 1.0 can be conjoined, giving raise to a *consistent* constraint model.

Table 2. An example of input constraint set processing

(a) Input

Constraint	supp	conf	IF
Init(a)	1.0	1.0	1.0
Participation(a)	1.0	1.0	1.0
CoExistence(a, d)	1.0	1.0	1.0
End(d)	1.0	1.0	1.0
NotChainSuccession(b, d)	1.0	0.9	0.8
NotChainSuccession(a, d)	0.75	0.5	0.5
ChainResponse(b, c)	1.0	0.9	0.8
NotChainSuccession(a, b)	0.9	0.7	0.6
NotChainSuccession(a, c)	0.8	0.7	0.6
ChainResponse(b, a)	0.75	0.9	0.9

(b) Processed output

	i	Constraint	supp	conf	IF
M^{S}_{list}	1	Init(a)	1.0	1.0	1.0
	2	End(d)	1.0	1.0	1.0
	3	CoExistence(a, d)	1.0	1.0	1.0
	4	ChainResponse(b, c)	1.0	0.9	0.8
	5	NotChainSuccession(b, d)	1.0	0.9	0.8
M^{U}_{list}	1	NotChainSuccession(a, b)	0.9	0.7	0.6
	2	NotChainSuccession(a, c)	0.8	0.7	0.6
	3	NotChainSuccession(a, d)	0.75	0.5	0.5
	4	AlternateResponse(b, a)	0.75	0.9	0.9

Even though constraints in M^S are guaranteed to be conflict-free, they could still contain redundancies. Therefore, the following part of the algorithm is dedicated to the elimination of redundant constraints from this set. To check redundancies, we employ the characterisation of constraints in terms of FSAs. Instead, constraints in M^U may contain both redundancies and inconsistencies. Table 2b presents the partition of M into M^S and M^U.

First, we initialise an FSA A to be the identity element w.r.t. automata product. In other words, A is initialised to accept any sequence of events that map to a task in the log alphabet. This automata incrementally incorporates those constraints that are maintained in the filtered model. To set up the redundancy elimination in M^S as well as the redundancy and inconsistency elimination in M^U, we then order their constitutive constraints according the the following criteria (in descending order of priority): (i) descending support (this is trivial for M^S, since all constraints have a support of 1.0); (ii) category – consider first existence constraints, then positive relation constraints, and finally negative constraints; (iii) descending confidence; (iv) descending interest factor. This ranking is of utmost importance, as it determines the priority with which constraints are analysed. The priority, in turn, implicitly defines the "survival expectation" of a constraint, as constraints that come later in the list are more likely to be pruned if they are either redundant or conflicting.

We briefly explain the reason for this multi-dimensional ranking. Support is the first criterion adopted, because we prefer to preserve those constraints that are satisfied in the most part of the log. The category criterion is instead driven by the expertise acquired in the last years in the context of DECLARE mining [15, 20]. In particular, we tend to preserve those constraints that have the potential of inducing the removal of a massive amount of other constraints, due to redundancy. As an example, consider the case of the *Init* template: Given $\rho \in \mathfrak{A}$, if $Init(\rho)$ holds true, then also the relation constraint $Precedence(\rho, \sigma)$ is guaranteed to hold true, for every $\sigma \in \mathfrak{A} \setminus \{\rho\}$. This means that, in the best case, $|\mathfrak{A}| - 1$

constraints will be removed because they are all redundant with $Init(\rho)$. Similarly, consider the positive relation constraint $ChainResponse(\rho, \sigma)$: It implies $NotChainSuccession(\rho, \sigma')$ for every $\sigma' \in \mathfrak{A} \setminus \{\rho, \sigma\}$. Thus, $ChainResponse(\rho, \sigma)$ has the potential of triggering the removal of $|\mathfrak{A}| - 2$ negative constraints due to redundancy. The last criteria adopted pertain confidence and interest factor, in order to prefer those constraints whose parameters occur in most traces. In Algorithm 1, the computation of this ranking is encapsulated inside function "sortBySupportCategoryConfidenceIF", which returns a list of constraints ordered according to the aforementioned criteria. In Table 2b, the result of the sorting is reported.

After the sorting, constraints are iteratively considered for inclusion in the refined model, by iterating through the corresponding ranked lists. Constraints in the list of M^S, i.e., $C_i^{M^S} \in M_{list}^S$, are only checked for redundancy, whereas constraints in M^U, $C_i^{M^U} \in M_{list}^U$, are checked for both redundancy and consistency. For every constraint $C_i^{M^S} \in M_{list}^S$, redundancy is checked by leveraging language-inclusion. In particular, this is done by computing the FSA $A^{C_i^{M^S}}$ for $C_i^{M^S}$, and then checking whether its generated language $\mathscr{L}\left(A^{C_i^{M^S}}\right)$ is included inside $\mathscr{L}(A)$, which considers the contribution of all constraints maintained so far. If this is the case, then the constraint is dropped. Otherwise, A is extended with the contribution of this new constraint (by computing the product $A \times A^{C_i^{M^S}}$), and $C_i^{M^S}$ is added to the set M^R of constraints to be returned. In the example of Table 2b, $CoExistence(\mathsf{a}, \mathsf{d})$ is analysed after the existence constraints $Init(\mathsf{a})$ and $End(\mathsf{d})$, based on the preliminary sorting operation. It thus turns out to be redundant, because $Init(\mathsf{a})$ and $End(\mathsf{d})$ already specify that both a and d will occur in every trace. Therefore, they will necessarily always co-occur.

Redundancy and consistency checking of the constraints $C_i^{M^U} \in M_{list}^U$ is performed by the "resolveConflictAndRedundancy" procedure (Algorithm 2). The procedure checks the consistency of those constraints that are not redundant. The redundancy is, again, checked based on the language inclusion of the language generated by the currently analyzed constraint $\mathscr{L}\left(A^{C_i^{M^U}}\right)$ in $\mathscr{L}(A)$, where A is the automaton that accumulates the contribution of all constraints that have been kept so far. The consistency is checked through a language emptiness test, performed over the intersection of $\mathscr{L}\left(A^{C_i^{M^U}}\right)$ and $\mathscr{L}(A)$. This is done by checking that $\mathscr{L}\left(A \times A^{C_i^{M^U}}\right) \neq \emptyset$. In case a conflict is detected, we do not immediately drop the conflicting constraint, but we try, instead, to find a more relaxed constraint that retains its intended semantics as much as possible, but does not incur in a conflict. To do so, we employ the constraint subsumption hierarchy (cf. Section 2.2). In particular, we employ the relaxation operator to retrieve the parent constraint of the conflicting one, and we recursively invoke the "resolveConflictAndRedundancy" procedure over the parent. The recursion terminates when the first non-conflicting ancestor of the conflicting constraint is found, or when the top of the hierarchy is reached.

The two cases are resp. covered in the example of Table 2b by *ChainResponse*(b, a), replaced by *AlternateResponse*(b, a), and by *NotChainSuccession*(a, d), which is removed because a non-conflicting ancestor does not exists. Note that *NotChainSuccession*(a, d) is to be eliminated because of the interplay of the other two *NotChainSuccession* constraints, *Init*(a) and *End*(d). *ChainResponse*(b, a) is in conflict with *ChainResponse*(b, c).

If the constraint under analysis is a coupling constraint, then we know that it is constituted by the conjunction of a corresponding pair of forward and backward constraints. In this situation, it could be the case that all the relaxations of the coupling constraint along the subsumption hierarchy continue to be conflicting, but the conflict would be removed by just considering either its forward or backward component (or a relaxation thereof). Consequently, we also recursively invoke the "resolveConflictAndRedundancy" procedure on these two components.

Finally, a last complete pass over constraints in M^R is done, to check again whether there are subsumption-hierarchy redundancies. If so, M^R is pruned accordingly.

5   Experiments and Results

Our experimentation is based on the application of the proposed approach to the event log provided for the BPI challenge 2012. In the first set of experiments, we use MINERful to mine the log. We discover the set of constraints with a support higher than 75%, a confidence higher than 12.5%, and an interest factor higher than 12.5%. The discovered constraints are 306. The total execution time is of 9,171 milliseconds. By applying the proposed algorithm, we obtain 130 constraints in total. In the original set of 306 there are 2 conflicting constraints that make the entire model inconsistent. These constraints are *NotChainSuccession*(A_PREACCEPTED, W_Completeren aanvrag), conflicting with *ChainResponse*(A_PREACCEPTED, W_Completeren aanvrag), and *NotChainSuccession*(W_Completeren aanvraag, A_ACCEPTED), conflicting with *ChainResponse*(W_Completeren aanvraag, A_ACCEPTED) for similar reasons. Note that the percentage of reduction over the set of discovered constraints (that was already pruned based on the subsumption hierarchy) is of 58%.

In the second set of experiments, we have applied the Declare Maps Miner to mine the log. We discovered the set of constraints with a support higher than 75% confidence higher than 12.5% and interest factor higher than 12.5%. The set of discovered constraints pruned based on the diverse pruning techniques provided by the tool contains 69 constraints. By applying the proposed algorithm starting from this set, we obtain 41 constraints (with an execution time of 2,764 milliseconds). The percentage of reduction is still of around 40%.

Figure 2 shows the number of discovered constraints using MINERful. In particular, the plot shows the percentage of templates that are redundant and then pruned by the proposed algorithm and the ones that are not redundant and, therefore, discovered. For some templates, it is easy to explain why a high percentage of constraints become redundant. For example, *CoExistence* constraints

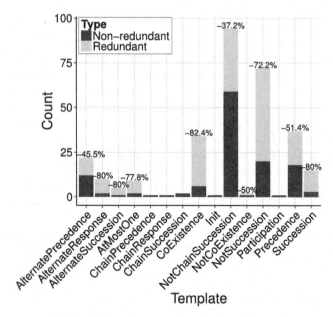

Fig. 2. Redundancy reduction w.r.t. templates

are more often pruned because they are weaker than others and are transitive so that very often their transitive closures become redundant [16]. For example, if *CoExistence*(a, b), *CoExistence*(b, c), and *CoExistence*(a, c) are valid, one of them is always redundant. On the other hand, other constraints, like the ones based on "chain" templates are stronger and not transitive and then pruned less often.

In general, redundant constraints can be pruned based on very complex reduction rules. For example, from our experiments, we derived that *AtMostOne*(A_FINALIZED) becomes redundant due to the presence in combination of *AtMostOne*(A_PARTLYSUBMITTED), *Participation*(A_PARTLYSUBMITTED), and *AlternatePrecedence*(A_PARTLYSUBMITTED, A_FINALIZED). Indeed, *Participation*(A_PARTLYSUBMITTED) and *AtMostOne*(A_PARTLYSUBMITTED) combined ensure that A_PARTLYSUBMITTED occurs exactly once. Then *AlternatePrecedence*(A_PARTLYSUBMITTED, A_FINALIZED) ensures that either A_FINALIZED does not occur or if it occurs it is preceded by the unique occurrence of A_PARTLYSUBMITTED without the possibilities of other occurrences of A_FINALIZED in between. Another example is *NotSuccession*(W_Nabellen offertes, A_SUBMITTED), which is redundant with the combination of *Init*(A_SUBMITTED), *AtMostOne*(A_PARTLYSUBMITTED), *Participation*(A_PARTLYSUBMITTED), and *ChainSuccession*(A_SUBMITTED, A_PARTLYSUBMITTED). Indeed, *AtMostOne*(A_PARTLYSUBMITTED) and *Participation*(A_PARTLYSUBMITTED) combined ensure that A_PARTLYSUBMITTED occurs exactly once. This constraint in combination with *ChainSuccession*(A_SUBMITTED, A_PARTLYSUBMITTED) and *Init*(A_SUBMITTED) ensures that A_SUBMITTED occurs only once at the beginning of every trace and, therefore, it can never occur after any other activity.

All experiments were run on a machine equipped with an Intel Core i5-3320M, CPU at 2.60GHz, quad-core, Ubuntu Linux 12.04 operating system. The tool has been implemented in Java SE 7 and integrated with the MINERful declarative process miner. It can be downloaded at: www.github.com/cdc08x/MINERful.

6   Related Work

Our research relates to three streams of research: Consistency checking for knowledge bases, research on process mining, and specifically research on DECLARE. Research in the area of knowledge representation has considered the issue of consistency checking. In particular, in the context of Knowledge-based configuration systems, Felfernig et al. [10] have challenged the problem of finding the core cause of inconsistencies within the knowledge base during its update test, in terms of minimal conflict sets (the so-called diagnosis). The proposed solution relies on the recursive partitioning of the (extended) CSP problem into subproblems, skipping those that do not contain an element of the propagation-specific conflict [13]. In the same research context, the work described in [11] focuses on the detection of non-redundant constraint sets. The approach is again based on a divide-and-conquer approach, that favours however those constraints that are ranked higher in a lexicographical order. Differently from such works, we tend to exploit the characteristics of DECLARE templates in a sequential exploration of possible solutions. As in their proposed solutions, though, we base upon a preference-oriented ranking when deciding which constraints to keep in the returned set.

The problem of consistency arises in process mining when working with behavioural constraints. Constraint sets as those of the α algorithm [1] and its extension [23] or behavioural profiles [21,22] are per construction consistent. DCR graphs are not directly discussed from the perspective of consistency [19], but benefit from our work due to their grounding in Büchi automata.

More specifically, our work is related to research on DECLARE and strategies to keep sets small and consistent. In [17], the authors present an approach based on the instantiation of a set of candidate DECLARE constraints that are checked with respect to the log to identify the ones that are satisfied in a higher percentage of traces. This approach has been improved in [15] by reducing the number of candidates to be checked through an apriori algorithm. In [16], the same approach has been applied for the repair of DECLARE models based on log and for guiding the discovery task based on apriori knowledge provided in different forms. In this work, some simple reduction rules are presented. These reduction rules are, however, not sufficient to detect redundancies due to complex interactions among constraints in a discovered model as demonstrated in our experimentation.

In [2,3], the authors present an approach for the mining of declarative process models expressed through a probabilistic logic. The approach first extract a set of integrity constraints from a log. Then, the learned constraints are translated into Markov Logic formulas that allow for a probabilistic classification of the traces. In [4,14], the authors present an approach based on Inductive Logic Programming techniques to discover DECLARE process models. These approaches are not equipped with techniques for the analysis of the discovered models like the one presented in this paper.

In [7,8], the authors introduce a two-step algorithm for the discovery of DECLARE constraints. As a first step, a knowledge base is built, with information about temporal statistics gathered from logs. Then, the statistical support of constraints is computed, by querying that knowledge base. Also these works introduce a basic way to deal with redundancy based on the subsumption hierarchy of DECLARE templates that is non capable to deal with redundancies due to complex interactions of constraints.

In [6], the authors propose an extension of the approach presented in [7,8] to discover target-branched DECLARE constraints, i.e., constraints in which the target parameter is replaced by a disjunction of actual tasks. Here, as well as redundancy reductions based on the subsumption hierarchy of DECLARE constraints, also different aspects of redundancy are taken into consideration that are characteristic of target-branched DECLARE, such as set-dominance.

7   Conclusion

In this paper, we addressed the problems of redundant and inconsistent constraint sets that are potentially generated by declarative process mining tools. We formalised the problem based on the notion of automata-product monoid and devised the corresponding analysis algorithms. The evaluation based on our prototypical implementation shows that typical constraint sets can be further pruned such that the result is consistent and locally minimal. Our contribution complements research on declarative process execution and simulation and provides the basis for a fair comparison of procedural and declarative representations.

In future research, we aim at extending our work towards other perspectives of processes. When mining declarative constraints with references to data and resources, one of the challenges will be to identify comparable notions of subsumption and causes of inconsistency. We also plan to follow up on experimental research comparing Petri nets and DECLARE. The notions defined in this paper help design declarative and procedural process models that are equally consistent and minimal, such that an unbiased comparison would be feasible.

References

1. van der Aalst, W.M.P., Weijters, T., Maruster, L.: Workflow mining: Discovering process models from event logs. IEEE Trans. Knowl. Data Eng. **16**(9), 1128–1142 (2004)
2. Bellodi, E., Riguzzi, F., Lamma, E.: Probabilistic declarative process mining. In: Bi, Y., Williams, M.-A. (eds.) KSEM 2010. LNCS, vol. 6291, pp. 292–303. Springer, Heidelberg (2010)
3. Bellodi, E., Riguzzi, F., Lamma, E.: Probabilistic logic-based process mining. In: CILC (2010)

4. Chesani, F., Lamma, E., Mello, P., Montali, M., Riguzzi, F., Storari, S.: Exploiting inductive logic programming techniques for declarative process mining. T. Petri Nets and Other Models of Concurrency **2**, 278–295 (2009)
5. Chomsky, N., Miller, G.A.: Finite state languages. Information and Control **1**(2), 91–112 (1958)
6. Di Ciccio, C., Maggi, F.M., Mendling, J.: Discovering target-branched declare constraints. In: Sadiq, S., Soffer, P., Völzer, H. (eds.) BPM 2014. LNCS, vol. 8659, pp. 34–50. Springer, Heidelberg (2014)
7. Di Ciccio, C., Mecella, M.: A two-step fast algorithm for the automated discovery of declarative workflows. In: CIDM, pp. 135–142. IEEE (2013)
8. Di Ciccio, C., Mecella, M.: On the discovery of declarative control flows for artful processes. ACM Trans. Manage. Inf. Syst. **5**(4), 24:1–24:37 (2015)
9. van Dongen, B.F.: Real-life event logs - a loan application process. BPIC (2012)
10. Felfernig, A., Friedrich, G., Jannach, D., Stumptner, M.: Consistency-based diagnosis of configuration knowledge bases. Artif. Intell. **152**(2), 213–234 (2004)
11. Felfernig, A., Zehentner, C., Blazek, P.: Corediag: eliminating redundancy in constraint sets. In: DX, pp. 219–224 (2011)
12. Gisburg, S., Rose, G.F.: Preservation of languages by transducers. Information and Control **9**(2), 153–176 (1966)
13. Junker, U.: QUICKXPLAIN: preferred explanations and relaxations for overconstrained problems. In: AAAI, pp. 167–172 (2004)
14. Lamma, E., Mello, P., Montali, M., Riguzzi, F., Storari, S.: Inducing declarative logic-based models from labeled traces. In: Alonso, G., Dadam, P., Rosemann, M. (eds.) BPM 2007. LNCS, vol. 4714, pp. 344–359. Springer, Heidelberg (2007)
15. Maggi, F.M., Bose, R.P.J.C., van der Aalst, W.M.P.: Efficient discovery of understandable declarative process models from event logs. In: Ralyté, J., Franch, X., Brinkkemper, S., Wrycza, S. (eds.) CAiSE 2012. LNCS, vol. 7328, pp. 270–285. Springer, Heidelberg (2012)
16. Maggi, F.M., Bose, R.P.J.C., van der Aalst, W.M.P.: A knowledge-based integrated approach for discovering and repairing declare maps. In: Salinesi, C., Norrie, M.C., Pastor, Ó. (eds.) CAiSE 2013. LNCS, vol. 7908, pp. 433–448. Springer, Heidelberg (2013)
17. Maggi, F.M., Mooij, A.J., van der Aalst, W.M.P.: User-guided discovery of declarative process models. In: CIDM, pp. 192–199 (2011)
18. Prescher, J., Di Ciccio, C., Mendling, J.: From declarative processes to imperative models. In: SIMPDA, vol. 1293, pp. 162–173. CEUR-WS.org (2014)
19. Reijers, H.A., Slaats, T., Stahl, C.: Declarative modeling–an academic dream or the future for BPM? In: Daniel, F., Wang, J., Weber, B. (eds.) BPM 2013. LNCS, vol. 8094, pp. 307–322. Springer, Heidelberg (2013)
20. Schunselaar, D.M.M., Maggi, F.M., Sidorova, N.: Patterns for a log-based strengthening of declarative compliance models. In: Derrick, J., Gnesi, S., Latella, D., Treharne, H. (eds.) IFM 2012. LNCS, vol. 7321, pp. 327–342. Springer, Heidelberg (2012)
21. Weidlich, M., Mendling, J., Weske, M.: Efficient consistency measurement based on behavioral profiles of process models. IEEE Trans. Software Eng. **37**(3), 410–429 (2011)
22. Weidlich, M., Polyvyanyy, A., Desai, N., Mendling, J., Weske, M.: Process compliance analysis based on behavioural profiles. Inf. Syst. **36**(7), 1009–1025 (2011)
23. Wen, L., van der Aalst, W.M.P., Wang, J., Sun, J.: Mining process models with non-free-choice constructs. Data Min. Knowl. Discov. **15**(2), 145–180 (2007)

Business Process Models and Analytics

Avoiding Over-Fitting in ILP-Based Process Discovery

Sebastiaan J. van Zelst[(✉)], Boudewijn F. van Dongen,
and Wil M.P. van der Aalst

Department of Mathematics and Computer Science,
Eindhoven University of Technology, Eindhoven, The Netherlands
{s.j.v.zelst,b.f.v.dongen,w.m.p.v.d.aalst}@tue.nl

Abstract. The aim of process discovery is to discover a process model based on business process execution data, recorded in an event log. One of several existing process discovery techniques is the ILP-based process discovery algorithm. The algorithm is able to unravel complex process structures and provides formal guarantees w.r.t. the model discovered, e.g., the algorithm guarantees that a discovered model describes all behavior present in the event log. Unfortunately the algorithm is unable to cope with exceptional behavior present in event logs. As a result, the application of ILP-based process discovery techniques in everyday process discovery practice is limited. This paper addresses this problem by proposing a filtering technique tailored towards ILP-based process discovery. The technique helps to produce process models that are less over-fitting w.r.t. the event log, more understandable, and more adequate in capturing the dominant behavior present in the event log. The technique is implemented in the ProM framework.

Keywords: Process mining · Process discovery · Integer linear programming · Filtering

1 Introduction

Process mining [1] aims to assist in the improvement and understandability of business processes. The basic input of process mining is process execution data, stored in an *event log*. We identify three process mining branches. *Process discovery* aims at constructing a process model given an event log. *Conformance checking* aims at assessing the conformance of an event log to a given process model. *Process enhancement* aims at extending, improving or repairing existing process models using the two aforementioned disciplines as a basis. In process mining, a process model's quality is evaluated w.r.t. four essential quality dimensions [2]. *Replay fitness* describes to what extent a model is able to reproduce the behavior present in an event log. *Precision* describes what fraction of the behavior allowed by a model is present in an event log. *Generalization* describes to what extent a model is able to reproduce future, unseen, behavior of a process. *Simplicity* describes the (perceived) complexity of a process model.

© Springer International Publishing Switzerland 2015
H.R. Motahari-Nezhad et al. (Eds.): BPM 2015, LNCS 9253, pp. 163–171, 2015.
DOI: 10.1007/978-3-319-23063-4_10

The ILP-based process discovery algorithm [3] encodes an event log as a set of linear inequalities that act as a core constraint body of a number of integer linear programs (ILPs) aimed at process model construction. The algorithm ensures perfect replay fitness, i.e., all behavior present in the event-log can be reproduced by the resulting process model. Under the assumption that the event log only holds frequent behavior, the algorithm works well. Real event logs typically include low-frequent exceptional behavior, e.g. caused by employees deviating from some normative process. As the algorithm guarantees perfect replay-fitness, it guarantees that the resulting model allows for all exceptional behavior present in the event log. In practice this leads to models that are incapable of capturing the dominant behavior present in the event log.

To leverage the strict replay-fitness guaranteed by the ILP-based process discovery algorithm we present a filtering technique that exploits the underlying data abstraction used within the ILP formulation. Using a simple running example we show that the approach enables us to filter exceptional behavior from event logs and results in models that do not have perfect replay-fitness w.r.t. the input data. However, the models are simpler and less over-fitting. To evaluate the technique we have applied it on a set of artificially generated event logs with varying levels of exceptional behavior.

The outline of this paper is as follows. In Section 2 we motivate the need for an ILP-based process discovery algorithm able to cope with the presence of exceptional behavior. In Section 3 we explain the effect of exceptional behavior. In Section 4 we introduce the concept of sequence encodings. In Section 5 we present a sequence encoding based filtering technique. In Section 6 we evaluate the approach in terms of its effects on model quality. Section 7 concludes the paper.

2   Motivation

The ILP-based process discovery algorithm uses Petri nets without arc-weights[1] as a process model formalism. Petri nets allow for expressing complex control flow patterns within event data, a valuable property from a business management perspective. Consider the two models depicted in Figure 1a and Figure 1b

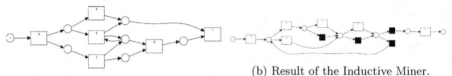

(a) Result of the ILP-based algorithm.

(b) Result of the Inductive Miner.

Fig. 1. Process discovery results of the conventional ILP-based discovery and the Inductive Miner [4] based on a log consisting of milestone pattern based behavior.

---

[1] We assume the reader to be acquainted with of Petri nets and refer to [1] for an overview.

which depict the result of applying the ILP-based process discovery algorithm and the Inductive Miner [4] on event log $L = [\langle a,c,d,e,f \rangle^{10}, \langle a,c,b,d,f \rangle^{10},$ $\langle a,c,e,d,f \rangle^{10}, \langle a,e,c,d,f \rangle^{10}]^2$. L contains behavior generated by a model exhibiting a *milestone pattern* [5]. The ILP-based discovery algorithm allows us to discover the milestone pattern whereas the inductive miner neglects the pattern and results in an under-fitting Petri net, i.e., it allows for much more behavior compared to the behavior present in the event log. This is due to the fact that the inductive miner assumes that the resulting model is *block-structured*.

Many process discovery algorithms assume models to be (semi)-structured or assume that only local dependencies exist amongst activities. As a side effect, the algorithms are not able to find complex control flow patterns. Examples of such techniques are the Heuristics miner [6], the Fuzzy miner [7] and the Genetic miner [8]. A selection of patterns that the ILP-based process discovery algorithm is able to reproduce are patterns like *interleaved parallel routing, critical section* and *arbitrary cycles*.

The impact of exceptional behavior present in event logs becomes clear when regarding the two Petri nets depicted in Figure 2. The models are discovered using conventional ILP-based process discovery. The event log used to discover the model in Figure 2a only consists of traces that fit the model presented, i.e. no exceptional behavior. The event log used for discovery of the model in Figure 2b is a slightly manipulated version of the event log used for Figure 2a. The event log contains little exceptional behavior, i.e., 5% of the traces in the event log is manipulated. Clearly, the model depicted in Figure 2b is not capturing the dominant behavior present in the event log.

The ILP-based process discovery algorithm allows for finding complex patterns within business process event data yet at the same time the algorithm suffers drastically from the presence of exceptional behavior in event logs. Therefore we need means to cope with exceptional behavior in order to enable the

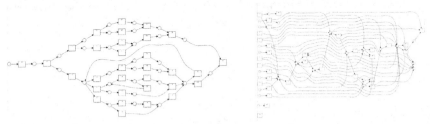

(a) Resulting model using an event log without exceptional behavior.

(b) Resulting model using an event log with a minimal amount of exceptional behavior.

Fig. 2. Discovered Petri nets after applying conventional ILP-based process discovery on event logs with and without the presence of exceptional behavior in the event log.

---

[2] For event logs we use the notion of a multiset of traces, using a control-flow perspective.

algorithm to discover models that more accordingly represent the dominant behavior present in an event log.

3 Exceptional Behavior and ILP-Based Discovery

The essential component of the ILP-based process discovery algorithm is a set of linear inequalities, based on the event log, that is used as a basic ILP constraint body. The global constraint expressed by these inequalities is best explained by the following sentence: *Any place present in the resulting Petri net must allow for each event in the input event log to be executed.* This leads to the fact that every trace in the log is completely reproducible by the resulting process model, i.e. replay fitness is perfect. It is also the root cause of the algorithm's behavior w.r.t. to exceptional behavior, e.g. Figure 2.

Consider event log $L = [\langle a,b,c,d,e,g \rangle^{105}, \langle a,c,b,d,e,g \rangle^{98}, \langle a,b,c,d,e, f,e,g \rangle^{87}, \langle a,c,b,d,e,f,e,g \rangle^{117}]$ which could be a result of 407 executions of the process model depicted in Figure 3a. Consider place p_5 having an incoming arc from transition c and an outgoing arc to transition d. As place p_5 is not having an outgoing arc to transitions a,b,c,e,f and g it does not interfere with firing these transitions at any point in time. The outgoing arc of place p_5 allows for firing d, only after firing transition c. This is in line with the event log because if event d occurs, it is always (indirectly) preceded by event c. In fact, each place within the Petri net allows for the execution of every activity in L. Hence, the Petri net is discoverable by the ILP-based process discovery algorithm.

Consider the addition of the single trace $\langle a,b,d,e,g \rangle$ to event log L, resulting in L', consisting of 408 traces. Arguably we can deem the newly added trace as exceptional behavior. The newly added trace can not be executed by the Petri net depicted in Figure 3a due to the presence of p_5, as it prevents transition d from firing as long as transition c has not fired. Consequently, given event log L' which only consists of one additional exceptional trace $\langle a,b,d,e,g \rangle$ w.r.t. event log L, the ILP-based process discovery algorithm is unable to find the Petri net of Figure 3a. If we replace p_5 by p_5' (Figure 3b), the resulting Petri net is again able to execute every activity in L'.

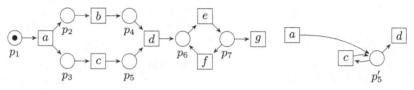

(a) Petri net corresponding to example event log L.   (b) Place p_5'.

Fig. 3. A Petri net corresponding to event log L, discoverable by the ILP-based process discovery algorithm (3a) and an alternative place p_5' for place p_5 given L' (3b).

4   Sequence Encoding

The exact construction of the linear inequalities used by the ILP-based process discovery algorithm is outside of the scope of this paper, hence we refer to [3,9]. It suffices to know that the set of linear inequalities is solely based on the *prefix closure* of the event log. The prefix closure of L' is the set of sequences $\overline{L'}$ s.t. each sequence in $\overline{L'}$ is either a prefix of a sequence in L' or a prefix of a sequence in $\overline{L'}$. Extrapolation of trace frequency information present in the event log to the prefix closure is trivial, i.e., $\overline{L'} = [\epsilon^{408}, \langle a \rangle^{408}, \langle a, b \rangle^{193}, \langle a, c \rangle^{215}, \langle a, b, c \rangle^{192},$ $\langle a, b, d \rangle, \langle a, c, b \rangle^{215} ..., \langle a, b, c, d, e, f, e, g \rangle^{87}, \langle a, c, b, d, e, f, e, g \rangle^{117}]$.

Each non-empty sequence in $\overline{L'}$ is mapped to a linear inequality, representing an ILP constraint. These linear inequalities can be represented by a pair consisting of the Parikh-based multiset representation of the sequence's prefix and the last event of the sequence. Such tuple is deemed a *sequence encoding*. The Parikh-based multiset representation of a sequence is just a mutliset denoting the number of occurrences of each element in the sequence, e.g. given sequence $\langle a, b, b, c \rangle$, its Parikh-based multiset representation is $[a, b^2, c]$. Computing sequence encodings is straightforward, e.g. for $\langle a \rangle$ we have $([], a)$, for $\langle a, b \rangle$ we have $([a], b)$, for $\langle a, c, b, d, e, f, e, g \rangle$ we have $([a, b, c, d, e^2, f], g)$, etc. Different sequences can have the same sequence encoding and therefore map to the same constraint. Consider $\langle a, b, c, d \rangle$ and $\langle a, c, b, d \rangle$ both mapping to $([a, b, c], d)$. The sequence encoding of ϵ is defined as $([], \epsilon)$.

5   Sequence Encoding Filtering

The presence of $\langle a, b, d, e, g \rangle$ in L' causes the ILP-based process discovery algorithm to be unable to find place p_5 of the Petri net depicted in Figure 3a. As the body of constraints of the ILP-based process discovery algorithm, i.e., the set of linear inequalities, specifies this behavior, we need means to remove the inequalities related to $\langle a, b, d, e, g \rangle$ from the constraint body. We do so by constructing a directed acyclic graph where each sequence encoding, i.e., each constraint, acts as a vertex. The sequence encoding $([], \epsilon)$ always acts as a root vertex. Two vertices are connected by an arc if the arc's source could be a prefix of the arc's target. The arcs are labeled using sequence frequencies present in the prefix closure of the event log. An example of such graph, based on $\overline{L'}$ is depicted in Figure 4.

In $\overline{L'}$ the empty sequence ϵ acts as a prefix of $\langle a \rangle$. Hence $([], \epsilon)$ has an outgoing arc to $([], \langle a \rangle)$ labeled with 408, i.e., in 408 cases ϵ acts as a prefix of $\langle a \rangle$. Sequence $\langle a \rangle$ on its turn acts as a prefix of $\langle a, b \rangle$ and $\langle a, c \rangle$, thus, $([], a)$ is connected to $([a], b)$ and $([a], c)$. The edge weights of the arcs from $\langle a \rangle$ to $\langle a, b \rangle$ and $\langle a, c \rangle$ are related to the number of times $\langle a \rangle$ acts as a prefix of $\langle a, b \rangle$, $\langle a, c \rangle$ respectively. Applying the previous rationale on all nodes yields the graph as presented in Figure 4.

After constructing the graph, we traverse it in a breadth-first manner and cut off branches that represent exceptional behavior. We start at its root and assess what outgoing arcs have a too low arc weight given some decision function.

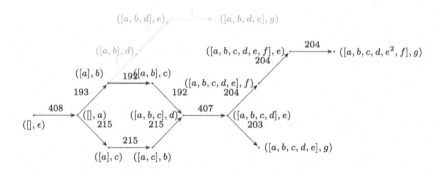

Fig. 4. Sequence encoding graph based on event log $\overline{L'}$. Filtering affected the branch starting at $([a], b)$ and ending in $([a, b, d, e], g)$.

Once we have decided what outgoing arcs should remain we traverse each of these arcs. From the end-point of such arc we again evaluate all outgoing arcs. Only those constraints corresponding to a vertex present in the filtered sequence encoding graph will be added to the ILP constraint body. The decision function that decides whether we cut off a certain branch is a parameter of the approach.

In the implementation of the algorithm we have adopted the following app-roach. For each vertex that we decide to keep, we always include the outgoing edge with the maximum edge label value. Additionally we include all other edges e that have a lower (or equal) value than (to) the maximum value, as long as the difference of e's value w.r.t. the maximum is within some bounded range. The bounded range is typically some fraction of the maximum, this fraction is deemed the cut-off coefficient c_c. As an example we apply this technique on the graph depicted in Figure 4 with $c_c = 0.25$.

The root has one arc and thus we keep this arc. Traversing the arc leads us to vertex $([], a)$ which has two outgoing arcs. The outgoing arc from $([], a)$ with the maximum label is the arc to $([a], c)$, labeled 215. This arc will be kept in the graph. The bounded range for any other arc starting from vertex $([], a)$ is computed by multiplying the cut-off coefficient with the maximum value for this node, i.e., the bounded range is $0.25 \times 215 = 53.75$. Any edge going out of $([], a)$ that has a value greater than or equal to $215 - 53.75 = 161.25$ is kept in the graph. In this case the arc from $([], a)$ to $([a], b)$ will remain as it has a value of 193. In vertex $([a], b)$ we identify that we keep the edge to $([a, b], c)$, which has the maximum label. We only keep outgoing arcs from $([a, b], c)$ with a label value greater than or equal to $192 - 0.25 \times 192 = 144$. As a result we will drop the edge to $([a, b], d)$ as it only has a label value of 1. The result of repeating the filtering procedure on all vertices is visualized Figure 4 where the filtered branch, i.e., starting at $([a], b)$ and ending in $([a, b, d, e], g)$, is graying out. Note that using the aforementioned approach all constraints related to (prefixes of) $\langle a, b, d, e, g \rangle$ are remove from the constraint body. As a consequence, place p_5 in

Figure 3a becomes a feasible place again. Thus, the model depicted in Figure 3a can be found using sequence encoding filtering applied on L'. As the model does not allow for $\langle a, b, d, e, g \rangle$, we no longer guarantee perfect replay fitness w.r.t. L'.

6   Evaluation

For evaluation we used an implementation of sequence encoding filtering present in the *HybridILPMiner*[3] package within the *ProM framework* (http://www. promtools.org). Here we discuss effects on model quality. For a quantification of the effect on ILP solve time we refer to [9]. The event logs used for evaluation are artificially generated event logs originating from a study related to the impact of exceptional behavior on rule-based approaches in process discovery [10]. The event logs contain different levels of exceptional behavior and are based on two ground truth event logs. The ground truth event logs, *a22f0n00* and *a32f0n00*, are free of exceptional behavior, i.e. all traces fit the originating model. *a22f0n00* consists of 22 different event classes whereas *a32f0n00* consists of 32 different event classes. Out of each ground truth event log a total of four new logs is generated, consisting of either 5%, 10%, 20% or 50% of manipulated traces. Manipulation of traces is performed by either tail/head of sequence removal, random part of sequence body removal or interchange of two randomly chosen events [10].

We primarily focus on precision, i.e. the amount of behavior allowed by the model also present in the event log. If all behavior allowed by the model is present in the event log, precision is maximal and equals 1. The more behavior is allowed by the model that is not present in the event log, the lower the precision value will be. By definition, the conventional ILP-based process discovery algorithm will result in models that allow for all behavior present in the event log. Thus, if we use the conventional algorithm on a manipulated event log, the resulting model will allow for all exceptional behavior. As the exceptional behavior is not present in the ground truth events log, computing precision of the resulting model based on the ground truth log is expected to be low. On the other hand, if we discover models using an algorithm that is more able to handle the presence of exceptional behavior, we expect the algorithm to allow for less exceptional behavior and, w.r.t. the ground truth model, we expect a higher precision value.

In Figure 5 the results of applying the conventional ILP-based process discovery algorithm and three different sequence encoding filtering instantiations for each event log are depicted. We used the branch cut-off technique as described in Section 5 with cut-off coefficients $\frac{1}{4}$, $\frac{1}{2}$, $\frac{3}{4}$. We measured both the replay-fitness and precision based on the ground truth event logs. Replay-fitness of the discovered models w.r.t. the ground truth event logs using all four approaches remains 1 in all cases[4]. Due to the incapability of handling exceptional behavior of the conventional algorithm, as expected, precision drops rapidly. For the sequence

---

[3] https://svn.win.tue.nl/repos/prom/Packages/HybridILPMiner/Branches/ experiments/2015_bpm_ilp_filtering-0.2.1/

[4] One exception for SEF with $c_c = \frac{1}{2}$, where replay fitness equals 0.99515.

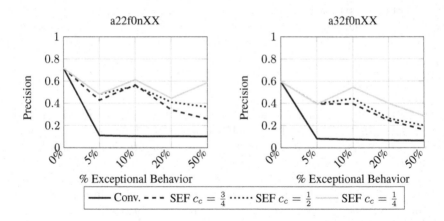

Fig. 5. Precision measurements based on event logs with exceptional behavior. Conventional ILP-based process discovery (Conv.) and sequence encoding filtering (SEF) was used for porcess model discovery.

encoding filtering we identify the $\frac{1}{4}$ variant to outperform the other two. This is explained by the fact that this variant is the most rigorous filter and removes the most constraints. It is clear that the decrease of precision for the sequence encoding based approaches is less severe compared to the conventional approach. This is in line with the rationale presented before, i.e., we expect the filtering based approaches to be more able in handling exceptional behavior. Therefore, we conclude that the filtering based models discover Petri net patterns that more accurately represent the dominant behavior in the input event log. Thus, the newly presented techniques allow us to successfully apply filtering whilst using ILP-based process discovery as a basis.

7   Conclusion

The work presented in this paper is motivated by the observation that the existing ILP-based process discovery algorithm is unable to cope with exceptional behavior in event logs. ILP-based process discovery has several advantages, but the inability to abstract from infrequent exceptional behavior makes it unusable in real-life settings. We presented the sequence encoding filtering technique which enables us to apply filtering exceptional behavior within the ILP-based process discovery algorithm. The technique allows us to find models with acceptable trade-offs w.r.t. replay fitness and precision. We showed that the technique enables us to find Petri net structures in data consisting of exceptional behavior, using ILP-based process discovery as an underlying technique.

References

1. van der Aalst, W.M.P.: Process Mining: Discovery, Conformance and Enhancement of Business Processes. Springer (2011)
2. Buijs, J.C.A.M., van Dongen, B.F., van der Aalst, W.M.P.: On the role of fitness, precision, generalization and simplicity in process discovery. In: Meersman, R., Panetto, H., Dillon, T., Rinderle-Ma, S., Dadam, P., Zhou, X., Pearson, S., Ferscha, A., Bergamaschi, S., Cruz, I.F. (eds.) OTM 2012, Part I. LNCS, vol. 7565, pp. 305–322. Springer, Heidelberg (2012)
3. Werf, JMEMvd, Dongen, BFv, Hurkens, C.A.J., Serebrenik, A.: Process Discovery using Integer Linear Programming. Fundamenta Informaticae **94**(3), 387–412 (2009)
4. Leemans, S.J.J., Fahland, D., van der Aalst, W.M.P.: Discovering block-structured process models from event logs - a constructive approach. In: Colom, J.-M., Desel, J. (eds.) PETRI NETS 2013. LNCS, vol. 7927, pp. 311–329. Springer, Heidelberg (2013)
5. van der Aalst, W.M.P., ter Hofstede, A.H.M., Kiepuszewski, B., Barros, A.P.: Workflow Patterns. Distributed and Parallel Databases **14**(1), 5–51 (2003)
6. Weijters, A.J.M.M., Ribeiro, J.T.S.: Flexible Heuristics Miner (FHM). In: Proceedings of the IEEE Symposium on Computational Intelligence and Data Mining, CIDM 2011, part of the IEEE Symposium Series on Computational Intelligence 2011, Paris, France, pp. 310–317, April 11–15, 2011
7. Günther, C.W., van der Aalst, W.M.P.: Fuzzy mining – adaptive process simplification based on multi-perspective metrics. In: Alonso, G., Dadam, P., Rosemann, M. (eds.) BPM 2007. LNCS, vol. 4714, pp. 328–343. Springer, Heidelberg (2007)
8. Buijs, J.C.A.M., van Dongen, B.F., van der Aalst, W.M.P.: A Genetic Algorithm for Discovering Process Trees. In: Proceedings of the IEEE Congress on Evolutionary Computation, CEC 2012, Brisbane, Australia, pp. 1–8, June 10–15, 2012
9. van Zelst, S.J., van Dongen, B.F., van der Aalst, W.M.P.: Filter Techniques for Region-Based Process Discovery. Technical Report 15–4, BPM Center.org (2015)
10. Maruster, L., Weijters, A.J.M.M., van der Aalst, W.M.P., van den Bosch, A.: A Rule-Based Approach for Process Discovery: Dealing with Noise and Imbalance in Process Logs. Data Min. Knowl. Discov. **13**(1), 67–87 (2006)

Estimation of Average Latent Waiting and Service Times of Activities from Event Logs

Takahide Nogayama[1]([✉]) and Haruhisa Takahashi[2]

[1] Department of Cloud and Security, IBM Research, Tokyo, Japan
nogayama@jp.ibm.com
[2] Department of Information and Communication Engineering,
University of Electro-Communications, Tokyo, Japan
takaharuroka@uec.ac.jp

Abstract. Analysis of performance is crucial in the redesign phase of business processes where bottlenecks are identified from the average waiting and service times of activities and resources in business processes. However, such averages of waiting and service times are not readily available in most event logs that only record either the start or the completion times of events in activities. The transition times between events in such logs are the only performance features that are available. This paper proposes a novel method of estimating the average latent waiting and service times from the transition times that employs the optimization of the likelihood of the probabilistic model with expectation and maximization (EM) algorithms. Our experimental results indicated that our method could estimate the average latent waiting and service times with sufficient accuracy to enable practical applications through performance analysis.

Keywords: Process mining · Performance analysis · Latent waiting and service times · Convolution of gamma distributions · EM algorithm

1 Introduction

The role of *process mining* has become much more important in the redesign phases of *business processes*. Recent developments in process mining have been based on the *Process-Aware Information System* (PAIS) [5] including the *Workflow Management* (WFM) system and the *Business Process Management* (BPM) system, which record business events as *event logs*. Process models and performance data extracted from observed event logs have played significant roles in business process improvement, redesign, re-engineering, and optimization.

Performance analysis that deals with time and frequency is especially crucial in improvements to business processes to reduce labor costs and to increase customer satisfaction. Event logs typically observed on PAIS contain the assignment, start, and end times of events in activities, from which useful statistics can be inferred. We can easily calculate the *average waiting time* and the *average*

© Springer International Publishing Switzerland 2015
H.R. Motahari-Nezhad et al. (Eds.): BPM 2015, LNCS 9253, pp. 172–179, 2015.
DOI: 10.1007/978-3-319-23063-4_11

service time of individual activities or resources from such event logs to discover bottlenecks in business processes.

The *average of activity transition times*, which are differences between the source end and destination start times, provides information on how many time resources are consumed outside of activities. However, the domain that can be improved is limited to inside the activities in most cases. Hence, the average transition time needs to be split into two parts, i.e., the source and destination activity related parts, to know how much of the transition time the activities consume in two cases:

1. When activity transition times tend to be very long, the source or destination activity must be a bottleneck.
2. The duration of activities cannot be known when only a single timestamp is observed for each activity. These types of event logs usually arise from non-PAIS. For example, legacy BPMS may only recode the end time, and Kuo et al. [7] faced start times only from logs in the clinical system of a hospital.

Such problems with incompleteness become more serious in non-PAIS. Nevertheless, the analysis of such incomplete event logs is indeed required by BPM system vendors. In fact, if the vendor can demonstrate promising improvements to business processes based on logs from the existing non-PAIS when customers of a vendor consider system migration from non-PAIS to PAIS, customers can easily be encouraged to accept the proposal for migration by the vendor.

We modeled the latent average waiting and service times of event logs under two assumptions:

1. The probability distribution of time duration only depends on the present state, and not on the previous sequence of events that preceded it, which are so called Markov properties.
2. The transition times are composed of latent waiting and service times, and individual time durations are i.i.d. with Gamma distributions.

We aimed at estimating the parameters of Gamma distributions for latent waiting and service times based on the *maximum likelihood estimation (MLE)*. Since these were latent variables, the *EM (expectation maximization) algorithm* was applied to infer the parameters. We evaluated our method with artificially generated data, and an event log "teleclaim" referred to by van der Aalst [1].

Performance analysis is discussed in Section 2 in terms of process mining. Observable and unobservable performance indicators are described in Section 3. The probabilistic model is defined in Section 4, and it is estimated in Section 5. Finally, the experimental results are presented in Section 6.

2   Related Work

A number of studies and tools have been developed to summarize performance data from workflow logs or event logs. Ferreira [6] gathered the minimum, maximum, and average activity durations of health care processes to analyze the lengths of stays by patients in a hospital. Lanz et al. [8] have accurately defined various time patterns that could be observed from event logs.

Performance summary data can also be utilized in the running process, i.e., in so called "operational support". The prediction of the remaining lead time in instances of the running process has been presented by van der Aalst et al. [2,3]. Sindhgatta et al. [11] assigned the tasks of a running process to appropriate workers by analyzing the average service time of activities. Rogge-solti and Kasneci [9] used the average service time of activities to detect anomalies in the instance of running processes.

Activities in business processes have been analyzed using queueing models in some literature [10,12] based on rich event logs that contain several types of events such as 'Entry', 'Assign', 'Start' and 'End'. Arrival processes and the number of services (operators) need to be described beforehand in these models. Nevertheless, difficulties arise since the arrival processes can vary by the behavior of the preceding activities, and the number of available operators in the back office can vary by a day or weeks as well as the time zone of the day.

Since assumptions about the arrival processes and the number of services are usually not recorded in event logs, they are determined based on the experience of data analysts. We tried to make our method work with as few assumptions as possible to avoid making estimations with incorrect assumptions. Our proposed method estimated latent waiting and service times without any assumptions about the arrival processes or the number of services. We only assumed that the time intervals were distributed with Gamma distributions because it includes rich and flexible expressions.

3   Performance Indicators of Activities Deliverable from Event Logs

Event sequences provide us some performance indicators of activities due to the difference in the two timestamps between two events. When an event sequence with a timestamp (e.g., in Fig. 1) is given, some indicators can be explicitly derived such as waiting time, service time, activity duration, and transition time.

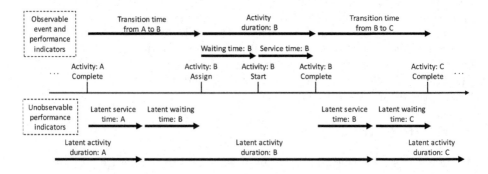

Fig. 1. Observable and unobservable performance indicators on event log.

The timestamps when one activity passes control to another are not explicitly recorded. We assumed that the *latent service time*, i.e., the first part of the transition time, would be controlled by the source activity, and the *latent waiting time*, i.e., the last part of the transition time, would be controlled by the destination activity in this research.

4   Probabilistic Model

We used the *gamma distribution* as the probability density function of the latent waiting and service times because it has enough flexibility to model the time duration composed in the practice of several small activities. For example, the underwriting activity in the insurance industry includes understanding of incoming applications, measuring of risk exposures, and determining of premiums that need to be charged to insure the client against risk. Its probability density function over a probabilistic variable $X > 0$ is defined by $p(X; q, \alpha) = X^{q-1} e^{-\frac{X}{\alpha}} / \Gamma(q) \alpha^q$ with a shape parameter $q > 0$ and a scale parameter $\alpha > 0$ where $\Gamma(q)$ is the *gamma function* $\Gamma(q) = \int_0^\infty z^{q-1} e^{-z} dz$. We write this as $X \sim G(q, \alpha)$.

We assumed that the transition time from a source to different destinations would share the same latent service time at the transition source. In addition, the transition time from different sources to one destination shares the same latent waiting time at that transition destination. For example, Fig. 2 illustrates the transition time and their latent waiting and service times on an XOR-split gateway. We expect that latent times can be estimated if we simultaneously solve the inverse problem.

Let $\mathcal{A}$ be the set of activities, and $\mathcal{T}$ be the set of transitions. Further, let T_{ij} be the random variable of the transition time from $i \in \mathcal{A}$ to $j \in \mathcal{A}$, S_i be the random variable of the latent service time of activity $i \in \mathcal{A}$, and W_j be the random variable of the latent waiting time of activity $j \in \mathcal{A}$. From the assumption in Section 1, $S_i \sim G(q_i, \alpha_i)$, $W_j \sim G(r_j, \beta_j)$, and $T_{ij} = S_i + W_j$ for all $(i, j) \in \mathcal{T}$ (see Fig. 3). The probabilistic density function of T_{ij} can be obtained from convolutional integration $p(S_i; q_i, \alpha_i) * p(W_j; r_j, \beta_j)$ as:

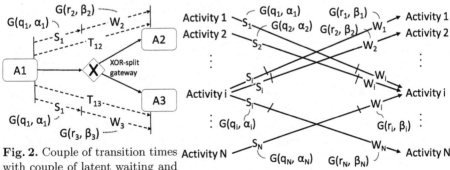

Fig. 2. Couple of transition times with couple of latent waiting and single shared latent service times on XOR-split gateway.

Fig. 3. Probabilistic model focusing on activity i.

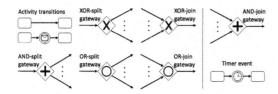

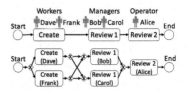

Fig. 4. Examples of BPMN notations. Time periods of notations on left can be considered as sum of two latent times following gamma distribution. Time periods of notations on right do not match our model well.

Fig. 5. Sequential process (Top) and generated XOR-split/join gateways (Bottom) by changing an activity identifier from name to name + resource.

$$p(T_{ij}; \boldsymbol{\theta}_{ij}) = \frac{e^{-T_{ij}/\beta_j}}{\Gamma(q_i)\Gamma(r_j)\alpha_i^{q_i}\beta_j^{r_j}} f(T_{ij}, \boldsymbol{\theta}_{ij}) \tag{1}$$

where we define $\boldsymbol{\theta}_{ij}$ as the vector $(q_i, \alpha_i, r_j, \beta_j)$, and $f(x, \boldsymbol{\theta}) = \int_0^x z^{q-1}(x-z)^{r-1}e^{(\frac{1}{\beta}-\frac{1}{\alpha})z}dz$.

This probabilistic model can describe the Business Process Model and Notation (BPMN) on the left of Fig. 4. However, it cannot adequately describe the AND-join gateway and time event on the right of Fig. 4. Another limitation of this model is that the transition time on stand alone sequential process, like that at the top of Fig. 5, is always split into the same two distributions. However, it is possible to generate XOR-split/join gateways by changing the definition of an activity identifier from name to name + resource.

5   Estimation of Parameters

Let $\boldsymbol{\Theta}$ be a vector $(q_1, \ldots, \alpha_1, \ldots, r_1, \ldots, \beta_1, \ldots)$ that includes all shape and scale parameters. Suppose the transition times t_{ijk} $((i,j) \in \mathcal{T}, k = 1, \ldots, n_{ij})$ are independent and observed to be identically distributed, we aim to find an estimator $\widehat{\boldsymbol{\Theta}}$ which would be as close to the true value $\boldsymbol{\Theta}_0$ as possible by using MLE. The estimators give us the *average latent waiting and service times* of activity i as $\widehat{r_i}\widehat{\beta_i}$ and $\widehat{q_i}\widehat{\alpha_i}$ respectively. The log likelihood function becomes:

$$\log L = \sum_{(i,j)\in\mathcal{T}} \sum_{k=1}^{n_{ij}} \log p(t_{ijk}; \boldsymbol{\theta}_{ij}) \tag{2}$$

However, the parameters that maximize this function are impossible to solve explicitly with equation transformations.

The EM algorithm [4] is a general technique for finding maximum likelihood solutions to probabilistic models that have latent variables. The observed variables in this case are T_{ij} and the latent variables are S_i. Note that W_j vanishes with $W_j = T_{ij} - S_i$. The EM algorithm iteratively maximizes the likelihood with the expectation and maximization steps.

In the expectation step, we construct a function:

$$\mathcal{Q}(\boldsymbol{\Theta},\boldsymbol{\Theta}') = \sum_{(i,j)\in\mathcal{T}}\sum_{k=1}^{n_{ij}}\int_0^{t_{ijk}} p(S_i|\,t_{ijk};\,\boldsymbol{\theta}_{ij})\log p(t_{ijk}\,,S_i;\,\boldsymbol{\theta}'_{ij})dS_i$$

to approximate the log likelihood (2), where the joint probability $p(T,S;\,\boldsymbol{\theta}) = p(S;\,l,\alpha)\,p(T-S;\,m,\beta) = \frac{S^{q-1}(T-S)^{r-1}}{\Gamma(q)\Gamma(r)\alpha^q\beta^r}e^{-\frac{T}{\beta}}e^{\left(\frac{1}{\beta}-\frac{1}{\alpha}\right)S}$ and the posterior probability $p(S|\,T;\,\boldsymbol{\theta}) = p(T,S;\,\boldsymbol{\theta})/p(T;\,\boldsymbol{\theta}) = \frac{S^{q-1}(T-S)^{r-1}}{f(T,q,\alpha,r,\beta)}e^{\left(\frac{1}{\beta}-\frac{1}{\alpha}\right)S}$.

In the maximization step, we find a new parameter $\boldsymbol{\Theta}'$ that maximizes $\mathcal{Q}$ while holding the old parameter $\boldsymbol{\Theta}$. The optimal point satisfies $\frac{\partial\mathcal{Q}}{\partial\boldsymbol{\Theta}'} = \boldsymbol{0}$. By substituting $\frac{\partial\mathcal{Q}}{\partial\alpha'_i} = 0$ into $\frac{\partial\mathcal{Q}}{\partial q'_i} = 0$, and $\frac{\partial\mathcal{Q}}{\partial\beta'_j} = 0$ into $\frac{\partial\mathcal{Q}}{\partial r'_j} = 0$, we obtain:

$$\psi(q'_i)-\log(q'_i)-\frac{1}{\displaystyle\sum_{j\in\mathcal{A}}n_{ij}}\sum_{j\in\mathcal{A}}\sum_{k=1}^{n_{ij}}\frac{g(t_{ijk},\boldsymbol{\theta}_{ij})}{f(t_{ijk},\boldsymbol{\theta}_{ij})}+\log\left(\frac{1}{\displaystyle\sum_{j\in\mathcal{A}}n_{ij}}\sum_{j\in\mathcal{A}}\sum_{k=1}^{n_{ij}}\frac{f_1(t_{ijk},\boldsymbol{\theta}_{ij})}{f(t_{ijk},\boldsymbol{\theta}_{ij})}\right)=0 \quad (3)$$

$$\psi(r'_j)-\log(r'_j)-\frac{1}{\displaystyle\sum_{i\in\mathcal{A}}n_{ij}}\sum_{i\in\mathcal{A}}\sum_{k=1}^{n_{ij}}\frac{h(t_{ijk},\boldsymbol{\theta}_{ij})}{f(t_{ijk},\boldsymbol{\theta}_{ij})}+\log\left(\frac{1}{\displaystyle\sum_{i\in\mathcal{A}}n_{ij}}\sum_{i\in\mathcal{A}}\sum_{k=1}^{n_{ij}}\frac{f_2(t_{ijk},\boldsymbol{\theta}_{ij})}{f(t_{ijk},\boldsymbol{\theta}_{ij})}\right)=0 \quad (4)$$

where we have defined $g(x,\boldsymbol{\theta}) = \int_0^x z^{q-1}(x-z)^{r-1}e^{\left(\frac{1}{\beta}-\frac{1}{\alpha}\right)z}\log z\,dz$, $h(x,\boldsymbol{\theta}) = \int_0^x z^{q-1}(x-z)^{r-1}e^{\left(\frac{1}{\beta}-\frac{1}{\alpha}\right)z}\log(x-z)dz$, $f_1(x,\boldsymbol{\theta}) = f(x,q+1,\alpha,r,\beta)$, $f_2(x,\boldsymbol{\theta}) = f(x,q,\alpha,r+1,\beta)$, and $\psi(x)$ is the *digamma function* $\frac{d}{dx}\ln\Gamma(x)$. The optimal shape parameters q'_i and r'_j are given by solving these nonlinear one variable equations. Then, by substituting the shape parameters into $\frac{\partial\mathcal{Q}}{\partial\alpha'_i} = 0$ and $\frac{\partial\mathcal{Q}}{\partial\beta'_j} = 0$, we obtain the optimal scale parameters:

$$\alpha'_i = \frac{1}{q'_i\displaystyle\sum_{j\in\mathcal{A}}n_{ij}}\sum_{j\in\mathcal{A}}\sum_{k=1}^{n_{ij}}\frac{f_1(t_{ijk},\boldsymbol{\theta}_{ij})}{f(t_{ijk},\boldsymbol{\theta}_{ij})}\,,\quad \beta'_j = \frac{1}{r'_j\displaystyle\sum_{i\in\mathcal{A}}n_{ij}}\sum_{i\in\mathcal{A}}\sum_{k=1}^{n_{ij}}\frac{f_2(t_{ijk},\boldsymbol{\theta}_{ij})}{f(t_{ijk},\boldsymbol{\theta}_{ij})}. \quad (5)$$

6   Experimental Results

We implemented our method and the synthetic log generator by using GNU Octave. The programming language was required to support a numerical integration and a root-finding algorithm.

6.1   Synthetic Log

We evaluated our method using artificially generated random numbers with three gamma distributions whose parameters were known in a business process of Fig. 6. We generated random numbers $s_1^1,\ldots,s_1^{200}$ as the instance of

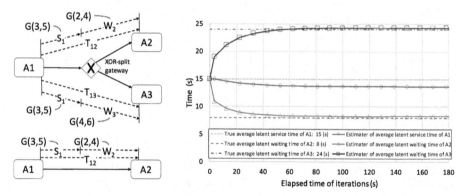

Fig. 6. XOR-split gateway (Top) and stand alone sequential process (Bottom) to generate synthetic logs.

Fig. 7. Estimators of each iteration with the synthetic log data generated on process in Fig. 6 (Top).

latent service time $S_1 \sim G(3,5)$, $w_2^1, \ldots, w_2^{100}$ as the instance of latent waiting time $W_2 \sim G(2,4)$, and $w_3^1, \ldots, w_3^{100}$ as the instance of latent waiting time $W_3 \sim G(4,6)$. Based on $t_{12}^i = s_1^i + w_2^i$ and $t_{13}^i = s_1^{i+100} + w_3^i$ for each $i = 1, \ldots, 100$, We then created transition times $t_{12}^1, \ldots, t_{12}^{100}$ and $t_{13}^1, \ldots, t_{13}^{100}$.

For the XOR-split gateway shown by the top of Fig. 6, two hundreds of transition times from A1 to A2 and A1 to A3 were generated. Fig. 7 illustrates the history of the estimators over iterations. The estimators converged with values close to the true average latent waiting and service times as the iteration progressed.

For the sequential process shown by the bottom of Fig. 6, one hundred of transition times from A1 to A2 were generated. The estimaters of the average latent waiting time of A1 and service time of A2 were the same value, the half of the sample average of transition times from A1 to A2, and not close to the true values. This result suggests that our method cannot decompose latent times from stand alone transition times as we discussed in Section 4.

6.2   Teleclaim Log

We evaluated our method with an event log "teleclaim" referred to by van der Aalst [1] that describes the handling of claims in an insurance company. It contains an instance of an XOR-split gateway from an "Incoming Claim" activity to a "B check" and an "S check" activities. The average transition time from an "Incoming Claim" to the "B check" and the "S check" were 2518 (s) for the former and 936 (s) for the latter.

We found that the estimator of the average latent service time of an "Incoming Claim" was 508 (s) from the results in this experiment. The estimator of the average latent waiting time of the "B check" and the "S check" were 1415 (s) for the former and 105 (s) for the latter. These results indicate the "Incoming Claim" incurred a relatively heavy time cost after the activity is completed.

7 Conclusion

We proposed three unobservable performance indicators, i.e., the latent waiting and service times and the latent activity duration. These indicators are not only useful in the performance analysis but also in predicting the time of a new sequence of activities that was not observed in event logs. We also proposed a statistical algorithm to estimate averages of such unobservable indicators with some assumptions.

We considered that these assumptions were reasonable in practice and our method could be applied to various event logs. The estimators obtained with our method were in good agreement with the true average latent times in the experimental results with artificially generated numbers.

Decomposition of transition times on AND-join gateway remains as one of the key issues to be clarified. Experiments with event logs that include a large number of events and gateways are also required as future work.

References

1. van der Aalst, W.M.P.: Process Mining: Discovery, Conformance and Enhancement of Business Processes, vol. 136. Springer (2011)
2. van der Aalst, W.M.P., Pesic, M., Song, M.: Beyond process mining: from the past to present and future. In: Pernici, B. (ed.) CAiSE 2010. LNCS, vol. 6051, pp. 38–52. Springer, Heidelberg (2010)
3. van der Aalst, W.M.P., Schonenberg, M.H., Song, M.: Time prediction based on process mining. Information Systems $36(2)$, 450–475 (2011)
4. Dempster, A.P., Laird, N.M., Rubin, D.B.: Maximum likelihood from incomplete data via the EM algorithm. Journal of the royal statistical society. Series B $39(1)$, 1–38 (1977)
5. Dumas, M., van der Aalst, W.M.P., ter Hofstede, A.H.M.: Process-Aware Information Systems: Bridging People and Software through Process Technology. Wiley (2005)
6. Ferreira, D.R.: Performance analysis of healthcare processes through process mining. ERCIM News 89, 18–19 (2012)
7. Kuo, Y.H., Leung, J.M.Y., Graham, C.A.: Simulation with data scarcity: Developing a simulation model of a hospital emergency department. In: Proceedings of the 2012 Winter Simulation Conference, pp. 1–12. IEEE (2012)
8. Lanz, A., Weber, B., Reichert, M.: Time patterns for process-aware information systems. Requirements Engineering $19(2)$, 113–141 (2014)
9. Rogge-Solti, A., Kasneci, G.: Temporal anomaly detection in business processes. In: Sadiq, S., Soffer, P., Völzer, H. (eds.) BPM 2014. LNCS, vol. 8659, pp. 234–249. Springer, Heidelberg (2014)
10. Senderovich, A., Weidlich, M., Gal, A., Mandelbaum, A.: Queue mining – predicting delays in service processes. In: Jarke, M., Mylopoulos, J., Quix, C., Rolland, C., Manolopoulos, Y., Mouratidis, H., Horkoff, J. (eds.) CAiSE 2014. LNCS, vol. 8484, pp. 42–57. Springer, Heidelberg (2014)
11. Sindhgatta, R., Dasgupta, G.B., Ghose, A.: Analysis of operational data for expertise aware staffing. In: Sadiq, S., Soffer, P., Völzer, H. (eds.) BPM 2014. LNCS, vol. 8659, pp. 317–332. Springer, Heidelberg (2014)
12. Zerguini, L.: On the estimation of the response time of the business process. In: 17th UK Performance Engineering Workshop, University of Leeds (2001)

A Structural Model Comparison for Finding the Best Performing Models in a Collection

D.M.M. Schunselaar[1]([✉]), H.M.W. Verbeek[1], H.A. Reijers[1,2],
and W.M.P. van der Aalst[1]

[1] Eindhoven University of Technology, P.O. Box 513,
5600 MB Eindhoven, The Netherlands
{d.m.m.schunselaar,h.m.w.verbeek,h.a.reijers,w.m.p.v.d.aalst}@tue.nl
[2] VU University Amsterdam, De Boelelaan 1105,
1081 HV Amsterdam, The Netherlands
h.a.reijers@vu.nl

Abstract. An improvement or redesign of a process often starts by modifying the model supporting the process. Analysis techniques, like simulation, can be used to evaluate alternatives. However, even a small number of design choices may lead to an explosion of models that need to be explored to find the optimal models for said process. If the exploration depends on simulation, it often becomes infeasible to simulate every model. Therefore, for throughput time, we define a notion of *monotonicity* to reduce the number of models required to be simulated whilst the optimal models are still found.

1 Introduction

While improving or redesigning a business process, one can model each part of the process in various ways. Even if each part has a limited number of variants, the combination of options may cause an explosion of possible models. This set of possible models, we call a *model collection*. As a redesigner is often not interested in just any model, she would like to have qualitative and quantitative information on the models in the model collection such that she can select the most suitable models, assuming one or more relevant performance criteria. In this paper, we are particulary interested in the throughput time (sometimes called flow time, sojourn time, or lead time) of a model and the best models are those models having a significant lower throughput time than the other models. Unfortunately, brute-force approaches require the simulation of each model, which is a time-consuming endeavour. Therefore, we present a technique to reduce the amount of models needed to be simulated, whilst the best models are still found. We have chosen throughput time as this is a well-understood and often studied Key Performance Indicator (KPI) which can only be deduced from

D.M.M. Schunselaar, H.M.W. Verbeek, H.A. Reijers, W.M.P. van der Aalst—This research has been carried out as part of the Configurable Services for Local Governments (CoSeLoG) project (http://www.win.tue.nl/coselog/).

© Springer International Publishing Switzerland 2015
H.R. Motahari-Nezhad et al. (Eds.): BPM 2015, LNCS 9253, pp. 180–188, 2015.
DOI: 10.1007/978-3-319-23063-4_12

the dynamic behaviour of a model contrary to some other KPIs, e.g., number of control-tasks, which can be deduced from the structure of the model.

The aforementioned reduction is achieved by defining a *monotonicity* notion, which provides a partial order over the models. If we take the model collection on the left-hand side of Fig. 1, where each dot corresponds to a model, our particular monotonicity notion may allow for the partial order on the right-hand side of the same figure. Our monotonicity notion is based on the structure of the process models and gives a so-called *at-least-as-good* relation. If we can deduce monotonicity between a model M and a model M', then we know that the throughput time of M is at-least-as-good as the throughput time of M'. By having such a partial order, we can limit our search for the optimal models, i.e., to the models A and B in Fig. 1. We know that models not considered have poorer or equal throughput performance. In Fig. 1, if we have simulated A and B and A is better than B, then we know that all models connected to B via the partial order do not need to be simulated as A is *better than* all of them. In this paper, the structural comparison between two models is done using a *divide-and-conquer* approach. In this approach, each model is seen as a collection of weighted *runs* (runs are sometimes called process nets [1], or partial orders). Based on the structures of two runs, we can decide whether one run is at-least-as-good as the other run. Then, using the run weights, representing the execution likelihood, we can decide whether one model is at-least-as-good as another model.

This paper is organised as follows: In Sect. 2, we present our runs, models, and model collections. Our monotonicity notion is presented in Sect. 3. Finally, we conclude our paper with related work (Sect. 4) and the conclusions (Sect. 5). A more extensive version of this paper can be found in [2].

2   Model Collection

In this paper, a model collection consists of models, while a model itself consists of weighted runs [1] (see Fig. 2). A run specifies the partial order of activities needed to be executed for a particular case and does not contain any choices. A run consists of *vertices* which are labelled with activities. In Fig. 2, we have a run P_1 with a vertex v_1 labelled with activity a. Next to this, a run specifies the

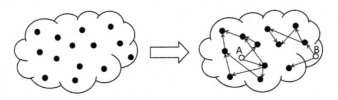

Fig. 1. Using monotonicity, we can transform the model collection on the left to the partially ordered model collection on the right. As a result, fewer alternatives need to be explored.

causal relationship between the vertices by means of edges. The edge between the vertices v_4 and v_5 in run P_1' means that e can only start once vertex v_4 executing d has been completed. We have abstracted from the transitive closure of the edges. The transitive closure of the edges we call paths. We have chosen this representation for our models as this fits better with our divide-and-conquer technique. In [1], an algorithm is presented to transform a Petri net into a collection of runs. By limiting the number of times an iteration is executed, it is possible to obtain a finite set of runs.

A model consists of runs and these runs combined define the behaviour of a model. As not every run must be equally probable, we define a weight function (w) within the model. Furthermore, a model specifies which resources can execute which activity (ar), e.g., in model M in Fig. 2, activity a can be executed by resources r_1 and r_6.

Note that a resource can execute only one activity, but multiple resources can execute the same activity. We require that a resource can only perform a single activity to guarantee that we can compare the resource utilisation of both models and thus the queue time per activity based on the structure. This is due to the fact that even a small increase in the resource utilisation can have a significant effect on the throughput time.

A model collection consists of models, a set of activities (A), a set of resources (R), a random variable describing the inter-arrival time of new cases (K_a), and a function giving the processing time of each activity (K_{PT}). Note that our model collection is less general than most other model collections as our model collection is a body of scenarios for executing the same process.

3   Throughput Time

As mentioned before, we focus on the throughput time. The throughput time of a single case is the time between arrival of this case and the moment the case

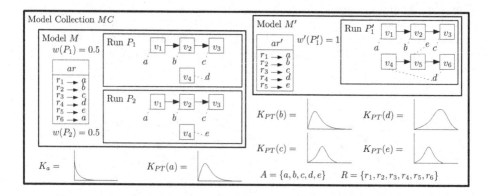

Fig. 2. An example model collection.

Fig. 3. Example throughput time KPIs for the models from Fig. 2.

is finished. We consider the situation where the model and runs are in steady state.

To save space, within this section, MC is a model collection, M and M' are models from MC, P and P' are runs from M and M' respectively.

We are interested in the best models, that is, the models which have a significantly lower throughput time, which requires the comparison of two random variables. For this comparison, we use the Cumulative Distribution Function (CDF) of the throughput time which we also use as our notion of throughput time KPI. Note that our approach is not limited to this definition of the throughput time KPI. Any definition works as long as it is monotone, i.e., if the throughput time increases, then the KPI should decrease.

Definition 1 (Throughput time KPI). *Let K_{TT} be the random variable describing the throughput time, let $\mathbb{P}(K_{TT} \leq x)$ be the probability that K_{TT} is at-most x, then the throughput time KPI, denoted by F_{TT}, is defined as: $\forall_x (F_{TT}(x) = \mathbb{P}(K_{TT} \leq x))$.*

Since our models consist of a collection of runs with a weight function, we define the throughput time of a model as the weighted sum of the throughput times of the runs. The at-least-as-good relation is defined as:

Definition 2 (At-least-as-good). *Let F_{TT} and F'_{TT} be two values for the throughput time, then the former is at-least-as-good as the latter if $\forall_x (F_{TT}(x) \geq F'_{TT}(x))$.*

By having that the throughput time KPI of M is above that of M', i.e., the probability that it stays below a certain point x is greater, we guarantee that in general M has a lower throughput time. It is, however, still possible that for an individual case the throughput time of M' is better than M. We are, however, interested in an overall comparison.

Taking the models from the collection in Fig. 2, Fig. 3 shows the possible throughput time KPIs for the models. By having that the KPI of M is above M', we conclude that M is at-least-as-good as M'. For the runs and vertices, we can draw similar graphs and also for runs and vertices it holds that if one KPI is above that of the other, then the former is at-least-as-good as the latter.

We define the at-least-as-good relation first between runs and show how this can be deduced based on the structures of the runs. Afterwards, we show how the at-least-as-good relation between runs can be leveraged to the model.

3.1   At-Least-as-Good Runs

Informally when comparing the structures of the runs P and P', if P has fewer work, or has more flexibility in the order of executing activities, then P can do things faster than P' (assuming M has not less resources per activity). We operationalise this by comparing the vertices in P and P' (fewer vertices is fewer work), and by comparing the edges (flexibility in the ordering). Next to this, we need to make the requirement that we only compare vertices with the same label. When comparing two runs, we abstract from the respective models these runs are part of. In the comparison of two models, we shall elaborate on this.

Since which resource can execute which activity is defined on model level, we first introduce when a model M is at-least-as-good as M' with respect to the resource allocation, denoted by $M \geq_{ar} M'$. This is if every activity in M can be performed by at least the same resources as that activity in M'.

Definition 3 (Structurally at-least-as-good runs). *Let $M \geq_{ar} M'$, and let map be an injective mapping from vertices in P to vertices of P', then we say P is structurally at-least-as-good as P' given mapping map (denoted by $P \geq_s^{map} P'$) if and only if: (1) every vertex in P is mapped onto some vertex in P', (2) every path in P is mapped to some path in P', and (3) every vertex in P is mapped onto a vertex in P' labelled with the same activity. We say P is structurally at-least-as-good as P' (denoted by $P \geq_s P'$), if a mapping map exists such that $P \geq_s^{map} P'$.*

For Def. 3, we take two runs and compute the partial order, e.g., if we take P_1 and P_1' from Fig. 2, we obtain the partial orders in Fig. 4 (we have given the vertices from P_1' different names). Between these partial orders, we create a mapping which does not need to be unique, e.g., v_4 could also have been mapped onto v_6'. Taking also ar and ar' from Fig. 2 into account, we say P_1 is structurally at-least-as-good as P_1' since there exists a mapping such that: (a) each vertex in P_1 is mapped onto a vertex in P_1', (b) P_1 has fewer edges in the partial order, and (c) on model level, a can be executed by r_1 and r_6.

The throughput time of a vertex consists of the *queue time* and the *processing time*. Queue time is the time between the moment that a work item arrives at v and the moment the resource *starts* working it. The processing time is the

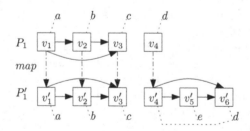

Fig. 4. The partial orders of the runs P and P' with a mapping *map* such that $P \geq_s^{map} P'$. Note that a mapping where v_4 is mapped onto v_6' would also have been fine.

time between when a resource *starts* working on a particular work item at v and the moment it is *finished*. This requires us to compare the queue times of the vertices. Therefore, we make the following assumptions:

1. the amount of arriving cases per time unit is exactly the same per run;
2. there is a single First In First Out (FIFO) queue per activity from which resources execute work items. This FIFO queue contains all the work items currently in the queues of the vertices labelled with a particular activity;
3. having more resources for an activity cannot increase the queue time of the FIFO queue for that activity if the amount of cases per time unit stays exactly the same.

Assumptions 1 and 3 allow us to compare the queue times for a particular activity. This is not yet enough for comparing the queue times between two vertices, e.g., it might be that the queue time on activity level is smaller, but, at a particular vertex, it could have increased. By having the FIFO queue, we prevent this from happening.

3.2   At-Least-as-Good Models

After showing the at-least-as-good relation between runs, we now define our at-least-as-good relation between models. The at-least-as-good relation between models holds if we can find a valid *matching graph* between the runs of the models. Graphically, a matching graph can be seen as a bipartite graph (Fig. 5). The runs of M are on the left-hand side and the runs of M' are on the right-hand side together with their weights. An edge between two runs indicates that the run on the left-hand side is at-least-as-good as the run on the right-hand side, e.g., P_1 is at-least-as-good as P_1'. As the weight of a run gives the probability of this run occurring it also gives the fraction of cases arriving for this run. Therefore, we have weights on the edges in the matching graph indicating the weight of the runs when they are compared. For instance, the 0.5 between P_2 and P_1' indicates that in the comparison of P_2 and P_1', we give them both a weight of 0.5.

As the weights on the edges in the matching graph indicate the weight of the runs when they are compared, we need to guarantee that the sum of the weights on the outgoing edges of a run is always that of the actual weight of that run. The same holds for the weights of the incoming edges of a run. The weights in the matching graph should be in $[0, 1]$. A (valid) matching graph is defined as:

Definition 4 ((Valid) Matching Graph). *Let $M \geq_{ar} M'$, then the matching graph, between M and M', denoted by $match_{M,M'}$, is a weighted collection of directed edges between vertices in M and vertices in M'. We say $match_{M,M'}$ is valid if and only if:*

- *if there is an edge between two runs in the matching graph, then the first is structurally at-least-as-good as the latter;*
- *the weights of the outgoing edges are the same as the weight of the run;*
- *the weights of the incoming edges are the same as the weight of the run.*

Using the matching graph, it becomes possible to structurally compare models with each other. If we are able to obtain a valid matching graph, we can conclude that one model is at-least-as-good as another model.

4   Related Work

By analysing redesign alternative encapsulated in a model collection, our work can be positioned on the intersection of *model collections*, and *performance evaluation*. We first discuss work from each of the two areas and then discuss work on the intersection.

In [3], the authors list the research areas within model collections. Often these model collections lack sufficient information for quantitative analysis, i.e., the context is missing, e.g., the arrival process of new cases, duration of activities, etc. If the model collection is viewed from a specific context, then our technique can be most beneficial in querying the collection of models. For instance, in PQL [4], the user can specify she is interested in models where an activity A is eventually followed by an activity B. As there might be a large amount of models returned from a query, our technique can be used to structurally order these models based on the throughput time. In this way, the user is immediately presented with the most promising models whilst adhering to the earlier specified structural requirements.

Within performance evaluation, the idea of monotonicity is not new and in queueing theory it has already been pursued [5]. In [5], the notion of monotonicity is similar but they focus on the parameters of the network and not the topology of the network. The work in [6] is similar to the work in [5] but now defined on continuous Petri nets. Since runs can be translated to Petri nets, this might be an interesting approach to use in the at-least-as-good relation between runs.

In [7], an approach is presented to evaluate when certain changes to the structure of the process model are appropriate. Starting from commonalities in reengineered processes, the paper deduces under which circumstances a change to the structure of the model is beneficial. The majority of the authors' ideas is not tailored towards throughput time but some ideas can be applied to our setting. These ideas are mainly on how resources perform their tasks.

So-called Knock-Out systems are discussed in [8] and heuristics for optimising these are defined. A Knock-Out system is a process model where after each task or group of tasks in case they are in parallel a decision is made to continue with the process or to terminate. The goal is to rearrange the tasks in such a way that

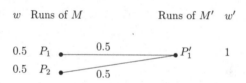

Fig. 5. An example valid matching graph.

the resource utilisation and flow time (throughput time) are optimised whilst adhering to constraints on the order of tasks encoded in precedence relations. By having an approach starting from a single model, this approach is not directly applicable to comparing two models.

In [9], a tool called KOPeR (Knowledgebased Organizational Process Redesign) is presented. KOPeR starts from a single model and identifies redesign possibilities. These redesign possibilities are simulated to obtain performance characteristics. This approach is not tailored towards directly comparing two models to determine which is at-least-as-good but our approach can be used to discard models prior to simulation.

In [10], process alternatives are analysed which have been obtained by applying redesign principles. Similar to the work in [9], our approach can aid in reducing the amount of to-be-analysed redesign options.

In our previous work, we have presented *Petra* a toolset for analysing a family of process models [11]. A family of process models is similar to a model collection but models are closer related. The work here can improve *Petra* by a-priori sorting the process models and only analyse the models most promising.

5 Conclusion

We have shown an approach to structurally compare the models within a model collection resulting in an at-least-as-good relation between models based on throughput time. This at-least-as-good relation can be used to minimise the effort to simulate a collection of highly similar models. This is particularly useful if redesigning an existing process where different improvement opportunities exist. Our approach poses a number of restrictions on the resources. In particular, we demand that resources can only execute a single activity and that they are truly dedicated to the process in question.

For future work, an interesting question is which of our assumptions can be relaxed to allow for the inclusion of a wider set of models to be considered. In particular, we want to look into whether runs have to be directed or whether they are also allowed to be undirected. This would allow us to compare different sequences of tasks and greatly increase our applicability. Furthermore, we want to extend the preliminary experimentation presented in [2] with models better reflecting reality.

References

1. Desel, J.: Validation of process models by construction of process nets. In: van der Aalst, W.M.P., Desel, J., Oberweis, A. (eds.) Business Process Management. LNCS, vol. 1806, pp. 110–128. Springer, Heidelberg (2000)
2. Schunselaar, D.M.M., Verbeek, H.M.W., van der Aalst, W.M.P., Reijers, H.A.: A Structural Model Comparison for finding the Best Performing Models in a Collection. Technical Report BPM Center Report BPM-15-05, BPMcenter.org (2015)

3. Dijkman, R.M., La Rosa, M., Reijers, H.A.: Managing Large Collections of Business Process Models - Current techniques and challenges. Computers in Industry **63**(2), 91–97 (2012)
4. ter Hofstede, A.H.M., Ouyang, C., La Rosa, M., Song, L., Wang, J., Polyvyanyy, A.: APQL: a process-model query language. In: Song, M., Wynn, M.T., Liu, J. (eds.) AP-BPM 2013. LNBIP, vol. 159, pp. 23–38. Springer, Heidelberg (2013)
5. Suri, R.: A Concept of Monotonicity and Its Characterization for Closed Queueing Networks. Operations Research **33**(3), 606–624 (1985)
6. Mahulea, C., Recalde, L., Silva, M.: Basic Server Semantics and Performance Monotonicity of Continuous Petri Nets. Discrete Event Dynamic Systems **19**(2), 189–212 (2009)
7. Buzacott, J.A.: Commonalities in Reengineered Business Processes: Models and Issues. Manage. Sci. **42**(5), 768–782 (1996)
8. van der Aalst, W.M.P.: Re-engineering Knock-out Processes. Decision Support Systems **30**(4), 451–468 (2001)
9. Nissen, M.E.: Redesigning Reengineering Through Measurement-Driven Inference. MIS Quarterly **22**(4), 509–534 (1998)
10. Netjes, M.: Process Improvement: The Creation and Evaluation of Process. Ph.D thesis, Eindhoven University of Technology (2010)
11. Schunselaar, D.M.M., Verbeek, H.M.W., Aalst, W.M.P. van der, Reijers, H.A.: Petra: a tool for analysing a process family. In: CEUR Workshop Proceedings of the PNSE 2014, vol. 1160, pp. 269–288 (2014). http://ceur-ws.org/Vol-1160/

Context-Sensitive Textual Recommendations for Incomplete Process Model Elements

Fabian Pittke[1]([✉]), Pedro H. Piccoli Richetti[2], Jan Mendling[1],
and Fernanda Araujo Baião[2]

[1] Institute of Information Business, WU Vienna, Austria
{fabian.pittke,jan.mendling}@wu.ac.at
[2] Department of Applied Informatics, Federal University of the State of Rio de
Janeiro, Rio de Janeiro, Brazil
{pedro.richetti,fernanda.baiao}@uniriotec.br

Abstract. Many organizations manage repositories of several thousand process models. It has been observed that a lot of these models have quality issues. For the model collections we have worked with, we found that every third model contains elements with incomplete element names. While prior research has proposed techniques to close gaps on the structural level, approaches that address the naming of incompletely specified model elements are missing. In this paper, we propose three strategies for naming process elements and a context-sensitive ranking to present the most relevant naming recommendations to the user. We prototypically implemented our approach and conducted an extensive user experiment with real-world process models in order to assess the usefulness of the recommendations. The results show that our approach fulfills its purpose and creates meaningful recommendations.

Keywords: Incompleteness of model elements · Context-sensitive recommendations · Business process models

1 Introduction

Nowadays, the management and documentation of business processes have become common practice in companies and led to an increasing adoption of BPM ideas [1]. In fact, the increasing adoption of BPM has stimulated the use of process models in different scenarios, such as providing knowledge for action [2], analyzing and redesigning real-world processes [3], or specifying system requirements and components [4]. However, in order to use these process models in such scenarios, they need to satisfy specific requirements with regard to layout, level of detail, and element labeling, which is typically not the case in practice [5].

A frequent problem of process models is their incompleteness with regard to the underlying business processes [6]. In general, the process model may be incomplete with regard to the structural and the textual content [7]. *Structural incompleteness* refers to missing elements of a process model, such as events,

© Springer International Publishing Switzerland 2015
H.R. Motahari-Nezhad et al. (Eds.): BPM 2015, LNCS 9253, pp. 189–197, 2015.
DOI: 10.1007/978-3-319-23063-4_13

activities, or flows relations. *Textual incompleteness* involves incomplete names of the aforementioned elements or of the model itself. While structural incompleteness has been addressed in prior research [8,9], there is the problem of textual incompleteness, which we observed in every third model of the collections we worked with. In particular, automatic support is needed for collections of several thousand models in which hundreds of activities may be incomplete [10]. So far, prior research has addressed the textual incompleteness only by automatically detecting violations according to naming conventions in multilingual repositories [11] or by automatically creating a missing name for an entire process model [12].

In this paper, we define the issue of incomplete model elements as a recommendation problem and propose an approach that supports modelers in closing these gaps. More specifically, our contribution is a two-step approach for recommending complete element names and for ranking them according to the context that is given by the process model. The first step creates a list of potential naming recommendations by applying three strategies with increasing level of context. The second step ranks these recommendations according to their appropriateness for the given process model. In order to demonstrate the capabilities and usefulness of our approach, we conducted a user experiment with real-world process models.

The paper is structured as follows. Section 2 provides an introductory example and illustrates the problem of incomplete process model elements. Section 3 introduces our approach for creating and ranking recommendations for incomplete model elements. Section 4 applies this approach to real-world process models and shows the result of a user evaluation. Section 5 reflects upon related work on process model auto-completion, before Section 6 closes the paper.

2   Problem Illustration

In order to discuss the problem of incomplete model elements and their consequences, we use the *Group Retirement* process of the SAP Reference model [13] in EPC notation (see Figure 1). Here, we omitted the events and only indicate them with dashed control-flow edges. The process begins with the creation of a master record for the respective asset. Depending on the result, the process continues with either processing the related asset acquisition, the transfer to the client, or the retirement. If one of these activities has been conducted, we assume the process to finish.

Figure 1 also highlights two bold-edged tasks that appear to be incomplete. The task *Transfer to a client* informs the reader about a transfer that needs to be conducted to complete the process. However, it is unclear if a particular object, e.g. an asset, needs to be transferred to the client or if a transfer itself needs to be planned, executed, or put into action. Depending on the situation, it would be more consistent to either name the task *Transfer of Asset to a Client* or *Transfer Processing to a Client*. Similarly, the task *Retirement* does not specify whether a particular object, for instance an asset or a asset group, needs to be

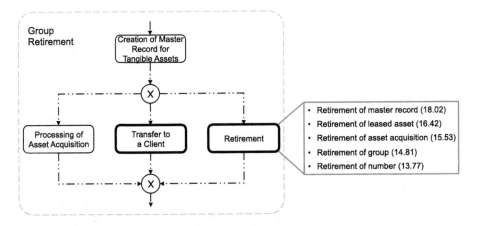

Fig. 1. Group Retirements Process Adapted from [13] with Incomplete Activities and Ranked Recommendations

retired. Apparently, both tasks fail to specify a particular action or an object as demanded by process modeling guidelines [14,15]. This not only hampers model understanding, but also leads to feedback loops between analysts and developers [16] or wrong business decisions [17].

3 Conceptual Approach

We define the issue of incomplete activities as a problem of creating and ranking recommendations for the incomplete elements [18]. We consider those elements to be incomplete if they fail to specify essential information, such as action and business object, as demanded by several studies [14,15]. The key feature of our recommendation *creation* approach is the incorporation of several context layers. Specifically, we distinguish three layers of context:

- Layer I: Local Process Model: The local context strategy considers all actions and business objects of a single process model as potential recommendations.
- Layer II: Process Model Collection: This strategy considers all process models of a repository and infers the missing business objects or actions from them.
- Layer III: External Corpora: This strategy uses a general text corpus to search for terms which frequently co-occur with the missing element.

With regard to the *ranking* of recommendations, we employ the sense clustering method of Richetti et al. [19] and apply it to all activity labels from a process model. Then, as an adaptation from the work of Bracewell et al. [20], we calculate the similarity of the recommended item with all sense clusters to obtain a ranking score that reflects the appropriateness of the recommendation to the model. This procedure is shown in Algorithm 1.

4   Evaluation

Evaluation Setup. To demonstrate the capabilities of our approach, we conduct an extensive user evaluation which aims to assess the usefulness of the recommendations. For this purpose, we outline our evaluation setup in terms of test data, prototypical implementation, evaluation design, and evaluation metrics.

Regarding the *test data*, we selected two process model collections of varying size, domain and expected quality of element naming. Table 1 summarizes the main characteristics of these process models, i.e. the SAP Reference Model [13] and the AI collection (see http://bpmai.org).

For the *prototypical implementation*, we used Java 1.7 to implement our approach. Based on the list of incomplete activities from our test collections, we created a set of potential recommendations by using the previously discussed strategies and creating a ranking of these recommendations. As far as the external corpora strategy is concerned, we used the publicly accessible version of the ANC corpus, which contains 15 million words of contemporary American English. Moreover, we also used the Stanford Tagger and Parser (see http://nlp.stanford.edu/software/) to retrieve the typed dependencies, i.e. verb object and passive sentence constructs, to identify frequent co-occurrences of words. For the ranking algorithm, we selected the Lin semantic similarity measure as it correlates best with human judgment [21].

Algorithm 1. Ranking Created Recommendations for a Process Model

---

1: **rankRecommendations(RecommendationList** R, **ProcessModel** p)
2:   $rankedRecommendations \leftarrow \emptyset$
3:   $activityLabels \leftarrow$ extractTextLabels(p)
4:   $senseClusters \leftarrow$ retrieveSenseClusters($activityLabels$)
5:   **for all** $r \in R$ **do**
6:     **for all** $C \in senseClusters$ **do**
7:       sim_p += $sim(r, C)$
8:     $rankedRecommendations \leftarrow (r, sim_p) \cup rankedRecommendations$
9:   $sortDescendingBySimValue(rankedRecommendations)$
10: **return** $rankedRecommendations$

Table 1. Demographics of the Test Collections

Characteristic	SRM	AI
No. of Models	604	1,091
No. of Activities	2,432	8,339
No. of Incomplete Activities	311	741
No. of Affected Models	184	381
Avg. No. Incomplete Activities	1.69	1.96
Modeling Language	EPC	BPMN
Domain	Independent	Academic Training
Standardization	High	Medium

Table 2. Performance of Recommendation Creation

	Local	Collection	External	Total
Useful Recommendations	58	58	33	149
Useless Recommendations	46	51	36	133

Concerning the *evaluation design*, we require the decision of humans whether a recommendation is useful given a specific process model as context. Since we face a considerably large number of incomplete labels together with an enormous list of recommendations (1052 incomplete labels with approx. 28600 recommendations), we utilize a statistical sampling among the recommendations and let the user evaluate a representative subset. Following the recommendations of Piegorsch [22] for the Jeffrey interval, we draw a random sample of 282 recommendations. Finally, we asked 5 users (2 modeling novices and 3 modeling experts) to provide us with their decision for the sample. Each user was provided with an incomplete activity and the corresponding process model in which this activity was highlighted. The participants were then asked to provide feedback for each recommendation on a 4-point-Likert-scale from *very useless (-2)* to *very useful (+2)*.

As far as *evaluation metrics* are concerned, we use precision and recall to assess the recommendations [18]. As it is fairly easy to achieve a recall of 1 (by presenting all recommendations to the user), we further distinguish between three situations: i) the most highly ranked, ii) the five most highly ranked (Top 5), and iii) all recommendations are shown to the user (Top 10). Thus, we report on the usefulness of the recommendations in general (Top 10 scenario), and on the performance of the ranking (Top 1 and Top 5 scenario). Moreover, we may also have a closer look at the performance of the recommendation creation strategies.

Results of Recommendation Creation. The performance results of the recommendation creation strategies are summarized in Table 2. The numbers show that the strategies are capable to create a large amount of relevant and useful recommendations. Apparently, the local context and the model collection strategy perform best in producing useful recommendations.

Results of Recommendation Ranking. The results of the ranking technique are shown in Table 3. In the Top 5 scenario, the number 0.57 indicates that at least two out of five Top 5 recommendations fit to the model context and are also regarded as a useful recommendation for the incomplete activity. In the Top 1 setting, the precision even amounts to 0.74 which implies that the first recommendation is already useful in three out of four cases. Depending on the setting, recall ranges between 0.15 and 0.58 which shows that even if our techniques did not create any meaningful recommendations on the first or the five highest ranked recommendations, more useful items may be included when looking at the following 5 recommendations. In the Top 10 scenario, the

Table 3. Recommendation Performance Results

	Top 1	Top 5	Top 10
No. Relevant & Retrieved	23	86	149
No. Non-relevant & Retrieved	8	66	133
No. Relevant & Not retrieved	126	63	0
Precision	0.74	0.57	0.53
Recall	0.15	0.58	1

Table 4. Top 5 Recommendations for the Group Retirement Process

Activity	Top 5 Recommendations	Ranking
Transfer to a Client	Transfer Time Specifications to a Client	25.76
	Transfer Balance Sheet Items to a Client	19.51
	Transfer Planned Sales Quantities to a Client	18.87
	Transfer Group to a Client	18.26
	Transfer Personnel Costs to a Client	16.24
Retirement	Retirement of Master Record	18.02
	Retirement of Leased Asset	16.42
	Retirement of Asset Acquisition	15.53
	Retirement of Group	14.81
	Retirement of Number	13.77

precision value of 0.53 indicates that at least half of the recommendations are useful for the given process models in our user experiment. Overall, we consider the performance of our techniques as satisfactory to address the problem at hand.

In addition to the quantitative results, we also discuss qualitative results of our recommendation techniques. Table 4 shows the five highest ranked recommendations for the two incomplete activities of Fig. 1. In general, we can infer from the context of the process model that the two activities *Transfer to a Client* and *Retirement* are most likely applied to the business objects *Group* or *Asset*. Looking at the results of our techniques, we do spot two recommendations that incorporate these two business objects. Moreover, the techniques also provide additional recommendations that make also sense in the process model, such as *Balance Sheet Items* or *Planned Sales Quantities* in case of the first activity.

5 Related Work

We discuss related work based on the classification of Kluza et al. [7], i.e. structural and textual recommendations. *Structural recommendations* propose a new model fragment to the users and connects it with already existing fragments of the process model. There is a plethora of recommendation methods available that employ different techniques. Prior research proposed similarity metrics [23], a combination of business rules and structural constraints [24], the π-calculus in combination with ontologies [25], a tagging-based approach [26], or Bayesian networks [27] for the recommendation task. Moreover, prior research also proposed modeling editors that support the user and provide recommendations based on the existing process model that was modeled so far [8,9]. Although these approaches provide model fragments including a naming, they need to rely on existing knowledge bases such as the model repository. Thus, naming errors in the knowledge base also appear in the recommendations and are multiplied when users follow these recommendations. Instead, our approach contributes to the overall quality of the knowledge base because it supports modelers in correcting process model elements with missing information.

Textual recommendations involve the recommendation of model element names based on existing process model elements. Leopold et al. proposed several naming strategies for individual model fragments or process models [12]. The authors build on linguistic features, such as dominating objects or conjunctions, to infer a suitable name. In contrast to these approaches, we do not focus on the recommendation of a general name of a process model fragment, but instead on the naming of single elements which improves the overall quality of results .

6   Conclusion

In this paper, we proposed a novel approach to address the problem of incomplete process model elements which occurs in every third process model of a model repository. In particular, we introduced three different strategies that exploit the local process model, the collection, and external sources to come up with a set of initial recommendations. In order to filter useful recommendations, we further ranked them according to their fitness to the process model context. Both aspects have been implemented in a research prototype and evaluated in an extensive user experiment by sampling process models from real world process model repositories. The quantitative and qualitative evaluation demonstrate the capabilities of creating meaningful recommendations and stimulates further endeavors for practice and research.

In future research, we first want to include additional aspects of process models, such as events and roles, in the creation of recommendations. Moreover, we also plan to enhance our techniques with machine learning approaches to improve the overall recommendation results. Second, we intend to evaluate our approach in a professional environment. In such an environment, process modelers will use our technique as a complement when designing process models. For this purpose, we want to gain a cooperation partner from practice. We hope that the research of this paper resembles an important step towards the quality assurance of process models.

References

1. Sinur, J., Hill, J.B.: Magic quadrant for business process management suites. Gartner RAS Core Research Note, 1–24 (2010)
2. Krogstie, J., Sindre, G.: Jørgensen, H.: Process models representing knowledge for action: a revised quality framework. Eur. J. Inf. Syst. **15**(1), 91–102 (2006)
3. Davenport, T.H., Short, J.E.: The new industrial engineering: Information technology and business process redesign. Sloan Mgmt. Review **31**(4), 11–27 (1990)
4. Dumas, M., Van der Aalst, W.M., Ter Hofstede, A.H.: Process-aware information systems: bridging people and software through process technology. Wiley (2005)
5. Mendling, J.: Empirical Studies in Process Model Verification. In: Jensen, K., van der Aalst, W.M.P. (eds.) Transactions on Petri Nets and Other Models of Concurrency II. LNCS, vol. 5460, pp. 208–224. Springer, Heidelberg (2009)
6. Mendling, J., Leopold, H., Pittke, F.: 25 challenges of semantic process modeling. Int. Journal of Inf. Systems and Software Eng. for Big Companies **1**(1), 78–94 (2015)
7. Kluza, K., Baran, M., Bobek, S., Nalepa, G.J.: Overview of recommendation techniques in business process modeling. Knowledge Eng. and Software Eng., 46–57 (2013)
8. Clever, N., Holler, J., Shitkova, M., Becker, J.: Towards auto-suggested process modeling-prototypical development of an auto-suggest component for process modeling tools. In: EMISA, pp. 133–145 (2013)
9. Koschmider, A., Oberweis, A.: Recommendation-based business processes design. In: Handbook on Business Process Management 1. Springer, pp. 323–336 (2015)
10. Rosemann, M.: Potential Pitfalls of Process Modeling: Part A. Business Process Management Journal **12**(2), 249–254 (2006)
11. Leopold, H., Eid-Sabbagh, R.H., Mendling, J., Azevedo, L.G., Baião, F.A.: Detection of naming convention violations in process models for different languages. Decision Support Systems **56**, 310–325 (2013)
12. Leopold, H., Mendling, J., Reijers, H.A., La Rosa, M.: Simplifying process model abstraction: Techniques for generating model names. Inf. Sys. **39**, 134–151 (2014)
13. Keller, G., Teufel, T.: SAP(R) R/3 Process Oriented Implementation: Iterative Process Prototyping. Addison-Wesley (1998)
14. Mendling, J., Reijers, H.A., van der Aalst, W.M.P.: Seven Process Modeling Guidelines (7PMG). Information and Software Technology **52**(2), 127–136 (2010)
15. Mendling, J., Reijers, H.A., Recker, J.: Activity Labeling in Process Modeling: Empirical Insights and Recommendations. Inf. Sys. **35**(4), 467–482 (2010)
16. Gordijn, J., Akkermans, H., van Vliet, H.: Business modelling is not process modelling. In: Mayr, H.C., Liddle, S.W., Thalheim, B. (eds.) ER Workshops 2000. LNCS, vol. 1921, pp. 40–51. Springer, Heidelberg (2000)
17. Barjis, J.: The importance of business process modeling in software systems design. Science of Computer Programming **71**(1), 73–87 (2008)
18. del Olmo, F.H., Gaudioso, E.: Evaluation of recommender systems: A new approach. Expert Systems with Applications **35**(3), 790–804 (2008)
19. Richetti, P.H.P., Baião, F.A., Santoro, F.M.: Declarative process mining: reducing discovered models complexity by pre-processing event logs. In: Sadiq, S., Soffer, P., Völzer, H. (eds.) BPM 2014. LNCS, vol. 8659, pp. 400–407. Springer, Heidelberg (2014)
20. Bracewell, D.B., Russell, S., Wu, A.S.: Identification, expansion, and disambiguation of acronyms in biomedical texts. In: Chen, G., Pan, Y., Guo, M., Lu, J. (eds.) ISPA-WS 2005. LNCS, vol. 3759, pp. 186–195. Springer, Heidelberg (2005)

21. Lin, D.: An information-theoretic definition of similarity. ICML **98**, 296–304 (1998)
22. Piegorsch, W.W.: Sample sizes for improved binomial confidence intervals. Computational Statistics & Data Analysis **46**(2), 309–316 (2004)
23. Hornung, T., Koschmider, A., Oberweis, A.: A recommender system for business process models. In: Workshop on Information Technologies & Systems (2009)
24. Hornung, T., Koschmider, A., Oberweis, A.: Rule-based autocompletion of business process models. In: CAiSE Forum, vol. 247 (2007)
25. Markovic, I., Pereira, A.C.: Towards a formal framework for reuse in business process modeling. In: ter Hofstede, A.H.M., Benatallah, B., Paik, H.-Y. (eds.) BPM Workshops 2007. LNCS, vol. 4928, pp. 484–495. Springer, Heidelberg (2008)
26. Hornung, T., Koschmider, A., Lausen, G.: Recommendation based process modeling support: method and user experience. In: Li, Q., Spaccapietra, S., Yu, E., Olivé, A. (eds.) ER 2008. LNCS, vol. 5231, pp. 265–278. Springer, Heidelberg (2008)
27. Bobek, S., Baran, M., Kluza, K., Nalepa, G.J.: Application of bayesian networks to recommendations in business process modeling. In: AIBP@ AI* IA, pp. 41–50 (2013)

Extracting Configuration Guidance Models from Business Process Repositories

Nour Assy[✉] and Walid Gaaloul

Computer Science Department, Telecom SudParis,
UMR 5157 CNRS Samovar, Évry, France
nour.assy@telecom-sudparise.eu

Abstract. *Configurable process models* are gaining a great importance for the design and development of reusable business processes. As these processes tend to be very complex, their configuration becomes a difficult task. Therefore, many approaches propose to build decision support systems to assist users selecting desirable configuration choices. Nevertheless, these systems are to a large extent *manually created* by domain experts, which is a time-consuming and tedious task. In addition, relying solely on the expert knowledge is not only error-prone, but also challengeable. In this paper, we propose to learn from past experience in process configuration in order to automatically extract a *configuration guidance model*. Instead of starting from scratch, a configuration guidance model assists analysts creating business-driven support systems.

1 Introduction

Motivated by the "Design by Reuse" paradigm, *configurable process models* are recently gaining momentum due to their capability of explicitly representing the common and variable parts of similar processes into one customizable model [1]. However, configurable process models cannot be freely configured as the derived variants have to be *correct*. Besides the structural and behavioral correctness [2], the configured variants need to be valid considering specific domain constraints. For instance, in a hotel reservation process, if the "online reservation" activity is excluded from the model, the "online payment" activity would be excluded, otherwise the derived variant would not be optimal or consistent. While automated approaches have been proposed for configuring process models in a structurally and semantically correct manner [3], existing domain-based approaches [4–7] still require a significant manual work.

Inspired by the need to integrate the users' experience in process configuration [1,8], we propose in this paper to benefit from previous experience in process configuration in order to automatically extract configuration guidance models. Our aim is to learn from the experience gained through past process configurations in order to extract useful and implicit knowledge that assist analysts deriving business-driven decision support systems. Following the requirements identified in [1] for a successful process configuration technique, a configuration guidance model targets to answer the following three questions: (1) *When* a

ⓒ Springer International Publishing Switzerland 2015
H.R. Motahari-Nezhad et al. (Eds.): BPM 2015, LNCS 9253, pp. 198–206, 2015.
DOI: 10.1007/978-3-319-23063-4_14

configuration decision can be taken for a configurable element? (2) *How* an element is configured given the previously selected choices? (3) *How often* a specific decision has been made?

With respect to these questions, we define a configuration guidance model as a tree-like structure with dependencies' relations and frequency information. First, the tree structure allows a "hierarchical" ordering of the configuration steps in a parent-child fashion. That is, the parent element is configured before the child element (answer of the *when*). Second, two types of dependencies relations, inclusion and exclusion, may exist between the configurable elements (i.e. tree elements), (2) between their configuration choices and (3) between the configurable elements and the configuration choices (answer of the *how*). And last, the configuration choices and dependencies relations are labeled with frequency information that reveal the probability of their presence in previous process configurations (answer of the *how often*).

The remainder of the paper is organized as follows: Section 2 introduces our configuration guidance model. In section 3, we present our automated approach to extract configuration guidance models from existing business process repositories. Related work is discussed in section 4, and we conclude in section 5.

2   Configuration Guidance Model

In this section, we give some definitions on configurable process models and introduce our configuration guidance model.

A configurable process model, is a business process model with configurable elements. A configurable element is an element whose configuration decision is made at design-time [1]. An example of a configurable process model for a simple travel booking process modeled with the configurable BPMN (c-BPMN) is illustrated in Fig. 1. The configurable elements are graphically modeled with thick lines. They are the active elements of a process modeling notation. In case of c-BPMN, configurable elements can be *activities* and/or *connectors*. A configurable activity can be included (i.e. *ON*) or excluded (i.e. *OFF*) from the process model. A configurable connector has a generic behavior which is restricted by configuration. It can be configured by (1) changing its type while preserving its behavior and/or (2) restricting its incoming (respectively outgoing) branches in case of a join (respectively split) [1]. For example, the configurable "*OR*" can be configured to any connector's type while a configurable "*AND*" can be only configured to an "*AND*". We denote by $c_1 \sqsubseteq c_2$ iff the behavior of c_1 is subsumed by that of c_2. For example $AND \sqsubseteq OR^c$, $AND \sqsubseteq AND^c$, $Seq \sqsubseteq XOR^c$ etc.

Definition 1 gives the formal definition of a configuration.

Definition 1 (Configuration *Conf*). *A configuration of a configurable node* n^c *denoted as* $Conf_{n^c}$ *is defined as:*

- *if* n^c *is an activity then* $Conf_{n^c} \in \{ON, OFF\}$;
- *if* n^c *is a connector then* $Conf_{n^c} \in \{(c', s) : (c', s) \in CT \times 2^S\}$ *where:*

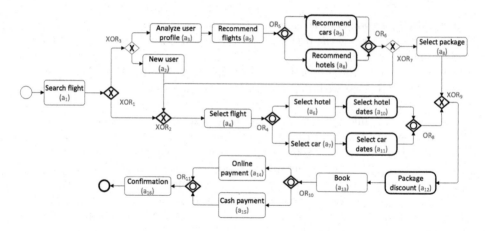

Fig. 1. An example of a configurable travel booking process

- $CT = \{OR, AND, XOR, Seq\}$ and $c' \sqsubseteq c$,
- $S = \bullet c$ *(respectively $S = c\bullet$) in case c is a join (respectively split) connector where $\bullet c$ (respectively $c\bullet$) is the set of elements in the incoming branches (respectively outgoing branches) of c.*

We denote by $\mathbb{C}_{n^c}$ the set of all configurations of the configurable element n^c according to Definition 1. For example, in Fig. 1, $\mathbb{C}_{OR_4} = \{(OR, \{a_6, a_7\}), (XOR, \{a_6, a_7\}), (AND, \{a_6, a_7\}), (Seq, \{a_6\}), (Seq, \{a_7\})\}$.

A configuration guidance model is a tree-like structure with inclusion and exclusion dependencies relations. An excerpt of the configuration guidance model for the configurable process in Fig. 1 is illustrated in Fig. 2. The tree structure allows for a "hierarchical" ordering of the configurable elements of a process model in a parent-child fashion, that is the parent element is configured before the child element (see Section 3.1). The tree elements are graphically modeled with circles. Each tree element has multiple configuration choices (see Definition 1). In our approach, we compute the probability of selection of each configuration option (see Section 3). Graphically, the configuration choices are modeled with rectangles attached to their configurable elements.

The configuration guidelines represented as inclusion and exclusion relations are graphically modeled with dotted lines and have their probability of certainty. The probability of certainty expresses to which extent an inclusion or exclusion relation is valid. Three types of inclusion relations (denoted as I_R) may exist (i) between the configurable elements (denoted as I_{c-c}), (ii) between the configuration choices (denoted as I_{cf-cf}) and (iii) between the configurable elements and the configuration choices (denoted as I_{c-cf}). The same holds for the exclusion relations E_R (see section 3.2).

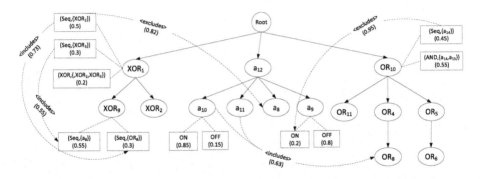

Fig. 2. An excerpt of the extracted configuration guidance model

3   Deriving Configuration Guidance Models

In this section, we present our automated approach for extracting configuration guidance models from business process repositories. Let P^c be a configurable process model and $\mathbb{P} = \{P_i : i \geq 1\}$ a set of previously derived variants from P^c. The processes in $\mathbb{P}$ can be collected by computing a similarity value (e.g. [9]). P^c and $\mathbb{P}$ are used as inputs by our algorithm (see Algorithm 1) to generate a configuration guidance model denoted as $\mathcal{G}_M^c = (\mathcal{T}^c, \mathbb{C}^*, I_R, E_R)$ where $\mathcal{T}^c$ is the tree hierarchy, $\mathbb{C}^*$ is the set of elements' configurations, I_R is the set of inclusion relations and E_R is the set of exclusion relations. The algorithm consists of a preliminary step (Line 3) then proceeds in two main steps (Lines 4-9).

Algorithm 1. Building a configuration guidance model

1: **input:** P^c, $\mathbb{P}$
2: **output:** $\mathcal{G}_M^c = (\mathcal{T}^c, \mathbb{C}^*, I_R, E_R)$
3: get inclusion associations $\mathcal{A}_\rightarrow$ and exclusion associations $\mathcal{A}_{\rightarrow\neg}$
   {**extract tree hierarchy**}
4: derive probabilistic dependency matrix $M_P = getProbabilisticMatrix(\mathcal{A}_\rightarrow)$
5: derive implication graph $G_\rightarrow = getImplicationGraph(M^p)$
6: generate tree hierarchy $\mathcal{T}^c = getTreeHierarchy(G_\rightarrow)$
   {**derive model additional information**}
7: derive configurations' probability $\mathcal{P}_{conf} = Sup(conf) : conf \in \mathbb{C}^*$
8: derive inclusion relations I_R from $G_\rightarrow$ and $\mathcal{A}_\rightarrow$
9: derive exclusion relations E_R from $\mathcal{A}_{\rightarrow\neg}$

In the preliminary step, the sets of positive and negative configuration associations denoted as $A_\rightarrow$ and $A_{\rightarrow\neg}$ respectively are extracted from $\mathbb{P}$ using *Apriori* [10], a well known algorithm for deriving association rules. This step has been elaborated in our previous work [11] and is briefly explained in the following. A positive configuration association is in the form of $conf_1 \rightarrow conf_2$

where $conf_1$ and $conf_2$ are configuration choices of different configurable elements and $conf_1 \rightarrow conf_2$ means that $conf_1$ and $conf_2$ co-occur frequently together. An example of a positive configuration association is: $Conf_{a_{10}} = ON \rightarrow Conf_{OR_8} = (Seq\{a_{10}\})$. A negative configuration association is in the form of $conf_1 \rightarrow \neg conf_2$ and means that the occurrence of the configuration $conf_1$ excludes that of $conf_2$. An example of a negative configuration association is: $Conf_{OR_{10}} = (Seq, \{a_{14}\}) \rightarrow \neg Conf_{a_9} = ON$. Well known metrics, such as *support*, *confidence* and *Conditional Probability Increment Ratio (CPIR)* are used by Apriori in order to (1) prune the set of extracted configurations to the frequently ones using a minimum support threshold, (2) generate the highly probable configuration associations using a minimum confidence threshold and (3) mine negative associations using a minimum CPIR threshold.

3.1   Extracting Tree Hierarchy

The tree hierarchy T^c consists of parent-child relations between the configurable elements. An element n_1^c is a candidate parent of a child element n_2^c if the configuration of n_2^c highly depends on that of n_1^c. The dependencies relations between the configurable elements can be derived from their configuration choices. In fact, the more are their configuration choices dependent, the more are the configurable elements dependent. The dependency of a configuration choice $conf_2$ on another configuration choice $conf_1$ corresponds to their conditional probability $P(conf_2|conf_1)$ which can be derived from the confidence of their positive configuration association $conf_1 \rightarrow conf_2 \in A_\rightarrow$. It is computed as:

$$P(conf_2|conf_1) = \frac{P(conf_1 \cap conf_2)}{P(conf_2)} = \frac{Sup(conf_1 \cup conf_2)}{Sup(conf_2)} = C(conf_1 \rightarrow conf_2) \tag{1}$$

where $P(conf_1 \cap conf_2)$ is the probability of co-occurrence of $conf_1$ and $conf_2$; $P(conf_2)$ is the probability of occurrence of $conf_2$. The probabilities are derived from the support metric computed by Apriori. Having the dependencies probabilities between the configuration choices, the conditional probability between two configurable elements n_1^c and n_2^c is computed as:

$$P(n_2^c|n_1^c) = \frac{\sum_j P(conf_{n_{2_j}^c}|n_1^c)}{\#conf_{n_{2_j}^c}} = \frac{\sum_j \frac{\sum_i P(conf_{n_{2_j}^c}|conf_{n_{1_i}^c})}{\#conf_{n_{1_i}^c}}}{\#conf_{n_{2_j}^c}} \tag{2}$$

where $P(n_2^c|n_1^c)$ is the average of the conditional probabilities between the configuration choices of n_1^c and n_2^c. $\sum_j P(conf_{n_{2_j}^c}|n_1^c)$ is the sum of the conditional probabilities between each configuration choice $conf_{n_{2_j}^c}$ of n_2^c and the configurable element n_1^c. The probability $P(conf_{n_{2_j}^c}|n_1^c)$ is in turn defined as the average of the conditional probabilities between the configuration choice $conf_{n_{2_j}^c}$ and each configuration choice $conf_{n_{1_i}^c}$ of n_1^c. It can be computed by dividing the sum of the conditional probabilities between $conf_{n_{2_j}^c}$ and each $conf_{n_{1_i}^c}$ of n_1^c by the number of $conf_{n_{1_i}}$ such that $P(conf_{n_{2_j}^c}|conf_{n_{1_i}^c}) \neq 0$; $\#conf_{n_{2_j}^c}$ is the number of the configuration choices of n_2^c such that $P(conf_{n_{2_j}^c}|n_1^c) \neq 0$.

The conditional probabilities between each pair of configurable elements are computed and stored in a *dependency probabilistic matrix* denoted as M_P. M_P is a $m \times m$ matrix where m is the number of configurable elements. An entry (i, j) in M_P corresponds to the conditional probability $P(n_j^c|n_i^c)$ where n_j^c is the element in the jth column and n_i^c is the element in the ith row. We say that a configurable element n_2^c depends on another element n_1^c denoted as $n_1^c \rightarrow n_2^c$ iff $P(n_2^c|n_1^c) \geq minP$ where $minP$ is a given threshold.

The derived dependencies' relations with their probabilities are modeled in a graph, called *implication graph* $G_\rightarrow$ [12]. The nodes in $G_\rightarrow$ correspond to the configurable elements. A weighted edge exists from a node n_1^c to n_2^c iff $n_1^c \rightarrow n_2^c$; the edge's weight is the probability $P(n_2^c|n_1^c)$. An excerpt of $G_\rightarrow$ derived from a set of dependencies relations is illustrated in Fig. 3a. Having $G_\rightarrow$, the tree

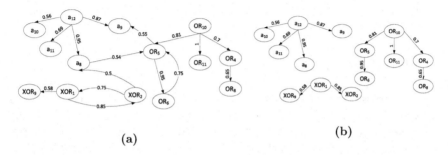

(a)   (b)

Fig. 3. (a) An implication graph and (b) its derived optimal spanning tree

hierarchy corresponds to extracting a spanning tree (called arborescence for directed graphs) [12]. Since, there exist multiple possible spanning trees, we aim at deriving the optimal hierarchy that maximizes the dependencies' relations weights. The problem can be mapped to finding the *minimal spanning tree* which can be solved using existing algorithms such as Edmonds' algorithm [13] and efficient implementations such as [14]. Figure 3b illustrates an excerpt of the optimal spanning tree extracted from the implication graph in Fig. 3a which contains multiple trees. In this case, an artificial root node is added and connected to them in order to obtain the tree hierarchy in Fig. 2.

3.2   Deriving Additional Model Information

In this section, we complete the remaining configuration guidance model information, i.e. the configuration choices probabilities and the inclusion/exclusion relations and their probabilities. The configuration choices $\mathbb{C}^*$ are the set of configurations extracted by Apriori and and their probabilities are equal to the Apriori computed support. For example, in Fig. 2, the configuration $(Seq, \{XOR_2\}) \in \mathbb{C}^*$ has a probability $P = 0.5$. The three types of inclusion relations and their probabilities are defined as follows [1]

- $I_{c-c} = \{n_1^c \rightarrow n_2^c\}$: $n_1^c, n_2^c \in N^c \wedge n_1^c \rightarrow n_2^c \in G_\rightarrow \setminus T^c$, i.e. the inclusion relations between the configurable elements are those that are present in the implication graph but have been excluded when deriving the tree hierarchy. The probability $\mathcal{P}_R(n_1^c \rightarrow n_2^c) = P(n_2^c|n_1^c)$.
- $I_{cf-cf} = \{conf_1 \rightarrow conf_2\}$: $conf_1 \in \mathbb{C}_{n_x^c}, conf_2 \in \mathbb{C}_{n_y^c} \wedge (conf_1 \rightarrow conf_2 \in A_\rightarrow) \wedge (\exists conf_1' \in \mathbb{C}_{n_x^c}, conf_2' \in \mathbb{C}_{n_y^c} : conf_1' \rightarrow conf_2' \notin A_\rightarrow)$, i.e. the inclusion relations between the configuration choices are those that appear in the positive configuration associations but whose configurable elements are not fully dependent. $\mathcal{P}_R(conf_1 \rightarrow conf_2) = P(conf_2|conf_1)$.
- $I_{c-cf} = \{n^c \rightarrow conf\}$: $n^c \in N^c, conf \in \mathbb{C}^* \wedge \forall conf' \in \mathbb{C}_{n^c} : conf' \rightarrow conf \in A_\rightarrow$. The probability $\mathcal{P}_R(n^c \rightarrow conf) = P(conf|n^c)$, i.e. an inclusion relation exists between a configurable element n^c and a configuration choice $conf$ iff each configuration choice of n^c has a dependency relation to $conf$. The same holds for the relations $conf \rightarrow n^c \in I_{c-cf}$. The probability $\mathcal{P}_R(n^c \rightarrow conf) = P(conf|n^c)$.

4   Related Work

Business process variability modeling [15] is an emergent topic that is being increasingly addressed by academic and industrial researchers for enabling design-time process flexibility. Our work is based on configurable process models proposed in [1]. The authors in [1] define the requirements for a configurable process modeling technique. They highlight the need for configuration guidelines that may include the configuration steps order, the interrelationships between the configuration decisions and the frequency information that come from system users. In our work, we follow these requirements and propose an automated approach to learn a configuration guidance model depicting such information.

La Rosa et al. [4] propose a questionnaire-driven approach for configuring reference models. They describe a framework to capture the system variability based on a set of questions defined by domain experts and answered by designers. Asadi et al. [7] and Gröner et al. [6] propose to use feature models for modeling the variability and the configuration constraints. The constraints are defined by experts and formalized in Description Logic expressions. Templates and configuration rules are used by Kumar et al. [5] in order to configure a reference process template using configuration rules which are defined and validated by experts.

In summary, existing approaches for assisting the configuration of process models require an expensive manual work from experts. These approaches are only based on the expert knowledge while, as highlighted in [1,8], a successful process configuration has to integrate the experience gained through previous

---

[1] The exclusion relations can be derived in the same way using $A_{\rightarrow\neg}$.

configurations. Therefore, in this paper, we address this research gap by proposing an automated approach for assisting the configuration of process models using previously configured processes.

5 Conclusion and Future Works

In this paper, we proposed an automated approach for extracting configuration guidance models from process model repositories. Our work is motivated by the need of (1) automated approaches on the one hand and (2) information originating from previous process configurations on the other hand in the creation of configuration decision support systems. Experimental results show that we generate accurate configuration guidance models.

The current limitation of our approach lies in the the lack of an empirical evaluation. In this regard, we are currently conducting experiments in order to evaluate the accuracy of our extracted configuration guidance models. In parallel, we are working with industrial partners and our team members in order to validate the approach from a business perspective.

References

1. Rosemann, M., van der Aalst, W.M.P.: A configurable reference modelling language. Inf. Syst. **32**(1), 1–23 (2007)
2. van der Aalst, W.M.P.: The application of petri nets to workflow management. Journal of Circuits, Systems, and Computers **8**(1), 21–66 (1998)
3. van der Aalst, W.M.P., Lohmann, N., Rosa, M.L.: Ensuring correctness during process configuration via partner synthesis. Inf. Syst. **37**(6), 574–592 (2012)
4. La Rosa, M., van der Aalst, W., Dumas, M., ter Hofstede, A.: Questionnaire-based variability modeling for system configuration. Software & Systems Modeling **8**(2), 251–274 (2009)
5. Kumar, A., Yao, W.: Design and management of flexible process variants using templates and rules. Comput. Ind. **63**(2), 112–130 (2012)
6. GröNer, G., BošKović, M.: Silva Parreiras, F., GašEvić, D.: Modeling and validation of business process families. Information Systems **38**(5), 709–726 (2013)
7. Asadi, M., Mohabbati, B., Gröner, G., Gasevic, D.: Development and validation of customized process models. Journal of Systems and Software **96**, 73–92 (2014)
8. Gottschalk, F.: Configurable Process Models. Ph.D thesis, Eindhoven University of Technology, December 2009
9. Weidlich, M., Mendling, J., Weske, M.: Efficient consistency measurement based on behavioral profiles of process models. IEEE Trans. Softw. Eng. **37**(3), 410–429 (2011)
10. Agrawal, R., Srikant, R.: Fast algorithms for mining association rules in large databases. In: VLDB, pp. 487–499 (1994)
11. Assy, N., Gaaloul, W.: Configuration rule mining for variability analysis in configurable process models. In: Franch, X., Ghose, A.K., Lewis, G.A., Bhiri, S. (eds.) ICSOC 2014. LNCS, vol. 8831, pp. 1–15. Springer, Heidelberg (2014)

12. She, S., Lotufo, R., Berger, T., Wasowski, A., Czarnecki, K.: Reverse engineering feature models. In: ICSE (2011)
13. Edmonds, J.: Optimum Branchings. Journal of Research of the National Bureau of Standards **71B**, 233–240 (1967)
14. Gabow, H.N., Galil, Z., Spencer, T., Tarjan, R.E.: Efficient algorithms for finding minimum spanning trees in undirected and directed graphs. Combinatorica **6**(2), 109–122 (1986)
15. Rosa, M.L., van der Aalst, W.M., Dumas, M., Milani, F.P.: Business process variability modeling: A survey. ACM Computing Surveys (2013)

BPM in Industry

Web-Based Modelling and Collaborative Simulation of Declarative Processes

Morten Marquard[1], Muhammad Shahzad[1,2], and Tijs Slaats[1,3(✉)]

[1] Exformatics A/S, Dag Hammarskjölds Allé 13, 2100 Copenhagen Ø, Denmark
{mmq,ts}@exformatics.com
http://www.exformatics.com
[2] TEO International, Islamabad, Pakistan
muhammad.shahzad@teo-intl.com
[3] IT University of Copenhagen, Copenhagen, Denmark

Abstract. As a provider of Electronic Case Management solutions to knowledge-intensive businesses and organizations, the Danish company Exformatics has in recent years identified a need for flexible process support in the tools that we provide to our customers. We have addressed this need by adapting DCR Graphs, a formal declarative workflow notation developed at the IT University of Copenhagen. Through close collaboration with academia we first integrated execution support for the notation into our existing tools, by leveraging a cloud-based process engine implementing the DCR formalism. Over the last two years we have taken this adoption of DCR Graphs to the next level and decided to treat the notation as a product of its own by developing a stand-alone web-based collaborative portal for the modelling and simulation of declarative workflows. The purpose of the portal is to facilitate end-user discussions on how knowledge workers really work, by enabling collaborative simulation of processes. In earlier work we reported on the integration of DCR Graphs as a workflow execution formalism in the existing Exformatics ECM products. In this paper we report on the advances we have made over the last two years, we describe the new declarative process modelling portal, discuss its features, describe the process of its development, report on the findings of an initial evaluation of the usability of the tool, resulting from a tutorial on declarative modelling with DCR Graphs that we organized at last years BPM conference and present our plans for the future.

Keywords: Declarative modelling · DCR graphs · Web-based process modelling · Collaborative process simulation · Process flexibility · Knowledge work

Authors listed alphabetically. This work has been supported by the Danish Agency for Science, Technology and Innovation through an industrial PhD grant. We gratefully acknowledges helpful comments from Søren Debois, Thomas Hildebrandt and anonymous reviewers.

© Springer International Publishing Switzerland 2015
H.R. Motahari-Nezhad et al. (Eds.): BPM 2015, LNCS 9253, pp. 209–225, 2015.
DOI: 10.1007/978-3-319-23063-4_15

1   Introduction

Former secretary of labor in the Clinton administration, Robert Reich, argued that the competitiveness of nations depends on the education and skills of its people and on the infrastructure connecting people with one another [25]. He segmented the work force into three types of work: (1) routine production services, (2) "in-person" services and (3) "symbolic- analytic" services. Today we often refers to symbolic analysts as knowledge workers [3,6], the employees which contribute to most of the economic growth in developed economies. Supporting these knowledge workers and ensuring easy and smooth collaboration is important to compete globally. Enabling knowledge workers to work smarter, rather than just harder, involves various IT infrastructures to ensure communication and collaboration.

Traditional process initiatives, typically seen in the automobile industry, focus on routine production services [25]. While increasing productivity and cutting costs in primary industries is important to compete globally, it is even more important to provide similar support for knowledge workers. Comparing tools and processes used in the automobile industry with knowledge intensive industries reveals a great disparity: the infrastructure supporting routine production services is much more advanced what is found supporting knowledge workers. Often knowledge workers use email as their primary communication and collaboration tool, and studies shows that knowledge workers on average spend 28 percentage of the time reading and responding to emails [16]. This is hardly efficient and makes it hard to compete in a global economy, especially as knowledge workers in the developing countries have cheap and easy access to secretaries and other in-person services, and therefore will be better serviced than knowledge workers in the developed countries. The engineers, doctors and financial analysts in the western world simply need to work harder as they cannot leverage cheap primary services. Therefore, providing infrastructure and technologies for knowledge workers which automate their more mundane tasks is critical to compete globally. McKinsey Global Institute estimate a productivity gain of 20-25 percentage on average knowledge workers by using modern *social technologies* [16].

Efforts to make knowledge workers more productive often involve attempts to transfer and adopt the technologies used in routine production services, in particular process technologies are commonly based on the industry standard Business Process Management Notation (BPMN) [23,34]. The BPMN notation is founded in the concept of flow; the idea that to describe the behaviour of a process one needs to describe how control passes (flows) between its activities. It has been observed however that the flow-based paradigm is not ideal for knowledge-centred processes: knowledge workers deal with very diverse problems which rarely "fit the mould", instead of being given predefined sequences of tasks they often need to decide themselves what actions they should take based on their expert knowledge. The IT systems that support them therefore need to be able of offering a large degree of flexibility. [21,26,35] Such flexible processes exhibit a large degree of variability, exhibited in flow-based models by many different possible paths and states, which leads to so-called *spaghetti models* which are no longer understandable by users.

As an alternative a new *declarative* or *constraint-based* paradigm has been proposed[8, 12, 22, 24, 30]. The declarative paradigm is grounded in the idea that one should only model the constraints (or business rules) of a process and then derive the possible paths from the constraints. Any execution allowed by the constraints is a valid execution of the process model, i.e. the workers are given maximal flexibility within the rules.

Exformatics is a Danish software developer providing Electronic Case Management (ECM) solutions to knowledge-intensive businesses and organizations such as LEGO, ISS, ministries and government institutions. Already from their founding they have realised the need for flexible processes support in their tools and in initial versions this was solved by very rough process definitions that only grouped tasks within specific phases, but otherwise left maximal flexibility to the users. They realised that this approach lacked the ability of adding more meaningful rules and constraints to their processes and through participation in a Danish knowledge network *Infinit* [1], which supports interaction and dissemination between academia and industry they came into contact with the Process Models group at the IT University of Copenhagen (ITU) which was working on related issues and in particular has developed the DCR Graphs notation [5, 8, 10, 19]. DCR Graphs is a declarative notation for flexible processes that sets itself apart from other declarative notations such as Declare by utilizing only a very small set of constraints, yet yielding high formal expressive power. In addition it offers a straightforward run-time semantics formalized as transformations of the graphs, which means that its visual representation can be used both at design-time to represent process definitions and at run-time to represent process instances, in a similar manner as Petri-nets.

Exformatics became very interested in the work on DCR Graphs and how they could employ the notation to leverage flexible processes. Therefore they initiated a close collaboration with the researchers at ITU, facilitated through various Danish funding mechanisms supporting university-industry collaboration [4]. Most notable among these was a 3 years industrial PhD project, where Exformatics employed a PhD student to do research on flexible process notations while at the same time being enrolled at ITU.

During this project DCR Graphs were first integrated into the existing ECM tools as a formalism for process-control by implementing a cloud-based process engine based on the DCR Graphs semantics[28]. At the same time the student also developed a prototype tool for the graphical modelling of DCR Graphs which was well received within the company and opened the road to further adaptation of DCR Graphs not only as an internalized notation for standardized processes, but also as a graphical notation for designing processes as a part of business consultancy services, in essence making DCR Graphs a product of their own.

Engaging end-users in the process dialogue is hard as process notations can be hard to understand for the users, but lack of end-user engagement often leads to process implementations not supporting the real business needs. Misunderstandings over the semantics of notations and assumed implicit behaviour that is not explicitly modelled lead to users interpreting processes in different ways, ultimately leading to failure of many process initiatives. In order to avoid such issues we aimed to include extensive support for collaborative process simulation in our tools. To ensure employee engagement we allow the users to *play* the processes like a computer game among co-workers. The team of co-workers can define the process using a declarative process-model and immediately start process simulation in order to verify whether the modelled processes meet their expectations and the real world needs. End-users often asks questions like *what happens if...* or *can we do ...*, such questions can be simulated in the tool and subsequently the process model can be adjusted to meet the increased understanding of the process. Rather than requiring modellers to "know" a precise and correct model from day one, we empower them to iteratively model the processes through an increased understanding of the (possibly changing) business rules and requirements.

To support such flexible, interactive and run-time adaptable process modelling activities and facilitating end-user discussions on how knowledge workers really work we developed a stand-alone web-based collaborative portal for the modelling and simulation of declarative workflows. This paper focuses on this new declarative process portal. We start by giving a short introduction to DCR Graphs. We then give a detailed overview of the portal and its features, discuss the development processes that led to its creation and discuss initial efforts at evaluating the usability of the portal. We finalize by discussing our plans for the future, both in terms of new features to the portal and new avenues of research.

1.1   Related Work

Several web-based commercial tools exist for the modelling of business processes; such as Signavio, IBM Blueworks Live and Oracles Business Process Management Suite. However, to our knowledge DCRGraphs.net is the first web-based modelling tool aimed in particular at constraint-based notations for flexible processes.

The latest version of BPMN [23] includes support for so-called *ad hoc subprocesses*, providing a method for adding pockets of flexibility to a BPMN diagram and supporting constraints similar to the condition and response relation of DCR Graphs [9]. In addition there is an currently ongoing effort by the Object Management Group to develop a new standard notation aimed in particular at case management and adding support for flexible processes to BPMN, called the Case Management Model And Notation (CMMN) [22]. The work on CMMN is strongly inspired on the research on the Guard-Stage-Milestone (GSM) model [13] developed at IBM Research, which in turn is based on earlier work on artifact-centric business processes [2]. While GSM is foremost a data-centric model it has some declarative influences as well, the main elements of the notation are *stages* containing tasks, which are either active or inactive based on *guards* defined on the stage. The acceptance criteria of a stage are modelled through *milestones*, which can in turn be part of the guards of other stages. Compared to GSM, DCR Graphs put more focus on the behaviour of tasks and events than on the data of the process.

Declarative process languages came to prominence in the BPM community through the development of the Declare notation [24,31,33]. Declare consists of a relatively large set of constraints typically found in business processes, which are traditionally mapped to Linear Temporal Logic(LTL) formulae, although other formalizations also exist [15,17,18]. DCR Graphs differ from Declare in the number of symbols used in the notation: Declare uses a large number of constraint templates, each with their own symbol whereas DCR Graphs are limited to 5 elementary relations. Also, because the runtime semantics of DCR Graphs are given in terms of transformations on their marking, it is straightforward to visualize and reason about the simulation of DCR Graphs. Exformatics adopted DCR Graphs because of their close research collaboration with ITU, giving them direct access to the researchers behind the notation, because they preferred a more concise notation and put particular importance into reasoning about the runtime of processes through simulation. We are not aware of any published work reporting on industrial use of Declare.

2   Hierarchical DCR Graphs

In this section we exemplify DCR Graphs and their semantics using an abstracted version of the main case management process of the Exformatics ECM system. In figure 1 we start with the root process. The main building blocks of a DCR Graph are the events (or activities), drawn as a box with a bar on top. The box contains the name of the activity and the bar contains the roles that are able of executing it. Our process has a single role: the case manager. Activities can be grouped together by nesting them under a super-activity, in which case only the atomic activities are executable. Such groupings are a graphical shorthand for applying constraints or properties to multiple activities at once: in our process the super-activity Case having the role Case Manager

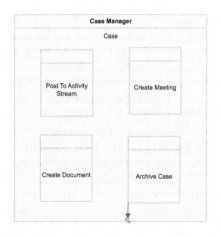

Fig. 1. Root Case Management Process

means that the case manager is able of executing every atomic activity nested under it. Constraints or business rules can be added to the model by adding one of five relations, drawn as directed arrows between activities. The root process contains a single relation, the *exclusion* relation ($\rightarrow\%$) from Archive Case to *Case*. The exclusion relation is used to remove activities from the process, for example to close tasks that should no longer be executable, or to model an exclusive choice between two activities. Because the super-activity Case acts as a grouping the exclusion relation applies to all five of the underlying activities. This means that after archiving the case no further actions can be taken as it removes all activities from the process. Following the declarative paradigm unconstrained activities can be done at any time and any number of times, therefore the process supports many different runs: one could for example upload two

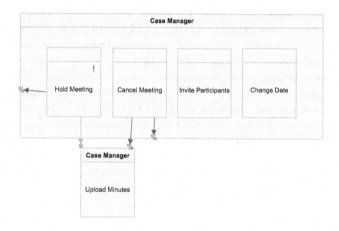

Fig. 2. Meeting Sub-process

documents, create a meeting, upload another document and finally archive the case. Note that while `Archive Case` closes the process by removing all activities, it is not required to happen and the previous example run would also have been valid if it had not ended by archiving the case.

Figure 2 shows the process for organizing a meeting. Similarly to the previous example we use the exclusion relation to remove activities from the process when they are no longer relevant: the activities `Invite Participants`, `Change Date`, `Hold Meeting` and `Cancel Meeting` are grouped together and removed by either holding or cancelling the meeting. Only after holding the meeting is it possible to upload the minutes of the meeting, this is modelled by the condition relation ($\rightarrow\bullet$) which states that before `Upload Minutes` can be done we first need to have done `Hold Meeting`. `Cancel Meeting` excludes this activity since it does not make sense to upload minutes for a meeting that was cancelled. Finally the goal of the meeting sub-process is that we either eventually hold the meeting or cancel it. This is modelled by making `Hold Meeting` a *pending response*, drawn by adding a blue exclamation mark to the activity box. A pending response denotes that an activity should either happen or be removed from the process before we can finish or close the process; in our example either `Hold Meeting` needs to be done or `Cancel Meeting` needs to exclude it.

Figure 3 shows the process for managing a document in the ECM. To edit the document a user needs to check it out, the file is then locked until it is checked in

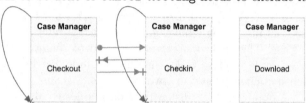

Fig. 3. Document Handling Sub-process

again. This is modelled using first the exclusion relation to exclude each activity when they happen (meaning they can only be done once at a time) and the

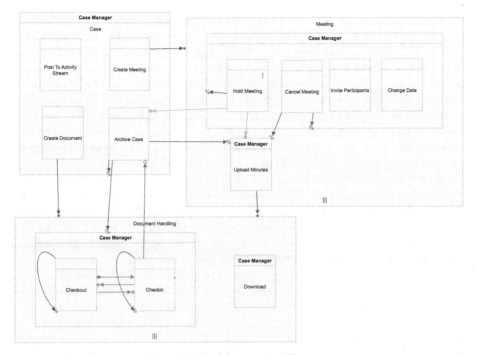

Fig. 4. Case Management Process

two new *include relations* (→+) between the two activities. The include relation is used to add removed activities back into the process, so in this case, when `Checkout` happens, it removes itself and adds `Checkin` to the process and vice versa. Finally when a file is checked out we always want it to be checked in again before the process can finish. We model this through the *response relation* (•→) which is a dynamic version of the pending response that we introduced earlier. It denotes that after `Checkout` is executed we require `Checkin` to be executed (or excluded) at least once before we can close the process. It is always possible to download the document through the unconstrained `Download` activity.

Finally we would like to tie all these process together into a single process describing the handling of a case in the ECM system. For this we use an extension called *hierarchical DCR (Hi-DCR) Graphs*, which adds a notion of spawnable multi-instance sub-processes. Figure 4 shows the case management process as a Hi-DCR Graph. The main new concept are the two new sub-processes `Meeting` and `Document Handling`, drawn as a box without a bar on top of it. These are essentially DCR Graphs inside the root process that need to be initialized through the new *spawn relation* (→*), creating a new copy of the sub-process for each time it is spawned. In the example the activity `Create Meeting` spawns a new copy of `Meeting` each time it is executed and `Create Document` and `Create Minutes` create a new `Document Handling` process each time they are executed.

When one has a relation between an activity of a sub-process and an activity of its parent, the relation will apply to each instance of the activity. For example a case can not be archived while there are pending meetings; this is modelled by adding a condition from `Hold Meeting` to `Archive Case`, meaning that while there is at least one `Hold Meeting`-activity that has not yet been executed or excluded (by cancel meeting), it is impossible to execute `Archive Case`. In a similar manner it should not be possible to archive the case while documents are checked out. We model this through the *milestone relation* ($\rightarrow\diamond$), which blocks an activity as long as some other activity is pending. Because of the response relation from `Checkout` to `Checkin`, there will be a pending response on the latter whenever the file is checked out. The milestone from `Checkin` to `Archive Case` ensures that as long as there is at least one instance of `Checkin` that is pending, we can not archive the case. Finally, to archive the case, `Archive Case` excludes all instances of all activities in `Document Handling`, except for `Download` as it should still be possible to download files. All instances of `Upload Minutes` are also excluded, it is not necessary to exclude the other activities in `Meeting` as this will already have been done by holding or cancelling the meeting and unless one of these has been executed the case can not be archived.

The example DCR Graphs from figures 1, 2 and 3 are all available on DCR-Graphs.net, the Hi-DCR Graph in figure 4 was drawn using the development version of the portal which is not yet ready for release.

3   The DCR Graphs Process Portal

The DCR Graphs Portal [1] provides an online web based tool for the modelling, sharing and simulation of DCR graphs.

To use the portal one can register as a new user or log in using a LinkedIN or Facebook account. After registering users can maintain their profile, create DCR Graphs, connect to friends and colleagues and simulate DCR Graphs either individually or collaboratively with other users. Users can communicate with each other through a main *activity stream* (similar to Facebook's news feed) and local activity streams for each DCR Graph.

The portal contains a graphical web-based editor which supports the modelling of all aspects of a DCR Graph, such as the activities, relations, roles and data. A number of unique features have been added to help improve the presentation and understanding of the modelled processes: activities and relations can be assigned a numerical *level*, which can be used to control the level of detail at which one wishes to view the model. In addition activities and relations can be assigned one or more groups and a model can be filtered based on these groups or specific roles. To facilitate discussion and collaboration among co-workers, easy access to the activity stream of the graph has been provided from within the editor. The editor also supports revisions management, tracking all changes and providing users the ability to designate major versions. Older versions can be viewed graphically and rolled-back to. There is a wizard available to rapidly create a new graph. The editor supports importing XML files (following the standard provided in [28]) and can export DCR Graphs as XML, SVG and

---

[1] www.dcrgraphs.net

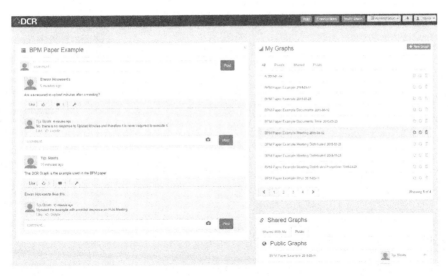

Fig. 5. Portal

PNG files. Models can be shared with friends an co-workers or made publicly available to all users of the portal.

From the editor the user can start to simulate a model. When initiating a new simulation the user can assign a user to each of the roles of the model, these can be human users or automated users. To simulate a model individually one simply leaves all the roles assigned to oneself, but by inviting friends or co-workers one can start a collaborative simulation with different people playing different roles in the process. Currently two automated users are provided, an eager user that will perform any available activity that is either required or has not yet been done before and a lazy user that only performs activities which are currently required. By assigning all roles to automated users one can start a fully automated simulation. Simulations can be paused, at which point it is possible to dynamically edit the model, resumed and restarted and a record of each simulation is kept in the system which can be viewed and replayed. During simulation the runtime of the DCR Graph is updated and visualized on-the-fly, enabled activities which have either not been executed before, or are currently required are given a green border to highlight them to the user. In addition there is a task list which displays all enabled or pending activities, grouped in the following order: 1) enabled and pending event, 2) pending but blocked events, 3) enabled events which have not been executed earlier and 4) enabled events which have been executed earlier (but can be repeated). The activities executed are logged in the Execution Log, which can be used later to replay the simulation. The task list also displays the current accepting state of the process, i.e. whether the process can be considered completed or more activities need to be executed to finish the process. The participants in the process are listed during simulation with the roles they play in the current simulation.

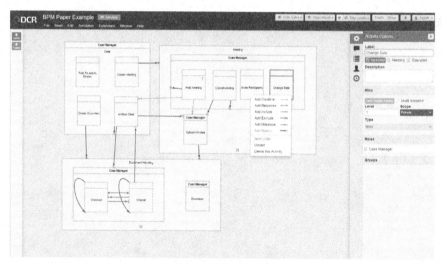

Fig. 6. Editor

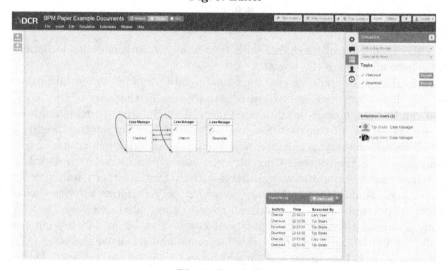

Fig. 7. Simulation

In order to support private usage by customers and universities (for which academic licensing possibilities are available) we've extended the portal to support private organizations with their own users, graphs, etc. This enables organisations to set up their own version of the portal, inviting their employees and students and model and share processes within a closed community. Users can belong to several organisations, including the *public* organisation which is available to all users by default.

In order to enable and encourage 3rd party development, such as student projects, we provide an application plug-in framework for the portal. We foresee a series of additional features such as model checking (dead- and live-lock checking) and extended process visualisation being facilitated by this framework.

The framework has recently been used to develop an app supporting flow-based visualizations of DCR Graphs and searching for suitable "happy paths" based on different search criteria as part of a research project performed in cooperation with the IT university of Copenhagen and a Danish credit institution. More details on the framework can be found at the wiki[2].

4   Development of the DCR Portal

Development of the portal has been carried out using the Scrum methodology, through close co-operation between the development team at TEO International in Pakistan and the design team at Exformatics in Denmark. We used short 2 to 3 week sprints with frequent updates of the portal. Different technologies have been used to achieve the solution so far, including: JavaScript with Raphaël, jQuery, Microsoft .NET with MVC 4, REST services and the existing DCR Process Engine which was developed in a mix of C# and F#. We are currently working on the 10th major version of the portal, which will include support for sub-processes.

The DCR Editor is purely a JavaScript application which utilizes REST services developed in .NET to communicate with the web-server. The editor uses the Raphaël Library to visualize the graphs in SVG-format. Simulation of the graphs uses DCR process engine services which have been upgraded over the time to support newly added features. The wrapper of the Editor, which provides listing of the graphs, sharing, activity stream and friendship functionalities is developed in MVC 4 .NET. Simulation in Editor uses realtime notifications, updates with the help of Signal R which uses WebSockets where possible. The editor utilizes caching techniques to minimize the requests to server and improve the performance of the product.

5   Evaluation

At last years BPM conference we organized a tutorial on flexible business process modelling using DCR Graphs where we first gave an introduction to DCR Graphs, exemplifying the notation through a demo of the process portal, then asked the audience to try out the portal for themselves by doing a number of exercises and finally requested their feedback in the form of a questionnaire.

---

[2] wiki.dcrgraphs.net

Twelve people filled out the questionnaire, eleven identified as researchers and one as a practitioner. On average the attendants had been active in the BPM field for 5 years, ranging from 6 months to 14 years. Five people had previous experience with DCR Graphs, whereas 9 people had previous experience with declarative modelling notations in general.

Table 1. Understandability of Concepts

	Very Easy	Easy	Neutral	Hard	Very hard
Events (Activities)	4	5	2	1	
Roles	5	5	1	1	
Condition Relation	2	7	2		
Response Relation	2	5	3	2	
Inclusion Relation	1	2	4	5	
Exclusion Relation	1	4	5	2	
Pending response	1	5	4	1	
Nesting		6	2	3	

In the first set of questions we asked the audience if they found the underlying concepts of DCR Graphs hard or easy to understand. We specifically asked them to only comment on the understandability

Table 2. Understandability of Notation

	Very Easy	Easy	Neutral	Hard	Very hard
Events(Activities)	3	7	2		
Roles	3	4	4	1	
Condition Relation		6	3	3	
Response Relation		8	2	2	
Inclusion Relation		5	5	2	
Exclusion Relation		6	5	1	
Pending response		7	3	2	
Nesting	1	6	2	3	

of the concept and not the graphical notation used. The results are shown in table 1, perhaps not surprisingly most found activities (9) and roles (10) easy or very easy to understand. Of the relations the participants found the condition the easiest to understand, 9 people scored it easy or very easy, followed by the response (7), exclusion (5) and finally inclusion (3). It is noteworthy that despite being closely related the audience found the inclusion relation significantly harder to understand then the exclusion relation, we conjecture that the exclusion more closely matches familiar concepts such as mutual exclusion, whereas the inclusion relation was more novel to the audience.

In the next set of questions we asked the audience to rate the understandability of the graphical notation. Table 2 shows the results,

Table 3. Usability of the Tool

	Very Easy	Easy	Neutral	Hard	Very hard
Modelling Screen		11	1		
Adding Friends	1	6	2	1	
Individual simulation		11	1		
Collaborative simulation		6	2	1	

overall activities and roles were found to be easy or very easy to understand, whereas the users were more neutral about the notation of the relations. The condition and response scored higher then the inclusion and exclusion, we conjecture that this may be because many attendants were already familiar with the precedence and response constraints in Declare.

In our final set of questions, whose results are shown in table 3, we focussed on the tool itself and asked the participants to rate the usability of its various components. Both the modelling and simulation functionality scored high, with 11 people finding them easy to use and the final participant being neutral on their usability. Adding connections scored a little less well, with 7 people finding this part of the tool easy or very easy to use. Collaborative simulation scored only slightly lower, with 6 participants finding it easy to use, out of 9 people answering this particular question.

The portal has been used for teaching a process modelling course at ITU, with 75 users signed up. While we have not organized a similar questionnaire for the students, overall the experience has been positive and no major issues were encountered in using the portal. More recently we also initiated a collaboration with the Federal University of the State of Rio de Janeiro (UNIRIO) where they use the portal for teaching a similar course.

6   Future Work

We recognize that it is too early to draw strong conclusions from the questionnaire based on a small number of academic participants. In the near future we plan to run multiple industrial workshops following the same structure as the tutorial, both as a method for raising awareness of the portal and attracting potential new customers and as a way to receive additional feedback from actual practitioners which will allow us to make stronger claims regarding its usability.

Further initiatives focus on:

Sub-processes
The ability to split processes into sub-processes which can be instantiated and executed separately from the parent process. Experience from previous use cases [7] shows that sub-processes are important to model processes in an easy to describe and understandable way. Work on this item is already ongoing and we expect to have sub-processes included in the live version of the portal by the summer of 2015.

Verification
Various algorithms have been developed to analyse DCR graphs for dead- and live-lock [11,20]. Adding such analysis to the portal is important not only to support modelling DCR Graphs in the design phase, but also to support run-time adaptation of DCR Graphs within production systems such as the Exformatics Electronic Case Management tool. When the user adds new activities and/or constraints the resulting model should be checked for live- and dead-lock.

Gamification

As suggested by Keith Swenson, author of various books on Adaptive Case Management [29], we intend to investigate adding *gamification* features to the portal by allowing participants to *earn* points and credits through active participation in the various aspects of the portal, for example helping other users with relevant questions or modelling and publishing popular models of common processes.

Collaborative Editing

Several users, in particular students (who commonly work in groups), have requested support for the collaborative editing of process models. As this goes well along with collaborative simulation this is a feature we're likely to add in the near future.

Time

An extension to DCR Graphs supporting time and deadlines has been proposed in the past [11]. We aim to support this extension in the portal, both as a part of the editor and simulation, for which we will provide the ability to scale, manually progress and pause time so that long-term processes can be simulated more quickly.

Resources and Stochastic Models

DCR Graphs provide a constraint-based notation that allows one to describe and find all possible paths through a model, but to assist the users enacting the process it would be useful to inform them which paths the most efficient, similarly to how a route-finding tool such as Google Maps can find the fastest route between two points based on maps that describe any possible path. Simply finding the path requiring the least amount of activities is in most cases not enough, as not all activities consume the same amount of resources. To improve the ability of the portal to find efficient solutions for a process it would be useful if we could model the resources consumed by activities (for example time, machinery, personnel and/or financial means) and the probability that activities out of the users control (for example external or automated activities) will occur.

Process Mining

We plan to integrate various process mining [32] techniques into the tool, allowing users to conformance check logs based on a DCR Graphs model and supporting process discovery of DCR Graphs models. In addition we intend to use process mining techniques in combination with the previously mentioned support for resources and stochastic models to support advanced methods for process improvement where the portal predicts efficient paths through a process based on an analysis of previous behaviour.

Hybrid Techniques

A common pitfall of declarative notations is that practitioners are more familiar and accustomed to flow-based approaches such as BPMN diagrams, swim-lanes and flow-charts, making them hesitant to fully adopt a completely new paradigm. We are therefore investigating adding hybrid techniques [14, 27, 36] to the portal which will allow users to use DCR Graphs in combination with some of the flow-based models that they are used to.

7   Conclusion

Over the last few years Exformatics has taken large steps in adopting declarative process notations and techniques: they have employed the notation as a modelling tool in projects with customers, developed a declarative process engine based on the DCR Graphs notation and deployed said process engine as part of a recent customer project. More recently they have developed a new stand-alone solution, the DCR Graphs process portal, which provides an easily accessible web-based modelling and simulation tool for declarative processes. The portal has a strong social aspect, supporting communication between the different stakeholders about their models and the ability to jointly simulate models in a collaborative setting. In this paper we described the portal and its development, together with the underlying Hierarchical DCR Graphs language, an extension of the original DCR Graphs language that offers support for multi-instance sub-processes.

There are many avenues for possible future work and Exformatics will continue to invest heavily in both declarative and hybrid process technologies. They have entered into a new collaboration initiative with IT University of Copenhagen (ITU), are partly funding a postdoctoral researcher over the next two years, are directly hiring a part-time researcher who is also employed at ITU and have joined as a partner on a number of research funding applications on declarative and hybrid process notations and technologies. Furthermore Exformatics participates in various industry initiatives, currently with a major Danish financial institution which has worked with process modelling for many years but are looking into declarative notations to provide more flexible process models.

References

1. Innovations netværk for it. http://www.infinit.dk/
2. Bhattacharya, K., Gerede, C., Hull, R., Liu, R., Su, J.: Towards formal analysis of artifact-centric business process models. In: preparation, pp. 288–304 (2007)
3. Davenport, T.H., Jarvenpaa, S.L., Beers, M.C.: Improving knowledge work processes. Sloan management review (1996)
4. Debois, S., Hildebrandt, T., Marquard, M., Slaats, T.: Bridging the valley of death - a success story on danish funding schemes paving a path from technology readiness level 1 to 9. In: Proceedings of the 2nd International Workshop on Software Engineering Research and Industrial Practice (SER&IP 2015)
5. Debois, S., Hildebrandt, T., Slaats, T.: Hierarchical declarative modelling with refinement and sub-processes. In: Sadiq, S., Soffer, P., Völzer, H. (eds.) BPM 2014. LNCS, vol. 8659, pp. 18–33. Springer, Heidelberg (2014)
6. Drucker, P.F.: Management Challenges for the 21st Century. HarperBusiness (2001)
7. Dubois, S., Hildebrandt, T., Marquard, M., Slaats, T.: A case for declarative process modelling: Agile development of a grant application system (2014)
8. Hildebrandt, T., Mukkamala, R.R.: Declarative event-based workflow as distributed dynamic condition response graphs. In: Post-Proceedings of PLACES 2010 (2010)

9. Hildebrandt, T., Mukkamala, R.R., Slaats, T.: Designing a cross-organizational case management system using dynamic condition response graphs. In: 2011 15th IEEE International Enterprise Distributed Object Computing Conference (EDOC), pp. 161–170, 29–september 2, 2011
10. Hildebrandt, T., Mukkamala, R.R., Slaats, T.: Nested dynamic condition response graphs. In: Arbab, F., Sirjani, M. (eds.) FSEN 2011. LNCS, vol. 7141, pp. 343–350. Springer, Heidelberg (2012)
11. Hildebrandt, T., Mukkamala, R.R., Slaats, T., Zanitti, F.: Contracts for cross-organizational workflows as timed dynamic condition response graphs. Journal of Logic and Algebraic Programming (JLAP), May 2013
12. Hull, R., Damaggio, E., De Masellis, R., Fournier, F., Gupta, M., Heath III, F.T., Hobson, S., Linehan, M., Maradugu, S., Nigam, A., Sukaviriya, P.N., Vaculin, R.: Business artifacts with guard-stage-milestone lifecycles: managing artifact interactions with conditions and events. In: Proc. of DEBS 2011, pp. 51–62. ACM, New York (2011)
13. Hull, R., Damaggio, E., Fournier, F., Gupta, M., Heath III, F.T., Hobson, S., Linehan, M., Maradugu, S., Nigam, A., Sukaviriya, P., Vaculin, R.: Introducing the guard-stage-milestone approach for specifying business entity lifecycles (invited talk). In: Bravetti, M. (ed.) WS-FM 2010. LNCS, vol. 6551, pp. 1–24. Springer, Heidelberg (2011)
14. Maggi, F.M., Slaats, T., Reijers, H.A.: The Automated discovery of hybrid processes. In: Sadiq, S., Soffer, P., Völzer, H. (eds.) BPM 2014. LNCS, vol. 8659, pp. 392–399. Springer, Heidelberg (2014)
15. Maggi, F.M., Montali, M., Westergaard, M., van der Aalst, W.M.P.: Monitoring business constraints with linear temporal logic: an approach based on colored automata. In: Rinderle-Ma, S., Toumani, F., Wolf, K. (eds.) BPM 2011. LNCS, vol. 6896, pp. 132–147. Springer, Heidelberg (2011)
16. Bughin, J., Dobbs, R., Roxburgh, C., Sarrazin, H., Sands, G., Chui, M., Manyika, J., Westergren, M.: The social economy: Unlocking value and productivity through social technologies (2012)
17. Montali, M.: Specification and Verification of Declarative Open Interaction Models: aLogic-Based Approach. Lecture Notes in Business Information Processing, vol. 56. Springer (2010)
18. Montali, M., Pesic, M., van der Aalst, W.M.P., Chesani, F., Mello, P., Storari, S.: Declarative specification and verification of service choreographiess. ACM Transactions on the Web (TWEB) 4(1), 3 (2010)
19. Mukkamala, R.R.: A Formal Model For Declarative Workflows - Dynamic Condition Response Graphs. PhD thesis, IT University of Copenhagen, March 2012
20. Mukkamala, R.R., Hildebrandt, T., Slaats, T.: Towards trustworthy adaptive case management with dynamic condition response graphs. In: Proceedings of the 17th IEEE International EDOC Conference, EDOC 2013 (2013)
21. Mulyar, N.A., Schonenberg, M.H., Mans, R.S, van der Aalst, W.M.P.: Towards a Taxonomy of Process Flexibility (Extended Version) (2007)
22. Object Management Group. Case Management Model and Notation, version 1.0. Webpage, May 2014. http://www.omg.org/spec/CMMN/1.0/PDF
23. Object Management Group BPMN Technical Committee. Business Process Model and Notation, version 2.0. http://www.omg.org/spec/BPMN/2.0/PDF
24. Pesic, M., Schonenberg, H., van der Aalst, W.M.P.: DECLARE: full support for loosely-structured processes. In: Proceedings of the 11th IEEE International Enterprise Distributed Object Computing Conference, p. 287. IEEE Computer Society (2007)

25. Reich, R.B.: The Work of Nations: Preparing Ourselves for 21st Century Capitalism. Vintage Books (1992)
26. Reichert, M., Weber, B.: Enabling Flexibility in Process-Aware Information Systems: Challenges, Methods, Technologies. Springer, Berlin-Heidelberg (2012)
27. Reijers, H.A., Slaats, T., Stahl, C.: Declarative modeling–an academic dream or the future for BPM? In: Daniel, F., Wang, J., Weber, B. (eds.) BPM 2013. LNCS, vol. 8094, pp. 307–322. Springer, Heidelberg (2013)
28. Slaats, T., Mukkamala, R.R., Hildebrandt, T., Marquard, M.: Exformatics declarative case management workflows as dcr graphs. In: Daniel, F., Wang, J., Weber, B. (eds.) BPM 2013. LNCS, vol. 8094, pp. 339–354. Springer, Heidelberg (2013)
29. Swenson, K.D.: Mastering the Unpredictable: How Adaptive Case Management Will Revolutionize the Way That Knowledge Workers Get Things Done. Meghan-Kiffer Press (2010)
30. van der Aalst, W.M.P., Pesic, M., Schonenberg, H.: Declarative workflows: Balancing between flexibility and support. Computer Science - R&D $23(2)$, 99–113 (2009)
31. van der Aalst, W., Pesic, M., Schonenberg, H., Westergaard, M., Maggi, F.M.: Declare. Webpage 2010. http://www.win.tue.nl/declare/
32. van der Aalst, W.M.P.: Process Mining: Discovery, Conformance and Enhancement of Business Processes, 1st edn. Springer Publishing Company, Incorporated (2011)
33. van der Aalst, W.M.P., Pesic, M.: DecSerFlow: towards a truly declarative service flow language. In: Bravetti, M., Núñez, M., Zavattaro, G. (eds.) WS-FM 2006. LNCS, vol. 4184, pp. 1–23. Springer, Heidelberg (2006)
34. Völzer, H.: An overview of BPMN 2.0 and its potential use. In: Mendling, J., Weidlich, M., Weske, M. (eds.) BPMN 2010. LNBIP, vol. 67, pp. 14–15. Springer, Heidelberg (2010)
35. Weber, B., Reichert, M., Rinderle-Ma, S.: Change patterns and change support features - enhancing flexibility in process-aware information systems. Data and Knowledge Engineering $66(3)$, 438–466 (2008)
36. Westergaard, M., Slaats, T.: Mixing paradigms for more comprehensible models. In: Daniel, F., Wang, J., Weber, B. (eds.) BPM 2013. LNCS, vol. 8094, pp. 283–290. Springer, Heidelberg (2013)

Case Analytics Workbench: Platform for Hybrid Process Model Creation and Evolution

Yiqin Yu[1(✉)], Xiang Li[1], Haifeng Liu[1], Jing Mei[1], Nirmal Mukhi[2], Vatche Ishakian[3], Guotong Xie[1], Geetika T. Lakshmanan[5], and Mike Marin[4]

[1] IBM Research, Beijing, China
{yuyiqin,lixiang,liuhf,meijing,xieguot}@cn.ibm.com
[2] IBM Analytics Group, Tarrytown, NY, USA
nmukhi@us.ibm.com
[3] IBM T.J. Watson Research Center, Cambridge, MA, USA
vishaki@us.ibm.com
[4] IBM Analytics Group, Costa Mesa, CA, USA
mikemarin@us.ibm.com
[5] Audible, Inc., Cambridge, MA, USA
geetikal@audible.com

Abstract. Hybrid process models are considered an attractive approach for modeling knowledge-intensive processes. A hybrid process model combines both imperative and declarative modeling, which can handle both the structured and the flexible parts of a business process. However, it is difficult and time-consuming to create and refine a hybrid process model due to its structure complexity and case variability. This paper introduces the Case Analytics Workbench, an end-to-end system to accelerate hybrid process model creation and evolution by combining declarative and imperative process mining, event log clustering and human interaction in a cloud environment. We validated the effectiveness and applicability of our system by performing two case studies from insurance and health care industry respectively.

Keywords: Hybrid process model · CMMN · Process mining · Clustering

1 Introduction

Business process modeling plays a significant role in the domain of business process management, which is the activity of representing the processes of an enterprise, so that they can be executed, analyzed and improved. Imperative modeling approaches, such as the XML process definition language (XPDL) [35], the web services business process execution language (BPEL) [26], and the business process model and notation (BPMN) [27], have been the dominant manner for modeling processes. These approaches model every possible sequence of activities in a business process to provide a structured model.

Along with the emerging of knowledge-intensive processes, the imperative approaches meet challenges. As defined in [33], the conduct and execution of

©Springer International Publishing Switzerland 2015
H.R. Motahari-Nezhad et al. (Eds.): BPM 2015, LNCS 9253, pp. 226–241, 2015.
DOI: 10.1007/978-3-319-23063-4_16

knowledge-intensive processes are heavily dependent on knowledge workers performing various interconnected knowledge intensive decision-making tasks, which are information centric and require substantial flexibility [5]. Declarative modeling approaches such as Declare [2], DCR Graphs [3] and SCIFF [15] have been proposed recently to support the required flexibility [1]. With declarative models, only the essential characteristics are described in the model, and constraints between activities are explicitly defined to restrict banned behaviors.

However, a study [31] among experts shown that the declarative modeling language is not a process modeling language that can be used to model entire business processes in practice. It also indicated that in most processes at least parts of the process are better represented by the imperative approach. As an overall consideration, the hybrid modeling approach, combining imperative and declarative modeling approaches, appears as a more attractive way to model the entire business processes.

From the aspect of human effort, to create and refine a hybrid process model is not a trivial work especially for knowledge-intensive processes. First, the modeler should get an overall perspective about the process model. It will become more difficult along with the increasing structure/information complexity of the process. Second, there will be a learning curve for modeler to get hold of new hybrid modeling languages and guidelines. Third, to keep the hybrid model up-to-date, the modeler should be able to run process mining methods and explain the results properly for model refinement. Finally, the modeler would also call other analytics methods to provide customized modeling.

In order to ease the workload of process modelers and accelerate the hybrid process model creation and evolution, we introduce an end-to-end system named Case Analytics Workbench, which

- Combines declarative and imperative process mining results to extract data-driven evidences and automatically synthesize them with the original hybrid model,
- Implements an industry oriented hybrid modeling approach which uses CMMN [24, 28] to model the declarative parts and BPMN [27] to model the imperative parts with the consideration of applicability and extendibility,
- Leverages event log clustering to support customized process modeling,
- Provides rich user interactions and visualizations to facilitate the model creation and evolution process, and
- Is integrated with a case management [6, 9, 32] product IBM Case Manager (ICM) [13, 36].

We also performed two real world case studies from insurance and health care industries to show the capability of workbench on process model creation and evolution.

2   Related Work

Although a formal definition of hybrid process models has not come to a broad agreement, there is already existing industrial and academic works about modeling of hybrid processes and hybrid model creation. ICM [13, 36] is an industrial product for case modeling and execution that implement hybrid process models. The declarative constraints between hierarchical container tasks and tasks are defined as preconditions. And the process tasks that contain a set of restricted connected steps form the imperative parts. In ICM, graphical user interfaces are developed for modelers to manually create and refine hybrid models, but neither process mining methods nor data analytics components are involved yet. As a successful implementation in industry, we refer to the main structure of the hybrid model in ICM, but extend it to a more generalized way. That is, to use CMMN to model the declarative part and keep it as the main structure of the model, and to use BPMN as the imperative modeling language and keeps them in process tasks.

Hermans [12] introduced a comprehensive hybrid process modeling approach containing 1) a hybrid modeling language, which combines BPMN as imperative modeling language and Declare as declarative language, 2) An iterative process of creating a hybrid process model, and 3) a set of user guidelines for hybrid process model creation. A new element named block is introduced to wrap either declarative or imperative sub-processes. Different from our hybrid model structure, block elements can be freely organized in a hybrid model. Other than process mining approaches for such hybrid model are not mentioned in the paper. Another hybrid modeling approach implemented in CPN Tools 4 [18, 29] combines the places and transitions of colored Petri nets with the constraints of the Declare and DCR Graphs languages. The work in [4] produced a hybrid process model that combine control flow and business rules modeling, and the work in [7] introduced a hybrid process model that combine behavioral and informational models.

Since most of the existing process mining techniques can only generate a process model that is either procedural or declarative, Maggi et al [23] introduced a hybrid process mining approach which can automatically discover imperative sub-processes and declarative sub-processes by dividing event logs into structured and unstructured sequences. Suppose the support of sub-processes by event logs and correlation with specified goal could be calculated, this kind of process mining engine can be treated as a source of evidence for the workbench.

3   Case Analytics Workbench

Fig. 1 illustrates the high-level architecture of the workbench, which is divided into four main modules. The first and fundamental module is the Case Model Management Module (see Fig. 2), which contains a model storage component, a model manager component and an editor component. This module allows a user to interact with a case model for model creation, editing, saving and transformation.

To retrieve evidences from data, three additional modules are designed. Goal of the Data Management Module is to handle (diverse of) process execution logs, transform them to formal event log formats, and further process them with clustering. The Process Mining Module consumes event logs from the Data Management Module to run declarative and imperative process mining methods. In addition to presenting the mining results to the user for better insight and understanding, the Evidence Management Module collects the mining results as model evidences through respective evidence adaptors. This module supports storage, visualization, filtering and synthesis of these evidences as shown in Fig. 2.

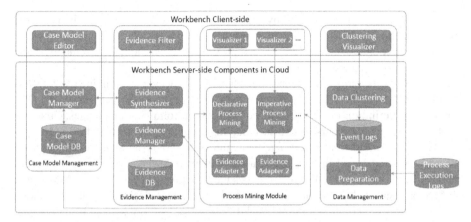

Fig. 1. High-level architecture of the workbench

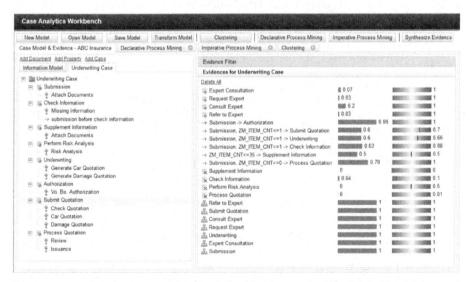

Fig. 2. The main UI of the workbench. The left panel is a case model editor, and the right panel is an evidence management panel showing the list of evidences as well as a filter.

From the aspect of deployment, the workbench follows a roughly framework of Model-View-Controller (MVC) [17], which can be separated to two parts: server-side components which are deployed in cloud environment, and the client-side components maintain the business logic and support user interface rendering. Benefiting from the cloud environment, analysis components can be more effective by leveraging abundant space and memory resources on the cloud. They are built with unified forms such as Bluemix [14] services and APPs, which makes them standardized for invocation and distribution. We will provide more detail about each module next.

3.1   Case Model Definition

Referencing the requirements of hybrid modeling language described in [12], the hybrid modeling language should 1) support imperative modeling elements, 2) support declarative modeling elements, 3) support hierarchical modeling elements, 4) be executable, and 5) be graphically intuitive.

Considering the applicability and extendibility, we decide to combine existing imperative and declarative language other than to develop a new language [31]. We produce the definition of Case Model to address the following challenges. First, according to the requirements of hybrid modeling language, we need to find a declarative language and an imperative language and they should be able to be integrated together. Second, according to the goal of widely industry applicability and rapid industry use, we should use industry-oriented languages. Naturally, CMMN and BPMN are identified as the industrial oriented standards as declarative and imperative language, respectively. In our case model, CMMN elements are used to form the main structure, which contain elements such as Case, Stage, Human Task, Process Task and Sentry (Constraint) element, and BPMN elements are defined under Process Task elements.

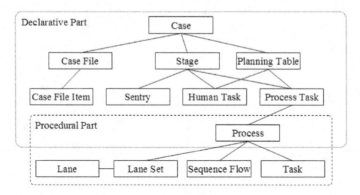

Fig. 3. Main elements of Case Model.

Definition 1 (Case Model). A Case Model (CM) (Fig. 3) is a hybrid process model with contracted and BPMN-extended CMMN in which

- The hierarchical declarative part is composed by CMMN elements including Stage, Planning Table, Sentry, Human Task and Process Task,
- Imperative parts are defined by BPMN elements under Process Task elements such as Lane, Lane Set, Sequence Flow and Task (To distinguish from Task elements in CMMN, we rename this Task element as Step), and
- Data elements are defined by using Case File, Case File Item elements in CMMN.

3.2   Data Management and Clustering

The Data Management Module serves as prerequisite for the Process Mining Module, in which the data preparation component consumes process execution logs from diverse sources and converts to event logs. Data clustering component is also assembled to this module to enhance the analysis of event logs.

3.2.1 Data Clustering

The goal of the clustering methods is to group processes together based on their execution patterns. Events related to a particular case are grouped together to reflect a given process instance. We use timestamps to define an order of occurrence of events. Each event is then mapped uniquely to a single Unicode character. Thus, every trace is transformed into a Unicode string representation, where the order of the Unicode characters is determined by the order of events within the process trace.

We apply DBScan Clustering algorithm [10] to cluster the set of string based trace representations. The reason we chose DBScan is to allow for arbitrary number of clusters to form and extends seamless to run in a Map reduce framework [11]. By default, DBScan implementations use Euclidean distance between points, which in our case each point is a sequence of characters. To overcome this issue, we adopt Levenshtein distance [19] instead of the Euclidean distance. As an instance of string edit distance, Levenshtein distance has been used in process mining and clustering event logs [40].

Levenshtein distance measures the difference between two string sequences of arbitrary lengths (not necessarily the same). It does so by calculating the number of operations required to transform one string into another. Thus, it provides a good measure of similarity for finding similar execution patterns. DBScan requires the initialization of two parameters.

MinPts: determines the number of points required to form a cluster. We set this parameter to 1, which means that every trace can possibly be a standalone cluster. It also means that clusters containing a single trace can be considered as outliers.

epsilon: represents the distance threshold between two points that can be considered similar.

To find the optimal epsilon is achieved through user experiments combined with subjective expectations of what should correspond to a good cluster outcome [38]. A typical way to aid the user is to provide suggestions for epsilon by calculating the mean or median distance based on a sample set of available traces.

The clustering algorithm outputs a group of clustered traces — share similar execution sequence based on Levenshtein distance — which are then presented to the user using the cluster visualization tool. Users have the option to drill down into the cluster to visualize for example, a particular event sequence.

3.3   Process Mining

The Process Mining Module contains at least one engine for declarative process mining and one for imperative process mining. Remember the process-mining method for each engine is not restricted to what is described in this paper. Take imperative process-mining engine as an example, those mining methods that can consume event logs and mine BPMN-based processes can be wrapped into the engine and convert its results to evidences.

3.3.1 Declarative Process Mining

A declarative process-mining engine mines declarative elements from the event logs such as human tasks and constraints. According to the definition of Case Model, The declarative part is hierarchical. That is to say, the same step can be planned in different tasks, and a task can also be defined in different stages. However, in an event trace, each event is defined in step level, and its task and stage information is normally unavailable, which may result in ambiguity of mapping an event to the correct task in the model. Here works in [20] are applied to align each event trace with the model before performing process mining, and types of variations are extended to additional tasks, absent tasks, additional constraints and violated constraints.

Additional and Absent Activities Discovery. This task is achieved by building a Hidden Markov Model (HMM) [30] to annotate each event in the event logs with a task in the model. The structure of HMM is derived from the process model, where a hidden state represents a task and an observation corresponds to an event in step level [20]. As the process model is incomplete and events that are not defined in the model may occur, we also create an "unknown" observation to match these events. The probabilities of the HMM are initially assigned according to the hierarchy and dependencies of the model, and refined from a set of training event traces by applying the Baum-Welch algorithm [30]. Then we can align a given event trace with the HMM by using the Viterbi algorithm [30], which finds the globally optimal sequence of tasks. After alignment, we can directly detect two types of variations: additional activities, which are frequently executed in the event log but not defined in the model, and absent activities, which are defined in the model but rarely or never executed in the event logs.

Additional Constraints Discovery. The event-condition-action (ECA) based constraints are discovered from an event trace by applying our modified association rule mining algorithm [21]. The algorithm uses the metrics of support (that is the proportion of traces satisfying a constraint) to measure the frequency of a candidate constraint, as well as the normalized odds ratio to quantify its correlation with the achievement of case goal. For each task, the best ECA rule, which is frequent and significantly more likely to lead to the goal achievement, is translated into the constraint of the task. Note that in a CMMN-based model, both temporal dependencies (on part) and data conditions (if part) of the tasks should be formally represented as constraints, which can be defined based on ECA rules [8].

Violated Constraints Discovery. Because the semantics of ECA rules can not be used for verification, while traditional linear temporal logic (LTL) can not capture the data conditions of tasks, we redefine the constraints using first-order LTL (FO-LTL) [25], which is constructed by combining first-order formulas by temporal and Boolean operators. For detecting the violated constraints, we translate each FO-LTL constraint into a Büchi automaton[25]. If an event trace can not be accepted by the automaton, then the trace violates the constraint. Base on the checking results of each event trace, we calculate the support of each constraint, as well as its correlation (normalized odds ratio) with the achievement of case goal.

3.3.2 Imperative Process Mining

The imperative process-mining component extracts from event logs information about the events for each process task. This produces a set of typed and time-stamped events. We exploited this data in two ways: First, we used the standard flexible heuristic miner [34]. This returns the results of the mining (a BPMN specification) to the workbench as evidence, to be considered and combined with evidence from other analyses in order to refine or create the complete model.

Our second approach was to create aggregate behavioral view of the process. The goal here was to provide a visual representation of the execution of typical processes. In order to achieve this, we combine the individual process trace into a single aggregate trace. The aggregate trace consists of tasks, with their average, minimum and maximum start and end times. All timestamps are expressed relative to the start of the case, in order to have a normalized basis for aggregation of the data. Additionally, the percentage of cases in which a particular task was executed (which would be relevant in case the task was discretionary or created on an ad hoc basis) is included in the aggregation. Similar to the data for each task, the list of steps within each task is aggregated. The algorithm to compute this aggregation is simple, and amenable to parallelization (we discuss this further below). This aggregation, represented in JSON format, is provided to a timeline visualizer created for the purpose of providing visual insights about historical data for the workbench users.

3.4   Evidence Management Module

Evidence Manager. This component collects evidences from diverse of adapters that convert process-mining results to evidences.

Definition 2 (Evidence). Evidence is a piece of model elements with support information (see Table 1) about how strongly this piece should be synthesized to the model and where and how it could be synthesized.

Table 1. The main attributes of Evidence

Key	Value	Sample
name	The name of an evidence	Request Expert
modelEleId	The aligned model element id of an evidence	347834-123347
modelType	The model type of an evidence	Task
evidenceType	The analysis type of an evidence	Additional
supportDegree	The support degree of an evidence	0.25
goalCorrelation	The goal correlation of an evidence	3.42
content	The content of an evidence	/
parentModelId	The parent model id of an evidence	Underwriting Case

Evidence Synthesizer. Evidence synthesizer automatically aligns the case model and evidences together, and recommends the synthesis operations against the base model [39]. First, with the adapted modeling evidences from various sources, we need to synthesize them together in order to recommend refinement operations against the base case model. Because a task can be defined in multiple stages and data sets usually do not include explicit stage labels for each task, evidences may not have labeling information either (note that evidences derived from the declarative process engine have been aligned with the case model already). Thus, a critical task is to assign those evidences with unknown stage labels into appropriate stages. We adopt a K-means clustering method to solve the problem where we cluster task evidences relying on their context attributes including performer role, information required, information updated, temporal relationships with other activities, and K is the number of stages, and the members of one cluster are assigned into the same stage. We represent the alignment result as a Consolidated Model View (CMV) where the original model is a tree and aligned evidences are put into appropriate branches. Fig. 4 depicts an example of CMV where the case model has three stages and three activities a1, a2 and a3, and five evidences are aligned with the case model. Activity a3 have a predefined precondition of a2 and a vetoing precondition evidence $E1^-(a2, a3)$. Note that multiple evidences from different sources may target to the same case model element. We call them *peer evidences*, and a voting evidence $E1^+(a4)$ and vetoing evidence $E2^-(a4)$ are such examples as they both target to a4 (which is actually a newly discovered task from the data). Other three evidences are noted as *unique evidences*.

After a consolidate model view is formed, we recommend three types of synthesis operations for a given case model (CM) as follows:

- ADD(Tx): Adding a newly discovered element Tx to the CM where Tx can be either a task or a precedence constraint between two existing activities in the CM.
- DEL(Tx): Deleting an existing element Tx in the CM.
- UPD(Tx, Mandatory): Changing behavior of task Tx from optional to mandatory (the default execution behavior of an task in a CM is optional)

The main idea of recommending synthesis operations is as follows: (1) For an unique evidence the algorithm recommends an ADD or DEL operation depending on whether it is a voting or vetoing evidence and whether its strength exceeds the predefined thresholds; (UPD operation is generated if strong voting evidences are associated with an existing task); (2) For peer evidences targeting to the same element, it firstly merges them to a virtual unique evidence and then applies the same rule as (1) to recommend operations accordingly. The merging process determines if the virtual unique evidence is voting or vetoing depending on the strength of each peer, and assigns a reconciled strength with it. Note that because the strengths of evidences from different analytic sources may be measured using different metrics and each source may have different power in reconciliation, our algorithm allows setting different source weights for evidences when reconciling the conflicts among peers.

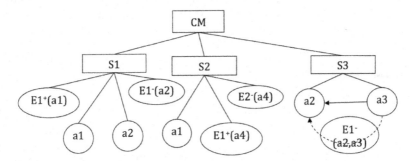

Fig. 4. An example of consolidated model

4   Case Studies

In this section, we will report two real world use cases, which come from insurance and health care industry respectively to demonstrate and evaluate the capability of the workbench. The first case will describe how the different components in workbench are orchestrated to help the modeler to create an underwriting process model in a convenient manner, and the second case will be about the refinement of complex hybrid model.

The workbench server-side was deployed on IBM Bluemix, which is a cloud-based platform for building, managing and running diverse of apps. Database components of the workbench server-side were deployed as Bluemix Services by using SQL Database Service [16] in Bluemix as well as Cloudant, and other components were deployed as Bluemix APPs providing RESTful APIs.

4.1   Case Study 1: Underwriting Process Creation and Derivation

This case study was designed as underwriting processes improvement and optimization which is from real requirements of an insurance company. A raw case model (Fig. 2) is firstly created with the main skeleton containing "structural" and "activity" elements such as Case, Stage, Task and Step elements.

Data Preparation and Clustering. 4300 historical execution logs of the underwriting process are collected from the insurance company lasting from August to December 2013. This kind of data was then transformed to formal event logs via the data preparation component. Event log clustering could also be triggered in order to derive distinctive views from the original model. As the result, two clusters were generated, one of which contain 2038 case instances such as "Generate Auto quote → Check quote → Handle pending quotation request", "Check quote → Generate Auto quote → Consult Expert → Handle pending quotation request" and the other contain 2267 instances such as "Check quote → Generate property quote → Handle pending quotation request". From the clustering results, the user is able to discern that cluster 0 corresponds to auto insurance cases (since there are no steps relating to property insurance underwriting), while cluster 1 corresponds to property insurance cases.

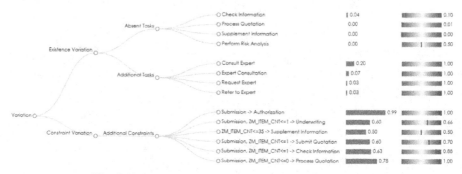

Fig. 5. Visualization of declarative process mining results

Process Mining. Fig. 5 shows the results of declarative process-mining method which also took the raw case model as input and set the goal as "Cycle time less than two days". For better understanding, all the results was visualized in a Dendrogram, which clearly shown the structure of variation types. Each result was shown as a leaf node of the Dendrogram with its main attributes including support degree (visualized as the length of a blue bar and a succedent support degree number) and correlation with goal achievement (visualized as the position of a black line on the colored bar and a succedent correlation number). We observed that some reasonable and meaningful elements that were not defined in the raw model, such as the additional tasks (e.g., "Consult Expert") as well as the additional constraints, were discovered by the declarative process-mining engine. The imperative process-mining engine also mined reasonable sub-processes for some tasks and converted them to evidences. As seen in the evidence management panel in Fig. 2, the last seven evidences were converted from imperative process-mining results. For example, the Submit Quotation evidence marked with a workflow icon contains a sub-process "start → car quotation → check quotation → end".

Evidence and Evidence Synthesis. Evidences shown in Fig. 2 were converted from the results of both the declarative and imperative process-mining engines. Before running the automatic evidence synthesis engine, "strong" evidences whose support is larger than 0.3 and goal correlation is larger than 0.5 are selected via the filter. The UI of synthesis is shown in Fig. 6(a). The evidence synthesizer component provided the recommendations of model refinement, and the user selected and finally confirmed the modifications to generate the final model as shown in Fig. 6(b).

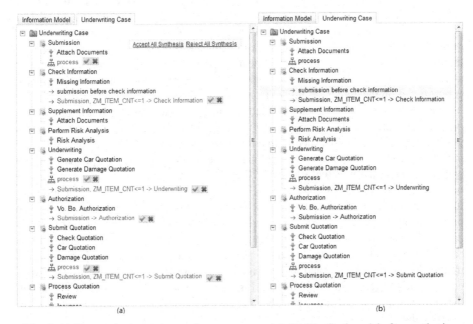

Fig. 6. (a) The synthesis overlay on the raw case model; (b) The final model after synthesis.

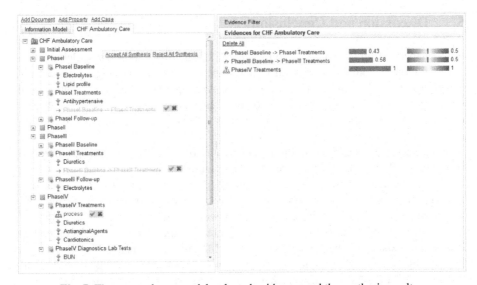

Fig. 7. The care pathway model, selected evidences and the synthesis results.

4.2   Case Study 2: Care Pathway Refinement

We also performed a real world case study for care pathway refinement. A care pathway is a standardized process that consists of multiple care stages corresponding to different disease progression conditions, where each stage contains various clinical tasks and their constraints. Due to its strong requirement on flexibility and ad hoc variation, we think the hybrid approach will be suitable to model complex care pathways. In this study, an initial care pathway, which was derived from a clinical guideline for the management of congestive heart failure (CHF) [37], was manually built as a case model using our workbench. Then we refined this model for a specific patient cohort based on the evidences mined from the real electronic medical records (EMR).

The process-mining engines provided meaningful evidences for the improvement of the care pathway. For example, in the original care pathway derived from the guideline, some constraints specify that the baseline tests have to be performed before initiating treatments. However, as shown in Fig. 7, our declarative process-mining engine detected that in actual EMR data, the treatments were usually initiated without performing the baseline tests before. Clinicians gave a reasonable explanation for these violations. In real world care practice, clinicians can give treatments based on past medical histories that are not recorded in EMR; therefore, these constraints are not required and can be ignored in some cases. Besides, we also applied the results of care pathways mined by the imperative process-mining approach [38]. Though the treatment actions were defined in the original case model, their orders were not explicitly specified. Therefore, as shown in Fig. 7, we manually selected fragments from the care pathway model found in [38], and added the possible sequences into the refined model.

5   Discussion and Conclusion

In this paper, we presented a solution to accelerate the hybrid process model creation and evolution by combining declarative and imperative process mining with event log clustering. An end-to-end system named Case Analytics Workbench was built up in the cloud environment allowing users to check analysis results and interact with case models, and real world case studies are designed from insurance and health care industry.

From the system design point of view, the cloud-based architecture brings adaptivity and extendibility for different use case design. For example, in the introduced case studies, different components were assembled in different manners. Case Study 1 leveraged Data Clustering component to group event logs that have similar patterns, while evidences in Case Study 2 are from embedded declarative process-mining engine as well as external imperative process-mining engine. The cost of component decoupling exists. As the Data Management Module is independent with process-mining engines, to transmit data among them will be a burden for the network if the volume of data is relatively large. There should be advanced mechanism to deal with the data transmission in each process-mining engine.

From the applicability point of view, running of case studies and their results made strong impressiveness to specialists include business process administrators, BPM specialists, BPM product managers and developers, as well as clinical physicians. Most of them gave positive feedbacks about the combination of diverse process mining methods and the involvement of clustering method. They also agreed that the process of creating or improving a business process model should include the user interaction, and our mechanism of user interaction, including the visualization of analytics results and the design of interaction mode, is also appreciated by the specialists.

For further evaluation, a thorough empirical evaluation is still needed which should involve different modelers to complete a hybrid modeling task integrally. As the workbench is just a modeling tool but can not run the generated models, the applicability of models is also not well evaluated. Generated models should be further transformed and exported to other practical business process management platforms such as ICM and do empirical evaluation during the runtime of model.

Considering the hybrid process modeling approach, there are also further considerations. Firstly, due to the modeling limitations of CMMN and BPMN, we clearly distinguished the declarative part (Stage and Task elements) from the imperative part (Step elements in Process Task) in our definition of case model, which worked well in our case studies. In some other cases, however, there is no significant border between the model elements where these two modeling manners should be applied, and a more flexible hybrid process model could be designed. Besides, our current platform use the GSM-based model [8] to represent both temporal and data-aware constraints for the declarative part of model, which can only support limited categories of temporal constraints. A potential solution is to integrate the data-aware extended model of Declare [22], which supports much more types of temporal constraints and data conditions.

The Process Mining Module could also be enhanced by developing more process-mining engines such as works in [23] and [41]. Each engine could be treated as one source of evidences. Along with the increasing of diverse engines, fusion of evidences from them will become a challenge for the Evidence Management Module.

References

1. van der Aalst, W.M.P., et al.: Declarative workflows: Balancing between flexibility and support. Computer Science - Research and Development **23**(2), 99–113 (2009)
2. van der Aalst, W.M.P., Pesic, M., Schonenberg, H.: Declarative workflows: Balancing between flexibility and support. Computer Science - R&D **23**(2), 99–113 (2009)
3. Hildebrandt, T., Mukkamala, R.R.: Declarative event-based workflow as distributed dynamic condition response graphs. Places **2010**, 59–73 (2010)
4. Charfi, A., Mezini, M.: Hybrid web service composition: business processes meet business rules. In: 2nd International Conference on Service Oriented Computing, pp. 30–38. ACM, New York (2004)
5. Di Ciccio, C., et al.: Knowledge-Intensive Processes: Characteristics, Requirements and Analysis of Contemporary Approaches. Journal on Data Semantics (2014)

6. Clair, L.C., et al.: Dynamic Case Management — An Old Idea Catches New Fire. Forrester, Cambridge (2009)
7. Cull, R., Eldabi, T.: A hybrid approach to workflow modelling. Journal of Enterprise Information Management **23**(3), 268–281 (2010)
8. Damaggio, E., Hull, R., Vaculín, R.: On the equivalence of incremental and fixpoint semantics for business artifacts with guard-stage-milestone lifecycles. In: Rinderle-Ma, S., Toumani, F., Wolf, K. (eds.) BPM 2011. LNCS, vol. 6896, pp. 396–412. Springer, Heidelberg (2011)
9. Davenport, T., Nohria, N.: Case Management and the Integration of Labor. MIT Sloan Management Review **35**(2), 11–23 (1994)
10. Ester, M., et al.: A density-based algorithm for discovering clusters in large spatial databases with noise. In: 2nd International Conference on Knowledge Discovery and Data Mining, pp. 226–231. AAAI Press (1996)
11. He, Y., et al.: MR-DBSCAN: an efficient parallel density-based clustering algorithm using mapreduce. In: Proceedings of the 2011 IEEE 17th International Conference on Parallel and Distributed Systems, pp. 473–480. IEEE Computer Society, Washington, DC (2011)
12. Hermans, V.C.T.: A hybrid process modeling approach. Eindhoven University of Technology (2014)
13. IBM: Case Manager. http://www-03.ibm.com/software/products/en/casemana (Accessed: March 13, 2015)
14. IBM: IBM Bluemix. http://www-01.ibm.com/software/bluemix/ (Accessed: March 13, 2015)
15. Montali, M.: Declarative Open Interaction Models. In: Montali, M. (ed.) Specification and Verification of Declarative Open Interaction Models. LNBIP, vol. 56, pp. 11–45. Springer, Heidelberg (2010)
16. IBM: SQL   Database.   https://console.ng.bluemix.net/?ace_base=true/#/store/cloudOEPaneId=store&serviceOfferingGuid=0d5a104d-d700-4315-9b7c-8f84a9c85ae3&fromCatalog=true (Accessed: March 13, 2015)
17. Krasner, G., Pope, S.: A Description of the Model-View-Controller User Interface Paradigm in the Smalltalk-80 System. Journal of Object Oriented Programming **1**(3), 26–49 (1988)
18. Westergaard, M., Slaats, T.: CPN Tools 4: A Process Modeling Tool Combining Declarative and Imperative Paradigms. BPM Demos 2013 (2013)
19. Levenshtein, V.I.: Binary codes capable of correcting deletions, insertions, and reversals. Soviet Physics Doklady **10**(8), 707–710 (1966)
20. Li, X., et al.: Automatic variance analysis of multistage care pathways. In: Lovis, C., et al. (eds.) e-Health - For Continuity of Care - Proceedings of MIE 2014, the 25th European Medical Informatics Conference, August 31-September 3, Istanbul, Turkey, pp. 715–719 (2014)
21. Li, X., et al.: Mining temporal and data constraints associated with outcomes for care pathways. In: The 15th World Congress on Health and Biomedical Informatics, MEDINFO 2015 (Accepted)
22. Maggi, F.M., Dumas, M., García-Bañuelos, L., Montali, M.: Discovering data-aware declarative process models from event logs. In: Daniel, F., Wang, J., Weber, B. (eds.) BPM 2013. LNCS, vol. 8094, pp. 81–96. Springer, Heidelberg (2013)
23. Maggi, F.M., Slaats, T., Reijers, H.A.: The automated discovery of hybrid processes. In: Sadiq, S., Soffer, P., Völzer, H. (eds.) BPM 2014. LNCS, vol. 8659, pp. 392–399. Springer, Heidelberg (2014)

24. Marin, M., et al.: Data centric BPM and the emerging case management standard: a short survey. In: La Rosa, M., Soffer, P. (eds.) Business Process Management Workshops. LNBIP, vol. 132, pp. 24–30. Springer, Heidelberg (2013)
25. De Masellis, R., Su, J.: Runtime enforcement of first-order LTL properties on data-aware business processes. In: Basu, S., Pautasso, C., Zhang, L., Fu, X. (eds.) ICSOC 2013. LNCS, vol. 8274, pp. 54–68. Springer, Heidelberg (2013)
26. OASIS: Web Services Business Process Execution Language Version 2.0. OASIS
27. OMG: Business Process Model and Notation (BPMN), version 2.0.2. OMG (2014)
28. OMG: Case Management Model and Notation, version 1.0. OMG (2014)
29. Westergaard, M., Slaats, T.: Mixing paradigms for more comprehensible models. In: Daniel, F., Wang, J., Weber, B. (eds.) BPM 2013. LNCS, vol. 8094, pp. 283–290. Springer, Heidelberg (2013)
30. Rabiner, L.R.: A tutorial on hidden markov models and selected applications in speech recognition. Proc. IEEE **77**(2), 257–286 (1989)
31. Reijers, H.A., Slaats, T., Stahl, C.: Declarative modeling–an academic dream or the future for BPM? In: Daniel, F., Wang, J., Weber, B. (eds.) BPM 2013. LNCS, vol. 8094, pp. 307–322. Springer, Heidelberg (2013)
32. Swenson, K.D.: Mastering the Unpredictable: How Adaptive Case Management Will Revolutionize the Way That Knowledge Workers Get Things Done. Meghan-Kiffer Press (2010)
33. Vaculin, R., et al.: Declarative business artifact centric modeling of decision and knowledge intensive business processes. In: The Fifteenth IEEE International Enterprise Computing Conference (EDOC 2011), pp. 151–160. IEEE (2011)
34. Weijters, A.J.M.M., Ribeiro, J.T.S.: Flexible Heuristics Miner (FHM). In: Proceedings of the IEEE Symposium on Computational Intelligence and Data Mining, CIDM 2011, Part of the IEEE Symposium Series on Computational Intelligence 2011, April 11-15, Paris, France, pp. 310–317 (2011)
35. WfMC: XML Process Definition Language (XPDL), vversion 2.2. Workflow Management Coalition (2012)
36. Zhu, W., et al.: Advanced Case Management with IBM Case Manager. IBM Redbooks (2012)
37. Hunt, S.A., Abraham, W.T., Chin, M.H., et al.: ACC/AHA 2005 guideline update for the diagnosis and management of chronic heart failure in the adult. Circulation **112**(12), 154–235 (2005)
38. Lakshmanan, G.T., Rozsnyai, S., Wang, F.: Investigating clinical care pathways correlated with outcomes. In: Daniel, F., Wang, J., Weber, B. (eds.) BPM 2013. LNCS, vol. 8094, pp. 323–338. Springer, Heidelberg (2013)
39. Liu, H., Li, X., Yu, Y., Mei, J., Xie, G., Perer, A., Fei, W., Hu, J.: Synthesizing analytic evidences to refine care pathways. In: Medical Informatics Europe Conference (2015)
40. Becker, M., Laue, R.: A comparative survey of business process similarity measures. Computers in Industry **63**(2), 148–167 (2012)
41. Ekanayake, C., Dumas, M., García-Bañuelos, L., La Rosa, M.: Slice, Mine and Dice: Complexity-Aware Automated Discovery of Business Process Models. In: Daniel, F., Wang, J., Weber, B. (eds.) BPM 2013. LNCS, vol. 8094, pp. 49–64. Springer, Heidelberg (2013)

A Clinical Pathway Mining Approach
to Enable Scheduling of Hospital Relocations
and Treatment Services

Karsten Helbig[✉], Michael Römer, and Taïeb Mellouli

Department of Management Information Systems and Operations Research,
Martin-Luther-University Halle-Wittenberg, Halle, Germany
{karsten.helbig,michael.roemer,mellouli}@wiwi.uni-halle.de

Abstract. As discussed in numerous studies, clinical pathways of patients form
an appropriate tool for describing hospital processes and thereby provide a basis
for increasing the effectiveness of hospitals. Developing pathways led to a considerable research investigating IT-techniques to support pathway generation.
However, previous research neglected finding pathways designed to support
scheduling of hospital relocations and treatment services. To close this gap, we
first introduce a clinical pathway concept consisting of both pathway structure
and pathway constraints suitable for scheduling tasks. Second, we provide a
pathway mining method for automatically extracting corresponding pathways
from standard hospital billing data required for the German §21-KHentgG. Applying our approach to a real world dataset of a university hospital, we illustrate
the results using a pathway for malignant neoplasm of prostate containing feasible time windows and precedence relations of treatments, durations at attended
wards as well as possible process improvements stimulated from the results.

Keywords: Clinical pathway · Hospital · Process mining · Scheduling

1 Introduction

Hospitals in Germany cause costs of 76bn Euro per year, which is approx. 25% of the
total costs of the German health care system [1]. In order to reduce healthcare costs,
the German Diagnosis Related Groups (DRG) system was established in 2003. Since
then, hospitals are under considerable cost and quality strain by earning a case-based
lump-sum. Today, every third hospital is still unprofitable [2]. Badly managed patient
flows lead to an inefficient use of human and material resources, increasing costs and
decreasing quality of medical care [3]. One of the most promising methods to achieve
an efficient patient flow management is the use of clinical pathways (CP) [3].

A CP is a specific set of time-constrained treatment services and ward relocations to
be performed to cure a disease between a patient's admission and discharge. The aim of
using CP is to increase the transparency and the standardization of medical processes in
order to enable scheduling and controlling [4]. However, developing CP is a complex
and time-consuming task. As a result, only few CP are used in day-to-day hospital

©Springer International Publishing Switzerland 2015
H.R. Motahari-Nezhad et al. (Eds.): BPM 2015, LNCS 9253, pp. 242–250, 2015.
DOI: 10.1007/978-3-319-23063-4_17

operations. Due to heavily interdependent treatment services, using none or just a few CP within some kind of patient scheduling system becomes an obstacle to finding a best possible allocation of hospital resources. In order to obtain CP for nearly every disease treated by a hospital, IT support is indispensable.

Because of the great potential of employing CP, in recent years much effort has been taken to develop methods to automatically identify pathways. Existing methods for pathway mining focus on explicit descriptive characterizations of CP. Since they neglect implicit path feasibility information such as time windows of treatments or precedence constraints, they typically struggle with the heterogeneity and the variability of hospital-wide treatment processes and, cannot be used for scheduling.

Based on recent research in pathway mining and hospital-wide scheduling, this paper has two aims to improve business process management in hospitals: (1) Introduce a scheduling-focused CP concept composed of pathway structure and pathway constraints and (2) to develop a pathway mining method which is able to automatically extract CP corresponding to this CP concept from a standardized billing data each German hospital is obliged to create once a year according to the §21-KHentgG.

2   Related Work

Studies show significant improvements in medical care quality and economic factors like costs by employing CP in clinical operations management [5, 6]. In order to leverage this potential throughout the entire hospital, one pathway for every kind of treatment is needed. Unfortunately, due to the highly complex, ad hoc and multidisciplinary nature of hospital processes, the development of a specific CP containing all necessary constraints of all treatments to cure an illness is a difficult and time-consuming task [7].

To support the development of CP, IT-based pathway mining methods have been designed in the recent years. These methods can be classified into process mining, mining from clinical guidelines and other techniques like data mining or machine learning.

In process mining, process models are extracted from execution logs [8]. Since the billing data used in this paper is similar to event logs, our novel path mining method can be classified as a process mining approach. For this reason, the following review focusses on this class of approaches for pathway mining.

Process mining methods have successfully been employed to identify changes in treatment processes and differences to given guidelines or clinical best practices [9]. Furthermore, they have been used to find particularly conspicuous and deceitful patient cases automatically [7, 10]. Notwithstanding, there is a great need of new process mining approaches. After analyzing several common process mining techniques, none of them was able to meet all requirements for using them in practice or to identify good models even for well-defined clinical processes [11, 12].

Huang et al. face these criticisms and develop a new approach based on a dynamic programming algorithm which splits the observed time periods into continuous and overlapping intervals. Their approach is able to find frequent medical behavior patterns in each specific time interval in a given event log file. In a case study valid pathway summaries are found showing the global and time interval specific structure of current medical treatment processes [13].

Another approach developed by *Huang et al.* is based on an unsupervised probabilistic clustering technique called Latent Dirichlet Allocation. The patterns encompass a set of treatment activities forming the essential features of the CP [14]. In experiments with a real word data set, the temporal structure of discovered CP patterns could be extracted successfully by considering a treatment's timestamps [15].

To sum up, the mentioned approaches have a descriptive character and are able to show how current treatment processes are performed in hospitals. Nevertheless, none of these approaches is able to find CP that can be used for scheduling patient treatment services and relocations since they lack scheduling-relevant information like time or precedence constraints between single CP steps. Furthermore, the heterogeneity of patient case data from highly variable treatment processes is one of the most challenging problems in process mining approaches [7, 11, 12, 15, 16]. To find homogenous case groups, the use of clustering techniques is advised [16]. Unfortunately, using a clustering algorithm is likely to mix up heterogeneous patient cases resulting in CP that will never occur in reality, cannot be used for scheduling and could even decrease hospital process transparency.

To bridge this gap, we describe a process mining approach which is able to find homogenous cases and plausible CP for elective inpatients (pre-planned, non-emergency cases) that meet scheduling-relevant requirements, addressing the two main challenges of process mining techniques: (1) strongly heterogeneous patient cases with a great variability in treatment processes and (2) event data from various IT-systems with different structure and content [7, 11, 12, 15–17].

3   Concept of Scheduling-Focused Clinical Pathways

The CP scheduling problem aims at improving the patient flow and hospital resource allocation by finding a best possible hospital-wide schedule for each patient avoiding bottlenecks, waiting times etc. As a result, for each patient it is known where and when which kind of treatment will be performed and how long the patient will stay on certain wards during his hospitalization if no complications arise [18, 19].

Regarding the findings related to this scheduling problem, a time granularity of one day is considered to be sufficient [18, 19]. Thus, a clinical pathway comprises a set of day-based steps (ward relocations and medical treatments). Consequently, we propose that the result of CP mining should contain two separate interrelated components leading to an implicit pathway characterization: First, **the pathway structure** containing a set of daily pathway steps which are categorized into **relocations** and **treatments** together with their timely occurrence relative to the hospital admission. Second, a set of **pathway constraints** ensure feasible scheduling results while allowing some flexibility in scheduling which can be used for optimization (see Fig 1). Details of required resources are part of the scheduling process and beyond our scope.

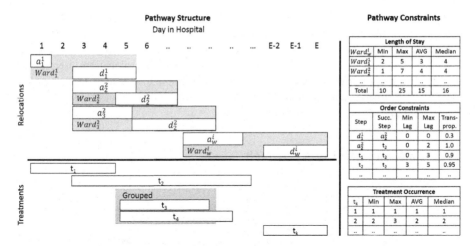

Fig. 1. Concept of Scheduling Based Pathways

Relocations describe the sequence of wards a patient has to pass and the stay time on each ward. A relocation i consists of two events (admission a_w^i and discharge d_w^i) corresponding to the start and end day of the stay on ward w. Possible values are integer values showing the day of this event during hospitalization corresponding to the hospital admission $a_w^1 = 1$. The time between two events corresponds to the length of stay in days on a ward using resource capacity (e.g. one bed). To provide more scheduling flexibility, it is possible to consider more than one ward as a relocation candidate. In Fig. 1, for example, either admission a_2^2 or a_3^2 could be selected after discharge d_1^1.

Treatments t_k are aggregated packages of activities required to cure an illness. Each treatment can be performed within one day if all relevant resources are available. If two or more have to take place at the same day, they can be "grouped".

The timing of each relocation and treatment is constrained by the given feasible time frame relative to the admission day. The frame is bounded by the first and the last observed occurrence of a step within all cases. This supports a flexible treatment scheduling respecting patients and resource requirements later on.

Pathway constraints include the length of stay, precedence constraints and treatment occurrences. The length of stay specifies how much time a patient should at least (Min) and at most (Max) spend on a ward w at relocation i. In order to improve transparency, the average (AVG) and the median length of stay (Median) is considered for each individual ward as well as for the total stay time of the whole pathway.

The feasible time windows of all steps are computed on the basis of multiple cases. This can lead to overlapping permissible windows (see Fig. 1 treatment t_1 and t_2). Given this overlapping, precedence constraints are necessary to ensure a medically correct order of all steps after scheduling. These constraints consist of precedence relations as well as minimum (Min Lag), maximum (Max Lag) waiting time-lags and relative transition frequencies between successive steps. If the Min Lag equals zero, the two steps might occur at the same day. We use relative transition frequencies to ensure medically correct CP. To avoid CP biased by some exceptions in treatment processes, we use thresholds for the minimum relative transition frequency (e.g. occurrence of 90% in all cases) which have to be satisfied in order to consider a given transition. Transition frequencies between wards show valid relocation alternatives. Finally, treatment occurrences ensure that each treatment t_k is at least (Min_{tk}) and at most (Max_{tk}) times contained in a CP. Average (AVG_{tk}) and median ($Median_{tk}$) occur is again computed for transparency purposes.

4   Pathway Mining Approach

```
1  caseGroupList = getHomogenousGroups(leadingDiagnosis,admissionWard)
2     for each group in caseGroupList:
3        while i <= max(countRelocationStates(group)):
4           wardList = getWardsAtRelocationState(i,group)
5           for each ward in wardList:
6              wardKeyFigDict[i,ward] = computeWardKF(i,ward,group)
7           i = i+1
8        totalLOSKeyFiguresDict = getTotalLOSKF(group)
9        treatmentList = getAllTreatments(group)
10       for each treat in treatmentList:
11          treatmentKeyFigures[treat] = getTreatKF(group)
12          listOfDays = getDaysOfOccurrence(treat, group)
13          treatDays[treat] = getFeasDays(listOfDays)
14       posGroups = getAllPossibleTreat-Groups(treatmentList)
15       for each (treat-A, treat-B) in posGroups:
16          if getGroupValue(treat-A, treat-B) >= groupThreshold:
17             listOfFoundGroups.add(treat-A, treat-B)
18       for each (pred,succ) in getAllPossibleStepOrders(group):
19          transFreq = getTransitionFrequency(pred,succ)
20          if transFreq >= precedenceThreshold then:
21             orderDict[pred,succ] = getOrderKF(pred,succ,group)
```

The above shown CP mining algorithm identifies pathway structures and constraints based on homogenous case groups received from a §21-KHentgG[1] billing data set. A homogenous case group is a collection of patient cases sharing the same illness and a similar treatment. In line (L) 1 we extract all of these case groups, assuming that all possible treatments of a certain illness have to start at the same ward within a hospital and show a similar set of operations and procedures (OPS). Thus we first select all elective cases with the same leading diagnosis[2] and an admission on the same ward. After that we compute binary OPS profiles of all selected cases. All cases that now share the same OPS profile are considered as a homogenous case group.

To find all **relocations,** we first compute the maximum number of relocation steps of a group (L 3). Based on this, we extract the list of possible wards in chronological order (L 4). In L 5, we compute the key figures Min, Max, AVG and Median of length of stay (LOS) on each ward as well as the feasible day-based time windows for

---

[1] An overview of the entire §21-KHentgG dataset, all case related data and an example data set can be found at: http://www.g-drg.de/cms/Datenlieferung_gem._21_KHEntgG

[2] Each case can have plenty of diagnoses, but only one leading diagnosis. This diagnosis is the medical reason for hospitalization.

admission and discharge to/from these wards relative to the first admission. Similar key figures are computed in L 8 for the total LOS for the whole case group[3].

In L 9 to 13, we extract all **treatments** within the case group, the key figures Min, Max, AVG and Median of the occurrence of each treatment as well as the list of feasible days (relative to the first admission) for each treatment. Start and end of the feasible time interval are computed in L 13 as min/max of all observed occurrences.

In order to obtain all groups of treatments to be scheduled at the same day, we first determine all pairs of steps which occurred at the same day (L 14). Based on these, we compute the relative group value by counting the number of real occurrences of both treatments at the same day divided by the amount of possible occurrences at the same day, which is the minimum of the occurrence of both treatments (L 16). To avoid groupings due to exceptional treatments, a given *groupThreshold* has to be met to create a hard-constrained grouping (L 17).

To identify precedence constraints, we compute the transition frequency of each possible pairing of case steps (L 18 to 19). We compute the transition frequency of two steps by counting how many times a certain daily-based pair occurred divided by the number of how many times the pair *could have* occurred within the group. The value of possible occurrences is the value of how many times both steps occur within all cases. To ensure valid relocation sequences after scheduling, we compute the transition frequency for two wards depending on the number of relocations in the case. Possible wards at stage $i+1$ are feasible only if a relocation from the former ward at stage i has been observed. In order to avoid precedence constraints based on few individual patient treatments, a given *precedenceThreshold* has to be met within all cases to create significant constraints (L 20 to 21).

5   Results

The following results are based on a real-world billing dataset of a German university medical center from 2011 involving approx. 40.000 inpatient cases.

Since we pursue the goal of developing a general pathway mining method, we tested our approach on several leading diagnoses. In order to facilitate the discussion of the results, the following presentation focuses on the diagnosis C61[4] (Malignant neoplasm of prostate) forming the leading diagnosis with the third largest amount of inpatients, admitted 504 times in 2011. We chose ward HA2200 for further path mining because 97 % of all patients were admitted there.

After extracting the OPS profiles of all 492 cases, we received the homogenous case groups by hierarchical Ward clustering using the Jaccard coefficient to compute the distance matrix and cutting the results at a height of zero such that only equal items are within a cluster. This ensures that different kinds of treatments are not mixed up within one cluster. Altogether, the Ward clustering resulted in 112 equal cases contained in three big clusters with 85, 75 and 50 cases and four medium-sized

---

[3] In order to simplify accessing the figures later on, we store them in [key: value] dictionaries:

[4] All diagnosis are stored as IDC-10 strings within the dataset.

clusters with 11 to 27 cases. One third of all cases (131) are assigned to clusters with 2 to 10 cases and 71 clusters contain a single case. In the following, we discuss the results mining a 13-case cluster containing interesting results and exhibiting a complex treatment process. The parameters *groupThreshold* and *precedenceThreshold* were set to 0.95 and 0.9. Fig. 2 shows the path mining results. This CP contains 5 treatments including a surgery. The stay time is between 8 and 19 days, with an average of 11 and no further relocation. The DRG of the cases is M01B and has an average stay time of 9.9 days in Germany[5].

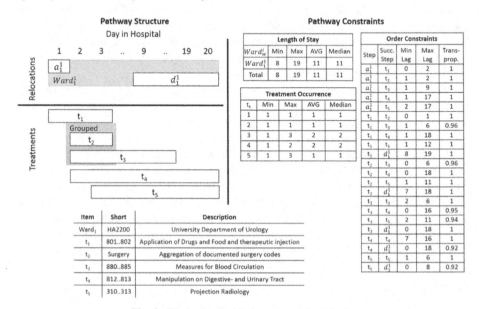

Fig. 2. CP obtained with the presented method

It is notable that the surgery in our cases is done at day 2 or 3. If the surgery could be performed at the first day of hospitalization, the length of stay may be reduced. The found precedence constraint between t_2 and d_1^1 with a min lag of 7 days underlines this guess. A closer look at the data reveals that the average stay time of cases with surgery at the second day is approximately 11 days, instead of 14 days. Another interesting insight for managing patient flows is the insight of grouping the surgery (t_2) and "measures of blood circulation" (t_3). If it is known ahead that the resources required for t_3 are unavailable at a certain time, the admission of patients should be shifted accordingly in order to avoid waiting time. The pathway mining results were discussed the case manager of the ward HA2200. She recognized the structure of our mined treatments processes and confirmed our scheduling-related interpretations like shifting the surgery on the first day and that a surgery could only be done if all preparing OPS have been done before.

---

[5] http://medcode.ch/de/de/drgs/G-DRG-2012/M01B

6   Conclusion

In 2012, every third German hospital was unprofitable [2]. One of most promising ways to improve hospital efficiency is the implementation of CP [3]. In this paper, we propose a scheduling-focused CP concept and an algorithm to automatically extract CP from standardized billing data. Summarizing the results, our method is able to identify real-world treatment processes from standardized hospital billing data. Regarding the aims of this paper, the unique contributions of our approach are: First, our scheduling-based CP concept identifies structures and dependencies instead of merely computing key figures. This new level of transparency enables discussing reasons and solutions for inefficient treatment processes. Second, our CP ensure a valid patient scheduling by only considering homogenous case groups and scheduling-related information.

In future research, we will combine our CP components (structure and constraints) with resource information in order to develop a new kind of hospital-wide scheduling system for elective patient flows. This system will be validated in cooperation with the university hospital. With our results we hope to make an important step on the path to realizing the vision of being "[..] able to derive (partial) treatment process models merely by pushing a button"[12].

References

1. Publikation - Gesundheit - Statistisches Bundesamt (Destatis) - Gesundheit - Ausgaben - Fachserie 12 Reihe 7.1.1 - 2011 - Statistisches Bundesamt (Destatis) (2011)
2. Augurzky, B.: Krankenhaus Rating Report 2013: Krankenhausversorgung zwischen Euro-Krise und Schuldenbremse. medhochzwei-Verl., Heidelberg (2013)
3. Villa, S., Barbieri, M., Lega, F.: Restructuring patient flow logistics around patient care needs: implications and practicalities from three critical cases. Health Care Manag. Sci. **12**, 155–165 (2009)
4. Jacobs, B.: Ableitung von klinischen Pfaden aus evidenzbasierten Leitlinien am Beispiel der Behandlung des Mammakarzinoms der Frau (2007)
5. Cerrito, P.: Clinical Data Mining to Discover Optimal Treatment Patterns. In: Pardalos, P.M., Georgiev, P.G., Papajorgji, P., Neugaard, B. (eds.) Systems Analysis Tools for Better Health Care Delivery, pp. 99–130. Springer, New York (2013)
6. Huang, Z., Dong, W., Duan, H., Li, H.: Similarity Measure Between Patient Traces for Clinical Pathway Analysis: Problem, Method, and Applications. IEEE J. Biomed. Health Inform. **18**, 4–14 (2014)
7. Rebuge, Á., Ferreira, D.R.: Business process analysis in healthcare environments: A methodology based on process mining. Inf. Syst. **37**, 99–116 (2012)
8. van der Aalst, W.M.P.: Process mining: discovery, conformance and enchancement of business processes. Springer, Heidelberg (2011)
9. Peleg, M., Soffer, P., Ghattas, J.: Mining process execution and outcomes – position paper. In: Hofstede, A., Benatallah, B., Paik, H.-Y. (eds.) Business Process Management Workshops, pp. 395–400. Springer, Heidelberg (2007)
10. Yang, W.-S., Hwang, S.-Y.: A process-mining framework for the detection of healthcare fraud and abuse. Expert Syst. Appl. **31**, 56–68 (2006)

11. Kaymak, U., Mans, R., van de Steeg, T., Dierks, M.: On process mining in health care. Presented at the October (2012)
12. Lang, M., Bürkle, T., Laumann, S., Prokosch, H.-U.: Process mining for clinical workflows: challenges and current limitations. Stud. Health Technol. Inform. **136**, 229–234 (2008)
13. Huang, Z., Lu, X., Duan, H.: On mining clinical pathway patterns from medical behaviors. Artif. Intell. Med. **56**, 35–50 (2012)
14. Huang, Z., Lu, X., Duan, H.: Latent treatment topic discovery for clinical pathways. J. Med. Syst. **37**, 1–10 (2013)
15. Huang, Z., Dong, W., Ji, L., Gan, C., Lu, X., Duan, H.: Discovery of clinical pathway patterns from event logs using probabilistic topic models. J. Biomed. Inform. (2013)
16. Song, M., Günther, C.W., van der Aalst, W.M.P.: Trace clustering in process mining. In: Ardagna, D., Mecella, M., Yang, J. (eds.) Business Process Management Workshops, pp. 109–120. Springer, Heidelberg (2009)
17. Mans, R.S., van der Aalst, W.M., Vanwersch, R.J., Moleman, A.J.: Process mining in healthcare: data challenges when answering frequently posed questions. In: Lenz, R., Miksch, S., Peleg, M., Reichert, M., Riaño, D., ten Teije, A. (eds.) ProHealth 2012 and KR4HC 2012. LNCS, vol. 7738, pp. 140–153. Springer, Heidelberg (2013)
18. Gartner, D., Kolisch, R.: Scheduling the hospital-wide flow of elective patients. Eur. J. Oper. Res. (2013)
19. Helbig, K.: Zeitplanung für Patientenpfade unter Berücksichtigung von Betten, Behandlungskapazitä ten und Fairnesskriterien. Tagungsband 15 Interuniv. Doktorandenseminar Wirtsch. Univ. Chemnitz Dresd. Freib. Halle-Wittenb. Jena Leipz. 34–44 (2011)

A Framework for Benchmarking BPMN 2.0 Workflow Management Systems

Vincenzo Ferme$^{(\boxtimes)}$, Ana Ivanchikj, and Cesare Pautasso

Faculty of Informatics, University of Lugano (USI), Lugano, Switzerland
{vincenzo.ferme,ana.ivanchikj,cesare.pautasso}@usi.ch
http://www.benchflow.inf.usi.ch

Abstract. The diverse landscape of Workflow Management Systems (WfMSs) makes it challenging for users to compare different solutions to identify the ones most suitable to their requirements. Thus a comparison framework that would define common grounds in many different aspects, such as price, reliability, security, robustness and performance is necessary. In this paper we focus on the performance aspect, and we present a framework for automatic and reliable calculation of performance metrics for BPMN 2.0 WfMSs. We validate the framework by applying it on two open-source WfMSs. The goal is to contribute to the improvement of existing WfMSs by pinpointing performance bottlenecks, and to empower end users to make informed decisions when selecting a WfMS.

Keywords: BPMN 2.0 · Workflow management systems · Benchmarking

1 Introduction

With the growth in the variety of Workflow Management Systems (WfMSs) companies face a difficult decision when selecting a suitable system for their Business Process Management (BPM) projects. The main differences among WfMSs consist of: the supported executable modeling languages (e.g., WS-BPEL, BPMN 2.0), the integration with external systems and tools (e.g., Web service APIs for monitoring and business intelligence [3]), their performance [12], robustness [6], operating costs and other non-functional requirements. In this paper, we address the need to assess alternative WfMSs based on the runtime performance of the Business Process (BP) execution by their Workflow Engine (WfE). Such assessment would empower BPM adopters to map their requirements to the available solutions and BPM vendors and developers to improve their technology offerings. Our framework for benchmarking BPMN 2.0 WfMSs ensures the reliability of the benchmarking process. It does so by structurally defining and controlling the environment under which the performance experiments are carried out and their results analyzed, while taking into account the main requirements of a good benchmark [5]. The decision to focus on BPMN 2.0 (BPMN2 hereinafter) is due to its growing support by commercial and academic WfMSs. As initial validation of the framework we use it for a simplistic performance test of two WfMSs.

© Springer International Publishing Switzerland 2015
H.R. Motahari-Nezhad et al. (Eds.): BPM 2015, LNCS 9253, pp. 251–259, 2015.
DOI: 10.1007/978-3-319-23063-4_18

2 Related Work

The need for benchmarking WfMSs has been identified many times. In 2000, Weikum et al. [4] propose a benchmark for comparing the performance of different commercial WfEs by measuring their throughput to study the impact of the database component. Ten years later, SOABench [1] defines one of the first performance comparisons for WS-BPEL WfEs. It assumes that the performance of a WS-BPEL WfE can be reduced to its response time. A recent review by Röck et al. [12], of the work undertaken so far for benchmarking WS-BPEL WfEs, highlights: the lack of an extensive evaluation of different WfEs, the unclear definition of the workload mix (i.e., the mix of process models executed by the System Under Test (SUT)) and the load functions (i.e., the functions describing how the requests to start and interact with the BP instances are sent to the SUT), as well as the narrowly focused metrics for characterizing system's performance. There exist many commercial and open-source performance measurement frameworks [11], some dedicated to generic Web Applications (e.g, Faban (http://faban.org), JMeter (http://jmeter.apache.org)), and others to middlewares [1], [8]. However, to the best of our knowledge, no ready-to-use open-source solutions exist for comprehensive benchmarking of BPMN2 WfMSs. There exist similar tools [1], [7], however they do not implement performance benchmarking (e.g., Betsy [7]), or they use virtual machines to deploy the SUT (e.g., SOABench [1]), introducing additional overhead possibly impacting the performance.

3 The BenchFlow Benchmarking Framework

As opposed to other software systems, benchmarking WfMSs introduces additional challenges derived from: 1) the system deployment complexity due to their distributed nature; 2) the high number of configuration parameters affecting their performance; 3) the absence of a standard interface to interact with the WfMSs and to access execution data; 4) the asynchronous execution of the processes; and 5) the complexity of the execution behaviours that can be expressed by modern modeling and execution languages such as BPMN2. The system deployment complexity and the high number of configuration options require to integrate the configuration and the deployment of the SUT, i.e., the WfMS, as part of the performance test definition. It is the only way to scale out the large number of tests needed to comprehensively evaluate the WfMSs performance. The absence of a standard interface makes abstractions necessary for handling many different WfMSs by the framework. The asynchronous execution of processes makes it challenging to collect the measures directly on the SUT side since the client is only aware of the response time of the requested task's queuing, whereas it remains unaware of its actual execution status and execution time. The complexity of the possible behaviours that can be expressed needs to be tackled by proposing a model-driven approach that, starting from a BPMN model and a set of WfMS configurations, has to instantiate the infrastructure necessary to perform the test.

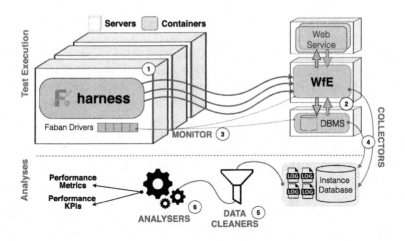

Fig. 1. BenchFlow Framework Architecture

The BenchFlow framework builds upon Faban, an established and tested "performance workload creation and execution framework", to design the load drivers and issue the load to the WfMS. The load driver, which is executed by the harness, provides the infrastructure needed to define the simulated users and their interaction with the WfE. BenchFlow also exploits Docker (https://www.docker.com) as a containerization technology, to enable the automatic deployment and configuration of the WfMS and to ensure that the experimental results can be reproduced. As shown in Fig.1, a WfMS can be tested with BenchFlow only if: 1) its API can be used for automation of the test execution [13]. The API should feature: deployment of BP models, start of a BP instance execution, access to the list of pending user and manual tasks and ability to complete them, and sending events to the running BP instances; 2) its logs or instance database (DB) include performance data about the BP instances' execution. These can be queried to calculate WfMS performance metrics. BenchFlow aims to minimise the effort of adding a new WfMS to the framework and executing performance tests on it. To add a new WfMS, users need to: provide a containerized version of the WfMS (this should be published in a public registry if the results are meant to be reproduced), integrate the custom WfE interfaces, provide the queries that BenchFlow can run to assess the completion of the BP instances execution and to extract the raw performance data.

3.1 Performance Test Execution

The WfMSs are automatically deployed and undeployed using Docker (Fig. 1.1 and 1.2). Each component involved in the benchmark (the WfE, the instance

DB, the Web services and Faban load drivers) are packaged as Docker images to be deployed and executed on different servers connected by a dedicated local network so that interferences are minimized. Docker enables the repeatability of the benchmark execution, since it freezes the system state so that every test runs from exactly the same initial conditions. Containerization technologies introduce some overhead in system's performance that can be detrimental for the performance tests. However a recent reliable performance analysis of Docker [2] has shown that, if carefully configured, Docker reaches near-zero overhead.

After the WfMS is deployed, the workload can be applied. The workload is defined by standard BPMN2 models and BenchFlow provides already defined workload packages and artifacts. These consist of a mix of BPMN2 models that have to be deployed in the WfE. They are characterized by their features (e.g., which BPMN2 language constructs they use), and the simulated behaviour of the users instantiating them and interacting with them, as well as the simulated behaviour of the Web Services called by the WfE. Each WfMS uses a custom mechanism for deployment, instantiation and interaction with tasks. We abstract common interaction interfaces, and then map them to the actual ones implemented by each WfMS. Faban drivers issue the load to the WfMS, and we expose its API by means of a Domain Specific Language (DSL), similarly to what has been done in other performance frameworks and generic application performance testing (e.g., https://github.com/flood-io/ruby-jmeter). The use of a DSL simplifies the definition of a reusable workload package encapsulating the simulated behaviour of the interacting users and external services.

3.2 Performance Analyzes

BenchFlow automatically collects all the data needed to compute performance metrics, and to check the correct execution of the tests (e.g., errors by different WfMS components). The client-side data (e.g., the response time of BP instance start requests) are collected by Faban and integrated with the server-side data collected by BenchFlow. The server-side data is collected from the execution logs from all the different containers realizing the WfMS, as well as from the instance DB populated by the WfMS during the test execution. In order to avoid interferences during the test execution, we collect (Fig. 1.4) all the data only after the WfMS completes the execution of the issued load. This is determined by first monitoring the CPU utilization of the running Docker container, and then when the container is idle, by checking if the number of completed BP instances matches the number of BP instances started by the load driver (Fig. 1.3). We exploit the logs to identify execution errors, and containers' statistics (obtained through Docker *stats* API) and the instance DB data to compute the performance metrics included in BenchFlow (Fig. 1.6). Each WfMS has its own internal representation and structure for the logs and the instance DB data. In order to define the metrics computation and the performance analyzes only once for all WfMSs we map these logs and data to a uniform representation (Fig. 1.5).

4   Evaluation: Preliminary Scalability Experiment

In this section we present the results of using BenchFlow to evaluate the scalability of two open-source WfMSs as the number of users increases. The load issued to the WfMS and the selected performance metrics are not exhaustive.

Fig. 2. Experiment Business Process Model

4.1   Experiment Description and Set-Up

This performance testing experiment is based on the following elements [11]:

1) *Workload:* the instances of the BP models set executed by the WfE during the experiment. Given the limited scope of this experiment we use only one simple BP model presented in Fig. 2. The Script task is an empty script. The Timer event defines a wait time of 2s before allowing the process to continue.

2) *Load Function:* the function handling system's load. In our case the Load function determines how the BP instances are initiated by a variable number of simulated users (since we are testing system's scalability), growing from 5 to 150 concurrent users. Due to experiment's simplicity the load driver executes the Load function only once when the test starts. The duration of the load function is 300s with 30s of *ramp-up period*. The ramp-up period defines the transition from none to all simulated users being active. This means that it takes 30s before all users start issuing requests for BP instance instantiation. For example, in an experiment with 5 users, a new simulated user is created every 6s during the ramp-up period. After becoming active each user issues one BP instance start request per second.

3) *Test environment*: the characteristics of the hardware used to run the experiment. We use three servers (Fig. 1): one for the harness executing the load driver, one for the WfE and one for the Database Management System (DBMS). We deploy the WfE on the least powerful machine (12 CPU Cores at 800Mhz, 64GB of RAM) to ensure that the machine where we deploy the Load driver (64 CPU Cores at 1400MHz, 128GB of RAM) can issue sufficient load and that the DBMS (64 CPU Cores at 2300MHz, 128GB of RAM) can handle the requests from the WfE. After each test we verify the absence of measurement noise by checking the environment metrics (CPU, RAM and network usage) and the WfE logs to ensure that all the BP instances are completed.

We run the experiment on two open-source WfMSs supporting native execution of BPMN2. We test them on top of Apache Tomcat 7.0.59 using Oracle Java 8 and MySQL Community Server 5.5.42. We use the default configuration as specified on vendors' websites.

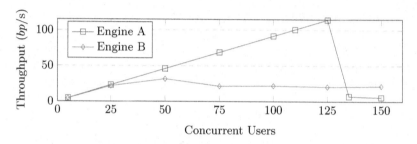

Fig. 3. Throughput

4.2   Results

The first metric we analyze is the *Throughput* $= \frac{\#BPInstances(bp)}{Time(s)}$ [9, ch. 11]. As per Fig. 3 Engine B does not scale well after 25 and the throughput starts degrading after 50 users. Engine A can handle a load up to 125, with the throughput decreasing abruptly with 135-150 users. Thus the Capacity of the WfEs can be estimated to less than 135 for Engine A and less than 50 users for Engine B.

The BP *instance duration* is the time difference between the start and the completion of a BP instance. It is presented in the box and whisker plot in Fig. 4(a) for Engine A and Fig. 4(b) for Engine B. This type of plot displays the analyzed data into quartiles where the box contains the second and third quartile, while the median is the line inside the box. The lines outside of the box, called whiskers, show the minimum and maximum value of the data [10]. The measurements show that Engine A scales better since it starts having an unexpected behaviour after 125 concurrent users, while the first execution performance problems of Engine B appear at 50 users, as evident from the instance duration increase of one order of magnitude. In Fig. 5 we report Engine A's CPU utilization for each of the tests. It is interesting to notice that while the instance duration increases substantially starting from 135 concurrent users (Fig. 4 (a)), the CPU utilization decreases, indicating that the slowdown of the WfE is not caused by lack of resources. The same has been verified by checking the CPU/RAM utilization of the DBMS.

After noticing a bottleneck in performance scaling, we investigate the causes. Since only two constructs, a Script task and a Timer event, are used in the experiment BP model, we test the WfE performance in handling each of them individually. The test processes used consist of a Start event, the tested construct and an End event. As per the previously gathered information we focus on the critical number of users (125/135 for Engine A and 25/50 for Engine B). We use the *delay* metric which compares the expected to the actual duration of the construct execution. The expected duration of the Timer is 2s, while the empty Script task should take 0s to complete. The delay measurements (Fig. 6) show that both WfEs handle the Script task efficiently with an average delay below 10ms. The same does not hold for the Timer. For Engine A, the average delay of the Timer at 135 users is by three orders of magnitude greater than at 125 users.

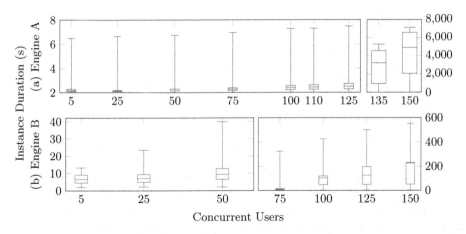

Fig. 4. Aggregated Process Instance Duration Comparison

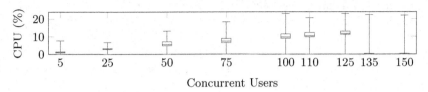

Fig. 5. Aggregated CPU Usage (Engine A)

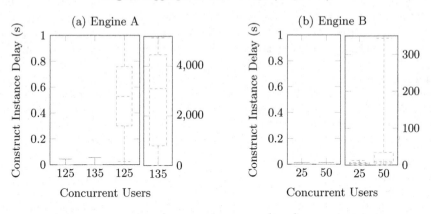

Fig. 6. Script Task (———) and Timer Event (- - - -) feature comparison

For Engine B, the delay increases by two orders of magnitude between 25 and 50 users. The observed system behaviour could be due to an excessive overhead introduced by concurrently handling many Timers, which could cause growth in the Timers queue thus postponing their execution and increasing their delay.

5   Conclusion and Future Work

The BenchFlow framework greatly simplifies the performance benchmarking of BPMN2 WfMSs, by abstracting the heterogeneity of their interfaces and automating their deployment, the data collection and the metrics and Key Performance Indicators (KPIs) computation. It does so by relying on Faban and Docker, and by verifying the absence of noise in the performance measurements. While the complexity of BPMN2 makes it challenging to benchmark the performance of the WfMSs implementing it, the benefits of doing so are evident. The first experimental results obtained with a simple BP model running on two popular open-source WfMSs have uncovered important scalability issues. We have discussed the identified performance bottlenecks with the WfMS vendors who have clarified the probable cause. Namely, in Engine A we have used a different DBMS configuration in the setup of the system. In Engine B the goal of the default configuration is a fast setup, not optimisation. The discussion has emphasised the need of defining a systematic methodology for obtaining a ready to use setup of the WfMS from the vendors. Developers can use these results to improve the WfMSs, while end users can decide which WfMS to deploy depending on how many concurrent users they have, and carefully set their configuration.

As a next step we plan to release the framework to the community to gain empirical evidence about its benefits and limitations. We will also continue the experiments to measure the performance of additional real-world WfEs. The ultimate goal is to give a fair comparison of commercial BPMN2 WfMSs by means of a small set of KPIs [13], which we intend to derive by defining and aggregating a set of raw metrics. We also plan to extend the BenchFlow framework towards other non-functional quality attributes, e.g., reliability, security and robustness.

Acknowledgments. This work is partially funded by the Swiss National Science Foundation with the BenchFlow - A Benchmark for Workflow Management Systems (Grant Nr. 145062) project. The authors would like to thank Paul Holmes-Higgin, Frank Leymann, Sebastian Menski, Daniel Meyer, Tijs Rademakers, Bernd Rücker, and Marigianna Skouradaki for the insightful discussions and feedback.

References

1. Bianculli, D., Binder, W., et al.: Automated performance assessment for service-oriented middleware: a case study on BPEL engines. In: 19th WWW, pp. 141–150. ACM, Raleigh (2010)
2. Felter, W., Ferreira, A., Rajamony, R., Rubio, J.: An updated performance comparison of virtual machines and linux containers. Tech. rep, IBM, July 2014
3. Garro, J.M., Bazán, P.: Constructing and monitoring processes in BPM using hybrid architectures. IJACSA **3**(4), 78–85 (2014)
4. Gillmann, M., Mindermann, R., et al.: Benchmarking and configuration of workflow management systems. In: Scheuermann, P., Etzion, O. (eds.) CoopIS 2000. LNCS, vol. 1901, pp. 186–197. Springer, Heidelberg (2000)
5. Gray, J.: The Benchmark Handbook for Database and Transaction Systems, 2nd edn. Morgan Kaufmann, San Francisco (1992)

6. Harrer, S., Wirtz, G., Nizamic, F., Lazovik, A.: Towards a robustness evaluation framework for BPEL engines. In: 7th SOCA, pp. 199–206. IEEE, Matsue (2014)
7. Harrer, S., et al.: Automated and isolated tests for complex middleware products: the case of BPEL engines. In: 7th ICSTW, pp. 390–398. IEEE, Cleveland (2014)
8. IBM: IBM Rational Performance Tester. http://www.ibm.com/software/products/en/performance
9. Lazowska, E.D., et al.: Quantitative System Performance: Computer System Analysis Using Queueing Network Models. Prentice-Hall, Upper Saddle River (1984)
10. McGill, R., Tukey, J.W., Larsen, W.A.: Variations of box plots. The American Statistician **32**(1), 12–16 (1978)
11. Molyneaux, I.: The Art of Application Performance Testing: From Strategy to Tools. O'Reilly Media Inc., Sebastopol (2014)
12. Röck, C., et al.: Performance benchmarking of BPEL engines: a comparisonframework, status quo evaluation and challenges. In: 26th SEKE, Pittsburgh(2014)
13. Skouradaki, M., Roller, D.H., et al.: On the road to benchmarking BPMN 2.0 workflow engines. In: 6th ICPE, pp. 301–304. ACM, Austin (2015)

Process Compliance and Deviations

Visually Monitoring Multiple Perspectives of Business Process Compliance

David Knuplesch[1]([✉]), Manfred Reichert[1], and Akhil Kumar[2]

[1] Institute of Databases and Information Systems, Ulm University, Ulm, Germany
{david.knuplesch,manfred.reichert}@uni-ulm.de
[2] Smeal College of Business, Pennsylvania State University, State College, PA, USA
akhilkumar@psu.edu

Abstract. A challenge for any enterprise is to ensure conformance of its business processes with imposed compliance rules. The latter may constrain multiple perspectives of a business process, including control flow, data, time, resources, and interactions with business partners. However, business process compliance cannot completely be decided at design time, but needs to be monitored during run time as well. This paper introduces a comprehensive framework for visually monitoring business process compliance. As opposed to existing approaches, the framework supports the visual monitoring of all relevant process perspectives based on the extended Compliance Rule Graph (eCRG) language. Furthermore, it not only allows detecting compliance violations, but visually highlights their causes as well. Finally, the framework assists users in monitoring business process compliance and ensuring a compliant continuation of their running business processes.

Keywords: Business process compliance · Compliance monitoring

1 Introduction

Correctness issues of business process models have been intensively discussed for more than a decade. While early work focused on syntactical correctness and soundness constraints (e.g., absence of deadlocks and lifelocks), the compliance of business processes with semantic constraints has been increasingly considered during the recent years. Usually, *compliance rules* stem from domain-specific requirements, e.g., corporate standards or legal regulations [1], and need to be ensured in all phases of the process life cycle [2,3]. In this context, approaches dealing with the compliance of business processes during their execution are covered by the notion of *compliance monitoring*. In general, events of running business processes need to be considered to detect run-time violations of compliance rules and to notify users accordingly (cf. Fig. 1).

In general, two kinds of compliance monitoring need to be distinguished–reactive and proactive. Regarding *reactive monitoring*, the system only reports

---

This work was done within the research project C³Pro funded by the German Research Foundation (DFG) under project number RE 1402/2-1.

© Springer International Publishing Switzerland 2015
H.R. Motahari-Nezhad et al. (Eds.): BPM 2015, LNCS 9253, pp. 263–279, 2015.
DOI: 10.1007/978-3-319-23063-4_19

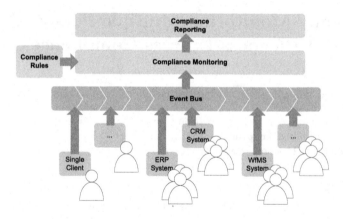

Fig. 1. Compliance Monitoring [4]

a compliance violation once it has occurred. By contrast, *proactive monitoring* aims to preventively avoid any violation; e.g., by recommending appropriate tasks, which still need to be executed to meet the compliance rule, to users.

As example consider the event log from Fig. 2, which refers to an order-to-delivery process [5]: Compliance rule c_1, shown on the right, is satisfied in one case, but violated in another. In particular, the depicted log refers to two different request items related to customers *Mr. Smith* and *Mrs. John*. These items, in turn, trigger two different instances of compliance rule c_1. In both cases, the amount is greater than 10,000 € and hence a solvency check is required (cf. c_1). However, the latter was only performed for the request item of Mr. Smith, but not for the one of *Mrs. John*, i.e., c_1 is violated in the latter case. In addition to the violation of c_1, compliance rule c_2 is violated twice. While the violated

#	date	time	type	id	details
37	1/7/2013	15:27	receive	124	Request
38	1/7/2013	15:27	write	124	customer = Mr.Smith
39	1/7/2013	15:27	write	124	amount = 15.000€
40	1/7/2013	15:27	end	124	*Request*
55	1/7/2013	18:03	receive	592	Request
56	1/7/2013	18:03	write	592	customer = Mrs.John
57	1/7/2013	18:03	write	592	amount = 27.000€
58	1/7/2013	18:03	end	592	*Request*
77	2/7/2013	15:43	start	234	SolvencyCheck (Mrs. Brown)
78	2/7/2013	15:43	read	234	customer = Mr.Smith
79	2/7/2013	15:54	write	234	rating= high
80	2/7/2013	15:55	end	234	*SolvencyCheck*
91	2/7/2013	18:13	start	453	Approval (Mr. Muller)
92	2/7/2013	18:14	read	453	customer = Mr.Smith
93	2/7/2013	18:14	read	453	rating = high
94	2/7/2013	18:17	write	453	result= granted
95	2/7/2013	18:18	end	453	*Approval*
96	2/7/2013	18:19	start	642	Approval (Mrs. Brown)
97	2/7/2013	18:20	read	642	customer = Mrs.John
98	2/7/2013	18:23	write	642	result = granted
99	2/7/2013	18:23	end	642	*Approval*

Compliance rules

c_1 When a ***request item*** with an amount ***greater than 10,000*** is ***received from an agent***, the request must not be approved unless the solvency of the respective customer is checked. The latter task must be started ***at maximum three days*** after the receipt. Furthermore, task **approval** and task **solvency check** must be performed ***by different staff members***.

c_2 After approval of a ***request item***, the agent must be informed about the result ***within one day***.

c_3 After starting the production related to a particular ***order*** the latter may only be changed ***by the head of production***.

Fig. 2. Event log of order-to-delivery processes and compliance rules

instance of rule c_1 will never be successfully completed, the violations of c_2 still may be healed by informing the *agent* about the results of the approvals. The compliance rule examples further indicate that solely monitoring control flow dependencies between tasks is not sufficient to ensure compliance at run time. In addition, constraints with respect to the data, time, and resource perspectives of a business process as well as the interactions this process has with partner processes need to be monitored as well [6–9]. For example, the data perspective of compliance rule c_1 is addressed by the *request item* and its *amount*. In turn, receiving the *request item* (cf. c_1) corresponds to an interaction with a business partner. Furthermore, the phrase *"by different staff members"* deals with the resource perspective, whereas the condition *"at maximum three days"* refers to the time perspective. To meet practical demands, compliance monitoring must not omit these process perspectives.

Altogether, the following requirements need to be addressed:

RQ1. As a fundamental challenge of any compliance monitoring approach, compliance violations must be reliably detected and reported to the appropriate parties by using alerts, emails, text messages, or other notification mechanisms. Furthermore, compliance-aware user guidance is needed to avoid rule violations.

RQ2. Since compliance is not restricted to the control flow perspective solely, the time, resource and data perspectives of a business process as well as its interactions with business partners need to be considered during compliance monitoring as well.

RQ3. In general, the execution of a business process may trigger multiple instances of the same compliance rule. On one hand, this highlights the need for being able to identify the causes of a specific compliance violation as well as for providing proper user feedback [10]. On the other, this mightlead to situations in which a compliance rule is fulfilled or violated multiple times in the context of a particular process instance. Accordingly, any compliance assessment must reflect the relation between fulfilled and violated instances of compliance rules.

RQ1-RQ3 cover the essential *compliance monitoring functionalities* (CMFs) as proposed in [4]. Therefore, they may be used to compare existing approaches for monitoring business compliance. However, [4] also states that existing approaches only partially meet the CMFs. In particular, the combination of an expressive language (RQ2) and full traceability (RQ3) is not well understood yet.

This paper extends the work, we presented in [5] in order to provide a comprehensive framework addressing RQ1-RQ3. In particular, it adds detailed algorithms for compliance rule monitoring based on the visual *extended Compliance Rule Graph (eCRG)* language [8,9]. The current state of a particular eCRG is reflected through a set of visual rule markings. The latter not only indicate compliance violations, but may also be utilized for recommending the next process tasks to be executed to ensure compliance (RQ1). Furthermore, these markings allow us to clearly differ between fulfilled and violated instances of an eCRG and also pro-

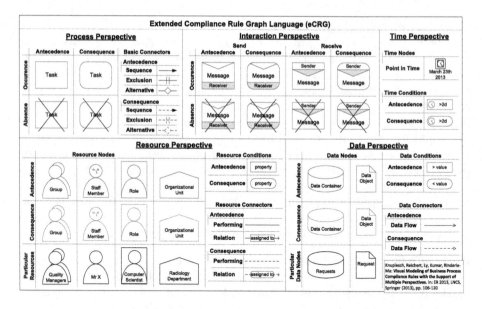

Fig. 3. Elements of the eCRG language [8,9]

vide a suitable basis for compliance metrics (RQ3). Note that the eCRG language supports the time, resource and data perspectives as well as interactions with business partners (RQ2). We evaluate the algorithms based on a proof-of-concept prototype, which was also applied to real world compliance scenarios we had obtained from one of our case studies in the healthcare domain [9].

The remainder of this paper is organized as follows: Section 2 introduces the *extended Compliance Rule Graph* (eCRG) language. The monitoring framework as well as algorithms that manage the markings of an eCRG are introduced in Section 3. Section 4 validates the framework and presents its proof-of-concept prototype. Section 5 discusses related work. Section 6 concludes the paper and provides an outlook on future research.

2   Fundamentals

This paper utilizes the extended Compliance Rule Graph (eCRG) language we developed for modeling compliance rules [8,9]. The eCRG language is based on the Compliance Rule Graph (CRG) language [10]. As opposed to CRG, eCRG not only focuses on the control flow perspective, but also provides integrated support for the resource, data and time perspectives as well as for the interactions with business partners. To cover the various perspectives, the eCRG language allows for *attachments* in addition to *nodes* and *connectors* (i.e. edges). Nodes, connectors and attachments may be partitioned into an *antecedence pattern* and one or several related *consequence patterns*. Both patterns are modeled using *occurrence* and *absence nodes*, which either express the occurrence or absence of certain events (e.g. related to the execution of a particular task) or which refer

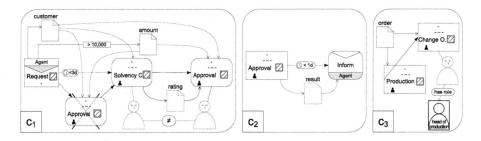

Fig. 4. Modeling compliance rules $c_1 - c_3$ with the eCRG language

to process entities (e.g. data objects). In turn, edges and attachments are used to refine the specification of the elements they are affiliated to (e.g., by specifying control flow dependencies). Furthermore, an eCRG may contain *instance nodes* referring to particular objects that exist independently from the respective rule (e.g. *Mr. Smith, postnatal ward, physician*). Note that instance nodes are neither part of the antecedence nor the consequence pattern. Fig. 3 provides an overview of eCRG elements, which are applied in Fig. 4 to model the compliance rules from Fig. 2. In this paper, we refer to the following elements of an eCRG:

- *Nodes*: These include, for example, *TaskNodes, MessageNodes, PointInTimeNodes, DataObjects*, and *ResourceNodes*.
- *Edges*: These include, for example, *SequenceFlowEdges, DataFlowEdges, PerformingEdges, ResourceRelations*, and *DataRelations*.
- *Attachments*: These include, for example, *DataConditionAttachments, ResourceConditionAttachments*, and *TimeConditionAttachments*.

In this context, two elements a and b of an eCRG have the *same dependency level* ($a \triangleq b$), if they are elements of the same pattern. In turn, an attachment or edge c *corresponds to* a node d, if c directly or indirectly constrains d. Finally, set $\Lambda := Nodes \cup Edges \cup Attachments$ contains all elements of an eCRG. For a more formal eCRG specification, we refer to [11,12].

3 eCRG Compliance Monitoring

This section introduces the framework for visually monitoring multiple perspectives of business process compliance at runtime. As discussed in Sect. 1, compliance monitoring is based on streams of events occurring during the execution of business processes. In particular, it aims to determine or prevent compliance violations. For this purpose, the framework annotates and marks the elements of an eCRG with text, colors and symbols during the processing of events. These markings not only provide a basis for determining the state of compliance of a particular rule, but also highlight the causes of occurring compliance rule violations.

States of Compliance Rules. When monitoring the compliance of running processes, compliance rule instances may be in different states. Fig. 5 outlines the

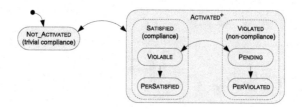

Fig. 5. States of compliance rules

states supported by the framework. The most fundamental state is NOT_ACTIVA-TED, i.e., the compliance rule does not apply to the running process instance so far. In turn, state ACTIVATED expresses that the compliance rule is applicable to the process instance. Furthermore, this state includes the sub-states SATISFIED and VIOLATED (cf. Fig. 5). State SATISFIED is further partitioned into sub-states VIOLABLE and PERSATISFIED (i.e., permanently satisfied), whereas state VIOLATED includes sub-states PENDING and PERVIOLATED (i.e., permanently violated). As explained in the context of the example, business processes may trigger (i.e. activate) multiple instances of a compliance rule. Hence, a compliance rule may be in state ACTIVATED multiple times as indicated by superscript "+" in Fig. 5. However, each of these *activations* of a compliance rule may be in a different sub-state. For example, the event log of the example from Fig. 2 activates compliance rule c_1 twice (cf. Fig. 2). While the first activation is in state PERSATISFIED, the second one is in final state PERVIOLATED.

Events. As the framework enables compliance monitoring for multiple process perspectives (cf. RQ2), it not only monitors events referring to the start and end of tasks. In addition, it considers events that correspond to the sending and receiving of messages as well as data flow events. Furthermore, events may include temporal information as well as information about involved resources. Table 1 summarizes the event types supported by the framework. Each entry refers to the time the event occurred and to a unique identifier. The latter enables us to correlate start, end and data flow events of the same task or message. Note that we presume correct event streams; i.e., they do not deviate from the real process. Further, events are provided in ascending order.

eCRG Markings. To monitor the state of a compliance rule, we mark the elements of an eCRG (cf. Sect. 2, [8,9]) with symbols, colors and text (cf. Fig. 6). Such a *marking of an eCRG* highlights whether or not the events corresponding to a node have occurred so far. Further, a marking describes whether conditions corresponding to edges and attachments are satisfied, violated, or still may be evaluated.

Table 1. Supported Events

Task events	Message events	Data flow events
start(time, id, tasktype, performer)	send(time, id, message)	write(time, id, value $\xrightarrow{param}$ source)
end(time, id, tasktype, performer)	receive(time, id, message)	read(time, id, value $\xleftarrow{param}$ source)
	end(time, id, message)	

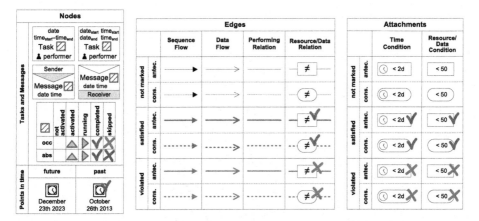

Fig. 6. Fundamental markings of eCRG elements

Let $\mathcal{R}$ be the set of resources, Ω be the set of data objects, $\mathcal{I}$ be the set of identifiers, and   be the set of point in times. Further, let ϵ be the *empty value*. Then: A marking M can be described with the following functions:

- $M.mark : \Lambda \rightarrow \{\square = \epsilon, \triangle, \blacktriangleright, \checkmark, \times\}$ marks the elements of the eCRG as *not-marked* $\square$, *activated* $\triangle$, *running* $\blacktriangleright$, *satisfied* (or *completed*) $\checkmark$, and *violated* (or *skipped*) $\times$ (cf. Fig. 6),
- $M.res : \Lambda \rightarrow \mathcal{R} \cup \{\epsilon\}$ assigns resources to the elements of the eCRG,
- $M.val : \Lambda \rightarrow \Omega \cup \{\epsilon\}$ assigns values to each element of the eCRG,
- $M.id : \Lambda \rightarrow \mathcal{I} \cup \{\epsilon\}$ assigns unique identifiers to the elements of the eCRG,
- $M.start(M.end) : \Lambda \rightarrow \quad \cup\{\epsilon\}$ assigns starting (ending) times to the elements.

The functions of the *initial marking* 0 assign ϵ (and $\square$ respectively) to all elements of an eCRG, except the ones of the *instance pattern* that are mapped to the particular resource, data value or point in time they refer to. Since there may be multiple activations of a particular compliance rule, the *state of an eCRG* is a set $\mathcal{M}$ of markings.

Fig. 7 shows two markings for compliance rule c_1 from Fig. 2. On the left, marking F highlights the fulfillment of c_1 for the request of Mr. Smith. In turn, marking K on the right emphasizes how markings support users in proactively ensuring compliance. In particular, K indicates which data values the task *solvency check* shall read and how task *approval* shall be performed afterwards in order to satisfy c_1.

Event Processing. This section describes the processing of events with an eCRG.[1] Fig. 8 provides an overview. First, all markings are prepared for the processing. Second, effects of these preparations (i.e., changed markings) are propagated onto connected elements. Third, the actual *event handling* takes place. Fourth, effects of the latter step are propagated to connected elements as well. Note that the first two steps may be applied without the last two ones, e.g., to calculate the current state of a compliance rule at an arbitrary point in time.

---

[1] [11] provides a formal specification of the operational semantic of the eCRG language.

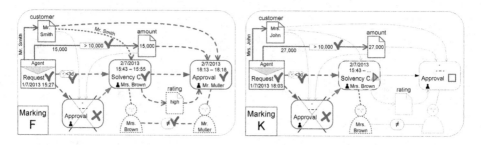

Fig. 7. Examples of markings for compliance rule c_1

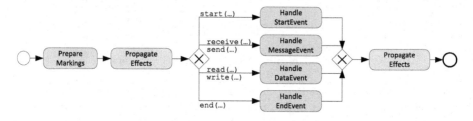

Fig. 8. Processing of start, message, data, and end events

In general, not only the occurrence of events, but also elapsing time can violate compliance, e.g, when the maximum time distance between two tasks becomes violated. To ensure that related issues are not ignored, Listing 1 updates the time perspective of markings before the latter process an event. In particular, point in time nodes are changed to ✓, if they lie in the past now, whereas time condition attachments on task nodes or sequence flow edges are skipped (✗) if they are no longer satisfiable.

Listing 2 deals with the handling of start and message events. In particular, markings of activated task or message nodes, which match the event, are re-set from △ to ▶. Accordingly, identifiers, resources and starting times are set. Note

---

Listing 1. Prepare Markings (with respect to the time perspective)

```
1  prepareMarking(M, event(time,...))
2     ForEach(pitn ∈ PointInTimeNodes with M.mark(pitn) = □)
3        If (pitn ≤ time )  M.mark(pitn) := ✓;

4     ForEach(tc ∈ TimeConditionAttachments with M.mark(tc) = □)
5        If (tc is attached to tn ∈ TaskNodes and M.mark(tn) = ▶)
6           If (∀t ≥ time: tc(t_s(t), t) = false) M.mark(tc) := ✗;

7        ElseIf (tc is attached to sf = (n1, n2) ∈ SequenceFlowEdges and
                M.mark(n1) = ✓)
8           If (∀t ≥ time: tc(t_e(n1), t) = false) M.mark(tc) := ✗;

9     Return M;
```

Listing 2. Handle Events

```
1  handleStartEvent(M, start/send/receive(time, id, type, performer))
2  |   M := ∅;

3  |   ForEach(σ ⊆ {tn|tn ∈ TaskNodes and M.mark(tn) = △ and typeOf(tn) =type} )
4  |   |   ForEach(tn ∈ σ)
5  |   |   |   M' := copy(M);
6  |   |   |   M'.mark(tn) := ▶; M'.start(tn) :=time;
7  |   |   |   M'.id(tn) =id; M'.res(tn) :=performer;
8  |   |   M := M ∪ {M'};

9  |   Return M;

10 handleMessageEvent(M, send/receive(time, id, type))
11 |   M := ∅;

12 |   ForEach(σ ⊆ {tn|tn ∈ MessageNodes and M.mark(tn) = △ and typeOf(tn) =type} )
13 |   |   ForEach(tn ∈ σ)
14 |   |   |   M' := copy(M);
15 |   |   |   M'.mark(tn) := ▶; M'.start(tn) :=time; M'.id(tn) =id; ;
16 |   |   M := M ∪ {M'};

17 |   Return M;

18 handleEndEvent(M, end(time, id, type, performer))
19 |   ForEach(tn ∈ TaskNodes with M.id(tn) = id)
20 |   |   M.mark(tn) := ✓; M.end(tn) :=time;

21 |   Return {M};

22 handleDataEvent(M, write/read(time, id, value ——param——> source))
23 |   ForEach(df = (n, x) ∈ DataflowEdges with M.id(n) = id and M.mark(n) = ▶)
24 |   |   If (typeOf(df) =param)
25 |   |   |   M.mark(df) := ✓; M.val(df) :=value;

26 |   Return {M};
```

that start and message events are handled non-deterministically; i.e., the changes are applied to copies of the original marking that is maintained (cf. Fig. 9.2). Further, Listing 2 specifies the handling of data events. In particular, the corresponding data flow edges of running task (message) nodes are annotated with the data value passed (cf. Figs. 9.4 and 9.5). Finally, the handling of end events is addressed in Listing 2 as well. In particular, the markings of corresponding nodes in state running (▶) are set to completed (✓); their ending time is set accordingly. (cf. Fig. 9.A)

Effects of preparing and handling events must be propagated to ensure correct markings (e.g., activation of subsequent task nodes) as well as to detect contradictory markings related to the data and resource perspectives. In particular, data values are propagated along data flow edges to connected data objects. In turn, resources are propagated from task nodes via resource edges to connected resource nodes. The propagation fails, if a resource or data object node is set to a different value before. In this case, the respective edge is skipped (✗). Furthermore, conditions and relations are evaluated as soon as possible. If any element of the eCRG, which corresponds to a task or message node, becomes skipped

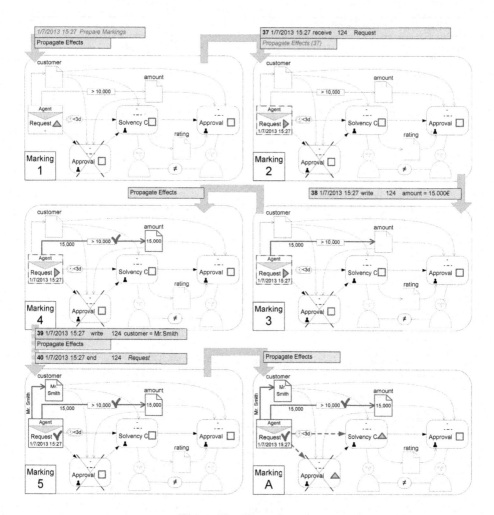

Fig. 9. Handling of events

(e.g., due to a failed data or resource propagation, or a violated condition), the task or message node will be skipped as well. Then, outgoing sequence flows of completed nodes will be marked as satisfied ($\checkmark$). In turn, non-marked incoming edges of already started nodes as well as edges from and to skipped nodes will be skipped. Task and message nodes will be activated ($\triangle$) when all incoming sequence flows, these nodes depend on, are satisfied. In turn, task or message nodes will be skipped ($\times$) if they depend on sequence flows being skipped as well. Note that the latter might result in the cascading skipping of other sequence flow edges (cf. Listing 3).

Table 2 illustrates the set of markings that results after processing the event stream from Fig. 2 for compliance rule c_1. In turn, Figs. 10-13 highlight conflicts

Listing 3. Propagate Effects

```
1  effectPropagation(M)
2      ForEach(pfr = (tn, r) ∈ PerformingEdges with M.mark(pfr) = □ and
       M.res(tn) ≠ ε)
3          M.mark(pfr) := ✓; M.res(pfr) := M.res(tn);
4          If(M.mark(r) = □)
5              If(r ≜ pfr) M.mark(r) := ✓; M.res(r) := M.res(tn);
6          ElseIf (M.res(pfr) ≠ M.res(r)) M.mark(pfr) := ✗;

7      ForEach(rr = (r₁, r₂) ∈ ResRelations with M.mark(r₁) = M.mark(r₂) = ✓)
8          If(rr(r₁, r₂) = true) M.mark(rr) = ✓ Else M.mark(rr) = ✗

9      ForEach(df = (n, o) ∈ DataFlowEdges with M.mark(df) = ✓)
10         If(M.mark(o) = □)
11             If(o ≜ df) M.mark(o) := ✓; M.val(o) := M.val(df);
12         ElseIf (M.val(df) ≠ M.val(o)) M.mark(df) := ✗;

13     ForEach(dr = (o₁, o₂) ∈ DataRelations with M.mark(o₁) = M.mark(o₂) = ✓)
14         If(dr(o₁, o₂) = true) M.mark(dr) := ✓ Else M.mark(dr) := ✗

15     ForEach(att ∈ Attachments with M.mark(att) = □ and M.mark(@(att)) = ✓)
16         If(att(@(att)) = true) M.mark(att) := ✓ Else M.mark(att) := ✗;

17     ForEach(x, y ∈ AllElements with x ≜ y and y corresponds to x)
18         If(M.mark(y) = ✗ and M.mark(x) ≠ ✗) M.mark(x) := ✗;

19     ForEach(sf = (n₁, n2) ∈ SequenceFlowEdges with M.mark(sf) = □)
20         If(M.mark(n₁) = ✓) M.mark(sf) = ✓;
21         If(M.mark(n₁) = ✗ or M.mark(n₂) ∈ {▶, ✓, ✗}) M.mark(sf) = ✗;

22     ForEach(n ∈ TaskNodes ∪ MessageNodes with M.mark(n) = □)
23         If(∀sf = (n, n₂) ∈ SequenceFlowEdges with sf ≜ n holds M.mark(sf) = ✓)
24             M.mark(n) = △;

25     Repeat
26         M' = M;
27         ForEach(sf = (n₁, n2) ∈ SequenceFlowEdges with M.mark(sf) = □)
28             If(M.mark(n₁) = ✗ or M.mark(n₂) ∈ {▶, ✓, ✗}) M.mark(sf) = ✗;

29         ForEach(n ∈ TaskNodes ∪ MessageNodes with M.mark(n) = □)
30             If(∃sf = (n, n₂) ∈ SequenceFlowEdges with sf ≜ n and M.mark(sf) = ✗)
31                 M.mark(n) = ✗;
32             If(∃sf = (n₂, n) ∈ SequenceFlowEdges with sf ≜ n and M.mark(sf) = ✗)
33                 M.mark(n) = ✗;

34     Until (M = M');
35     Return M;
```

regarding the data (Fig. 10), control flow (Fig. 12), resource (Fig. 11), and time (Fig. 13) perspectives. Note that conflicting markings only highlight why the considered events do not constitute a fulfillment of a particular compliance rule, but they do not necessarily lead to a violation of the latter.

Table 2. Markings after processing the event log from Fig. 2

#	Request		Approval (CA)			Solvency Check			Approval (CO)			cust.	cust.→ App.(CA)	cust.→ Solv.C	amount	rating
1	△		□			□			□			ε	ε	ε	ε	ε
A!	✓	124	△			△			□			Smith	ε	ε	15.000	ε
B!	✓	592	△			△			□			John	ε	ε	27.000	ε
C	✓	124	✗			✓	234	Brown	△			Smith	ε	Smith	15.000	high
D	✓	592	△			✗	234	Brown	✗			John	ε	Smith	27.000	ε
E	✓	592	✗	453	Muller	△			□			John	Smith	ε	27.000	ε
F	✓	124	✗			✓	234	Brown	✓	453	Muller	Smith	ε	Smith	15.000	high
G	✓	124	✓	453	Muller	△			□			Smith	Smith	ε	15.000	high
H	✓	124	✗			✓	234	Brown	✗	642	Brown	Smith	ε	Smith	15.000	ε
I	✓	592	✓	642	Brown	△			□			John	John	ε	27.000	ε
J	✓	124	✗	642	Brown	△			□			Smith	John	ε	25.000	ε

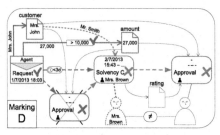

Fig. 10. Data conflict

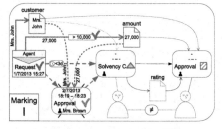

Fig. 12. Control flow conflict

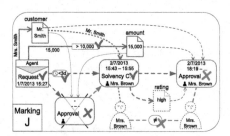

Fig. 11. Resource conflict

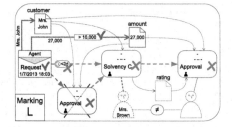

Fig. 13. Time conflict

Compliance assessments and metrics. Based on the described set of markings, we can identify the different *activations* of an eCRG and derive their state of compliance. In turn, *activations* correspond to the minimal markings, which satisfy the antecedence pattern, but do not satisfy any element of the antecedence absence pattern (cf. Sect. 2). In particular, an activation is satisfied if there exists another marking extending the activation and satisfying the consequence pattern. We omit a formal specification here and refer to [11] instead.

Table 3. Compliance assessments and metrics

#	Extensions	ACTIVATED	VIOLABLE	PENDING	PERSATISF.	PERVIOL.
A	{C,F,G,J}	39-...		39-95	95-...	
B	{D,E,H,I}	58-...		58-99		99-...

date	time	μ_1	μ_2
1/7/2013	15:00	n.d.	n.d.
2/7/2013	15:00	0%	100%
2/7/2013	18:18	50%	50%
2/7/2013	19:00	50%	0%

Table 3 highlights the properties of both activated markings A and B along the log from Fig. 2. In particular, Table 3 shows that c_1 is activated twice; once satisfied and once violated. Furthermore, Table 3 indicates the events that complete the activations (39 and 58), the fulfillment (95), and the violation (99). Note that it is easy to specify metrics based on the states of compliance based on the number of activated markings in a particular compliance state PROPERTY: $\#(\mathcal{M}, \text{PROPERTY}) := |\{M \in \mathcal{M}|\text{PROPERTY}(M)\}|$; e.g., Table. 3 refers to the

$$\text{compliance rate } \mu_1 := \frac{\#(\mathcal{M}, \text{SATISFIED})}{\#(\mathcal{M}, \text{ACTIVATED})} \quad \text{and}$$

$$\text{critical rate } \mu_2 := \frac{\#(\mathcal{M}, \text{VIOLABLE}) + \#(\mathcal{M}, \text{PENDING})}{\#(\mathcal{M}, \text{ACTIVATED})}.$$

4   Evaluation

The eCRG language has been evaluated with respect to different aspects (cf. [8, 12]). In particular, its expressiveness allows modeling different sets of compliance patterns (e.g. [13]). In turn, a case study in the medical domain revealed that a

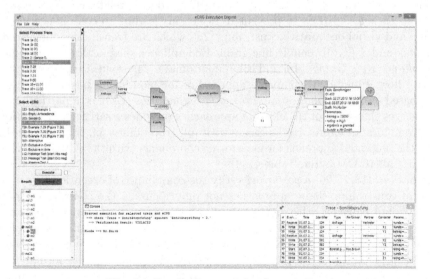

Fig. 14. Proof-of-concept implementation

business analyst was able to properly use eCRG [9]. Finally, current empirical studies indicate that there is *no significant difference* between computer experts and business analysts in understanding eCRGs.

To verify the feasibility of the presented compliance monitoring framework, we implemented an advanced proof-of-concept prototype [14]. The latter incrementally processes event logs, unfolds the markings (cf. Sect. 3), and visualizes them. Note that the prototype supports additional features, not discussed in this paper due to space limitations; e.g., beyond end-start control flow constraints, start-start, start-end, and end-end constraints are supported as well. We applied the prototype to different scenarios including the presented order-to-delivery example as well as real world compliance scenarios obtained in the context of a case study in the healthcare domain [9]. Note that the benefits of the framework come with the cost of a high, up-to exponential computational complexity of $O(|\text{EVENTS}|^{|\text{NODES}|})$. Fig. 14 provides a screenshot of the eCRG execution engine.

5 Related Work

In recent years, business process compliance has gained increasing attention and several surveys have been provided [7,15,16]. Accordingly, interest in *compliance monitoring* and *continous auditing* [17] has increased as well. [18] enriches process models with a semantic layer of internal controls. In [19,20], the detailed architecture of an online auditing tool (OLAT) is described. The latter allows monitoring the operations of an organization in detective, corrective and preventive modes. The broad spectrum of techniques enabling compliance monitoring include *behavioural profiles* [21] (i.e., to utilize ordering relations), *Supervisory Control Theory* [22] (i.e., to prevent from actions leading to compliance violations), and visual declarative constraints [23], which are transformed into *Event Calculus* and *LTL*. To enable fine-grained compliance diagnostics at run-time, *Compliance Rule Graphs* [10] and colored automata [24] are utilized, focusing on control flow. Finally, [4] compares approaches for monitoring business compliance based on 10 *compliance monitoring functionalities* (CMF). In particular, it emphasizes that none of the existing approaches provides a satisfactory solution that combines an expressive language with full traceability (cf. RQ2+RQ3). In turn, the presented approach for monitoring compliance with the eCRG language supports all 10 CMFs (cf. Table 4) [4].

However, [13,25,26] *a posteriori* verify the compliance of execution logs with a set of constraints. Some approaches not only focus on the control flow perspective, but consider other perspectives as well. *A priori* or *design time* compliance checking is addressed by a multitude of approaches, which commonly apply model checking; e.g., [27–30]. Some of them use visual compliance rules and address multiple perspectives. To specify compliance rules, formal languages (e.g., LTL [28]), pattern-based approaches (e.g., [13,31]) are applied.

Table 4. Compliance Monitoring Functionalities [4]

Approach	CMF 1 time	CMF 2 data	CMF 3 resources	CMF4 non atomic	CMF 5 life-cycle	CMF 6 multi-instance	CMF 7 reactive mgmt	CMF 8 proactive mgmt	CMF 9 root cause	CMF 10 compl. degree
Mubicon LTL [24]	+/-	-	-	+	-	-	+	+	+	+/-
Mubicon EC [36]	+	+/-	+	+	+	+	+	-	+/-	+/-
ECE Rules [37]	+	+/-	+	+	-	-	+	-	+/-	+
SCT [22]	+/-	-	+	+	+	-	-	+	-	-
SeaFlows [10]	+/-	+/-	+/-	+	+/-	+	+	+	+	+/-
eCRG Monitoring	+	+	+	+	+	+	+	+	+	+

Further, visual notations [10, 27] as well as methodologies to relate the latter with informal and textual specifications [32] have been proposed. Note that declarative languages [33, 34] can be also applied to specify compliance rules. Finally, the integration of business process compliance throughout the entire process lifecycle [2, 3] as well as monitoring of performance measures in the context of artifact-centric process models in real-time [35] have been addressed.

6   Summary and Outlook

In recent years, business process compliance has gained an increasing interest. A multitude of approaches focus on compliance monitoring at run time [10, 17–19, 24, 36]. However, existing approaches do not provide a satisfactory solution that combines an expressive language with full traceability [4].

To remedy this drawback, we proposed, developed and demonstrated a compliance monitoring framework that utilizes the extended compliance rule graph (eCRG) language, which enables the visual modeling of compliance rules with the support of the control flow, data, time, and resource perspectives as well as interactions with partners (RQ2). In particular, the presented approach marks eCRG with text, color and symbols to visually highlight the current state of compliance, whereas the informally presented operational semantics specifies how observed events evolve these markings (RQ1) Finally, formal criteria for compliance assessments are provided in a related report [11] and compliance metrics were introduced (RQ3). As opposed to existing approaches, the framework combines full traceability with an expressive visual notation. Moreover, we provide a proof-of-concept implementation that was applied to different scenarios.

Beyond the identification and highlighting of particular compliance violations in detail, another important task is to summarize and present the latter in abstract compliance reports. Hence, we aim at a user-friendly navigation through different levels of granularity. Furthermore, we will conduct further empirical studies as well as usability experiments.

References

1. Governatori, G., Sadiq, S.: The journey to business process compliance. In: Handbook of Research on BPM. IGI Global, pp. 426–454 (2009)
2. Knuplesch, D., Reichert, M.: Ensuring business process compliance along the process life cycle. Technical Report 2011–06, Ulm University (2011)

3. Ly, L.T., et al.: Integration and verification of semantic constraints in adaptive process management systems. Data & Knowl. Eng. **64**(1), 3–23 (2008)
4. Ly, L.T., et al.: A framework for the systematic comparison and evaluation of compliance monitoring approaches. In: EDOC 2013, pp. 7–16. IEEE (2013)
5. Knuplesch, D., Reichert, M., Kumar, A.: Towards visually monitoring multiple perspectives of business process compliance. In: CAiSE 2015 Forum, pp. 41–48
6. Cabanillas, C., Resinas, M., Ruiz-Cortés, A.: Hints on how to face business process compliance. JISBD **2010**, 26–32 (2010)
7. Knuplesch, D., Reichert, M., Mangler, J., Rinderle-Ma, S., Fdhila, W.: Towards compliance of cross-organizational processes and their changes. In: La Rosa, M., Soffer, P. (eds.) BPM Workshops 2012. LNBIP, vol. 132, pp. 649–661. Springer, Heidelberg (2013)
8. Knuplesch, D., Reichert, M., Ly, L.T., Kumar, A., Rinderle-Ma, S.: Visual modeling of business process compliance rules with the support of multiple perspectives. In: Ng, W., Storey, V.C., Trujillo, J.C. (eds.) ER 2013. LNCS, vol. 8217, pp. 106–120. Springer, Heidelberg (2013)
9. Semmelrodt, F., Knuplesch, D., Reichert, M.: Modeling the resource perspective of business process compliance rules with the extended compliance rule graph. In: Bider, I., Gaaloul, K., Krogstie, J., Nurcan, S., Proper, H.A., Schmidt, R., Soffer, P. (eds.) BPMDS 2014 and EMMSAD 2014. LNBIP, vol. 175, pp. 48–63. Springer, Heidelberg (2014)
10. Ly, L.T., Rinderle-Ma, S., Knuplesch, D., Dadam, P.: Monitoring business process compliance using compliance rule graphs. In: Meersman, R., Dillon, T., Herrero, P., Kumar, A., Reichert, M., Qing, L., Ooi, B.-C., Damiani, E., Schmidt, D.C., White, J., Hauswirth, M., Hitzler, P., Mohania, M. (eds.) OTM 2011, Part I. LNCS, vol. 7044, pp. 82–99. Springer, Heidelberg (2011)
11. Knuplesch, D., et al.: An operational semantics for the extended compliance rule graph language. Technical Report 2014–6, Ulm University (2014)
12. Knuplesch, D., et al.: On the formal semantics of the extended compliance rule graph. Technical Report 2013–05, Ulm University (2013)
13. Ramezani, E., Fahland, D., van der Aalst, W.M.P.: Where did i misbehave? Diagnostic information in compliance checking. In: Barros, A., Gal, A., Kindler, E. (eds.) BPM 2012. LNCS, vol. 7481, pp. 262–278. Springer, Heidelberg (2012)
14. Beck, H.: Automatisierte Überwachung von Business Process Compliance Regeln mit Daten-, Zeit-, Ressourcen- und Interaktions-Aspekten. Master Thesis, Ulm University, Germany (2014)
15. Becker, J., et al.: Generalizability and applicability of model-based business process compliance-checking approaches. BuR - Business Research **5**(2), 221–247 (2012)
16. Fdhila, W., Rinderle-Ma, S., Knuplesch, D., Reichert, M.: Change and compliance in collaborative processes. In: SCC 2015 (2015)
17. Alles, M., Kogan, A., Vasarhelyi, M.: Putting continuous auditing theory into practice: Lessons from two pilot implementations. Inf. Sys. **22**(2), 195–214 (2008)
18. Namiri, K., Stojanovic, N.: Pattern-based design and validation of business process compliance. In: Meersman, R., Tari, Z. (eds.) OTM 2007, Part I. LNCS, vol. 4803, pp. 59–76. Springer, Heidelberg (2007)
19. van der Aalst, W.M.P., et al.: Conceptual model for online auditing. Decision Support Systems **50**(3), 636–647 (2011)
20. Accorsi, R.: An approach to data-driven detective internal controls for processaware information systems. DUMW **2012**, 29–33 (2012)

21. Weidlich, M., Ziekow, H., Mendling, J., Günther, O., Weske, M., Desai, N.: Event-based monitoring of process execution violations. In: Rinderle-Ma, S., Toumani, F., Wolf, K. (eds.) BPM 2011. LNCS, vol. 6896, pp. 182–198. Springer, Heidelberg (2011)
22. Santos, E.A.P., Francisco, R., Vieira, A.D., de F.R. Loures, E., Busetti, M.A.: Modeling business rules for supervisory control of process-aware information systems. In: Daniel, F., Barkaoui, K., Dustdar, S. (eds.) BPM Workshops 2011, Part II. LNBIP, vol. 100, pp. 447–458. Springer, Heidelberg (2012)
23. Maggi, F.M., Montali, M., van der Aalst, W.M.P.: An operational decision support framework for monitoring business constraints. In: de Lara, J., Zisman, A. (eds.) Fundamental Approaches to Software Engineering. LNCS, vol. 7212, pp. 146–162. Springer, Heidelberg (2012)
24. Maggi, F.M., Montali, M., Westergaard, M., van der Aalst, W.M.P.: Monitoring business constraints with linear temporal logic: an approach based on colored automata. In: Rinderle-Ma, S., Toumani, F., Wolf, K. (eds.) BPM 2011. LNCS, vol. 6896, pp. 132–147. Springer, Heidelberg (2011)
25. Baumgrass, A., Baier, T., Mendling, J., Strembeck, M.: Conformance checking of RBAC policies in process-aware information systems. In: Daniel, F., Barkaoui, K., Dustdar, S. (eds.) BPM Workshops 2011, Part II. LNBIP, vol. 100, pp. 435–446. Springer, Heidelberg (2012)
26. Outmazgin, N., Soffer, P.: A process mining-based analysis of business process work-arounds. Soft. & Sys. Mod., 1–15 (2014)
27. Awad, A., Weidlich, M., Weske, M.: Specification, verification and explanation of violation for data aware compliance rules. In: Baresi, L., Chi, C.-H., Suzuki, J. (eds.) ICSOC-ServiceWave 2009. LNCS, vol. 5900, pp. 500–515. Springer, Heidelberg (2009)
28. Knuplesch, D., Ly, L.T., Rinderle-Ma, S., Pfeifer, H., Dadam, P.: On enabling data-aware compliance checking of business process models. In: Parsons, J., Saeki, M., Shoval, P., Woo, C., Wand, Y. (eds.) ER 2010. LNCS, vol. 6412, pp. 332–346. Springer, Heidelberg (2010)
29. Knuplesch, D., Reichert, M., Fdhila, W., Rinderle-Ma, S.: On enabling compliance of cross-organizational business processes. In: Daniel, F., Wang, J., Weber, B. (eds.) BPM 2013. LNCS, vol. 8094, pp. 146–154. Springer, Heidelberg (2013)
30. Knuplesch, D., et al.: Ensuring compliance of distributed and collaborative workflows. In: CollaborateCom 2013, pp. 133–142. IEEE (2013)
31. Turetken, O., Elgammal, A., van den Heuvel, W.J., Papazoglou, M.: Capturing compliance requirements: A pattern-based approach. IEEE Software, 29–36 (2012)
32. Sunkle, S., Kholkar, D., Kulkarni, V.: Toward better mapping between regulations and operational details of enterprises using vocabularies and semantic similarity. In: CAiSE 2015 Forum, pp. 229–236
33. Pesic, M., Schonenberg, H., van der Aalst, W.M.P.: DECLARE: full support for loosely-structured processes. EDOC **2007**, 287–300 (2007)
34. Hildebrandt, T., Mukkamala, R.R., Slaats, T.: Nested dynamic condition response graphs. In: Arbab, F., Sirjani, M. (eds.) FSEN 2011. LNCS, vol. 7141, pp. 343–350. Springer, Heidelberg (2012)
35. Liu, R., Vaculín, R., Shan, Z., Nigam, A., Wu, F.: Business artifact-centric modeling for real-time performance monitoring. In: Rinderle-Ma, S., Toumani, F., Wolf, K. (eds.) BPM 2011. LNCS, vol. 6896, pp. 265–280. Springer, Heidelberg (2011)
36. Montali, M., et al.: Monitoring business constraints with the event calculus. ACM Trans. Intell. Syst. Technol. **5**(1), 17:1–17:30 (2014)
37. Bragaglia, S., et al.: Fuzzy conformance checking of observed behaviour with expectations. In: AI*IA 2011, pp. 80–91 (2011)

Managing Controlled Violation of Temporal Process Constraints

Akhil Kumar[1(✉)], Sharat R. Sabbella[2], and Russell R. Barton[1]

[1] Smeal College of Business, Penn State University, University Park,
State College, PA 16802, USA
{akhil,rbarton}@psu.edu
[2] Sharat Industries, R.A Puram, Chennai 600028, India
sharatreddy.sil@gmail.com

Abstract. Temporal workflows are becoming increasingly important in many real-world applications. In such workflows, activity durations and times are specified and it is necessary to ensure both at design time and run time that temporal constraints are not violated. However, in real-time workflows, such as in a medical process or emergency situations, some violations are unavoidable. Hence, a more nuanced view of violations should be taken. Here we introduce the notion of controlled violations as the ability to monitor a running process and develop an approach based on constraint satisfaction to determine the best schedule for its completion in a way so as to minimize the total penalty from the violations. The violations are evaluated in terms of metrics like number of violations, delay in process completion, and penalty of weighted violations. We also relate our work to the concept of controllability in literature and show how it can be checked using our method. Finally, the expressive power of our approach is discussed.

1 Introduction

Many real-world workflows need to run under time constraints. In modeling such time-aware processes [3,4,10,18,13], the duration of each activity (or task) is provided as a range, or just a lower or upper limit. For example in a medical process the duration of the patient admission activity is, say, between 10 and 20 minutes. By associating such durations with each activity one can determine expected minimum and maximum times for each execution path of the workflow from start to end. Moreover, deviations from the expected times can be monitored, and appropriate messages and alerts can be generated to draw attention. Another aspect of temporal workflows relates to inter-activity constraints that impose restrictions on the elapsed time between one activity and another. Further they may be specified with reference to the start or finish time of the respective activities. A variety of temporal constraints can be imposed on a workflow [11]. While general types of semantic constraints have been studied in literature [9,16,17], there is less work on temporal constraints.

Some examples of such constraints that arise in a medical process (say for a fracture treatment) are:

- A radiologist's report must be submitted within 24 hours of a CT scan
- If surgery is needed it must take place within a week of the radiologist's report

©Springer International Publishing Switzerland 2015
H.R. Motahari-Nezhad et al. (Eds.): BPM 2015, LNCS 9253, pp. 280–296, 2015.
DOI: 10.1007/978-3-319-23063-4_20

- Antibiotics must be taken for 3 days before surgery
- A blood thinner like Aspirin must be stopped 24 hours before surgery
- The patient must recover in the hospital for 2 days before being discharged
- The total time from patient admission to discharge should not exceed 7 days

A temporal workflow should represent various temporal patterns and relationships among activities. Temporal patterns and ways of reasoning with them are discussed in [1,2]. To some extent, planning a temporal workflow is like scheduling with concepts like early (late) start times and finish times for various activities [6,7]. Another concept in the context of temporal workflows is the idea of controllability [4,8,10,15] which relates to the flexibility present in a workflow schedule. The work on controllability is based on the notion of conditional simple temporal networks [20] which were developed in the context of planning. A workflow that allows activity durations to fall anywhere within their allowed range and still complete successfully is said to be *dynamically controllable*. Algorithms for dynamic controllability are discussed in [8,10,15].

In this paper, we take the view that the prescribed time duration ranges for an activity should not be very strict. Some unexpected delays may occur for various reasons at run time (e.g. patient admissions is backed up; CT machine has broken down, etc.) and lead to violations of constraints. If a task deviates slightly from its range, it does not mean that the workflow is uncontrollable. The natural question to pose then is: how will this deviation or violation affect the rest of the workflow? If the effect is small then the workflow can continue normally. Our goal in this paper is to develop a model that can take into account the possibility of violation of various constraints and explore the tradeoffs among the violations. Thus, if antibiotics medication has to be taken for three days before surgery and this will delay the surgery, there is a tradeoff between reducing the duration of the medication and delaying the surgery.

The novel aspect of our work is that we allow for constraints to be violated by introducing relaxation variables in our model, thus allowing for "graceful degradation." Our approach is based on constraint satisfaction with respect to an objective function. Each temporal constraint (both intra-activity and inter-activity) can be expressed as a linear equation(s). By checking if the constraints are consistent one can verify if they will all be satisfied. These variables assume values equal to the amount of violation in a constraint to force satisfaction. At the same time we also associate penalties with each violation, e.g. for every time unit of delay in start of surgery beyond the guidelines. Finally, these penalties are aggregated and minimized in an objective function.

There are several contributions of this work. First, we develop a new approach to temporal workflow consistency and illustrate it in detail. Second, we introduce the notion of controlled violations of constraints and show how it can be applied in practice along with "what-if" analysis. Third, we relate our work to controllability and show how our method can be used to check for controllability. Finally, we argue that this approach is complete in terms of expressiveness since it can cover a variety of temporal patterns.

This paper is organized as follows. In section 2 we discuss a basic model for describing temporal constraints and show how it can be translated into structural and temporal constraint equations. Then, in Section 3, we describe how the approach was implemented and tested. Later, Section 4 extends our approach for managing violations of constraints and develops a formal optimization model based on penalties. Section 5 discusses how our approach can be extended to more complex control flow structures involving overlapping and repetitive activities. Finally, Section 6 discusses related work, and the last section gives the conclusions and shares some thoughts for future work.

2   Modeling Approach

2.1   A Simple Temporal Model

To create a temporal model of a process two types of constraint models are combined: (1) a basic structural constraint model, and (2) temporal constraint model. The structural constraints capture the control flow of the process to coordinate the proper sequence in which the tasks occur. The temporal flow model considers the permitted durations of each activity and the minimum or maximum gaps between them.

Def. 1. A general temporal process model TP can be represented as:

$$TP = (\mathcal{T}, \mathcal{A}, \mathcal{X}, \mathcal{E}, \mathcal{TI}, \mathcal{C})$$

Where

$\mathcal{T}$: set of task nodes, T1, T2, …

$\mathcal{A}$: set of AND control nodes, A1, A2, …

$\mathcal{X}$: set of XOR control nodes, X1, X2, …

$\mathcal{E}$: set of edges among the nodes in $\{\mathcal{T}, \mathcal{A}, \mathcal{X}\}$

$\mathcal{TI}$: set of task duration ranges:$\{(i, Dimin, Dimax),…\}$

C: set of additional inter-task constraints.

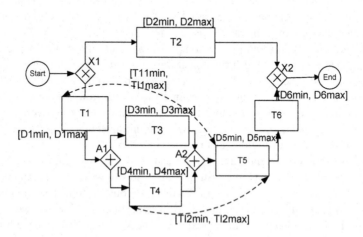

Fig. 1. A basic temporal model with XOR and AND connectors

Fig. 1 gives an example of a simple temporal model. It shows the control flow, along with [min,max] durations of each task and inter-task constraints. It can be expressed as:

$\mathcal{T}$: {T1, T2, ..., T6}
$\mathcal{A}$: { A1, A2}
$\mathcal{X}$: { X1, X2, X3, X4}
$\mathcal{E}$: {(start, X1), (X1, T1), (X1, T2), (T1, A1), (A1, T3), (A1, T4), (T3, A2), (T4, A2),...}
$\mathcal{TI}$: {(T1, D1min, D1max), (T2, D2min, D2max), (T3, D3min, D3max), ...}
$\mathcal{C}$: {(T1, T5, S, S, TI1min, TI1max), (T4, T5, S, F, TI2min, TI2max) }

Note that while we only consider durations of, and delays between pairs of, activities, *fixed time activities* can also be modeled by setting their relative time with respect to the start of a process and converting them into delays with respect to the start activity.

2.2.1 A Constraint Satisfaction Approach
Next we show how to map the above model into a series of constraint equations that can be solved using a constraint satisfaction approach. We need to consider two types of constraints: *structural flow constraints* and *temporal constraints*. The flow constraints capture the coordination sequence among tasks, while the temporal constraints specify the durations for a task and also the inter-task gaps or delays.

2.2 Structural Constraints (SC)
Structural constraints are represented by structural equations to capture the flow of a process. Each node in a process is represented by a binary 0-1 variable.

Def. 2. Structural constraint representation. SC constraints are represented by structural balance equations of a process. The equations for *sequence, choice and parallel* patterns are shown in Fig. 2. All processes also have two special tasks or events, "Start" and "End." We add a constraint "**Start = 1**" to denote that the process is triggered. Also, constraint "**End = 1**" must hold true to indicate proper completion of a process instance.

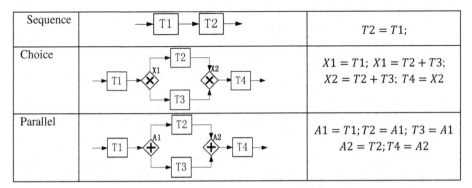

Sequence		$T2 = T1;$
Choice		$X1 = T1;\ X1 = T2 + T3;$ $X2 = T2 + T3;\ T4 = X2$
Parallel		$A1 = T1; T2 = A1;\ T3 = A1$ $A2 = T2; T4 = A2$

Fig. 2. Structural balance equations for process modeling structures

Additional structural patterns are described in Table 1.

2.2.2   Basic Temporal Constraints (TC)

The temporal constraints express a variety of temporal relationships. Here we consider three types of constraints: flow constraints, task duration constraints and the inter-task gap constraints. We will discuss each one separately.

Def. 3. Temporal Flow (TF) constraints. These constraints are derived from the edge set $\mathcal{E}$.   For every node ni and successive node pair (ni, nj) in $\mathcal{E}$, we add a constraint as:

$$TSi \leq TFi$$
$$TFi \leq TSj$$

where

TSi: start time of node i relative to the start time of the workflow instance

TFi: finish time of node i relative to the start time of the workflow instance

Table 1. Additional structural constraints

Constraint	Meaning	Formal Specification
mandatory (Ti)	Task Ti must be executed.	$Ti = 1$
prohibited (Ti)	Task Ti must <u>not</u> to be executed.	$Ti = 0$
coexist (Ti, Tj)	Both or none of Ti and Tj are executed.	$Ti = Tj$
choice $(T1,$ $T2,$ ..., $Tn, m)$	Exactly m of $T1, T2,$ ..., Tn should be executed.	$T1 + T2 + \cdots + Tn = m$
exclusion (Ti, Tj)	At most one of Ti or Tj can be executed.	$Ti + Tj \leq 1$

Def. 4. Task duration (TD) constraints. These constraints ensure that the duration of an activity i lies between the permitted range [Dimin, Dimax]. They are specified as:
Dimin $\leq$ TFi – TSi $\leq$ Dimax.

Def. 5. Inter-task (TI) constraints. These constraints ensure that the gap or delay between the start (end) of an activity pair (i,j) lies between the permitted range [Gij_min, Gij_max]. They are specified as:
Gij_min $\leq$ TFi (TSi) $\leq$ TSj (TFj) $\leq$ Gij_max

Def. 6. Duration constraints for A and X connectors.

(i)   For X connectors, the duration is XFi – XSi = 0.
(ii)   For A-split connectors also, AFi – ASi = 0.
(iii)   For A-join connectors, AFj = Max(TFi), $\forall$TFi s.t. (TFi, AFj) $\in$ $\mathcal{E}$.

Next, we define temporal consistency and show that our approach is correct. It is also possible to give non-zero times to the X and A connector durations, and our approach will not be affected by it.

Def. 7. Temporal consistency. A temporal process model is temporally consistent if for every valid and complete execution path (from start to end) there exists a solution that satisfies the duration and inter-task constraints.

Lemma 1: Combining the SC and TC constraints and solving them leads to a temporally consistent solution.

Proof sketch. To argue correctness of our formulation, we note that the SC constraints ensure that: (i) a structurally valid set of tasks is selected; and (ii) that it represents a complete process instance from start to end (by Def. 2). Moreover, with the TC constraints, we define: (i) the durations for *all* tasks and connectors (by Def. 4, 6); and (ii) the finish-start time relationships between task-task, task-connector, connector-task and connector-connector (by Defs. 3 and 5). Since all variables for task and connector start/finish times are included in the formulation, *all possible paths* are evaluated. Hence, a solution to this system of equations will be a temporally consistent and structurally correct solution. If no solution is found, then it implies that one does not exist.

This is a *weak consistency* in that it shows that a schedule exists for the temporal workflow for one combination of durations for each activity. It does not show that all combinations of durations in the allowed range will lead to a valid solution as in *dynamic controllability* [8]. Moreover, solving this system of equations will give one solution but other solutions can be found by assigning specific values to certain variables.

2.3   Additional Temporal Constraints

Table 2 gives a summary of various kinds of temporal constraints, categorized in three groups: *basic constraints, overlap constraints* and *repetition constraints*. The constraints 1 and 2 are the basic ones discussed above. Constraints 3-5 are overlap constraints. Finally, constraints 6-9 are repetition constraints. This shows that we can also represent more complex constraints involving combined durations of activities and overlap among activities, as well as express loops and restrict the number of times a loop is repeated. All of these constructs have practical applications which will be discussed later. We will also argue completeness of our approach later too.

Table 2. Summary of modeling constructs for temporal constraints

	Constraint	Meaning	Formal Specification
B a s i c	1. Duration of a task Tj	Duration of a task Tj is between t1 and t2	$tmin \leq TFi - TSi \leq tmax$
	2. Minimum (maximum) gap between (Ti, Tj)	Specify minimum (maximum) gap between two tasks	$TSj - TFi \geq g (\leq g)$
O v e r l a p	3. (CO) Combined overlap $(Ti, Tj, Tk, ...)$	Duration for which all n tasks are overlapping with one another	$Min(TFi, TFj, TFk, ...) -$ $Max(TSi, TSj, TSk, ...)$
	4. (CD) Combined duration $(Ti, Tj, Tk, ...)$	Duration from the start of the first to start, to the end of the last to finish (Time span)	$Min(TSi, TSj, TSk, ...) -$ $Max(TFi, TFj, TFk, ...)$
	5. Pair-wise overlap $(Ti, Tj, Tk, ...)$	Duration for which at least two or more tasks overlap	$\sum(TFi - TSi) - CD$
R e p e t i t i o n	6. rt-dependency $(Ti^{(o)}, Ti^{(o+1)}, g)$	Occurrences o, o+1 of a repeatable task Ti should be separated by time gap (g)	$TSi^{(o+1)} - TFi^{(o)} \geq g$
	7. Alternating (Ti, Tj)	Every occurrence k of (Ti, Tj) alternates	$TFi^{(k)} \leq TSj^{(k)}$
	8. Maximum number of repetitions of a loop	Task Ti must not repeat more than r times.	$\sum Ti^{(k)} \leq r$
	9. Max repetitions in a time interval	No more than two successive occurrences must occur within a duration D	For all $k = 1, 2, ...$ $TSi^{(k+2)} - TSi^{(k)} > D$

3   Building and Solving the Constraint Satisfaction Model

Above we presented a general approach for constructing a set of structural and temporal constraint equations to describe a temporal process model. The two sets of constraints are combined to obtain a complete model and solved to check for consistency by a constraint satisfaction tool such as CPLEX [5].   If a solution is found it means that the model is temporally consistent; otherwise, it is not.

To illustrate our approach, the example in Fig. 3 of a patient suspected of having a proximal femoral fracture will be used as a running example. This figure shows a simplified clinical pathway in BPMN notation. This process model consists of 14 tasks coordinated by sequential flows along with choice and parallel structures in BPMN notation. Briefly, after a patient is admitted (T1), she undergoes anamnesis and examination (T2). Depending upon the result of the examination, if the patient is under suspicion of having a proximal femoral fracture, she has to take a CT scan test (T5); otherwise, she is diagnosed further and prepared for therapy (T3), followed by customized therapy A (T4). Alternatively, depending on the results of her imaging diagnosis (T6), she is either treated with therapy B (T7) or by surgery (T11). If surgery is needed, then it must be scheduled (T8), and two prerequisite tasks surgical planning (T9) and administering pain medication (T10), are carried out. Recovery (T12) follows surgery (T11). Finally, the case is documented (T13) and the patient is discharged (T14).

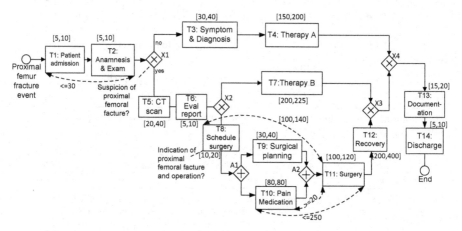

Fig. 3. A medical process for proximal femur fracture

The duration for each task is written in square brackets adjacent to it (in time units). If a value is blank it does not apply. An inter-task constraint is represented by a dashed line connecting the pair of tasks to which it applies. In Fig. 3, there is a constraint between T1 and T2 that requires that T2 must finish no more than 30 time units after the start of T1. When the dashed line connects the left boundary of a task, it means that the constraint applies to its start time, while if it connects the right boundary of a task it applies to its finish time.

Following the general approach described above, the formulation is given in Fig. 4. It shows four groups of constraints. These constraints form a system of equations in 14 binary task variables (T1, T2, ...) for the presence or absence of the 14 tasks and 14 start (TS1, TS2, ...) and 14 finish time (TF1, TF2, ...) floating point variables for the 14 tasks also. In addition there are corresponding variables for the connector nodes as well such as X1, XS1, XF1, ..., A1, AS1 AF1, ... All the TD and TI constraints are preceded by a condition check to see if the task(s) to which they apply are activated in the process path. Otherwise, the conditions would not apply.

This system of equations can be solved for constraint satisfaction. However, in general this problem will have an infinite number of solutions since we are dealing with floating point variables for generality. Hence, we added an objective function to create a mixed integer programming formulation (MILP), where the objective is to **minimize** the finish time of the last task 'End'.

We used the tool CPLEX to solve the formulation. CPLEX is a well-known tool for solving such MILP models. It offers several operators such as *if-then, min, max, count*, etc. for representing various constraints.

```
Minimize TS['End']        //Minimize end time of process
s.t.
//Structural constraints (SC)
Start. Start = 1;
End. End = 1;
SF1. T2 = T1;
SF2. X1 = T2;
SF3. T3+T5 = X1;
SF4. T4=T3; T15=T5; X2 = T15;
...
//Temporal flow constraints (TF)
TF1. TF1 ≥ TS1;
TF2. TS2 ≥ TF1;
TF3. XS1 ≥ TF2;
...
//Temporal duration constraints (TD)
TD1. T1 == 1 => TF1 – TS1 ≥ 5;
TD2. T1 == 1 => TF1 – TS1 ≤ 10;
...
//Temporal inter-task constraints (TI)
TI1. T1 == 1 && T2 == 1 => TF2 – TS1 ≤ 30;
TI2. T11 == 1 && T8 == 1 => TS11 – TS8 ≥100;
TI3. T11 == 1 && T8 == 1 => TS11 – TS8 ≤140;
TI4. T11 == 1 && T10 == 1 => TF11 – TS10 ≤250;
TI5. T11 == 1 && T10 == 1 => TS11 –TF10 ≥ 20;
```

Fig. 4. A (partial) formulation of a temporal workflow

3.1   Design Time Solution

Fig. 4 shows the (partial) formulation for the process model of Fig. 3. To create this formulation we combine the TF, TD, TI and connector duration constraints (see Def. 3-6). In addition, we add the objective function.

We used CPLEX to solve this MILP model and got an objective function value of 210. This is a design time solution showing that the problem is feasible. Tasks 1-4, 13-14 are present in this solution. This corresponds to the path in Fig. 3 where the upper outgoing branch is taken at X1. The solution also shows the start and finish times of each activity in this solution.

Clearly, other outgoing branches could have been taken at X1 and then at X2. To find a design time solution that shows whether these paths are feasible and the actual solution, we can force the lower outgoing path at X1 by adding a constraint T5 = 1. This produced a solution with an objective function value of 465 and included tasks 1-2, 5-6, and 8-14. Finally, we tried forcing a solution with the upper outgoing branch at X2 by adding T7 = 1. In this case the objective function value is 255 and it includes tasks T1-T2, T5-T7, and T13-T14.

3.2   Run-Time Solution

Above we developed an "ideal," design time solution that can be planned even before the process starts running. At run time changes have to be made to the formulation in a running process based on its actual progress. So, say we have just completed task T8 (schedule surgery) and while its scheduled completion time was 45, the actual completion time was 65 because the scheduling became complicated for various reasons and manual intervention was needed. We wish to find out what constraints if any will be violated on account of this delay and how the process will run from here on. Hence, we make changes to the formulation in the following steps:

(i)   Add the start and finish times of each task that has been completed.

(ii)   Remove any duration constraints for these tasks as they do not apply any more. Next, we solve the formulation again to see if a feasible solution can be found. If so, it will give us the new schedule taking into account the runtime delay.

Run-Time Scenario 1. Consider the situation where task T8 is delayed. Its normal duration is [10,20], but in this case it has taken 30 time units as shown below:

$$TS1= 0; \; TS1 = 5; \; TS5=10; \; TS6=30; \; TS8= 35;$$
$$TF1=5; \; TF2=10; \; TF5=30; \; TF6= 35; \; TF8 = 65;$$

To analyze the subsequent run-time behavior of this process, we add these constraints to our formulation and remove the duration constraints for these tasks (i.e. 1,2,5,6, 8) since they are already completed. Upon solving the new formulation, a new solution with a finish time for the process of 485 is found. When we set TF8 = 75 the finish time became 495. However, when we set TF8 = 85, no solution was found. On further inspection it was realized that constraint TI3 (see Fig. 4) was being violated.

In general, if a design-time solution exists, but a run-time solution is not found then it means that the problem has become infeasible on account of either duration or inter-task constraints. In this situation it is helpful to know the reason for the violation and its extent. For instance we would like to know that a certain constraint C1 is violated by X1 time units. To deal with such situations we will introduce the notion of constraint violations in the next section.

Process changes. Our approach can also deal with process changes easily. If the process changes through insertions and deletions of activities, or if activity durations are modified, only the link and activity information file needs to reflect these changes and then a new formulation can be generated easily with our program. Moreover, it is very easy to force certain branches in the process, say, at an X-split connector, by adding a constraint like Ti = 1 where Ti is the first task on the desired path.

"What-if" analysis. Further, various kinds of what-if analyses can be performed with this approach. To find the maximum possible duration of a task (say, T5) without violating any constraints, we modify the objective function to: **Maximize (T5-TS['End'])**, and solve the new MILP.   We can also assign specific duration values to a combination of tasks and check if these values still lead to a feasible solution.

4   Model for Temporal Constraint Violations

4.1   Relaxation Variables

So far, we assumed that every constraint was *strict* and could not be violated. The main idea for dealing with violations is to introduce relaxation variables for each constraint in such a way that if a constraint is violated then the variable takes on a positive non-zero value, and otherwise it is 0. Thus a duration constraint such as, say, "schedule surgery" (T8) with a duration of [10, 20] is expressed as:

$$TF8 - TS8 \geq 10$$

By introducing a constraint variable $CD8$, we may rewrite this constraint as:

$$TF8 - TS8 + CD8 \geq 10$$

Now, CD8 is simply a relaxation variable that assumes a non-negative value. If the actual duration of T8 is less than 10, say, the duration is 5, then CD8 = 5. Thus the constraint is satisfied and CPLEX can find a solution for the formulation.   CD8 is an example of a lower bound relaxation variable. The upper bound constraint in our example on the duration of T8 is 20. In this case a similar relaxation variable, say $CD8'$ is introduced as follows:

$$TF8 - TS8 - CD8' \leq 20$$

Notice that the negative sign before $CD8'$ means that the relaxation allows us to satisfy the upper bound constraint by again assuming a positive value. If the duration lies between 10 and 20, then $CD8'$ is 0.

Relaxation for *inter-task constraints* is modeled in the same way.   Constraint TI2 of Fig. 4, for instance, is:

$$TS11 - TS8 \geq 100$$

Again, by adding a new relaxation variable, say, $CI2$ we can rewrite this constraint as:

$$TS11 - TS8 + CI2 \geq 100$$

The corresponding upper bound constraint TI3 in Fig. 4 is relaxed by another relaxation variable $CI3$ as follows:

$$TS11 - TS8 - CI3 \leq 140$$

Run-Time Scenario 2. When we revised these constraints by adding the relaxation variables in the ILP formulation, and solved it for the case where TF8=85, we found a solution with an objective function value of 505 for TF14. Moreover, the value for $CI3$ was 10 indicating that constraint TI3 was violated by 10 time units due to the delay in completion of T8.

Relaxation can also be applied to TF and TD constraints if some flow and duration requirements are not very strict. In addition, the amount of relaxation can be restricted by imposing limits on the amount of violation that is allowed. Thus, we could add a constraint like CD10 $\leq$ 20 to specify that the maximum lower end relaxation allowed in the duration range constraint for pain medication (T10) is 20. Thus, the duration of the pain medication can be decreased from 80 to 60, but no more.

4.2   Controlled Violation with Penalties

Our notion of controlling a temporal process subject to violations is that it is not sufficient to simply detect a violation and stop there. It is necessary to explore the effects of a violation that has occurred further and suggest corrective action.   In the above example for Run-time scenario 2 we noticed that the delay in the surgery scheduling activity leads to the violation of constraint TI3 by 10 and also an overall delay of 50 in the completion of the process. Hence, it is necessary to explore further to see if there is any corrective action possible to: (1) rectify the violation in constraint TI3 by making changes to the succeeding tasks; (2) reduce the delay in completion time of the process. It is also useful here to distinguish between strict and violable constraints.

Run-Time Scenario 3. If, say, the constraint TI3 is strict, then we would like to see whether there is an alternative solution that would restore TI3 but force changes in another constraint. In order to check for this we remove the relaxation variable CI3 for the constraint TI3 to make it a strict constraint and add relaxation variables to the remaining constraints TI1, TI2, TI4, TI5. In addition we also add the corresponding relaxation variables CI1, CI2, CI4 and CI5 to the objective function because we wish to minimize the extent of the violation. Now, we found a solution in which CD10 = 10 and TF14 = 495. This means that by reducing the duration of Pain medication (T10) by 10 time units, we are able to satisfy constraint TI3 and find a solution.

4.3   Associating Penalties with Slack Variables

Above in Run-time scenario 3, we assumed that the objective function was:

$$\textbf{Minimize } TS['End'] + \sum CDi + \sum CIi$$

This means we added the violations due to each relaxation variable taking a non-zero value to the finish time of the process. However, this objective function treats each violation equally. In real practice, it is likely that the various constraint violations might have a differential impact on the outcome. Hence, in general a different penalty may be assessed for the violation of each constraint. Such penalties would be determined by the domain experts. Therefore the revised objective function should be:

$$\text{Minimize } TS['End'] + \sum PDi * CDi + \sum PIi * CIi$$

Run-Time Scenario 4. In our running example, a doctor may feel that violation of constraint CI5 is less important than a violation of the other constraints.   Hence, we could assign say a penalty of just 0.5 to CI5 and of 1 to the other constraints. When we rerun the MILP with this change we get a solution in which CI5 = 20. Now the process completion time TF[14] drops to 485.   Clearly, since the penalty for CI5 is smaller the optimal solution is one which relaxes this constraint.

In general, each constraint may have a different penalty assigned to it based on the domain knowledge. In this way it is possible to evaluate the tradeoffs between different constraints and find different solutions at run time.

5   Further Extensions

A key feature of our optimization based approach is that a variety of temporal patterns can be handled with this method. The various patterns were organized in Table 2 into three categories: basic, overlap and repetition. So far the focus of this paper was on the basic patterns. Now, we will discuss the other two in some detail.

5.1   Overlap Patterns

Overlap patterns allow constraints that specify a minimum or maximum amount of overlap between two or more activities. Take the example in Fig. 5 that is a variant of our running example in Fig. 3. Here we have added a second pain medication (T15) in parallel with the first one (T10), but with the additional requirement that *two medications (say, aspirin and marcumar) may be taken together only for 20 time units*.

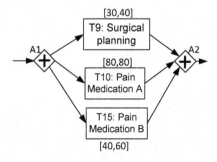

Fig. 5. An example to illustrate the overlap constraint

To capture this idea, we can write a constraint such as:

$$\text{Min(TF10, TF15)} - \text{Max(TS10, TS15)} \leq 20$$

Overlap Scenario 1. We modified the MILP formulation to include this change and solved it for design time. CPLEX still gave us a best solution of 465 for the revised process. On further inspection, it was realized that the new task T15 is scheduled in such a way that TS10=45; and TS15=105. Further, TF10=125; and TF15=145. Since there is a gap of 20 between T10 and its successor T11 by inter-task constraint TI5, the allowed maximum overlap of 20 between T10 and T15 ensures that the total process time does not increase. However, if we increase the overlap between T10 and T15 to 0, then the process completion time increases to 485.

In general, for n overlapping tasks, the combined period overlap among (when at least two or more tasks overlap is given by:

$$\text{Min}(TF_i, \ TF_j, \ TF_k, \ ...) - \text{Max}(TS_i, \ TS_j, \ TS_k, \ ...)$$

It should also be noted that containment is a special case of overlap. If task i is contained in task j then TSi $\geq$ TSj; and TFi $\leq$ TFj.

5.2   Repetition Patterns

Repetitive patterns also arise frequently and must be handled appropriately. One form of this pattern is shown in Fig. 6 in the context of our running example.

Repetition Scenario 1. In the example of Fig. 6 a CT scan is performed and then evaluated. If there was a problem in the scan and the report was not complete, the scan must be repeated. However, the repetitions must be separated by an interval of 150. Moreover, there cannot be more than three repetitions.

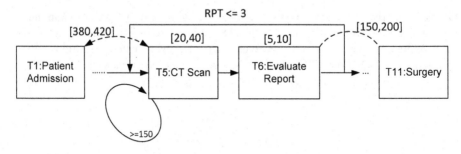

Fig. 6. Modeling a loop pattern

Such patterns can be expressed in our framework. In general, the successive incarnations of task T5 (and, similarly, of T6) are denoted as $T5^{(1)}, T5^{(2)}, T5^{(3)}, ...$ They take on binary values just like other tasks. Now, $1 \leq T5^{(1)} + T5^{(2)} + T5^{(3)} \leq 3$. Also, the start and finish times of these incarnations are related as: $TS5^{(i+1)} \geq TF6^{(i)}$; and the temporal condition between successive iterations of the T5 loop is: $TS5^{(i+1)} - TS5^{(i)} \geq 150$, $i \geq 1$. Finally, as shown in Fig. 6, T5 itself is a super task that can still relate to other tasks through inter-task constraints. Thus, we need additional constraints in our formulation to capture the semantics of T5 (and T6) as tasks in themselves:

$$T5 == 1 => T5^{(1)} + T5^{(2)} + T5^{(3)} \geq 1$$
$$T5 == 1 => TS5 = Min(TS5^{(1)}, TS5^{(2)}, TS5^{(3)})$$
$$T5 == 1 => TF5 = Max(TF5^{(1)}, TF5^{(2)}, TF5^{(3)})$$

Now, T5 (and T6) relate to the other tasks as shown in the Fig. 6. Once these constraints are incorporated we can solve the optimization model in the same way as the models without loops. The main limitation with our approach in theory is that it requires a cap on the number of repetitions. However, in actual practice such a limit always exists as in the situation described here.

6   Discussion and Related Work

The approach presented above is general and extensible. Not only does it apply to structured processes with AND and XOR connectors, it can also be extended to new types of connectors such as inclusive ORs by defining the formal structural balance equations for them. It would simply require changing Def. 2. Moreover, this approach applies to unstructured processes as well where split and join connectors are not well-nested or matched since we treat each connector separately. The MILP problem is NP-complete; however, very efficient solution techniques for it are known.

Although a formal proof is beyond the scope of our current work, yet we can informally argue completeness of our approach in terms of expressive power as follows. With the overlap feature we can describe any reasonable interval of time by combining durations of multiple tasks and the delays between them. Further we can write constraints across intervals, like "interval 1 is larger than interval 2." Moreover, we can handle repetitions. This gives us a powerful capability for modeling temporal constraints that covers the space of possibilities from a modeling point of view.

The first efforts towards developing temporal patterns are due to Allen [1] who developed a general theory of action and time for reasoning about actions based on temporal logic. He also introduced relationships like *before, equal, meets, overlaps, during, starts* and *finishes* as a way of relating two or more time intervals, and then reasoning about them. However, the work of Allen was not done in the context of workflows. Temporal reasoning in the context of workflows is discussed in [1]. By far, the early efforts on introducing time into workflow systems were due to Sadiq, et al. [18] and Eder, et al. [6,7]. The approach in [6,7] relies on ideas from project planning and critical path methods to determine various metrics like earliest start date, latest finish date, etc. for various activities. Zhao and Stohr [22] also developed a framework and algorithms for temporal workflow management in the context of a claims handling system based on turnaround time prediction, time allocation and task prioritization. They used reward functions to guide workers' behavior.

Lanz et al. presented several time patterns (TP) that represent temporal constraints of time-aware processes [12,13]. These patterns are in four groups: durations and time lags; restricting execution times; variability; and recurrent process elements. Most research however has focused on the first group. The approach of [12,13] and others towards dealing with time-aware processes have relied on the conditional simple temporal networks (CSTN) as a representational technique [20]. These networks allow a mapping from time points at which observations are taken to propositional statements attached to nodes. These statements are checked for their truth values at the observation times and the corresponding actions at the nodes are performed if the statements are true. The propositions are Boolean combinations of simple range constraints. Techniques for checking such networks are discussed in the work of Combi et al. [8] where they have also extended the CSTN's to CSTNU's (CSTNs with uncertainty) which are more general CSTNs. In CSTNUs the uncertainly arises from the fact that some contingent edges become applicable only if a condition is satisfied.

CSTNs were developed in the context of planning problems and have also been applied to workflows. Since the main idea is to partition the nodes in a CSTN based on the truth values of propositions, they do not always follow a workflow like structure. The idea of constraint violation and relaxation that we presented here does not exist in the context of CSTNs. Moreover, to the best our knowledge, extensions like overlap and iteration using special functions like max and min are also not present since they restrict the constraints to simple range constraints.

Another related concept in the context of temporal workflows is that of dynamic controllability [10,20,15]. In this view, a temporal workflow consists of *contingent links* whose actual duration is determined by nature within a given range, and *agent-controlled links* whose actual value is under the control of and determined by an agent at execution time. The actual values of the durations of the contingent links are known only at run-time. A CSTN or CSTNU network corresponding to a workflow process is dynamically controllable if there exists a viable agent strategy to successfully complete the execution of the workflow for all combinations of values of the contingent link durations. Algorithms for ensuring controllability are described in [4, 8,10,20,15]. It is not possible to compare our approach directly with dynamic controllability because in our formulation there are no contingent links. All our task duration and inter-task duration ranges are determined based on, say, medical (or some other kind of) guidelines. However, it would be interesting to explore how our approach can be applied to solve the dynamic controllability problem as part of future work.

Another interesting constraint based approach for modeling clinical pathways is discussed in [21]. It considers resources and various scheduling patterns with setup costs and temporal constraints, but it does not use a process focus and does not provide a solution methodology.

7   Conclusions

We presented a new approach for temporal process modeling based on constraint satisfaction. It can be used to check temporal consistency at both design and run times. A unique aspect of our approach is that it can allow controlled violation of constraints by allowing relaxation of some constraints and associating penalties with the violations. It was illustrated with a realistic example of a clinical workflow. However, the approach is general. We also showed that it can express a variety of temporal patterns and deal with changes in the process.

Further investigation is needed to compare our approach with the ones based on dynamic controllability and CSTN networks. More work is also needed in developing methods for associating the right penalties with constraints and optimal ways of recovering from violations. Compensation and substitution based methods may also be used for this purpose and costs can be included in the model as well. As an example, in a process running late, it may be possible to substitute an expensive procedure or diagnostic test that runs faster, say, in two days versus another less expensive one that takes four days. There is also need for faster solution techniques for the MILP formulation.

Finally, activity durations, path choices, violation types, degrees and frequencies, and temporal patterns can all be statistically characterized. This would allow for a stochastic approach to managing constraint violations along the lines of the work in [19].

Acknowledgment. This research was supported in part by the Smeal College of Business. Sabbella was supported in part by a grant from HP while he was a student at Penn State.

References

1. Allen, J.F.: Towards a general theory of action and time. Artificial Intelligence **23**(2), 123–154 (1984)
2. Bettini, C., Wang, X.S., Jajodia, S.: Temporal reasoning in workflow systems. Distrib. Para. Dat. **11**(3), 269–306 (2002)
3. Chen, J., Yang, Y.: Temporal dependency based checkpoint selection for dynamic verification of temporal constraints in scientific workflow systems. ACM Trans. on Soft Eng. and Methodol. **20**(3), 9:1–9:23 (2011)
4. Combi, C., Gozzi, M., Posenato, R., Pozzi, G.: Conceptual modeling of flexible temporal workflows. TAAS **7**(2), 19:1–19:29 (2012)
5. CPLEX, Reference manual. IBM corporation (2009)
6. Eder, J., Euthimios, P., Pozewaunig, H., Rabinovich, M.: Time management in workflow systems. In: Proc. BIS 1999, pp. 265–280 (1999)
7. Eder, J., Gruber, W., Panagos, E.: Temporal modeling of workflows with conditional execution paths. In: Ibrahim, M., Küng, J., Revell, N. (eds.) DEXA 2000. LNCS, vol. 1873, pp. 243–253. Springer, Heidelberg (2000)
8. Hunsberger, L., Posenato, R., Combi, C.: The dynamic controllability of conditional STNs with uncertainty. In: Proc. PlanEx 2012 (2012)
9. Kumar, A., Yao, W., Chu, C.: Flexible Business Process Compliance with Semantic Constraints using Mixed-Integer Programming. INFORMS Journal on Computing **25**(3) (Summer 2013)
10. Lanz, A., Posenato, R., Combi, C., Reichert, M.: Controllability of time-aware processes at run time. In: Meersman, R., Panetto, H., Dillon, T., Eder, J., Bellahsene, Z., Ritter, N., De Leenheer, P., Dou, D. (eds.) OTM 2013. LNCS, vol. 8185, pp. 39–56. Springer, Heidelberg (2013)
11. Lanz, A., Reichert, M., Weber, B.: A formal semantics of time patterns for process aware information systems. Tech. Rep. UIB-2013-02, University of Ulm (2013)

12. Lanz, A., Weber, B., Reichert, M.: Time patterns for process-aware information systems. Req. Eng. **19**(2), 113–141 (2014)
13. Lanz, A., Reichert, M.: Dealing with changes of time-aware processes. In: Sadiq, S., Soffer, P., Völzer, H. (eds.) BPM 2014. LNCS, vol. 8659, pp. 217–233. Springer, Heidelberg (2014)
14. Marjanovic, O., Orlowska, M.E.: On modeling and verification of temporal constraints in production workflows. Knowl. and Inf. Syst. **1**(2), 157–192 (1999)
15. Morris, P.H., Muscettola, N., Vidal, T.: Dynamic control of plans with temporal uncertainty. In: Nebel, B. (ed.) The Seventeenth International Joint Conference on Artificial Intelligence (IJCAI 2001), pp. 494–502. Morgan Kaufmann (2001)
16. Reichert, M., Weber, B.: Enabling Flexibility in Process-aware Information Systems: Challenges, Methods, Technologies. Springer (2012)
17. Rinderle, S., Reichert, M., Dadam, P.: Correctness criteria for dynamic changes in workflow systems: A survey. Data & Knowl. Eng. **50**(1), 9–34 (2004)
18. Sadiq, S.W., Marjanovic, O., Orlowska, M.E.: Managing change and time in dynamic workflow processes. Int'l J. Coop. Inf. Syst. **9**(1–2), 93–116 (2000)
19. Shu, J., Barton, R.: Managing supply chain execution: monitoring timeliness and correctness via individualized trace data. Prod. and Ops. Mgmt. **21**, 715–729 (2012)
20. Tsamardinos, I., Vidal, T., Pollack, M.: CTP: A new constraint-based formalism for conditional, temporal planning. Constraints **8**(4), 365–388 (2003)
21. Wolf, A.: Constraint-based modeling and scheduling of clinical pathways. In: Larrosa, J., O'Sullivan, B. (eds.) CSCLP 2009. LNCS, vol. 6384, pp. 122–138. Springer, Heidelberg (2011)
22. Zhao, J., Stohr, E.: Temporal workflow management in a claim handling system. In: Proceedings of Work Activities Coordination and Collaboration (WACC 1999), San Francisco, CA, USA, pp. 187–195 (1999)

Complex Symbolic Sequence Encodings for Predictive Monitoring of Business Processes

Anna Leontjeva[1]([✉]), Raffaele Conforti[2], Chiara Di Francescomarino[3],
Marlon Dumas[1], and Fabrizio Maria Maggi[1]

[1] University of Tartu, Tartu, Estonia
{anna.leontjeva,marlon.dumas,f.m.maggi}@ut.ee
[2] Queensland University of Technology, Brisbane, Australia
raffaele.conforti@qut.edu.au
[3] FBK-IRST, Trento, Italy
dfmchiara@fbk.eu

Abstract. This paper addresses the problem of predicting the outcome of an ongoing case of a business process based on event logs. In this setting, the outcome of a case may refer for example to the achievement of a performance objective or the fulfillment of a compliance rule upon completion of the case. Given a log consisting of traces of completed cases, given a trace of an ongoing case, and given two or more possible outcomes (e.g., a positive and a negative outcome), the paper addresses the problem of determining the most likely outcome for the case in question. Previous approaches to this problem are largely based on simple symbolic sequence classification, meaning that they extract features from traces seen as sequences of event labels, and use these features to construct a classifier for runtime prediction. In doing so, these approaches ignore the data payload associated to each event. This paper approaches the problem from a different angle by treating traces as complex symbolic sequences, that is, sequences of events each carrying a data payload. In this context, the paper outlines different feature encodings of complex symbolic sequences and compares their predictive accuracy on real-life business process event logs.

Keywords: Process mining · Predictive monitoring · Complex symbolic sequence

1 Introduction

Process mining is a family of methods for analyzing business processes based on *event logs* consisting of *traces*, each representing one execution of the process (a.k.a. a *case*). A trace consists of a sequence of (possibly timestamped) events, each referring to an execution of an activity (a.k.a. an *event class*). Events in a trace may have a payload consisting of attributes such as the resource(s) involved in the execution of an activity or other data recorded with the event.

© Springer International Publishing Switzerland 2015
H.R. Motahari-Nezhad et al. (Eds.): BPM 2015, LNCS 9253, pp. 297–313, 2015.
DOI: 10.1007/978-3-319-23063-4_21

Predictive business process monitoring [14] is a category of process mining methods that aims at predicting at runtime and as early as possible the outcome of a case given its current (incomplete) trace. In this context, an outcome may be the fulfillment of a constraint on the cycle time of the case, the validity of a temporal logic constraint, or any predicate over a completed case. For example, in a sales process, a possible outcome might be the placement of a purchase order by a potential customer, whereas in a medical treatment process, a possible outcome is the recovery of the patient upon completion of the treatment.

Existing approaches to predictive monitoring [7,14] essentially map the problem to that of early sequence classification [24]. The idea is to train a classifier over the set of prefixes of historical traces. This classifier is used at runtime in order to predict the outcome of an ongoing case based on its current (incomplete) trace. A key step is to extract features from prefixes of historical traces. In this respect, existing approaches treat traces as simple symbolic sequences, meaning sequences of symbols, each representing an event but without its payload. When data is taken into account, only the latest payload of data attributes attached to the event at the end of each trace prefix is included in the feature vector of the classifier, but the evolution of data attributes as the case unfolds is ignored.

This paper investigates an alternative approach where traces are treated as complex symbolic sequences, that is, sequences of events each carrying a data payload consisting of attribute-value pairs. A crucial design choice in this approach is how to encode a complex symbolic sequence in terms of vectors of features. In this respect, the paper proposes two complex sequence encodings. The first encoding is based on indexes. This encoding specifies, for each position in the case, the event occurring in that position and the value of each data attribute in that position. The second encoding is obtained by combining the first one with an encoding based on Hidden Markov Models (HMMs), a well-known generative probabilistic technique. As this work deals with the problem of case classification, a discriminative HMM approach is adopted. In particular, separate HMMs are trained for each possible outcome (e.g., one HMM for positive cases and one for negative cases). Then, the likelihood of a trace prefix to belong to each of these two models is measured. The difference in likelihoods is expressed in terms of odds-ratios, which are then used as features to train the classifier. The proposed methods are evaluated in terms of their accuracy at different points in a trace based on two real life logs: (i) a patient treatment log provided for the BPI challenge 2011 [1] and (ii) an insurance claim process log from an insurance company [22].

The paper is structured as follows. Section 2 reviews previous work on predictive business process monitoring and introduces HMMs, which are used later in the paper. Section 3 presents the proposed methods while Section 4 discusses their evaluation. Finally, Section 5 draws conclusions and outlines future work.

2   Background and Related Work

This section provides an overview of existing predictive business process monitoring approaches (Section 2.1) and briefly introduce Hidden Markov Models (HMMs), which we use for complex symbolic sequence encoding (Section 2.2).

2.1   Predictive Monitoring: The Related Work

Existing techniques for predictive business process monitoring can be broadly classified based on the type of predicted outcome. In this respect, a first group of works concentrates on the time perspective. In [2,3], the authors present a set of approaches in which annotated transition systems, containing time information extracted from event logs, are used to: (i) check time conformance while cases are being executed, (ii) predict the remaining processing time of incomplete cases, and (iii) recommend appropriate activities to end users working on these cases. In [10], an ad-hoc predictive clustering approach is presented, in which context-related execution scenarios are discovered and modeled through state-aware performance predictors. In [20], the authors use stochastic Petri nets for predicting the remaining execution time of a process.

A second group of works focuses on approaches that generate predictions and recommendations to reduce risks. For example, in [7], the authors present a technique to support process participants in making risk-informed decisions, with the aim of reducing the process risks. Risks are predicted by traversing decision trees generated from the logs of past process executions. In [16], the authors make predictions about time-related process risks, by identifying (using statistical principles) and exploiting indicators observable in event logs that highlight the possibility of transgressing deadlines. In [21], an approach for Root Cause Analysis through classification algorithms is presented. Decision trees are used to retrieve the causes of overtime faults on a log enriched with information about delays, resources and workload.

An approach for prediction of abnormal termination of business processes is presented in [12]. Here, a fault detection algorithm (local outlier factor) is used to estimate the probability of a fault to occur. Alarms are provided for early notification of probable abnormal terminations. In [6], Castellanos et al. present a business operation management platform equipped with time series forecasting functionalities. This platform allows for predictions of metric values on running process instances as well as for predictions of aggregated metric values of future instances (e.g., the number of orders that will be placed next Monday). Predictive monitoring focused on specific types of failures has also been applied to real case studies. For example, in [8,15], the authors present a technique for predicting "late show" events in transportation processes. In particular, they apply standard statistical techniques to find correlations between "late show" events and external variables related to weather conditions or road traffic.

A key difference between these approaches and our technique is that they rely either on the control-flow or on the data perspective for making predictions at runtime, whereas we take both perspectives into consideration. The two perspectives have been considered together only in [14], where a framework for the predictive monitoring of constraint fulfillment and violation has been proposed. In this approach, however, only the payload of the last executed event is taken into account, while neglecting the evolution of data values throughout the execution traces. The present paper aims at addressing this latter limitation by treating the input traces as complex symbolic sequences.

2.2   Hidden Markov Models

Hidden Markov Models (HMMs) [18] are a class of well-studied models of sequential observations that have been widely applied in the context of sequence classification [24]. HMMs are probabilistic generative models, meaning that there is an assumption that an observed sequence is generated by some process that needs to be uncovered via probabilistic reasoning. The idea behind HMM is that a sequence consists of observed events, generated by some hidden factors. Assume, for example, that two coins – a fair one and a biased one – are tossed in some unknown order. Only a sequence of heads and tails can be observed. Our goal is to figure out which parts of the sequence were produced by the fair and which by the biased coin. This process can be described by:

- observed events $O = \{O_1, O_2, ..., O_T\}$ - resulting sequence consisted of heads and tails;
- set of discrete symbols - the finite *alphabet size* $V = \{V_1, V_2, ..V_{|M|}\}$ - {head, tail} in our example;
- number of hidden states N, where each state is denoted as $S = \{S_1, S_2, ..S_{|N|}\}$ - represented by fair and biased coin in our example;
- vector of initial probabilities π - how often, in general, each coin is chosen;
- matrix of emission probabilities B - probabilities for each symbol to occur in a particular hidden state - for example, the probability of tails of the biased coin;
- matrix transition probabilities A - probability to move from one state to another or to stay in the same state - transition probabilities answer the question "how often the coins were switched".

The common HMM construction procedure is to specify parameters N and V and to train a model $\lambda = \{A, B, \pi\}$ using a maximum likelihood method such as the standard Baum-Welch algorithm [18].

3   Predictive Monitoring: The Proposed Approach

In this section, the proposed approach for predictive monitoring is described. In particular, in Section 3.1, an overview of the entire approach is given. In Section 3.2, the core part of the proposed approach is introduced, i.e., the encoding of log cases as complex symbolic sequences.

3.1   Overview

Fig. 1 shows an overview of the proposed approach. To predict the outcome of an ongoing case, its current (incomplete) trace (say of length n) is encoded using complex symbolic sequences. As explained in detail in Section 3.2, a complex symbolic sequence carries information about the control flow and the data flow of the trace.

In the approach, a log of historical (completed) cases is supposed to be available. From these cases, all the prefixes of length n are extracted and, in turn,

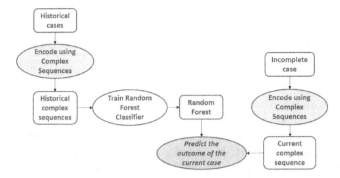

Fig. 1. Overview of the proposed approach.

encoded in the form of complex symbolic sequences. In addition, these sequences are labeled using a binary or categorical value according to their outcome. These "historical complex symbolic sequences" are used to train a classifier. The current ongoing trace is then used to query the classifier that returns the label that is the most probable outcome for the current case according to the information derived from the historical cases. In this work, we use random forest as classifier that belongs to the class of ensemble methods [5]. At the core of the method is the concept of decision tree. However, instead of training a single tree on a dataset, it grows a pre-defined number of trees and let them vote for the most popular outcome. Random forest is easy to train as it requires less input parameters to tune compared to other classification algorithms.[1] Moreover, it has shown superior results over other well-known classification algorithms like support vector machines (SVM) and generalized boosted regression models (GBM) [19,23] in several cases [9]. A comparison of the performances of these algorithms when applied to one of the datesets used in this paper is shown in Fig. 8.

3.2 Complex Symbolic Sequence Encodings

Each case of a log corresponds to a sequence σ_i of events describing its control flow. Each event is also associated with data in the form of attribute-value pairs. Moreover, each completed case is associated to an outcome - a *label*, which can assume binary or categorical values. We represent a case in the following form:

sequence(event{associated data},...,event{associated data}): label

As running example, we consider the log in Fig. 2 pertaining to a medical treatment process. Each case relates to a different patient and the corresponding sequence of events indicates the activities executed for a medical treatment of that patient. In the example, *consultation* is the first event of sequence σ_1. Its data payload "{33, radiotherapy}" corresponds to the data associated to

---

[1] Random forest requires two parameters: Number of trees to grow (ntrees) and number of features to use for each tree (mtry).

σ_1 (consultation{33, radiotherapy},...,ultrasound{33, nursing ward}):false

...

σ_k (order rate{56, general lab},..., payment{56, clinic}):true

Fig. 2. Running example.

attributes *age* and *department*. Note that the value of *age* is static: It is the same for all the events in a case, while the value of *department* is different for every event. In the payload of an event, always the entire set of attributes available in the log is considered. In case for some event the value for a specific attribute is not available, the value *unknown* is specified for it.

The goal of predictive business process monitoring is to build a classifier that learns from a set of historical cases L how to discriminate classes of cases and predict as early as possible the outcome of a new, unlabeled case. More specifically, we are interested in automatically deriving a function f that, given an ongoing sequence σ_x provides a label for it, i.e., $f : (L, \sigma_x) \rightarrow \{label_x\}$. To achieve this goal, a random forest classifier is trained on all sequence prefixes of the same length of σ_x derived from historical cases in L. In order to train the classifier, each (prefix) sequence σ_i, $i = 1...k$ has to be represented through a feature vector $g_i = (g_{i1}, g_{i2}, ...g_{ih})$.

In the most straightforward encodings, sequences are treated as simple symbolic sequences, while additional information related to data and data flow is neglected. This work combines and exploits both the control and the data flow dimension by considering the sequences as complex symbolic sequences. In particular, two different encodings (the *index-based* encoding and the *HMM-based* encoding) are taken into consideration. In the following sections, first, four classical baseline encodings are sketched and then the two new encodings are illustrated in detail.

Table 1. Baseline encodings for the example in Fig. 2.

(a) *boolean* encoding.

	consultation	ultrasound	...	payment	label
σ_1	1	1	...	0	false
...					
σ_k	0	0	...	1	true

(b) *frequency-based* encoding.

	consultation	ultrasound	...	payment	label
σ_1	2	1	...	0	false
...					
σ_k	0	0	...	4	true

(c) *simple index* encoding.

	event_1	...	event_m	label
σ_1	consultation		ultrasound	false
...				
σ_k	order rate		payment	true

(d) *index latest payload* encoding.

	age	event_1	...	event_m	...	department_last	label
σ_1	33	consultation		ultrasound	...	nursing ward	false
...							
σ_k	56	order rate		payment	...	clinic	true

3.3   Baselines

The first two approaches we use as baselines in our experiments describe sequences of events as feature vectors, where each feature corresponds to an event class (an activity) from the log. In particular, the *boolean* encoding represents a sequence σ_i through a feature vector $g_i = (g_{i1}, g_{i2}, ...g_{ih})$, where, if g_{ij} corresponds to the event class e, then:

$$g_{ij} = \begin{cases} 1 & \text{if } e \text{ is present in } \sigma_i \\ 0 & \text{if } e \text{ is not present in } \sigma_i \end{cases}$$

For instance, the encoding of the example reported in Fig. 2 with the *boolean* encoding is shown in Table 1a. The *frequency-based* encoding, instead of boolean values, represents the control flow in a case with the frequency of each event class in the case. Table 1b shows the *frequency-based* encoding for the example in Fig. 2.

Another way of encoding a sequence is by taking into account also information about the order in which events occur in the sequence, as in the *simple index* encoding. Here, each feature corresponds to a position in the sequence and the possible values for each feature are the event classes. By using this type of encoding the example in Fig. 2 would be encoded as reported in Table 1c.

The fourth baseline encoding adds to the simple index baseline the data of the latest payload. Here, data attributes are treated as static features without taking into consideration their evolution over time. Table 1d shows this encoding for the example in Fig. 2.

Table 2. Encodings for the example in Fig. 2.

(a) *index-based* encoding.

	age	event_1	...	event_m	...	department_1	...	department_m	label
σ_1	33	consultation		ultrasound		radiotherapy		nursing ward	false
...									
σ_j	56	order rate		payment		general lab		clinic	true

(b) *HMM-based* encoding.

	age	event_1	...	event_m	...	department_1	...	department_m	LLR_event	...	LLR_department	label
σ_1	33	consultation		ultrasound		radiotherapy		nursing ward	0.12	...	0.56	false
...												
σ_j	56	order rate		payment		general lab		clinic	4.3	...	1.7	true

3.4   Index-Based Encoding

In the *index-based* encoding, the data associated with events in a sequence is divided into static and dynamic information. Static information is the same for all the events in the sequence (e.g., the information contained in case attributes), while dynamic information changes for different events (e.g., the information contained in event attributes). The resulting feature vector g_i, for a sequence σ_i, is:

$$g_i = (s_i^1, .., s_i^u, event_{i1}, event_{i2}, ..event_{im}, h_{i1}^1, h_{i2}^1...h_{im}^1, ..., h_{i1}^r, h_{i2}^r, ...h_{im}^r),$$

where each s_i is a static feature, each $event_{ij}$ is the event class at position j and each h_{ij} is a dynamic feature associated to an event. The example in Fig. 2 is transformed into the encoding shown in Table 2a.

3.5   HMM-Based Encoding

The core idea of HMMs is to provide an abstraction of the information contained in a sequence. However, in general, HMMs are used to *describe* sequential data, not to *classify* it. Moreover, they usually deal only with simple symbolic sequences. The aim of the proposed approach, in contrast, is to be able to *discriminate* between *complex symbolic sequences* with respect to their outcome and make predictions for new, unlabeled sequences.

In order to overcome these limitations of HMMs, we propose some extensions. In order to shift from generative (descriptive) to discriminative models, we take an approach similar to the one presented in [11,13]. Here, the main idea is to use *discriminative HMMs* to represent a sequence through a measure that captures in some way the relation of the sequence with its outcome. To deal with complex symbolic sequences, the data associated to events is separated into static and dynamic information and the evolution of each dynamic feature (and the sequence of event classes) is expressed as a simple symbolic sequence. In addition, to encode a case with *HMM-based* encoding, a training set is needed to train the HMMs. In particular, the following steps need to be performed:

- the sequences of event classes and sequences related to each dynamic feature of both the case to be encoded and to the ones in the training set are transformed into simple symbolic sequences;
- the simple symbolic sequences of each dynamic feature (or event class) from the training set are partitioned according to the labels of the cases they belong to. For example, in the binary case one subset corresponds to all sequences that have a positive label and another subset to the sequences with a negative label;
- for each subset of simple symbolic sequences corresponding to a dynamic feature (or event class), a HMM is trained. For example, in the binary case two different HMMs, $HMM_{positive}$ and $HMM_{negative}$, are generated;
- for each simple symbolic sequence derived from the case to be encoded, the log-likelihood ratio (LLR) is computed. LLR expresses the likelihood of the sequence to belong to one of the trained models. In the binary case, it shows the likelihood of the sequence to belong to the model describing the positive sequences ($HMM_{positive}$) over the likelihood to belong to the HMM of the negative ones ($HMM_{negative}$). Intuitively, the greater the value of LLR is, the greater is the chance that the sequence belongs to a case with a positive outcome. For a case σ_i, and for a given dynamic feature (or event class) h_j, the corresponding log-ratio is defined as:

$$LLR(\sigma_i^{h_j}) = log\left(\frac{HMM(\sigma_i^{h_j})_{positive}}{HMM(\sigma_i^{h_j})_{negative}}\right),$$

where $\sigma_i^{h_j}$ is the simple symbolic sequence extracted from σ_i related to h_j. The information contained in a simple symbolic sequence is, hence, condensed into one number, expressing the relationship of the sequence with a given label value.

The result of applying this procedure to all the information that can be considered as a simple symbolic sequence in a case (sequences of event classes and dynamic data) is a set of LLR values, which are added to the feature vector obtained with the *index-based* encoding. In particular, the input vector for the classifier is, in this case:

$$g_j = (s_j^1, .., s_j^u, event_{j1}, event_{j2}, ..event_{jm}, h_{j1}^1, ...h_{jm}^1, ..., h_{j1}^r, ...h_{jm}^r, LLR_j^1, ..LLR_j^r),$$

where each s_i is a static feature, each $event_{ij}$ is the event class at position j and each h_{ij} is a dynamic feature associated to an event. Each LLR_j^i is the log-likelihood ratio computed based on the simple symbolic sequence corresponding to an event class or a dynamic feature of the original case. Table 2b shows an encoding for the example in Fig. 2 obtained by using log-likelihood ratio values.

4   Evaluation

In this section, we provide a description of the carried out experimentation. In particular, our evaluation focuses on the following research questions:

RQ1. Do the proposed encodings provide *reliable* results in terms of predictions?
RQ2. Do the proposed encodings provide reliable predictions at *early* stages of the running case?
RQ3. Are the proposed encodings *stable* with respect to the quality of the results provided at different stages of the running case?

The three questions focus on three intertwined aspects. The first one relates to the quality of the results (in terms of prediction correctness) provided by the proposed encodings. The second one investigates how early the encodings are able to provide reliable results. The third one focuses on the stability of the quality of the results when computed at different stages of an ongoing case. In the following, we describe the experiments carried out to answer these research questions.

4.1   Datasets

We conducted the experiments by using two real-life logs: The BPI challenge 2011 [1] log (herein called dataset$_1$) and an event log (herein called dataset$_2$) of an Australian insurer. The former log pertains to a healthcare process and describes the executions of a process related to the treatment of patients diagnosed with cancer in a large Dutch academic hospital. Each case refers to the treatment of a

Table 3. Case study datasets.

Log	# Cases	# Events	# Event Classes
dataset$_1$	1,143	150,291	624
dataset$_2$	1,065	16,869	9

different patient. The event log contains domain specific attributes that are both case attributes and event attributes in addition to the standard XES attributes.[2] For example, *Age, Diagnosis,* and *Treatment code* are case attributes (that we consider as static features) and *Activity code, Number of executions, Specialism code,* and *Group* are event attributes (that we consider as dynamic features). The second log relates to an insurance claims handling process and covers about one year of completed cases. The insurance claims log includes only event attributes like *Claim type, Claim reason,* and *Amount.* Table 3 summarizes the characteristics of the two logs (number of cases, number of events, and number of event classes).

4.2   Evaluation Measures

In order to assess the goodness-of-fit for the trained classifiers, we used the Area Under the ROC Curve (AUC) measure [4]. A ROC curve is defined starting from a standard notion of confusion matrix, i.e., the matrix in which each column represents the predicted outcomes of a set of cases, while each row represents the actual outcomes and cells represent:

- true-positive (T_P: cases with positive outcomes predicted correctly);
- false-positive (F_P: cases with negative outcomes predicted as positive);
- true-negative (T_N: cases with negative outcomes predicted correctly);
- false-negative (F_N: cases with positive outcomes predicted as negative).

To draw a ROC curve, two derivatives of the confusion matrix should be defined, i.e., the true positive rate (TPR), represented on the y-axis, and the false positive rate (FPR), represented on the x-axis of the ROC curve. The TPR (or recall), $\frac{TP}{(TP+FN)}$, defines how many positive outcomes are correctly predicted among all positive outcomes available. On the other hand, the FPR, $\frac{FP}{(FP+TN)}$, defines how many negative outcomes are predicted as positive among all negative outcomes available. AUC condenses the information provided by a ROC curve into a single measure of performance. A classifier of the random guess, expressed as a ROC curve, is represented by a diagonal line with AUC of 0.5, while the perfect classifier would score AUC of 1 and is represented by the ROC curve crossing the coordinates $(0, 1)$ - where $FPR = 0$ and $TPR = 1$.

The measure we use to evaluate the earliness of a prediction is based on the number of events that are needed to achieve a minimum value for AUC. Finally,

---

[2] XES (eXtensible Event Stream) is an XML-based standard for event logs proposed by the IEEE Task Force on Process Mining (www.xes-standard.org).

Table 4. Distribution of labels in the datasets.

LTL	# Positive cases	# Negative cases
φ_1	459	684
φ_2	894	249
φ_3	260	883
φ_4	320	823
γ_1	788	277

we use standard deviation to evaluate the stability of the results computed at different stages of an ongoing case.

4.3   Evaluation Procedure

In our experimentation, first, we have ordered the cases in the logs based on the time at which the first event of each case has occurred. Then, we have split the logs in two parts. We have used the first part (80% of the cases) as training set, i.e., we have used these cases as historical data. Note that the training set was used differently in the experiments based on the different encodings. For most of them, the entire training set was used to train the random forest classifier. The only exception is the HMM-based encoding that uses 75% of the training set for training the HMMs and 25% for training the random forest. We have used the remaining cases (remaining 20% of the whole log) as a test set (used as ongoing cases).

Next, we have defined 4 temporal constraints corresponding to the following linear temporal logic rules [17] over event classes in $dataset_1$:

- $\varphi_1 = \mathbf{F}(\text{"tumor marker } CA - 19.9\text{"}) \vee \mathbf{F}(\text{"ca} - 125 \text{ using meia"})$,
- $\varphi_2 = \mathbf{G}(\text{"}CEA - \text{tumor marker using meia"} \rightarrow \mathbf{F}(\text{"squamous cell carcinoma using eia"}))$,
- $\varphi_3 = (\neg\text{"histological examination} - biopsies nno\text{"})\mathbf{U}(\text{"squamous cell carcinoma using eia"})$,
- $\varphi_4 = \mathbf{F}(\text{"histological examination} - \text{big resectiep"})$.

and we have used them to label cases in the training set from $dataset_1$ as compliant or non-compliant (one labeling for each rule). This set of (realistic) rules encompasses all the main linear temporal logic operators. Cases in the training set of $dataset_2$ have been labeled with respect to a constraint corresponding to a rule γ_1 formalizing a regulation internal to the insurance company. This rule requires a claimant to be informed with a certain frequency about the status of his or her claim. The distribution of labels in the datasets is shown in Table 4.

In our experiments, a few input parameters had to be chosen. For random forest classifier, the number of trees was fixed to 500 and the optimal number of features to use for each tree (mtry) was estimated separately using 5-fold cross-validation on the training set. The optimal number of hidden states for HMMs was estimated in a similar way. In particular, the original training set was split, in turn, into training and testing cases and, using these cases, different parameter configurations were tested. The optimal ones – with highest AUC, were chosen for the experiments.

In order to measure the ability of the models to make accurate predictions at an early stage, we computed the AUC values using prefixes ranging from 2 to 20. This choice is justified by the observation that for the defined formulas, encodings based on the sole control flow are able to provide correct predictions after about 20 events.

4.4   Results and Discussion

Figures 3-6 show the trend of the AUC values when predicting the compliance of cases in the test set from dataset$_1$, with respect to φ_1-φ_4. In particular, each plot shows the evolution of the AUC values for the encodings under examination when using the first 20 prefixes of each case in the test set. In Fig. 3, we plot the AUC trend for predictions over the fulfillment of φ_1. For very early predictions the baseline based on the latest data payload gives an AUC that is comparable to the one obtained with complex symbolic sequences. However, for longer prefixes, when more data is available referring to the trend of the attribute values attached to events, this information is exploited by the encodings based on complex symbolic sequences that diverge from the baseline that remains approximately constant. Note that starting from prefixes of length 7 the AUC for both the encodings based on complex symbolic sequences is above 0.9.

Similar trends can be observed in Figures 4-5 referring to the case labeling based on the compliance with respect to φ_2 and φ_3. In the last plot, in Fig. 6, referring to the case labeling based on the compliance with respect to φ_4, the divergence of the encodings based on complex symbolic sequences with respect to the one that considers only the latest data payload is more evident. Here, the HMM-based encoding slightly outperforms the one that considers only indexes.

Fig. 7 shows the AUC trend obtained for the case labeling based on the compliance with respect to γ_1 of cases in dataset$_2$. We can observe that also for this dataset, for early predictions the baseline encoding based on the latest data payload gives a good AUC, while the other baselines have a lower AUC. For slightly longer prefixes (between 6 and 13), the AUC values of all the baseline encodings is comparable with the one of the encodings based on complex symbolic sequences. From prefixes of length 11 the AUC values for the boolean encoding and for the one based on the latest data payload decrease again. This case study shows that, although baseline encodings can perform very well for certain prefix lengths, their performance is not stable. On the other hand, encodings based on complex symbolic sequences are able to provide a reasonable AUC (around 0.8 in this case) even for short prefixes and to keep it constant or slightly improve it for longer prefixes.

Summing up, the case studies show that the baseline based on the latest data payload and the encodings based on complex symbolic sequences provide, in general, reliable predictions. Table 5, reporting the average AUC values for all the encodings under examination, confirms these results. However, while the baseline encoding is not always able to reach an average AUC value of 0.8, the two encodings based on complex symbolic sequences have an average AUC that

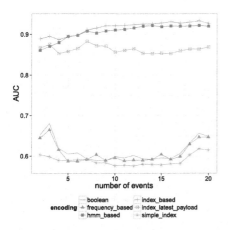

Fig. 3. AUC values using prefixes of different lengths. Labeling based on compliance with respect to φ_1.

Fig. 4. AUC values using prefixes of different lengths. Labeling based on compliance with respect to φ_2.

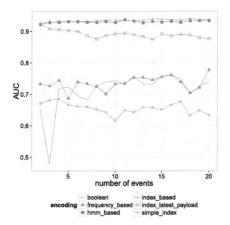

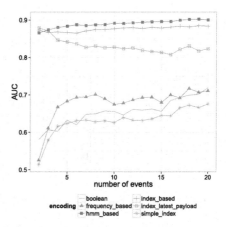

Fig. 5. AUC values using prefixes of different lengths. Labeling based on compliance with respect to φ_3.

Fig. 6. AUC values using prefixes of different lengths. Labeling based on compliance with respect to φ_4.

is always higher than 0.82. Based on these results, we can, hence, positively answer **RQ1**.

Our experimentation also highlights that some of the presented encodings are able to provide reliable predictions at a very early stage of an ongoing case. As shown in Table 6 (left), the baseline based on the latest data payload and the encodings based on complex symbolic sequences are able to provide an AUC

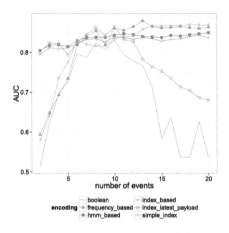
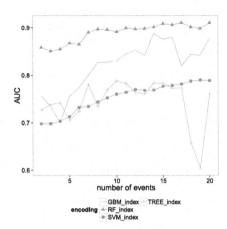

Fig. 7. AUC values using prefixes of different lengths. Labeling based on compliance with respect to γ_1.

Fig. 8. AUC values using different classification algorithms. Labeling based on compliance with respect to φ_1.

Table 5. AUC trends. Bold values show the highest average AUC values (higher than 0.8) and the lowest AUC standard deviation values (lower than 0.02).

encoding	mean across prefixes					st. deviation across prefixes				
	φ_1	φ_2	φ_3	φ_4	γ_1	φ_1	φ_2	φ_3	φ_4	γ_1
boolean	0.614	0.610	0.714	0.655	0.690	0.027	**0.018**	0.063	0.036	0.111
frequency-based	0.609	0.610	0.735	0.679	**0.816**	0.025	0.021	0.022	0.043	0.084
simple index	0.590	0.627	0.656	0.631	**0.814**	**0.013**	0.025	**0.018**	0.036	0.080
index latest payload	**0.863**	**0.908**	**0.892**	**0.831**	0.787	**0.009**	**0.008**	**0.012**	**0.018**	0.060
index-based	**0.917**	**0.928**	**0.935**	**0.876**	**0.828**	**0.016**	**0.006**	**0.004**	**0.006**	**0.013**
HMM-based	**0.907**	**0.932**	**0.931**	**0.890**	**0.835**	**0.018**	**0.009**	**0.003**	**0.010**	**0.013**

Table 6. Min. number of events needed for an AUC > 0.8 (left) and > 0.9 (right).

encoding	min(prefix) for $AUC = 0.8$					min(prefix) for $AUC = 0.9$				
	φ_1	φ_2	φ_3	φ_4	γ_1	φ_1	φ_2	φ_3	φ_4	γ_1
boolean					8					
frequency-based					6					
simple index					6					
index latest payload	2	2	2	2	2		2	2		
index-based	2	2	2	2	3	7	2	2		
HMM-based	2	2	2	2	2	7	2	2	18	

higher than 0.8 in all the cases under examination at a very early stage of an ongoing case (starting from prefixes of length 2 in most of the cases). This is not the case for the other baseline encodings. The encodings based on complex symbolic sequences are also able in most of the cases to reach an AUC higher

Table 7. Execution times per prefix length in seconds.

	HMM Training					RF Training					Predictions				
	2	5	10	15	20	2	5	10	15	20	2	5	10	15	20
index-based avg						1.08	5.05	26.29	79.20	176.65	0.23	1.43	6.46	13.37	24.21
index-based s.d.						0.09	0.22	2.46	5.54	12.28	0.05	0.13	0.57	0.78	1.72
HMM-based avg	23.14	34.11	49.03	65.95	83.51	0.99	4.88	26.55	81.74	186.41	0.24	1.45	6.34	13.69	26.40
HMM-based s.d.	1.24	2.53	4.02	4.75	8.23	0.20	0.55	1.18	6.25	11.22	0.05	0.14	0.56	0.92	2.96

than 0.9, though not always and at a very early stage of an ongoing case. In fact, both these encodings require 7 events for predicting the fulfillment of φ_1. The HMM-based encoding is the only one able to predict the fulfillment of φ_4 with an AUC of 0.9 (after 18 events). Starting from these observations, we can positively answer **RQ2**.

Finally, the experiments highlight that some of the encodings have a trend that is more stable than others when making predictions at different stages of the ongoing cases. Table 5 shows that the encodings based on complex symbolic sequences have the most stable AUC trends (the standard deviation for AUC is lower than 0.02 in all the cases). This is not always true for the baseline encodings. We can then provide a positive answer to **RQ3**.

Execution Times All experiments were conducted using R version 3.0.3 on a laptop with processor 2,6 GHz Intel Core i5 and 8 GB of RAM. Table 7 shows the average execution time (in seconds) and the standard deviation (with respect to the time needed to predict the fulfilment for each of the investigated rules) required by the index-based and the HMM-based methods for different prefix lengths. The execution times for constructing the classifiers (off-line) is between 1.08 seconds and 186.41 seconds across all the experiments for the index-based encoding and between 0.99 and 186.41 seconds for the HMM-based encoding. Note that, in addition, the HMM-based encoding also requires time for training the HMMs, ranging from 23.14 to 83.51 seconds. At runtime, the process time for making a prediction on a given prefix of a case is in the order of milliseconds for the runtime prediction on short cases (in the order of seconds for longer cases).

5   Conclusion

The paper has put forward some potential benefits of approaching the problem of predictive business process monitoring using complex symbolic sequence encodings. The empirical evaluation has shown that an index-based encoding achieves higher reliability when making early predictions, relative to pure control-flow encodings or control-flow encodings with only the last snapshot of attribute values. The evaluation has also shown that encodings based on HMMs may add in some cases an additional margin of accuracy and reliability to the predictions, but not in a significant nor systematic manner.

A threat to validity is that the evaluation is based on two logs only. Although the logs are representative of real-life scenarios, the results may not generalize to other logs. In particular, the accuracy may be affected by the definition of *positive outcome*. For logs different from the ones used here and other notions of outcome, it is conceivable that the predictive power may be lower. A direction for future work is to evaluate the methods on a wider set of logs so as to better understand their limitations.

The methods considered in this paper are focused on the problem of intra-case predictive monitoring, where the aim is to predict the outcome of one individual ongoing case seen in isolation from others. A macro-level version of this problem is the *inter-case predictive monitoring*, where the goal is to make predictions on the entire set of ongoing cases of a process, like for example predicting what percentage of ongoing cases will be delayed or end up in a negative outcome. Initial work on inter-case predictive monitoring [7] has approached the problem using control-flow encodings plus the last snapshot of attribute values. An avenue for future work is to investigate the use of complex symbolic sequence encodings in this context.

Acknowledgments. This research is partly funded by the ARC Discovery Project "Risk-aware Business Process Management" (DP110100091) by the EU FP7 Programme under grant agreement 609190 - "Subject-Orientation for People-Centred Production", and by the Estonian Research Council and by ERDF via the Software Technology and Applications Competence Centre – STACC.

References

1. 3TU Data Center: BPI Challenge 2011 Event Log (2011). doi:10.4121/uuid: d9769f3d-0ab0-4fb8-803b-0d1120ffcf54
2. van der Aalst, W.M.P., Pesic, M., Song, M.: Beyond process mining: from the past to present and future. In: Pernici, B. (ed.) CAiSE 2010. LNCS, vol. 6051, pp. 38–52. Springer, Heidelberg (2010)
3. van der Aalst, W.M.P., Schonenberg, M.H., Song, M.: Time prediction based on process mining. Inf. Syst. **36**(2), 450–475 (2011)
4. Bradley, A.P.: The use of the area under the roc curve in the evaluation of machine learning algorithms. Pattern Recognition **30**(7), 1145–1159 (1997)
5. Breiman, L.: Random forests. Machine Learning **45**(1), 5–32 (2001)
6. Castellanos, M., Salazar, N., Casati, F., Dayal, U., Shan, M.-C.: Predictive business operations management. In: Bhalla, S. (ed.) DNIS 2005. LNCS, vol. 3433, pp. 1–14. Springer, Heidelberg (2005)
7. Conforti, R., de Leoni, M., Rosa, M.L., van der Aalst, W.M.P., ter Hofstede, A.H.M.: A recommendation system for predicting risks across multiple business process instances. Decision Support Systems **69**, 1–19 (2015)
8. Feldman, Z., Fournier, F., Franklin, R., Metzger, A.: Proactive event processing in action: a case study on the proactive management of transport processes. In: Proc. of DEBS, pp. 97–106. ACM (2013)
9. Fernández-Delgado, M., Cernadas, E., Barro, S., Amorim, D.: Do we need hundreds of classifiers to solve real world classification problems? The Journal of Machine Learning Research **15**(1), 3133–3181 (2014)

10. Folino, F., Guarascio, M., Pontieri, L.: Discovering context-aware models for predicting business process performances. In: Meersman, R., Panetto, H., Dillon, T., Rinderle-Ma, S., Dadam, P., Zhou, X., Pearson, S., Ferscha, A., et al. (eds.) OTM 2012, Part I. LNCS, vol. 7565, pp. 287–304. Springer, Heidelberg (2012)
11. Goldszmidt, M.: Finding soon-to-fail disks in a haystack. In: Proc. of HotStorage. USENIX (2012)
12. Kang, B., Kim, D., Kang, S.H.: Real-time business process monitoring method for prediction of abnormal termination using knni-based lof prediction. Expert Syst, Appl. (2012)
13. Leontjeva, A., Goldszmidt, M., Xie, Y., Yu, F., Abadi, M.: Early security classification of skype users via machine learning. In: Proc. of AISec, pp. 35–44. ACM (2013)
14. Maggi, F.M., Di Francescomarino, C., Dumas, M., Ghidini, C.: Predictive monitoring of business processes. In: Jarke, M., Mylopoulos, J., Quix, C., Rolland, C., Manolopoulos, Y., Mouratidis, H., Horkoff, J. (eds.) CAiSE 2014. LNCS, vol. 8484, pp. 457–472. Springer, Heidelberg (2014)
15. Metzger, A., Franklin, R., Engel, Y.: Predictive monitoring of heterogeneous service-oriented business networks: the transport and logistics case. In: Proc. of SRII Global Conference. IEEE (2012)
16. Pika, A., van der Aalst, W.M.P., Fidge, C.J., ter Hofstede, A.H.M., Wynn, M.T.: Predicting deadline transgressions using event logs. In: La Rosa, M., Soffer, P. (eds.) BPM Workshops 2012. LNBIP, vol. 132, pp. 211–216. Springer, Heidelberg (2013)
17. Pnueli, A.: The temporal logic of programs. In: Proc. of FOCS, pp. 46–57. IEEE (1977)
18. Rabiner, L.: A tutorial on hidden markov models and selected applications in speech recognition. Proceedings of the IEEE **77**(2), 257–286 (1989)
19. Ridgeway, G.: Generalized boosted models: A guide to the gbm package. Update **1**(1) (2007)
20. Rogge-Solti, A., Weske, M.: Prediction of remaining service execution time using stochastic petri nets with arbitrary firing delays. In: Basu, S., Pautasso, C., Zhang, L., Fu, X. (eds.) ICSOC 2013. LNCS, vol. 8274, pp. 389–403. Springer, Heidelberg (2013)
21. Suriadi, S., Ouyang, C., van der Aalst, W.M.P., ter Hofstede, A.H.M.: Root cause analysis with enriched process logs. In: La Rosa, M., Soffer, P. (eds.) BPM Workshops 2012. LNBIP, vol. 132, pp. 174–186. Springer, Heidelberg (2013)
22. Suriadi, S., Wynn, M.T., Ouyang, C., ter Hofstede, A.H.M., van Dijk, N.J.: Understanding process behaviours in a large insurance company in australia: a case study. In: Salinesi, C., Norrie, M.C., Pastor, Ó. (eds.) CAiSE 2013. LNCS, vol. 7908, pp. 449–464. Springer, Heidelberg (2013)
23. Suykens, J.A., Vandewalle, J.: Least squares support vector machine classifiers. Neural Processing Letters **9**(3), 293–300 (1999)
24. Xing, Z., Pei, J., Keogh, E.J.: A brief survey on sequence classification. SIGKDD Explorations **12**(1), 40–48 (2010)

Emerging and Practical Areas of BPM

Business Process Management Skills and Roles: An Investigation of the Demand and Supply Side of BPM Professionals

Patrick Lohmann[✉] and Michael Zur Muehlen

School of Business, Stevens Institute of Technology,
Castle Point on Hudson, Hoboken, NJ 07030, USA
{patrick.lohmann,michael.zurmuehlen}@stevens.edu

Abstract. Business Process Management (BPM) as a discipline covers a wide spectrum of tasks, from the definition of strategic process objectives to the technical implementation of process execution infrastructure. This paper compares and contrasts the process roles demanded by industry with the backgrounds of BPM professionals. We perform a content analysis of advertised job positions in order to compare the skill sets demanded by industry with those found in an extensive study of BPM practitioner profiles. Our findings suggest several discrete roles: Chief Process Officer, Process Owner, Process Architect, Process Consultant, and Process Analyst. We find that while consultants and analysts are the most sought-after positions, they also represent the largest pool of available BPM professionals on the market. Roles that indicate a higher level of maturity such as Process Architects are solicited much less frequently, but are used by job seekers as advertising labels. We find Chief Process Officers to be a desirable role from an organizational maturity perspective, but also the rarest and highest qualified role on the supply side. Our findings provide initial insight for BPM education programs and potential BPM career trajectories.

Keywords: BPM capability · BPM education · BPM maturity · BPM role modeling

1 Introduction

Business processes integrate and coordinate organizational workflows in order to create and deliver customer value [2]. Business Process Management (BPM) is a dynamic capability that comprises the skills and knowledge necessary to govern and change business processes [14]. BPM has become a distinguishing feature of companies that succeed in competitive industries. Zara's ability to quickly refresh its clothing collections [5], Disney's competency to derive multiple revenue streams from its movies [16], or Uber's global expansion of ride-sharing services [8] are just some examples of companies that demonstrate maturity regarding their BPM capability. Proponents of BPM maturity models regard higher organizational

© Springer International Publishing Switzerland 2015
H.R. Motahari-Nezhad et al. (Eds.): BPM 2015, LNCS 9253, pp. 317–332, 2015.
DOI: 10.1007/978-3-319-23063-4_22

maturity as a precondition for the effective and repeatable execution of process change projects, the systematic gathering of actionable process performance metrics, and a better alignment between organizational workflows and their supporting execution infrastructure [4,18].

BPM maturity models receive widespread attention as an assessment tool to evaluate the level of sophistication of BPM activities and to decide on further action for underdeveloped activities [17]. The BPM Capability Framework (see Fig. 1) is a maturity model comprised of 30 capabilities necessary to govern and change business processes [18]. Unlike other BPM maturity models that either focus on the discovery of opportunities for the improvement of processes such as the Process and Enterprise Maturity Model [4], or that describe prescriptive guidelines for the management of particular processes such as the Business Process Maturity Model [21], the BPM Capability Framework is a maturity model designed to establish BPM as a structured practice for the process-oriented management of companies [18]. Although it is recognized as rigorously researched and practically relevant, the framework provides little practicable advice on when and where to develop the suggested capabilities [17].

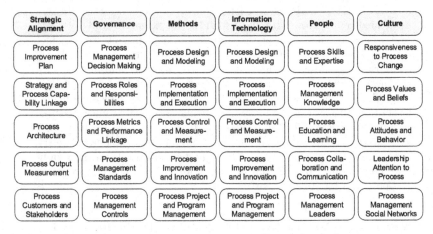

Strategic Alignment	Governance	Methods	Information Technology	People	Culture
Process Improvement Plan	Process Management Decision Making	Process Design and Modeling	Process Design and Modeling	Process Skills and Expertise	Responsiveness to Process Change
Strategy and Process Capability Linkage	Process Roles and Responsibilities	Process Implementation and Execution	Process Implementation and Execution	Process Management Knowledge	Process Values and Beliefs
Process Architecture	Process Metrics and Performance Linkage	Process Control and Measurement	Process Control and Measurement	Process Education and Learning	Process Attitudes and Behavior
Process Output Measurement	Process Management Standards	Process Improvement and Innovation	Process Improvement and Innovation	Process Collaboration and Communication	Leadership Attention to Process
Process Customers and Stakeholders	Process Management Controls	Process Project and Program Management	Process Project and Program Management	Process Management Leaders	Process Management Social Networks

Fig. 1. The BPM Capability Framework [18]

Starting from a strategic decision to pursue BPM, a company typically develops BPM capabilities through a mix of learning experience and investments in people and technology. BPM investments typically involve the deployment of dedicated personnel responsible for carrying out BPM activities, organized in a special function such as a Center of Excellence, which should ensure a focal point for the accumulation of BPM knowledge [2,22] although it must be mentioned that not all companies succeed in this type of setup. It may also involve the hire of skilled BPM professionals from the labor market to acquire or enhance capabilities and to further train existing personnel [22]. The aim of this paper is to investigate the types of BPM professionals demanded by process functions and to compare them with the market of process professionals. The questions that motivated this study are: *(RQ.1) What skills do companies seek in BPM professionals? (RQ.2) Are there distinct roles of BPM professionals, as evidenced by sought-after skill bundles? (RQ.3) To what extent do BPM professionals on the market match these roles?*

Several studies suggest positions and associated responsibilities required by mature process functions. Melenowsky and Hill [10] (Gartner Research) provide a list of responsibilities of the Process Director, Process Architect, Process Consultant, and Process Analyst. Antonnucci and Goeke [1] validate these roles by surveying 111 BPM practitioners associated with the Association of Business Process Management Professionals. Olding and Searle [13] (Gartner Research) extend Melenowsky and Hill's findings with the Process Champion, Executive Sponsor, Process Owner, and Process Project Manager. While these studies provide a comprehensive survey of process roles found in industry, what they not address is how these individual roles contribute to BPM maturity. We believe this missing link between people-based skills and organizational BPM capability is one reason why companies show different returns on BPM investment during their journey to becoming truly process-oriented [12], being confronted with unnecessary uncertainty regarding where to develop BPM capabilities. A critical decision to be made addresses the question of when to deploy new process positions and when to further train existing BPM personnel in their roles what (new) skills in order to progress in BPM maturity.

Given the dominance of prior studies surveying BPM practitioners, this paper supplements the existing BPM governance body of knowledge and investigates the question of roles and skills using descriptive data. We performed a content analysis of BPM positions advertised by companies on a major national employment website *(Monster.com)*. We also conducted a survey of key process roles identified in these job advertisements using public résumés posted by BPM professionals on the largest business-oriented social network *(LinkedIn.com)* to get a better understanding of the demographics of BPM professionals assuming certain process positions in industry. The remainder is structured as follows. In the next section we describe the research methods used for data collection and analysis. We then summarize our analysis of advertised BPM positions in section 3 and suggest a classification of process roles and their contribution of BPM capabilities, as derived from the job advertisements. In section 4 we present the demographic characteristics of BPM professionals, as derived from their publicly available résumés. We discuss our findings in section 5 and conclude with study limitations and suggestions for future research.

2   Data Collection and Analysis

We employed Content Analysis as the research method. Content Analysis is often used to identify the skills companies seek in Information Systems professionals [3,11]. It is a technique that allows for making rigorous and replicable inferences from (textual) data based on a specified coding scheme that reflects the research context. Content Analysis can be characterized as a soft positivism scientific approach [6,9], meaning it is designed to interpretively reveal preexisting variables in the data. The coding scheme may be derived from existing theory, expert experience, or prior research [7]. The coding variables must be mutually exclusive and provide an exhaustive account of the research context. This means, the coding scheme must be unambiguous and cover all relevant aspects of BPM [7].

2.1 Sampling of Advertised BPM Positions

We collected job advertisements from Monster.com that were published between October 29, 2013 and December 6, 2013. Monster.com is generally recognized among the largest and most often cited employment websites [15]. In order to avoid restricting the search to specific job titles, we searched for the following keywords: *Business Process Management, Process Management*, and *BPM*. The search resulted in a total of 900 job advertisements. We rejected 447 duplicates and those that were not BPM-related such as positions of the Industrial Engineer or Manufacturing Analyst. In order to analyze the remaining 161 job advertisements, we adopted the BPM Capability Framework as the coding scheme for two reasons. Firstly, the suggested capabilities satisfy the requirements of being mutually exclusive and exhaustive. The framework was developed through a series of Delphi studies with internationally renowned BPM experts from academia and industry with the goal to develop a holistic view of BPM, covering such critical success factors as Strategic Alignment, Governance, Methods, Information Technology (IT), People, and Culture [18]. Secondly, the capabilities allow to generalize from the job advertisements without loosing too much details about the skills, qualifications, knowledge requirements, or responsibilities required of the BPM position advertised. We iteratively coded each advertisement and assigned a coding variable when we identified a match of a word, phrase, or sentence with a capability. We normalized the frequency of each variable in an advertisement, treating the occurrence of a variable as a binary decision [7].

2.2 Sampling of Profiles of BPM Professionals

We collected résumés of BPM professionals from LinkedIn.com between February 3, 2015 and February 26, 2015. While LinkedIn allowed us to identify individuals who self-declare their relationship to a process position, the proprietary Dun & Bradstreet database (*Data.com*) allowed us to cross-reference certain individuals to determine their official job title. In order to establish the baseline population, we searched both databases for the process roles identified in the BPM job advertisements: *Chief Process Officer, Process Owner, Process Architect, Process Consultant, Process Analyst*, both with and without the prefix *Business*. We also searched for related job families in order to establish the relative frequency of process-related jobs. These job families included the *(General) Manager, Process Manager, Enterprise Architect, Business Architect, Business Consultant*, and *Business Analyst*. Having established the relative frequency of each position, we randomly collected 225 résumés of individuals with the roles of the Chief Process Officer (25), Process Owner (50), Process Architect (50), Process Consultant (50), and Process Analyst (50). For each résumé we coded the industry sector and country of the employer, the prior work experience until the individual attained the process position, the experience in the process position, the educational background, and prior and subsequent job titles (in cases where the position was no longer the current position), as well as whether the individual had switched companies to attain the position. We excluded résumés with incomplete work histories, education profiles, or mismatched job titles. For Process Owners, however, we also included individuals whose title was different from *Process Owner*, but who stated in their résumés the ownership of a specific business process.

3 Process Roles and Skills Demanded by Industry

The skills advertised in the BPM positions are heat-mapped in Fig. 2. Process improvement and innovation is a major area of concern for companies, followed by process design and modeling skills. In theory, process improvement and innovation are two distinct skills. The purpose of process improvement is to modify and existing process. It refers to the ability to continuously adjust day-to-day business operations. Process innovation regards to the ability of either replacing an existing process with a redesigned, new one or deploying a new process in a previously underdeveloped area. 124 job advertisements seek process improvement skills, while just 16 expect process innovation experience. 90 advertisements seek (Lean) Six Sigma experience for process improvement.

The skill sets companies expect in the BPM positions suggest several discrete process roles (see Table 1). Most job advertisements refer to the Process Consultant position (75), followed by Process Analyst (56). Ten advertisements try to fill a position that relates to the Chief Process Officer. Seven job advertisements refer to the Process Architect position and three advertisements seek a Process Owner. We summarize the skills required of these positions in the following, but omit the Process Owner from further analysis because of the too small number of job advertisements.

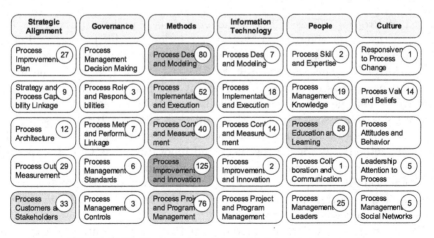

Fig. 2. Skills Described in the BPM Job Advertisements

Table 1. Classification of process roles and job titles. We classified an advertised BPM position as *Other* when it addressed some BPM capabilities, but the described skill set had too little in common with those of the remaining process roles.

Process Role	Job Titles (Number of Occurrences)	Total
Chief Process Officer	Business Process Director, Director Continuous Improvement, Director of Process Improvement, Director of Programs, Director of Process Management, Global Process Excellence Manager, Senior Manager IT Strategy and Planning, Vice President Operations, Manager Quality Improvement, Vice President Quality Management and Improvement	10
Process Owner	Business Process and Quality Manager, Supply Chain Manager, Senior IAM Process Manager	3
Process Architect	Business Process Architect, Business Architect, Business Architect Lead, IT Architect, Manager Enterprise IT Business Alignment (3)	7
Process Consultant	Improvement Manager (11), BPM Project Manager (8), Senior Business Analyst (7), Lean-Six Sigma Black Belt (5), Business Process Consultant (4), IT Consultant (3), Process Improvement Manager (3), BPM Program Manager (3), Improvement Lead (2), Senior Business Systems Analyst (2), Senior Healthcare Consultant (2), Senior Quality Engineer (2), Manufacturing Engineering Manager (2), Business Process Reengineering Expert, Business Advisor, Business Analysis Manager, Improvement Consultant, Improvement Specialist, IT Lean Manager, Logistics Specialist, Management Systems Facilitator, Manager of Quality, Operational Excellence Consultant, Operational Excellence Manager, Organizational Improvement Consultant, Process Engineering Manager, Process Expert, Process Improvement Specialist, Senior IT Consultant, Senior Manager Business Process Control, Senior Quality Analyst, Senior Process Engineer, Senior Supply Chain Analyst, Six Sigma Site Leader	75
Process Analyst	Business Analyst (16), Quality Engineer (8), Improvement Engineer (6), Process Analyst (6), IT Analyst (4), Business Process Analyst (3), Process Engineer (3), Functional Analyst (2), Improvement Analyst (2), IT Business Analyst (2), Business Systems Analyst, Solutions Analyst, Solutions Engineer, Systems Analyst	56
Other	Production Unit Manager, Manager Business Sales, Pharmacy Director, Application Administrator, Business Model Professional, IT Global Lead, Sourcing Manager, IT Risk Management Consultant, Business Intelligence Administrator, Software Engineer	10

3.1   The Chief Process Officer

The Chief Process Officer (CPO) is advertised as a position that drives the BPM practice in the company. A typical description found expects the CPO to *"define quality requirements with business executives to align strategy, resources, goals, priorities, and overall improvement."* The CPO is accountable for ensuring a continuous process of process improvement and innovation. As head of the process function, the advertisements describe the CPO as a positions that models process roles and associated activities, and that allocates BPM personnel to process change projects. The advertisements also require the CPO to identify the right methodology for improvement and innovation. The CPO is expected to keep abreast with current Industry standards and technology trends. Given prior practical BPM experience, the CPO may be responsible for developing and conducting workshops that enhance organization-wide process-awareness, as several job advertisements recognize.

Fig. 3 illustrates the skills required of the CPO. As an executive position, the advertisements see the CPO as a position that builds coalitions and consensus

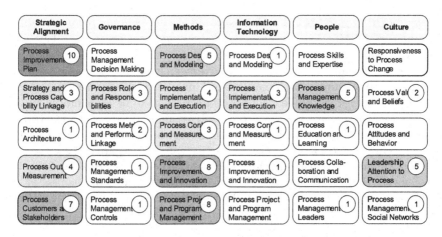

Strategic Alignment	Governance	Methods	Information Technology	People	Culture
Process Improvement Plan `10`	Process Management Decision Making	Process Des and Modeling `5`	Process Des and Modeling `1`	Process Skills and Expertise	Responsiveness to Process Change
Strategy and Process Capability Linkage `3`	Process Role and Responsibilities `3`	Process Implementation and Execution `4`	Process Implementation and Execution `3`	Process Management Knowledge `5`	Process Val and Beliefs `2`
Process Architecture `1`	Process Metr and Performa Linkage `2`	Process Con and Measurement `3`	Process Con and Measurement `1`	Process Education and Learning `1`	Process Attitudes and Behavior
Process Out Measurement `4`	Process Management Standards `1`	Process Improvement and Innovation `8`	Process Improvement and Innovation `1`	Process Collaboration and Communication `1`	Leadership Attention to Process `5`
Process Customers a Stakeholders `7`	Process Management Controls `1`	Process Proj and Program Management `8`	Process Project and Program Management	Process Management Leaders `1`	Process Management Social Networks `1`

Fig. 3. Skills Required of the Chief Process Officer

for business improvement and innovation among business executives, promoting a customer- and stakeholder-orientation in process change projects. The CPO contributes to the long-term strategy planning, evaluating business process capabilities against the achievement of strategic goals. The advertisements mention decision-making authority for setting and executing the process improvement plan. Several job advertisements also require the CPO to possess *"strong project management skills, with experience in organizing, planning, and executing large-scale projects from vision through implementation, involving internal personnel, contractors, and vendors."* The CPO is expected to work with technology companies in order to *"identify and drive technology-based process improvement opportunities."*

3.2 The Process Architect

The Process Architect is advertised as a position that is responsible for maintaining the link between strategy and process capabilities. A typical advertisement expects the Process Architect to *"develop roadmaps for business and supporting applications [...] that align the business and IT to resolve any risks, gaps, dependencies, and drive strategic investment recommendations."* The job titles suggest that the Process Architect is typically a Business Architect or (sometimes) an IT Architect. Having oversight over the enterprise architecture from either a process or technology angle, the Process Architect is expected to manage synergies across process improvement and innovation alternatives, ensuring that different process change projects are executed in concert. Some job advertisements assign responsibility for organizing the process improvement plan to the Process Architect.

Fig. 4 illustrates the skills required of the Process Architect. Expected to be an experienced Process Analyst, the Process Architect is described as a role that brings business- or technology-architectural oversight for process modeling and documentation into the lines of business. For example, a typical advertisement describes the Process Architect as a position that *"drive[s] [the] organizational adoption of BPM concepts and technology, and work[s] with the BPM practition-ers to mature BPM delivery methodology and adapt best practices."* This may comprise the set-up of regular process design and modeling reviews into the business units, as demanded by several job advertisements. The Process Architect recommends opportunities for improved and innovative process design based on the process architecture, while the IT Architect seems to be accountable for the actual delivery of process change projects. If business rules are modeled, their maintenance and implementation may also be part of the accountabilities of the Process Architect and IT Architect, respectively. In this regard, we see the first signs of an emerging Decision Architect role that consolidates Business Decision Management (BDM) [20] activities and that advises the lines of business in the creation and maintenance of integrated decision models to *"ensure [the] optimal standardization and re-use of decisions across [processes]".*

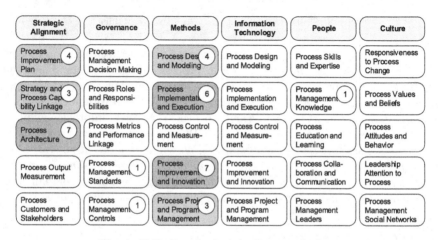

Strategic Alignment	Governance	Methods	Information Technology	People	Culture
Process Improvement Plan ④	Process Management Decision Making	Process Des ④ and Modeling	Process Design and Modeling	Process Skills and Expertise	Responsiveness to Process Change
Strategy and Process Capability Linkage ③	Process Roles and Responsibilities	Process Implementation and Execution ⑥	Process Implementation and Execution	Process Management Knowledge ①	Process Values and Beliefs
Process Architecture ⑦	Process Metrics and Performance Linkage	Process Control and Measurement	Process Control and Measurement	Process Education and Learning	Process Attitudes and Behavior
Process Output Measurement	Process Management Standards ①	Process Improvement and Innovation ⑦	Process Improvement and Innovation	Process Collaboration and Communication	Leadership Attention to Process
Process Customers and Stakeholders	Process Management Controls ①	Process Proj and Program Management ③	Process Project and Program Management	Process Management Leaders	Process Management Social Networks

Fig. 4. Skills Required of the Process Architect

3.3   The Process Consultant

The Process Consultant is described as a position that *"assist[s] process owners and improvement teams in the definition, documentation, measurement, analysis, improvement and control of business processes."* The Process Consultant delivers process education and learning, promoting process values and beliefs among business managers. As an advisor to the Process Owner, the Process Consultant is a position that evaluates needs for improvement and supports the Process Owner in the creation of business cases for process change.

Fig. 5 illustrates the skills required of the Process Consultant. The Process Consultant is either as a Business or IT Consultant. Those that seek a business-oriented Process Consultant can be further grouped according to their view on improvement. Having an outside look on such external value drivers as quality [2], the Process Consultant is expected to develop key performance indicators that measure customer satisfaction and to recommend process change opportunities

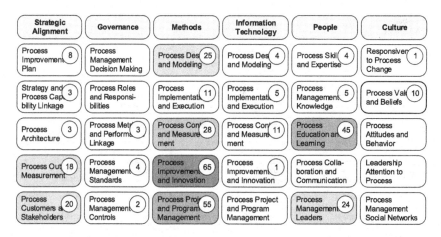

Strategic Alignment	Governance	Methods	Information Technology	People	Culture
Process Improvement Plan (8)	Process Management Decision Making	Process Design and Modeling (25)	Process Design and Modeling (4)	Process Skill and Expertise (4)	Responsiveness to Process Change (1)
Strategy and Process Capability Linkage (3)	Process Roles and Responsibilities	Process Implementation and Execution (11)	Process Implementation and Execution (5)	Process Management Knowledge (5)	Process Values and Beliefs (10)
Process Architecture (3)	Process Metrics and Performance Linkage (3)	Process Control and Measurement (28)	Process Control and Measurement (11)	Process Education and Learning (45)	Process Attitudes and Behavior
Process Output Measurement (18)	Process Management Standards (4)	Process Improvement and Innovation (65)	Process Improvement and Innovation (1)	Process Collaboration and Communication	Leadership Attention to Process
Process Customers and Stakeholders (20)	Process Management Controls (2)	Process Project and Program Management (55)	Process Project and Program Management	Process Management Leaders (24)	Process Management Social Networks

Fig. 5. Skills Required of the Process Consultant

that contribute to improved customer experience. In contrast, the advertisements that emphasize such internal value drivers as operational efficiency [2] expect the Process Consultant to apply more methodology-driven approaches for improvement, focusing on (statistical) data-driven process control and measurement to reduce variations in business operations. In this regard, the Process Consultant is seen as a position that *"facilitate[s] and collaborate[s] with cross-functional teams to create and evaluate recommendations to improved process design."* Example job titles for this type of Process Consultant focusing on executing the process improvement plan are *Lean Six Sigma Black Belt, Improvement Manager*, or *BPM Project Manager*.

The job advertisements seeking technology-oriented Process Consultants describe a position that is responsible for the technical implementation of process change projects. In this regard, the Process Consultant is expected to *"facilitate the design of integrated software solutions [...] and drive the definition, testing, training, and implementation of functional requirements."* This involves the definition of technology assets and resources necessary for process execution, but also the recommendation of process changes by applying Lean practices to the technology landscape, as several job advertisements describe. Some advertisements also mention involvement in the development and implementation of process control and measurement efforts, bringing into the team knowledge about the technical infrastructure enacting business processes.

3.4   The Process Analyst

The Process Analyst is typically a Business Analyst or (sometimes) an IT Analyst, as the job titles suggest. Fig. 6 illustrates the skills required of the Process Analyst. Liaising with the lines of business, a typical advertisement expects the Process Analyst to *"analyze business and user needs, and document specifications to meet those needs, [and] conduct user testing or processes to understand data input to a process step, the process decisions, and the data output to a*

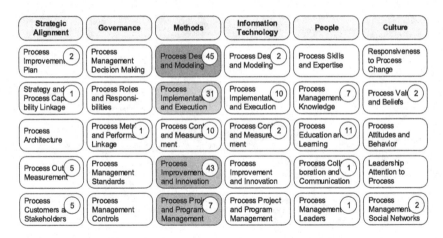

Fig. 6. Skills Required of the Process Analyst

process step." Modeling major process decisions to be made for process compli-cation, we see first signs of an emerging Decision Analyst role that *"analyze[s], determine[s], implement[s] and test[s] decision models to meet business require-ments"*, and that *"actively seek[s] out ways to improve processes, reduce risk, increase productivity, and lower costs"* through the automation of operational decisions utilizing BDM concepts.

Some job advertisements see the Process Analyst as an assistant to the Pro-cess Consultant, being involved in process data-driven process improvement projects. In this regard, the Process Analyst is seen as a position responsible for the development and implementation of process control and measurement within a business unit. A job title found for this type of Process Analyst is *Quality Engineer.* While the business-oriented Process Analyst is seen as a posi-tion that creates process (and/or decision) specifications, the job advertisements describe the technology-oriented Process Analyst as a position that analyzes the underlying process execution (and/or decision services) infrastructure as part of the technical implementation of process change projects. We find that when companies demand modeling skills they are much more likely to advertise for Process Analysts than Process Modelers. The Process Analyst is also expected to ensure process standardization, including the training of business units in changed process designs and process-related software.

4   Profiles of BPM Professionals on the Market

Given the process roles identified from the advertised BPM positions, we find Process Analysts ($\sim$ 61K) to be the largest group among BPM professionals on LinkedIn, followed by Process Consultants ($\sim$ 27,8K). Compared to the total population of Business Analysts ($\sim$ 1M) and Business Consultants ($\sim$ 295K), they only make a diminishing small subset of these more general roles. Process Architects are less frequent ($\sim$ 4,8K), but represent about 12% of the total popu-lation of Enterprise Architects and 36% of Business Architects. Process Owners

Table 2. Frequency of Process Roles in Résumés

Process Role	Population		Sample Work	Sample Role
	Global	United States	Exp. [Years]	Exp. [Months]
Chief Process Officer	241	91	21.2	33.7
Process Owner	12,501	3,924	19.5	39.2
Process Architect	4,776	2,155	19.4	47.8
Process Consultant	27,779	10,809	14.5	47.3
Process Analyst	60,972	24,877	14.4	46.7
Reference Role	**Population**			
	Global	United States		
Manager	39,627,963	16,499,740		
Process Manager	69,676	24,887		
Enterprise Architect	38,792	18,966		
Business Architect	13,293	4,758		
Business Consultant	295,381	102,235		
Business Analyst	1,019,176	437,842		

($\sim$ 12,5K) represent about 18% of the total population of Process Managers. Detailed results, including the average prior work as well as role experience of our sample population, are shown in Table 2.

4.1 The Chief Process Officer

The CPO has an average work experience of 21 years before being promoted and holds this position for about 34 months. The position is filled by an internal candidate in 75% of the companies, predominantly by an individual from Operations or IT. If the CPO has a background in the IT function, the position is most often assumed by an executive with IT leadership authority such as *Chief Information Officer (CIO)*. In contrast, if the CPO has a career in Operations, the role holder seems to be also *Chief Operations Officer (COO)*. The educational background found most often is Finance and Economics. While some hold a PhD or advanced degree such as MBA or MS, most are BS graduates. The CPO is the rarest role on LinkedIn. Many of the role holders can also be found in Dun & Bradstreet's executive directory, which suggests that CPO is a bona-fide executive position and companies may see this position as a stepping stone for other C-level careers. We find that when CPO was a former position of an individual, the subsequent position is most often that of a Chief Executive Officer or COO. Surprisingly, none of the role holders have a held such previous positions in the process function as Process Architect or Process Analyst. This raises the question whether process-oriented leadership and general management skills are more important than actual BPM experience.

4.2 The Process Owner

The Process Owner has an average work experience of 19 years and holds this position for about 39 months. The position is generally filled internally by a senior executive from the line of business. It is therefore not surprising that we collected only three job advertisements for this position. The Process Owner mostly holds an MBA or MS in a business-related field. While the CPO seems to be either a full-time position or a part-time role of the CIO or COO, the Process Owner is a senior-level, part-time role with job titles such as *Senior VP & Business Process Owner Procurement* or *Senior VP & Business Process Owner Demand to Supply*. Most Process Owners are assigned to classical Enterprise Resource Planning (ERP)-type business processes such as Order-to-Cash, Purchase-to-Pay, Procurement-to-Pay, or Plan-to-Inventory. We also see Process Owners responsible for such processes as Supply Chain or Accounts Payable. Industries that promote this position seem to be ERP-heavy sectors such as Chemicals, Electronics, as well as Healthcare, but we also find Pharmaceuticals nominating Process Owners for heavily regulated research and approval processes such as Regulatory Compliance Tracking or (Pre-)Clinical Trials.

4.3 The Process Architect

The Process Architect has an average work experience of 19 years and holds this position for about 48 months. The Process Architect generally has a background outside of the line of business, typically in consulting, project management, and (sometimes) business analysis. The Process Architect had to switch companies in 80% of the cases in order to attain this position. The educational background is very diverse, from Management via Information Systems, Industrial and Systems Engineering to Computer Science. Some Process Architects are certified as Project Management Professionals, ITIL, or (Lean) Sig Sigma Black Belt. Many individuals declaring themselves as Process Architects seem to be architects for specific process-aware information systems, being employed by technology vendors such as SAP, IBM, or PegaSystems. In this regard, we find job titles such as *IBM Architect* or *SAP Business Process Architect*. Further, we see some evidence that job seekers use the role title as a marketing label to advertise their BPM skills. The title also seems to be used by individuals employed by management consulting companies to bolster their BPM credentials, as the job profile described in their résumés tend to reflect more the skill set required of a Process Consultant or Process Analyst.

4.4 The Process Consultant

The Process Consultant has an average work experience of 14 years and holds this position for about 47 months. The position tends to be filled externally by a candidate with a background in Sales or Business Development and who has held a mid-level management position. We also see individuals being internally promoted, holding job titles such as *Process Improvement Consultant* or *Process Consultant Lean Six Sigma*. In this regard, the Process Consultant has a background in project management or industrial engineering, being certified as Project Management Professionals or (Lean) Six Sigma Green or Black Belt. Only a small number of Process Consultants actually have a prior career in business analysis or an outside management consulting company. The industries appointing Process Consultants relate to a variety of sectors such as Chemicals, Finance, Healthcare, Insurance, or Telecommunications.

4.5   The Process Analyst

The Process Analyst has an average work experience of 14 years and holds this position for about 47 months. The positions is generally held by prior Business Analysts that have evolved into a more process-oriented role. In order to attain this positions, individuals had to switch companies in 65% of the sample. 50% of the Process Analysts hold an advanced degree such as MBA and MS, while the remainder as BS graduates. The educational background is typically Information Systems, Computer Science, or Business Accounting. A variety of industries employ Process Analysts such as Consumer Goods, Food, Energy, Healthcare, or Pharmaceuticals. However, 14 years of prior work experience means that the Process Analyst is not an entry-level position, but requires work experience and business domain knowledge.

5   Discussion and Conclusion

The purpose of this paper is to investigate the types of BPM practitioners demanded by companies and to compare these with the market situation of available process professionals, answering the three questions questions *(RQ.1– RQ.3)*. Firstly, we sought to identify the skills companies seek in BPM professionals by analyzing advertised BPM positions. Secondly, we classified these positions into distinct process roles based on similar skill sets and revealed that different roles address different subsets of BPM capabilities. Thirdly, we investigated the demographics of BPM professionals to better understand the characteristics of key process positions in industry. While we generally find a match between the demand and supply side of BPM professionals, we see a mismatch with the Process Architect. This means, we see a lot of Process Architects on the market, but just a few positions openly advertised. This raises the question whether companies have not reached a level of BPM maturity that necessitates the skills and knowledge of this role or whether they rely on external consulting contracts to acquire the architecture skills on an ad-hoc basis.

5.1   Insights for Practice

While actively managing roles and skills is a complicated challenge for the CPO to mature BPM that goes beyond the scope of this paper [14], it seems that companies are confronted with a chicken-and-egg dilemma of BPM maturity. This means, it is unclear whether BPM maturity is a pre-requisite for the existence of certain process roles, or whether it is more the effect of their organizational existence. Our analysis of advertised BPM positions suggests the latter causality, meaning that the appointment of skilled people attaining certain process roles may lead to progress in BPM maturity. While this would imply BPM maturity to be a function of the strategic commitment to (dis-)invest in human capital more than process-aware information systems (PAIS) [19], we see some evidence for this proposition in industry, where a change in a Chief Executive Officer position is associated with the shutdown of the company's BPM Center of Excellence.

To maintain BPM maturity generally warrants both industry-specific business knowledge and technology expertise in order to effectively decide on what BPM projects to execute as well as appropriate methodology for their efficient delivery [18]. Our findings suggest that BPM professionals in their roles either address method or (business) process-related skills and knowledge. The profiles of BPM professionals also suggest their roles to be either vendor- (i.e., technology-) or business-driven, which leads to a taxonomy of roles. Fig. 7 illustrates this classification as well as possible career trajectories via demanded skills of advertised BPM positions and existing careers of BPM professionals.

Method-oriented vs. process-oriented roles: *Method-oriented* roles require skills and experience in approaches and techniques that enable the consistent execution of the process management lifecycle across a business process portfolio. Examples of this type of roles are the Process Architect, who harmonizes and standardizes BPM concepts and activities across the company, and the method-oriented Process Consultant who focuses on the exploitation of processes through the use of process-data driven improvement techniques such as Six Sigma or Lean Management to increase operational efficiency. *Process-oriented* roles require analytical skills and business or technology expertise in order to translate or implement business or regulatory requirements into process capabilities. Examples of this type of roles are the CPO who works with business executives on strategic business (process) objectives, the Process Consultant who advises Process Owners on tactical business process objectives, and the Process Analyst who liaises with the business units on operational issues that involve process change.

Technology-driven vs. business-driven roles: Process roles may be defined by best practice recommendations of technology vendors and specializations of BPM professionals, being certified experts in PAIS such as IBM, SAP, or PeopleSoft. Examples of this type of *technology-driven* roles are IBM Architect or SAP Business Process Consultant, but also Process Owners appointed to control classical ERP-type business processes such as Purchase-to-Pay or Order-to-Cash that can be characterized by low innovativeness. In contrast, *business-driven* roles are appointed for business processes that are less generic, but allow

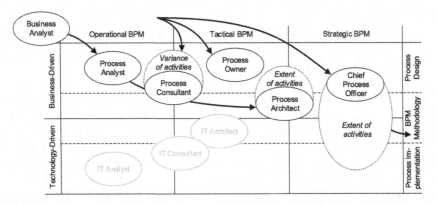

Fig. 7. A Classification of Process Roles and Possible Career Trajectories

a company to distinguish itself from its competitors or to maintain regulatory compliance. Examples for this type of roles are Process and Decision Analysts, Process Consultants, or Process Owners appointed to control and proactively change highly regulated or idiosyncratic processes such as Clinical Trials, (Trade) Clearing & Settlement, or Client On-boarding, but also Supply Chain that shape competitive advantage.

We see some evidence that clearly defined career paths of BPM professionals are not yet widespread, as 65% of Process Analysts and 80% of Process Architects had to switch companies in order to attain these positions. Moreover, some roles tend to be hired with internal candidates such as Process Owner or CPO, while others such as Process Architect or Process Consultant are more often hired from the outside. Although we see mixed results with regard to the hiring of Process Analysts, this position is not an entry-level position for university graduates but a specialization of the Business Analyst. We believe Process Analysts would make good Process Architects given their skills gained as an analyst, but would require further education in BPM methodology and fundamentals of PAIS. Those Process Analysts that assist methodology-oriented Process Consultants require further education and certification in Six Sigma or Lean Management to assume this position. There exists a different career trajectory for the CPO, where leadership and general managerial skills seem to outweigh specific BPM expertise. However, the range of skills and expertise required of the this position are more diverse than this paper implies, ranging from the strategic supply chain design to the technical management of process implementations. Indeed, we expect to see different types of CPOs in industry.

5.2 Limitations and Future Research

To our knowledge, this is the first paper to use descriptive data to clarify the relationship between organizational BPM capabilities and individual-level skills and roles. The process roles found in practice generally match those discussed in the academic literature and our research approach that aims towards generalizability invites the academic and practitioner BPM community to further verify or falsify our interpretations of the contribution of people-based roles to BPM maturity. It must be mentioned that both the advertised BPM positions as well as BPM practitioner profiles reside largely in the United States, even though they represent less than half of the population for the identified process roles on LinkedIn. We believe a global study would be very valuable, but possess certain logistical challenges. In order to obtain a representative global sample, we would have to take into account different country terminologies as well as localized language settings for international LinkedIn sites and other professional network sites (e.g., Xing.com). While our study focuses on the U.S. population, we believe it represents a fair sample of BPM professionals in English-speaking countries, and our analysis of CPOs has a broad global footprint. We believe that specifically the chicken-and-egg causality dilemma of BPM maturity as well as the Process Architect and Chief Process Officer roles warrant further academic investigation, as their skill sets and career trajectories differ from the other roles analyzed.

References

1. Antonucci, Y.L., Goeke, R.J.: Identification of appropriate responsibilities and positions for business process management success: Seeking a valid and reliable framework. Business Process Management Journal **17**(1), 127–146 (2011)
2. Franz, P., Kirchmer, M.: Value-Driven Business Process Management: The Value-Switch for Lasting Competitive Advantage. McGraw-Hill (2013)
3. Gallivan, M.J., Truex, D.P., Kvasny, L.: Changing patters in it skill sets 1988–2003: A content analysis of classified advertising. The Data Base for Advances in Information Systems **35**(3), 64–87 (2004)
4. Hammer, M.: The process audit. Harvard Business Review **85**(4), 111–123 (2007)
5. Hansen, S.: How zara grew into the world's largest fashion retailer (2012). http://www.nytimes.com/2012/11/11/magazine/how-zara-grew-into-the-worlds-largest-fashion-retailer.html
6. Kirsch, L.J.: Deploying common systems globally: The dynamics of control. Information Systems Research **15**(4), 374–395 (2004)
7. Krippendorff, K.: Content Analysis, 3rd. edn. SAGE Publications (2013)
8. MacMillan, D., Schechner, S., Fleisher, L.: Investors push uber's valuation past $40 billion (2014)
9. Madill, A., Jordan, A., Shirley, C.: Objectivity and reliability in qualitative analysis: Realist, contextualist and radical constructionist epistemologies. British Journal of Psychology **91**(1), 1–20 (2000)
10. Melenowsky, M.: Role definition and organizational structure: Business process improvement. Tech. Rep. G00141487, Gartner Research (2006)
11. Müller, O., Schmiedel, T., Gorbacheva, E., vom Brocke, J.: Towards a typology of business process management professionals: Identifying patterns of competencies through latent semantic analysis. Enterprise Information Systems (2014)
12. Neubauer, T.: An empirical study about the status of business process management. Business Process Management Journal **15**(2), 166–183 (2009)
13. Olding, E., Searle, S.: Role definition and organizational structure: Business process improvement. Tech. Rep. G00219408, Gartner Research (2011)
14. Pöppelbuss, J., Plattfaut, R., Niehaves, B.: How do we progress? an exploration of alternate explanations for bpm capability development. Communications of the Association for Information Systems **36**(1), 1–22 (2015)
15. Prabhakar, B., Litecky, C.R., Arnett, K.P.: It skills in a tough job market. Communications of the ACM **48**(10), 91–94 (2007)
16. Roger, C.: Big hero 6 proves it: Pixar's gurus have brought the magic back to disney animation (2014). http://www.wired.com/2014/10/big-hero-6/
17. Röglinger, M., Pöppelbuss, J., Becker, J.: Maturity models in business process management. Business Process Management Journal **18**(2), 328–346 (2012)
18. Rosemann, M., de Bruin, T., Power, B.: Business Process Management: Practical Guidelines to Successful Implementations, chap. BPM Maturity. Elsevier (2006)
19. Simpson, D.: Making capabilities strategic. McKinsey Quarterly **3**, 59–63 (2014)
20. Taylor, J., Raden, N.: Smart Enough Systems: How to Deliver Competitive Advantage by Automating Hidden Decisions. Prentice Hall (2007)
21. Weber, C.V., Curtis, B., Gardiner, T.: Business process maturity model. Tech. Rep. Version 1, Object Management Group (2008). http://www.omg.org/spec/BPMM/1.0/
22. Zollo, M., Winter, S.G.: Deliberate learning and the evolution of dynamic capabilities. Organization Science **13**(3), 339–351 (2002)

BPMN Task Instance Streaming for Efficient Micro-task Crowdsourcing Processes

Stefano Tranquillini[1]([⊠]), Florian Daniel[1,2], Pavel Kucherbaev[1], and Fabio Casati[1]

[1] University of Trento – DISI, Via Sommarive 9, I-38123 Povo, (TN), Italy
{tranquillini,daniel,kucherbaev,casati}@disi.unitn.it
[2] Tomsk Polytechnic University, Belinskya Street 30, 634050 Tomsk, Russia

Abstract. The Business Process Model and Notation (BPMN) is a standard for modeling and executing business processes with human or machine tasks. The semantics of tasks is usually discrete: a task has exactly one start event and one end event; for multi-instance tasks, all instances must complete before an end event is emitted. We propose a new task type and streaming connector for crowdsourcing able to run hundreds or thousands of micro-task instances in parallel. The two constructs provide for task streaming semantics that is new to BPMN, enable the modeling and efficient enactment of complex crowdsourcing scenarios, and are applicable also beyond the special case of crowdsourcing. We implement the necessary design and runtime support on top of Crowd-Flower, demonstrate the viability of the approach via a case study, and report on a set of runtime performance experiments.

Keywords: Crowdsourcing processes · Task instance streaming · BPMN

1 Introduction

BPMN [15] is the most representative example of the state of the art in business process modeling. Its core modeling constructs are tasks and control flow connectors. Both constructs follow semantics that stem from their roots in office automation: tasks are *atomic*. They express indivisible pieces of work that have a well-defined start and end, and do not provide insight into what is going on inside a task while in execution. In the basic setting, one task corresponds to one runtime instance of the task. However, the notation also supports *multi-instance tasks* that allow the execution of multiple runtime instances either in parallel or in sequence. State-of-the-art engines commonly implement multi-instance tasks following the same atomic start/end semantics of basic tasks (the end event fires only when all instances have completed), although the BPMN specification [15] also envisions intermediate instance termination events for complex behavior definitions (p. 432).

There are however modeling scenarios that would benefit from more transparency, in order to be executed more efficiently. This is, for instance, the case

© Springer International Publishing Switzerland 2015
H.R. Motahari-Nezhad et al. (Eds.): BPM 2015, LNCS 9253, pp. 333–349, 2015.
DOI: 10.1007/978-3-319-23063-4_23

of processes that run multiple instances of tasks in parallel. An extreme example is *crowdsourcing*, that is, the outsourcing of a unit of work to a crowd of people via an open call for contributions [8]. Thanks to the availability of crowdsourcing platforms, such as Amazon Mechanical Turk (https://www.mturk.com) or CrowdFlower (http://www.crowdflower.com), the practice has experienced a tremendous growth over the last years and demonstrated its viability in different fields, such as data collection and analysis or human computation – all practices that leverage on *micro-tasks*, which are tasks that ask workers to complete simple assignments (e.g., label an image or translate a sentence) in exchange for an optional reward (e.g., few cents or dollars). The power of crowdsourcing is represented by the crowd, which may be huge and span the World, and its ability to process even thousands of task instances in short time in parallel.

However, not all types of work can easily be boiled down to simple micro-tasks, most platforms still require significant amounts of manual work and configuration, and there is only very limited support for structured work, that is, work that requires the integration of different tasks and multiple actors, such as machines, individuals and the crowd. We call these kinds of structured work *crowdsourcing processes*, since they require the coordination of multiple tasks, actors and operations inside an integrated execution logic [17].

Crowdsourcing processes therefore represent a problem where business process management (BPM) is expected to excel. The modeling and efficient enactment of crowdsourcing process is however still not well supported [11]. In particular, BPMN does not provide the right means to model processes that are as simple as, for example, asking the crowd to upload a thousand images in one task and then to label them in another task. The labeling task would start only once all images have been uploaded, not benefiting from the evident parallelization opportunities of the scenario. The tokens of Petri Nets [18] would allow one to deal with this kind of dynamic state, but BPMN does not support tokens.

In [17], we proposed BPMN4Crowd, a BPMN extension for the modeling of crowdsourcing processes that can be executed on our own crowdsourcing platform, the Crowd Computer; the approach uses the standard task termination semantics of BPMN. In this paper, we instead study the problem of micro-task parallelization in generic BPMN engines, making the following contributions:

- An extension of BPMN with a *new task and connector type* that provides full support for the streaming of outputs of completed micro-task instances to subsequent micro-task instances without requiring an overall task end event.
- An implementation of a *runtime environment* for crowdsourcing processes with micro-task instance streaming. The environment is distributed over a BPMN engine for the coordination of work, a state-of-the-art crowdsourcing platform for the micro-tasks, and an intermediate middleware.
- An implementation of a visual *design environment* with support for the extended BPMN modeling notation and the translation of extended models into standard BPMN for the engine and configuration instructions for the crowdsourcing platform and the middleware.

– A demonstration of the viability of the approach via a concrete crowdsourcing *case study* complemented by a *performance analysis* reporting on the execution time improvements that can be achieved.

2   Crowdsourcing Processes

2.1   Scenario: Transcription of Receipts

The reimbursement of a business trip, such as the attendance of a scientific conference, is subject to the documentation of the incurred expenses. This documentation are the receipts that can be scanned and transcribed for the processing of the reimbursement. Transcribing a receipt is a small task that can be crowdsourced at low cost and with fast response times.

Let's imagine we would like to support the following crowdsourcing process: The admin reimbursing the travel expenses initiates the process by feeding it with the receipts (e.g., 40) collected from traveling employees. This causes the process to upload photos/images of the receipts onto an online crowdsourcing platform and to instantiate a transcription request for each individual receipt. Since the work by workers cannot be trusted in general, for each 2 transcriptions the process creates another task for the crowd that asks workers to check the transcriptions and fix them if necessary. Checking and fixing takes less time than transcribing, so each worker can process 2 items. Another task is used to classify the receipts, e.g., into flight tickets, hotel receipts, restaurant receipts, or similar. Classifying is simple, and it is reasonable to ask a worker to classify 4 receipts. The two tasks can be performed in parallel once transcriptions are available. Upon completion, an automatic email notifies the admin about the results.

2.2   Crowdsourcing Processes and Streaming Opportunities

The described scenario presents all the characteristics of a crowdsourcing process as defined in the introduction, which indicates a process that, next to optional human and machine tasks, also contains tasks executed by the crowd, so-called crowd tasks. A *crowd task* represents a set of micro-tasks that are jointly performed by the *crowd* via an online *crowdsourcing platform*. A *micro-task* is performed by an individual *worker*, is commonly interpreted as a task that requires limited skills and limited time (from seconds to few minutes), and is remunerated with limited rewards (from cents to few dollars). Crowd tasks can be seen like BPMN multi-instance tasks that typically require large numbers of instances to be performed in parallel (we focus on micro-tasking and do not further study the case of contest- or auction-based crowdsourcing models). For example, the above scenario asks for 40 transcriptions, 20 controls of transcriptions (2 per task), and 10 classifications of receipts (4 per task).

Figure 1 illustrates the dependencies among the crowd tasks of the scenario and the benefits that could be achieved if the process supported the streaming of micro-task instances. With the term *micro-task instance streaming* we denote

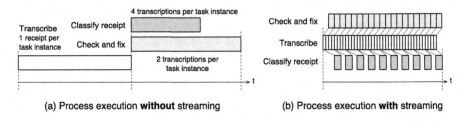

Fig. 1. The parallelization benefits of task instance streaming in crowdsourcing

the streaming of micro-task instance end events while the respective crowd task is still in execution, that is, other micro-task instances of the crowd task are still in execution. Completed instances can be streamed, that is, their end events and output data, from a crowd task A to a crowd task B, causing the instantiation of micro-tasks of B as soon as the necessary number of micro-task instances of A have completed. For example, the transcription of 4 receipts causes the instantiation of 1 classification and 2 checks. The number of instances to be created thus depends on the data transformation logic between two crowd tasks: *grouping* outputs reduces the number of micro-task instances of the subsequent crowd task; *multiplying* outputs or *splitting* grouped outputs increases the number of micro-task instances of the subsequent crowd task. Data transformations may be needed to accommodate the mismatch between output and input data sizes of different crowd tasks, as exemplified in our reference scenario. The goal of grouping/splitting is usually that of keeping the overall effort of a micro-task constant in response to changing efforts required to process an input data item, e.g., one transcription requires roughly the same effort as four classifications of receipts. Multiplying outputs creates redundancy that can be used to increase the quality of outputs, e.g., a same receipt can be given to two different workers and their outputs can be checked for consistency.

3   Assumptions and Approach

This work assumes that the crowdsourcer has working knowledge of both business process modeling with BPMN and crowdsourcing with a micro-tasking platform like CrowdFlower. Human and machine tasks are enacted by the business process engine running the BPMN process; crowd tasks are enacted by the crowdsourcing platform. The design of the UIs for the crowd tasks is done by the crowdsourcer inside the crowdsourcing platform. The platform provides programmatic access (via API) to the following abstract micro-task management functions: `uploadData` to associate micro-tasks with input data, `startInstance` to instantiate micro-tasks, `getInstanceStatus` to query the runtime status of micro-task instances, and `getInstanceOutput` to download results produced by a worker. For instance, both CrowdFlower and Amazon Mechanical Turk provide implementations of these abstract functions.

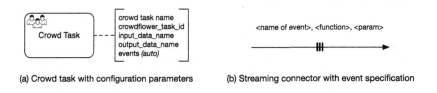

(a) Crowd task with configuration parameters   (b) Streaming connector with event specification

Fig. 2. Proposed modeling convention for micro-task instance streaming in BPMN

The approach to provide support for crowdsourcing processes is similar to the one already successfully adopted in prior works [6]: In order to provide insight into micro-task instance terminations, we extend the syntax and semantics of BPMN with two new modeling constructs, a *crowd task* and a *streaming connector*, that are specifically tailored to the needs of crowdsourcing. The streaming connector answers the need for a novel *data passing technique* that supports the grouping, splitting and multiplication of streaming data as well as the passing of data between the process and the crowd tasks. We complement the language with a *visual editor* that allows the crowdsourcer to model his crowdsourcing process and equip the editor with a process *deployment tool* that transforms the process model with extended semantics into (i) a standards-compliant *BPMN process* and (ii) a set of *configurations* able to steer the crowdsourcing platform and to establish a communication channel between the platform and the engine. The extended BPMN process model contains the necessary logic for micro-task and communication management. Data streaming among crowd tasks is implemented via a simple *middleware* placed in between the BPMN engine and the crowdsourcing platform and able to monitor micro-task instance completions and to group, split or multiply respective output data. As soon as the monitor detects an expected number of micro-task instance completions, it assembles the respective data and sends to the process engine a *message* that can be intercepted by the process. Reacting to messages allows the process to create micro-task instances of dependent crowd tasks and to progress.

The goal is to provide crowdsourcing support as an extension of existing BPM practice, so as to be able to leverage on modeling conventions and software infrastructure that are already familiar to the BPMN-skilled crowdsourcer.

4   Streaming Crowd Tasks

Next, we introduce the BPMN modeling constructs that enable the modeling of crowsourcing processes, we discuss the options we have to transform crowdsourcing processes into standard BPMN processes, and we describe the concrete runtime infrastructure we implemented to support process execution.

4.1   Modeling Micro-task Instance Streaming

Modeling crowdsourcing processes requires expressing tasks for the crowd and the propagation of outputs between workers. We propose to satisfy these requirements with two new constructs (Figure 2): crowd tasks and streaming connectors.

Crowd tasks are tasks that represent micro-tasks to be executed by workers inside a crowdsourcing platform. We identify crowd tasks using a crowd logo in the top left corner of the BPMN task construct. Crowd tasks cannot be expressed as simple multi-instance tasks, since these do not provide insight into the completion of task instances and can therefore not be used to implement the expected streaming logic. The deployment and execution of crowd tasks further asks for a mediation between the process engine and the crowdsourcing platform, an aspect that goes beyond the conventional semantics of tasks in BPMN. We therefore opt for a new construct for crowd tasks that (i) provides for the execution of multiple instances of micro-tasks equipped with respective instance completion events, (ii) the deployment of the micro-tasks' input data on the crowdsourcing platform, and (iii) the start of the micro-task instances.

Streaming connectors connect two crowd tasks A and B and express that they are "followed" multiple times at runtime. How many times, depends on the *data transformation function* (Figure 3). If A has l micro-task instances and the connector *groups* m instances, B has l/m micro-task instances; if it *multiplies* instances of A by n (creating n copies by value) B has $l \times n$ micro-task instances. If it *splits* the outputs of A into its l items, B has l micro-task instances. The *flat* function hands items over as they are.

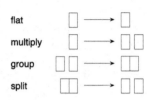

Fig. 3. Streaming data transformation functions.

The choice of a new type of connector is again justified by the need to express a logic that is not yet captured by any of the other BPMN constructs: the connector actually represents events (one for each individual data object generated by the data transformation function) that can only be handled by the internal logic of the subsequent crowd task B, which creates a micro-task for each event it receives from A. In addition, the event carries the output data produced by A, which task B uses to provide its micro-tasks with the necessary inputs. This turns the streaming connector into a data streaming connector for crowd tasks.

With the help of these two new constructs and the common constructs of BPMN, we are now able to model the crowdsourcing process described in our reference scenario as illustrated in Figure 4. The process starts with a common human task for uploading the receipts, followed by a crowd task for their transcription. The `Check and improve` and `Classify receipt` crowd tasks are executed in parallel and followed by a machine task sending the notification email with the results. The first crowd task takes as input the 40 receipts and produces respective transcriptions as output. Similarly, the outputs of the checking and classification crowd tasks are used as inputs of the final machine task. The very novel aspect of the model is the use of the streaming connector from the first to the other two crowd tasks. `Check and improve` is executed once for each couple

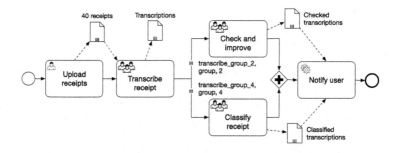

Fig. 4. Extended BPMN model of the receipt transcription crowdsourcing process

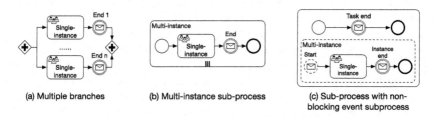

(a) Multiple branches   (b) Multi-instance sub-process   (c) Sub-process with non-blocking event subprocess

Fig. 5. Model transformation options

of transcriptions (note the annotation of the connector) and `Classify receipt` once for each four transcriptions. Due to the data flow nature of the streaming connector there is no need to explicitly model data objects exchanged between crowd tasks. The data object in output of a crowd task (e.g., `Transcriptions`) is filled during task execution and is ready only when the last instance of its micro-tasks has completed, which also corresponds to the completion of the crowd task itself. This complies with the conventional semantics of BPMN.

4.2   Model Transformation

To provide BPMN modelers with an as familiar as possible modeling paradigm, we leverage on a standard BPMN engine and let it manage all and only those process execution aspects that are needed to coordinate the work of actors, machines, and the crowd. To do so we transform the process model created with abstract crowd tasks and streaming connectors into a BPMN-compliant model that can be executed and managed by an engine extended with runtime support for crowd tasks. The challenge is to overcome the mismatch between the requirement of providing insight into the execution of micro-task instances and the assumption that tasks are atomic. Next, we show how we approach the model transformation, then we focus on propagating and transforming data.

Transforming the crowdsourcing-specific constructs into executable BPMN constructs may be achieved in several ways. In particular, we identify the three approaches depicted in Figure 5 to make explicit the *multiplicity of task instances* at both model and execution level:

(a) *Parallel branches:* The straightforward option to execute several tasks independently in parallel is to create multiple parallel branches, each one executing a single crowd task instance in the crowdsourcing platform. The termination of instances can be captured via dedicated events by the streaming middleware. This approach in principle gives access to the results of each task instance individually. Yet, it is not convenient, since the number of branches to be created is proportional to the number of micro-tasks of the crowd task, and the process model is only hard to read and manage. Especially the number of required instances may be large and can explode when more than a single crowd task is to be streamed. The approach also makes execution expensive, since all the branches are instantiated as soon as the process execution reaches the preceding gateway.

(b) *Multi-instance sub-processes:* This transformation option overcomes the problem of having several branches with the same logic modeled in parallel. The multi-instance sub-process behaves similar to the parallel branches: the full number of expected sub-processes is instantiated together at runtime when the first instance of the sub-process is started. However, the model is more modular, uses only one event type, and is better readable and maintainable.

(c) *Non-blocking event sub-processes:* To limit the number of parallel instances of sub-processes, it is possible to use a sub-process with a non-blocking event sub-process. The event sub-process is instantiated only upon a respective start event, and it does not block or alter the execution of the parent process. The start events can be generated dynamically at runtime as soon as the necessary input data are available; the `Instance end` event communicates task instance completions, the `Task end` event terminates the parent sub-process when all the instances have been processed.

Option (c) stands out as the most efficient transformation of the streaming constructs. However, although part of the BPMN standard, non-blocking event sub-processes are not (yet) reliably supported by state-of-the-art BPMN engines (our implementation is based on the open-source BPM platform Activiti). We therefore follow option (b), the multi-instance sub-processes, to transform models into executable format.

Given the resulting event-based nature of micro-task instance streaming, propagating data among crowd tasks requires (i) having access to the *data items* produced by each micro-task instance, (ii) enabling the *grouping/splitting/multiplication* of data items, and (iii) progressing the process based on *events*. Figure 6(a) shows a model pattern making use of the streaming connector; Figure 6(b) shows its transformed, executable model. *Connector-crowd task pairs* are mapped depending on their nature (streaming connectors connect crowd tasks only):

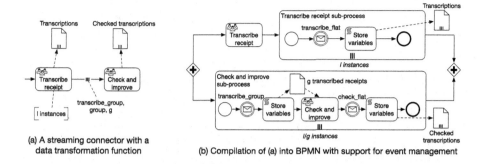

(a) A streaming connector with a
data transformation function

(b) Compilation of (a) into BPMN with support for event management

Fig. 6. Implementing micro-task instance streaming with data transformations

- *Standard control flow connectors followed by a crowd task* are transformed into one crowd task representing the execution of the micro-tasks inside the crowdsourcing platform and a multi-instance sub-process intercepting the respective micro-task instance terminations. The events to be intercepted are generated by the streaming middleware and contain the output data of the terminated micro-tasks. The `Store variables` script task takes the received data items and stores them in the global data object (if needed).
- *Streaming connectors followed by a crowd task* are transformed into a multi-instance sub-process that first intercepts instance terminations of the preceding micro-tasks and then runs the own micro-task instances and intercepts their terminations. Again, upon reception of each event the two script tasks store the respective data into a data object. The first script task uses a local data object, the second one fills again the global data object.

Note how the source sequence of crowd tasks is transformed into parallel branches of sub-processes that are synchronized via events. Incidentally, this resembles the streaming logic illustrated in Figure 1(b) also graphically.

In the executable model, crowd tasks have the following execution semantics: (i) read the data items specified as input, (ii) upload data to crowdsourcing platform, (iii) bind micro-task completions to suitable events in the middleware, (iv) start micro-tasks for each data item. The middleware and crowdsourcing platform start execution in parallel to the process engine. The engine waits for events from the middleware and processes them as specified in the model.

The model transformation logic further provides a convenient way to implement the **data transformation functions** illustrated in Figure 3. The key lies in the sensible use of events and the configuration of the streaming middleware:

- *Flat*: Micro-task instances are streamed as they terminate without applying any data transformation. This requires the generation and handling of one event for each termination. For instance, the `transcribe_flat` event in Figure 6(b) intercepts all instances of the `Transcribe receipt` micro-task.
- *Group*: Micro-task instance terminations are streamed only in groups. This requires the middleware to buffer instance terminations till the required

number of terminations is reached and to emit an event that carries the collection of data items produced by the grouped instances. The process reacts to group events, like in the case of the `transcribe_group` event in Figure 6(b).

- *Split*: Micro-task instances are streamed as they terminate and their output data collections are split into their constituent elements, requiring the middleware to emit multiple events per termination. This function only applies to micro-tasks that produce collections of data items in output, as for instance the task `Classify receipt` in our reference scenario (four classifications).
- *Multiply*: The implementation of this data transformation function is similar to the split function, with the difference that data items are forwarded as they are, yet multiple events with data copied by value are generated and handled as separated events in the process.

Thanks to this mapping logic, it is further possible to compute at transformation time the **number of instances** of each sub-process in the final model, starting from the number of micro-tasks of the first crowd task in the source model. We already discussed the necessary arithmetic in Section 4.1.

For a complete understanding of the proposed transformation logic, it is important to recall that the streaming connector can only be used between two crowd tasks and to note that a crowd task followed by a standard control flow connector implements the standard semantics of BPMN: the control flow connector is enacted only once all the micro-task instances of the preceding crowd task have terminated. This convention may lead to independent "islands" of streaming areas inside a process if multiple crowd tasks are separated by standard control flow constructs. For example, the crowdsourcing process modeled in Figure 4 could make use of other crowd tasks after the notification of the user about the completion of the transcription of the receipts. Each of these islands is transformed into a set of parallel branches and woven into the regular control flow structure of the source model as exemplified in Figure 6.

4.3 Runtime Environment

Figure 7 illustrates the software architecture we implemented to run crowdsourcing processes. It is composed of three main blocks: (i) a *BPMN engine* where the processes are executed; (ii) a *streaming middleware* that manages the events and transforms data; and (iii) *CrowdFlower*, the crowdsourcing platform where micro-tasks are deployed and executed. To model a crowdsourcing process, the developer uses the *IDE* (an extension of the Activiti Modeler) that supports the *modeling extensions* presented previously. The process model is then *transformed* into an executable process and deployed into the BPMN engine. The engine is equipped with a *runtime extension* for the interaction with the middleware. Human actors and Web services are managed by the engine (Activiti, http://activiti.org) using its own user interface and service adapters.

The streaming middleware is composed of three blocks: The *micro-task launcher* deploys micro-tasks via the CrowdFlower API, given a task identifier, respective input data (if any), and a task template. The *message handler*

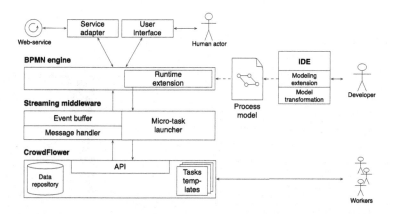

Fig. 7. Architecture of runtime environment for crowdsourcing processes with streaming support. The middleware deploys micro-tasks and manages events and data.

and *event buffer* receive webhook calls from the CrowdFlower API when a task instance is completed, buffer output data, and create events for the BPMN engine.

CrowdFlower is the crowdsourcing platform where the streaming middleware deploys the micro-tasks for execution by the crowd. To enable the runtime deployment in CrowdFlower, *task templates* are designed at process modeling time and linked via suitable parameters to the crowd tasks in the BPMN model. Each template has to be designed to handle the correct number of data items in input. For example, the `Check and improve` template has two forms, one for each receipt to be processed. At runtime, the launcher feeds the templates with data from the BPMN engine, which are then available to workers as micro-tasks.

5 Case Study and Evaluation

5.1 Modeling and Implementation

Modeling the process shown in Figure 4 in the extended Activity Modeler is a conventional BPMN modeling exercise with three exceptions: First, the crowd tasks make use of a new, dedicated modeling construct that allows the modeler to clearly identify them inside the model and to configure it's internal logic (remember Figure 2(a)). Second, streaming connectors are modeled as control flow connectors with a suitable annotation, as shown in Figure 2(b). The annotation turns the connector into a streaming connector. Third, the input and output data objects of each crowd task are set again via suitable parameters. The resulting model is almost identical to Figure 4, except for the missing notation for the streaming connector and the data objects that are referenced via parameters.

One of the key configurations of the crowd tasks is their binding with their task templates in CrowdFlower. This requires creating three task templates for

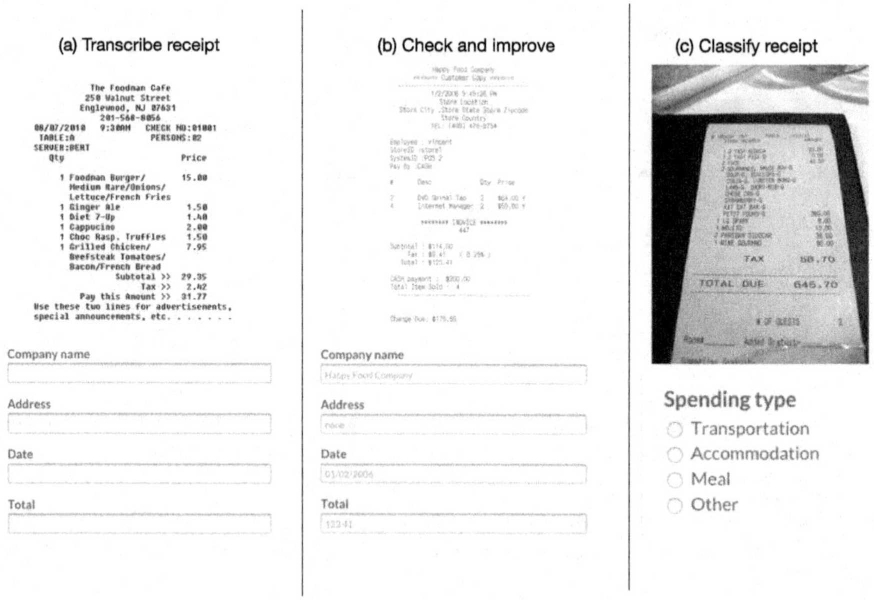

Fig. 8. Screen shots of the three micro-task pages as rendered in CrowdFlower

the process and setting the `crowdflower_task_id` for each crowd task. The templates are created to accept as input and to provide as output the correct data expected by the process execution. The screen shots in Figure 8 show an excerpt of the three templates instantiated with concrete receipts. For all the tree templates we set the reward to 10 dollar cents, which is high for this type of micro-task, so as to attract more workers and have results in a short time.

Given the process model and the implemented task templates, it is possible to transform the process into its executable form. Specifically, Figure 9 shows the transformed model of Figure 4. In line with the transformation logic described previously, the three crowd tasks are transformed into three parallel branches containing the sub-processes managing the instances of the micro-tasks completed in CrowdFlower. The topmost branch corresponds to the original `Transcribe receipt` task and feeds the other two branches with events that group two and four micro-task completions, respectively. The numbers of instances are also computed, and the process is ready for execution.

5.2   Performance Evaluation

To evaluate the performances of this implementation, we performed a set of experiments in which we focused on the crowd tasks only (the process without the `Upload receipts` and `Notify user` tasks). We uploaded the 40 receipts manually, and ran the process 6 times: 3 times without streaming and 3 times with streaming (as illustrated in Figure 1). We ran the two settings on two

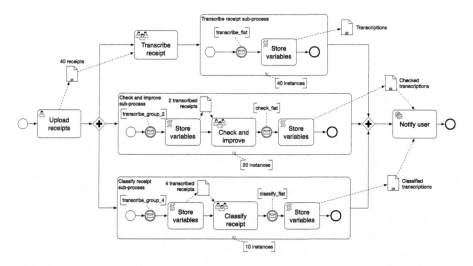

Fig. 9. Transformed BPMN process model with the micro-task instance streaming logic resolved into a set of crowd tasks for micro-task deployment and event handlers and multi-instance sub-processes for instance management and data transformation.

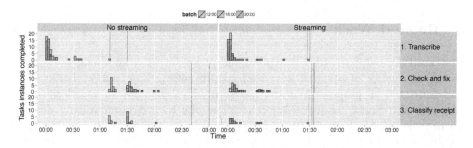

Fig. 10. Performance analysis of no streaming vs. streaming. The colored vertical lines indicate the end of the respective micro-task execution (the deployed batches).

different days (Thursday and Friday, 19/20 March, 2015) in three different batches at 12:00, 16:00, and 20:00 CET, and stopped micro-tasks after max 1.5 hours of execution. Independently of streaming or not, our experience has shown that a same micro-task can be executed within very different times (from minutes to hours). In order to prevent overlapping batches, we applied the cut-off time and manually completed outstanding instances. The cost of each execution was of approximately 8 USD, with a reward of 0.10 USD per micro-task instance.

The runtime behavior of the process executions is illustrated in Figure 10, which plots the histogram of micro-task instances performed per time unit (2:25 minutes, for best readability) for each crowd task. In all tasks, the majority of micro-task instances is completed during the productivity peak immediately after deployment, and almost all instances are completed within one hour.

However, in some runs the last one or two instances took several hours to complete, and the figure applies the cutoff of 1.5 hours (for presentation purposes). We did not compare the quality of outputs between the streaming and non-streaming conditions, which is out of the scope of this work (speed).

The charts clearly show the benefit of streaming: approximately 90% of all receipts passed through all three crowd tasks within the first 10 minutes of execution, while in the no streaming condition the same amount of receipts passed only through the transcription task. With streaming, it takes only a couple of minutes to transcribe, check and fix, and classify the first receipt; without streaming it takes about one and a half hours. The two peaks in the no streaming condition happen in correspondence of the respective terminations of the prior transcription task. Note that without streaming almost all micro-task instances are processed very fast, while with streaming the last few instances are more dispersed in time. This is in line with the findings by Chilton et al. [5] that workers tend to select micro-tasks (i) that appear on the first two pages in the crowdsourcing platform and (ii) that have a high number of instances. The last few instances of a micro-task, especially in the streaming setting where micro-tasks are deployed at the rate of individual instances, the last condition is not met. With hundreds or thousands of instances, the benefits of streaming however clearly outweigh this shortcoming.

6   Related Work

The need for support for crowdsourcing processes is acknowledged by the recent emergence of a set of advanced crowdsourcing approaches: Turkit [13] and AutoMan [3] propose dedicated programming languages (a JavaScript-like language and Scala, respectively) that allow one to programmatically deploy micro-tasks on Mechanical Turk and to pass data among them. AutoMan, in particular, allows the crowdsourcer to define confidence levels for the quality of results and automatically manages the scheduling and pricing of micro-tasks as well as the acceptance and rejection of results. Jabberwocky [1] is a MapReduce-based human computation framework that consists of (i) a human and machine resource layer (Dormouse), (ii) a parallel programming framework (ManReduce), and (iii) a high-level scripting language for micro-task definition (Dog). CrowdDB [7] is an SQL-extension that allows one to embed crowd interrogations into SQL queries. Based on schemas and annotations of tables in a database, it transforms queries into workflows of crowd tasks for Mechanical Turk, generates appropriate user interfaces, and manages data integration. AskSheet [16] is a Google Spreadsheet extension with functions that allow the spreadsheet to leverage on crowdsourced work. For instance, data enrichment micro-tasks deployed on Mechanical Turk can be used to check prices or products in given grocery stores. Turkomatic [12] delegates not only work to the crowd but also work management operations. The crowdsourcer and workers alike can arbitrarily split micro-tasks into subtasks, aggregate subtasks, or perform them. The result is a self-managed workflow executed in Mechanical Turk. CrowdForge

[10] is a Django-based crowdsourcing framework for composite tasks similar to Turkomatic that however follows the Partition-Map-Reduce approach. Each step in the resulting process is a crowd task performed on Mechanical Turk. Crowd-Searcher [4] is a crowdsourcing system that leverages on reusable design patterns and on tasks performed by machines or people on crowdsourcing platforms or on Facebook.

In the specific context of business process management, CrowdLang [14] is a BPMN-inspired programming language with crowdsourcing-specific constructs. It helps one to design and run composite tasks using tasks performed by both machines and people sourced from various crowdsourcing platforms. Similarly, CrowdWeaver [9] allows the crowdsourcer to visually design workflows of both crowd tasks deployed on CrowdFlower and machine tasks. Finally, in our own prior work we proposed Crowd Computer [17], a BPMN-based design and run-time environment for complex crowdsourcing processes and the design of custom crowdsourcing models (e.g., from micro-tasking to auctions and contests). Composite tasks are expressed graphically as business processes and may make use of human, crowd and machine tasks as well as the full power of BPMN.

None of these approaches, however, supports the streaming of micro-task instances. To the best of our knowledge, only Appel et al. [2] focused on event stream processing in the context of BPMN. The focus of their work is on so-called event stream processing units that represent machine tasks processing real-time data streams. The focus of our work is specifically on the peculiarities of crowd work and the typical data transformations that characterize that domain.

7   Conclusion

The work described in this paper advances the state of the art in business process management with three contributions: an *extension of BPMN* for the modeling of streaming crowdsourcing processes, a BPMN engine with support for *crowd tasks*, and a *streaming middleware* able to overcome the impedance mismatch between the business process engine and the crowdsourcing platform. The analyzed case study demonstrates the convenience of the new modeling constructs and the runtime performance gains that can be achieved.

One of the limitations of the implementation so far is the lack of support for non-blocking event sub-processes, due to the lack of a respective implementation in the BPMN engine we used as starting point. Without being able to dynamically create sub-process instances at runtime, the modeler must guarantee at design time that all data transformations (splitting and grouping) can be mapped to a correct number of respective runtime events, e.g., the process in Figure 4 requires multiples of 4 data items in input. From a modeling point of view, it is currently possible to branch streaming connectors but not to join them again (joins can be implemented using the standard control flow connectors of BPMN). This limitation is due to the fact that this kind of join is no longer a simple join of the control flow but a join of data streams. Joining them asks for joining data items with different multiplicities or group sizes. This asks for logics to deal with redundancy (e.g., averaging outputs) and the correlation of data items. Another limitation that is intrinsic to the approach is that we can control only those aspects of the process execution that are handled by the BPMN engine; we do not have control over the execution semantics of the crowdsourcing platform, e.g., of how micro-tasks are instantiated, managed, canceled, assigned to workers, etc. We can thus not manage exceptions that are internal to the crowdsourcing platform, e.g., micro-tasks that are never completed.

In our future work, we intend to solve these shortcomings and to support the joining of data streams using different join logics, to provide for a model transformation that is fully integrated into the modeling environment, and to integrate support for micro-task instance streaming into our prior work on the Crowd Computer. We intend to conduct additional experiments with hundreds or thousands of micro-tasks to stress-test and fine-tune the runtime environment. In order to attack the high variance of micro-task durations, we want to understand better the reasons for slow durations, so as to dynamically re-deploy problematic micro-tasks and to speed up overall execution times.

The data and streaming middleware of this work are open-sourced on https:// github.com/Crowdcomputer/ and can be adapted to different BPM engines, crowdsourcing platforms, and application domains.

Acknowledgment. This work was partially supported by the project "Evaluation and enhancement of social, economic and emotional wellbeing of older adults" under the agreement no. 14.Z50.310029, Tomsk Polytechnic University.

References

1. Ahmad, S., Battle, A., Malkani, Z., Kamvar, S.: The jabberwocky programming environment for structured social computing. In: UIST 2011, pp. 53–64 (2011)
2. Appel, S., Frischbier, S., Freudenreich, T., Buchmann, A.: Event stream processing units in business processes. In: Daniel, F., Wang, J., Weber, B. (eds.) BPM 2013. LNCS, vol. 8094, pp. 187–202. Springer, Heidelberg (2013)
3. Barowy, D.W., Curtsinger, C., Berger, E.D., McGregor, A.: Automan: a platform for integrating human-based and digital computation. SIGPLAN Not. **47**(10), 639–654 (2012)
4. Bozzon, A., Brambilla, M., Ceri, S., Mauri, A., Volonterio, R.: Pattern-based specification of crowdsourcing applications. In: Casteleyn, S., Rossi, G., Winckler, M. (eds.) ICWE 2014. LNCS, vol. 8541, pp. 218–235. Springer, Heidelberg (2014)
5. Chilton, L.B., Horton, J.J., Miller, R.C., Azenkot, S.: Task Search in a human computation market. In: HCOMP 2010, pp. 1–9 (2010)
6. Daniel, F., Soi, S., Tranquillini, S., Casati, F., Heng, C., Yan, L.: Distributed orchestration of user interfaces. Inf. Syst. **37**(6), 539–556 (2012)
7. Franklin, M.J., Kossmann, D., Kraska, T., Ramesh, S., Xin, R.: CrowdDB: answering queries with crowdsourcing. In: SIGMOD 2011, pp. 61–72 (2011)
8. Howe, J.: Crowdsourcing: why the power of the crowd is driving the future of business, 1st edn. Crown Publishing Group, New York (2008)
9. Kittur, A., Khamkar, S., André, P., Kraut, R.: Crowdweaver: visually managing complex crowd work. In: CSCW 2012, pp. 1033–1036 (2012)

10. Kittur, A., Smus, B., Khamkar, S., Kraut, R.E.: Crowdforge: crowdsourcing complex work. In: UIST 2011, pp. 43–52 (2011)
11. Kucherbaev, P., Daniel, F., Tranquillini, S., Marchese, M.: Composite crowdsourcing processes: challenges, approaches, and opportunities. IEEE Internet Computing, conditionally (2015). http://bit.ly/1BtjMTy (accepted)
12. Kulkarni, A., Can, M., Hartmann, B.: Collaboratively crowdsourcing workflows with Turkomatic. In: CSCW 2012, pp. 1003–1012 (2012)
13. Little, G., Chilton, L.B., Goldman, M., Miller, R.C.: Turkit: human computation algorithms on mechanical turk. In: UIST 2010, pp. 57–66 (2010)
14. Minder, P., Bernstein, A.: *CrowdLang*: a programming language for the systematic exploration of human computation systems. In: Aberer, K., Flache, A., Jager, W., Liu, L., Tang, J., Guéret, C. (eds.) SocInfo 2012. LNCS, vol. 7710, pp. 124–137. Springer, Heidelberg (2012)
15. O.M.G. (OMG): Business Process Model and Notation (BPMN) version 2.0. (2011). http://www.omg.org/spec/BPMN/2.0
16. Quinn, A.J., Bederson, B.B.: AskSheet: efficient human computation for decision making with spreadsheets. In: CSCW 2012, pp. 1456–1466 (2012)
17. Tranquillini, S., Daniel, F., Kucherbaev, P., Casati, F.: Modeling, Enacting and Integrating Custom Crowdsourcing Processes. ACM Trans. Web **9**(2), May 2015
18. van der Aalst, W.M.P.: The Application of Petri Nets to Workflow Management. Journal of Circuits, Systems, and Computers **8**(1), 21–66 (1998)

Goal-Aligned Categorization of Instance Variants in Knowledge-Intensive Processes

Karthikeyan Ponnalagu[1,3]([✉]), Aditya Ghose[3], Nanjangud C. Narendra[2], and Hoa Khanh Dam[3]

[1] IBM Research India, Bangalore, India
karthikeyan.ponnalagu@in.ibm.com
[2] Cognizant Technology Solutions, Bangalore, India
ncnaren@gmail.com
[3] University of Wollongong, Wollongong, Australia
aditya.ghose@gmail.com, hoa@uow.edu.au

Abstract. Discovering and reasoning about deviations of business process executions (from intended designs) enables organizations to continuously evaluate their execution/performance relative to their strategic goals. We leverage the observation that a deviating process instance can be viewed as a valid variant of the intended process design provided it achieves the same goals as the intended process design. However, organizations often find it difficult to categorize and classify process execution deviations in a goal-based fashion (necessary to decide if a deviation represents a valid variant). Given that industry-scale knowledge-intensive processes typically manifest a large number of variants, this can pose a problem. In this paper, we propose an approach to help decide whether process instances in execution logs are valid variants using the goal-based notion of validity described above. Our proposed approach also enables analysis of the impact of contextual factors in the execution of specific goal-aligned process variants. We demonstrate our approach with an Eclipse-based plugin and evaluate it using an industry-scale setting in IT Incident Management with a process log of 25000 events.

Keywords: Variability · Goals · Business Process Mining

1 Introduction

A business process management framework seeks to ensure that the desired outcomes are achieved from the execution of business processes in the organization [9]. Typically, any industry-scale business process admits multiple variants, each of which ideally help achieve goals in an organizational goal model. Therefore, adequate management of process models with large scale variations, mandates treating each process variant as an independent model entity [12,25]. Currently, there is an increasing trend of unintended deviations specifically in the execution of Knowledge intensive processes [7] from optimal paths. Discovering such deviations (both accepted and unaccepted) and reasoning them in terms of organization's objectives remain a challenge. In time or resource constrained domains such

© Springer International Publishing Switzerland 2015
H.R. Motahari-Nezhad et al. (Eds.): BPM 2015, LNCS 9253, pp. 350–364, 2015.
DOI: 10.1007/978-3-319-23063-4_24

as Incident Management and other call center support scenarios, not addressing such a challenge will result in adverse business impact. Works such as [28] focus on minimizing such deviations through dedicated change patterns. This we see as an important aspect of *variability management (VM)* and specifically in business process management. VM has received considerable research and industry attention over the past decade [6] due to increasing need for differing alignments to organization's strategies and goals. In the context of organization's goal alignment, an adequate (and formal) definition of what makes a process instance a variant of another has remained elusive [14]. In our earlier paper [24], we have proposed a formal goal oriented variability management approach towards enabling this. However, mining and classifying goal alignments of executed process instances from process logs is still required to continuously improve process designs [26] and governing goal models [22]. Such bottom-up exercises enable organizations to ensure better goal adherence of process executions [8]. Therefore, our main objective in this paper is to propose a formal approach to mine, validate, categorize and reason variants of knowledge-intensive processes [7] using contextual factors with the underpinning of a goal model.

1.1   Preliminaries

A *knowledge-intensive process* is a sequence of *automated or human tasks*, with each task producing an *effect* in the form of a state transition. Effects are viewed as : *normative* - as they state required outcomes (i.e., goals); and *descriptive* in that they describe the normal, and predicted, subset of all possible outcomes. We assume that the effect annotations have been represented in conjunctive normal form (CNF) [15].

A *goal O* $=< G, R >$ is basically an organization level root goal, which is a formal assertion (a condition or a partial state description) that an organization seeks to realize. The root goal O is refined into a set of sub goals, where each sub goal can further be refined depending on the complexity of function associated with a goal. Here G denotes the set of goals that satisfies O , and $R \subseteq 2^G$ denotes the set of refinements that exist between a parent goal and child goal. We define the *goals* of a business process as a combination $G_1 \wedge G_2 \wedge \ldots \wedge G_n$ of boolean conditions in CNF, all of which need to be satisfied at the end of the process execution. We leverage the goal refinement procedure discussed in our earlier work [10] to refine the overall goals of a business process alternatively using conjunctive and disjunctive clauses, until all sub-goals have been completely specified to the user's satisfaction.

A *process goal model* thus refined is captured as a directed hyper graph [4]. A hyper edge $e \in E$ is merely a set of vertex, i.e. e $\subseteq$ V , such that $\mid e \mid \geq 2$. While we subscribe to the KAOS methodology for goal decomposition, we leveraged the hyper graph representation for distinguishing OR-refinements ($\mid e \mid = 2$) from AND-refinements ($\mid e \mid \geq 2$). Given that, there will be a single parent goal and one or more child goal as nodes, the hyper graph we generate is of type backward hyperarc, or B-arc. Here, $Tail(\varepsilon)$ denotes the set of **from vertex**, and $Head(\varepsilon)$ denotes the set of **to vertex**. If there is only one **from vertex** , the hyperarc is referred to as a backward hyperarc, or B-arc. Execution of resource constrained processes such as incident management may deviate due to periodic changes ("Friday afternoon preceding a long weekend there are fewer agents available) or due to changing external factors(e.g., " competitors offering increased warranty period with free support"). Such changes impact the selection of one process variant over another and it is vital to detect and analyze them. Correlating variants with contextual factors enables the correct matching between processs vairant and context, which is another interesting outcome of our work.

1.2 Key Contributions

In this paper, we propose a bottom-up approach for goal oriented classification of process variant instances discovered from execution logs. The benefit of our approach is to clearly categorize valid process instances based on their specific goal alignments. We assume the following inputs to our proposed approach: (a) a goal model hyper graph with goals and associated decomposition of sub goals (AND, OR) represented as a collection of boolean conditions in conjunctive normal form (CNF) [15] and (b) an event log containing multiple process instance execution data. With this, we achieve the following: 1. Identification of unique process variants executed out of this process design. 2. Alignment of each process variant(and its associated instances) with a specific OR-refinement sub goal in the goal decomposition model. 3. Discover the contextual factors to reason the goal alignments of each process variant.

This paper is organized as follows. We discuss the related work in this area in section 5. Section 2 discusses our evaluation setting, which is drawn from IT incident and problem management. In section 3, we discuss how we leverage goal oriented variability models to categorize process instances in terms of goal alignment. We also discuss the impact of contextual factors associated with valid clusters of process instances. In Section 4, we evaluate our proposed approach by running experiments on an real world industry setting. We conclude the paper in section 6.

2 Running Example

We consider an industrial setting involving IT incident resolution process as our running example. This is illustrated in Fig. 1. We have leveraged the eclipse based BPMN modeling tool for capturing the process design. End effect annotations are associated with each task in the process design. We consider the goal model depicted in Fig. 2 to validate and categorize the executed process instances of this process. Like the process annotation exercise, each leaf goal in the goal decomposition model is annotated with corresponding end effects achieved by realizing the goal. The "VAGAI" tool is designed to parse the process design and the goal model along with the annotations. The annotations are basically clauses in CNF form and the terms are specific to Incident Management domain in this case. The goal model mandates the following : When a new incident

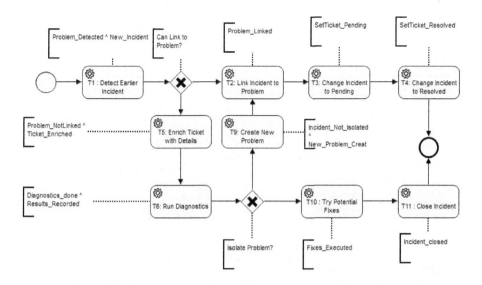

Fig. 1. Annotated Incident Resolution Process in VAGAI Tool

is reported, it needs to be determined whether there was an earlier reported incident matching with this new incident. If there is a match, then the new incident is linked with the problem of the matched incident. Basically a problem is a higher level classification for a group of incidents. Depending on the status of the linked problem,the new incident is either stated as unresolved or in progress. If there exists no similar incident or no linked problem, then the reported system or application is subjected to a standard list of diagnostic tests to enrich the incident description. If the reported issue is solved, the incident is closed. An AND link in Fig. 2 specifies that all sub-goals of a goal need to be satisfied for the goal to be satisfied; an XOR link specifies that the sub-goals are mutually exclusive, and only one is needed to satisfy the goal.

3   Goal-Driven Variant Mining

We describe the goal-driven variant mining approach in detail in this section. We leverage the *event log* associated with the process execution machinery to establish correlation between goals and process instances. We note that an event log can be viewed as being composed of 2 kinds of events: (1) events that record the execution of activities and (2) events that record state changes in the objects impacted by a process. In some circumstances, there is a one-to-one correspondence between the execution of a task and a state change in an object impacted by the process, but often the execution of a task leads to potentially many state transitions in multiple objects. Our intent is to leverage events of the second kind, by viewing these as representations of the *effects* of a process. Without

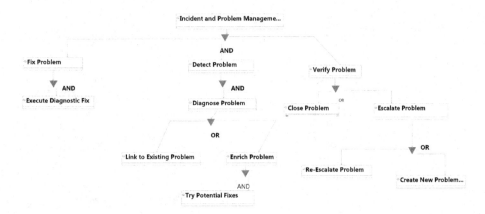

Fig. 2. Example Goal Model

loss of generality, we will view each *effect event* as a pair $\langle \phi, t \rangle$ where ϕ is an effect assertion in the underlying first-order language (referring to the state of an object impacted by the process) and t is a time-stamp. The underlying first-order language is in effect an ontological schema that is domain-specific.

Our focus here is on determining the goals (in an organization's goal model) that a given process instance helps satisfy. This in turn determines whether that process instance is a *valid variant* of another process instance or of a process design. To determine goal satisfaction, we need access to the *end effects* that accrue when a process instance executes to completion (we then check if these end effects entail the goals in question). The determination of the end effects of a process instance can be straightforward if the event logging machinery logs both *changes* and *non-changes* (i.e., we periodically log the states of all objects of interest). In such settings, the final set of object states represent the end effects of the process instance. More commonly, though, we can expect the event logging machinery to log only the *changes* (but not the *non-changes*). In such settings, we need specialized techniques to determine which changes *persist* and which are overriden by subsequent changes. We use techniques developed in the literature on *reasoning about action* for this purpose, where *state update operators* are used to determine how a knowledge-base describing a state of the world is updated as a consequence of the execution of an action. A number of state update operators have been reported in the literature, such as the Possible Models Approach [29] and the Possible Worlds Approach [11]. Our overall strategy is as follows. We define a *partial state* to be the set of effect assertions that hold after the execution of one task and prior to the execution of the next (we assume that the same object is not concurrently impacted by multiple process instances, so that we are able to segregate the effects of distinct process instances). Note that we can obtain effect assertions from effect events merely by removing the associated time-stamp. Given a partial state S and a set of effect assertions e obtained from effect events accruing from the execution of a task, the resulting partial state is given by $S \oplus e$ where $\oplus$ is a state update operator. In our work, we use the Possible Worlds Approach for state update (although any other state update operator could be validly used instead). This $\oplus$ operator is defined as follows (we assume, in the following, that each effect assertion is written in the Conjunctive Normal Form). We also use a knowledge-base KB of domain constraints. If $S \cup e \cup KB$ is consistent, then $S \oplus e = S \cup e$. Otherwise, $S \oplus e = e \cup \{s \mid s \subseteq S, s \cup e \cup KB$ is consistent, and there does not exist any s' where $s \subset s' \subseteq S$ such that $s' \cup e \cup KB$ is consistent$\}$. We start with an initial partial state description (which may potentially be empty) and incrementally update it (using $\oplus$) until we reach the partial state immediately following the final task in the process instance. These represent the *end effects* of the process instance. Note that the output of the state update operator is potentially non-deterministic. Thus we might obtain multiple sets of end of effects. We could perform goal satisfaction analysis with each of these (as in some of our definitions below), or we could do additional sensing to determine which of these competing sets of end effects actually transpired.

Correlating Processes with Goal Models: An organizational goal model provides an effective basis for categorizing (and hence developing a deeper understanding of) each process instance that we encounter in a log of past process executions. By correlating each process instance (and indeed, each process model) with a goal in the organizational goal model, we can obtain insight into the intent underpinning that particular instance, and, as shown below, also understand which process models/instances it was a variant of. We will correlate a process instance to its *maximally refined correlated goal* in the organizational goal model, as defined below. Given a goal model (AND-OR goal graph) $\mathcal{G}$, a goal G_i will be referred to as the *maximally refined correlated goal* for a process instance p if and only if all of the following conditions hold:

- Condition C1: For every set of end effects e of p, $e \models G_i$.
- Condition C2: There exists no goal G'_i in $\mathcal{G}$ that can be obtained via (AND/OR-) refinement of G_i such that for every set of end effects e of S_j, $e \models G'_i$.

Determining Valid Variants: We now need to define formally the conditions under which we will deem a process instance to be a *valid variant* of another process instance, or of another process design. Multiple competing intuitions can be brought to bear in defining these. We will explore three of these below. We will assume that the test for validity of a variant is a commutative binary test involving a pair of process instances and/or designs (recall that a process design can also be annotated with post-conditions/effects at design time and thus subject to similar analysis). Let E be the set of sets of end effects of one process and E' be the corresponding set for the other process.

Post-condition Entailment: For every $e' \in E'$, there exists an $e \in E$ such that $e' \models e$ and for every $e \in E$, there exists an $e' \in E'$ such that $e' \models e$. This notion makes no reference to the organizational goal model, but requires instead that

---

Algorithm 1. *GoalAlign*

1: Input Goal Model - G,List of Event Groups - L, Map [Event Group,List[Goals]] M1, Map [Event Group,Goal] M2, List PIGA.
2: **for all** event groups $S_1..S_n$ in L **do**
3:    **for all** goals $G_1..G_m$ in Goal Model G **do**
4:       bEntailed = CheckGoalEntailment(G_i, S_i)
5:       if (bEntailed = true)
6:       Add S_i as key, G_i as value in M1
7:       M1.put(S_i,G_i,)
8:    **end for**
9:    M2.Put(S_i,getMaxCorrelatedGroup(M1,S_i))
10: **end for**
11: PIGA.add(M2)
12: Return PIGA

---

all end effects of one process to be realized by another for the pair to be deemed to be variants. This may be an overly strong condition in some settings.

Goal Entailment: Both processes share the same maximally refined correlated goal G in the organizational goal model. This is a weaker notion, requiring that processes realize the same goal to be deemed to be variants.

Disjunctive Entailment: There exists a goal G in the organizational goal model such that for every $e' \in E'$, $e' \models G$ and for every $e \in E$, $e \models G$. A corollary of this condition is that both processes have maximally refined correlated goals which are related via a sequence of OR-refinements to a common ancestor goal in the goal model. The variants thus represent alternative ways of realizing the common ancestor goal.

Analyzing how a Process Instance Realizes a Goal: The end effects of a process instance can be a rich source of information on how that instance realized a particular goal. We could investigate the reasons for different (non-functional) performance profiles of different instances (for example, why certain instances executed quickly or cheaply, while others took a longer time). We could investigate differences in levels of client satisfaction for different process instance variants. Key to this analysis is the ability to correlate the precise set of end effects of a process that contributed to the realization of a particular goal. To this end, we define the notion of a *goal-realizing effect group* to be a minimal subset of the set of end effects that realize a given goal. Given a set of end effects E of a process and a goal G, the *goal-realizing effect group gr* for G is a set of effect assertions such that: (1) $gr \subseteq E$, (2) $gr \models G$ and (3) there exists no gr' where $gr' \subseteq E$, $gr' \subset gr$ and $gr' \models G$. A goal-realizing effect group provides a valuable unit of analysis, as we shall demonstrate in the section on empirical evaluation.

Process Instance Goal Alignment (PIGA) In this section, we discuss identification of correlation or alignment of event transitions with goals termed as

Process Instance Goal alignment (PIGA). PIGA is formalized basically as a conjunctive normal form satisfiability (CSAT) problem, which is NP-complete. Therefore, given a *goal-realizing effect group* S, finding correlation with a goal G in formal terms is simply finding the truth assignments in the CNF expression of G using the cumulative end effects of S. The Algorithm 1 outlines the steps for generating PIGA. We take the list of state transitions and the goal decomposition model as input. We create two map objects M1, M2 to store the set of goal event correlations in the form of key value pairs. The function `CheckGoalEntailment` takes a goal (annotated with intended set of effects in CNF) and a event group (annotated with actual set of effects) to compute the entailment as a truth satisfactory exercise. For each event group in the process log, we validate the truth assignments of all goals in the goal model. We repeat this for all groups in the process log. Each event group and the list of correlated goals will be stored as a key value pair in Map M1. The function `getMaxCorrelatedGroup` takes this map M1 and identify the maximally correlated group (based on satisfying the conditions C1, C2 and C3) for each goal. We repeat this evaluation for each of the mined process instance to identify the "valid process instances". The representation of each process instance as a list of *maximally refined correlated goals* constitutes the completion of generating Process Instance Goal Alignment (PIGA). At the end of this exercise, if any of the mandatory sub goals of root goal G is not correlated, it implies that the process instance P is not correlated with the goal G and is rejected.

Correlating Process Variants with Contextual Factors: An additional class of analyses becomes feasible as a consequence of oour approach - one that identifies correlations between contextual factors and process variants. These correlations (which are easy to establish via the application of association rule mining) can lead to recommendation rules which suggest which process variant might be most appropriate under a given set of contextual conditions.

4   Evaluation

The purpose of the evaluation is to establish that our approach is useful in achieving the following:

- Correctly identifying valid variants of processes via reference to a goal model.
- Effectively categorizing process instance variants via their goal correlations.
- Associating contextual factors with identified process variants that can provide guidance in selecting the correct variant for the context.

For our evaluation, we considered a process log consisting of 25000 events, representing part of the execution history of a help desk division in an IT organization dealing mainly with end user technical issues. The process log contains 1400 process instances with an of average 14 events per case. Fig. 3 plots the number of process instances against the number of state transitions (effects) per instance, where all the process instances involve incident resolution. The

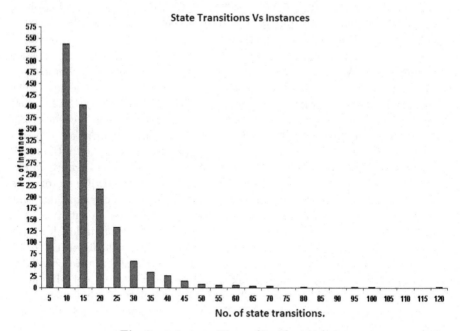

Fig. 3. state transitions of incident tickets

figure suggests that some incident resolution process instances involve considerable work (a large number of effects) while others involve very little (a small number of effects). These variations can be due to the complexity of the incidents, but may also suggest that there is poor matching between the incident and the process variant being used to deal with it. Each process instance in the log indicates how after receiving a complaint from a customer, an incident ticket is created and how subsequent state transitions (effects) are achieved by the (human) agent assigned to the incident ticket, till the ticket is closed. Our intention is to determine whether these instances are goal aligned, which of these are variants of each other and the contextual factors that guide the choice of a variant (many of these instances conform to the process design in Fig. 1). The organizational goal model is depicted in Fig. 2.

The evaluations is done on a 64 bit Windows 7 machine with Intel Celeron @ 1.07 Ghz, 4 GB RAM on which the VAGAI tool was executed. For our evaluation, we have borrowed the same terminology that have been used in the event records for annotating the goal model and process model using our tool as illustrated in Fig. 1. The terminology based on a well known standard called Common Information Model (CIM)[1]. This enables leveraging the VAGAI tool to evaluate goal correlation for each process instance(containing set of state transitions) with the annotated goal model depicted in Fig. 2.

---

[1] dmtf.org/standards/cim

First, we start with evaluating the generation of PIGA with a sample set of process instances from the running example. In Table 1, we observe that the process instance INS0001 helps achieve three distinct goals ("Detect Problem", "Fix Problem", "Verify Problem") with three corresponding goal-realizing effect groups GR1, GR2 and GR3 respectively. Each group correlates with one of the mandatory sub-goals in the goal model in Fig. 2. Therefore, INS0001 is a valid goal preserving process instance of Fig. 1 as it satisfies the conditions C1 and C2. Similarly, the instance INS0096 associated with groups GR1, GR7,GR10 is also a valid process instance. However, unlike INS0096, INS0001 is a variant realization of process design in Fig. 1 as the groups GR2, GR3 are alternate realizations of goals Fix Problem and Verify Problem respectively. Now let us look at some examples of invalid process instances such as INS0015 and INS0024. Even though in these instances, logically the tickets are closed, there is no entailment of both the mandatory sub-goals Fix Problem, Verify Problem. Similarly the instances INS0033, INS0066 are not valid instances as they don not entail the goal Verify Problem. The verification of fix was not performed in these instance. Instances such as these were false positives, that were declared as correct execution in the manual auditing of process executions, as the tickets were actually termed as closed.

Let us compare the process instances INS0001 and INS0034 in Table 1. By observing their correlation groups alignment to mandatory sub-goals, we establish that both are valid process instances that adhere to the root goal in 2. We can obviously infer that these two instances are not executed similarly. In the case of INS0001, the identified solution is locally applied by the support executive and only confirmed by the user. But in the case of INS0034, given the nature of the customer system, the customer is instructed to follow the guidelines to apply the fix and fixing is subsequently confirmed. These two are two different realizations of the goal and belong to two categories (Remote fix, Local fix with guidance) of process variations. We establish that the instance INS0001 is a derived variant of the instance INS0034.

The tool runs in an iterative mode to evaluate all the 1400 process instances given in the process log for goal alignment. The generated PIGA for all the 1562 event instances contains a total of 74 goal-realizing effect groups. Out of which, 55 groups were correlating with a mandatory sub-goal from the goal model depicted in Fig. 2. This resulted in only 681 instances being categorized as valid instances out of the total set. The remaining instances were termed as invalid as they do not correlate all the mandatory goals.

Subsequent to the categorization of valid process instances into different data sets, we proceed to identify context factors that can be associated with each category. For this, we transformed the free text ticket description and summary fields into high frequency parse tokens leveraging the tool discussed in [21]. We restricted the number of such tokens associated with each state transition to a maximum of 5. When a maximally refined correlation group is constructed, we extract the high frequency tokens from individual records and associate with the group. For each event group, the contextual factors with maximum

Table 1. Process Instance Goal Alignment

Event Groups	State Transitions	Instance ID	Goal
GR1	(Start,Open Notification, Ticket Opened, Acknowledge Notification, Investigation Started)	INS0001,INS0015, INS0034,INS0066, INS0096	Detect Problem
GR2	(Tech Note Identified, Solution Identified, Fixing Started, Pending Customer, Incorrect Solution, Tech Note Identified, Solution Identified, Fixing Started, Pending Customer)	INS0001	Fix Problem
GR3	(Service Restored, Ticket Closed)	INS0001	Verify Problem
GR4	(Start,Open Notification Not Sent, System Alerted, Notification Sent, Ticket Opened, Acknowledge Notification, Investigation Started, Problem Identified)	INS0024	Detect Problem
GR6	(Start, Open Notification Not Sent, System Alerted, Notification Sent, Ticket Opened, Acknowledge Notification, Investigation Started, Problem Identified)	INS0033	Detect Problem
GR7	(Tech Note Identified, Solution Identified, Fixing Started, Problem Fixed)	INS0033,INS0066, INS0096	Fix Problem
GR9	(Reassigned-Additional Work, Solution Identified, Customer Notified)	INS0034	Fix Problem
GR10	Customer Confirmed, Ticket Closed	INS0034,INS0096	Verify Problem

support and confidence is associated. As we observe in Table 2, most of customer self-help fixes have been contributed by remote system connection issues. Also issues due to third party software have been raised taking considerable effort in diagnosing and closing the problem. Most of the escalation issues have been contributed by either wrong email addresses or wrong ticket assignments. For the instance INS0034, we can identify that Email Notification, Remote Connection Issues and Manual Solution Fix are the associated contextual factors. We can infer that the factors Remote Connection Issues and Manual Solution Fix leads to adherence of goal Fix Problem. Such observations can eventually lead to augmenting the current goal model with creating additional OR-Refinement child goals for the goal Fix Problem.

We discuss the generalization of our approach and the threats to its validity as follows. Firstly, we expect that the semantic annotations of process models, goal models in terms of the end effects are precisely applied for any given domain. We demonstrated this in our prototype implementation, by leveraging standard property fields associated with the tasks or goals to specify the annotations. Secondly, the validation of goal alignment is two staged, one between the process model and goal model, the other between the goal model and state transition groups from mined process instances. In our tool, we subject the process model and goal model to a basic level of validation for completeness and correctness in terms of the specified annotations.This is basically to validate whether a given goal model is the right candidate for validating a larger data set of process

Table 2. Categorization of variant instances based on goal alignment

Goal Aligned Groups	Category	Associated Variant Instances	Contextual factor		
			Name	Max.Support	Max. Confidence
5	Customer Self-Fix	62	Remote Connection Issues	.07	.9
20	Execute Diagnostic Fix	155	Known Solution, Email Sent	.08	1.0
9	Discard Incidents	11	Third party Vendor Issues	.09	0.9
10	Define New Problems	51	Event Trace Missing	.07	.8
1	Escalate Problem	10	Wrong Ticket Assignment	.009	0.6
6	Enrich Existing Problem	5	Additional Diagnostics	.05	0.7
4	Pending Closer	31	Wrong Email Note	0.06	.9

instance records. Our approach in this aspect is generalized and is not restrictive to process models or goal models of any scale or any domain. This is clearly demonstrated with the scale of our case study involving 1400 process instances. Therefore, we argue that the threat to its validity (both construct and internal) in terms of systematic errors or data measurement is minimal. The only limitation we foresee is by leveraging our approach with incompletely annotated goal model or not using a valid semantic matching tool. But ensuring the completeness of annotations and correctness of matching can help address this limitation by establish correct correlation between a goal model and process instance.

5   Related Work

The area of process mining leverages data mining techniques on one hand, and process modeling and analysis techniques on the other hand [27]. The existing works in the area of process mining have efficiently focused on the data mining aspects [3,26] such as control flow discovery, process artifact evolution and model conformance. In comparison, we focus on concept and goal conformance drift that arises with evolutionary changes in process executions. [20] discusses techniques for extracting categories from process model repositories. In [5], a configurable process model as a family of process variants is discovered from a collection of event logs. Approaches for process variability support at design time, such as Provop [13], focus on managing large collections of process variants of a single process model. In comparison, in our proposed approach, we validate and categorize the discovered family of variants with the underpinning of goal model. Our approach can leverage works such as [17] that focus on enriching process designs with goal driven configurations. This is a crucial aspect in knowledge-intensive processes, where there can be significant drift from valid(goal aligned) work flows due to manual errors and environmental constraints. [18] focus on alignments to generate a well-defined classification problem per decision point. In contrast, we leverage the goal model and its OR-refinement decomposition to generate categories of process deviations before hand and associate case instances mined from event logs to one of these categories. Works such as [23] propose techniques, where the mined event correlations from instances are utilized to construct a common reference model. Our approach compliments such work to derive event correlation groups that are aligned to the goal decomposition model. In addition, we also augment different OR-refinement sub goals through correlation and provide goal driven assessment of differentiation between the variant models derived from the common process model. Our proposed approach leverage and compliment work on goal annotated process modeling [2] by extending the notion of goal entailment through semantic end effect annotations and subsequent correlation. In [16], the authors propose the use of probabilistic models for discovering the intentions behind the execution traces and to compare them to the prescribed intentional process model. We focus on a different category of process models which are mostly user knowledge driven but subscribe to a well defined process model with predefined decision points. In [19], the authors clearly establish the need for a general framework for mining and correlating business process characteristics from event logs. Our proposed work subscribe to such a notion and propose goal alignment to provide additional reasoning on process characteristics. In [1], the authors thoroughly analyze various process variability approaches and our proposed approach compliments such frameworks for successful validation and reasoning for generation of different process variants.

6   Conclusion

Organizations increasingly tend to analyze the adherence of the day to day execution of internal business processes with their stated goals. The emergence of Knowledge-intensive processes have enabled dynamic adaptations to process execution, but also contributed to arising challenges of non-conformance and misalignment to organization goals and strategies. In this paper, we have proposed a goal oriented process variability mining and categorization approach. This bottom-up approach enables the organizations to study the depth and breadth of goal adherence in their organizations. In our future work, we would like to study the impact of any proposed change in the goal decomposition model on process execution based on the PIGA model and also focus on goal augmentation based on instance variants.

References

1. Ayora, C., Torres, V., Weber, B., Reichert, M., Pelechano, V.: Vivace: A framework for the systematic evaluation of variability support in process-aware information systems. Information and Software Technology **57**, 248–276 (2015)

2. Becker, J., Pfeiffer, D., Räckers, M., Falk, T., Czerwonka, M.: Semantic business process modelling and analysis. In: Handbook on Business Process Management 1, pp. 187–217. Springer (2015)
3. Beheshti, S.-M.-R., Benatallah, B., Motahari-Nezhad, H.R.: Enabling the analysis of cross-cutting aspects in ad-hoc processes. In: Salinesi, C., Norrie, M.C., Pastor, Ó. (eds.) CAiSE 2013. LNCS, vol. 7908, pp. 51–67. Springer, Heidelberg (2013). http://dx.doi.org/10.1007/978-3-642-38709-8_4
4. Borici, A., Thomo, A.: Semantic graph compression with hypergraphs. In: 2014 IEEE 28th International Conference on Advanced Information Networking and Applications (AINA), pp. 1097–1104. IEEE (2014)
5. Buijs, J.C.A.M., van Dongen, B.F., van der Aalst, W.M.P.: Mining configurable process models from collections of event logs. In: Daniel, F., Wang, J., Weber, B. (eds.) BPM 2013. LNCS, vol. 8094, pp. 33–48. Springer, Heidelberg (2013)
6. Czarnecki, K., Grünbacher, P., Rabiser, R., Schmid, K., sowski, A.: Cool features and tough decisions: a comparison of variability modeling approaches. In: Proceedings of the Sixth International Workshop on Variability Modeling of Software-Intensive Systems, pp. 173–182. ACM (2012)
7. Di Ciccio, C., Marrella, A., Russo, A.: Knowledge-intensive processes: Characteristics, requirements and analysis of contemporary approaches. Journal on Data Semantics, 1–29 (2014)
8. Dreiling, A., Recker, J.C.: Towards a theoretical framework for organizational innovation. In: Proceedings of the 17th Pacific Asia Conference on Information Systems. Association for Information Systems (2013)
9. Dumas, M., La Rosa, M., Mendling, J., Reijers, H.A.: Fundamentals of business process management. Springer, Berlin (2013)
10. Ghose, A.K., Narendra, N.C., Ponnalagu, K., Panda, A., Gohad, A.: Goal-driven business process derivation. In: Kappel, G., Maamar, Z., Motahari-Nezhad, H.R. (eds.) Service Oriented Computing. LNCS, vol. 7084, pp. 467–476. Springer, Heidelberg (2011)
11. Ginsberg, M.L., Smith, D.E.: Reasoning about action i: A possible worlds approach. Artificial Intelligence **35**(2), 165–195 (1988)
12. Hallerbach, A., Bauer, T., Reichert, M.: Capturing variability in business process models: the provop approach. Journal of Software Maintenance and Evolution: Research and Practice **22**(6–7), 519–546 (2010)
13. Hallerbach, A., Bauer, T., Reichert, M.: Capturing variability in business process models: the provop approach. J. Softw. Maint. Evol. **22**, 519–546 (2010). http://dx.doi.org/10.1002/smr.v22:6/7
14. Heath, D., Singh, R., Shephard, B.: Approaching strategic misalignment from an organizational view of business processes. In: 2013 46th Hawaii International Conference on System Sciences (HICSS), pp. 4055–4064. IEEE (2013)
15. Carbonell, J.: Context-based machine translation. In: Proceedings of the 7th Conference of the Association for Machine Translation in the Americas, pp. 19–28 (2006)
16. Khodabandelou, G., Hug, C., Deneckere, R., Salinesi, C.: Supervised intentional process models discovery using hidden markov models. In: 2013 IEEE Seventh International Conference on Research Challenges in Information Science (RCIS), pp. 1–11. IEEE (2013)
17. Lapouchnian, A., Yu, Y., Mylopoulos, J.: Requirements-driven design and configuration management of business processes. In: Alonso, G., Dadam, P., Rosemann, M. (eds.) BPM 2007. LNCS, vol. 4714, pp. 246–261. Springer, Heidelberg (2007). http://dx.doi.org/10.1007/978-3-540-75183-0_18

18. de Leoni, M., van der Aalst, W.M.: Data-aware process mining: discovering decisions in processes using alignments. In: Proceedings of the 28th annual ACM symposium on applied computing, pp. 1454–1461. ACM (2013)

19. de Leoni, M., van der Aalst, W.M.P., Dees, M.: A general framework for correlating business process characteristics. In: Sadiq, S., Soffer, P., Völzer, H. (eds.) BPM 2014. LNCS, vol. 8659, pp. 250–266. Springer, Heidelberg (2014)

20. Malinova, M., Dijkman, R., Mendling, J.: Automatic extraction of process categories from process model collections. In: Lohmann, N., Song, M., Wohed, P. (eds.) BPM 2013 Workshops. LNBIP, vol. 171, pp. 430–441. Springer, Heidelberg (2014)

21. Mani, S., Sankaranarayanan, K., Sinha, V.S., Devanbu, P.T.: Panning requirement nuggets in stream of software maintenance tickets. In: Proceedings of the 22nd ACM SIGSOFT International Symposium on Foundations of Software Engineering, (FSE-22), pp. 678–688 (2014)

22. Messai, N., Bouaud, J., Aufaure, M.-A., Zelek, L., Séroussi, B.: Using formal concept analysis to discover patterns of non-compliance with clinical practice guidelines: a case study in the management of breast cancer. In: Peleg, M., Lavrač, N., Combi, C. (eds.) AIME 2011. LNCS, vol. 6747, pp. 119–128. Springer, Heidelberg (2011)

23. Motahari-Nezhad, H., Saint-Paul, R., Casati, F., Benatallah, B.: Event correlation for process discovery from web service interaction logs. The VLDB Journal **20**(3), 417–444 (2011). http://dx.doi.org/10.1007/s00778-010-0203-9

24. Ponnalagu, K., Narendra, N.C., Ghose, A., Chiktey, N., Tamilselvam, S.: Goal oriented variability modeling in service-based business processes. In: Basu, S., Pautasso, C., Zhang, L., Fu, X. (eds.) ICSOC 2013. LNCS, vol. 8274, pp. 499–506. Springer, Heidelberg (2013)

25. Reichert, M., Hallerbach, A., Bauer, T.: Lifecycle management of business process variants. In: Handbook on Business Process Management 1, pp. 251–278. Springer (2015)

26. van der Aalst, W., Adriansyah, A., de Medeiros, A.K.A., Arcieri, F., Baier, T., Blickle, T., Bose, J.C., van den Brand, P., et al.: Process mining manifesto. In: Daniel, F., Barkaoui, K., Dustdar, S. (eds.) BPM Workshops 2011, Part I. LNBIP, vol. 99, pp. 169–194. Springer, Heidelberg (2012)

27. Van Der Aalst, W.M., Weske, M.: To interorganizational workflows. Seminal Contributions to Information Systems Engineering: 25 Years of CAiSE, p. 289 (2013)

28. Weber, B., Zeitelhofer, S., Pinggera, J., Torres, V., Reichert, M.: How advanced change patterns impact the process of process modeling. In: Bider, I., Gaaloul, K., Krogstie, J., Nurcan, S., Proper, H.A., Schmidt, R., Soffer, P. (eds.) BPMDS 2014 and EMMSAD 2014. LNBIP, vol. 175, pp. 17–32. Springer, Heidelberg (2014)

29. Winslett, M.: Reasoning about action using a possible models approach. Urbana **51**, 61801 (1988)

Process Monitoring

Process Mining on Databases: Unearthing Historical Data from Redo Logs

Eduardo González López de Murillas[1,2(✉)], Wil M.P. van der Aalst[1], and Hajo A. Reijers[1]

[1] Department of Mathematics and Computer Science, Eindhoven University of Technology, P.O. Box 513, 5600 MB Eindhoven, The Netherlands
{e.gonzalez,w.m.p.v.d.aalst,h.a.reijers}@tue.nl
[2] Lexmark Enterprise Software, Gooimeer 12, 1411DE Naarden, The Netherlands

Abstract. Process Mining techniques rely on the existence of event data. However, in many cases it is far from trivial to obtain such event data. Considerable efforts may need to be spent on making IT systems record historic data at all. But even if such records are available, it may not be possible to derive an event log for the case notion one is interested in, i.e., correlating events to form process instances may be challenging. This paper proposes an approach that exploits a commonly available and versatile source of data, i.e. *database redo logs*. Such logs record the writing operations performed in a general-purpose database for a range of objects, which constitute a collection of *events*. By using the relations between objects as specified in the associated data model, it is possible to turn such events into an event log for a wide range of case types. The resulting logs can be analyzed using existing process mining techniques.

Keywords: Process mining · Database · Redo log · Historical data · Trace creation · Transitive relations · Data model

1 Introduction

Process mining heavily depends on event data. But to get proper data, it is either necessary (i) to build a customized storage facility oneself or (ii) to rely on data that is already stored by existing IT systems. The former approach requires extensive knowledge of the application domain and a potentially hybrid technology landscape to create a facility that records all possible events that are related to a pre-defined notion of a case. This is potentially costly and not very flexible.

The second approach requires the transformation of available data – which is not specifically stored for process mining purposes – into an event log. Approaches exist to accomplish this for the data stored in and generated by SAP systems [6,13,14], EDI messages [4], and ERP databases in general [16]. Some efforts for generalization have been made here, as can be seen in [15]: XESame is a tool that allows transforming database records into events, traces

© Springer International Publishing Switzerland 2015
H.R. Motahari-Nezhad et al. (Eds.): BPM 2015, LNCS 9253, pp. 367–385, 2015.
DOI: 10.1007/978-3-319-23063-4_25

and logs, prior definition of the mappings between database elements and log concepts like timestamp, case, activity and resource. Nonetheless, the drawback of these approaches is that they are restricted to the specific IT system or data format that they are developed for.

Artifact-centric approaches are more generic and also fit within the second strategy [3,5,8–11]. These techniques provide a way to get insights into the contents of a database, showing the life-cycle of objects without presenting *data convergence* (one event is related to multiple cases) and *data divergence* (several events of the same type are related to a single case) issues, as happens in classical log extraction. However, both issues are not fully solved in the artifact field. In fact, one could argue that the key problems are evaded by restricting the contents of a single artifact, in order to avoid data divergence, and hiding data convergence in the discovered relations between them.

The technique explained in this paper, based on the ideas introduced in [1], also relies on the use of existing data. However, it exploits so-called *redo logs* that several Data Base Management Systems (DBMSs), like Oracle RDBMS and MySQL, maintain for data integrity and recovery reasons. This source of data has the potential to create a full historic view on what has happened during the handling a wide range of data objects. Note that by simply looking at the regular content of a DBMS, one cannot see which events led to its current state. Fortunately, redo logs provide an opportunity to learn about the historical evolution of data on the basis of a generic-purpose data source, exactly tuned to the purpose of the process mining analysis one wishes to perform.

Redo logs already contain a list of events, but the challenge is how to correlate these events to create the traces one is interested in. In this paper, we explain how to create a trace on the basis of a configurable concept of a case (i.e. the process instance), exploiting the relations expressed in the data model of the DBMS in question. The result is a log which represents a specific point of view on the objects in the database, including the stages of their historical evolution and the causal relations between them.

The analysis technique presented in this paper can be used, whenever redo logs are available, as an alternative to building a specific recording facility. The approach is also generic, in the sense that it can be used to extract data from a technology that is used by a wide variety of organizations. Additionally, it is a viable alternative for artifact-centric approaches, since it allows for a much richer behavior discovery due its incorporation of the data model to infer causal relations between events. Finally, the nature of the extracted logs (events with unique IDs and availability of data schemas) opens the door to developing new discovery techniques that could exploit the additional information that databases provide, in order to solve data convergence and divergence issues.

The paper is structured as follows. Section 2 presents a walkthrough of the approach on a simple example to explain the various phases of creating an event log. Section 3 provides the formalization of the important concepts that this work builds upon. Section 4 describes the tool that implements these concepts to generate an event log. Section 5 provides an example case to show how the technique can be flexibly applied to solve a range of business questions. Finally, Section 6 presents the conclusion and future work.

2 Walkthrough

The aim of this work is to analyze database redo logs, which can be seen as a list of modifications performed on the database content, so that we use these to generate event logs. These event logs will be used to perform process mining analyses like process discovery, conformance checking, and process enhancement. To explain the idea of redo log analysis, a step by step walk-through using a simple case is performed in this section.

Let us consider as an example a database that stores information on a portal for selling concert tickets. At this point, we will focus on three tables only: *customer*, *booking*, and *ticket*. These tables contain information about the customers of the portal, the bookings made by these customers, and the tickets being booked by them.

2.1 Event Extraction

An example of a fragment of a redo log is shown in Table 1. This fragment contains six changes made to the records of the three tables. Each of these events indicates (a) the time at which it occurred, (b) the operation performed and on which table this was done, (c) an SQL sentence to redo the change, and (d) another SQL sentence to undo it. We claim that these basic fields provide enough information to reconstruct the state of the database at any intermediate stage. Also, they allow us to perform an in-depth analysis to detect patterns on the behavior of the process or processes that rely on the support by this database.

The first thing we need to do is to transform each of the records in the redo log in Table 1 to an event that we can manipulate. To do so, it is necessary to split the contents of redo and undo sentences into different attributes. Table 2 shows the attributes for each event extracted from the *redo* and *undo* columns in Table 1. The rows with the symbol = for "Value after event" indicate that the value for an "Attribute name" did not change after the event. Also, the values between braces {} in the "Value before event" column were extracted not from the present event but from previous ones. This is, for instance, the case in the second event: It is an update on the name of the customer, the record of which was already inserted in the first event in the table. Finally, the values between parentheses () identify the ones that could not be extracted directly from the redo log, but only from the database content itself. This is because those columns were not modified in that event, as is the case in events 4 and 6, where only the field "ticket:booking_id" is updated. Therefore, the other values remain equal and it is not necessary to specify them in the *redo* and *undo* sentences. It is still necessary to identify on which row of the database the change must be applied. To do so, the redo log system provides a *RowID* identifier to find it. In addition to

Table 1. Fragment of a redo log: each line corresponds to the occurrence of an event

#	Time + Op + Table	Redo	Undo
1	2014-11-27 15:57:08.0 + INSERT + CUSTOMER	insert into "SAMPLEDB". "CUSTOMER" ("ID", "NAME", "ADDRESS", "BIRTH_DATE") values ('17299', 'Name1', 'Address1', TO_DATE('01-AUG-06', 'DD-MON-RR'));	delete from "SAMPLEDB". "CUSTOMER" where "ID" = '17299' and "NAME" = 'Name1' and "ADDRESS" = 'Address1' and "BIRTH_DATE" = TO_DATE('01-AUG-06', 'DD-MON-RR') and ROWID = '1';
2	2014-11-27 16:07:02.0 + UPDATE + CUSTOMER	update "SAMPLEDB". "CUSTOMER" set "NAME" = 'Name2' where "NAME" = 'Name1' and ROWID = '1';	update "SAMPLEDB". "CUSTOMER" set "NAME" = 'Name1' where "NAME" = 'Name2' and ROWID = '1';
3	2014-11-27 16:07:16.0 + INSERT + BOOKING	insert into "SAMPLEDB". "BOOKING" ("ID", "CUSTOMER_ID") values ('36846', '17299');	delete from "SAMPLEDB". "BOOKING" where "ID" = '36846' and "CUSTOMER_ID" = '17299' and ROWID = '2';
4	2014-11-27 16:07:16.0 + UPDATE+ TICKET	update "SAMPLEDB". "TICKET" set "BOOKING_ID" = '36846' where "BOOKING_ID" IS NULL and ROWID = '3';	update "SAMPLEDB". "TICKET" set "BOOKING_ID" = NULL where "BOOKING_ID" = '36846' and ROWID = '3';
5	2014-11-27 16:07:17.0 + INSERT + BOOKING	insert into "SAMPLEDB". "BOOKING" ("ID", "CUSTOMER_ID") values ('36876', '17299');	delete from "SAMPLEDB". "BOOKING" where "ID" = '36876' and "CUSTOMER_ID" = '17299' and ROWID = '4';
6	2014-11-27 16:07:17.0 + TICKET + UPDATE	update "SAMPLEDB". "TICKET" set "ID" = '36876' where "BOOKING_ID" IS NULL and ROWID = '5';	update "SAMPLEDB". "TICKET" set "ID" = NULL where "BOOKING_ID" = '36876' and ROWID = '5';

it, an extra column C has been added, which encodes a numeric vector for each event representing which columns had its value (1) not modified, (2) changed from a value to NULL, (3) from NULL to a value or (4) inserted/updated.

2.2 Exploiting the Data Model

After extracting the events from the redo log, the next step required is to obtain the data model from the database. This will be a main ingredient used to correlate events. Finding these correlations will tell us which sets of events can be grouped into traces to finally build an event log. Obtaining the data model involves querying the tables, columns, and keys defined in the database schema. Figure 1 shows the extracted data model. For the selected tables *customer*, *booking* and *ticket*, we see that two key relations exist between them: (a) *(booking_customer_fk, customer_pk)* and (b) *(ticket_booking_fk, booking_pk)*. This means that we must use the first pair of keys (a) to correlate *customer* and

Table 2. Fragment of a redo log: each line corresponds to the occurrence of an event

#	Attribute name	Value after event	Value before event	C
1	Customer:id	17299	-	4
	Customer:name	Name1	-	4
	Customer:address	Address1	-	4
	Customer:birth_date	01-AUG-06	-	4
	RowID	=	1	-
2	Customer:id	=	{17299}	1
	Customer:name	Name2	Name1	4
	Customer:address	=	{Address1}	1
	Customer:birth_date	=	{01-AUG-06}	1
	RowID	=	1	-
3	Booking:id	36846	-	4
	Booking:customer_id	17299	-	4
	RowID	=	2	-
4	Ticket:booking_id	36846	NULL	3
	Ticket:id	=	(317132)	1
	Ticket:belongs_to	=	(172935)	1
	Ticket:for_concert	=	(1277)	1
	RowID	=	3	-
5	Booking:id	36876	-	4
	Booking:customer_id	17299	-	4
	RowID	=	4	-
6	Ticket:booking_id	36876	NULL	3
	Ticket:id	=	(317435)	1
	Ticket:belongs_to	=	(173238)	1
	Ticket:for_concert	=	(1277)	1
	RowID	=	5	-

booking events, and the second pair of keys (b) to correlate *booking* and *ticket*
events. Both pairs (a) and (b) must be used to correlate the events of the three
tables.

When using pairs of primary and foreign keys, we can consider the attributes
referred by them as *equivalent* for our purposes, i.e. relating to the same event.
We will do so to actually relate events that belong to different tables, but use
different column names (attributes in the events) to store the same values. Therefore, attributes *customer:id* and *booking:customer_id* are considered to be equivalent, and the same can be said of the pair *booking:id* and *ticket:booking_id*. Then,
using these equivalences and observing the *value after event* column in Table 2,
we see that every event is related to at least one other event by means of some
attribute value. That is the case, for instance, for events 1 and 2, given that
they share the same value for the attribute *customer:id*. Also, event 3 is related
to events 1, 2 and 5, sharing the same value for the attributes *customer:id* and
booking:customer_id, and to event 4, sharing the same value for the attributes
booking:id and *ticket:booking_id*. Event 6 is related to event 5 by means of the
attributes *booking:id* and *ticket:booking_id* as well. A graph in which events are

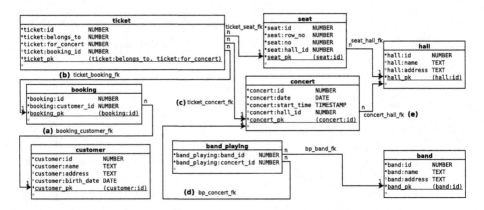

Fig. 1. Database schema for the *Ticket selling* example.

(a) Connected graph of related events.   (b) Graphs for the two final traces.

Fig. 2. Traces as graphs of related events (events e1 to e6 refer to Table 2.

the vertexes and edges show relations between them would look like the one in Figure 2a. This graph helps to understand the structure of a trace we wish to extract. What needs to be taken care of still is that it contains events of two *different* ticket bookings (events 3-4 and events 5-6), which is behavior that we would like to see separately.

2.3   Process Instance Identification

To decide which events go into which traces, it is necessary to define which view is desired to obtain on a process. In this case, let us assume that it is interesting to see how tickets are booked by customers. Using relations Fig 1.a and Fig 1.b, we can say that individual traces should contain behavior for the same user, booking and ticket: our *case* notion. Applying that notion, we see that events 1 and 2 point to a single customer. Events 3 and 4 point to a single pair of booking and ticket, and still relate to the customer of events 1 and 2. However, events 5 and 6 represent a different pair of booking-ticket but do relate to the customer in events 1 and 2. Therefore, this leads to two separated but not disjoint graphs in which events 1 and 2 are common, as observed in Figure 2b. Each of these graphs represent the structure of a trace for a separate case in our event log.

From the initial change log $CL = \langle e1, e2, e3, e4, e5, e6 \rangle$ we obtain two traces $t1 = (e1, e2, e3, e4)$ and $t2 = (e1, e2, e5, e6)$ following the above reasoning. In this case, applying a discovery algorithm to these two traces will result in a very simple sequential model. In Section 5, we will present samples of questions and answers to understand the process extending the same technique to a more extensive dataset and choosing different views on the data. This way we can find patterns and obtain interesting insights regarding the observed behavior. What follows now is the formal basis that precisely captures the ideas discussed so far.

3   Formalizations

The basic idea to use redo logs for the creation of an event log has been introduced in the previous section. This section provides a formal description of the underlying notions. Some of the notation used in this part originate from [1]. First, we need to define the *data model*.

Definition 1 (Data Model). *Assume V to be some universe of values. A data model is a tuple $DM = (C, A, classAttr, val, PK, FK, keyClass, keyRel, keyAttr, refAttr)$ such that*
  - *C is a set of class names,*
  - *A is a set of attribute names,*
  - *$classAttr \in C \rightarrow \mathcal{P}(A)$ is a function mapping each class onto a set of attribute names. A_c is a shorthand denoting the set of attributes of class $c \in C$, i.e., $A_c = classAttr(c)$,*
  - *$val \in A \rightarrow \mathcal{P}(V)$ is a function mapping each attribute onto a set of values. $V_a = val(a)$ is a shorthand denoting the set of possible values of attribute $a \in A$,*
  - *PK is a set of primary key names,*
  - *FK is a set of foreign key names,*
  - *PK and FK are disjoint sets, that is $PK \cap FK = \emptyset$. To facilitate further definitions, the shorthand K is introduced, which represents the set of all keys: $K = PK \cup FK$,*
  - *$keyClass \in K \rightarrow C$ is a function mapping each key name to a class. K_c is a shorthand denoting the set of keys of class $c \in C$ such that $K_c = \{k \in K \mid keyClass(k) = c\}$,*
  - *$keyRel \in FK \rightarrow PK$ is a function mapping each foreign key onto a primary key,*
  - *$keyAttr \in K \rightarrow \mathcal{P}(A)$ is a function mapping each key onto a set of attributes, such that $\forall k \in K : keyAttr(k) \subseteq A_{keyClass(k)}$,*
  - *$refAttr \in FK \times A \nrightarrow A$ is a function mapping each pair of a foreign key and an attribute onto an attribute from the corresponding primary key. That is, $\forall k \in FK : \forall a, a' \in keyAttr(k) : (refAttr(k, a) \in keyAttr(keyRel(k)) \wedge (refAttr(k, a) = refAttr(k, a') \implies a = a')$.*

Definition 2 (Notations). *Let $DM = (C, A, classAttr, val, PK, FK, keyClass, keyRel, keyAttr, refAttr)$ be a data model.*
  - *$M^{DM} = \{map \in A \nrightarrow V \mid \forall a \in dom(map) : map(a) \in V_a\}$ is the set of mappings,*

- $O^{DM} = \{(c, map) \in C \times M^{DM} \mid dom\,(map) = classAttr\,(c)\}$ *is the set of all possible objects of DM.*

A data model defines the structure of objects in a database. Such objects can belong to different classes and varied relations can exist between them. A collection of possible objects constitutes an *object model*.

Definition 3 (Object Model). *Let DM = (C, A, classAttr, val, PK, FK, keyClass, keyRel, keyAttr, refAttr) be a data model. An object model of DM is a set $OM \subseteq O^{DM}$ of objects. $\mathcal{U}^{OM}\,(DM) = \mathcal{P}\,(O^{DM})$ is the set of all object models of CM.*

The objects in an *object model* must have a specific structure according to a certain *data model*. Also, some rules apply to ensure that the *object model* respects the rules stated by the *data model*. This is covered by the notion of a *valid object model*.

Definition 4 (Valid Object Model). *Let DM = (C, A, classAttr, val, PK, FK, keyClass, keyRel, keyAttr, refAttr) be a data model. $VOM \subseteq \mathcal{U}^{OM}\,(DM)$ is the set of valid object models. We say that $OM \in VOM$ if the following requirements hold:*

- $\forall (c, map) \in OM : (\forall k \in K_c \cap FK : (\exists (c', map') \in OM :$
  $keyClass(keyRel(k)) = c' \wedge (\forall a \in keyAttr(k) :$
  $map(a) = map'(refAttr(k, a)))))$, *i.e., referenced objects must exist,*
- $\forall (c, map), (c, map') \in OM : (\forall k \in K_c \cap PK : ((\forall a \in keyAttr(k) :$
  $map(a) = map'(a)) \implies map = map'))$, *i.e., PK and UK values must be unique.*

Different vendors offer *DataBase Management Systems* (DBMSs) like Oracle RDBMS, Microsoft's SQL server, MySQL, etc. All of them allow to store *objects* according to a specific *data model*. The work of this paper focuses on the analysis of redo logs, being conceptually independent of the specific implementation. These redo logs can contain information about changes done either on the data or the structure of the database. We will focus here on the changes *on data*, which include insertions of new objects, updates of objects, and deletions. Each of these changes represent an event, which has a type (Definition 5) and mappings for the value of objects before and after the change (Definition 6). Also, the combination of an event and a specific time stamp represents an *event occurrence* (Definition 7).

Definition 5 (Event Types). *Let DM = (C, A, classAttr, val, PK, FK, keyClass, keyRel, keyAttr, refAttr) be a data model and VOM the set of valid object models. $ET = ET_{add} \cup ET_{upd} \cup ET_{del}$ is the set of event types composed of the following pairwise disjoint sets:*

- $ET_{add} = \{(\oplus, c) \mid c \in C\}$ *are the event types for adding objects,*
- $ET_{upd} = \{(\oslash, c) \mid c \in C\}$ *are the event types for updating objects,*
- $ET_{del} = \{(\ominus, c) \mid c \in C\}$ *are the event types for deleting objects.*

Definition 6 (Events). *Let $DM = (C, A, classAttr, val, PK, FK, keyClass, keyRel, keyAttr, refAttr)$ be a data model, VOM the set of valid object models and $map_{null} \in \{\emptyset\} \to V$ a function with the empty set as domain. $E = E_{add} \cup E_{upd} \cup E_{del}$ is the set of events composed of the following pairwise disjoint sets:*

- *$E_{add} = \{((\oplus, c), map_{old}, map_{new})) \mid (c, map_{new}) \in O^{DM} \land map_{old} = map_{null}\}$*
- *$E_{upd} = \{((\oslash, c), map_{old}, map_{new})) \mid (c, map_{old}) \in O^{DM} \land (c, map_{new}) \in O^{DM}\}$*
- *$E_{del} = \{((\ominus, c), map_{old}, map_{new})) \mid (c, map_{old}) \in O^{DM} \land map_{new} = map_{null}\}$*

Definition 7 (Event Occurrence, Change Log). *Let $DM = (C, A, classAttr, val, PK, FK, keyClass, keyRel, keyAttr, refAttr)$ be a data model, VOM the set of valid object models and E the set of events. Assume some universe of timestamps TS. $eo = (e, ts) \in E \times TS$ is an event occurrence. $EO(DM, E) = E \times TS$ is the set of all possible event occurrences. A change log $CL = \langle eo_1, eo_2, ..., eo_n \rangle$ is a sequence of event occurrences such that time is non-decreasing, i.e., $CL = \langle eo_1, eo_2, ..., eo_n \rangle \in (EO(DM, E))^*$ and $ts_i \leq ts_j$ for any $eo_i = (e_i, ts_i)$ and $eo_j = (e_j, ts_j)$ with $1 \leq i < j \leq n$.*

Definition 8 (Effect of an Event). *Let $DM = (C, A, classAttr, val, PK, FK, keyClass, keyRel, keyAttr, refAttr)$ be a data model, VOM the set of valid object models and E the set of events. For any two object models $OM_1 \in VOM$ and $OM_2 \in VOM$ and event occurrence $eo = (((op, c), map_{old}, map_{new}), ts) \in EO(DM, E)$, we denote $OM_1 \overset{eo}{\to} OM_2$ if and only if $OM_2 = \{(d, map) \in OM_1 \mid map \neq map_{old} \lor op = \oplus\} \cup \{(c, map_{new}) \mid op \neq \ominus\}$.*

Event e is permissible in object model OM, notation $OM \overset{e}{\to}$, if and only if there exists an OM' such that $OM \overset{e}{\to} OM'$. If this is not the case, we denote $OM \overset{e}{\not\to}$, i.e., e is not permissible in OM. If an event is not permissible, it will fail and the object model will remain unchanged. Relation $\overset{e}{\Rightarrow}$ denotes the effect of event e. It is the smallest relation such that (a) $OM \overset{e}{\Rightarrow} OM'$ if $OM \overset{e}{\to} OM'$ and (b) $OM \overset{e}{\Rightarrow} OM$ if $OM \overset{e}{\not\to}$.

When, in Definition 8, we say that $OM_1 \overset{eo}{\to} OM_2$, it means that OM_2 must contain (1) all the objects in OM_1 except the one that the event occurrence eo refers to, and (2), the object inserted if eo is an insertion or the modified object if it is an update. If eo is a deletion, the object is not included in OM_2.

Definition 9 (Effect of a Change Log). *Let $DM = (C, A, classAttr, val, PK, FK, keyClass, keyAttr, refAttr)$ be a data model, VOM the set of valid object models, E the set of events and $OM_0 \in VOM$ the initial valid object model. Let $CL = \langle e_1, e_2, ..., e_n \rangle \in (EO(DM, E))^*$ be a change log. There exist object models $OM_1, OM_2, ..., OM_n \in VOM$ such that $OM_0 \overset{e_1}{\Rightarrow} OM_1 \overset{e_2}{\Rightarrow} OM_2... \overset{e_n}{\Rightarrow} OM_n$. Hence, change log CL results in object model OM_n when starting in OM_0. This is denoted by $OM_0 \overset{CL}{\Rightarrow} OM_n$.*

Definitions 1 to 9 establish the basis to understand data models, events and change logs, among other concepts. However, a mechanism to relate events to each other to build traces is still missing. For that purpose, and as one of the main contributions of this paper, the concept of *trace id pattern* is introduced. Then, subsequent definitions will be presented to show the trace building technique.

In a classical approach, the notion of case id is given by an attribute common to all the events in a trace. If traces do not exist yet, they can be created grouping events by the value of the selected attribute. However, in our setting, we have a collection of events of different classes with disjoint attribute sets. This means that it will be impossible to find a single common attribute to be used as case id. A *trace id pattern* substitutes the idea of a case id attribute for a set of attributes and keys. By its use, it becomes possible to find a common set of attributes between events of different classes using foreign-primary key relations. This relations establish the equivalence between pairs of attributes. The example presented in Section 2.2 illustrates this idea using the pair of keys *customer_pk* and *booking_customer_fk* to set the equivalence between the attributes *customer:id* and *booking:customer_id*. Each *trace id pattern* configures a view of a process to focus on, determining also which is the central element of the view, called *root*. This *root* element will determine the start event for each trace and will allow, in further steps, to build traces according to such a view.

Definition 10 (Trace ID Pattern). *Let DM = (C, A, classAttr, val, PK, FK, keyClass, keyRel, keyAttr, refAttr) be a data model. A Trace ID Pattern on DM is a tuple $TP_{DM} = (TPA, TPK, ROOT)$ such that*
- *$TPA \subseteq A$ is a subset of the attributes in the data model,*
- *$TPK \subseteq K$ is a subset of the keys in the data model,*
- *$ROOT \in TPK$ is a key of the data model.*

To find the equivalence between different *attribute names*, we define a *canonical mapping* (Definition 11), i.e., a way to assign a common name to all the attributes linked, directly or transitively, through foreign-primary key relations. To show a simple example, the canonical mapping of the attribute *booking:customer_id* would be *customer:id* since both are linked through the foreign-primary pair of keys *booking_customer_fk* and *customer_pk*.

Definition 11 (Canonical Mapping). *Let DM = (C, A, classAttr, val, PK, FK, keyClass, keyRel, keyAttr, refAttr) be a data model and TP = (TPA, TPK, ROOT) a trace id pattern on DM. A canonical mapping $canon \in A \rightarrow A$ is a function mapping each attribute to its canonical attribute such that:*

$$canon(a) = \begin{cases} a & \text{if } a \notin \bigcup_{k \in FK} keyAttr(k), \\ canon(refAttr(fk, a)) & \text{if } a \in \bigcup_{k \in FK} keyAttr(k). \\ with fk \in \{k \in FK \mid a \in keyAttr(k)\} \end{cases}$$

The combination of a *trace id pattern* and the *canonical mapping* results in the *canonical pattern attribute set*, i.e., the set of canonical attributes for each of the elements (keys and attributes) configured in the *trace id pattern*. This allows us to obtain a minimum set of attributes to identify traces, avoiding the presence of attributes which, despite being different, map to the same canonical form.

Definition 12 (Canonical Pattern Attribute Set). *Let $DM = (C, A, clas-sAttr, val, PK, FK, keyClass, keyRel, keyAttr, refAttr)$ be a data model and $TP = (TPA, TPK, ROOT)$ a trace id pattern on DM. The canonical pattern attribute set of TP is a set $CPAS^{TP} = \{canon(a) \mid a \in TPA \cup (\bigcup_{k \in TPK} keyAttr(k))\}$.*

Definition 13 (Notations II). *Let $DM = (C, A, classAttr, val, PK, FK, keyClass, keyRel, keyAttr, refAttr)$ be a data model, TS some universe of timestamps and $eo = (((op, c), map_{old}, map_{new}), ts)$ an event occurrence. We define the following shorthands for event occurrences:*

- *$eventClass(eo) = c$ denotes the class of an event occurrence,*
- *$time(eo) = ts$ denotes the timestamp of an event occurrence,*
- *$mapVal_{eo}$ denotes the right mapping function to obtain the values of the event in an event occurrence such that*

$$mapVal_{eo} = \begin{cases} map_{new} & \text{if } op \in \{\oplus, \oslash\}, \\ map_{old} & \text{if } op = \ominus \end{cases}$$

Each trace we want to build represents a process instance. However, a process instance, which is formed by *event occurrences*, needs to comply with some rules to guarantee that they actually represent a meaningful and valid trace. The first thing we need to accomplish is to build a set of traces that do not contain too much behavior according to the selected view (*trace id pattern*). We will call this the set of *well-formed traces*.

Definition 14 (Traces, Well-Formed Traces). *Let $DM = (C, A, classAttr, val, PK, FK, keyClass, keyRel, keyAttr, refAttr)$ be a data model, $TP_{DM} = (TPA, TPK, ROOT)$ a trace id pattern on DM, CL a change log of event occurrences and $T = \{t \in \mathcal{P}(\{eo_i \mid 1 \leq i \leq n\})\}$ the set of possible traces on that change log. $WFT^{CL} \subseteq T$ is the set of well-formed traces such that $WFT^{CL} = \{t \in T \mid (\forall eo_i, eo_j \in t : \forall a_i \in A_{eventClass(eo_i)}, a_j \in A_{eventClass(eo_j)} : (a_i \in dom(mapVal_{eo_i}) \wedge a_j \in dom(mapVal_{eo_j}) \wedge \{canon(a_i), canon(a_j)\} \subseteq CPAS^{TP} \wedge canon(a_i) = canon(a_j)) \implies mapVal_{eo_i}(a_i) = mapVal_{eo_j}(a_j))\}$, i.e., the traces that do not contain event occurrences with different values for an attribute of which its canonical form is in the canonical pattern attribute set.*

The same way that a *trace id pattern* configures a view of the process, each process instance will be represented by a unique *trace id*. This concept (Definition 15) allows us to distinguish different traces. These traces aggregate events holding relations that can exist even between *events* of different *classes*.

Definition 15 (Trace ID). *Let $DM = (C, A, classAttr, val, PK, FK, keyClass, keyRel, keyAttr, refAttr)$ be a data model, $TP_{DM} = (TPA, TPK, ROOT)$ a trace id pattern on DM and $t \in WFT$ a well-formed trace. $TID_t^{TP} \subseteq CPAS^{TP} \times V$ is a set of pairs attribute-value for a trace t according to a trace id pattern TP such that $TID_t^{TP} = \{(a, v) \in CPAS^{TP} \times V \mid eo \in t \wedge a = canon(b) \wedge b \in dom(mapVal_{eo}) \wedge v = mapVal_{eo}(b)\}$.*

The second goal of the trace building process is to avoid the creation of traces containing events that do not belong to the same instance, according to the selected view (*trace id pattern*). Definition 17 sets such rules. Some of these rules require a way to find connections between events. Such connections or properties are stated in Definition 16 as *trace id properties*.

Definition 16 (Trace ID Properties). *Let $DM = (C, A, classAttr, val, PK, FK, keyClass, keyRel, keyAttr, refAttr)$ be a data model, $TP_{DM} = (TPA, TPK, ROOT)$ a trace id pattern on DM, $\{t, t'\} \subseteq WFT$ are two well-formed traces and $\{TID_t^{TP}, TID_{t'}^{TP}\}$ their corresponding trace ids. We define the following properties*

- $TID_t^{TP} \sim TID_{t'}^{TP} \iff \exists (a, v) \in CPAS^{TP} \times V : (a, v) \in TID_t^{TP} \wedge (a, v) \in TID_{t'}^{TP}$, *i.e., TID_t^{TP} and $TID_{t'}^{TP}$ are related if and only if an attribute exists with the same value in both trace ids,*
- $TID_t^{TP} \cong TID_{t'}^{TP} \iff \forall ((a, v), (a', v')) \in TID_t^{TP} \times TID_{t'}^{TP} : (a = a' \wedge v = v') \vee (a \neq a')$, *i.e., TID_t^{TP} and $TID_{t'}^{TP}$ are compatible if and only if for each common attribute the value is the same in both trace ids,*
- $TID_t^{TP} \bowtie TID_{t'}^{TP} \iff TID_t^{TP} \sim TID_{t'}^{TP} \wedge TID_t^{TP} \cong TID_{t'}^{TP}$, *i.e., TID_t^{TP} and $TID_{t'}^{TP}$ are linkable if and only if they are compatible and related,*
- $TID_t^{TP} \leq TID_{t'}^{TP} \iff TID_t^{TP} \subseteq TID_{t'}^{TP}$, *i.e., TID_t^{TP} is a subtrace of $TID_{t'}^{TP}$ if and only if all the attributes in TID_t^{TP} are contained in $TID_{t'}^{TP}$ with the same value,*

Definition 17 (Valid Traces, Event Logs). *Let $DM = (C, A, classAttr, val, PK, FK, keyClass, keyRel, keyAttr, refAttr)$ be a data model, $TP_{DM} = (TPA, TPK, ROOT)$ a trace id pattern on DM, CL a change log of event occurrences, WFT^{CL} the set of well-formed traces on that change log and $RootCAN \subseteq CPAS^{TP}$ is the set of canonical attributes of root such that $RootCAN = \{b \in CPAS^{TP} \mid \exists a \in keyAttr(ROOT) : canon(a) = b\}$. We define $VT(PT, CL) \subseteq WFT^{CL}$ as the set of valid traces for TP such that $VT(PT, CL) = \{t \in WFT^{CL} \mid \forall eo \in t : ((\forall c \in RootCAN : \exists (c, v) \in TID_{\{eo\}}^{TP}) \wedge (\nexists eo' \in t : time(eo') < time(eo))) \vee (TID_{\{eo\}}^{TP} \bowtie TID_{\{eo' \in t \mid time(eo') < time(eo)\}}^{TP}))\}$.*

Finally, we define an event log L^{PT} as the maximum subset of $VT(PT, CL)$ such that $\forall t, t' \in L^{PT} : (TID_t^{TP} \subseteq TID_{t'}^{TP} \implies t = t')$, i.e., the set of valid traces that does not contain any pair in which one of the traces is a subtrace of the other.

In the end, we guarantee that the resulting *event log* contains the minimum set of traces with the maximum behavior (L^{PT}) for a certain view *trace id pattern* TP). The traces in this *event log* start with an event containing values for the configured *root* element of the TP. Also, each of these traces contain events that are directly or transitively related ($\sim$) and compatible ($\cong$).

4 Implementation

The techniques presented in this paper allow for the extraction of events from any type of RDBMS with redo logs. Our implementation, however, is specific for

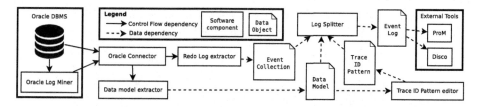

Fig. 3. Architecture of the Redo Log Inspector tool.

Oracle technology. We can obtain data models directly from an Oracle DBMS, which makes it possible to design the *trace id pattern* (Definition 10) needed to generate an event log in accordance to Definition 17 from an event collection. The Redo Log Inspector [1] tool that we developed to demonstrate the feasibility of our ideas, fully implements the approach described in the previous sections and provides a user interface to control all the aspects of the analysis.

The Redo Log Inspector is composed of different components (see Figure 3). It uses a *Oracle Connector* component to communicate with the Oracle database and with the Oracle Log Miner functions. This component is used by the *Redo Log extractor* to generate an *Event Collection* from the desired tables. The *Data model extractor* also makes use of the *Oracle connector* to automatically obtain a *Data Model*. This last element is used by the *Trace ID Pattern editor* to design the desired *Trace ID Pattern*. Then, the three objects (*Event collection, Data model* and *Trace ID Pattern*) are used by the *Log splitter* to compute the traces to form a *Event log*. Finally, the *Event log* can be analyzed with existing process mining tools, such as ProM[2] [2] and Disco[3]. Figure 4 shows a screenshot of the tool while splitting an event collection into traces using a Trace ID Pattern.

5   Demonstration

The database we will use to demonstrate our approach is part of an imaginary portal for selling concert tickets. As stated, the database stores information about customers, bookings, and tickets. In addition, the concert venues are represented in the database, along with the collection of seats they offer. Each concert is also stored in it, with the list of bands performing. Figure 1 shows the data schema of the database. It is composed of eight different tables with several columns each, and a number of relations between them:

- Concerts: date and start time of the concert and the venue in which it will take place.
- Band: name and address of bands, which could perform in different concerts.
- Band_playing: relates bands to concerts, indicating which ones will perform.
- Hall: details of the venues in which concerts can take place.

---

[1] Redo Log Inspector v1.0: http://www.win.tue.nl/~egonzale/projects/rlpm/
[2] ProM: http://www.promtools.org
[3] Disco: http://fluxicon.com/disco/

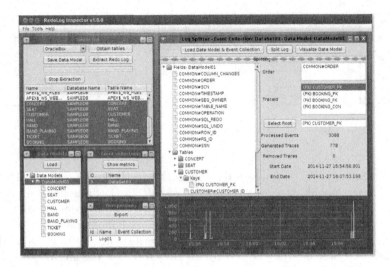

Fig. 4. Screenshot of the tool while splitting an event collection into traces.

- Seat: each of the seats available in a venue.
- Ticket: the product being sold to users. They link a concert to a specific seat in a venue. Also, they refer to a booking if they have been acquired.
- Booking: objects created by customers when buying tickets.
- Customer: address, name and birth date. Each entry represents an user account.

Tables may be linked to other tables by means of foreign keys. For instance, the table *ticket* contains a foreign key named *ticket_concert_fk*: It associates the column *ticket:for_concert* to the primary key of table *concert*, specifically the column *concert:id*. This field relates a *ticket* to a specific *concert* in a $n : 1$ relation, which means that a *ticket* must refer to a *concert*, but a *concert* can be related to many *tickets*.

In this database, like in many other settings, only the last state of the process is stored. This means we are able to answer questions of the following types:

1. How many concerts have been organized in the past?
2. Which venue has hosted most events in the last year?
3. What is the average number of tickets bought per customer in a month?

However, we would also like to find answers to other kinds of questions as well. In particular, we wish to pose questions that do not focus so much on the data facts, but on the underlying process that created and modified the data. Some of these questions are:

Q1. Which are the steps followed by a user to book a ticket?
Q2. Do customers book tickets before all the bands were confirmed?
Q3. Do bands ever cancel their performances in concerts?
Q4. Are venues being reserved before or after the bands have confirmed their performance?

It is evident that in order to find answers the inclusion of additional fields in the data schema would have been helpful. That data could be recorded explicitly in the database, adding timestamps to rows in every table and recording historical data of operations. It would be the equivalent of explicitly recording a *log* in the database. However, not every system has been designed to exploit the benefits of data and process mining. In other words, there are situations where we cannot rely on explicitly recorded logs of sorted events.

For instance, the fourth question could be answered querying the database only if the timestamps of execution of every operation are being recorded. However, Figure 1 shows that such timestamps are not present in the data schema of the proposed example. Something similar applies to the third question, which inquires if bands can cancel their performance at concerts. This requires the database to keep record of all the bands that were to perform in concerts and also the ones that canceled, for instance, by means of a status flag. Unfortunately the data schema does not store such information. What happens in case of a cancellation is that the corresponding entry will be removed from the table *band_playing*. This makes it impossible to know afterward which bands were once scheduled to perform but not anymore.

The focus of this section is to use database redo logs to answer the proposed questions using the technique presented in this paper. To do so, a dataset[4] of 8512 events has been generated based on a simulated environment interacting with the Oracle database presented in Figure 1. CPN tools [12] was used to model the creation of concerts and customers, the selling of tickets, and other operations on the elements of the database. The activities of such a process connect through a socket to a Java application managing the communication with an Oracle database. This way the environment of the system is simulated. This last one also generated the set of redo log files used to extract the events in our dataset. In the remainder the four questions are answered step-by-step.

5.1   Which are the Steps Followed by a User to Book a Ticket?

In order to answer this first question, we need to obtain the process describing the customer actions from the moment the selling portal is reached until the moment the ticket is sold. To do so, a log that contains traces showing that behavior has to be generated. This question will be answered in the next section in conjunction with the second one for the sake of brevity.

5.2   Could Customers Book Tickets Before all the Bands were Confirmed?

To answer this second question, two parts of the system must be involved: the ticket booking by customers and the concert organizing parts. For the first part, we can assume that the tables *customer*, *booking* and *ticket* must be involved in

---

[4] http://www.win.tue.nl/~egonzale/projects/rlpm/datasets/ticket-selling-dataset. zip

the process. Using the data schema in Figure 1, we see that tables *customer* and *booking* are linked by means of the pair of primary and foreign keys *customer_pk* and *booking_customer_fk* (Figure 1.a). Also, the tables *booking* and *ticket* are linked by means of the pair of keys *booking_pk* and *ticket_booking_fk* (Figure 1.b). Now, it is necessary to complete it with the concert organizing part. To do so, we have to relate each ticket to the concert it belongs to, and the later one to the bands playing. Observing Figure 1 we see that there is a relation between tables *ticket* and *concert* by means of the pair of keys *ticket_concert_fk* and *concert_pk* (Figure 1.c). Also, tables *concert* and *band_playing* share a relation by means of keys *concert_pk* and *bp_concert_fk* (Figure 1.d). Therefore, we should add these three keys to the Trace ID Pattern $TP = (TPA, TPK, ROOT)$, resulting in the following configuration:

- $TPA = \emptyset$,
- $TPK = \{customer\_pk, booking\_customer\_fk, booking\_pk,$ $ticket\_booking\_fk, concert\_pk, ticket\_concert\_fk, bp\_concert\_fk\}$,
- $ROOT = customer\_pk$.

Given that we want to cover the process from the moment a *customer* enters the system until the ticket is bought, it makes sense to select as root element of our Trace ID Pattern the primary key *customer_pk* in table *customer*. In other words, the customer is the case we want to follow through the process.

After this, the splitting process that follows generates a log with 149 cases. In this case the Inductive Miner [7] is used, and the log is replayed on it. Then, the activity *44+BAND_PLAYING+INSERT* is highlighted, which filters the log to show statistics using only the traces that contain the selected activity. The result is the annotated model in Figure 5. In it we observe that an insertion in the *customer* table can be followed either by modifications on it, or by an insertion in the *booking* table. An update in the *ticket* table can only be preceded by a *booking* creation. This means that, according to the evidence, the process followed by a customer to buy a ticket is as follows: (1) Create an account, which results in the insertion of a record in the table *customer*. (2) Create a booking, inserting a record in the table *booking*. (3) Buy the selected ticket, updating the *booking_id* field in the desired record in the table *ticket*. It can be also observed that modifications on the details of a customer profile can be made at almost any point in time, but not between the insertion of a booking and the update of a ticket. This suggests that both steps are performed automatically and in a strict sequence (Q1). To answer the second question it is interesting to see that insertions in the table *band_playing* can happen at any moment, before or after tickets are booked. This means that new bands are added to the concert not only after a concert is created, but also after a ticket has been booked. This does not require a causal relation in the sense that bands are added because a ticket is booked. However, it shows that both activities can happen in that order, answering the second proposed question (Q2).

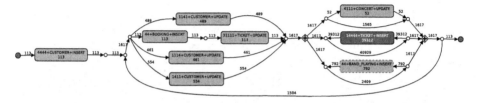

Fig. 5. Model of the ticket purchase and part of the concert organizing process.

5.3 Do Bands Ever Cancel Their Performance in Concerts?

To find out the answer to the third question, we should look at the *band_playing* table and see if any entry has been removed. This would not be possible when just inspecting the current content of the database. Fortunately, thanks to the redo logs, we can reconstruct the life-cycle of concerts. For the sake of brevity, the answer will be provided using the same experiment to answer the fourth question.

5.4 Are Venues Being Reserved Before or After the Bands have Confirmed Their Performance?

To solve the fourth question, we need to see how halls are being assigned to concerts at the same time that bands are being confirmed to perform on concerts. To do so, we have to focus on tables *concert, hall* and *band_playing*. Observing the data schema in Figure 1, we see that tables *concert* and *hall* are linked by means of the pair of primary and foreign keys *concert_hall_fk* and *hall_pk* (Figure 1.e). Also, there is a link between the tables *concert* and *band_playing* by means of the pair of keys *concert_pk* and *bp_concert_fk* (Figure 1.d). Therefore, we will use the four of them in our Trace ID Pattern $TP = (TPA, TPK, ROOT)$:

- $TPA = \emptyset$,
- $TPK = \{hall\_pk, concert\_hall\_fk, concert\_pk, bp\_concert\_fk\}$,
- $ROOT = concert\_pk$.

Knowing that concerts are the main object in this view, *concert_pk* will be selected as the root element. Splitting the dataset using these settings generates a log with 18 traces. Using the Inductive Miner and replaying the log, the annotated model in Figure 6 is obtained. It is evident that no deletions of records on

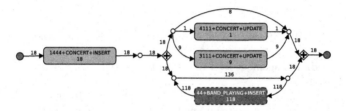

Fig. 6. Model showing the process of organizing a concert.

table *band_playing* have been recorded. Therefore, as far as we can tell, none of the bands ever canceled their performance within a concert (Q3). We can also see that *hall* column in concerts can be updated before, after, or at the same time that bands confirm their performance in concerts. Therefore, there are no restrictions on the order of both events (Q4).

6   Conclusion

This work proposes to systematically use database redo logs as a new source of event data. The benefits include the existence of a data model and the historical view we obtain from the database. This represents a considerable innovation compared to the analysis of plain database content. To make sense of the events and obtain logs, the new concepts of *trace id pattern* and *trace id* have been introduced, which enable the discovery of transitive relations between data objects and the causal dependencies of the data modifications. An innovative approach to group the events in traces has been provided as well. Also, the feasibility of the approach has been shown in the form of a prototype. This prototype has been applied on a synthetic dataset to demonstrate its potential usefulness to answer a range of business questions that could not be directly answered by querying the database.

The technique is characterized by some drawbacks. First, the splitting algorithm produces a log where the same event may appear in different traces. This causes the existing process discovery algorithms to generate statistics that must be interpreted from the view we selected on the process. This is due to the fact that they consider events to be unique and only present in a single trace, when, in our case, they can be repeated and be counted more than once. If not interpreted correctly, the numbers could lead to the wrong conclusions. Also, the algorithm produces a number of traces that in some cases exceed the number of original events. These traces need to be analyzed by the discovery algorithms to produce models. This means that, in the end, we are going through the log many times. It would be useful to reduce the analysis to a single pass through the event collection to compute the structures needed by the discovery algorithms, e.g. a *Directly-follows Graph*. The analysis of real-life event logs is an obvious next task. Performing a case study on non-artificial redo logs will, hopefully, support the value of the techniques presented in this paper.

References

1. van der Aalst, W.M.P.: Extracting event data from databases to unleash process mining. In: vom Brocke, J., Schmiedel, T. (eds.) BPM - Driving Innovation in a Digital World. Management for Professionals, pp. 105–128. Springer International Publishing (2015)
2. van der Aalst, W.M.P., van Dongen, B.F., Günther, C.W., Rozinat, A., Verbeek, E., Weijters, T.: Prom: the process mining toolkit. In: Proceedings of the BPM Demonstration Track (BPMDemos 2009), Ulm, Germany, September 8, 2009

3. Cohn, D., Hull, R.: Business artifacts: A data-centric approach to modeling business operations and processes. Bulletin of the IEEE Computer Society Technical Committee on Data Engineering **32**(3), 3–9 (2009)
4. Engel, R., van der Aalst, W.M.P., Zapletal, M., Pichler, C., Werthner, H.: Mining inter-organizational business process models from EDI messages: a case study from the automotive sector. In: Ralyté, J., Franch, X., Brinkkemper, S., Wrycza, S. (eds.) CAiSE 2012. LNCS, vol. 7328, pp. 222–237. Springer, Heidelberg (2012)
5. Fahland, D., de Leoni, M., van Dongen, B.F., van der Aalst, W.M.P.: Behavioral conformance of artifact-centric process models. In: Abramowicz, W. (ed.) BIS 2011. LNBIP, vol. 87, pp. 37–49. Springer, Heidelberg (2011)
6. Ingvaldsen, J.E., Gulla, J.A.: Preprocessing support for large scale process mining of sap transactions. In: ter Hofstede, A.H.M., Benatallah, B., Paik, H.-Y. (eds.) BPM Workshops 2007. LNCS, vol. 4928, pp. 30–41. Springer, Heidelberg (2008)
7. Leemans, S.J.J., Fahland, D., van der Aalst, W.M.P.: Discovering block-structured process models from event logs - a constructive approach. In: Colom, J.-M., Desel, J. (eds.) PETRI NETS 2013. LNCS, vol. 7927, pp. 311–329. Springer, Heidelberg (2013)
8. Lu, X.: Artifact-Centric Log Extraction and Process Discovery. Master's thesis, Technische Universiteit Eindhoven, The Netherlands (2013). http://repository.tue.nl/761324
9. Mueller-Wickop, N., Schultz, M.: ERP event log preprocessing: timestamps vs. accounting logic. In: vom Brocke, J., Hekkala, R., Ram, S., Rossi, M. (eds.) DESRIST 2013. LNCS, vol. 7939, pp. 105–119. Springer, Heidelberg (2013)
10. Nigam, A., Caswell, N.S.: Business artifacts: An approach to operational specification. IBM Systems Journal **42**(3), 428–445 (2003)
11. Nooijen, E.H.J., van Dongen, B.F., Fahland, D.: Automatic discovery of data-centric and artifact-centric processes. In: La Rosa, M., Soffer, P. (eds.) BPM Workshops 2012. LNBIP, vol. 132, pp. 316–327. Springer, Heidelberg (2013)
12. Ratzer, A.V., Wells, L., Lassen, H.M., Laursen, M., Qvortrup, J.F., Stissing, M.S., Westergaard, M., Christensen, S., Jensen, K.: CPN tools for editing, simulating, and analysing coloured Petri nets. In: van der Aalst, W.M.P., Best, E. (eds.) ICATPN 2003. LNCS, vol. 2679, pp. 450–462. Springer, Heidelberg (2003)
13. Roest, A.: A practitioner's guide for process mining on ERP systems : the case of SAP order to cash. Master's thesis, Technische Universiteit Eindhoven, The Netherlands (2012). http://repository.tue.nl/748077
14. Segers, I.: Investigating the Application of Process Mining for Auditing Purposes. Master's thesis, Technische Universiteit Eindhoven, The Netherlands (2007). http://repository.tue.nl/630348
15. Verbeek, H.M.W., Buijs, J.C.A.M., van Dongen, B.F., van der Aalst, W.M.P.: XES, XESame, and ProM 6. In: Soffer, P., Proper, E. (eds.) CAiSE Forum 2010. LNBIP, vol. 72, pp. 60–75. Springer, Heidelberg (2011)
16. Yano, K., Nomura, Y., Kanai, T.: A practical approach to automated business process discovery. In: 2013 17th IEEE International Enterprise Distributed Object Computing Conference Workshops (EDOCW), pp. 53–62, September 2013

Log Delta Analysis: Interpretable Differencing of Business Process Event Logs

Nick R.T.P. van Beest[1,3](✉), Marlon Dumas[2],
Luciano García-Bañuelos[2], and Marcello La Rosa[3,1]

[1] NICTA, Brisbane, Australia
nick.vanbeest@nicta.com.au
[2] University of Tartu, Tartu, Estonia
{marlon.dumas,luciano.garcia}@ut.ee
[3] Queensland University of Technology, Brisbane, Australia
m.larosa@qut.edu.au

Abstract. This paper addresses the problem of explaining behavioral differences between two business process event logs. The paper presents a method that, given two event logs, returns a set of statements in natural language capturing behavior that is present or frequent in one log, while absent or infrequent in the other. This log delta analysis method allows users to diagnose differences between normal and deviant executions of a process or between two versions or variants of a process. The method relies on a novel approach to losslessly encode an event log as an event structure, combined with a frequency-enhanced technique for differencing pairs of event structures. A validation of the proposed method shows that it accurately diagnoses typical change patterns and can explain differences between normal and deviant cases in a real-life log, more compactly and precisely than previously proposed methods.

1 Introduction

Process mining is a family of methods to extract insights from business process execution logs. One problem type addressed by process mining methods is *deviance mining* [1]: understanding differences between executions that lead to a positive outcome vs. those that lead to a negative outcome, such as understanding what differentiates executions of a process that fulfill a service-level objective vs. those that violate it.

In previous case studies [2,3], deviance mining has been approached using *model delta analysis*. The idea is to apply automated process discovery techniques to the traces of positive cases and to those of negative cases separately. The discovered process models are visually compared to identify distinguishing patterns. This approach does not scale up to complex logs. For example, Fig. 1 shows the models discovered by the Disco tool [4] for positive and negative cases of a patient treatment log at an Australian hospital – where a positive execution concerns a treatment that completes in less than a given timeframe. Manual comparison of these models is tedious and error-prone, calling for an automated method to distill differences that explain the observed deviance.

© Springer International Publishing Switzerland 2015
H.R. Motahari-Nezhad et al. (Eds.): BPM 2015, LNCS 9253, pp. 386–405, 2015.
DOI: 10.1007/978-3-319-23063-4_26

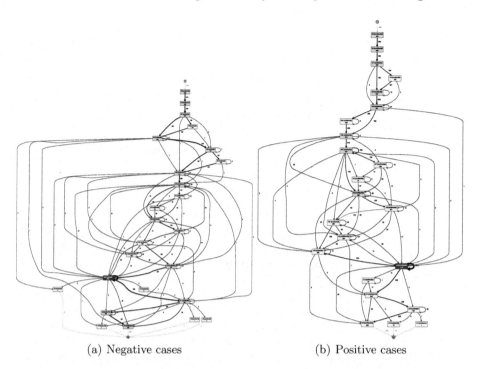

(a) Negative cases   (b) Positive cases

Fig. 1. Model discovered from a hospital log for positive and negative cases

This paper approaches the problem of deviance mining via a *log delta analysis* operation defined as follows: *Given two event logs L_1 and L_2, explain the differences between the behavior observed in L_1 and that observed in L_2.* As the output is intended to inform business analysts, it should be compact and interpretable. Accordingly, the proposed method produces a set of simple statements, each capturing a behavior observed (frequently) in one log but not observed (or observed less frequently) in the other.

The proposal relies on a novel approach to losslessly encode an event log as an *event structure* [5]: a directed acyclic graph where nodes represent event occurrences sharing a common history. We enhance this representation with frequency information to capture how often a given event occurrence is observed in the log. Given the frequency-enhanced event structures of two event logs, the method calculates their differences based on an extended version of a technique for event structure differencing [6]. The latter step leads to a set of statements capturing behavior that is observed with some frequency in one log and with lower frequency (or not at all) in the other log.

The proposal has been evaluated on artificial logs capturing different types of change patterns [7] and combinations thereof, as well as on the hospital log from which the models in Fig. 1 are generated. The evaluation puts forward advantages of the proposed approach over an alternative method based on sequence classification.

The paper is structured as follows. Section 2 discusses related work and introduces event structures. Sections 3 and 4 present the construction of event structures from logs and their differencing for the purpose of log delta analysis. Section 5 discusses the evaluation while Section 6 draws conclusions.

2   Background and Related Work

This section discusses previous work on deviance mining and introduces the notion of event structure used in the rest of the paper.

2.1   Deviance Mining

Approaches to deviance mining can be classified into two categories [1]: *model delta analysis* and *sequence classification*. As explained in Section 1, model delta analysis [2,3,8] requires manual comparison of automatically discovered process models. As such, it is error-prone and does not scale up to complex logs.

Sequence classification methods construct a classifier (e.g. a decision tree) that can determine with sufficient accuracy whether a given trace belongs to the positive or the negative class. The crux of these methods is the choice of features. In this respect, these methods fall into three categories: activity-based feature encoding, frequent sequence mining and discriminative sequence mining. In *activity-based feature encoding*, each trace is encoded as a vector containing one feature per activity referenced in the event log. The value of the feature corresponding to activity A is the number of times A appears in the trace. *Frequent sequence mining* methods [3,9,10] extract frequent patterns from the set of positive cases and that of negative cases separately. A possible pattern is that activity A occurs before activity B. Each pattern becomes a feature. The value of a feature for a trace is the number of times the pattern in question occurs in the trace. *Discriminative sequence mining* methods [11] operate similarly but extract patterns based on their discriminative power: a pattern is selected if it is a characteristic of positive cases but not of negative ones, or vice-versa.

In [1], we evaluated the above sequence classification methods on real-life logs. We found that a discriminative sequence mining method outperformed others (accuracy wise), but in all cases the obtained sets of rules were overly complex. For the patient treatment log in Section 1, between 106 and 130 rules are produced – each rule consisting of a conjunction of patterns possibly involving multiple activities. This observation motivates the development of a method to produce a compact set of statements explaining the differences between two groups of traces (e.g. positive vs. negative).

The problem of deviance mining could in theory be addressed based on the notion of behavioral profiles [12], where a process is represented via a matrix of behavioral relations between pairs of task labels. The idea would be to construct a behavioral profile for the normal cases and one for the deviant cases (as in model delta analysis), and then to calculate a difference between the two matrices. This approach however would be hindered by the fact behavioral profiles have limited expressive power: they sometimes fail to capture "task skipping" behavior and cannot distinguish an acyclic process with a similar process with an added cycle [12]. Thus the resulting difference statements would be incomplete. To avoid this limitation, the log delta analysis method adopts a more powerful representation of behavior, namely event structures.

2.2 Event Structures

A Prime Event Structure (PES) [5] is a graph of events, where an event e represents the occurrence of an action (e.g. task) in the modeled system (e.g. business process). If a task occurs multiple times in a run, each occurrence is represented by a different event. The order of occurrence of events is defined via binary relations: i) *Causality* ($e < e'$) indicates that event e is a prerequisite for e'; ii) *Conflict* ($e\#e'$) implies that e and e' cannot occur in the same run; iii) *Concurrency* ($e \parallel e'$) indicates that no order can be established between e and e'.

Definition 1 (Labeled Prime Event Structure [5]). *A* Labeled Prime Event Structure *over the set of event labels $\mathscr{L}$ is the tuple $\mathscr{E} = \langle E, \leq, \#, \lambda \rangle$ where*

- *E is a set of events (e.g. tasks occurrences),*
- *$\leq \subseteq E \times E$ is a partial order, referred to as* causality,
- *$\# \subseteq E \times E$ is an irreflexive, symmetric conflict relation,*
- *$\lambda : E \rightarrow \mathscr{L}$ is a labeling function.*

We use $<$ to denote the irreflexive causality relation. The concurrency relation *of $\mathscr{E}$ is defined as $\parallel = E^2 \setminus (< \cup <^{-1} \cup \#)$. Moreover, the* conflict relation *satisfies the principle of conflict heredity, i.e. $e\#e' \wedge e' \leq e'' \Rightarrow e\#e''$ for $e, e', e'' \in E$.*

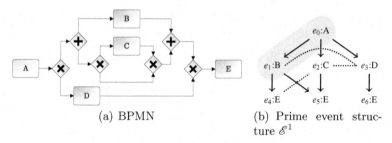

(a) BPMN   (b) Prime event structure $\mathscr{E}^1$

Fig. 2. Sample process model

For illustration, Fig. 10 presents side-by-side a BPMN process model and a corresponding PES $\mathscr{E}^1$. Nodes are labelled by an event identifier followed by the label of the represented task, e.g. "e_2:C" tells us that event e_2 represents an occurrence of task "C". The causality relation is depicted by solid arcs whereas conflict is depicted by dotted edges. For simplicity, transitive causal and hereditary conflict relations are not depicted. Every pair of events that are neither directly nor transitively connected are in a concurrency relation. Note that three different events refer to the task with label "E". This duplication is required to distinguish the different states where task "E" occurs.

A state of an event structure (a.k.a. *configuration*) is characterized by the set of events that have occurred so far. For example, set $\{e_0:A, e_1:B\}$ – highlighted in Fig. 2(b) – is the configuration where tasks A and B have occurred. In this configuration, event $\{e_3:D\}$ can no longer occur because it is in conflict with $\{e_1:B\}$. Meanwhile, events $\{e_2:C\}$ and $\{e_4:E\}$ can occur, but the occurrence of one precludes that of the other.

Definition 2 (Configuration). *Let $\mathscr{E} = \langle E, \leq, \#, \lambda \rangle$ be a prime event structure. A* configuration *of $\mathscr{E}$ is the set of events $C \subseteq E$ such that*
- *C is causally closed, i.e. $\forall e' \in E, e \in C : e' \leq e \Rightarrow e' \in C$, and*
- *C is conflict-free, i.e. $\forall e, e' \in C \Rightarrow \neg(e \# e')$.*

The local configuration *of an event $e \in E$ is the set $\lfloor e \rfloor = \{e' \mid e' \leq e\}$. Similarly, the (set of)* strict causes *of an event $e \in E$ is defined as $\lfloor e) = \lfloor e \rfloor \setminus \{e\}$.*

Set inclusion forms a partial order on configurations. We denote by $Conf(\mathscr{E})$ the set of all possible configurations of $\mathscr{E}$ and by $MaxConf(\mathscr{E})$ the subset of maximal configurations with respect to set inclusion. In the running example, $MaxConf(\mathscr{E}^1) = \{\{e_0, e_1, e_2, e_5\}, \{e_0, e_1, e_4\}, \{e_0, e_3, e_6\}\}$.

3   Constructing Event Structures from Logs

In an event log, events are related via a total order induced by their timestamps.

Definition 3 (Event log, Trace). *Let L be an* event log *over the set of labels $\mathscr{L}$, i.e. $L \in \mathbb{B}(\mathscr{L}^*)$. Let E be a set of event occurrences and $\lambda : E \to \mathscr{L}$ a labelling function. An event* trace *$\sigma \in L$ is defined in terms of an order $i \in [0, n-1]$ and a set of events $E_\sigma \subseteq E$ with $|E_\sigma| = n$ such that $\sigma = \langle \lambda(e_0), \lambda(e_1), \ldots, \lambda(e_{n-1}) \rangle$.*

Consider the event log in Fig. 3. The event log consists of 10 traces, with three instances of trace t_1 (cf. column "N"), two instances of t_2, etc. Herein, we write $\sigma = \langle A,B,C,E \rangle$ to refer to any of the three instances of t_1 such that $E_\sigma = \{e_0, e_1, e_2, e_3\}$ and $\{(e_0, A), (e_1, B), (e_2, C), (e_3, E)\} \subset \lambda$.

Trace	Ref	N
A B C E	t_1	3
A C B E	t_2	2
A B E	t_3	2
A D E	t_4	3

Fig. 3. Event log

To construct an event structure from a log, we start by transforming the log into a set of partially ordered runs by extracting concurrency relations between pairs of events. Several approaches have been proposed to extract concurrency relations between pairs of events from an event log [13,14]. Here, we use the so-called *alpha concurrency* approach [14], but other approaches can be applied instead. Alpha concurrency is a relation over event labels appearing in a log. Specifically, two event labels a and b are alpha-concurrent if a is sometimes observed immediately after b and vice-versa.

Definition 4 (Alpha concurrency [14]). *Let L be an event log over the set of event labels $\mathscr{L}$ and $\sigma \in L$ be a log trace. A pair of tasks with labels $a, b \in \mathscr{L}$*

are said to be in alpha directly precedes relation, *denoted* $A \prec_{\alpha(L)} B$, *iff there exists a trace* $\sigma = \langle \lambda(e_0), \lambda(e_1), \ldots, \lambda(e_{n-1}) \rangle$ *in* L, *such that* $A = \lambda(e_i)$ *and* $B = \lambda(e_{i+1})$. *A pair of tasks* $A, B \in \mathscr{L}$ *are* alpha concurrent, *denoted* $A \parallel_{\alpha(L)} B$, *iff* $A \prec_{\alpha(L)} B \wedge B \prec_{\alpha(L)} A$.

In the example log, $B \prec_\alpha C$ because of trace $t_1 = \langle A,B,C,E \rangle$ and $C \prec_\alpha B$ because of $t_2 = \langle A,C,B,E \rangle$, hence $B \parallel_\alpha C$. To construct partially ordered runs from traces, we take as input an oracle χ that defines a concurrency relation $\parallel_\chi$ over event occurrences (as opposed to event labels). Specifically, we use the concurrency relation $\parallel_\chi = \{(e, e') \mid \lambda(e) \parallel_{\alpha(L)} \lambda(e')\}$ for an event log L and its alpha concurrency relation $\parallel_{\alpha(L)}$. Given this, Def. 5 captures how traces are transformed into partially ordered runs.

Definition 5 (Transformation of a trace into a partially ordered run).
Let L be an event log over the set of event labels $\mathscr{L}$ and $\parallel_\chi$ be a concurrency relation. Moreover, let E be a set of event occurrences, $\lambda : E \to \mathscr{L}$ a labelling function. We say that event e_i directly precedes event e_{i+1}, denoted $e_i \lessdot e_{i+1}$, iff there exists a trace $\sigma = \langle \lambda(e_0), \lambda(e_1), \ldots, \lambda(e_{n-1}) \rangle$ in L with index $i \in [0, n-2]$. Thus, tuple $\pi = \langle E_\pi, \leq_\pi, \lambda_\pi \rangle$ is the partially ordered run corresponding to trace σ, induced by the concurrency relation $\parallel_\chi$ and the directly precedes relation $\lessdot$, where:

- *E_π is the set of events occurring in σ,*
- *$\leq_\pi$ is the causality relation defined as $\leq_\pi = E_\pi^2 \cap (\lessdot^+ \setminus \parallel_\chi)^*$, and*
- *$\lambda_\pi : E_\pi \to \mathscr{L}$ is a labelling function, i.e. $\lambda_\pi = \lambda|_{E_\pi}$.*

$\Pi_\chi(L)$ is the set of partially ordered runs induced by $\parallel_\chi$ over the traces in L.

The crux of the transformation of a trace into a run is the computation of the causality relation $\leq_\pi$. Fig. 4 illustrates how this is done for $t_1 = \langle A,B,C,E \rangle$. First, Fig. 4(a) presents the direct precedes relation $\lessdot$ for t_1, which is directly derived from the sequential order in the event trace. Fig. 4(b) presents the (irreflexive) transitive closure of $\lessdot$, that is, $\lessdot^+$. Note that the blue edges in Fig. 4(b) correspond to the transitive relations.

The set difference $\lessdot^+ \setminus \parallel_\chi$ results in removing the edge connecting B with C as shown in Fig. 4(c). We can then remove the edge connecting A with E (shown in grey) by computing the transitive reduction of the causality relation. The concurrency relation $\parallel_\pi$ for a partially ordered run π is derived from $\leq_\pi$, i.e. $\parallel_\pi = E_\pi^2 \setminus (<_\pi \cup <_\pi^{-1})$. Observe that $\parallel_\pi$ coincides with $\parallel_\chi$.

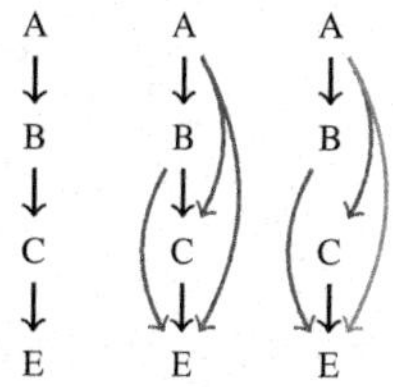

A partially ordered run resembles a prime event structure, with the exception that it does not have conflicting relations. This is because a run records the set of events that have actually occurred in an execution. Fig. 5 shows

(a)   (b)   (c)

Fig. 4. Transformation of t_1 into π_1

the set of partially ordered runs $\{\pi_1, \pi_2, \pi_3\}$ derived from the log in Fig. 3 and its corresponding alpha concurrency, where π_1 encodes the traces t_1 and t_2 and, therefore, is associated with 10 different cases. Similarly, π_2 encodes t_3, π_3 encodes t_4 and correspond to two and three cases respectively.

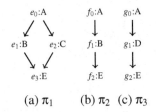

(a) π_1 (b) π_2 (c) π_3

Fig. 5. Partially ordered runs of the event log in Fig. 3

The merging of runs $\Pi(L)$ to derive a prime event structure relies on an equivalence relation $\sim$. This relation partitions the set of events $E = \cup_{\pi \in \Pi(L)} E_\pi$, in a way that preserves the labelling of events as well as their "computation context". Labelling preserving implies that all the events in an equivalence class have the same label. The "computation context" is again related with a configuration. Informally, we require that if two events $e, e' \in E$ are equivalent, written $e \sim e'$, all events in the local configuration of e have an equivalent event in the local configuration of e'. As is customary, we write $[e]_\sim = \{e' \mid e \sim e'\}$ to denote the equivalence class of event e and for simplicity, we write $[S]_\sim = \{[e']_\sim \mid e \in S\}$ to denote the set of equivalence classes for all the events in the set S. The following definition formalizes the intuition above.

Definition 6 (Configuration-based prefix merging equivalence).
Let $e_i \in E_{\pi_i}$ and $e_j \in E_{\pi_j}$ be event occurrences in two different partially ordered runs. The configuration-based prefix merging equivalence *is an equivalence relation $\sim$ over E, with the following properties:*

(i) $\sim$ is a reflexive, transitive and symmetric relation,
(ii) $e_i \sim e_j$ is label-preserving, i.e. $\lambda(e_i) = \lambda(e_j)$, and
(iii) $e_i \sim e_j$ is configuration preserving, i.e. $[\lfloor e_i \rfloor]_\sim = [\lfloor e_j \rfloor]_\sim$.

We now define a transformation to derive a prime event structure from an event log.

Definition 7 (Log-based Prime Event Structure). *Let L be an augmented event log. Let $\Pi(L)$ be its set of partially ordered runs. The prime event structure induced by equivalence relation $\sim$ is the tuple $\mathscr{E}(L)_\sim = \langle E_\sim, \leq_\sim, \#_\sim, \lambda_\sim \rangle$ s.t.*

- $E_\sim = \{ [e]_\sim \mid e \in \cup_{\pi \in \Pi(L)} E_\pi \}$,
- $\leq_\sim = \{ ([e]_\sim, [e']_\sim) \mid \exists \pi \in \Pi(L) : e \leq_\pi e' \}$,
- $\|_\sim = \{ ([e]_\sim, [e']_\sim) \mid \exists \pi \in \Pi(L) : e \|_\pi e' \}$,
- $\#_\sim = E_\sim^2 \setminus (\leq_\sim \cup \leq_\sim^{-1} \cup \|_\sim)$, *and*
- $\lambda_\sim = \{ ([e]_\sim, \lambda(e)) \mid [e]_\sim \in E_\sim \}$

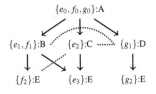

Fig. 6. PES induced by $\sim$ over the runs in Fig. 5

Let us now illustrate how the prime event structure for the set of runs in Fig. 5 is built. As usual, we assume that $\emptyset \in \sim$. It should be clear that $\{e_0, f_0, g_0\} \in \sim$: all those events share the label "A"; the events in the strict causes of each of those events form also an equivalence class (please consider that $\lfloor e_0 \rfloor = \lfloor f_0 \rfloor = \lfloor g_0 \rfloor = \emptyset$); and the causality relation is preserved (this result is trivial because only one event has been considered so far). Note that $[e_0]_\sim = [f_0]_\sim = [g_0]_\sim = \{e_0, f_0, g_0\}$. Let us now consider the set of events sharing the label "B", namely $\{e_1, f_1\}$. Note that $\lfloor e_1 \rfloor = \{e_0\}$ and $\lfloor f_1 \rfloor = \{f_0\}$ and since $[e_0]_\sim = [f_0]_\sim$, we can conclude that $\{e_1, f_1\}$ is configuration preserving. Moreover, the equivalence class $\{e_1, f_1\}$

preserves causal order because $e_0 \leq_{\pi_1} e_1$ and $f_0 \leq_{\pi_2} f_1$. Fig. 6 depicts the entire PES induced by $\sim$ over the set of runs in Fig. 5. To further illustrate the concepts, let us consider the set of events sharing the label "E", namely $\{e_3, f_2, g_2\}$. Please note that the partition $\{e_3, f_2, g_2\}$ has to be refined because their corresponding configurations do not coincide, e.g. $[\lfloor e_3 \rfloor]_\sim = \{[e_0]_\sim, [e_1]_\sim, [e_2]_\sim\}$ is different to $[\lfloor f_2 \rfloor]_\sim = \{[e_0]_\sim, [e_1]_\sim\}$. Therefore, one equivalence class for each of those events is required, i.e. $\{[e_3]_\sim, [f_2]_\sim, [g_2]_\sim\} \subset \sim$. One can easily check that the PES in Fig. 6 is isomorphic to the PES in Fig. 2(b) and, hence, the sample event log could have been generated by executing the process model depicted in Fig. 2(a).

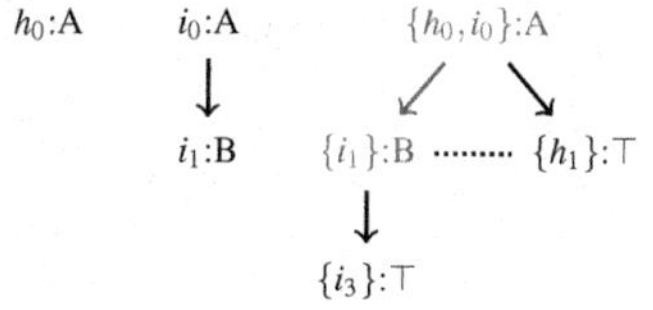

As formally proved later, Def. 7 ensures that each input run is represented as a configuration of the resulting PES. Unfortunately, it does not necessarily warranties that a run will be represented as a maximal configuration. To illustrate this issue, consider the event log $L^2 = \{\langle A \rangle, \langle A, B \rangle\}$. L^2 gives rise to two runs, namely π_4 and π_5, which are shown in Fig. 7. Moreover, the subgraph in red corresponds to $\mathscr{E}(L^2)$. One can easily verify that $Conf(\mathscr{E}(L^2) = \{\{[i_0]_\sim\}, \{[i_0]_\sim, [i_1]_\sim\}\}$ and $MaxConf(\mathscr{E}(L^2)) = \{\{[i_0]_\sim, [i_1]_\sim\}\}$. Since

(a) π_4 (b) π_5 (c) $\mathsf{E}\,\widehat{(L^2)}_\sim$

Fig. 7. Runs and PES for $\widehat{L^2}$

$h_0 \sim i_0$, we have that $\{[h_0]_\sim\}$ is also a configuration of $\mathscr{E}(L^2)$. Somehow, we can say that $\mathscr{E}(L^2)$ generalizes the behavior observed in L^2. In order to fix this limitation, we append an artificial end event to each trace in the input log, giving rise to an augmented log. Moreover, we use a special label, i.e. $\top$, to keep track of the artificial end events. Formally, for each $\sigma = \langle \lambda(e_0), \ldots, \lambda(e_{n-1}) \rangle$ from an event log L, we build a new trace $\hat{\sigma} = \langle \hat{\lambda}(e_0), \ldots, \hat{\lambda}(e_{n-1}), \hat{\lambda}(e_n) \rangle$ where e_n is a fresh event and $\hat{\lambda} = \lambda \circ \{(e_n, \top)\}$. We write $\widehat{L}$ to refer to the augmented log of L. Fig. 7(c) presents the PES for log $\widehat{L^2}$. One can easily check that the artificial event h_1 preserves the maximality of the configuration corresponding to the run π_4. The following Theorem formalizes the intuition above and one of the major contributions of this work: $\mathscr{E}(\widehat{L})$ is a lossless representation of L.

Theorem 1 (Lossless representation). *Let $\Pi(\widehat{L})$ be the set of partially ordered runs of the augmented event log $\widehat{L}$, and $E = \cup_{\pi \in \Pi} E_\pi$ its corresponding set of events. Moreover, let $\mathscr{E}(\widehat{L})_\sim = \langle E_\sim, \leq_\sim, \#_\sim, \lambda_\sim \rangle$ be the prime event structure induced by the equivalent relation $\sim$.*

For every run $\pi \in \Pi(\widehat{L})$ it holds $[E_\pi]_\sim \in MaxConf(\mathscr{E}(\widehat{L})_\sim)$.

Proof. We first prove that $[E_\pi]_\sim$ is a configuration of $\mathscr{E}(\widehat{L})_\sim$.
 - *(Causal closedness)* Take $e \in E_\pi$ and $f \in E \setminus E_\pi$ s.t. $e \sim f$. By Def. 6(iii), we have $[\lfloor e \rfloor]_\sim = [\lfloor f \rfloor]_\sim$, that is, all strict causes of event e form also an equivalence class $\sim$. Therefore, $[\lfloor e \rfloor]_\sim \subseteq E_\sim$ (cf. Def. 7). Recall $\lfloor e \rfloor = \{e' \mid e' <_\pi e\}$. Hence, $[E_\pi]_\sim$ is causally closed.

- *(Conflict freeness)* Take $e \in E_\pi$ and $f \in E \backslash E_\pi$ s.t. $\lambda(e) = \lambda(f)$ and $[\lfloor f \rfloor]_\sim \subseteq$ $[\lfloor e \rfloor]_\sim$. Assume that $[f]_\sim \#_\sim [e]_\sim$. Recall $[E_\pi]_\sim$ is causally closed and hence consistent with $\leq_\sim$. Since $\|_\sim$ is derived from $\|_\pi$, by construction of $\#_\sim$, we require $[f]_\sim \neq [e]_\sim$ or equivalently $\neg(f \sim e)$. If $[\lfloor f \rfloor]_\sim = [\lfloor e \rfloor]_\sim$, by Def. 6(ii) it holds $f \sim e$, reaching contradiction. Conversely, if $[\lfloor f \rfloor]_\sim \neq [\lfloor e \rfloor]_\sim$, then it holds $\neg(f \sim e)$ and $[f]_\sim \notin [E_\pi]_\sim$. Hence, $[E_\pi]_\sim$ is conflict free.

Next, we prove by contradiction that $[E_\pi]_\sim$ is a maximal configuration of $\mathscr{E}(\widehat{L})_\sim$. Let $z \in E_\pi$ be the artificial end event of π. Assume there exists a run $\pi' \in \Pi(\widehat{L})$, with $z' \in E_{\pi'}$, s.t. $[E_\pi]_\sim \subseteq [E_{\pi'}]_\sim$, i.e. $[E_\pi]_\sim$ is not maximal w.r.t. $\subseteq$, and $[E_{\pi'}]_\sim \in Conf(E_\sim)$. Note that $[\lfloor z \rfloor]_\sim \subseteq E_\sim$ and also $[\lfloor z' \rfloor]_\sim \subseteq E_\sim$. If $[\lfloor z \rfloor]_\sim = [\lfloor z' \rfloor]_\sim$, then $z \sim z'$, which preserves maximality. Conversely, if $[\lfloor z \rfloor]_\sim \neq [\lfloor z' \rfloor]_\sim$ (yet $[\lfloor z \rfloor]_\sim \subset [\lfloor z' \rfloor]_\sim$), then $\neg(z \sim z')$ and $[z]_\sim \#_\sim [z']_\sim$. Moreover, if $\{[z]_\sim, [z']_\sim\} \subseteq [E_{\pi'}]_\sim$, then $[E_{\pi'}]_\sim$ is not conflict free and, therefore, not a configuration, reaching contradiction. Hence, $[E_\pi]_\sim$ is maximal.   □

4   Comparing Event Structures

In this section, we describe our approach to identify and verbalize differences between two logs. These logs can concern two logs with variance, two logs from different organizations or one log with two classes: one regular, one deviant. The control-flow of both variants of the log is compared and verbalized in Section 4.1. Subsequently, the logs are transformed into a Frequency-enhanced Prime Event Structure (FPES) in Section 4.2, which allows to verbalize the branching frequency differences between the logs.

4.1   Control-Flow Comparison

In [6], we presented a technique for differencing pairs of event structures. This technique performs a *Partial Synchronized Product* (PSP) of the event structures, which is a synchronized simulation starting from the empty configurations. At each step, the events that can occur given the current configuration in each of the two event structures (i.e. the *enabled* events) are matched. If the events match, the simulation adds the matching events to the current configurations and continues. If an enabled event in the current configuration of one event structure does not match with an enabled event in the current configuration in the other event structure, a mismatch is declared. The unmatched event is "hidden" and the simulation jumps to the next matching configurations.

Fig. 9 presents an excerpt of the PSP for $\mathscr{E}^1$ and $\mathscr{E}^2$, shown in Fig. 10 and Fig. 8 respectively. Note that $MaxConf(\mathscr{E}^2) = \{\{f_0, f_1, f_2, f_4\}, \{f_0, f_3, f_5\}\}$. Clearly, all maximal configurations of $\mathscr{E}^2$ can be matched to configurations of $\mathscr{E}^1$. The right-hand leaf node in the PSP illustrates the matching of configuration $\{e_0, e_1, e_2, e_5\}$ from $\mathscr{E}^1$ and $\{f_0, f_1, f_2, f_4\}$ from $\mathscr{E}^2$. There, the set m records the fact that all the events in both configurations have been matched, lh records that none of the events from $\mathscr{E}^1$ (the one to the left of the "product") has been hidden, and rh records that no event from $\mathscr{E}^2$ has been hidden. Similarly, the

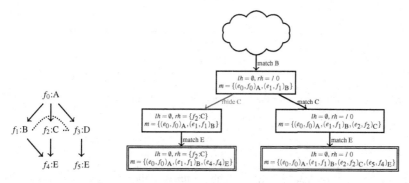

Fig. 8. PES $\mathscr{E}^2$ **Fig. 9.** Fragment of PSP of the PESs in Figs. 2(b) and 3

leaf node at the left-hand side corresponds to the best matching of configurations $\{e_0, e_1, e_4\}$ and $\{f_0, f_1, f_2, f_4\}$, respectively from $\mathscr{E}^1$ and $\mathscr{E}^2$. The cloud in the top indicates that some states precede to the matching of a pair of events sharing the label "B". The label on the edge from the cloud to the node just below records such matching. The configuration $\{e_0, e_1\}$ enables the occurrence of e_4:E, but that occurrence precludes the occurrence of e_2:C. This gives rise to a behavioral mismatch, that is resolved by hiding f_2:C. The red arrow in the PSP captures this hiding: the event f_2:C from $\mathscr{E}^2$ (right-hand side model in the product) is hidden. In the target box, m remains the same, i.e. no additional matching, whereas rh records the hiding of f_2:C. The reader is referred to [6] for further details on the technique.

In [7], a number of simple change patterns are catalogued (shown in Table 1). Each simple change will be used to identify the unique observation in the PSP, which is subsequently translated into a statement in natural language. However, change R3 concerns a branching frequency change instead of a control-flow change and will be discussed in Section 4.2. An overview of the control-flow changes is presented in Table 2.

Table 1. Change patterns applied to the base model to produce the variants.

Insertion	Resequentialization	Optionalization
1. Add / remove	1. Loop	1. Parallel / sequence
2. Duplicate	2. Skip	2. Conditional / sequence
3. Substitute	3. Change branching frequency	3. Synchronize

4.2   Frequency-Enhanced Comparison

In addition to control-flow variance, differences in branching probabilities are another type of variance that needs to be identified. To this end, we enhance the PES of a log with the branching frequencies as follows.

Table 2. Translation from PSP observations to natural language expressions.

I1	**PSP observation:** $match(a) \to rhide(b)$, with no other branch showing $match(b)$. **Verbalization:** In variant 2, b occurs after a, while in variant 1 it does not.
I2	**PSP observation:** $match(a) \to \ldots \to match(b) \to rhide(a)$. **Verbalization:** In variant 2, after the occurrence of b, a is duplicated, while in variant 1 it is not.
I3	**PSP observation:** $match(a) \to rhide(c) \to lhide(b)$. **Verbalization:** In variant 2, after the occurrence of a, b is substituted by c.
R1	**PSP observation:** $match(a) \to match(b) \to rhide(a) \to rhide(b)$. **Verbalization:** In variant 2, a is repeated multiple times, while in variant 1 it is not. In variant 2, b is repeated multiple times, while in variant 1 it is not.
R2	**PSP observation:** $lhide(a)$ in one branch and $match(a)$ in another branch. **Verbalization:** In variant 2, a can be skipped, while in variant 1 it cannot.
O1	**PSP observation:** $match(a) \to lhide(b) \to rhide(b)$. **PES observation:** (variant 1) a $\parallel$ b; (variant 2) a $\leq$ b. **Verbalization:** In variant 1, a and b are in parallel, while in variant 2, a precedes b.
O2	**PSP observation:** $rhide(a)$ in one branch and $lhide(b)$ in another branch. **Verbalization:** In variant 1, a precedes b, while in variant 2, a and b are mutually exclusive.
O3	**PSP observation:** $match(a) \to match(b) \to lhide(c) \to rhide(c)$. **PES observation:** (variant 1) a $\parallel$ b, a $\parallel$ c, b $\leq$ c; (variant 2) a $\parallel$ b, a $\leq$ c, b $\leq$ c. **Verbalization:** In variant 1, a is in parallel with b and c, while in variant 2, a is in parallel with b.

Definition 8 (Frequency-enhanced Prime Event Structure (FPES)).

Let $\mathscr{E}(L)_\sim = \langle E_\sim, \leq_\sim, \#_\sim, \lambda_\sim \rangle$ be the prime event structure induced by equivalence relation $\sim$ on the set of partially ordered runs $\Pi(L)$ of log L. A frequency-enhanced prime event structure is a tuple $\mathscr{F}(L)_\sim = \langle \mathscr{E}(L)_\sim, \mathscr{O}, \mathscr{P} \rangle$ where

- $\mathscr{O} : E \to \mathbb{N}$ is a function that associates an event $[e]_\sim$ with the number of times its event label occurs in the event log, and corresponds with the cardinality of the equivalence class, i.e. $\mathscr{O}([e]_\sim) = |[e]_\sim|$.
- $\mathscr{P} : E \times E \to [0,1]$ is a function that associates a pair of events $[e_1]_\sim$ and $[e_2]_\sim$ with the probability of occurrence of $[e_2]_\sim$ given that event $[e_1]_\sim$ has occurred. This function is defined as:
$$\mathscr{P}([e_1]_\sim, [e_2]_\sim) = \begin{cases} \mathscr{O}([e_2]_\sim)/\mathscr{O}([e_1]_\sim) & \text{if } [e_1]_\sim <_\sim^{red} [e_2]_\sim \\ 0 & \text{Otherwise} \end{cases}$$

Fig. 10 presents the FPES for the log L that we have used as our running example. For each event in the graph there is a grey circle close to the event indicating the corresponding number of occurrences (i.e. $\mathscr{O}$) on the input log.

For instance, event $\{e_2\}$:C occurs a total of five times. This value can be tracked back to the log as follows: e_2 comes from run π_1, which in turn comes from traces t_1 and t_2. Since t_1 and t_2 represent three and two cases each, we have a total of five occurrences. The branching frequency (i.e. $\mathscr{P}$) is also shown Fig. 10, with labels close to the edge representing a direct causal relation (i.e. $<_{\sim}^{red}$). Note that including transitive causal relations during the verbalization would result in a large number of difference statements. Most of them, however, would most likely be redundant. Therefore, we only consider direct causal relations.

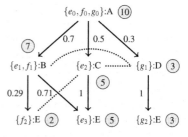

Fig. 10. FPES $\mathscr{F}(L)$

Algorithm 1. Obtain frequency differences

```
 1: function OBTAINDIFFERENCES(𝓕₁, 𝓕₂)
 2:     diffSet ← ∅
 3:     λ̄_{𝓕₁} ← GETEVENTDEPTHLABELSET(𝓕₁); λ̄_{𝓕₂} ← GETEVENTDEPTHLABELSET(𝓕₂)
 4:     BP₁ ← GETAVERAGEBRANCHINGPROBABILITYSET(𝓕₁, λ̄_{𝓕₁})
 5:     BP₂ ← GETAVERAGEBRANCHINGPROBABILITYSET(𝓕₂, λ̄_{𝓕₂})
 6:     for e, e' ∈ E_{𝓕₁} s.t. (⟨λ̄_{𝓕₁}[e], λ̄_{𝓕₁}[e']⟩ ↦ p₁) ∈ BP₁ do
 7:         for f, f' ∈ E_{𝓕₂} s.t. (⟨λ̄_{𝓕₂}[f], λ̄_{𝓕₂}[f']⟩ ↦ p₂) ∈ BP₂ do
 8:             if λ̄_{𝓕₁}[e] = λ̄_{𝓕₂}[f] ∧ λ̄_{𝓕₁}[e'] = λ̄_{𝓕₂}[f'] ∧ p₁ ≠ p₂ then   ▷ Probability mismatch?
 9:                 diffSet ← diffSet ∪ {(λ̄_{𝓕₁}[e], λ̄_{𝓕₁}[e'], λ̄_{𝓕₂}[f], λ̄_{𝓕₂}[f'], p₁, p₂)}
10:             end if
11:         end for
12:     end for
13: end function
14: function GETAVERAGEBRANCHINGPROBABILITYSET(𝓕, λ̄_𝓕)
15:     sums ← ∅; probs ← ∅
16:     for e, e' ∈ E_𝓕 s.t. e <_𝓕^{red} e' do
17:         sums[⟨λ̄_𝓕[e], λ̄_𝓕[e']⟩] ← sums[⟨λ̄_𝓕[e], λ̄_𝓕[e']⟩] + 𝓟_𝓕(e, e')   ▷ ∅ is interpreted as 0
18:     end for
19:     for e, e' ∈ E_𝓕 s.t. (⟨λ̄_𝓕[e], λ̄_𝓕[e']⟩ ↦ p) ∈ sums do
20:         probs[⟨λ̄_𝓕[e], λ̄_𝓕[e']⟩] ← p / |{e'' ∈ E_𝓕 | e'' < e' ∧ λ̄_𝓕[e''] = λ̄_𝓕[e]}|
21:     end for
22:     return probs
23: end function
24: function GETEVENTDEPTHLABELSET(𝓕)
25:     return { ⟨ e ↦ (λ_𝓕(e), |{e' | e' ≤ e ∧ λ_𝓕(e) = λ_𝓕(e')}|) ⟩ | e ∈ E_𝓕 }
26: end function
```

The logs to be compared are each transformed into an FPES according to Def. 8. Subsequently, Algorithm 1 is used to obtain the set of frequency differences. As FPESs contain all event occurrences, repeated activities in a trace show up as separate events in the FPES with shared labels. Hence, we first create a set $\bar{\lambda}$ for each FPES, which holds each label along with the depth of the event occurrence in the respective run, determined based on the causality relation between each of these events (lines 3 and 25). As such, labels that are in conflict (and hence occur on different branches) will not be counted as consecutive occurrences. Function GETAVERAGEBRANCHINGPROBABILITYSET (lines 4, 5 and 14) calculates the average branching frequency of an activity based on the frequencies of occurrence of events. For instance, the branching activity may occur in multiple mutually exclusive branches, whereas the originating activity may also correspond to multiple event occurrences. As such, the frequencies of the respective event occurrences of a particular label are summed (line 17) and divided by the number of originating event occurrences that lead to an event with that label (line 20).

Next a set of difference statements can be created between events using the average frequency obtained. The differences are verbalized by referring to the frequency of branching between two activities in one variant, versus the same branching in the other variant. Consider the two event structures from Fig. 2(b) and Fig. 8, which we refer to as variant 1 and variant 2 respectively. We are interested in the frequency differences between event A and D. In variant 1, the frequency is 0.5, while in variant 2 the frequency is 0.7. This results in the following: $(\langle e_0 \mapsto [A, 1]\rangle, \langle e_3 \mapsto [D, 1]\rangle, \langle f_0 \mapsto [A, 1]\rangle, \langle f_3 \mapsto [D, 1]\rangle, 0.5, 0.7) \in$ diffSet. Based on the diffSet, the branching frequency differences can be verbalized, as shown in Table 3.

Table 3. Translation from FPES observations to natural language expressions.

R3	**FPES observation**: (variant 1) $(a, b) = x_1$; (variant 2) $(a, b) = x_2$.
	Verbalization: In variant 1, after the occurrence of a the branching frequency to b is $<x_1 * 100>\%$, while in variant 2, after the occurrence of a the branching frequency to b is $<x_2 * 100>\%$.

Note that some differences between occurrence frequencies (R3) in the compared logs may be insignificant (cf. for example branching frequencies of 43.1% for variant 1 vs. 43.8% for variant 2). In addition, reported differences may include activities that only occur very rarely, e.g. in only 0.3% of all process instances. Accordingly, we apply a filter to the set of statements that removes those referring to frequency differences below a user-specified threshold.

Complexity analysis. The complexity of the approach has several elements. The transformation of the input event log into partially order runs (cf. Def. 5) is dominated by the computation of the transitive closure of the causality relation. This step has a complexity of $O(|\sigma_m|^3)$, where $|\sigma_m|$ is the length of the longest trace in the event log.

Prime event structures can be built using a partition-refinement approach via a breadth-first traversal of the graph induced by the direct causal relation of the event structure being computed. This traversal strategy guides the partitioning of events in a way that it eases the verification of the "preservation of configurations" required by $\sim$ (cf. Def. 6(ii)). Checking "preservation of configurations" is in worst case $O(|E|^2)$ and the breadth-first traversal is $O(|E| \cdot |<^{red}_{\sim}|)$. However, the complexity of this step is dominated by the computation of the transitive reduction of the causality relation in the resulting event structure, that is $O(|<^{red}_{\sim}|^3)$, which is used in subsequent steps.

The above steps are polynomial. It turns out that the overall complexity of the log-delta analysis method is dominated by the computation of the PSP, which relies on the well-known A* heuristic search algorithm. The state space to be explored by A* is $O(3^{|Conf(E_1)| \cdot |Conf(E_2)|})$, since each configuration from E_1 is associated with each configuration from E_2 via three possible operations (i.e. *match*, *lhide* and *rhide*). However, this worst case complexity only occurs when the event structures are completely different. Conversely, when the event structures are identical, the heuristic search converges in linear time. In our setting, the input logs are expected to exhibit a high overlap in behavior and hence a reasonable performance.

5   Evaluation

We implemented the proposed method in the Apromore platform[1]. Using this implementation, we conducted a two-pronged validation. First, using synthetic datasets we assessed the method's ability to diagnose variations corresponding to typical process change patterns and combinations thereof. Second, using a real-life log, we qualitatively assessed the difference diagnosis produced by the method and compared it to rules produced using a sequence classification method.

5.1   Evaluation on Synthetic Logs

We generated synthetic logs by simulating BPMN process models using the BIMP simulator[2]. As a *base model*, we used a textbook example of a loan application process [15] comprising a representative set of control-flow patterns: sequence, choice, skipping, parallelism and repetition (cf. Fig. 11). Subsequently, we generated nine variants of this model by applying each of the simple change patterns (Table 1). We performed a 1000-traces simulation of the base model and each of its variants. Next, we applied the delta analysis method to compare the log of the base model against the log of each variant.

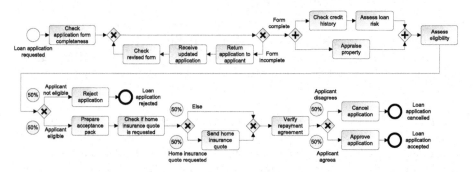

Fig. 11. Base model (branching probabilities are shown inside circles)

---

[1] Available at http://www.apromore.org/platform/tools
[2] http://bimp.cs.ut.ee

Next, we generated 6 logs by combining the 9 simple change patterns into composite (nested) changes. Specifically, we applied a randomly chosen change pattern from one of the three categories (say "I"), then nested a second pattern randomly chosen from another category (say "O") inside the fragment modified by the first pattern, and a third pattern randomly chosen from the last category ("R"). This led to one composite change (and corresponding log) for each permutation of the three categories. For example, a variant "IRO" was obtained by adding an activity ("Insert") then putting it in parallel with an existing activity ("Resequencing') and skipping the latter ("Optionalization").

Results: Table 4 shows the diagnosis produced for each of the nine variants corresponding to the simple changes. In all cases, the diagnosis matches the corresponding change pattern. Each diagnosis contains one statement per task affected by the change, e.g. in the case of R1 where the loop comprises three tasks, the diagnosis contains three statements. In R3, the branching frequencies in the diagnosis do not exactly match the ones in the BPMN diagrams, due to the stochastic nature of the simulation.

Table 5 shows the diagnosis for three of the six composite changes. For space reasons, we omit the other composite changes (all results are packaged with the software tool). As expected, the composite changes lead to more difference statements than the simple changes (cf. Table 4), but in every case the diagnosis matches the corresponding change. Some difference statements refer to minor variations in frequencies (e.g. one branch is taken 48.1% of times in one variant and 49.2% in the other). This again comes from the stochastic nature of the simulation. Such spurious statements can be filtered by setting the frequency delta threshold to e.g. 10% (cf. Section 4.2).

Execution times: Each log comparison took between 10.06 and 11.18 seconds on a laptop with Intel i7 2.5GHz, running JVM 8 with 16GB of allocated memory.

5.2   Evaluation on Real-Life Logs

We evaluated the method on the sub-logs of positive and negative cases of the patient treatment process discussed in Section 1 (Fig. 1). Variant 1 (448 cases, 7329 events) corresponds to the negative (slow) cases, while variant 2 (363 cases, 7496 events) corresponds to the positive cases. The logs cover a period of 1.5 years.

Results: An evaluation of sequence classification methods using this log is presented in [1], where it is shown that sequence classification methods require between 106 and 130 statements to explain the differences between these sub-logs. In contrast, our method requires 48 statements to explain all differences (without filtering) and 42 statements with a frequency delta threshold of 20%. Moreover, the statements produced by sequence classification approaches produce rules referring to the number of occurrences of a given event or event pattern in a variant, without specifying where exactly the difference occurs. For example,

Table 4. Simple changes and their verbalization.

I1 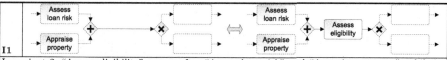	
In variant 2, "Assess eligibility" occurs after "Assess loan risk" and "Appraise property", while in variant 1 it does not occur.	
I2 	
In variant 2, after the occurrence of "Verify repayment agreement", "Assess loan risk" is repeated, while in variant 1 it is not.	
I3 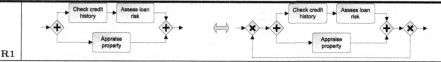	
In variant 2, after the occurrence of "Send home insurance quote", "Verify repayment agreement" is substituted by "Replaced activity".	
R1 	
In variant 2, "Check credit history" is repeated multiple times, while in variant 1 it is not.	
In variant 2, "Assess loan risk" is repeated multiple times, while in variant 1 it is not.	
In variant 2, "Appraise property" is repeated multiple times, while in variant 1 it is not.	
R2	
In variant 2, "Prepare acceptance pack" can be skipped, while in variant 1 it cannot.	
In variant 2, "Check if home insurance quote is requested" can be skipped, while in variant 1 it cannot.	
R3 	
In variant 1, after the occurrence of "Check if home insurance quote is requested" the branching frequency to "Send home insurance quote" is 50.2%, while in variant 2, after the occurrence of "Check if home insurance quote is requested" the branching frequency to "Send home insurance quote" is 24.7%.	
O1 	
In variant 1, "Assess loan risk" and "Appraise property" are in parallel, while in variant 2, "Assess loan risk" precedes "Appraise property".	
O2 	
In variant 1, "Check credit history" precedes "Assess loan risk", while in variant 2, "Check credit history" and "Assess loan risk" are mutually exclusive.	
O3 	
In variant 1, "Appraise property" is in parallel with "Check credit history" and "Assess loan risk", while in variant 2, "Appraise property" is in parallel with "Check credit history".	

Table 5. Composite changes and their verbalization.

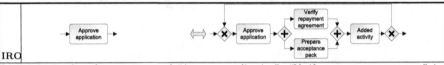

IRO

In variant 2, after the occurrence of "Approve application", "Verify repayment agreement" is repeated, while in variant 1 it is not.

In variant 2, "Prepare acceptance pack" is repeated after "Approve application", while in variant 1 it is not.

In variant 2, "Added activity" occurs after "Verify repayment agreement" and "Prepare acceptance pack", while in variant 1 it does not occur.

In variant 1, after the 1st occurrence of "Verify repayment agreement" the branching frequency to the 1st occurrence of "Approve application" is 48.1%; while in variant 2, after the 1st occurrence of "Verify repayment agreement" the branching frequency to the 1st occurrence of "Approve application" is 13.6%

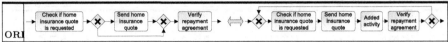

ORI

In variant 2 "Check if home insurance quote is requested" is repeated multiple times, while in variant 1 it is not.

In variant 1 "Send home insurance quote" can be skipped, while in variant 2 it is always executed.

In variant 2 "Send home insurance quote" is repeated multiple times, while in variant 1 it is not.

In variant 2 "Verify payment agreement" is repeated multiple times, while in variant 1 it is not.

In variant 2 "Added activity" occurs after "Send home insurance quote", while in variant 1 it does not occur.

In variant 1, after the occurrence of "Check if home insurance quote is requested" the branching frequency to "Send home insurance quote" is 47.7%; while in variant 2, after the execution of "Check if home insurance quote is requested" the branching frequency to "Send home insurance quote" is 15.9%.

In variant 1, after the 1st occurrence of "Verify repayment agreement" the branching frequency to the 1st occurrence of "Approve application" is 48.1%; while in variant 2, after the 1st occurrence of "Verify repayment agreement" the branching frequency to the 1st occurrence of "Approve application" is 32.0%.

In variant 1, after the execution of "Send home insurance quote" the branching frequency to the 1st occurrence of "Verify repayment agreement" is 100.0%; while in variant 2, after the execution of "Send home insurance quote" the branching frequency to the 1st occurrence of "Verify repayment agreement" is 42.8%.

In variant 1, after the 1st occurrence of "Verify repayment agreement" the branching frequency to the 1st occurrence of "Cancel application" is 51.9%; while in variant 2, after the 1st occurrence of "Verify repayment agreement" the branching frequency to the 1st occurrence of "Cancel application" is 23.2%.

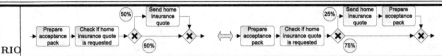

RIO

In variant 2, after the occurrence of "Send home insurance quote", "Prepare acceptance pack" is repeated, while in variant 1 it is not.

In variant 1, after the execution of "Check if home insurance quote is requested" the branching frequency to the 1st occurrence of "Verify repayment agreement" is 52.3%; while in variant 2, after the execution of "Check if home insurance quote is requested" the branching frequency to the 1st occurrence of "Verify repayment agreement" is 71.5%.

In variant 1, after the 1st occurrence of "Verify repayment agreement" the branching frequency to the 1st occurrence of "Approve application" is 48.1%; while in variant 2, after the 1st occurrence of "Verify repayment agreement" the branching frequency to the 1st occurrence of "Approve application" is 49.2%.

In variant 1, after the 1st occurrence of "Verify repayment agreement" the branching frequency to the 1st occurrence of "Cancel application" is 51.9%; while in variant 2, after the 1st occurrence of "Verify repayment agreement" the branching frequency to the 1st occurrence of "Cancel application" is 50.8%.

using the approach in [9], the following statements are produced – where "Nursing Progress Notes", "Nursing Primary Assessment", etc. refer to the number of occurrences of the corresponding tasks[3]:

- IF "Nursing Progress Notes" > 7.5 THEN variant 1.
- IF "Nursing Progress Notes" ≤ 7.5 AND "Nursing Primary Assessment" > 1.5 THEN variant 2.
- IF "Nursing Progress Notes" ≤ 5.5 AND "Pre Arrival Note" ≤ 0.5 AND "Blood tests" ≤ 1.5 THEN variant 2.

Meanwhile, our method produces statements that point to the exact state in the process where a behavioral difference occurs. For example:

- In variant 1, "Nursing Primary Assessment" is repeated after "Medical Assign Start" and "Triage Request", while in variant 2 it is not.
- In variant 2, "Blood tests" occurs after "Triage Request", while in variant 1 it does not occur.
- In variant 1, after the 1st occurrence of "Pathology" the branching frequency to the 2nd occurrence of "Nursing Primary Assessment" is 15.0%, while in variant 2, after the 1st occurrence of "Pathology" the branching frequency to the 2nd occurrence of "Nursing Primary Assessment" is 33.3%.

Execution time: The comparison of the two variants of the hospital log took 7.82 seconds, which is in the same order of magnitude as in the synthetic logs.

6   Conclusion

The paper presented a method for diagnosing the differences between two event logs via natural language statements capturing behavior present in one log but not in the other. This diagnostics is built on top of a lossless encoding of logs in the form of frequency-enhanced event structures. Based on this encoding, the method detects and diagnoses mismatching behavior, specifically: (i) events that occur in one log but not in the other; (ii) events occurring with different frequencies; (iii) events repeated in one log but not in the other; and (iv) behavioral relations that hold in one log but not in the other.

The validation on synthetic logs shows that the method accurately diagnoses typical change patterns, while the validation on a real-life log shows that it can explain differences between normal and deviant executions more compactly and precisely than sequence classification techniques considered in prior work (over 60% fewer statements).

A limitation of the method is that it does not fully recognize cyclic behavior. While the method detects that an activity occurs multiple times in traces of one log but not in those of the other, it does not identify the boundaries of

---

[3] Even though the number of occurrences is always an integer, some rules contain decimals because the decision tree learning algorithm may use decimals as split thresholds.

cycles. This leads to multiple difference statements concerning the same cycle (cf. change R1 in Table 4). Another limitation is that the method treats the input log as consisting of sequences of event labels, ignoring timestamps and event payloads. Hence, directions for future work include designing cycle-aware, temporal and data-aware extensions of the method.

The current transformation from traces to partially ordered runs relies on the alpha concurrency oracle. While useful in relatively simple scenarios, this oracle can sometimes confuse concurrency with loops [14]. Another direction for future work is to comparatively evaluate this oracle against alternative ones such as the one in [13].

Finally, we plan to evaluate the method with domain experts so as to assess the usefulness of the generated statements for understanding deviance in practical scenarios.

Acknowledgments. NICTA is funded by the Australian Government. This research is funded by the Australian Research Council Discovery Project DP15010-3356 and the Estonian Research Council.

References

1. Nguyen, H., Dumas, M., La Rosa, M., Maggi, F.M., Suriadi, S.: Mining business process deviance: a quest for accuracy. In: Meersman, R., Panetto, H., Dillon, T., Missikoff, M., Liu, L., Pastor, O., Cuzzocrea, A., Sellis, T. (eds.) OTM 2014. LNCS, vol. 8841, pp. 436–445. Springer, Heidelberg (2014)
2. Suriadi, S., Wynn, M.T., Ouyang, C., ter Hofstede, A.H.M., van Dijk, N.J.: Understanding process behaviours in a large insurance company in australia: a case study. In: Salinesi, C., Norrie, M.C., Pastor, Ó. (eds.) CAiSE 2013. LNCS, vol. 7908, pp. 449–464. Springer, Heidelberg (2013)
3. Lakshmanan, G.T., Rozsnyai, S., Wang, F.: Investigating clinical care pathways correlated with outcomes. In: Daniel, F., Wang, J., Weber, B. (eds.) BPM 2013. LNCS, vol. 8094, pp. 323–338. Springer, Heidelberg (2013)
4. Günther, C.W., Rozinat, A.: Disco: discover your processes. In: BPM 2012 Demos, CEUR, pp. 40–44 (2012)
5. Nielsen, M., Plotkin, G.D., Winskel, G.: Petri Nets, Event Structures and Domains, Part I. TCS **13**, 85–108 (1981)
6. Armas-Cervantes, A., Baldan, P., Dumas, M., García-Bañuelos, L.: Behavioral comparison of process models based on canonically reduced event structures. In: Sadiq, S., Soffer, P., Völzer, H. (eds.) BPM 2014. LNCS, vol. 8659, pp. 267–282. Springer, Heidelberg (2014)
7. Weber, B., Reichert, M., Rinderle-Ma, S.: Change patterns and change support features: Enhancing flexibility in process-aware information systems. DKE **66**(3), 438–466 (2008)
8. Partington, A., Wynn, M.T., Suriadi, S., Ouyang, C., Karnon, J.: Process mining of clinical processes: Comparative analysis of four australian hospitals. In: ACM TMIS (2014) (In press)
9. Jagadeesh Chandra Bose, R.P., van der Aalst, W.M.P.: Abstractions in process mining: a taxonomy of patterns. In: Dayal, U., Eder, J., Koehler, J., Reijers, H.A. (eds.) BPM 2009. LNCS, vol. 5701, pp. 159–175. Springer, Heidelberg (2009)

10. Swinnen, J., Depaire, B., Jans, M.J., Vanhoof, K.: A process deviation analysis – a case study. In: Daniel, F., Barkaoui, K., Dustdar, S. (eds.) BPM Workshops 2011, Part I. LNBIP, vol. 99, pp. 87–98. Springer, Heidelberg (2012)
11. Lo, D., Cheng, H., Han, J., Khoo, S.C., Sun, C.: Classification of software behaviors for failure detection: a discriminative pattern mining approach. In: KDD 2009, pp. 557–566. ACM (2009)
12. Weidlich, M., Mendling, J., Weske, M.: Efficient Consistency Measurement Based on Behavioral Profiles of Process Models. IEEE TSE **37**(3), 410–429 (2011)
13. Cook, J.E., Wolf, A.L.: Event-base detection of concurrency. In: FSE 1998, pp. 35–45. ACM (1998)
14. van der Aalst, W.M.P., Weijters, T., Maruster, L.: Workflow mining: discovering process models from event logs. IEEE TKDE **16**(9), 1128–1142 (2004)
15. Dumas, M., La Rosa, M., Mendling, J., Reijers, H.: Fundamentals of Business Process Management. Springer (2013)

Fast and Accurate Business Process Drift Detection

Abderrahmane Maaradji[1,3]([⊠]), Marlon Dumas[2], Marcello La Rosa[1,3], and Alireza Ostovar[3]

[1] NICTA, Canberra, Australia
Abderrahmane.Maaradji@nicta.com.au, m.larosa@qut.edu.au
[2] University of Tartu, Tartu, Estonia
marlon.dumas@ut.ee
[3] Queensland University of Technology, Brisbane, Australia
alireza.ostovar@qut.edu.au

Abstract. Business processes are prone to continuous and unexpected changes. Process workers may start executing a process differently in order to adjust to changes in workload, season, guidelines or regulations for example. Early detection of business process changes based on their event logs – also known as business process drift detection – enables analysts to identify and act upon changes that may otherwise affect process performance. Previous methods for business process drift detection are based on an exploration of a potentially large feature space and in some cases they require users to manually identify the specific features that characterize the drift. Depending on the explored feature set, these methods may miss certain types of changes. This paper proposes a fully automated and statistically grounded method for detecting process drift. The core idea is to perform statistical tests over the distributions of runs observed in two consecutive time windows. By adaptively sizing the window, the method strikes a trade-off between classification accuracy and drift detection delay. A validation on synthetic and real-life logs shows that the method accurately detects typical change patterns and scales up to the extent that it works for online drift detection.

1 Introduction

Business processes are prone to evolution in response to various factors, including changes in the regulatory environment, competitive environment, supply, demand and technology capabilities, as well as seasonal factors. Some process changes are planned and documented, but others may occur unexpectedly and remain unnoticed by some process stakeholders. For example, this may be the case of changes undertaken by the initiative of individual process workers in order to adapt to variations in workload or in resource capacity, changes brought about by replacement of human resources, changes in the frequency of certain types of (problematic) cases, or exceptions that in some cases give rise to new workarounds that over time solidify into norms. Undocumented process changes like those described above may over time affect process performance.

© Springer International Publishing Switzerland 2015
H.R. Motahari-Nezhad et al. (Eds.): BPM 2015, LNCS 9253, pp. 406–422, 2015.
DOI: 10.1007/978-3-319-23063-4_27

In this setting, process analysts and managers require methods and tools that allow them to detect and pinpoint process changes as early as possible. *Business process drift detection* [1–5] is a family of process mining techniques to detect changes based on observations of business process executions recorded in *event logs* consisting of *traces*, each representing one execution of the business process.

Existing methods for business process drift detection are based on the idea of extracting *features* (e.g. patterns) from traces. One possible feature is for example that task A occurs before task B in the trace, while another type of feature is for example that B occurs more than once in the trace. To achieve a suitable level of accuracy, these techniques either explore large feature spaces automatically or they require the users themselves to identify the specific features that are likely to characterize the drift – implying that the user already has an *a priori* idea of the characteristics of drift. In all cases, these methods may miss certain types of changes that are not covered by the types of features employed. Furthermore, the scalability of these techniques is hindered by the need to extract and analyze a potentially large set of high-dimensional feature vectors. As a result, existing techniques are not suitable for real-time drift detection.

This paper proposes a fully automated and scalable method for detecting concept drift in business process event logs. The core idea is to perform statistical hypothesis testing over the distributions of runs observed in two consecutive time windows. The underpinning assumption is that if a change occurs at a given time point, the distribution of runs before and after this time point will be statistically different, provided that the number of traces in the time window is sufficiently large for statistical testing. By adaptively sizing the window, the method strikes a trade-off between classification accuracy (F-score) and drift detection delay. The proposed method has been empirically evaluated on synthetic and real-life logs in order to assess its accuracy and scalability.

The paper is structured as follows. Section 2 discusses related work. Section 3 introduces the proposed method while Sections 4 and 5 present its evaluation on synthetic and real-life logs. Section 6 concludes the paper.

2 Related Work

Bose et al. [1,3] propose a method to detect process drifts based on statistical testing over feature vectors. This method is however not automated. Instead, the user is asked to identify the features to be used for drift detection, implying that the user has some knowledge of the possible nature of the drift. Furthermore, given the types of features supported, this method is unable to identify certain types of drifts such as inserting a conditional branch or a conditional move. Finally, this method requires the user to set a window size for drift detection. Depending on how this parameter is set, some drifts may be missed. This latter limitation is partially addressed in a subsequent extension [4], which introduces a notion of *adaptive window*. The idea is to increase the window size until it reaches a maximum size or until a drift is detected. However, this latter method requires that the user sets a minimum and a maximum window size. If the minimum window size is too small, minor variations (e.g. noise) may be misinterpreted as drifts (false positives). Conversely, if the maximum window size is too large, the execution time is affected and some drifts may go undetected.

Accorsi et al. [5] propose a drift detection method based on trace clustering. The idea is to cluster the traces based on the average distance between each pair of activities in the traces. Similar to Bose et al. [1,3], this method heavily depends on the choice of window size, such that a low window size leads to false positives while a high window size leads to false negatives (undetected drifts), as drifts happening inside the window go undetected. In addition the method is not designed to deal with loops, and may fail to detect types of changes that do not cause significant changes to the distances between activity pairs, e.g. changes involving an activity being skipped.

Carmona et al. [2] propose another process drift detection method based on an abstract representation of the process as a polyhedron. This representation is computed for prefixes in a random sample of the initial traces in the log. The method checks the fitness of subsequent prefixes of traces against the constructed polyhedron. If a significant number of these prefixes do not lie in the polyhedron, a drift is declared. To find a second drift after the first one, the entire detection process has to be executed from the start, thus hindering on the scalability of the method. In experiments we conducted with the logs used in Sections 4 and 5, the implementation of this method took hours to complete. Another drawback of this method is its inability to pinpoint the exact moment of the drift.

Burattin et al [6] address the problem of online discovery of process models from event streams. The goal is to discover a process model from the log and to update the discovered process model as new events are produced. The authors adapt an automated process discovery method, namely the Heuristics Miner, so as to handle incremental updates. Our proposal is complementary as it allows drifts to be detected accurately and efficiently, and can be used as an oracle to identify points in time when the process model should be updated.

The problem of drift detection has also been studied in a broader context in the field of data mining [7], where a widely studied challenge is that of designing efficient learning algorithms that can adapt to data that evolves over time (a.k.a. *concept drift*). This includes for example changes in the distributions of numerical or categorical variables. However, the methods developed in this context deal with simple structures (e.g. numerical or categorical variables and vectors thereof), while in business process drift detection we seek to detect changes in more complex structures, specifically behavioral relations between tasks (concurrency, conflict, loops). Thus, methods from the field of concept drift detection in data mining cannot be readily transposed to business process drift detection.

3   Drift Detection Method

From a statistical viewpoint, the problem of business process drift detection can be formulated as follows: *identify a time point when there is a statistically significant difference between the observed process behavior before and after this point*. A key design choice to turn this formulation into a decision procedure is to define what we mean by a *difference in the observed process behavior*. If we turn around this problem, the question becomes *when are two processes the same?* [8]. A number of equivalence notions have been proposed to address this question, borrowed from the field of concurrency theory [9]. One widely accepted notion of process equivalence is *trace equivalence*: two processes are the same if they have the same set of traces, thus they are different if their set of traces exhibits a (statistically significant) difference. However, this trace-based representation can be over-sensitive in our context because it does not capture concurrency. Indeed, any significant variation in the frequency of relative ordering of two activities that are anyways in parallel is treated as a drift. For example, if two activities b and c are in parallel, any significant variation in the frequency of occurrence of b followed by c vs. c followed by b gives rise to a drift, even though the parallel relation between these activities still holds. From this perspective, a more suitable approach is to reason in terms of runs (a.k.a. configurations) of a process, where concurrency is explicitly captured. For example, the two traces abcd and acbd characterize the process where a is followed by b and c in parallel and these are followed by d. In a run-based representation, only one run is needed to represent both traces: the run where a is followed by b and c in parallel and these are followed by d. As business processes typically contain concurrent activities, we opt for a run-based representation of logs and thus a notion of run-equivalence, known as *configuration equivalence* or *pomset equivalence* [9].

Given the above, we map the problem of process drift detection to that of finding a time point such that the set of runs before this point is statistically different from the set of runs after (for a given time window size). This formulation leads to a two-staged approach. First, we calculate a set of runs from a given sub-log, and then we apply statistical testing to find significant differences between the adjacent sets of runs. The next two sub-sections discuss these two stages in turn, while the third sub-section discusses the window size.

3.1   From Event Logs to Partial Order Runs

An event log consists of a set of traces, each capturing the sequence of events for a given case of the process ordered by timestamp. For example, $L = [\sigma_1^2, \sigma_2^3]$, where $\sigma_1 = \langle a, b, c, d \rangle$ and $\sigma_2 = \langle a, c, b, d \rangle$, defines a log containing 5 traces and a total of 20 events (for simplicity we used the simple event log representation [10]). It is formally defined as follow:

Definition 1 (Event log, Trace). *Let L be an* event log *over the set of labels $\mathcal{L}$, i.e. $L \in \mathbb{B}(\mathcal{L}^*)$. Let E be a set of event occurrences and $\lambda : E \to \mathcal{L}$ a labeling function. An* event trace *$\sigma \in L$ is defined in terms of an order $i \in [0, n-1]$ and a set of events $E_\sigma \subseteq E$ with $|E_\sigma| = n$ such that $\sigma = \langle \lambda(e_0), \lambda(e_1), \ldots, \lambda(e_{n-1}) \rangle$.*

While a trace defines a *total order* of events, encoding the concurrency relationship in it results into a partial order run. For simplicity, in the following we formalize the concurrency relationship using the *Alpha concurrency* from [11]. It is possible however to use a more accurate definition of concurrency such as the

Alpha+ [12] or *Alpha++* [13], or the one proposed in [14]. These alternative definitions do not suffer from the issue of confusing concurrency with short loops [12].

Definition 2 (Alpha concurrency). *Let L be an event log over the set of event labels $\mathcal{L}$ and $\sigma \in L$ be a log trace. A pair of tasks with labels $a, b \in \mathcal{L}$ are said to be in* alpha directly precedes relation, *denoted $A \prec_{\alpha(L)} B$, iff there exists a trace $\sigma = \langle \lambda(e_0), \lambda(e_1), \ldots, \lambda(e_{n-1}) \rangle$ in L, such that $A = \lambda(e_i)$ and $B = \lambda(e_{i+1})$. We say that a pair of tasks $A, B \in \mathcal{L}$ are* alpha concurrent, *denoted $A \parallel_{\alpha(L)} B$, iff $A \prec_{\alpha(L)} B \wedge B \prec_{\alpha(L)} A$.*

Note that the *Alpha concurrency* is a symmetric relation, and is applied over labels and not over event occurrences. For instance, we can identify that b $\prec_\alpha$ c from trace $\sigma_1 = \langle a, b, c, d \rangle$, and c $\prec_\alpha$ b from trace $\sigma_2 = \langle a, c, b, d \rangle$. Therefore, b and c are considered to be parallel, noted $b \parallel_\alpha c$.

In the following, we assume there exists an oracle χ which provides the concurrency relation $\parallel_\chi$. We will consider that $\parallel_\chi = \{(e, e') \mid \lambda(e) \parallel_{\alpha(L)} \lambda(e')\}$ for an event log L and its alpha concurrency relation $\parallel_{\alpha(L)}$.

As mentioned before, based on the concurrency relationship a trace is (losslessly) transformed to a *partial order* representation of its events. Definition 3 describes formally how, given a relation $\parallel_\chi$, a trace can be transformed into a partially ordered run.

Definition 3 (Transformation of a Trace Into a Run). *Let L be an event log over the set of event labels $\mathcal{L}$ and $\parallel_\chi$ be the concurrency relation provided by an oracle χ. Moreover, let E be a set of event occurrences, $\lambda : E \to \mathcal{L}$ a labelling function. We say that event e_i directly precedes event e_{i+1}, denoted $e_i \lessdot e_{i+1}$, iff there exists a trace $\sigma = \langle \lambda(e_0), \ldots, \lambda(e_1), \ldots, \lambda(e_{n-1}) \rangle$ in L with an order $i \in [0, n-1]$. Therefore, the tuple $\pi = \langle E_\pi, \leq_\pi, \lambda_\pi \rangle$ is the partially ordered run corresponding to trace σ, induced by the concurrency relation $\parallel_\chi$ and the directly precedes relation $\lessdot$, where:*

– *E_π is the set of events occurring in σ,*
– *$\leq_\pi$ is the causality relation defined as $\leq_\pi = E_\pi^2 \cap (\lessdot^+ \setminus \parallel_\chi)^*$,[1] and*
– *$\lambda_\pi : E_\pi \to \mathcal{L}$ is a labelling function, i.e. $\lambda_\pi = \lambda|_{E_\pi}$.*

We write $\Pi_\chi(L)$ to denote the set of all partially ordered runs induced by $\parallel_\chi$ over the set of traces in L.

In order to illustrate the operation of building a run from a trace, let us consider the example event log L and apply the definition step-by-step. We first compute the directly precedes relationship $\lessdot$ by representing the sequencing captured by the event traces, resulting in the set $\{(a_{\sigma_1}, b_{\sigma_1}), (b_{\sigma_1}, c_{\sigma_1}), (c_{\sigma_1}, d_{\sigma_1}), (a_{\sigma_2}, c_{\sigma_2}), (c_{\sigma_2}, b_{\sigma_2}), (b_{\sigma_2}, d_{\sigma_2})\}$. Second, we compute the (irreflexive) transitive closure $\lessdot^+$ by adding to the previous set the following new relations: $\{(a_{\sigma_1}, c_{\sigma_1}), (b_{\sigma_1}, d_{\sigma_1}), (a_{\sigma_1}, d_{\sigma_1}), (a_{\sigma_2}, b_{\sigma_2}), (c_{\sigma_2},$

Fig. 1. Example of a run (π_1)

---

[1] $+$ indicates the transitive closure and $*$ indicates the transitive reduction of a relation.

d_{σ_2}), $(a_{\sigma_2}, d_{\sigma_2})$}. Third, we compute the concurrency relation $\|_\chi$, and obtain $\{(b, c)\}$. Forth, we compute the causality relation $\leq_{\pi_1}$ for the run π_1 corresponding to trace σ_1 by computing set $<^+ \backslash \|_\chi$, which leads to removing the relation $(b_{\sigma_1}, c_{\sigma_1})$. Similarly, we remove $(c_{\sigma_2}, b_{\sigma_2})$ for $\leq_{\pi_2}$ for run π_2 from σ_2. Finally, we remove the unnecessary transitive relations $(a_{\sigma_1}, d_{\sigma_1})$ for π_1 and $(a_{\sigma_2}, d_{\sigma_2})$ for π_2 by applying the transitive reduction of the causality relation.

The result of this transformation applied on $\sigma_1 = \langle a, c, b, d \rangle$ is the run π_1 defined by the following causality relation $\leq_{\pi_1} = \{(a, b), (a, c), (b, d), (c, d)\}$ implicitly inferring that $b \|_\chi c$ (cf. Figure 1). Since each transformation of a trace in L results in the exact same run represented by π_1, we obtain that $\Pi(L) = [\pi_1^5]$.

Armed with this definition of run, we treat an event log as a continuous stream of traces. For each new trace we transform it to a run based on the alpha relationship that is dynamically computed on the basis of the traces observed until that point. Thus, the stream of traces is transformed into a stream of runs.

3.2   Statistical Testing Over Runs

In order to detect a drift in a stream of runs, we monitor any statistically significant change in the distribution of the most recent runs. This test is done on two populations of the same size built from the most recent runs in the stream. Basically the most recent runs are divided into a *reference* (less recent) and a *detection* (more recent) populations. Then, we evaluate the statistical hypothesis of whether or not the reference and detection populations are similar.

In this regard, we define two juxtaposed sliding windows, namely the reference and detection windows of length w, forming together the composite window of $2w$ most recent runs. Figure 2 depicts the two sliding windows over a stream of runs with a drift point. For every new run is observed in the stream, we slide both the reference and detection windows to the right in order to read the new run and perform a new statistical test. We keep iterating this process as long there are new runs observed in the stream.

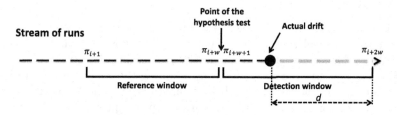

Fig. 2. Statistical test over two sliding windows

Since there is no a-priori knowledge of the run distributions (and their parameters) within the reference and detection windows population, we apply a nonparametric hypothesis statistical test. Moreover, given that an observation of the statistical variable is a run, the statistical test has to be applicable to a categorical variable. For these reasons, we selected the Chi-square test of independence between two variables.

The goal of a two-variable Chi-square test is to determine whether the reference variable and detection variable are similar. The reference variable (resp., the detection variable) is represented by the observations from the reference window (resp., the detection window). A contingency matrix is built to report the frequencies of each distinct run in each window. The Chi-square test is performed on this contingency matrix. The result of the test is the significance probability (the $P-value$). A drift is detected when the $P-value$ is less than the significance level α (the threshold), and localized at the point of juxtaposition of the reference and detection windows. The value of α is set to the typical value of the Chi-square statistical test, which is 0.05 [15].

The *delay d* shown in Figure 2 is a notion from concept drift in data mining [16]. It is not the distance between the actual drift and the location where the drift is detected. Rather, it indicates how long it takes for the statistical test to detect the drift after it has occurred, and is measured as the number of runs between the drift and the end of the detection window.

Since any statistical test is subject to sporadic stochastic oscillations, we introduced an additional filter to discard abrupt drops in the $P-value$. An abrupt stochastic oscillation is caused by the noise present in the event log, e.g. in the form of infrequent events or data gaps. Accordingly, we detect a drift only if a given number ϕ of successive statistical tests have a $P-value < \alpha$. In other terms, a persistent $P-value$ under the threshold is much more reliable than a sparse value happening abruptly. Our tests showed that a value of ϕ equal to $w/3$ provides the best results in terms of accuracy. More sophisticated approaches to filter out stochastic oscillations are however available, e.g. from the financial domain [17], and could be used instead.

The only independent parameter that needs to be manually set is the window size w. Below we discuss a technique to automatically modify this parameter as new runs are observed at runtime.

3.3   Adaptive Window

As discussed in Section 2, the choice of window size is critical in any drift detection method as a small window size may lead to false positives while a large one may lead to false negatives as well difficulty in locating the exact point of the drift. Our method strikes this trade-off by adapting the window size in order to have a more reliable statistical test. It is inspired by [18], where the authors provide rigorous guarantees on the performance of the adaptive window technique.

Our method is motivated by the fact that a low variation does not need too many data points to remain statistically representative, whereas a higher variation would need more data points to be statistically representative. In other words, if a high (resp. low) variation is captured within the composite window then we will need more (resp. less) observations to statistically express this distribution, and this is done by increasing (resp. decreasing) the window size.

The variation (named variability as well) of a statistical variable is a concept that aims to measure the dispersion of the observations. Regarding categorical data, [19] defined a set of properties and proposed a set of measures of variability (that can be alternatively used). We simply measure the variability of a given composite window by dividing the number of distinct runs (categories) by the number of the runs in this composite window (number of observations). In order to keep this rate constant from a statistical test to the next one, then the sliding composite window size needs to be adjusted if the number of distinct runs varies. Thus the evolution of the distinct number of runs over two consecutive statistical tests is captured and replicated on the window size based on a simple cross-multiplication.

Formally, given two consecutive statistics tests T_1 and T_2, the *evolution ratio* between T_2 and T_1 is defined as the ratio between the numbers of distinct runs in the composite window of T_2 over the number of distinct runs in the composite window of T_1. If the *evolution ratio* is equal to 1, this means that there was no evolution in the variation between T_1 and T_2. However, an *evolution ratio* less than 1 means that there is less variation in the T_2 composite window as compared to T_1, whereas an *evolution ratio* greater than 1 means the opposite.

The composite window size is adjusted according to the *evolution ratio*, specifically the new window size is equal to the current size multiplied by the ratio (cross-multiplication), i.e. $nextWindowSize = currentWindowSize \cdot evolutionRatio$. Every time that the reference and detection windows are shifted forward to incorporate a new run in the stream, the method adjusts the window size based on this formula. In order to initialize the procedure, we start with a given window size, which can be set empirically as discussed in the next section.

4   Evaluation on Synthetic Logs

We implemented the proposed method on top of the Apromore platform[2] and used this tool to assess the goodness of our method in terms of accuracy and scalability in a variety of settings. This tool can read a complete event log or a continuous stream of event traces. Each new trace is used to dynamically update the alpha-relationships for each pair of events, and then transformed to a partial order run, resulting in a stream of runs. This stream of runs is then used as input for the statistical test.

4.1   Setup

To assess accuracy we used two established measures in concept-drift detection in data mining [16], namely the *F-score*, measured as the harmonic mean of recall and precision, and the *mean delay*. The latter, computed as the average number of log traces after which a drift is detected, not only measures how late we detect the drift with regard to where it actually happens, but it also indicates how far in the log traces are read to be able to detect a drift.

---

[2] Available at http://apromore.org/platform/tools

To simulate the presence of a drift in a log, we generated a benchmark of 72 event logs by varying different parameters as follows. First, we used a textbook example of a business process for assessing loan applications [20] as the "base" model. This model, illustrated in Figure 3, has 15 activities, one start event and three end events, and exhibits different control-flow structures including loops, parallel and alternative branches.

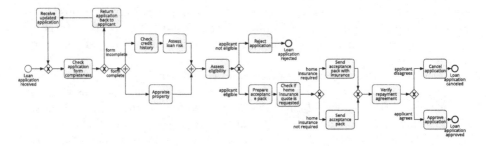

Fig. 3. Base BPMN model of the loan application process

Next, in order to assess the ability of our method to detect drifts determined by different types of control-flow changes, we systematically altered the base model by applying in turn one out of twelve *simple change patterns* described in [21].[3] These patterns, summarized in Table 1, describe different change operations commonly identified in business process models, such as adding, removing or looping a model fragment, swapping two fragments, or parallelizing two sequential fragments.

Table 1. Simple control-flow change patterns

Code	Simple change pattern	Category
re	Add/remove fragment	I
cf	Make two fragments conditional/sequential	R
lp	Make fragment loopable/non-loopable	O
pl	Make two fragments parallel/sequential	R
cb	Make fragment skippable/non-skippable	O
cm	Move fragment into/out of conditional branch	I
cd	Synchronize two fragments	R
cp	Duplicate fragment	I
pm	Move fragment into/out of parallel branch	I
rp	Substitute fragment	I
sw	Swap two fragments	I
fr	Change branching frequency	O

Further, in order to emulate more complex drifts, we organized the simple changes into three categories: Insertion ("I"), Resequentialization ("R") and Optionalization ("O") as shown in Table 1, so as to give rise to six possible *composite change patterns* by randomly applying one pattern from each category

---

[3] Non-applicable patterns such as inlining or extracting a subprocess were excluded.

in a nested way ("IOR", "IRO", "OIR", "ORI", "RIO", "ROI"). For example, the composite pattern "IOR" was obtained by first adding a new activity ("I"), then making this activity in parallel with an existing activity ("O") and finally by putting the whole parallel block into a loop structure ("R").

Finally, in order to vary the distance between drifts in the log, we generated four logs of 250, 500, 750 and 1,000 traces for the "base" model as well as for each of the 18 "altered" models, using the BIMP simulator,[4] and combined each group of 5 base logs with each group of 5 altered logs by alternating base and altered logs, in order to obtain four logs of sizes 2,500, 5,000, 7,500 and 10,000 traces for each of the 18 change patterns, leading to a total of 72 logs.[5] Figure 4 depicts an application of this operation to generate a log of 5,000 traces. Each log has 9 drifts located at multiples of 10% of the log size, thus with an inter-drift distance ranging from 250 to 1,000 traces (500 in the example). Knowing the number and position of each drift in the logs provides a gold standard against which we can evaluate the accuracy of our method.

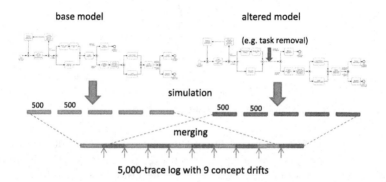

Fig. 4. Event log generation with embedded concept drift

4.2   Impact of Window Size on Accuracy

First, we evaluated the impact of the window size on accuracy. For this, we executed our method with different fixed window sizes ranging from 25 to 150 traces in increments of 25, against each of the 72 logs. Figure 5.a reports the F-score obtained with the four log sizes (2,500 to 10,000 traces), where for each log the F-score was averaged over the logs produced by the 18 change patterns. We observe that the F-score increases as the window size grows and eventually plateaus at a window size of 150. As expected, the more data points are included in the reference and detection windows, the more reliable is the statistical distribution, and thus the more accurate is the statistical test, leading to the detection

---

[4] http://bimp.cs.ut.ee

[5] All the BPMN models used for simulation, the synthetic logs and the detailed evaluation results are available with the software distribution

of all concept drifts (recall of 1), with few or no false positives (precision of 0.9 or above).

Not surprisingly, for a window size of 25 traces, the F-score is low (around 0.45). This is because the Chi-square does not converge if more than 20% of the data points have frequency below 5 [22], which is often the case with a window size of 25 traces, where the distinct runs might be as low as 5-10. This results in both low recall and precision. The drop in F-score at a window size of 150 for logs of 2,500 traces is not an inherent limitation of our method, but is due to having set a drift every 10% of the log, which equates to 250 traces for a log of 2,500 traces. Given that with a window size of 150 traces reference and detection windows aggregate 300 traces, in certain cases two drifts will be included within this set of traces. As a result, the method will treat the two drifts as one leading to a low recall.

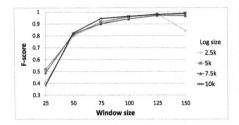 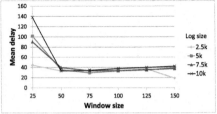

Fig. 5. F-score (a) and mean delay (b) obtained with different fixed window sizes.

Figure 5.b plots how the mean delay varies based on different window sizes, where the mean delay is averaged over the logs produced by the 18 different change patterns, according to the four log sizes. Interestingly, after an initial high mean delay, due to the unreliability of the statistical test with low numbers of data points, the mean delay grows very slowly as the window size increases. This shows that the method is very resilient in terms of mean delay to increases in windows size, having a relatively low delay of around 40 traces when the window size is 50 or above. Similar to the results for F-score, we observe a drop in the mean delay at a window size of 150, for logs of 2,500 traces. This positive effect is due to the second drift in the composite window of 300 traces being discovered before it happened with regards to the gold standard.

In summary, our method achieves high levels of accuracy both in terms of F-score (above 0.9) and mean delay (below 40 traces) in the presence of different types of drift and for different log sizes. This happens when employing a fixed window size that is at least 75 traces long, with the best trade off between F-score and mean delay being achieved with windows of 100 traces.

We also conducted experiments using the trace-based representation of logs (instead of the run-based one). We observed that the obtained accuracy with the trace-based representation was consistently lower than the one with runs. This observation confirms the intuition discussed in Section 3.

4.3   Impact of Adaptive Window Size on Accuracy

Next, we assessed the impact of the adaptive window method on F-score and mean delay. For this, we compared the results obtained with the fixed window size shown in Figure 5, averaged over the three log sizes of 5,000, 7,500 and 10,000 traces, with the results obtained using an adaptive window. For example, we compared the results obtained with a fixed window size of 25, with those obtained with an adaptive window initialized to 25 traces. We did not use the log size of 2,500 traces to avoid the effects of the interplay between window size and number of drifts observed in logs of this size in the previous tests.

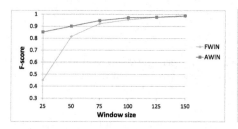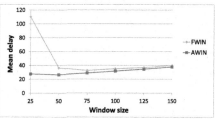

Fig. 6. F-score (a) and mean delay (b) obtained with different fixed window sizes (FWIN) vs. adaptive window sizes (AWIN).

Figure 6 reports the results of this comparison for F-score (a) and mean delay (b). The adaptive window method outperforms the fixed window method both in terms of F-score and mean delay. Indeed, the ability to dynamically change the window size based on the variation observed in the log (measured as the ratio between number of distinct runs and total number of runs in the combined window), allows us to obtain an adequate number of runs (not too small, not too large) in the reference and detection windows to perform the statistical test. This leads to a higher F-score, since more data points are automatically added to the window when the variation is high. At the same time, it leads to a lower mean delay as the window size is shrank when the variation is low, since in these cases a low number of runs is sufficient to perform the statistical test. As an advantage, the adaptive window method overcomes the low accuracy (both in terms of F-score and mean delay) obtained when fixing the window size to values as low as 25 traces (F-score of 0.85 instead of 0.45, and mean delay of 28 instead of 110). This enables the method to be employed in those scenarios where the distance between drifts in the log is expected to be very low (i.e. in the presence of very frequent drifts) and thus keeping the mean delay as low as possible becomes essential to identify as many drifts as possible.

4.4   Accuracy Per Change Pattern

As a further test on accuracy, we evaluated the relative levels of F-score and mean delay for each of the twelve simple change patterns and the six composite change patterns. For this we fixed the window size to 100 traces, which proved to provide the best trade off in terms of F-score and mean delay, and averaged the results obtained with the fixed window, and with the adaptive window initialized to 100 traces, over the three log sizes of 5,000, 7,500 and 10,000 traces.

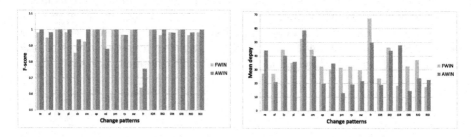

Fig. 7. F-score (a) and mean delay (b) per change pattern, obtained with fixed window size of 100 (FWIN) vs. adaptive window size initialized to 100 (AWIN).

Figure 7 shows the results. From these we can draw the following observations. First, the adaptive window method enhances F-score and mean delay for the majority of patterns (16 out of 18 for F-score and 12 out of 18 for mean delay), with the F-score often being 1. Second, the method experiences a sensibly lower F-score both for fixed and adaptive windows for the *frequency change* pattern ("fr"). This pattern modifies the frequency of certain event relations in the log. The low F-score is due to a low precision (lots of false positives). This is because our method is sensitive to frequency changes caused by the stochastic interference present in an event log. For example, even if the probabilities of taking two alternative branches in a process are observed to be 50% each in the entire log, when looking at an individual window, which is a small extract of the log, these probabilities are likely to be slightly different (e.g. they could be 40%-60% instead of 50%-50%). This interference tricks the detection of a frequency-based drift, but can be resolved by choosing a larger window size. For example, using a fixed window of 200 traces, we obtain an F-score of 0.98 (1 if using the adaptive window) for the "fr" pattern.

4.5   Execution Times

We conducted all tests on an Intel i7 2.20GHz with 16GB RAM (64 bit), running Windows 7 and JVM 8 with standard heap space of 512MB. The time required to update the alpha-relationships, extract the runs, and perform the Chi-square test, ranges from a minimum of 0.26 milliseconds to a maximum of 2.3 milliseconds with an average of 0.5 milliseconds. These results show that the method is suited for online concept drift detection, including scenarios where the inter-arrival time between completed traces is in the order of milliseconds.

4.6   Comparison with Baseline

Lastly, we compared the results obtained by our adaptive window method , with those obtained by the method of Bose et al. [1,3], since this is the most mature method for process drift detection available at the time of writing. Thus, we used the synthetic logs that we had previously generated for each of the 18 change patterns, set the window size to 100 and averaged the results over the three different log sizes of 5,000, 7,500 and 10,000 traces.

As discussed in Section 2, the method in [1,3] has the disadvantage that it requires to manually select the order relations between event labels to be used as features to build the feature space which in turn is required to detect the drifts. Thus, knowing the specific changes made in the altered models, we manually selected the most appropriate features for each log. Figure 8 shows the results of the comparison.

Our method outperforms the method in [1,3] both in terms of F-score and mean delay, achieving substantial F-score differences for ten change patterns, including "lp" (make fragment loopable/non-loopable), "cp" (duplicate fragment), "pm" (move fragment into/out of parallel branch) and composite patterns such as "IOR" and "RIO". This is due to the large number of false positives identified by method in [1,3]. Further, this method fails to identify drifts based on the following changes: "cb" (make fragment skippable/not skippable) and "cm" (move fragment into/out of conditional branch), even if appropriate features are chosen.

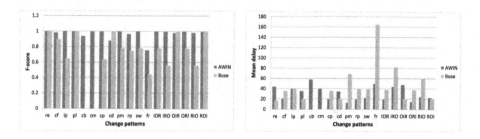

Fig. 8. F-score (a) and mean delay (b) per change pattern, obtained with our adaptive window method with size initialized to 100 (AWIN) vs. [1,3] with fixed window size of 100 (BOSE).

As a final test, we selected all features available from each log in order to simulate a fully-automated application of this method. However in this case the method fails to identify any drift due to a high level of false negatives, and construction of the feature space becomes an expensive task (over 15 minutes with window size of 100 traces).

5   Evaluation on Real-Life Log

We employed our method to detect concept drifts in an event log originated from the claims management system of a large Australian insurance company. The log

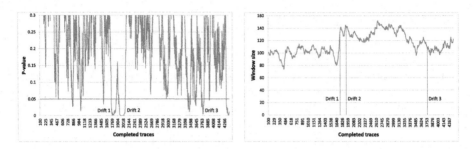

Fig. 9. Plot of the Chi-square test results (a) and adaptive window size (b).

consists of 4,509 traces with 29,108 total events of which 12 are distinct events. It records claim handling processes for motor insurance that were performed over a period of 13 months between 2011 and 2012.

We initialized the adaptive window to 100 traces. The method took 4.51 seconds to check the whole log and returned three drifts at 1,769, 1,911 and 3,763 traces, as shown by the results of the Chi-square test in Figure 9.a. In this plot we can also see a number of stochastic oscillations that were automatically filtered out by our method, as described in Section 3.2.

We then validated the results with a business analyst from the insurance company, who confirmed that the three drifts correspond to a new major release (Drift 1) and two minor releases (Drifts 2 and 3) of the claims management system. These releases led to various changes in the claim handling process supported by the system, e.g. the removal of a manual task for reviewing the claim correspondence and the replacement of a manual task for checking the invoice with an automated one, with the purpose of reducing the total number of open claims. The effects of these changes are confirmed by the distribution of the number of active cases over the log timeline, shown in Figure 10, which we have annotated with the position of the drifts identified by our method and the delays in reporting these drifts. We can see that each drift is associated with a drop in the number of active cases, which confirms the effectiveness of the new releases on process performance.

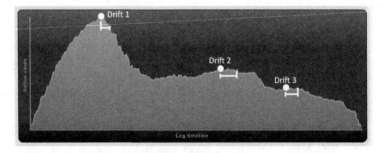

Fig. 10. The position and delay of the three drifts identified by our method, noted on active cases over log timeline

The delay in detecting the first two drifts is longer than the delay in detecting the last drift. This is due to a higher level of variation in the first part of the log (due to the more manual nature of the business process), which led our method to increase the size of the adaptive window. This is confirmed by Figure 9.b, which shows how the window size varies according to the number of completed traces. Here we can see that the detection of Drift 1 and 2 is associated with a larger window size (131 and 143) than the size used to detect Drift 3 (size 109).

6 Conclusion

The paper proposed a fully automated method for business process drift detection based on statistical testing of distributions of runs. The proposed method – especially in its "adaptive window" variant – accurately discovers typical process changes and combinations thereof, consistently outperforming a state-of-the art baseline. The evaluation results on a complex real-life log demonstrate the method's ability to detect drifts that correspond to user-recognizable process changes, as well as its scalability. The execution times in the order of milliseconds make it applicable for online drift detection.

In its present form, the proposed method treats event logs as consisting of sequences of event labels. In doing so, it does not take into account process execution data and resource allocations – usually encoded as event payloads. An avenue for future work is to make the method data-aware.

Another avenue for future research is to enhance the method in order to provide input to the user to understand the process change(s) underpinning a detected drift. One possibility to explain a drift is to present to the user the runs with the highest frequency differentials between the reference and the detection windows. This input may help the user to gain a partial and initial understanding of the process change(s), but it is unlikely to provide a comprehensive picture in the case of complex business processes. A possible direction to tackle this problem is to apply automated process discovery before and after the drift, and to use a process model comparison technique [23] in order to derive a diagnostics of the differences between the discovered pre-drift and the post-drift process models.

Acknowledgments. NICTA is funded by the Australian Government via the Department of Communications. This research is funded by the Australian Research Council Discovery Project DP150103356 and the Estonian Research Council.

References

1. Bose, R.P.J.C., van der Aalst, W.M.P., Žliobaitė, I., Pechenizkiy, M.: Handling concept drift in process mining. In: Mouratidis, H., Rolland, C. (eds.) CAiSE 2011. LNCS, vol. 6741, pp. 391–405. Springer, Heidelberg (2011)
2. Carmona, J., Gavaldà, R.: Online techniques for dealing with concept drift in process mining. In: Hollmén, J., Klawonn, F., Tucker, A. (eds.) IDA 2012. LNCS, vol. 7619, pp. 90–102. Springer, Heidelberg (2012)

3. Bose, R.J.C., van der Aalst, W.M., Zliobaite, I., Pechenizkiy, M.: Dealing with concept drifts in process mining. IEEE Transactions on NNLS **25**(1), 154–171 (2014)
4. Martjušev, J.: Efficient algorithms for discovering concept drift in business processes. Master's thesis, University of Tartu (2013)
5. Accorsi, R., Stocker, T.: Discovering workflow changes with time-based trace clustering. In: Aberer, K., Damiani, E., Dillon, T. (eds.) SIMPDA 2011. LNBIP, vol. 116, pp. 154–168. Springer, Heidelberg (2012)
6. Burattin, A., Sperduti, A., van der Aalst, W.M.: Control-flow discovery from event streams. In: 2014 IEEE Congress on Evolutionary Computation (CEC), pp. 2420–2427. IEEE (2014)
7. Gama, J., Žliobaitė, I., Bifet, A., Pechenizkiy, M., Bouchachia, A.: A survey on concept drift adaptation. ACM Computing Surveys (CSUR) **46**(4) (2014)
8. Hidders, J., Dumas, M., van der Aalst, W.M., ter Hofstede, A.H., Verelst, J.: When are two workflows the same? In: Proc. of CATS, pp. 3–11. Australian Computer Society (2005)
9. van Glabbeek, R., Goltz, U.: Equivalence notions for concurrent systems and refinement of actions. In: Kreczmar, A., Mirkowska, M. (eds.) Mathematical Foundations of Computer Science 1989. LNCS, vol. 379, pp. 237–248. Springer, Heidelberg (1989)
10. van der Aalst, W.: Process Mining: Discovery, Conformance and Enhancement of Business Processes. Springer (2011)
11. van der Aalst, W.M.P., Weijters, T., Maruster, L.: Workflow mining: discovering process models from event logs. IEEE TKDE **16**(9), 1128–1142 (2004)
12. de Medeiros, A.K.A., van der Aalst, W.M.P., Weijters, A.J.M.M.T.: Workflow mining: current status and future directions. In: Meersman, R., Schmidt, D.C. (eds.) CoopIS 2003, DOA 2003, and ODBASE 2003. LNCS, vol. 2888, pp. 389–406. Springer, Heidelberg (2003)
13. Wen, L., van der Aalst, W.M., Wang, J., Sun, J.: Mining process models with non-free-choice constructs. Data Mining and Knowledge Discovery **15**(2) (2007)
14. Cook, J.E., Wolf, A.L.: Event-based detection of concurrency. In: Proc. of FSE (1998)
15. Nuzzo, R.: Statistical errors. Nature **506**(13), 150–152 (2014)
16. Ho, S.S.: A martingale framework for concept change detection in time-varying data streams. In: Proc. of ICML, pp. 321–327. ACM (2005)
17. Murphy, J.J.: Technical analysis of the financial markets: A comprehensive guide to trading methods and applications. Penguin (1999)
18. Bifet, A., Gavalda, R.: Learning from time-changing data with adaptive windowing. In: SDM, vol. 7. SIAM (2007)
19. Wilcox, A.R.: Indices of qualitative variation. Technical report, Oak Ridge Nat. Lab (1967)
20. Dumas, M., La Rosa, M., Mendling, J., Reijers, H.: Fundamentals of Business Process Management. Springer (2013)
21. Weber, B., Reichert, M., Rinderle-Ma, S.: Change patterns and change support features-enhancing flexibility in process-aware information systems. DKE **66**(3), 438–466 (2008)
22. Yates, D., Moore, D., Starnes, D.S.: The practice of statistics: TI-83/89 Graphing Calculator Enhanced. Macmillan (2007)
23. Armas-Cervantes, A., Baldan, P., Dumas, M., García-Bañuelos, L.: Behavioral comparison of process models based on canonically reduced event structures. In: Sadiq, S., Soffer, P., Völzer, H. (eds.) BPM 2014. LNCS, vol. 8659, pp. 267–282. Springer, Heidelberg (2014)

Process Model Discovery II

Mining Project-Oriented Business Processes

Saimir Bala[✉], Cristina Cabanillas, Jan Mendling,
Andreas Rogge-Solti, and Axel Polleres

Vienna University of Economics and Business, Vienna, Austria
{saimir.bala,cristina.cabanillas,jan.mendling,
andreas.rogge-solti,axel.polleres}@wu.ac.at

Abstract. Large engineering processes need to be monitored in detail regarding when what was done in order to prove compliance with rules and regulations. A typical problem of these processes is the lack of control that a central process engine provides, such that it is difficult to track the actual course of work even if data is stored in version control systems (VCS). In this paper, we address this problem by defining a mining technique that helps to generate models that visualize the work history as GANTT charts. To this end, we formally define the notion of a project-oriented business process and a corresponding mining algorithm. Our evaluation based on a prototypical implementation demonstrates the benefits in comparison to existing process mining approaches for this specific class of processes.

Keywords: Process mining · Projects · Project mining · Version control systems

1 Introduction

Business process management plays an important role for improving the performance and compliance of various types of processes. In practice, many processes are executed with clear guidelines and regulatory rules, but without an explicit centralized control imposed by a process engine. In particular, it is often important to exactly know when which work was done. This is, for instance, the case for complex engineering processes in which different parties are involved. We refer to this class of processes as project-oriented business processes.

Such project-oriented business processes are difficult to control due to the lack of a centralized process engine. However, there are various unstructured pieces of information available to analyze and monitor their progress. One type of data that are often available these processes is event data from version control systems (VCS). While process mining techniques provide a useful perspective on how such event data can be analyzed, they do not produce output that is readily organized according to the project orientation of these processes.

This work has been funded by the Austrian Research Promotion Agency (FFG) under grant 845638 (SHAPE) and the European Union's Seventh Framework Programme under grant 612052 (SERAMIS).

© Springer International Publishing Switzerland 2015
H.R. Motahari-Nezhad et al. (Eds.): BPM 2015, LNCS 9253, pp. 425–440, 2015.
DOI: 10.1007/978-3-319-23063-4_28

In this paper, we define formal concepts for capturing project-oriented processes. These concepts provide the foundation for us to develop an automatic discovery technique which we refer to as *project mining*. The output of our project mining algorithm is organized according to the specific structure typically encountered in project-oriented business processes. With this work, we extend the field of process mining towards the coverage of this specific type of business process.

The paper is structured as follows. Section 2 describes the research problem and summarizes insights from prior research upon which our project mining approach is built. Section 3 defines the preliminaries of our work and presents an algorithm to mine project-oriented business processes. Section 4 describes the implementation of this algorithm and discusses the results from its application to VCS logs from a real-world engineering project. Section 5 highlights the implications of this work before Section 6 concludes.

2   Background

Here, we describe the addressed problem and related work.

2.1   Problem Description

The class of processes that we discuss in this paper are long-term engineering projects. These processes have specific requirements for monitoring. First, they are executed only once according to the specific needs of a particular project, and only partially according to recurring process descriptions. Second, they involve various actors that typically document their work in a semi-structured way using text and tables. Third, work in the project is usually subject to constraints regarding the start and end and the temporal order. Fourth, there is typically no process engine controlling the execution. Fifth, even though these limitations in terms of traceability exist, there are usually strong requirements in terms of tracking when which work was conducted.

In line with these observations, a *project-oriented business process* can be defined as an ad-hoc plan that specifies the tasks to be performed within a limited period of time and with a limited set of resources for achieving a specific goal. Unlike repetitive business processes for which notations such as BPMN [12] or EPC [1] are commonly used, project-oriented business processes may be properly represented with PERT or GANTT models. The concept is illustrated in Fig. 1.

Documentation is required not only explicitly as part of some activities but also to comply with norms and regulations that may require some evidence of the actions being performed in the organization. Documents are usually free of format or contain tables, at best. The unstructuredness of data makes it difficult to monitor processes and check rules on them. A starting point for analysis of project-oriented processes can be data logs that are stored in Software Configuration Management (SCM) systems that help tracking the evolution of data and restore information if needed [19]. However, hundreds of versions of

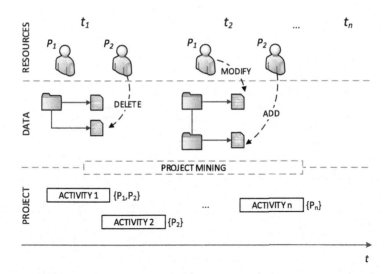

Fig. 1. Problem illustration

thousands of files are common in a single project [20], which makes it impractical to browse this data manually.

Let us see an example inspired by a real scenario of a process to write a project proposal that uses a Version Control System (VCS) to store the data. The project history, and hence, the data produced, starts when people begin to work on the proposal, which involves a description of the project goals and milestones, a division of tasks into work packages, an estimation of cost and resources required, etcetera. This information is spread in the repository over several folders containing different documents, which are later merged into a single file. If the proposal is accepted, the first step is to organize a kickoff meeting and assign specific resources to the work packages. A hierarchical set of folders is then created in the repository in order to store the information generated for each work package. As the project evolves over time, resources contribute by adding, removing or modifying information to the VCS repository. Project evolution is guided by specific norms that impose the execution of predefined steps. For instance, the European norm EN5016 requires a preliminary Reliability, Availability and Maintainability (RAM) analysis to support targets.

Table 1 depicts an excerpt of the log data generated, where the first column (on the left hand side) indicates the commit identifier, the second column indicates the person who committed changes, the third column indicates the commit date, and the fourth column indicates the files affected and the type of action performed among added (A), modified (M) and deleted (D). For the sake of simplicity, the table shows the log data of a specific time period and the actions related to a specific task, namely, *Define example*. That task was assigned to resource X and was supervised by resource Y and, later on, also by resource Z.

Table 1. Excerpt from VCS log data for the referenced time period

CID	Resource	Date	List of changes
1	Y	2014-11-12 11:57:46	A /example A /example/SHAPE/ToyStationExample.docx
...	...	...	...
3	X	2014-11-14 16:34:07	M /example/ToyStation.bpmn M /example/ToyStation.png
4	W	2014-12-15 13:49:11	D /example/Download
5	W	2015-01-08 16:06:41	A /example/Download2
6	X	2015-01-13 11:47:09	M /example/ToyStation_0Loop.bpmn M /example/ToyStation_nLoop.bpmn
7	Z	2015-01-16 16:50:29	A /example/ToyStation_0Loop.pdf A /example/ToyStation-feedbackZ.pdf

Existing frameworks, such as Subversion or Git, allow to access their logs in different ways. However, the covered information is limited to (roughly) that depicted in Table 1. Especially for big projects that are frequently updated over a large period of time, these logs are complex to analyze. Therefore, the problem to address is how to analyze and visualize the information produced in project-oriented business processes such that it can be represented in an understandable and manageable way by project experts and enable, a.o., the automation of mechanisms for compliance checking. The following properties of project-oriented process logs must be taken into account to achieve this goal: (i) VCS repositories consist of a hierarchy of folders and files which are logically organized such that work is grouped in a specific way; (ii) process activities are not registered in VCS log entries. Therefore, such information must be inferred by reasoning on the repository structure and/or the content of the log entries; (iii) the granularity of the events is unknown a priori and it needs to be defined before analyzing the data.

2.2   Related Work

The problem described has been addressed in the literature from different perspectives. The first category of related work tackles the problem by transforming it into a process mining problem. Consequently, approaches have been developed to preprocess VCS data such that process mining techniques can be applied, and hence, a business process can be derived from the log data. In this group, Kindler et al. [9,10] developed an algorithm for extracting software processes that are mapped to Petri Nets. Activities, which are not explicit in the logs, are discovered from their input and output artifacts. However, strong assumptions are made on the filenames as well as on the software process lifecycle. Rubin et al. in [15] addressed the problem of engineering processes that are not well documented and are usually unstructured. They provided a bridge from Kindler et al.'s approach to ProM [5] in order to mine different process perspectives, such as performance social network analyses. Rubin et al. [16] applied process mining to the touristic industry and obtained user processes from web client logs pursuing the goal of improving the software system by analyzing the underlying process. Poncin et al. [14] developed the FRASR framework for preprocessing software repositories to transform the VCS data to logs that conform to the process mining event log meta model [4] as utilized in ProM [5]. However, these approaches disregard the single-instance nature of project-oriented business processes and treat them as procedures that can be repeated over time.

The second category of related work focuses on the visualization of VCS data for different purposes. Several approaches study the interaction among developers over time from a visualization point of view. For instance, Ogawa and Ma [11] drew storyline pathways to show the story of each developer's contribution. Other approaches analyze and visualize VCS data at file level in order to discover file version evolution. Voinea and Telea [20] introduced an interactive navigation method to surf file version evolution as well as two methods to cluster versions of the same file in an abstraction layer. Wu et al. [22] also visualized the evolutions of entire projects at file level, emphasizing the evolution moments. Finally, several approaches study change prediction with the aim of discovering prediction patterns that can help in the process of software development [23,24]. The approaches mentioned in this category as well as others that apply similar techniques [3,6,8] focus on studying software evolution from different standpoints. However, the goal pursued differs in all cases from our goal in that they are not interested in discovering projects tasks out of the log data, and hence, they lack an explicit notion of work structure that we need to consider for our purpose.

Our approach combines ideas from both areas, as we aim at identifying tasks like in the approaches that rely on process mining, but we must cluster the data in an appropriate way, for which techniques developed in the approaches that pursue visualization may be adapted or extended.

3   Mining VCS Event Data

Here, we first formalize the notions encountered in the project mining setting. Then we develop an approach to acquire a hierarchical overview on the project from a repository perspective.

3.1   Preliminaries

Version control systems (VCSs) are used in projects to ensure reliable collaboration. We build our approach on VCS. Typically, the workflow in VCS is that people work on files (e.g., text, source code, spread sheets) and commit them to the central repository. Project participants comment on their commits so that other participants can better understand the nature of the changes to the files.

Let F be the universe of files. Files are organized in a file tree. Therefore, each file $f \in F$ has one parent file. The only file without a parent file is the root file. We capture this information in the parent relation $Parent : F \times F$.

For example, let $f_p \in F$ be the parent of file $f_c \in F$, then $(f_p, f_c) \in Parent$. The transitive closure on the parent files is given by the function $ancestor : F \rightarrow 2^F$ that returns the set of files along the path to the root.

When project members did a certain amount of work and want to save their current progress, they commit the changes to the VCS. We define changes on files as the events of interest on the lowest granularity.

Definition 1 (Event). *Let E be the set of events. An event $e \in E$ is a four-tuple (f, o, ts, k), where*

- *$f \in F$ is the affected file of the event.*
- *$o \in O = \{added, modified, deleted\}$ is the change operation on the file with obvious meaning.*
- *$ts \in TS = \mathbb{N}_0$ represents a unix time stamp marking the time of the event occurrence.*
- *$k \in \Sigma^*$ is a comment in natural language text.*

For events $e = (f, o, ts, k)$ we overload f, o, ts, and k to be used as accessor functions. For example, f is the function $f : E \rightarrow F$ mapping an event to its affected file.

Project participants can commit a number of changes to different files at one step. Therefore, we define the notion of commits as follows.

Definition 2 (Commit). *A commit C is a set of events sharing the same time stamp and comment, i.e., $\forall e, e' \in C : ts(e) = ts(e') \wedge k(e) = k(e')$. Additionally, each event in a commit affects different files, i.e., $\forall e, e' \in C : e \neq e' \rightarrow f(e) \neq f(e')$.*

Usually, it is in the hands of project participants, when they decide to commit changes to the VCS. In the extreme case, there could be only a single commit made in a project that adds all files to the repository. Note that this extreme practice would render the use of a VCS obsolete. On the contrary, it is common practice to regularly perform commits in order to securely store work progress and to reduce the chance of conflicts [7,13]. Conflicts occur, when another participant committed changes to a file that is being committed and can cause extra work. Based on these insights, we make the assumption that commits are regularly made during work.

Projects are decomposed into work packages. We assume a hierarchical work package structure of a project, such that a work package can have sub work packages. Further, the amount of work in a single work package need not be done in one single time span, but it can be split into several activities. Activities have a start and end time, and subsequent activities can have idle periods in between. Thus, we define projects as follows.

Definition 3 (Project). *A project P is a tuple $(W, S, A, \alpha, \omega, \beta)$, where*

- *W is the set of work packages in the project.*
- *$S \subseteq W \times W$ is the relation that hierarchically decomposes work packages into a tree structure.*
- *A is the set of activities that are conducted in the work packages.*

- $\alpha : A \rightarrow TS$ is the function that assigns a start time to activities. Activities are ordered by their start times.
- $\omega : A \rightarrow TS$ is the function that assigns an end time to activities.
- $\beta : A \rightarrow W$ is the mapping function that maps activities to their corresponding work packages.

Note that this definition reflects an activity centric view on projects. The definition deliberately omits further dimensions, e.g., costs, resources, risks. The idea is not to capture projects in every detail, but to focus on the work packages of a project to obtain an overview of the work that is being done. We are interested in when work has been started in a work package, and when work packages have been done. This information can be derived from the activities associated to the workpackages. An obvious assumption is that the work package starts with its first activity, and ends when its last activity is completed.

Based on these notions, we can define the task of *project discovery* as reconstructing the project P from a set of low level event data E. In the following, we present an approach to this problem.

3.2   Project Discovery Technique

For project discovery from the VCS commit history, we need to identify activities that are performed, associate the activities to work packages and recreate the work package structure of the project. Our aim is to create a hierarchical model that provides an overview of the project work. Therefore, we have to identify the start and end times of activities and of work packages before we can visualize the project work. The input to the technique is the log that is stored in the VCS. The challenge is that the raw log only records commits on the file system level and information on activity level is missing. However, we can deduce activity information from events based on the following assumptions.

A1: Meaningful file tree structure. The file tree structure in a project represents its work package structure. That is, the knowledge workers organize their work in a file hierarchy that reflects the project structure.

A2: Local changes. Activities in a work package affect only files of the work package folder, or in the corresponding sub-tree in the file tree structure.

A3: Frequent commits. Commits to the VCS are regularly performed, when conducting work in an activity.

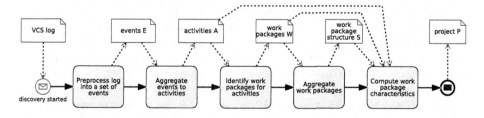

Fig. 2. Project discovery technique overview as BPMN process model.

Note that assumption A1 can be seen as a strong assumption on the file tree structure. Nevertheless, we argue that even if A1 is not entirely met, the aggregation of work information on the file tree hierarchy provides a valuable view on the project. Figure 2 shows the different steps of the technique. We describe each of them in detail.

Step 1: Preprocessing. The first step is to transform raw logs of version control systems (which might be grouped by commits) into a list of events as specified in Definition 1. This step is easily done by replicating the information on commit level to be contained in the events. The output is a set of events E.

Step 2: Aggregating events to activities. Given the set of events E that we gathered from a version control system, the next step is to identify the activities to which the events belong. Note that we do not know the activities of the project in advance, but need to infer them based on the events. Each event affects a single file in the file hierarchy.

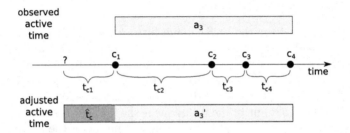

Fig. 3. Adjustment of activity start time α.

Based on assumption A2, we are interested in activities conducted in a work package, that is, we filter for the events that are contained in the given file or its children. For every file f of interest, we select the set of events affecting the file or its children as $E_f = \{e \in E \mid f = f(e) \lor f \in ancestor(f(e))\}$. The task is then to find the activities which emitted the set of events E_f. We rely on assumption A3, which states that during an activity, we expect multiple commits. Assumption A3 allows us to conclude that if we do not observe commits for a longer period of time, there is no activity being performed in the work package.

To this end, we adopt the abstraction technique by Baier et al. [2] and allow the domain expert to formulate rules for aggregating events to activities based on boundary conditions. Assuming that people frequently commit their progress (A3), we can specify a boundary condition based on the temporal distance to previous events. For example, we can specify that a time period of seven days without a commit is a boundary condition. As the result, we obtain the mapping from events to these activities, which we call $\gamma_f : E_f \to A_f$ in the remainder of the paper. The set of discovered activities identified for the work package based on given boundary conditions is then $A_f = \{a \mid e \in E_f, \gamma_f(e) = a\}$. We also define the inverse mapping, that is, the mapping from an activity to its events as $\gamma_f^{-1} : A_f \to 2^{E_f}$.

With the events mapped to activities, we need to find the temporal boundaries of the target activities. That is, we define the functions α and ω for each activity. The challenge here is that we do not know when an activity actually started, because the start of the activity is not recorded in the VCS. We can only observe the time of the first commit in that activity, but commits usually mark progress of an already running activity.

To address the challenge of missing start times, we impute the missing start time by prepending the expected active time $\hat{t}_c$ before a commit, as illustrated by Figure 3. This notion assumes that project participants commit their work progress after a certain amount of time. However, we cannot compute $\hat{t}_c$ by looking at the average commit rate in a work package, because this average is based on busy periods and idle periods. We need to factor out the idle periods in the computation of this measure. We know the end time of the activities, as the last commit marks the completion of work. Therefore, each activity a based on given boundary conditions has the associated end time $\omega(a) = \max(\{ts(e) \mid e \in \gamma_f^{-1}(a)\})$. Further, we write the first event's timestamp of an activity as the function $\alpha'(a) = \min(\{ts(e) \mid e \in \gamma_f^{-1}(a)\})$. Then, we define $c : A_f \to \mathbb{N}^+$ as the number of commits in one activity, formally $c(a) = |\{\mathcal{C} \mid e \in \mathcal{C} \wedge \gamma_f(e) = a\}|$.

With this information the expected active time between commits $\hat{t}_c$ is given as follows.

$$\hat{t}_c = \frac{\sum_{a \in A_f} (\omega(a) - \alpha'(a))}{\sum_{a \in A_f} (c(a) - 1)} \tag{1}$$

We assume that there is at least one activity spanning over at least two commits, i.e., $\exists a \in A_f \mid c(a) > 1$. Translated to our boundary condition, this assumption is that there is at least one week in each work package, in which there were at least two commits made. Otherwise, we set $\hat{t}_c$ to 0 for the current file f due to lack of information.

Given the expected active time between commits $\hat{t}_c$, we can finally adjust the start time of each activity. Therefore, we set the associated start time for each activity as $\alpha(a) = \alpha'(a) - \hat{t}_c$. That is, we subtract the expected active time from the first commit's timestamp.

We apply Step 2 to all files f in the file tree to get A_f. For the remainder of this paper, we define the function $\psi : A \to F$ that contains the mapping information of the discovered activities to their originating files. Finally, we set the activities A in the project to be the union of the activity sets per file $\bigcup_{f \in F} A_f$.

Steps 3 and 4: Mapping activities to work packages and aggregating. Once activities have been identified, we want to climb to the next abstraction layer: the work packages. Assumption A1 allows us to specify a one-to-one mapping $\kappa : F \to W$ between files in the file tree structure and work packages. More precisely, we construct the set of work packages W isomorphic to the set of files F, such that the *Parent* relation is preserved in the work package structure S relationship.

The mapping β of activities to work packages is simply $\beta(a) = \kappa(\psi(a))$. That is, the corresponding work package of the activity that was discovered for a file. In this way, we provide an activity based view on work packages, and we can aggregate on each level in the file system to see active periods of the corresponding hierarchy level.

Step 5: Computing work package characteristics. In this final step, we compute measures of interest for the discovered work packages. First, we obtain the temporal boundaries of a work package by the functions α and ω of the associated activities.

Let $\beta^{-1} : W \rightarrow 2^A$ be the inverse of the mapping function β of the project. The start and end time of a work package (α_W and ω_W) are functions from work packages to timestamps. The start time is defined as $\alpha_W(w) = \min(\{\alpha(a) \mid a \in \beta^{-1}(w)\})$, and the end time function of work packages ω_W is analogously defined using the maximum of the end times $\omega(a)$ of the activities. We call the duration of a work package τ that is the difference between ω_W and α_W.

Moreover, we are interested in the ratio of active working periods (i.e., the time spans of activities) to the total work package duration. This quantity helps to estimate the average work intensity in a work package.

Definition 4 (Coverage). *The coverage χ of work packages by activities is a function $\chi : W \rightarrow [0, 1]$ and is defined as follows.*

$$\chi(w) = \frac{\sum_{a \in \beta^{-1}(w)} (\omega(a) - \alpha(a))}{\tau(w)} \tag{2}$$

With this final step, we lifted the information hidden in low level events to a high-level Gantt chart perspective, with which project managers are familiar. In the following, we compare our technique to existing process mining approaches.

4   Evaluation

In this section we evaluate our solution to the project mining problem, and show results for the example presented in Section 2.

4.1   Experimental Setup

We evaluate our technique by a visual perspective and by comparison to possible different approaches. To this end we implemented our technique as a prototype. We used JAVA as a programming language to code the logic of our technique. For the visualization part we made use of custom SWT widgets provided by the

Nebula Project[1]. Our program can deal with logs from Subversion (SVN) [13] and Git[17], but it can be extended to other version control systems by providing an implementation of the preprocessing step discussed in Section 3.2. We ran the software in an Intel®Core ᵀᴹ i5-4570 CPU @ 3.20 GHz x 4 machine with 15.6 GiB of RAM and Linux kernel 3.13.0-46-generic 64-bit version.

4.2 Input Data Description

We tested our prototype with real-world log data taken from the SHAPE project. Logs were exported from the SVN and Git repositories of different projects. They come from the railway domain and describe engineering processes. Documentation stored in the repositories consists of manually produced text files, diagrams, and files coming from proprietary tools that are typically used in the domain.

We will display results for the SVN log that describes the process oriented project for SHAPE. Data span over one year, going from January 2014 to January 2015. This time window covers the phases of project definition and planning, and a part of the project execution. In the first phase, feasibility of the project was studied and budget, schedule and resources were determined. Proposal submission marked the end of this phase. The second phase started with a kickoff meeting in October 2014 and is still ongoing.

The total number of participants who actively contributed to the work packages stored in the SVN repository was 8 people in the beginning, with new resources joining the project after the kickoff date. The total number of files and directories counts up to 156 objects and 226 overall commit events. The total number of extracted change events after preprocessing (i.e. atomic changes on all the files) was 453.

The last part of the log data contains the task *Define example*, introduced in Section 2.1. For our showcase we assume that this task is contained in a work package named *example*.

4.3 Output Data

To monitor the project execution, we visualize the work progress that was done for each work package. Monitoring is performed by managers who want to have an overview on the project (which work packages are done, when and for how long, and where idleness or congestion occurs). Gantt charts offer a graphical representation for displaying schedules and jobs that were done on the various work packages [21] in a way that can easily be communicated to managers.

Figure 4 is a screenshot of how our tool presents the data. The tree structure on the left represents the *Parent* relation in the file tree. Events belonging to the same commit have the same color. On the top part of the chart we can see the result of merging events to activities with our aggregation method. Here we have merged the events of the example scenario on their highest abstraction level. The chart shows the three main activities and the idle times between them.

---

[1] https://www.eclipse.org/nebula/

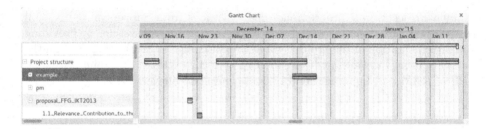

Fig. 4. Data representation from our tool. Atomic events are drawn as dot with a minimal duration and different color per commit.

On the other hand, in correspondence to expanded directories we show only their status before the aggregation. That is, every time a directory is fully expanded we apply a disaggregation into the corresponding activities. In this way, we can also show the finest granularity of work, i.e. the atomic events.

4.4 Project Analysis

Next, we apply our algorithm to the example case from Table 1 and check how it helps to identify work packages. The data is aggregated according to our threshold of seven days. We can observe three groups of events being temporally close to each other according to our threshold. That is, we expect the event data to be grouped into three activities.

The second step of our algorithm takes care of adjusting the starting time of the activities. Furthermore, we vertically order the events and activities in the Gantt chart according to the directory structure to show the mapping from the objects on the Gantt chart to each work package in the tree structure. The last step, computing work package characteristics is done automatically when we collapse a node of a tree.

Figure 5 shows a comparison of the case when we do not implement the activity adjustment to the case which adjusts it. In the upper part, activity

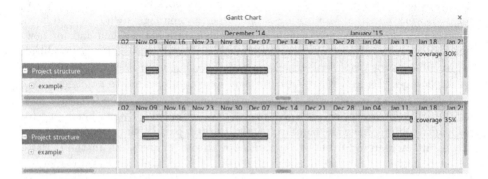

Fig. 5. Before and after the prepending the expected time before commit. Coverage factor increases when we adjust the starting times of the activities.

boundaries are based only on the first commit time that we see in the data. In the lower part, we observe that the start times were adjusted by approximately one day. The tool automatically adjusted the start time of the activities. As a consequence, the coverage factor increases because we expect that there was more work than what we observe by only considering the first commit time.

4.5 Coverage Tests on Available Open Projects

Finally, we apply our approach on different input data from open source projects. We are interested in exploring how the coverage factor varies in different existing projects. Hence, we take the work package w as our controlled variable and set it to the highest level of aggregation. Then, we analyze each project of the data set and observe the dependent variable $\chi(w)$. Another variable of interest is the $\hat{t}_c$ since it gives an idea of the average work speed (commit frequency) during active times.

Table 2. Coverage results for different open source projects

Log File name	Duration Days	Idle periods Number	Files Number	Commits Number	$\hat{t}_c$ Hours	$\chi(w)$ %
MiningCVS	24	0	89	63	9	100
Whitehall	1279	6	6539	15566	2	95
Petitions	834	17	1562	914	13	59
Study	624	13	7501	736	11	58
The Guardian	1667	59	12889	621	30	44
Book	414	15	154	592	5	32
Papers	1859	55	1791	649	20	30
Requirements	771	22	505	231	17	21
Yelp	206	6	24	54	20	20
Adobe	1076	13	356	237	24	15

The data we used stems from the following projects. *MiningVCS* is our tool. It consists of daily commits and was developed over 24 days. *Whitehall* is the code name for the Inside Government project, which aims to bring Government departments online in a consistent and user-friendly manner. *Petitions* is a Drupal 7 code base used to build an application on "We The People", the platform to create and sign petitions of the White House. *Study* is an SVN log about Healthcare domain, taken from SHAPE. *The guardian* is the log data from the Git repository of the well-known British national daily newspaper. *Book* is the log data that describes the writing of the book Crypto 101 by Laurens Van Houtven, taken from Git. *Papers* is taken from SHAPE project for building a paper archive. *Requirements* log data is taken from the the Git repository of OpenETCS and belongs to the railway domain. *Yelp* is the main Github page of Yelp were they showcase all their projects. *Adobe* is the Adobe Github Homepage v2.0, which is a central hub for Adobe Open sources projects.

Table 2 shows our experiments on the above-mentioned logs and the corresponding coverage factors. Projects that score a high coverage factor are characterized by continuous work. This can be further seen by looking at their average idle times $\bar{t}_{Idle}$. Let n_c be the number of commits per work package. We compute the average idle time as follows.

$$\bar{t}_{Idle} = \frac{\tau - n_c \cdot \hat{t}_c}{n} \ , \ n > 0 \tag{3}$$

where n is the number of idle times in the work package. If $n = 0$, then we trivially assign $\bar{t}_{Idle} = 0$, because there were no break periods over time.

Applying the formula to the above projects, we can observe how projects with a higher coverage factor have actually low values of $\bar{t}_{Idle}$. For instance, *Whitehall* scores a $\bar{t}_{Idle}$ of 11 days, whereas *Adobe* scores a $\bar{t}_{Idle}$ of 36 days. This supports the usage of the coverage factor χ as an indicator for work package time utilization.

5 Discussion

In this section we compare our method to other alternatives for mining data out of logs and interpret our results.

Well known tools that are used in academia and practice include ProM[5] and Disco[2]. Both tools require input data to be in the XES [18] format. Thus, we convert our data from the *Define example* case into XES. To show events per objects of the project structure, we choose the file path as the *caseId*. To flatten the logs we extract all the file paths and build a mapping from each file to the set of changes done to it.

Figure 6 depicts the results of the Dotted chart plugin of ProM applied to our log data. Also here, we observe different changes of each file of the repository. While the files and their corresponding events are shown, the plugin does not allow to rearrange the data in order to understand the file structure, nor does it allow to perform any kind of aggregation or connection between data, to observe them from a higher level perspective.

Figure 7 shows the results from mining our log data with the Disco tool. Here we can see a plot that displays the events that happen over time. The plot has some peeks in correspondence to active times of the *example* work package. They can be grouped in three clusters: an initial cluster with a few amount work, an intermediate cluster with the most significant part of the work, and a final cluster that again is not very active. In this way, clusters can be associated to activities. As a drawback, when the number of work packages and activities increase, the number of peeks grows and generate identifying clusters of activities by look at active (or idle) times becomes unworkable.

Our approach to mining the work progress of project-oriented business processes complements these techniques with metrics and a corresponding visualization that is informative to managers.

---

[2] http://fluxicon.com/disco/

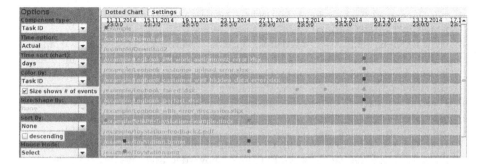

Fig. 6. Dotted chart from ProM

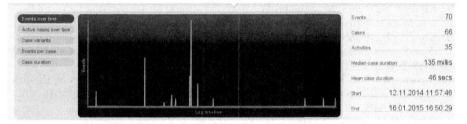

Fig. 7. Chart from Disco plotting the events over time.

6   Conclusion

In this paper we addressed the problem of mining and visualizing project-oriented business processes in a way that is informative to managers. We define an approach that takes VCS logs as input to generate Gantt charts. Our algorithm works under the assumptions that repositories reflect the hierarchical structure of the project, each work package is contained in a corresponding directory and project members commit their work regularly during active working times. The approach was implemented as a prototype and evaluated based on real-world data from open source projects.

In future work, we aim to extract further details of the VCS logs in order to calculate metrics that approximate the work effort. We plan to investigate on how the project mining approach is affected by project characteristics. Furthermore, we want to utilize statistical methods to better estimate the boundaries of the activities and work packages. Finally, we have already incorporated feedback from managers and plan to extend these to full user studies.

References

1. van der Aalst, W.: Formalization and verification of event-driven process chains. Information and Software Technology **41**(10), 639–650 (1999)
2. Baier, T., Mendling, J., Weske, M.: Bridging abstraction layers in process mining. Information Systems **46**, 123–139 (2014)
3. D'Ambros, M., Lanza, M.: A flexible framework to support collaborative software evolution analysis. In: Software Maintenance and Reengineering, pp. 3–12 (2008)

4. van Dongen, B.F., Van der Aalst, W.M.: A Meta Model for Process Mining Data. EMOI-INTEROP **160**, 30 (2005)
5. van Dongen, B.F., de Medeiros, A.K.A., Verbeek, H.M.W.E., Weijters, A.J.M.M.T., van der Aalst, W.M.P.: The ProM framework: a new era in process mining tool support. In: Ciardo, G., Darondeau, P. (eds.) ICATPN 2005. LNCS, vol. 3536, pp. 444–454. Springer, Heidelberg (2005)
6. Feldt, R., Staron, M., Hult, E., Liljegren, T.: Supporting software decision meetings: Heatmaps for visualising test and code measurements. In: 39th Conf. on Software Engineering and Advanced Applications, pp. 62–69. IEEE (2013)
7. Hou, Q., Ma, Y., Chen, J., Xu, Y.: An empirical study on inter-commit times in SVN. In: Int. Conf. on Software Eng. and Knowledge Eng., pp. 132–137 (2014)
8. Kagdi, H., Yusuf, S., Maletic, J.I.: Mining sequences of changed-files from version histories. In: Workshop on Mining Software Repositories, pp. 47–53. ACM (2006)
9. Kindler, E., Rubin, V., Schäfer, W.: Activity Mining for Discovering Software Process Models. Software Engineering **79**, 175–180 (2006)
10. Kindler, E., Rubin, V., Schäfer, W.: Incremental workflow mining based on document versioning information. In: Li, M., Boehm, B., Osterweil, L.J. (eds.) SPW 2005. LNCS, vol. 3840, pp. 287–301. Springer, Heidelberg (2006)
11. Ogawa, M., Ma, K.L.: Software evolution storylines. In: Proceedings of the 5th International Symposium on Software Visualization, pp. 35–42. ACM (2010)
12. OMG: BPMN 2.0. Recommendation, OMG (2011)
13. Pilato, C.M., Collins-Sussman, B., Fitzpatrick, B.W.: Version control with subversion. O'Reilly Media, Inc. (2008)
14. Poncin, W., Serebrenik, A., van den Brand, M.: Process mining software repositories. In: 2011 15th European Conference on Software Maintenance and Reengineering (CSMR), pp. 5–14. IEEE (2011)
15. Rubin, V., Günther, C.W., van der Aalst, W.M.P., Kindler, E., van Dongen, B.F., Schäfer, W.: Process mining framework for software processes. In: Wang, Q., Pfahl, D., Raffo, D.M. (eds.) ICSP 2007. LNCS, vol. 4470, pp. 169–181. Springer, Heidelberg (2007)
16. Rubin, V., Lomazova, I., van der Aalst, W.M.: Agile development with software process mining. In: Int. Conf. on Softw. and System Process, pp. 70–74 (2014)
17. Torvalds, L., Hamano, J.: Git: Fast version control system (2010). http://git-scm.com
18. Verbeek, H.M.W., Buijs, J.C.A.M., van Dongen, B.F., van der Aalst, W.M.P.: XES, XESame, and ProM 6. In: Soffer, P., Proper, E. (eds.) CAiSE Forum 2010. LNBIP, vol. 72, pp. 60–75. Springer, Heidelberg (2011)
19. Voinea, L., Telea, A.: An open framework for CVS repository querying, analysis and visualization. In: International Workshop on Mining Software Repositories (MSR 2006), pp. 33–39. ACM (2006)
20. Voinea, L., Telea, A.: Multiscale and multivariate visualizations of software evolution. In: Symposium on Software Visualization, pp. 115–124. ACM (2006)
21. Wilson, J.M.: Gantt charts: A centenary appreciation. European Journal of Operational Research **149**(2), 430–437 (2003)
22. Wu, J., Spitzer, C., Hassan, A., Holt, R.: Evolution spectrographs: visualizing punctuated change in software evolution. In: Workshop on Principles of Software Evolution, pp. 57–66, September 2004
23. Ying, A., Murphy, G., Ng, R., Chu-Carroll, M.: Predicting Source Code Changes by Mining Change History. IEEE Trans. Softw. Eng. **30**(9), 574–586 (2004)
24. Zimmermann, T., Weisgerber, P., Diehl, S., Zeller, A.: Mining version histories to guide software changes. In: Int. Conf. Software Engineering, pp. 563–572 (2004)

Efficient Process Model Discovery
Using Maximal Pattern Mining

Veronica Liesaputra[1], Sira Yongchareon[1(✉)], and Sivadon Chaisiri[2]

[1] Department of Computing and Information Technology, Unitec Institute of Technology,
Auckland, New Zealand
vliesaputra@unitec.ac.nz, sira@maxsira.com
[2] Faculty of Computing and Mathematical Sciences, University of Waikato,
Hamilton, New Zealand
sivadon@ieee.org

Abstract. In recent years, process mining has become one of the most important and promising areas of research in the field of business process management as it helps businesses understand, analyze, and improve their business
processes. In particular, several proposed techniques and algorithms have been
proposed to discover and construct process models from workflow execution
logs (i.e., event logs). With the existing techniques, mined models can be built
based on analyzing the relationship between any two events seen in event logs.
Being restricted by that, they can only handle special cases of routing constructs
and often produce unsound models that do not cover all of the traces seen in the
log. In this paper, we propose a novel technique for process discovery using
Maximal Pattern Mining (MPM) where we construct patterns based on the
whole sequence of events seen on the traces—ensuring the soundness of the
mined models. Our MPM technique can handle loops (of any length), duplicate
tasks, non-free choice constructs, and long distance dependencies. Our evaluation shows that it consistently achieves better *precision, replay fitness and
efficiency* than the existing techniques.

1 Introduction

Process mining has become a promising field of research that helps businesses better
understand, analyze, monitor and improve their workflow processes. Process discovery in particular is a core component of process mining that focuses on constructing
process models based on the analysis of processes using event log data produced from
information systems, such as workflow systems and business process management
systems. The discovered process models (e.g., in form of Workflow-net which is a
special class of Petri-net), can then be used for conformance checking, auditing, model enhancement, configuring a WFM/BPM system, and process improvement [1].

Since the mid-nineties, several techniques have been proposed to automatically
discover process models from event logs in both software processes and business
process domains [2, 3, 4]. Several algorithms are variants of the α-algorithm (e.g., in
[8, 9, 10, 11]), which can be seen as a well-known technique where process discovery
was first studied in the field. Nevertheless, due to the fact that the α-algorithms face
problems dealing with complicated routing constructs, noise, and incompletes [1],

©Springer International Publishing Switzerland 2015
H.R. Motahari-Nezhad et al. (Eds.): BPM 2015, LNCS 9253, pp. 441–456, 2015.
DOI: 10.1007/978-3-319-23063-4_29

more advanced techniques, such as region-based approaches (e.g., [21, 22, 25, 28]), heuristic mining [12], fuzzy mining [13], and genetic mining [37], have been proposed to tackle those aforementioned problems.

We argue that the existing algorithms for discovering process models are still unable to efficiently and accurately handle loops (of any length), duplicate tasks, concurrency, long dependencies and complex routing constructs. In fact, some of such algorithms may produce unsound models. To address these problems, we propose a novel process discovery technique called *Maximal Pattern Mining* (MPM). Instead of mining the relationship between two events, MPM mines a set of patterns that could cover all of the traces seen in an event log. We have implemented the algorithm and compared the results with the existing algorithms. Our evaluation shows that the MPM always produces sound process models with better *precision* and *replay fitness*. The processing time of our algorithm to mine and generate a process model is also significantly shorter than all the existing algorithms.

The remainder of the paper is organized as follows. Section 2 reviews and discusses the work that has been done in the process mining area. Section 3 proposes our MPM technique for process discovery and its algorithm. Section 4 discusses a technical evaluation and results. Finally, the conclusion and future works are given in Section 5.

2   Background and Related Work

In this section, we give some background and discuss related work in process mining, especially techniques for process discovery (a.k.a. control-flow discovery). Several discovery techniques have been developed based on algorithmic, machine learning, and probabilistic approaches. Very early process discovery approaches have been proposed by Cook and Wolf [3], Agrawal et al. [2], and Datta [4]. Cook and Wolf proposed RNet, Ktail and Markov software process discovery approach using event-based data based on statistical, algorithmic and probabilistic methods. Agrawal et al. and Datta studied graph-based discovery approaches in the context of workflow processes. Manilla and Meek [5] present a method for finding partial orders that describe the ordering relationships between the events in a collection of sequences and applying mixture modeling techniques to obtain a descriptive set of partial orders. However, their techniques cannot deal with concurrency, decision splits, synchronous and asynchronous joins, and other common issues found in a process mining field. Later, Schimm [6, 7] proposed a procedural approach using data mining techniques to mine a complete and minimal process algoschema from workflow logs that contains concurrent processes. However, the approach is restricted to block-structured processes. Van der Aalst et al. [8] proposed α-algorithm to learn structured workflow nets from complete event logs. However, the α-algorithm cannot cope with noise, incompleteness of workflow logs, short loops, and non-free choice constructs. Later, Alves de Medeiros et al. [9] developed α^+-algorithm, an improved version of the α-algorithm, which is capable of detecting short loops. Further, Wen et al. [10, 11] proposed α^{++}-algorithm to discover non-free choice constructs and β-algorithm to detect concurrency. Due to the fact that all the α-algorithms face a robustness problem, Weijters et al. [12] proposed Heuristics Miner by extending the α-algorithm to analyze the frequency of the three types of relationships between activities in a workflow log: direct dependency, concurrency, and not-directly connectedness. It is claimed that Heuristics Miner is able to mine short loops and non-local dependencies. In contrast to the α-algorithms, Gunther and van der Aalst [13] proposed Fuzzy Miner, an adaptive technique to discover behavior models from an event log using significance and correlation measures. Their technique is capable of mining unstructured processes. Asides from these techniques, Rembert and Omokpo [26] proposed a process discovery technique using the α-algorithm with Bayesian statistics to incorporate prior knowledge supplied by a domain expert to discover control-flow model in the presence of noise and uncertainty.

Herbst and Karagiannis [23] proposed a discovery algorithm to construct a stochastic activity graph and then convert it into a structured process model. Their algorithm can discover duplicate activities but not non-local dependencies. Folino et al. [24] proposed the Enhanced WFMiner algorithm to deal with noise, duplicate tasks and non-free choice. Ferreira and Gillblad [27] proposed a technique to tackle the problem of unlabeled event logs (without a case identifier) by using the Expectation–Maximization procedure. Van der Werf et al. [25] proposed a discovery technique using Integer Linear Programming (ILP) based on the theory of regions. Van der Aalst et al. [21] proposed a Finite State Machine (FSM) Miner/Petrify two-step approach to find a balanced trade-off between generalization and precision of discovered process models. The theory of region is used in their approach as a method to bridge FSM and Petri-Net models as also proposed in [22]. Sole and Carmona [28] presented an aggressive folding region-based technique, which is based on the theory of region, to reduce the total number of states of a transition system and speed up the discovery process.

Several machine leaning techniques have been used in the process discovery domain. Maruster et al. [14] proposed to use propositional rule induction, i.e., a uni-relational classification learner, to predict dependency relationships between activities from event logs that contain noise and imbalance. Ferreira and Ferreira [15] apply a combination of Inductive Logic Programming learning and partial-order planning techniques to discover a process model from event logs. In addition, Lamma et al. [16] applied Inductive Logic Programming to process discovery by assuming negative sequences while searching. Due to the limitations of local search, these approaches were unable to detect non-free choice constructs, duplicate tasks, and hidden tasks. Therefore, in order to discover such constructs, Buijs et al. [37] proposed a genetic algorithm which performs a global search based on the use of alignment fitness function to find the best matched models. Genetic Miner can detect non-local patterns and, due to its post-pruning step, it has a reasonable robustness. Similarly, Goedertier et al. [17] proposed AGNEsMiner to deal with problems such as expressiveness, noise, incomplete event logs, and the inclusion of prior knowledge by representing process discovery as a multi-relational classification problem [18] on event logs supplemented with Artificially Generated Negative Events (AGNEs). This technique can learn the conditions that distinguish between the occurrence of either a positive or a negative event. Furthermore, Greco et al. [19] proposed DWS mining to improve precision. The technique is implemented in an iterative procedure that refines the process model in each step, based on clustering of similar behavior patterns. In [20], Greco et al. proposed an approach for producing taxonomy of workflow models to capture the process behavior at different levels of abstraction by extending traditional discovery methods and an abstraction method.

Based on the above discussions, we have observed that only Genetic Miner [37] can tackle all the typical problems in process mining, i.e., noise, duplicate tasks, hidden tasks, non-free choice constructs, and loops. However, because of the nature of the genetic algorithm, it consumes more processing time and space in order to learn and construct a model. Mining efficiency is considered a major drawback of this approach in which it is undesirable, especially when it is applied to a complicated real-life log. To overcome such issues, we need to develop a better technique that can not only solve all of the typical process mining problems but also takes much less time to process.

3   Maximal Pattern Mining (MPM)

As discussed earlier, the well-known α-algorithm and its variants can be considered the most substantial techniques in the field of process mining [1, 8]. The model was built based on the relationship of an event A with the event's direct predecessors and successors. However, those algorithms have problems with complex control-flow constructs, such as non-free-choice constructs (where concurrency and choice meet), arbitrary nested loops, duplicate tasks, etc.

Bose et al. [33] proposes an algorithm to discover common patterns on events in traces, especially loops. Pattern similarity is calculated by using edit distance. Although their evaluation shows promising results, it was not clear how it would handle other control-flow constructs such as long distance dependencies and duplicate tasks, or how accurate and robust their algorithm is compared to other existing process-mining algorithms.

In this paper we use a similar pattern matching technique called *Maximal Pattern Mining* (MPM) to construct a workflow model. Instead of looking at the relationship between 2 events, we consider the whole sequence of events in all of the traces and find the optimal set of "regular expression"-like patterns that will cover them. Therefore, our algorithm can handle complex constructs such as non-free choice constructs, nested loops of any length (as opposed to short one or two length loops), duplicate tasks and long distance dependencies. It also uses a stricter rule than the edit distance uses in [33] to find similar patterns.

We overview and detail the MPM technique in Sections 3.1 and 3.2. Then, the assumptions and limitations of our technique are discussed in Section 3.3.

3.1   Overview

Let $T = \{t_0, t_1 \ldots t_n\}$ be the collections of all the traces in an event log in which they are ordered by the type of the events in the trace and then by the number of events in the trace. A trace t_n is an ordered sequence of events or completed tasks, $t_n = \langle z_0, z_1 \ldots z_m \rangle$. We denote $|t_n|$ as the number of events in a trace. An event z_m only contain 1 event type, i.e. $|z_m| = 1$. Possible event types include *create, schedule, assign, revoke, start, addFact, removeFact, updateFact,* and *complete* [17]. All the traces in T are not unique and a trace t_n may contain particular events more than once, i.e. it is possible to have $T = \{\langle a,b,c,b,b,c,d,e \rangle, \langle a,b,c,b,b,c,d,e \rangle, \langle a,b,b,c,e,d \rangle\}$.

Given an input T, our algorithm will first create a list of unique patterns $P = \{p_0, p_1 \dots p_i\}$ and then generate a graph based on P. The following sections will describe each of them.

A pattern $p_i = \langle e_0, e_1 \dots e_j \rangle$ is an ordered sequence of elements, $|p_i|$ is the number of elements in the pattern and $p_i.support$ is the number of traces covered by the pattern.

An element $e_j = \{v_0, v_1 \dots v_k\}$ contains k number of unique event types (i.e. $|e_j| = k$) and $e_j.loop$ is a list of $\langle v_k: w \rangle$ tuples that indicate whether v_k is self-looping ($w = \{v_k\}$) and/or is the last element of a sequence-loop ($w = \{e_x\ e_{x+1} \dots e_{x+y}\}$ and $e_{x+y} = v_k$). The *loop* list is ordered first by event value and then by the number of elements in w ($|w|$). An element's value v_k only contains 1 event type.

All the elements inside p_i may not be unique. For instance, given the $T = \{\langle a,b,c,b,b,c,d,e \rangle, \langle a,b,c,b,b,c,d,e \rangle, \langle a,b,b,c,e,d \rangle\}$ specified above, our algorithm will only produce 1 pattern in P. $p_0 = \langle e_0, e_1, e_2, e_3 \rangle$, where $e_0 = a$ and $e_0.loop = \emptyset$; $e_1 = b$ and $e_1.loop = \{<b: b>\}$; $e_2 = c$ and $e_2.loop = \{\langle c: \{bc\} \rangle\}$; and $e_3 = \{d, e\}$ and $e_3.loop = \emptyset$. Elements with more than one event type indicate a parallelization. In our example, e_3 shows that in the last 2 events of our model the values could be either *de* or *ed*. Because p_0 covers all the traces in T, $p_0.support = 3$.

Our graph algorithm will then generate the following model (Fig. 1) based on p_0. We use the operator AND to indicate the set of tasks that are running at the same time, and XOR to indicate a path selection.

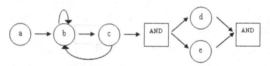

Fig. 1. The generated model for $\{\langle a,b,c,b,b,c,d,e \rangle, \langle a,b,c,b,b,c,d,e \rangle, \langle a,b,b,c,e,d \rangle\}$

The algorithm we use to construct the most optimal patterns for a given trace of events has five main components: finding self and/or sequence loops, storing the pattern in a vertical format, identifying events that should be done concurrently, investigating whether a trace is covered by a pattern in P, and pruning non-maximal patterns.

Loops. A sequence of elements $S = \langle s_0, s_1 \dots s_q \rangle$ is in a loop in the trace $t_n = \langle z_0, z_1 \dots z_m \rangle$ or in the pattern $p_i = \langle e_0, e_1 \dots e_m \rangle$ if and only if there is a sequence of elements such that for all $b \in \{0 \dots q\}$ and $q \leq (m - a)/2$, $z_{a+b} = s_b$ and $z_{a+q+b} = s_b$ or $e_{a+b} = s_b$ and $e_{a+q+b} = s_b$, where a is the starting index where S occurs in the trace or in the pattern ($0 \leq a \leq m$). The first phase of our pattern mining is to identify these loops. For every $S+$ occurring in t_n and p_i, we replace it with S and set the *loop* property of the last element in S. For instance, given a pattern $\langle a,b,c,d,\{e,f\},c,d,\{e,f\}c,d,\{e,f\}g \rangle$, the pattern becomes $\langle a,b,c,d,\{e,f\}g \rangle$ where the loop property for b is b, and the loop property for $\{e,f\}$ is $cd\{e,f\}$. We keep iterating on the pattern until there are no more loops in the pattern. All the loops in the pattern $\langle a,b,d,d,c,b,b,b,d,c,b,d,c,e \rangle$ will be identified in 2 iterations: 1) $\langle a,b,d^*,c,b^*,d,c,b,d,c,e \rangle$, 2) $\langle a,(b,d^*,c)^*,e \rangle$. By identifying loops first, MPM will be able to deduce that traces $\langle a,b,d,d,c,b,b,b,d,c,b,d,c,e \rangle$ and $\langle a,b,d,c,b,d,d,c,e \rangle$ are the same and are both covered by the pattern $\langle a,b,d,c,e \rangle$.

Vertical Representation. Existing process mining algorithms require several scans of the event log or need to maintain large amounts of intermediate candidates in the main memory to generate a process model [10, 11, 37, 18]. To alleviate this problem, MPM stores all patterns in the vertical format as an IdList in bitset representation [31] where each entry represents an element, the id of the trace where the element appears (*id*) and the positions (*pos*) where it appears. The support of a pattern is calculated by making joint operations with IdLists of smaller patterns. Thus, MPM would only need to perform a single scan through the log to generate IdLists of patterns containing single elements (see [31] for details). To make it more verbose, MPM uses the symbol $ to indicate the end of a trace. Given $T = \{\langle a,b,c,b,b,c,d,e,a\rangle, \langle a,b,b,c,e,d,a\rangle, \langle e,d,a\rangle\}$, the vertical representation (V_T) of it is represented as follow:

A		b		c		D		e		$	
id	pos	id	pos	id	pos	id	pos	id	pos	id	pos
0	0, 5	0	1	0	2	0	3	0	4	0	6
1	0, 5	1	1	1	2	1	4	1	3	1	6
2	2					2	1	2	0	2	3

Concurrency. A set of events $V = \{v_0, v_1 \ldots v_q\}$ are performed at the same time (or parallel) if and only if there are at least q number of unique traces with the following sequence $\langle z_0, z_1 \ldots z_{a-1}\, z_a, z_{a+1} \ldots z_{a+q}\, z_{a+q+1}, z_{a+q+2} \ldots z_m\rangle$, where the sequence $\langle z_0, z_1 \ldots z_{a-1}\rangle$ and $\langle z_{a+q+1}, z_{a+q+2} \ldots z_m\rangle$ have the same pattern across those traces, there are no events mentioned more than once in $\langle z_a, z_{a+1} \ldots z_{a+q}\rangle$, and for all $b \in \{0\ldots q\}$ and $q \leq (m - a)$, $z_{a+b} \subseteq V$, where a is the starting index where a combination of all the events in V occur ($0 \leq a \leq m$). Sequence $\langle z_0, z_1 \ldots z_{a-1}\rangle$ and $\langle z_{a+q+1}, z_{a+q+2} \ldots z_m\rangle$ may be $\emptyset$. Instead of $z_{a+b} = V$, we relax the criteria to $z_{a+b} \subseteq V$ with the assumption that if we see almost all of V possible events combination in T, it must just be the case that the trace log is incomplete. For example, given a set of traces $\{\langle a,b,c,d,e\rangle, \langle a,b,d,c,e\rangle, \langle a,c,d,b,e\rangle\}$. We first look at the first two traces where we get $\langle a,b,\{c,d\},e\rangle$ as it is possible to switch the position of task c and d around. We then compare it with the last trace where we get $\langle a,\{b,c,d\},e\rangle$ as we can switch the position of task c and d around with b. In the future, we may use the trace frequency to help us decide when we should use the strict or relaxed criteria.

Coverage. A pattern $p_i = \langle e_0, e_1 \ldots e_n\rangle$ specifies the sequence of patterns that covers some of the traces in T and it can be represented as a deterministic finite automata DFA_i with (a) well-defined start state, (b) one or more accepted states and (c) deterministic transitions across states on symbols of the event values. A trace $t_n = \langle z_0, z_1 \ldots z_m\rangle$ is covered by the pattern p_i if and only if the sequence of transitions for the elements of t_n from the start state results in an accept state. Fig. 2 illustrates the deterministic finite automaton for the pattern $\langle a,b,\{c,d\},e\rangle$ with the *loop* property for b to be b. We use > to indicate the start state and double circles for the accept state. The diagram shows that the pattern covers the following set of traces $\{\langle a, b, c, d, e\rangle, \langle a, b, d, c, e\rangle, \langle a, b, b, c, d, e\rangle, \langle a, b,...,b, c, d, e\rangle, \langle a, b,...,b, d, c, e\rangle\}$. However, it will reject the following set of traces $\{\langle a,b\rangle, \langle e\rangle, \langle a,b,h\rangle, \langle a,b,c,d\rangle, \langle a,b,b,d,c\rangle, \langle a,b,a,d,c,e\rangle\}$.

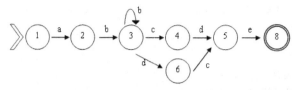

Fig. 2. The deterministic finite automata model for $p_i = \langle a,b,\{c,d\},e \rangle$

Maximal Patterns. A pattern p_i is said to be maximal if and only if there is no other pattern p_j in P that has the same start and accept states and covers the same or more traces in T. Given $P = \{\langle a,b,c,d \rangle, \langle a,\{b,c\},d \rangle, \langle a,b,c \rangle\}$, only p_1 and p_2 are maximal because p_0 is a sub-pattern of p_1.

Optionality. A sequence of elements $S_0 = \langle s_0, s_1 \ldots s_q \rangle$ in the pattern $p_j = \langle z_0 \ldots z_m, s_0, s_1 \ldots s_q, z_p \ldots z_r \rangle$ is in an XOR (optionality) relations with a sequence of elements $S_1 = \langle s'_0, s'_1 \ldots s'_t \rangle$ in the pattern $p_k = \langle z'_0 \ldots z'_n, s'_0, s'_1 \ldots s'_t, z_u \ldots z_v \rangle$ if and only if $z_m = z'_n$ and $z_p = z_u$. In some cases, z_m and z'_n could be a start state, and $z_p = z_u$ could be the accept state. For example, if $P = \{\langle a,b,c,d \rangle, \langle a,e,d \rangle, \langle g,f \rangle, \langle g,h \rangle\}$, the resulted graph will be $XOR(a \rightarrow XOR(b \rightarrow c, e) \rightarrow d, g \rightarrow XOR(f, h))$.

Noise (Frequent Patterns and Events). To further filter P from noisy data, we set a support threshold value, *thresh*, so that we will only keep frequent pattern p_i and event v_k, i.e. $p_i.support \geq thresh$ and $v_k.support \geq thresh$. All patterns and events are accepted if the threshold value is 0. To find out what the best threshold value is, we split the traces that we used for generating the pattern into 2 sets: training and validation. Our MPM algorithm generates maximal patterns only based on the traces found in the training sets. We then evaluate the performance of all the patterns generated by MPM on the traces of events in the validation set. If we are unhappy with the results, we change the threshold value of our algorithm, re-generate the pattern of the training traces based on the new threshold value and evaluate it on the validation traces. We keep doing this until we find the optimal threshold value.

3.2   Generating Maximal Patterns

The pseudo-code of the MPM algorithm is shown in Alg. 1. MPM takes as input an event log (T) and the support threshold value (*thresh*). For each trace t_n, it identifies all the loops, constructs the vertical representation of the log (V_T) and get the set of frequent events (E) as described in Section 3.1. Events in E, except for $\$$, are ordered from the most common to the least. For each event v in E, the procedure calls the EXPAND procedure with $\langle v \rangle$, E and *thresh*.

The EXPAND procedure takes as parameters a sequential pattern (p), a set of items (S) to be appended to p to generate candidates and minimum support value (*thresh*). Each item (s_i) in the set S is appended to p as the next sequential item of p. Each of the newly generated patterns are called p_i'. Because any infrequent sequential patterns cannot be extended to form a frequent pattern, the procedure uses IdList join operation [31] to calculate the number of traces where the pattern p_i' appears. If $p_i'.support \geq thresh$, p_i' is then used in a recursive call to EXPAND to generate patterns starting with p_i'. All the frequent p_i' are passed onto the RESOLVE procedure.

Algorithm 1. The procedure of the Maximal Pattern Mining algorithm

---

MPM (*T, thresh*)
   $V_T = \emptyset$
   FOR each trace $t_n \in T$
      t_n = SOLVE_LOOP (t_n)
      V_T = INSERT_TRACE (V_T, t_n)
   E = GET_FREQUENT_EVENTS (V_T)
   $P_T = \emptyset$
   FOR each event $v \in E$
      $P_T = P_T \cup$ EXPAND ($\langle v \rangle, E, thresh$)
   P_T = RESOLVE ($P_T, 0$)
   DRAW_GRAPH (P_T)

EXPAND (*p, S, thresh*)
   $S_T = \emptyset$
   $P_T = \emptyset$
   FOR each item $s_i \in S$
      $p_i' = p \cup s_i$
      IF $p_i'.support \geq thresh$ **THEN**
         $S_T = S_T \cup s_i$
   FOR each item $s_i \in S_T$
      $P_T = P_T \cup$ EXPAND ($p \cup s_i, S_T, thresh$)
   P_T = RESOLVE ($P_T, |p|$)
   Output P_T

RESOLVE (*FP, idx*)
   CP = Copy of FP
   FOR each item $p_i \in FP$
      FOR each item $p_j \in FP$ **AND** $i < j \leq FP$.length
         IF $p_i[idx] \neq \$$ **AND** $p_j[idx] \neq \$$ **AND**
            $p_i[idx ... p_i.$length$] = p_j[idx ... p_j.$length$]$ **THEN**
            p_i = SOLVE_CONCURRENCY (p_i, p_j)
            p_i = SOLVE_LOOP (p_i)
            Remove p_j from FP
         ELSE IF p_j is sub-pattern of p_i **THEN**
            Remove p_j from FP
         ELSE IF p_i is sub-pattern of p_j **THEN**
            Remove p_i from FP
            Go to the next item in FP
   IF $CP \neq FP$ **THEN**
      RESOLVE (FP, idx)
   Output FP

3.3   Assumptions and Limitations

An event in a transactional log usually contains information such as the event type/value (e.g. apply for a drivers licence or update patient information), the agent/performer that is doing the event, the requestor/client that initiates the whole sequence of events, timestamp and the data element being modified or accessed (e.g. the age of a patient, the driving test result). A trace of events is a sequence of events, sorted by the timestamp, done for a client. Because the goal of MPM is to find all possible orderings of the logged events in the system, only the event type/value are mined. Once we have organized the log into sets of traces, other information, such as timestamp and agent, are ignored. In this paper, the term event type and event value are used interchangeably.

In an experimental setting, we know the original model that our algorithm should strive to construct, the complete list of traces that the model could generate, and the instances in a log that are negative examples. But in real life scenarios no original models will be available; logs may contain noise such as mislabelled events and incorrectly logged sequences of events and exceptions. In fact, a particular trace of observed events does not have to be reproduced by the model. Furthermore, in a complex process with many possible paths, only a fraction of those paths may be present in the log, i.e., the log is incomplete. Thus, it is undesirable to construct a model that allows only for the observed instances in the log. Since we do not know which instance in the log is noise, we assume that every trace/event recorded in the log that appears no less than a user's specified threshold frequency is correct (positive examples). However, unobserved traces of events are not considered as negative examples. Our MPM algorithm can construct a model that can explain all the traces of events found in the log while also allowing for any unobserved behaviour.

As shown in Section 4.4., because we are always trying to solve loops before parallel tasks, just like α^{++}, AGNEs and Heuristic Miners, our algorithm is incapable of generating a model that can accurately represents duplicate tasks in a parallel process structure.

4   Experimental Result

In this paper, we evaluate the quality of the mined model produced by MPM, α^{++}, Genetic miner, Integer Linear Programming (ILP), AGNEs and heuristic miners according to logs that are mentioned in the respective publications. We did not perform the evaluation on α and α^+ as [10, 11] have reported that α^{++} can construct a model that handles more complex control-flow constructs.

4.1   Criteria

Buijs et al. [34] reviewed all the existing criteria used by various researchers to validate their process mining techniques and found that they all shared the notions of *simplicity, replay fitness, precision* and *generalization*. Therefore, we have also used these criteria along with *time* to evaluate the performance of our algorithm.

Replay fitness measures how well the model can generate the traces in the event log. Alignment distance function defined by van der Aalst, et al. [35] is used to calculate fitness of a process model. The generated process model should be simple, i.e. it only includes the necessary number of events and links to explain anything [35]. The *simplicity* measures defined in Buijs et al. [34] is used. *Precision* estimates how much the model accepts additional behaviour that is not seen in the log. Align precision metrics by Adriansyah, et al. [36] is used to test whether the generated model under-fits. In contrast to *Precision*, *generalization* addresses an overly precise model. As mentioned previously, it is not likely that a log is complete and noise-free. Therefore, the mined model should be robust enough so that the removal or addition of small percentage of traces in the log will not lead to a remarkably different model. Most importantly, processing time is also considered one of the critical criteria, we include the *time* taken by an algorithm to mine a process model as one of our quantitative criteria.

4.2   *k*-fold Cross Validation

Based on the existing techniques, evaluating the quality of a mined model is achieved by calculating the *replay fitness*, the *simplicity*, the *precision*, and the *generalization* measures of the model on all of the traces found in a log, and usually the log used during the evaluation is the same log that is used to build the model. However, it is well-known in the statistics and machine learning communities that it is a methodological mistake to learn and test the performance of a prediction function on the same data as the generated model will in all likelihood get 100% accuracy on the training data but perform very poorly on a new set of input data. This phenomenon is called *over-fitting*. To avoid over-fitting, the available data should be separated into a training data set that is used to generate the model, and a test data set that is used to evaluate the quality of the generated model. The most common approach to do this is called *k-fold cross validation* and this is the evaluation method that we use to evaluate the *generalization* measures of each model [35].

With *k*-fold cross validation, the log is split into *k* approximately equal sized partitions. Each partition is used exactly once as the test set while the remaining data is used as the training set. The performance of the algorithm is the average of the values computed on each iteration. For example, in 3-fold cross validation, the log is divided into 3 equal sized groups (A, B, C). First, the algorithm uses A and B as training data. The performance of the generated model (P_1) is then tested on C. Next, the algorithm uses B and C as training data, and evaluates the performance of the constructed model (P_2) on A. Finally, A and C are used as training data, and the performance of the generated model (P_3) is tested on B. The overall performance of the algorithm is measured by averaging P_1, P_2 and P_3. In our evaluation, we use 10-fold cross validation. Because k-fold cross validation ensures that our model does not over-fit the training data (i.e. the model is general enough), the performance measured in each iteration is *simplicity*, *replay fitness*, and *precision*. The overall performance of a technique on a log is calculated by averaging the performance of that technique on each fold.

In the process mining area, some researchers avoid over-fitting by evaluating the performance of their generated model on "noisy" logs. These logs are created by adding noise (such as artificial start and end events, incorrect event labelling, event mutation, traces addition and removal, etc.) to original logs. However, as mentioned previously, without an explicit reference model, we do not know which specific instances in the original logs is noise. Therefore, artificial logs may actually generate positive examples that we did not observe in the original log and we may incorrectly label them as negative instances [18]. This is also the reason why we do not think stratified k-fold cross validation, where we artificially create negative examples, as proposed by [30] is appropriate.

A one-way analysis of variance and paired t-tests is then used to examine statistically significant differences in the performance of each algorithm. This way we can generate a process model on several data sets.

4.3   Setup

Similar to other discovery algorithms, our MPM algorithm is implemented as a plugin of ProM [29]. In our evaluation, we use synthetics and real event log data to demonstrate the fact that the MPM algorithm can significantly improve the performance of the existing approaches, especially the α-algorithm and its variants. We do not use parameter fine-tuning or metadata to enhance the performance of our algorithm. We have also used the default settings for α++, genetic miner, ILP and AGNEs. To further extend the capability of Heuristic Miner, we configure it to discover long distance dependencies based on completed events' values and positions on a trace.

4.4   Synthetic Data

We compare the performance of MPM, α++, Genetic miner, ILP, AGNEs and Heuristic Miners on the artificial logs example that are used in [10, 11, 37, 18]. There are about 300 to 350 traces and maximum 10 unique events in each log.

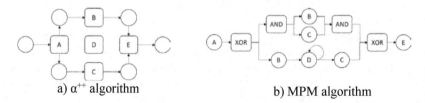

a) α++ algorithm   b) MPM algorithm

Fig. 3. Log $T = \{ABCE, ACBE, ABDDCE\}$

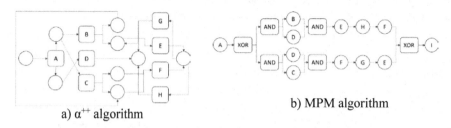

a) α++ algorithm   b) MPM algorithm

Fig. 4. Log T = {ABDEHFI, ADBEHFI, ACDFGEI, ADCFGEI}

Due to the fact that the α++ algorithm builds a process model based on the relationship between *any two* events so that it does not allow an event to occur more than once in the model, it requires additional heuristics to handle long distance dependencies, short loops (maximum of two events) and non-free-choice constructs (combination of choice and concurrency); and assumes that two or more events must occur concurrently if they have the same parents (i.e. bad precision). Therefore, it is possible for the α^{++} algorithm to produce *unsound* workflow nets as shown in Figures 3 and 4. Similarly, because Heuristic Miners also builds a casual matrix that represents the relationship between any two events, it cannot handle duplicate tasks as illustrated in Figure 5. Although AGNEs is more versatile than Heuristic Miners, it is still incapable of handling complex non-free choice constructs such as displayed in Figure 6.

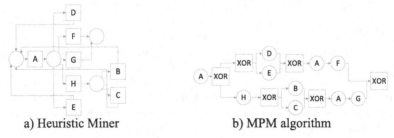

a) Heuristic Miner   b) MPM algorithm

Fig. 5. Log T = {ADAF, AEAF, AHBAG, AHCAG}

a)AGNES   b) MPM algorithm

Fig. 6. Log T = {ABC, ABDE, ADBE}

Our MPM algorithm discovers a process model by reading patterns from the *whole sequence* of events in traces. Thus, it has more stringent criteria than Heuristic Miners or α^{++}; it can handle duplicate tasks, long distance dependencies, loops of any length and non-free choice constructs. The process model discovered by MPM is always sound, and it is generally more accurate than the models mined by AGNEs, ILP, Heuristic Miners or α^{++}. However, MPM is incapable of generating a model that accurately represents duplicate tasks in a parallel process structure, as shown in Figure 7. Genetic Algorithm was the only algorithm that correctly mined this log.

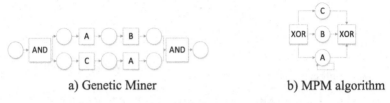

a) Genetic Miner   b) MPM algorithm

Fig. 7. Log T = {ACBA, ACAB, CAAB, CABA, ABCA}

As displayed in Table 1, ILP and MPM are the only algorithms that can consistently produce perfectly fitting models across all the synthetic data. Followed closely by Genetic, Heuristics and AGNEs miner. A paired t-test evaluation showed that there are significant differences at the 95% level in fitness performance between the ILP or MPM to α^{++}.

Table 1. The average *replay fitness, precision, simplicity* and run-time comparisons for the artificial logs

	Fitness	Precision	Simplicity	Time
α^{++}	0.7	0.5	1.0	250 ms
Genetic	0.9	0.9	0.7	1 hour
Heuristics	0.8	0.7	0.8	10 s
AGNEs	0.8	0.8	0.6	5 mins
ILP	1.0	0.6	0.9	2 mins
MPM	1.0	0.9	0.7	150 ms

ILP, α^{++} and Heuristic Miners tend to create overly general models making them much less precise. AGNEs can produce models that are more precise than α^{++}, ILP and Heuristic Miners so there is only a 90% level of significant difference between Genetic Algorithm and MPM to AGNEs.

Simplicity of Genetic Miner, AGNEs and MPM is rather low due to the duplication of several events. There are no significant differences at the 95% level in terms of the average simplicity between these algorithms compared to Heuristics miner. α^{++} and ILP are significantly better at the 95% level compared to Genetic Miner, AGNEs and MPM.

While Genetic Miner will sometimes produce a model that is more accurate than MPM, MPM can generate a similar model in significantly less time. Unlike ILP, MPM always generated sound model. Furthermore, MPM can incrementally build and improve the mined model in near real time as it receives new traces of events, i.e. the model becomes more accurate as it sees more unique traces of events.

4.5   Real-Life Log Data

Similar to the previous section, to evaluate the performance of MPM, α^{++}, Genetic miner, AGNEs, ILP and Heuristic Miners we used the real-life Hospital log obtained from [32]. For each log, we let each of the algorithms run for 5 days and if they exceeded that we counted them as DNF (Did Not Finish).

From Table 2, we can see a similar pattern to the one that we found with the synthetic data. Genetic Miner is the algorithm that takes the longest to finish. It takes at least 5 days for Genetic Miner to return any sort of result. Therefore, we could not comment on the simplicity, precision and replay fitness of the model generated by Genetic Miner. The worst performing algorithm in terms of fitness and precision is α^{++}. Even though the model generated by ILP can replay the trace log perfectly with just enough number of nodes, the model tend to under-fit. Unlike with the synthetic data, Heuristic Miners significantly outperforms AGNEs in terms of fitness, precision, simplicity and running time with the real-life log data analysis at the 95% level. Heuristic Miners could generate a model significantly faster than AGNEs, and the model is significantly more accurate and robust than that generated from AGNEs. We argue that this difference is caused by the introduction of incorrect false negative examples in AGNEs. Real-life logs contain much noise and tend to be incomplete. As such, it is fairly easy for AGNEs to regard an unobserved positive behaviour as a negative example. On the other hand, Heuristic Miners decides the relationship between two processes based on the probability of process B following process A given the evidence of prior processes as such it is more robust to noise. However, MPM is still significantly better than Heuristic Miners at the 95% in terms of fitness and run-time.

Table 2. Average *replay fitness, precision, simplicity* and run-time of different techniques across multiple logs

	Fitness	Precision	Simplicity	Time
α^{++}	0.3	0.4	0.9	10 mins
Genetic	DNF	DNF	DNF	>5 days
Heuristics	0.7	0.8	0.8	1 hour
AGNEs	0.5	0.6	0.3	20 hours
ILP	1.0	0.5	0.8	2 hours
MPM	0.9	0.9	0.7	9 mins

5   Conclusion and Future work

In this paper, we propose a novel technique called *Maximum Pattern Mining* (MPM) to discover a process model from event logs. We implemented our technique and evaluated it against the well-known process discovery algorithms: α^{++}, Genetic miner, ILP AGNEs and Heuristic Miners algorithms. The results from our experiments show that MPM performs better or comparable in terms of *fitness, precision, simplicity* and *run-time efficiency*. It can handle much more general cases, such as loops of any length and long distance dependencies. However to achieve high fitness and precision, MPM tends to use duplicate events in the model which caused low simplicity score. In the future, we will implement a graph that will allow users to define the tasks' abstraction level and hopefully increase MPM's simplicity score. As MPM was able to efficiently generate an accurate model from a real-life log in near real time, event-stream mining is feasible.

References

1. van der Aalst, W.M.P.: Process Mining: Overview and Opportunities. ACM Transactions on Management Information Systems **3**(2) article 7 (2012)
2. Agrawal, R., Gunopulos, D., Leymann, F.: Mining process models from workflow logs. In: Schek, H.-J., Saltor, F., Ramos, I., Alonso, G. (eds.) EDBT 1998. LNCS, vol. 1377, pp. 469–483. Springer, Heidelberg (1998)
3. Cook, J., Wolf, A.: Discovering models of software processes from event-based data. ACM Transactions on Software Engineering and Methodology **7**, 215–249 (1998)
4. Datta, A.: Automating the discovery of AS-IS business process models: probabilistic and algorithmic approaches. Information Systems Research **9**, 275–301 (1998)
5. Mannila, H., Meek, C.: Global partial orders from sequential data. In: Proceedings of the 6th ACM SIGKDD International Conference on Knowledge Discovery and Data Mining (KDD 2000), pp. 161–168 (2000)
6. Schimm, G.: Process miner - a tool for mining process schemes from event-based data. In: Flesca, S., Greco, S., Leone, N., Ianni, G. (eds.) JELIA 2002. LNCS (LNAI), vol. 2424, pp. 525–528. Springer, Heidelberg (2002)
7. Schimm, G.: Mining exact models of concurrent workflows. Computers in Industry **53**, 265–281 (2004)
8. van der Aalst, W.M.P., Weijters, A.J.M.M., Maruster, L.: Workflow mining: discovering process models from event logs. IEEE Transactions on Knowledge and Data Engineering **16**, 1128–1142 (2004)
9. Alves de Medeiros, A.K., van Dongen, B.F., van der Aalst, W.M.P., Weijters, A.J.M.M.: Process Mining: Extending the Alpha-Algorithm to Mine Short Loops. BETA Working Paper Series, vol. 113. TU Eindho- ven (2004)
10. Wen, L., van der Aalst, W.M.P., Wang, J., Sun, J.: Mining process models with non-free-choice constructs. Data Mining and Knowledge Discovery **15**, 145–180 (2007)
11. Wen, L., Wang, J., van der Aalst, W.M.P., Huang, B., Sun, J.: A novel approach for process mining based on event types. Journal of Intelligent Information Systems **32**, 163–190 (2009)
12. Weijters, A.J.M.M., van der Aalst, W.M.P., Alves de Medeiros, A.K.: Process Mining with the Heuristics Miner algorithm. BETA Working Paper Series, vol. 166. TU Eindhoven (2006)
13. Günther, C.W., van der Aalst, W.M.: Fuzzy mining – adaptive process simplification based on multi-perspective metrics. In: Alonso, G., Dadam, P., Rosemann, M. (eds.) BPM 2007. LNCS, vol. 4714, pp. 328–343. Springer, Heidelberg (2007)
14. Maruster, L., Weijters, A.J.M.M., van der Aalst, W.M.P., van den Bosch, A.: A rule-based approach for process discovery: dealing with noise and imbalance in process logs. Data Mining and Knowledge Discovery **13**, 67–87 (2006)
15. Ferreira, H., Ferreira, D.: An integrated life cycle for workflow management based on learning and planning. IJCIS **15**, 485–505 (2006)
16. Lamma, E., Mello, P., Montali, M., Riguzzi, F., Storari, S.: Inducing declarative logic-based models from labeled traces. In: Alonso, G., Dadam, P., Rosemann, M. (eds.) BPM 2007. LNCS, vol. 4714, pp. 344–359. Springer, Heidelberg (2007)
17. Goedertier, S., Martens, D., Vanthienen, J., Baesens, B.: Robust process discovery with ar-tificial negative events. Journal of Machine Learning Research **10**, 1305–1340 (2009)
18. Blockeel, H., De Raedt, L.: Top-down induction of first-order logical decision trees. Ar-tificial Intelligence **101**, 285–297 (1998)
19. Greco, G., Guzzo, A., Pontieri, L., Sacca, D.: Discovering expressive process models by clustering log traces. IEEE Transactions on Knowledge and Data Engineering **18**, 1010–1027 (2006)

20. Greco, G., Guzzo, A., Pontieri, L.: Mining taxonomies of process models. Data & Knowledge Engineering **67**, 74–102 (2008)
21. van der Aalst, W.M.P., Rubin, V., Verbeek, H.M.W., van Dongen, B.F., Kindler, E., Günther, C.W.: Process mining: a two-step approach to balance between underfitting and overfitting. Software and System Modeling **9**, 87–111 (2010)
22. Carmona, J., Cortadella, J., Kishinevsky, M.: New region-based algorithms for deriving bounded Petri nets. IEEE Transactions on Computers **59**, 371–384 (2010)
23. Herbst, J., Karagiannis, D.: Workflow mining with InWoLvE. Computers in Industry **53**, 245–264 (2004)
24. Folino, F., Greco, G., Guzzo, A., Pontieri, L.: Discovering expressive process models from noised log data. In: Proceedings of the 2009 International Database Engineering & Applications Symposium, pp. 162–172. ACM (2009)
25. van der Werf, J.M.E.M., van Dongen, B.F., Hurkens, C.A.J., Serebrenik, A.: Process discovery using integer linear programming. Fundamenta Informaticae **94**, 387–412 (2009)
26. Rembert, A.J., Omokpo, A., Mazzoleni, P., Goodwin, R.T.: Process discovery using prior knowledge. In: Basu, S., Pautasso, C., Zhang, L., Fu, X. (eds.) ICSOC 2013. LNCS, vol. 8274, pp. 328–342. Springer, Heidelberg (2013)
27. Ferreira, D.R., Gillblad, D.: Discovering process models from unlabelled event logs. In: Dayal, U., Eder, J., Koehler, J., Reijers, H.A. (eds.) BPM 2009. LNCS, vol. 5701, pp. 143–158. Springer, Heidelberg (2009)
28. Sole, M., Carmona, J.: Region-Based Folding in Process Discovery. IEEE Transactions on Knowledge and Data Engineering **25**(1), 192–205 (2013)
29. Günther, C.W., Verbeek, E.: XES Standard version 2 (2014). http://www.xes-standard.org/_media/xes/xesstandarddefinition-2.0.pdf
30. Rozinat, A., de Medeiros, A.K.A., Günther, C.W., Weijters, A.J.M.M., van der Aalst, W.M.P.: The need for a process mining evaluation framework in research and practice. In: ter Hofstede, A.H.M., Benatallah, B., Paik, H.Y. (eds.) BPM 2007. LNCS, vol. 9428, pp. 84–89. Springer, Heidelberg (2007)
31. Ayres, J., Flannick, J., Gehrke, J., Yiu, T.: Sequential pattern mining using a bitmap representation. In: Proc. 8th ACM Intern. Conf. Knowl. Discov. Data Mining, pp. 429–435. ACM (2002)
32. 3TU Data Center, BPI Challenge, Event Log, data.3tu.nl/repository/collection:event_logs_real
33. Bose, R.P.J.C., van der Aalst, W.M.: Abstractions in process mining: a taxonomy of patterns. In: Dayal, U., Eder, J., Koehler, J., Reijers, H.A. (eds.) BPM 2009. LNCS, vol. 5701, pp. 159–175. Springer, Heidelberg (2009)
34. Buijs, J.C.A.M., van Dongen, B. F., van der Aalst, W. M. P. : Quality Dimensions in Process Discovery: The importance of Fitness, Precision, Generalization and Simplicit., IJCIS **2**(1) (2014)
35. van der Aalst, W.M.P., Adriansyah, A., van Dongen, B.: Replaying History on Process Models for Conformance Checking and Performance Analysis. WIREs Data Mining and Knowledge Discover **2**(2), 182–192 (2012)
36. Adriansyah, A., Munoz-Game, J., Carmona, J., van Dongen, B.F., van der Aalst, W.M.P.: Measuring Precision of Modeled Behaviour. Information systems and e-Business Management (2015)
37. Buijs, J.C.A.M., van Dongen, B.F., van der Aalst, W.M.P.: A genetic algorithm for discovering process trees. In: IEEE Congress on Evolutionary Computation (CEC 2012), pp. 1–8. IEEE Computer Society (2012)

Log-Based Simplification of Process Models

Javier De San Pedro$^{(\boxtimes)}$, Josep Carmona, and Jordi Cortadella

Universitat Politècnica de Catalunya, Barcelona, Spain
{jspedro,jcarmona,jordicf}@cs.upc.edu

Abstract. The visualization of models is essential for user-friendly human-machine interactions during Process Mining. A simple graphical representation contributes to give intuitive information about the behavior of a system. However, complex systems cannot always be represented with succinct models that can be easily visualized. Quality-preserving model simplifications can be of paramount importance to alleviate the complexity of finding useful and attractive visualizations.

This paper presents a collection of log-based techniques to simplify process models. The techniques trade off visual-friendly properties with quality metrics related to logs, such as fitness and precision, to avoid degrading the resulting model. The algorithms, either cast as optimization problems or heuristically guided, find simplified versions of the initial process model, and can be applied in the final stage of the process mining life-cycle, between the discovery of a process model and the deployment to the final user. A tool has been developed and tested on large logs, producing simplified process models that are one order of magnitude smaller while keeping fitness and precision under reasonable margins.

1 Introduction

The understandability of a process model can be seriously hampered by a poor visualization. Many factors may contribute to this, being complexity a crucial one: models that are unnecessarily complex (incorporating redundant components, or components with limited importance) are often not useful for understanding the process behind. On the other hand, process models are expected to satisfy certain quality metrics when representing an event log: *fitness*, *precision*, *simplicity* and *generalization* [1]. In this paper we present techniques to simplify a process model while retaining the aforementioned quality metrics under reasonable margins. We focus on the simplification of Petri nets, a general formalism onto which several other process models can be essentially mapped.

Given a complex process model, one can simply remove arcs and nodes until a nice graphical object is obtained. However, this naive technique has two main drawbacks. First, the capability of the simplified model to replay the process executions may be considerably degraded, thus deriving a highly unfitting model. Second, the model components, arcs and places in a Petri net, are not equally important when replaying process executions, and therefore one may be interested in keeping those components that provide more insight into the real boundaries on what is allowed by the process (i.e., its precision).

© Springer International Publishing Switzerland 2015
H.R. Motahari-Nezhad et al. (Eds.): BPM 2015, LNCS 9253, pp. 457–474, 2015.
DOI: 10.1007/978-3-319-23063-4_30

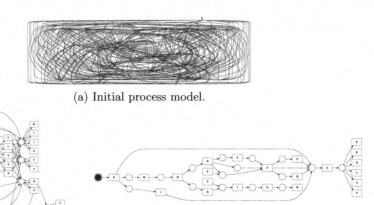

(a) Initial process model.

(b) Simplified fitting proc. model.   (c) Simplified series-parallel process model.

Fig. 1. Log-based simplification of an spaghetti-like process model.

Given a Petri net and an event log, this paper first ranks the importance of places and arcs using a simple simulation of the log by the Petri net, and then simplifies the model by retaining those arcs and places that are important in restricting the behavior allowed by the model. Several alternatives are presented, which render the preservation of fitness as a user decision, or extract certain Petri net subclasses (State Machines, Free-Choice) or structural subclasses (Series-Parallel graphs). The goal of these techniques is similar to that of [2]. However the techniques presented in this paper require a lower computational cost and exhibit better scalability when managing large problems, while producing results of competitive quality, as shown by the experimental results.

1.1   Motivating Example

We will illustrate one of the techniques presented in this paper with the help of an example. We have used the general-purpose tool dot [3] to render all the examples. Figure 1a reports a process model that has been discovered by the ILP miner from a real-life log, a well-known method for process discovery [4]. This miner guarantees perfect fitness (i.e., the model is able to reproduce all the traces in the log), but its precision value is low (31.5%) which indicates that the model may generate many traces not observed in the log.

Clearly, this model does not give any insight about the executions of the process behind. Hence, although it is a model having perfect fitness, some of the other quality metrics (precision, simplicity) are not satisfactory. Applying the simplification techniques of this paper, a process model can be transformed with the objective of improving its understandability. The process models at the bottom of Fig. 1 are the result of applying two of the techniques proposed in this paper. In Figure 1b the model is simplified while preserving as much as possible the quality metrics of the original model. The model has 6 times fewer places and arcs, making it much easier to understand. The resulting fitness is still perfect, but the precision has been reduced to 22.5%.

In Figure 1c we reduce the model to a *series-parallel graph*, further improving its simplicity and understandability. The fitness has been reduced to 64.1%, but on the other hand its precision has improved considerably (now 48.7%).

The paper is organized as follows. Section 2 introduces the required background of the paper. Section 3 gives an overview of the proposed simplification algorithms. In Section 4, a log-based technique to estimate the importance of arcs and places is described, which is used by some of the simplification algorithms, detailed in Section 5. Section 6 describes the remaining, non log-based simplification techniques. All techniques are evaluated in Section 7. Finally, related work and conclusions are discussed in Sections 8 and 9, respectively.

2   Preliminaries

2.1   Process Models

Process models are formalisms to represent the behavior of a process. Among the different formalisms, Petri nets are perhaps the most popular, due to its well-defined semantics. In this paper we focus on visualization of Petri nets, although the work may be adapted to other formalisms like BPMN, EPC or similar.

A Petri Net [5] is a 4-tuple $N = \langle P, T, \mathcal{F}, m_0 \rangle$, where P is the set of places, T is the set of transitions, $\mathcal{F} : (P \times T) \cup (T \times P) \rightarrow \{0, 1\}$ is the flow relation, and m_0 is the initial marking. A marking is an assignment of a non-negative integer to each place. If k is assigned to place p by marking m (denoted $m(p) = k$), we say that p is marked with k tokens. Given a node $x \in P \cup T$, its pre-set and post-set are denoted by $^\bullet x$ and $x^\bullet$ respectively.

A transition t is *enabled* in a marking m when all places in $^\bullet t$ are marked. When t is enabled, it can *fire* by removing a token from each place in $^\bullet t$ and putting a token to each place in $t^\bullet$. A marking m' is *reachable* from m if there is a sequence of firings $t_1 t_2 \ldots t_n$ that transforms m into m', denoted by $m[t_1 t_2 \ldots t_n \rangle m'$. A sequence $t_1 t_2 \ldots t_n$ is *feasible* if it is firable from m_0. A Petri net N is a: *Marked graph* if $\forall p \in P : |^\bullet p| = |p^\bullet| = 1$, *State machine* if $\forall t \in T : |^\bullet t| = |t^\bullet| = 1$ and *Free-Choice* if $\forall p_1, p_2 \in P : p_1^\bullet \cap p_2^\bullet \neq \emptyset \Rightarrow |p_1^\bullet| = |p_2^\bullet| = 1$.

2.2   Process Mining

A *trace* is a word $\sigma \in T^*$ that represents a finite sequence of events. An *event log* $L \in \mathcal{B}(T^*)$ is a multiset of traces[1]. Event logs are the starting point to apply process mining techniques, guided towards the discovery, analysis or extension

---

[1] $\mathcal{B}(A)$ denotes the set of all multisets over A.

of process models. *Process discovery* is one of the most important disciplines in process mining, concerned with learning a process model (e.g., a Petri net) from an event log. Although a novel discipline, there are several discovery techniques that have appeared in the last decade, most of them summarized in [1].

The second family of techniques in process mining is *conformance checking*, i.e., comparing observed and modeled behavior. There are four quality dimensions for comparing model and log: (1) *replay fitness*, (2) *simplicity*, (3) *precision*, and (4) *generalization* [1]. A model has a perfect replay fitness if all traces in the log can be replayed by the model from beginning to end. The *simplest* model that can explain the behavior seen in the log is the best model, a principle known as Occam's Razor. Fitness and simplicity alone are not sufficient to judge the quality of a discovered process model. For example, it is very easy to construct an extremely simple Petri net ("flower model") that is able to replay all traces in an event log (but also any other event log referring to the same set of activities). Similarly, it is undesirable to have a model that only allows for the exact behavior seen in the event log. A model is *precise* if it does not contain "too much" behavior that has not been observed in the log. A model that is not precise is "underfitting" [6]. In contrast to precision, a model should generalize and not restrict behavior to just the examples seen in the log.

In this paper, we consider simplifications that may preserve replay fitness which we will simply refer to as *fitness*. Metrics for fitness have been defined as indicators of how every trace in the log fits a model [7]. Likewise, metrics for precision exist in the literature [6].

Definition 1 (Fitting Trace and Log). *A trace $\sigma \in T^*$ fits a Petri net N if σ is a feasible sequence in N. An event log L fits N if for all $\sigma \in L$, σ fits N.*

3   Overview of Proposed Simplification Techniques

In this section, we introduce the 3 different approaches to the simplification problem that are the main contributions of this work. Figure 3 illustrates these approaches by applying each one to the input model shown in Fig. 2a. The first approach reduces the input to a Petri net that is visually close to a *series-parallel graph* [8] by removing the least important arcs and places (Fig. 2b). However, it has the greatest computational cost. We introduce a second approach that reduces the simplification problem to an Integer Linear Programming (ILP) optimization problem that is more efficient and optionally guarantees the preservation of fitness (Fig. 2c and 2d). These two techniques require an estimation of the importance of arcs and places. In Section 4 we explain how this scoring is computed, while Section 5 describes the techniques in more detail.

The third technique, however, does not consider any information from the log. Instead, the Petri net is projected into different structural classes: free choice (Fig. 2e) and state machine (2f). This approach is described in Section 6.

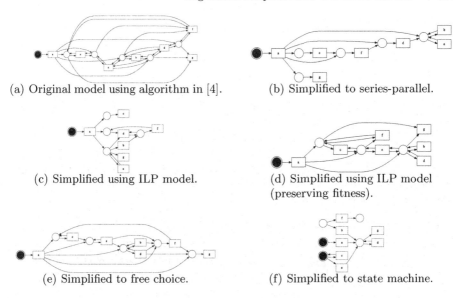

(a) Original model using algorithm in [4].   (b) Simplified to series-parallel.

(c) Simplified using ILP model.   (d) Simplified using ILP model (preserving fitness).

(e) Simplified to free choice.   (f) Simplified to state machine.

Fig. 2. Overview of the different simplification techniques.

4   Log-Based Arc Scores

Given a Petri net and an event log, in this section we introduce a technique to obtain a scoring of the arcs (and, indirectly, places) of the net with respect to their importance in describing the behavior underlying in the log.

The idea of the proposed technique is simple: when a Petri net replays a particular trace in the log, some arcs may have more importance than others for that particular trace. Hence, *triggering* and *utilization* scores will be defined to provide an estimation of the importance of the arcs in replaying the log. Arcs $\mathcal{F}(p,t) \neq 0$ with high trigger score correspond to frequent situations in the model where more behavior should not be allowed (i.e., the arc, and therefore p, is frequently disabling certain transitions to occur). By keeping these arcs/places in the model, one aims at deriving a model where precision is not degraded. Conversely, an arc $\mathcal{F}(t,p) \neq 0$ with high utilization score denotes a situation where transition t is frequently fired (thus frequently adding tokens to p), and therefore should not be removed to avoid degrading fitness.

Definition 2 (Trigger Arc). *Let $N = \langle P, T, \mathcal{F}, m_0 \rangle$ be a Petri net, σ a fitting trace for N, and $t' \in \sigma$ a transition represented by firing $m[t'\rangle m'$ in N. For any pair $p \in P$, $t \in T$, an arc $\mathcal{F}(p,t) \neq 0$ is trigger in $m[t'\rangle m'$ iff t is not enabled in m but enabled in m' and $m(p) < \mathcal{F}(p,t)$ but $m'(p) \geq \mathcal{F}(p,t)$.*

Intuitively, an arc $\mathcal{F}(p,t) \neq 0$ is trigger at every transition $t' \in \sigma$ in which t becomes enabled and p is in the set of places which, in that transition t', received the last tokens required for enabling t. Thus, a frequently-trigger arc indicates p is important in restricting the behavior allowed by the model, and that p or

$\mathcal{F}(p, t)$ cannot be removed without sacrificing precision. Note that for a single transition t there may be more than one trigger arc, even in the same transition $t' \in \sigma$. To use this information, we define a trigger score which characterizes the frequency of an arc in playing the trigger role. In the following definition, we include the score for arcs between transitions and places, the utilization score, which is based on the frequency of firing:

Definition 3 (Trigger/Utilization Score of an Arc). *Given a Petri net $N = \langle P, T, \mathcal{F}, m_0 \rangle$ and fitting log L, the trigger score of an arc $\mathcal{F}(p, t) \neq 0$, denoted by $\mathcal{T}(p, t)$, is the number of transitions from L in which $\mathcal{F}(p, t)$ is trigger. The utilization score of an arc $\mathcal{F}(t, p) \neq 0$, denoted by $\mathcal{U}(t, p)$, is the number of times transition t is fired in L.*

Given a log and a Petri net, obtaining the trigger/utilization scores can be done by *replaying* all traces in the log. Algorithm 1 shows how to compute trigger scores: for every transition in the log, the scores are updated by comparing the markings from the predecessor places of all newly enabled transitions.

Algorithm 1. TRIGGERSCORES

Input: An event log L and a Petri net $N = \langle P, T, \mathcal{F}, m_0 \rangle$
Output: A score $\mathcal{T}(p, t)$ for every arc $\mathcal{F}(p, t) \neq 0$
1 for $\sigma \in L$ do
2 | Let $m_0[t_1 \rangle m_1 [t_2 \rangle \ldots [t_n \rangle m_n = \sigma$
3 | for $i \leftarrow 1$ to n do
4 | | for $t \in T$ do
5 | | | if t *is enabled in* $m_i \wedge t$ *was not enabled in* m_{i-1} then
6 | | | | for $p \in {}^\bullet t$ do
   | | | | | // t is enabled in $m_i \implies m_i(p) \geq \mathcal{F}(p, t)$
7 | | | | | if $m_{i-1}(p) < \mathcal{F}(p, t)$ then $\mathcal{T}(p, t) \leftarrow \mathcal{T}(p, t) + 1$
8
9 return $\mathcal{T}$

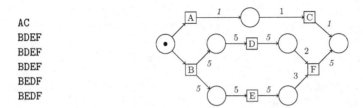

AC
BDEF
BDEF
BDEF
BEDF
BEDF

(a) Example trace   (b) Petri net with trigger/utilization scores

Fig. 3. Trigger and utilization score computation for an example trace and model.

Figure 3 shows the results of computing, on an example trace and model, both trigger and utilization scores. Utilization scores are shown in *italics*.

Finally, notice that in the definitions of this section we consider fitting traces. Given an unfitting trace (i.e., a trace that cannot be replayed by the model), an *alignment* between the trace and the model will provide a feasible sequence that is closest to the trace [7]. This allows widening the applicability of the scoring techniques of this section to any pair (log, model).

5 Simplification Techniques Using Log-Based Scores

5.1 Simplification to a Series-Parallel Net

A series-parallel net is one obtained by the recursive series or parallel composition of smaller nets. Series-parallel Petri nets are amongst the most comprehensible types of models. In a series-parallel net, forks and choices (and thus concurrency) are immediately visible. In fact, existing documentation often uses series-parallel nets as examples to illustrate concepts related to Petri nets.

For this reason, one of the main contributions in this work is a heuristic that reduces a complex Petri net into an almost series-parallel net. The algorithm iteratively removes the least important edges until the graph is either strictly series-parallel, or no additional reduction can be applied without losing the connectedness of the net. The importance of every arc is determined by their trigger score $\mathcal{T}(p,t)$, for place-transition arcs, and their utilization score $\mathcal{U}(t,p)$ for transition-place arcs. The approach is grounded in the notion of a set of reduction rules, explained below.

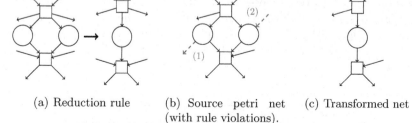

(a) Reduction rule   (b) Source petri net   (c) Transformed net
                          (with rule violations).
Fig. 4. Applying a transformation and transformation cost.

Reduction Rules. In [5] a set of reduction rules used for the analysis of large Petri net systems is introduced. Each of the transformations preserves liveness, safeness and boundedness of a Petri net. Thus, verification of these properties can be done in the simplified net instead of the original one. The transformations proposed are: *fusion of series places/transitions, fusion of parallel places/transitions* and *elimination of self-loop places/transitions*. A rule can be applied only when its preconditions are satisfied. An example of the *fusion of parallel places* rule can be seen in Fig. 4a.

Because of the construction of a series-parallel Petri net, it is possible to reduce such a net to a single place or transition by recursive application of these transformations. Therefore, every violation of the preconditions of a rule indicates a subnet which is not series-parallel.

To reduce a Petri net to a series-parallel skeleton, this work uses these reduction rules in an indirect way. We do not use the transformed Petri net that results from the application of the rules. Instead, the proposed method removes those arcs and places *which prevent the rules from being applied*. For every one of the reduction rules, a *transformation cost* is defined: the sum of the trigger and utilization scores of all the arcs that would need to be removed in order to apply such transformation. The transformation cost therefore models the importance of the arcs that would need to be removed.

Figure 4 shows an example rule, the computation of its transformation cost, and the resulting graph after applying the transformation rule. This rule can only be applied in this input Petri net if two arcs (dashed lines in Fig. 4b) are removed. Thus, the transformation cost is equal to the trigger score of arc (1) and utilization score of arc (2).

Algorithm. Algorithm 2 describes the main iteration of the method. Function `ApplicableTransformations` identifies all possible applications of the reduction rules, and computes the transformation cost for each of the possible applications.

At every iteration we select the transformation m with the least cost, that is, the one that requires removing the least amount of important arcs in order to be applied. Function `ApplyTransformation` applies such transformation m. If applying the transformation breaks the net into more than one connected component, the next best transformation is selected instead. Otherwise, function `PreconditionViolatingArcs` enumerates all the arcs that had to be removed in order to satisfy the preconditions of transformation m. Those arcs are removed them from the original Petri net N_0. The next iteration repeats the process on the transformed net N', finding new `ApplicableTransformations` only around the nodes that were changed on the previous iteration.

Algorithm 2. Series-Parallel algorithm

Input: A Petri net $N_0 = \langle P, T, \mathcal{F}, m_0 \rangle$, a trigger score $\mathcal{T}(p, t)$ for every (p, t) arc, and a
　　　　utilization score $\mathcal{U}(t, p)$ for every (t, p) arc
Output: A simplifed Petri net
1 $N \leftarrow N_0$
2 $M \leftarrow \text{ApplicableTransformations}(N)$
3 **while** $|M| > 0$ **do**
4 　　$m \leftarrow$ transformation with least cost from M
5 　　$N' \leftarrow \text{ApplyTransformation}(N, m)$
6 　　**if** N' *is disconnected* **then**
7 　　　　$M \leftarrow M \setminus \{m\}$
8 　　　　**continue**
9 　　$N_0 \leftarrow N_0 \setminus \text{PreconditionViolatingArcs}(N, m)$
10 　　$N \leftarrow N'$
11 　　$M \leftarrow \text{ApplicableTransformations}(N)$
12 **return** N_0

Once no additional reduction rules can be applied (e.g. because the net is now a single place or transition), the algorithm stops. The currently transformed graph is discarded, and the result of the algorithm is the simplified Petri net N_0. A final postprocessing step removes unneeded places (e.g. without incident arcs).

The nets generated by this heuristic are not necessarily fully series-parallel, since we never remove any arc that would result into an unconnected graph. This is the only method from this work that presents such a global guarantee, with the other methods providing weaker connectivity constraints. It is also possible to configure the method to generate strictly series-parallel models.

5.2   Simplification Using ILP Models

In this section we show a different approach to simplify a Petri net for visualization. The selection of which arcs to remove is seen as an optimization problem, and modeled as an Integer Linear Program (ILP). The use of ILP allows for highly efficient solving strategies. On the other hand, some constraints cannot be modeled using ILP. For example, the models attempt to preserve connectivity of the net at a localized level (i.e. ensuring transitions maintain at least one predecessor and successor place), but cannot guarantee global net connectivity.

The aim of the ILP model is to reduce the number of arcs as much as possible. The inputs are a Petri net $N = \langle P, T, \mathcal{F}, m_0 \rangle$, trigger scores $\mathcal{T}(p, t)$ and utilization scores $\mathcal{U}(t, p)$. We define a binary variable $S(p)$ for every $p \in P$, and a binary variable $A(p, t)$ or $A(t, p)$ for every arc in N. In a solution of this model, variable $S(p)$ is 0 when place p is to be removed from the input graph (similarly for arc variables $A(p, t)$ and $A(t, p)$). Below we describe the ILP model in detail.

$$\min \quad \sum_{\mathcal{F}(p,t)>0} A(p,t) + \sum_{\mathcal{F}(t,p)>0} A(t,p) \tag{1}$$

$$\text{s.t. } \forall p \in P : S(p) \iff \sum_{t \in p^\bullet} A(p,t) > 0 \land \sum_{t \in {}^\bullet p} A(t,p) > 0 \tag{2}$$

$$\sum_{\mathcal{F}(p,t)>0} \mathcal{T}(p,t) A(p,t) >= \Gamma \tag{3}$$

$$\sum_{\mathcal{F}(t,p)>0} \mathcal{U}(t,p) A(t,p) >= \Phi \tag{4}$$

$$\forall t \in T : \sum_{p \in t^\bullet} A(t,p) > 0 \land \sum_{p \in {}^\bullet t} A(p,t) > 0 \tag{5}$$

$$\forall p \in P : M(p) > 0 \implies S(p) \tag{6}$$

$$\forall t \in T, p \in P : \mathcal{F}(t,p) > 0 \land S(p) \implies A(t,p) \tag{7}$$

The objective function, Eq. 1, minimizes the number of preserved arcs. Constraint 2 encodes the relationship between A and S variables. A place is retained in the output net iff at least one predecessor or successor arc is retained.

The model ensures that the most important arcs, according to the trigger scores $\mathcal{T}$, are preserved. To implement this, constraint 3 imposes a minimum number of preserved arcs: where Γ can be configured as a percentage of the combined trigger score from all place transition arcs. A similar threshold constant Φ is imposed using the utilization score $\mathcal{U}$ for transicion place arcs (Eq. 4).

A fully connected graph cannot be guaranteed by the ILP model. Instead, Eq. 5 models a weaker constraint: every transition will preserve at least one predecessor and successor arc. In addition, every place marked in m_0 is always preserved, to avoid deriving a structurally deadlocked model (Eq. 6).

Preserving Fitness (Optional). The ILP model as described so far does not guarantee preservation of fitness from the original Petri net. A simple modification can ensure that the existing fitness is preserved, at the cost of being able to remove only a reduced number of arcs from the model. Following a well-known result in Petri net theory, removing only $\mathcal{F}(t, p)$ arcs never reduces the fitness of a model for any given log. Constraint 7 implements this restriction.

6   Simplification by Projection into Structural Classes

In this section we present ILP models to reduce Petri nets to two types of structural classes: free choice and state machines [5]. These methods do not require a log as they do not use trigger or utilization scores. Therefore, these proposals can be used to simplify Petri nets for visualization even when logs are not available, albeit their results may be of lower quality since scoring information is not used.

Note that [4] can also be configured to generate state machines or marked graphs, but this approach requires having a log. In addition, the models extracted may still be complex because of the requirement to preserve fitness.

6.1   Free Choice

In this method, we simplify Petri nets by converting them into free choice nets. This method preserves the fitness of the model, but reduces precision. While this reduction does not necessarily result in models simple enough for visualization, complexity is reduced while mantaining most structural properties. Thus, reducing a dense net into free choice both opens the door to efficient analysis and to further decomposition (state machine or marked graph *covers*) techniques [9].

We encode this definition as a set of constraints and create a ILP problem which maximizes the number of arcs. For every $p \in P, t \in T$, we define a binary variable $A(p, t)$ which indicates whether arc $\mathcal{F}(p, t)$ is preserved.

Equation 9 guarantees a free choice net. If $|p^\bullet| > 1$ (it is a choice) and $^\bullet|p^\bullet| > 1$ (it is not free), then p contains a non-free choice, and one of the conditions must be removed. Either only one of the successor arcs of p is preserved, eliminating the choice, or it is turned free by removing every predecessor arc of $p^\bullet$ except for the ones originating from p itself. Because $\mathcal{F}(t, p)$ arcs are never being removed, this simplification preserves fitness.

$$\max \qquad \sum_{\mathcal{F}(p,t)>0} A(p,t) \tag{8}$$

$$\forall p \in P : |p^\bullet| > 1 \wedge |^\bullet(p^\bullet)| > 1 \implies$$

$$\text{s.t.} \qquad \sum_{t \in p^\bullet} A(p,t) = 1 \quad \vee \quad \forall t \in p^\bullet, p' \in {}^\bullet t : p \neq p' \implies \neg A(p',t) \tag{9}$$

6.2   State Machine

In a state machine Petri net, every transition has exactly one predecessor arc and one successor arc. To encode this requirement into an ILP model, we again define a binary variable $A(p,t)$ or $A(t,p)$ for every arc in N.

$$\max \quad \sum_{\mathcal{F}(p,t)>0} A(p,t) + \sum_{\mathcal{F}(t,p)>0} A(t,p) \tag{10}$$

$$\text{s.t.} \ \forall t \in T : \sum_{\mathcal{F}(p,t)>0} A(p,t) = 1 \tag{11}$$

$$\forall t \in T : \sum_{\mathcal{F}(t,p)>0} A(t,p) = 1 \tag{12}$$

Constraints 11 and 12 encode the definition of a state machine. However, note that this method may reduce the fitness of the model. A similar ILP model can be created to extract a marked graph.

7   Experimental Evaluation

The methods proposed in this work have been implemented in C++. The ILP-based methods have been implemented using a commercial ILP solver, Gurobi [10]. To obtain the input models, the *ILP miner* [4] available in ProM 6.4 was used over a set of 10 complex logs. The publicly available dot utility [3] has been used to generate the visualizations of all the models of the paper. The measurements of fitness and precision have been done using alignment-based conformance checking techniques [7]. Both the logs and our implementation are publicly available at http://www.cs.upc.edu/~jspedro/pnsimpl/.

7.1   Comparison of the Different Simplification Techniques

In Section 5 (Fig. 3), an artificial model was used to illustrate the different simplification techniques presented in this work. Table 1 shows the details for each one of the simplified models.

Several metrics are used to evaluate the results from the simplification techniques. To evaluate the understandability and simplicity of a model, we use the size of the graph, in number of *nodes* and *arcs*, as well as the number of *crossings*. This is the number of arcs that intersect when the graph is embedded on a plane. Thus, a planar graph has no crossings. A graph with many crossing arcs is clearly a *spaghetti* that is poorly suited for visualization. To approximate the number of crossings, the *mincross* algorithm from dot [3] is used.

Table 1. Simplicity, precision and fitness comparison for models in Fig. 3.

	Nodes	Arcs	Crossings	Fitness	Precision
(*a*) Original net	13	35	7	100%	43.1%
(*b*) Series-parallel	13	17	0	100%	37.9%
(*c*) ILP model	12	16	0	68%	75.4%
(*d*) ILP (fitting)	11	21	0	100%	40.7%
(*e*) Free choice	13	24	1	100%	31.3%
(*f*) State machine	13	13	0	49.2%	81.3%

To measure how much the simplified Petri nets model the behavior of the original process we use *fitness* and *precision*, as defined in [7]. In this example, the series-parallel reduction offers perfect fitness, and only 5% loss of precision while removing half of the arcs and all crossings. However, the other methods also remain interesting. For example, the state machine simplification offers the best reduction in simplicity and increases the precision of the model to 80%, at the cost of reducing the fitness by 50%.

Figure 5 shows the Petri nets produced by the different techniques on a real-life log that is more *spaghetti*-like. The high number of crossings in the original model make it unsuitable for visualization. In this example, the series-parallel method no longer offers perfect fitness but still shows a good trade-off between complexity and fitness/precision. The other methods may be used if for example strict fitness preservation is required, at the cost of more complex models.

In Fig. 6, we compare numerically the techniques of this paper for the 10 logs. For most of the logs, the series-parallel reduction and the ILP-based techniques are able to reduce the number of crossing edges by several orders of magnitude (note the logarithmic scale), creating small visualizable graphs from models that would otherwise be impossible to layout. On the other hand, the simplification to free choice results in very large and complex models. As mentioned, the benefits of deriving free choice models come from the ability to apply additional reduction strategies. Simplifying to state machines generally produces poorly fitting models, but they tend to have very few crossings and high precision.

Figure 6 also includes a comparison with some of the previous work in the area: the *Inductive Miner* (IM) [11] and a *unfolding*-based method [2]. The IM is a miner guided towards discovering block-structured models and which we see as a promising technique (see Section 8) since it can be tunned to guarantee perfect fitness. Generally, models generated by the IM contain fewer crossings, caused by the addition of a significant number of *silent* transitions[2] which increase the

---

[2] A silent activity in the model is not related to any event in the log.

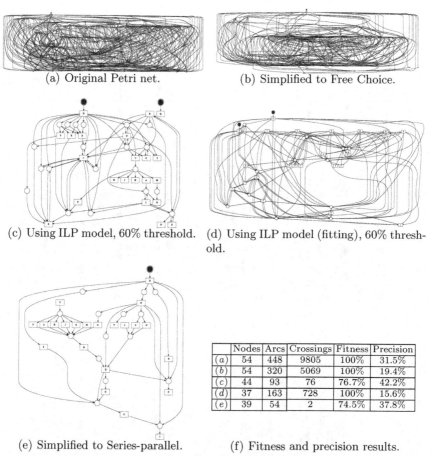

(a) Original Petri net.

(b) Simplified to Free Choice.

(c) Using ILP model, 60% threshold.

(d) Using ILP model (fitting), 60% threshold.

(e) Simplified to Series-parallel.

	Nodes	Arcs	Crossings	Fitness	Precision
(a)	54	448	9805	100%	31.5%
(b)	54	320	5069	100%	19.4%
(c)	44	93	76	76.7%	42.2%
(d)	37	163	728	100%	15.6%
(e)	39	54	2	74.5%	37.8%

(f) Fitness and precision results.

Fig. 5. Running all methods on real-life log (*incidenttelco*).

size of the model. For example, in the *incidenttelco* example the number of transitions of the model derived by the IM is 37, whilst the original model (and, correspondingly, those generated by the simplification techniques) has 22. The addition of silent activities can be beneficial for visualization, specially if the underlying process model is meant to be block-structured.

On the other hand, the unfolding procedure is more closely related to the methods proposed in this work. This technique uses an *unfolding* process to simplify an existing Petri net, and has been evaluated using the same nets as with our proposed methods. In general, it produces better results in terms of fitness and precision with respect to the ILP models, at the expense of longer computation time. When compared with the series-parallel method, the results in fitness and precision are comparable, but the unfolding method requires more computation time and the results are worst in terms of visualization.

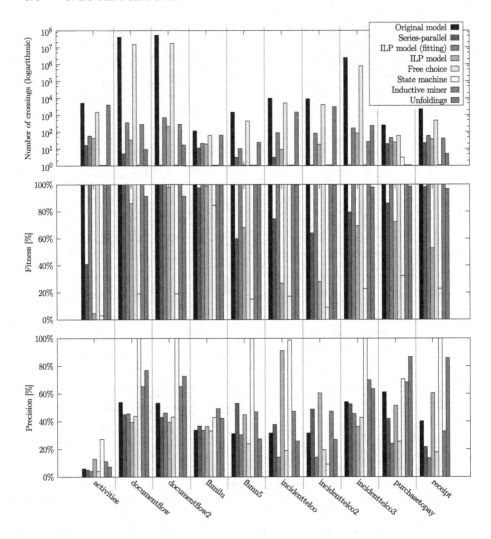

Fig. 6. Simplicity (logarithmic scale on the number of crossings), fitness and precision comparison between the different techniques using 10 real-life logs.

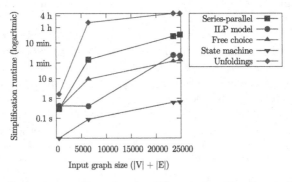

Fig. 7. Execution runtimes for the different simplification techniques.

In Fig. 7 we compare the runtimes of the different methods. The ILP solver resolved all the ILP simplification models in less than 1 minute, even for the largest of the input Petri nets from the test set (25K nodes and arcs). The series-parallel simplification, which is not ILP based, has a lower performance. However, there are many parts where the algorithm could be optimized. Still, the total execution runtime for the largest graph (25 minutes) was less than the 1 hour required for the miner in [4] to generate the input Petri net from the log, and significantly less than the 5 hours required by the unfolding technique presented in [2] (also shown in the plot).

The experiments presented in this section show the proposed simplification ILP models to be highly efficient and able to generate models that are orders of magnitude simpler than the original models. If additional simplification is required, the series-parallel method can be used with an increased runtime.

7.2   Effect of the Threshold Parameter on the ILP Model

The ILP simplification model presented in Section 5.2 contains a threshold parameter (Γ and Φ) which can be used to tune the complexity and size of the simplified models. In previous experiments and figures, a threshold was set manually so that models with approximately $2|T|$ arcs were generated (where T is the set of transitions from the input Petri net).

To illustrate how varying these thresholds affects the model complexity and quality, the ILP simplification model was executed for each of the input logs, with varying threshold parameters. Fig. 8 shows the number of crossings and the

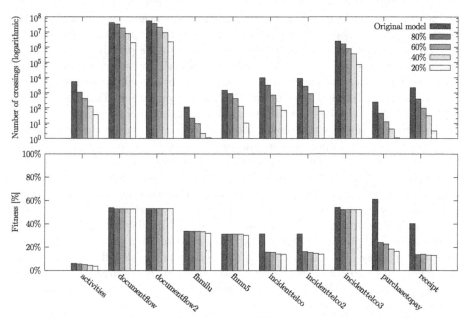

Fig. 8. Simplicity and fitness comparison using different thresholds for the ILP model.

fitness for each combination. Generally the fitness decreases with the threshold parameter, but there are some models where the trend reverses. This is because nothing in the model ensures that a log with a given threshold Γ will strictly capture all the behavior of a log simplified using Γ' with $\Gamma > \Gamma'$.

8   Related Work

The closest work to the methods of this paper is [2], where a technique was presented for the simplification of process models that controls the degree of precision and generalization. It applies several stages. First, a log-based unfolding of the model is computed, deriving a precise unfolded model. Second, this unfolding is then filtered, retainning only the frequent parts. Finally, a folding technique is applied which controls the generalization of the final model. Further simplifications can be applied, which help on alleviating the complexity of the derived model. There are significant differences between the two approaches: while in our case, the techniques rely on light methods and can be oriented towards different objectives, the approach in [2] requires the computation of unfoldings, which can be exponential on the size of the initial model [12]. Also, the filtering on the unfolding is done on simple frequency selection on the unfolding elements, while in this paper the importance of model elements is assessed with the frequency but also triggering information, which is related to the precision dimension. On the other hand, the techniques of this paper may need to verify model connectedness at each iteration. In conclusion, both techniques can be combined to further improve the overall simplification of a model.

The simplification of a process model should be done with respect to quality metrics, and in this paper we have focused on fitness and precision. An alternative to this approach would be to include these quality metrics in the discovery, a feature that has only been considered in the past by the family of genetic algorithms for process discovery [13–15]. All these techniques include costly evaluations of the metrics in the search for an optimal process model, in order to discard intermediate solutions that are not promising. This makes these approaches extremely inefficient in terms of computing time.

Furthermore, there exist discovery techniques that focus on the most frequent paths [16,17]. These approaches are meant to be resilient to noise, but on the other hand give no guarantees on the quality of the derived model. Additionally, these approaches are oriented towards less expressive models, which makes the simplification task easier than the one considered in this paper. A recent technique that is guided towards the discovery of block-structured models (*process trees*) and that addresses these issues may be a promising direction [11]. However, this technique is guided towards a particular class of Petri nets (workflow and sound), describing a very restricted type of behaviors. Finally, the techniques of this paper can be combined with abstraction mechanisms to further improve the visualization of the underlying process model.

9   Conclusions

A collection of techniques for the simplification of process models using log-based information has been presented in this paper. The techniques proposed tend to improve significantly the visualization of a process model while retaining its main qualities in relation with an event log. This contribution may be used on the model derived by any discovery technique, as an intermediate step between discovery and visualization. Also, the analysis of simplified models may be considerably alleviated (e.g., if deriving a free-choice net). The experiments done on dense models have also shown a significant simplification capability in terms of visualization metrics like density or edge-crossings.

Acknowledgments. This work as been partially supported by funds from the Spanish Ministry for Economy and Competitiveness (MINECO) and the European Union (FEDER funds) under grant COMMAS (ref. TIN2013-46181-C2-1-R) and by a grant from Generalitat de Catalunya (FI-DGR). We would also like to thank to Seppe van-den Broucke, Jorge Munoz-Gama and Thomas Gschwind for their great help in the experiments.

References

1. van der Aalst, W.M.P.: Process Mining - Discovery, Conformance and Enhancement of Business Processes. Springer (2011)
2. Fahland, D., van der Aalst, W.M.P.: Simplifying discovered process models in a controlled manner. Information Systems **38**(4), 585–605 (2013)
3. Gansner, E.R., Koutsofios, E., North, S.C., Vo, K.: A technique for drawing directed graphs. IEEE Trans. Software Eng. **19**(3), 214–230 (1993)
4. van der Werf, J.M.E.M., van Dongen, B.F., Hurkens, C.A.J., Serebrenik, A.: Process discovery using integer linear programming. In: van Hee, K.M., Valk, R. (eds.) PETRI NETS 2008. LNCS, vol. 5062, pp. 368–387. Springer, Heidelberg (2008)
5. Murata, T.: Petri nets: Properties, analysis and applications. Proceedings of the IEEE **77**(4), 541–574 (1989)
6. Muñoz-Gama, J., Carmona, J.: A fresh look at precision in process conformance. In: Hull, R., Mendling, J., Tai, S. (eds.) BPM 2010. LNCS, vol. 6336, pp. 211–226. Springer, Heidelberg (2010)
7. Adriansyah, A.: Aligning observed and modeled behavior. PhD thesis, Technische Universiteit Eindhoven (2014)
8. Valdes, J., Tarjan, R.E., Lawler, E.L.: The recognition of series parallel digraphs. SIAM J. Comput. **11**(2), 298–313 (1982)
9. Desel, J., Esparza, J.: Free choice Petri nets 40 (1995)
10. Gurobi Optimization: Gurobi Optimizer reference manual (2015)
11. Leemans, S.J.J., Fahland, D., van der Aalst, W.M.P.: Discovering block-structured process models from incomplete event logs. In: Ciardo, G., Kindler, E. (eds.) PETRI NETS 2014. LNCS, vol. 8489, pp. 91–110. Springer, Heidelberg (2014)
12. McMillan, K.L.: Using unfoldings to avoid the state explosion problem in the verification of asynchronous circuits. In: von Bochmann, G., Probst, D.K. (eds.) CAV 1992. LNCS, vol. 663, pp. 164–177. Springer, Heidelberg (1993)

13. van der Aalst, W.M.P., de Medeiros, A.K.A., Weijters, A.J.M.M.T.: Genetic process mining. In: Ciardo, G., Darondeau, P. (eds.) ICATPN 2005. LNCS, vol. 3536, pp. 48–69. Springer, Heidelberg (2005)
14. Buijs, J.: Flexible Evolutionary Algorithms for Mining Structured Process Models. PhD thesis, Technische Universiteit Eindhoven (2014)
15. Vázquez-Barreiros, B., Mucientes, M., Lama, M.: ProDiGen: Mining complete, precise and minimal structure process models with a genetic algorithm. Information Sciences **294**, 315–333 (2015)
16. Günther, C.: Process Mining in Flexible Environments. PhD thesis, Technische Universiteit Eindhoven (2009)
17. Weijters, A.J.M.M., Ribeiro, J.T.S.: Flexible heuristics miner (FHM). In: Computational Intelligence and Data Mining (CIDM), pp. 310–317 (2011)

Author Index

Assy, Nour 198

Baião, Fernanda Araujo 189
Bala, Saimir 425
Barkaoui, Kamel 55
Barton, Russell R. 280
Bunnell, Craig A. 35

Cabanillas, Cristina 425
Carmona, Josep 126, 457
Casati, Fabio 333
Chaisiri, Sivadon 441
Conforti, Raffaele 297
Cortadella, Jordi 457

Dam, Hoa Khanh 350
Daniel, Florian 333
de Murillas, Eduardo González López 367
De San Pedro, Javier 457
Debois, Søren 72
Di Ciccio, Claudio 144
Di Francescomarino, Chiara 297
Dumas, Marlon 297, 386, 406

Ferme, Vincenzo 251

Gaaloul, Walid 198
Gal, Avigdor 35
García-Bañuelos, Luciano 386
Ghose, Aditya 350
Guo, Qinlong 109

Helbig, Karsten 242
Hildebrandt, Thomas 72

Ioualalen, Malika 55
Ishakian, Vatche 226
Ivanchikj, Ana 251

Kadish, Sarah 35
Kheldoun, Ahmed 55
Knuplesch, David 263
Kucherbaev, Pavel 333
Kumar, Akhil 263, 280

La Rosa, Marcello 386, 406
Lakshmanan, Geetika T. 226
Leontjeva, Anna 297
Leopold, Henrik 90
Li, Xiang 226
Liesaputra, Veronica 441
Liu, Haifeng 226
Lohmann, Patrick 317

Maaradji, Abderrahmane 406
Maggi, Fabrizio Maria 144, 297
Mandelbaum, Avishai 35
Manderscheid, Jonas 19
Marin, Mike 226
Marquard, Morten 209
Mei, Jing 226
Mellouli, Taïeb 242
Mendling, Jan 35, 144, 189, 425
Montali, Marco 144
Mukhi, Nirmal 226

Narendra, Nanjangud C. 350
Nogayama, Takahide 172

Ostovar, Alireza 406

Pautasso, Cesare 251
Pittke, Fabian 189
Polleres, Axel 425
Ponce-de-León, Hernan 126
Ponnalagu, Karthikeyan 350

Reißner, Daniel 19
Reichert, Manfred 263
Reijers, Hajo A. 3, 90, 180, 367
Richetti, Pedro H. Piccoli 189
Rietzschel, Eric 3
Rogge-Solti, Andreas 35, 425
Röglinger, Maximilian 19
Römer, Michael 242

Sabbella, Sharat R. 280
Schunselaar, D.M.M. 180
Senderovich, Arik 35

Shahzad, Muhammad   209
Slaats, Tijs   72, 209

Takahashi, Haruhisa   172
Tranquillini, Stefano   333

van Beest, Nick R.T.P.   386
van der Aa, Han   90
van der Aalst, Wil M.P.   163, 180, 367
van Dongen, Boudewijn F.   163
van Zelst, Sebastiaan J.   163
vanden Broucke, Seppe K.L.M.   126
Vanderfeesten, Irene   3

Vanwersch, Rob J.B.   3
Verbeek, H.M.W.   180

Wang, Jianmin   109
Wen, Lijie   109

Xie, Guotong   226

Yan, Zhiqiang   109
Yongchareon, Sira   441
Yu, Philip S.   109
Yu, Yiqin   226

Zur Muehlen, Michael   317

Printed in the United States
By Bookmasters